SOLDIER OF
FORTUNE 500

SOLDIER OF
FORTUNE 500

A MANAGEMENT SURVIVAL GUIDE
FOR THE CONSULTING WARS

STEVE ROMAINE

Prometheus Books

59 John Glenn Drive
Amherst, New York 14228-2197

Published 2002 by Prometheus Books

Inquiries should be addressed to
Prometheus Books
59 John Glenn Drive
Amherst, New York 14228–2197
VOICE: 716–691–0133, ext. 207
FAX: 716–564–2711
WWW.PROMETHEUSBOOKS.COM

06 05 04 03 02   5 4 3 2 1

Library of Congress Cataloging-in-Publication Data

Romaine, Steve, 1955–
    Soldier of Fortune 500 : a management survival guide for the consulting wars / Steve Romaine.
        p. cm.
    Includes bibliographical references and index.
    ISBN 1–57392–995–6 (alk. paper)
    1. Business consultants. I. Title: Soldier of Fortune five hundred. II. Title.

HD69.C6 R65 2002
001—dc21
                                                                    2002069673

Printed in Canada on acid-free paper

Special thanks to editors Steven L. Mitchell and Peggy Deemer.

Also, Jan Bryniczka for his advice and suggestions,

Pete Lacovara for his contribution
to the summary and recommendations,

Randy Tatano for providing invaluable input,

and Grace and Maura Romaine for their love and patience.

In memory of Artie Fox, Howard Payne, and Bill Romaine—
Good company men with big hearts

Disclaimer

S OLDIER OF FORTUNE 500 is based on actual experiences and research of the author. It represents a concerted effort to present facts and attempts to refrain from embellishing on what actually transpired. Individual names have been changed, but the names of the institutions and consulting firms discussed in this book have not been altered. The presentation of events, as well as the opinions, suggestions, and conclusions drawn by the author, are all subject to his interpretation. There could potentially be other interpretations, and there also may have been additional information not available to the author that could have altered his point of view as well as any conclusions derived based on the subject material presented. The events described do not necessarily reflect the policy of the corporations where they took place. In some cases, the business models of the firms as described have changed. Personnel, vendor relationships, strategies, tactics, and conditions may also have changed since these events occurred.

Those who cannot remember the past are condemned to repeat it.
—George Santayana

TABLE OF
CONTENTS

CONTENTS

ACKNOWLEDGMENTS

Thanks to editors Steven L. Mitchell and Peggy Deemer for making this happen. Jan Bryniczka for reading early drafts and offering outstanding advice and suggestions. Pete Lacovara for his contribution to the final summary section and coining the title, *Soldier of Fortune 500*. Mitra Martin for creating a dynamite Web site (www.sof500.com—check it out) and for her help on the vendor consultant chart in the appendix. Rodger Doughty for ongoing help and support. Patrick Nolan of Villanova University, author of *The Jericho Mile*, who convinced me to change my major to English and advised me about the publishing industry. Leo O'Connor from Fairfield University who helped me meld my personal story into the bigger picture. Suzanne Cramond who convinced me to keep on writing and rewriting. Susan Tiller for helping me create the trail and avoid some of the land mines, and for introducing me to Ralph. Bernie Steele, one of a kind, who made me rethink accepted business practices and helped turn a bad work situation into a completely unexpected story of achievement through teamwork. Special thanks to Randy Tatano who provided invaluable input and encouragement. Grace and Maura Romaine for their love and patience. Also, Ray and Diana Sisler of Integrated Financial Solutions.

Don Hurley, Al Kaemmerlen, Brian Strong, Tom Kennedy, and the rest of former "Hurricanes" of IBM Branch 066 who tattooed on my head the importance of relationship marketing and stretching to the max, and who provided me with continuous "on-the-job" training. My Nations-Bank team for exhibiting "grace under pressure." Tina Co-Weeks for assisting with research, and Eileen Smith, Father Peter Towsley, Joe Fazio, and Dave Katz. Mike Conway, Walt Stewart, Steve Halley, Barb Potkay, Joel Bloom, Atul Kapoor, and Lou Weinstein for ongoing mentoring. Gary Stansell, Ron Belmont, George Molanari, Kay Stephenson, Kris Murthy, Myra Woods, and Brian McCollum for sharing ideas on more effective management practices. Donald A. Phin for the confidentiality agreement included in the appendix. for the The IBM–Newport News Shipbuilding team for making a Mets fan believe it can happen again. Harvard Business Press for suggesting that I reread *Liar's Poker* and *Barbarians at the Gate* and rewrite one more time. Christian Brothers Academy in Lincroft, New Jersey, and Fairfield Prep, in Fairfield, Connecticut. United Way which provides critical assistance to those in need and helped me establish invaluable business contacts by simply getting involved. And of course, Elisabeth Velander.

FOREWORD

The fallout after the implosion of the Texas-based energy company, Enron, turned many accepted business assumptions on their head. It wasn't just about financial reporting and the auditors. "Follow the money," and the trail leads directly to consultants and the business partners they often recommend. So what really happens when employees get downsized out of corporations? Lots of us become consultants. At times we are hired back to consult for big bucks with the very companies who let us go, as if we have somehow found new wisdom after hitting the street. Do you really think your company is safe when you hire an "independent" consultant, providing access to all kinds of information on your business, including information about your customers? Consultants are positioned perfectly to broker whatever we can get our hands on to vendors, telemarketers, competitors, or possibly individuals or organizations with even more devious intentions—something rarely considered before September 11, 2001. So what if we sign nondisclosure agreements. Who polices them? Who would know? Surprisingly, many managers treat us as if we were still company employees. We're not. Oftentimes our objectives are very different. Rarely are we screened the way employees are screened prior to being hired. Sometimes we have an attitude. They weren't loyal to me as a faithful employee, why should I be loyal now?

The best part about being a consultant is that our recommendations are almost always taken more seriously than if they had come from an employee. Some of the old-fashioned employee types who are still left in the company are onto us. Fortunately for the consulting profession, they rarely talk. Who would listen? It's the consultant who gets management's ear. Employees who attempt to speak out run the risk of joining the next wave of consultant-recommended layoffs. Sometimes it doesn't take that long before the outspoken employee is asked to leave.

During the last ten years, technology consultants, like me, almost always recommended "open systems" solutions. It didn't matter that open, by definition, is not secure—open systems meant lots more integration work for both us and our business partners. We also liked to rec- ommend outsourcing, arguing that we can help a client reduce costs. No one was ever very concerned if sometimes this meant that we subcon- tracted the work to little-known third parties, sometimes operating in remote and unstable parts of the world, at a cut rate, introducing a whole new level of risk. The important thing was quarterly earnings, and we were helping our client reduce costs and improve short-term profitability. More important, we were helping ourselves. For the corporate manager, it is now time that some of these generally accepted business assump- tions be reconsidered, including the proper use of consultants. The strength, security, and long-term viability of the corporation are at stake.

Consultants have been around as long as people have been paying for advice. In the 1990s, corresponding with the major downsizing pro- grams at many U.S. corporations, they have become significantly more visible in almost every part of the business. Corporations today are more dependent on consultants than ever before. In some companies consul- tants are used by senior managers the same way kids use MTV. Signing the contract is like powering on the remote control. Kick back and enjoy the ride.

Don't get me wrong. There are many very good, highly skilled, ethi- cally responsible consultants, but unlike other professions, there is no licensing requirement to become a consultant. Anyone can do it. We hear about malpractice suits in medicine and in the legal professions. Unlike auditing, the consulting industry has no generally accepted standards of professional business ethics, and yet, according to industry analysis firm International Data Corporation (IDC) projections, U.S. revenue for con- sulting was over $23 billion in 1997, close to 50 percent of the worldwide total. IDC-projected U.S. consulting revenue reached close to $40 billion in 2001.[1] No wonder auditing firms in pursuit of higher fees expand their services into consulting. Corporations, as well as the U.S. government, including its military apparatus, have become highly dependent on "work for hire" consultants.

By 2001, the dot-coms, which had helped the stock market soar at the end of the 1990s, had crumbled. There was debate about whether we were headed for recession. Then terrorists struck the World Trade Center and the Pentagon with hijacked passenger jets used as kamikaze missiles. Another passenger jet headed for Washington, D.C., was downed in Pennsylvania. The September 11 tragedies ended the debate about reces- sion. Many corporations posted significant losses for the quarter ending September 30, 2001, blaming it on these terrible tragedies. For example, as reported by the *Wall Street Journal*, Bank of America posted a 54 percent decline, "highlighting the challenges of a U.S. corporate-loan market that has deteriorated rapidly since Sept. 11."[2] While there is no question the terrorists' acts had a major impact, the inflicted tragedies were not the root cause of the economic fallout, but rather highlighted some fundamental problems. The year 2001 ended with the collapse in market value of Enron, a major success story of the nineties, with a devastating effect on stockholders and employees.[3] Allegations of mismanagement, falsifying financial statements, missing and destroyed documents, as well as conflict of interest issues with auditors and consultants from Arthur Andersen LLP surfaced. Surely some of the problems long ignored by Enron management extend to other companies as well. Now more than ever, these problems need to be addressed.

With so much money being earned in an unregulated profession, it should not be surprising that abuses have occurred. Consultants are involved and often dominate information technology (IT) projects in almost all Fortune 500 corporations. It is estimated by the Standish Group International Inc., the technology firm of advisors, that over 70 percent of IT projects fail by either missing deadlines, running well overbudget, failing to achieve objectives, or by being completely scrapped. Failed projects are believed to cost U.S. corporations and the government $145 billion a year.[4] Scanning the trade press, you would hardly know most technology projects fail. Most of the articles are written from the point of view of the consultants or managers responsible for hiring them.

Unfortunately, most managers do not recognize or want to admit that they recognize the obvious problems. For too long, consultants have gotten a free pass. It's time to understand what causes this crippling conspiracy of silence. More important, corporate managers need to better understand the dynamics of the consulting relationship and how to prevent these failures in project management, communication, and security from continuing. I hope that sharing some of my experiences will open some eyes and, for well-intentioned business managers, provide some guidance to help avoid becoming one of the causalities of the consultant wars.

The following is a factual account of experiences working as, with, and for consultants. It is based on actual experiences with several prominent U.S. corporations and consulting firms. The names of the individuals involved in the story have been changed. The names of the firms and their CEOs have not. These firms include International Business Machines Corporation (IBM), Gartner Group Inc., Pitney Bowes Inc., Chase Manhattan Bank Corporation, McKinsey & Company, NationsBank Corporation, Gemini Consulting, Newport News Shipbuilding Inc., and Andersen Consulting (which after years of legal rankling, split from

Arthur Andersen LLP, changed its name to Accenture Ltd., moved its headquarters to Bermuda, and went public on July 19, 2001).[5] While the primary focus is within the technology area, it is not about technology per se. Efforts were made to keep the technical jargon at a minimum and to focus instead on the dynamics that exist between consultants and employees of the corporation during contractual engagements. To assist the reader, there is a brief description of the cast of characters for easy reference in addition to a glossary of terms in the appendix. There is also a summary of observations at the conclusion of each chapter and a summary of recommendations in the last chapter.

The story essentially represents three distinct periods. The first is working for IBM in the early 1990s as the company transitioned from a business with minimal dependency on outside consultants to one where consultants begin to play a much more critical role. The second section is based on experiences in my own consulting practice where I worked with Fortune 500 clients such as Pitney Bowes, Chase Manhattan Bank, and IBM. These experiences gave me an opportunity to view the client-consultant relationship from a completely different perspective. It also provided a unique vantage point to watch and collaborate with larger and more prestigious consulting firms—learning what works with clients and what makes consulting firms successful in increasing their penetration within the corporation. The third and final section represents the period working as a senior vice president with NationsBank, a company highly dependent on consultants for the running of almost all facets of the business.

On April 13, 1998, NationsBank announced plans to merge with Bank of America Corporation. Approved by the regulators, the largest national bank in terms of both deposits and branches was created. Consultants became a critical behind-the-scenes partner for consolidating operations and other activities related to the merger. They had been deeply involved with both institutions for years. As NationsBank and Bank of America pursued aggressive acquisition strategies, consultants gained considerable control and influence. As a result, consultants and business partners replaced corporate employees, handling major banking operations for the new megacorporation. There are close to 30 million Bank of America customers. I doubt very many of these customers realized that some of their most private financial information was handled everyday by work-for-hire mercenaries, not friendly town bankers as one might assume.

It could be argued that my experiences represent unique and isolated events. Although this is possible, it is important to emphasize that these experiences took place over the course of seven years. There is a pattern that suggests that consultants now play a much more important role in the everyday working of corporations and in charting future strategic directions. They can play a very valuable role. And then again, . . .

NOTES

1. Marianne Hedin, "1997 Worldwide and U.S. Consulting Marketing and Trends," *IDC: Consulting and Management Services* (Framingham, Mass.: IDC, 1997), 1, 29.

2. Jathon Sapsford, "Bank of America's Profit Falls 54%, Highlighting Loan-Market Problems," *Wall Street Journal* 16 October 2001, C1.

3. Bethany McLean, "The Enron Disaster Lies, Arrogance, Betrayal," *Fortune*, 24 December 2001, 58–68.

4. Tom Field, "When Bad Things Happen to Good People," *CIO*, 15 October 1997, http://www.cio.com/archive.

5. "Briefing.com Story Stocks: Accenture," *CNET.com*, 19 July 2001, http://investor.cnet.com/investor/news/newsitem/0-9900-1028-6613330-0.html, accessed 11 January 2002.

CAST OF CHARACTERS

Barbara Albrecht

Senior vice president at NationsBank responsible for managing a new strategy group within the NationsBank Services Company. A former project manager, upon assuming her new role, she immediately contracts with external consultants to chart a "path forward" for the Transaction Services business unit. Transaction Services is a business unit within the NationsBank Services Company.

Tony Alvarez

Tandem marketing representative responsible for the NationsBank account. Tony is a likable guy who wins a major competitive bid. He also provides leadership in developing Tandem's response to the NationsBank engine request for information (RFI).

Bob Betts

Gemini consultant responsible for the infrastructure team. He tells Romaine he is not a technologist and has no previous banking experience. Betts travels to Paris to meet with Romaine during the Gemini country-profiling exercise.

Denny Billings

NationsBank executive vice president responsible for the Model Bank project. He eventually heads up the engine project as well and contracts with Andersen Consulting to assist in the design phase. He tells Romaine he will help him learn the ropes at NationsBank.

Tom Carter

Program manager for major Chase Manhattan project. Carter has a very successful track record in completing high-risk projects successfully and on time. He likes "being where the action is" and is well respected by both senior executives and his direct reports.

Michael Dellano

Chase Manhattan vice president and senior technology strategist. Mike came up through the ranks, starting as a keypunch operator. He believes in the importance of aligning a technology architecture to support corporate goals and provides education classes for senior executives down to system programmers. He will not approve a technology project unless it can be directly tied to a corporate goal. Mike was a external consultant before Chase rehired him. He believes in using consultants for specific projects but doesn't understand why well-paid executives hire consultants every time they need to make a decision.

Richard Edmonds

Technical-architecture consultant working for a Gemini affiliate in the United Kingdom. He is brought in during the last few weeks of the NationsBank engagement with Gemini to help complete the technical-infrastructure plan.

Ben Elders

Gemini partner responsible for a major contract with the Transaction Services line of business at NationsBank. The engagement is to assist in building a new strategy and a new technical-infrastructure plan to support it.

Betsy Fields

Director, NationsBank Strategic Technology Group (STG). The STG group that she oversees is responsible for advising NationsBank executives on new technology directions and investments. While she reports to the president of the services company, her responsibilities extend to the entire NationsBank enterprise. She believes it is important to be perceived as a team player first, before an agent of change. Fields encourages people within her organization to get more involved in business unit activities and begin to demonstrate the added value of the STG within the Services Company.

Dave Gibbons

Andersen Consulting partner responsible for the NationsBank engine project. He recruits Andersen consultants for the project who have a background in mainframe technology because this is the prevalent technology used for the NationsBank's Model Bank program. Model Bank is the program of most importance to NationsBank senior management directing the engine project.

Jerry Guston

Consultant who provides advice and counsel to the head of IBM's Networking Systems line of business. He was considered one of the top networking consultants in the business. At one point in his career, Jerry works for Gartner Group and becomes Will Logan's boss.

Toby Hobson

IBM branch manager in Norfolk, Virginia. He suggests that Romaine, who works for him, set up a meeting with his customer and the chairman of IBM. This sets off an unexpected chain of events.

Alan Johnson

President of the NationsBank Services Company. He runs a large, complex service organization that supports other business units. Al has a reputation for playing favorites with particular consultants and vendors. In spite of changes in the business, he continues to emphasize the importance of maintaining a strategic focus for the engine project.

Kevin Jones

Data center manager for Newport News Shipbuilding. Kevin works for Paul Young, the operations manager. He tells Romaine that Amdahl was meeting with Paul Young.

Jay Kittles

Andersen project manager for the NationsBank engine project. He has a background in banking and understands the importance of real-time electronic access for the future to compete in the emerging e-commerce market. He gradually loses influence on the project and falls out of the graces of Dave Gibbons, the Andersen partner in charge of the project.

Harvey Kraft

Responsible for managing electronic operations for the Transaction Services line of business at NationsBank. He eventually takes over as manager of strategy for the same line of business, replacing Barbara Albrecht. Harvey has a reputation for starting a fire in one place to get things going someplace else.

Joe Levy

Runs his own consulting business. A former IBM executive with World Trade organization, Joe left IBM to help develop a consulting practice for Gartner Group. The consulting practice was developed to complement Gartner's established research service.

Will Logan

Former Gartner Group consultant who joins Steve Romaine in his new company, Informed Technology Decisions. He is technically brilliant but has very strong, almost "religious" views when it comes to technology and refuses to compromise.

Sue Loggins

Attorney who becomes friends with Romaine. After he tells her about his current predicament, she suggests that she leave the bank.

Don Mangrove

A regional manager for the NationsBank Model Bank project, he eventually becomes the senior manager responsible for implementing the engine project. He has a close relationship with Denny Billings and has a reputation of being a good company man.

Peter Miles

Andersen consultant who works for Darlene Wittington in the Integration Services organization of NationsBank. He serves in a liaison role with the engine project. His background is in check processing.

Frank Nichols

As the director of information services for Newport News Shipbuilding, he has been a loyal customer of IBM's for years, but during the late '80s and early '90s Nichols believes that IBM has lost its focus on customer support. He creates a strong management team and is well respected by employees.

Ken Pollack

Andersen Consulting partner responsible for NationsBank Direct Bank initiative. Direct Bank is a program to develop integration with telephone banking with client/server technology.

Vincent Porter

Senior manager within the Strategic Technology Group of NationsBank. He becomes a member of the transaction engine project steering committee. Don also agrees to chair a subcommittee for the engine to create a strategic architecture plan and to keep difficult constituents from various business units in line.

Dan Price

NationsBank employee who works on technology architecture for the Transaction Services line of business. Dan is a former project manager and, while he demonstrates smarts and good instincts, is reluctant to take initiative. Dan is mired down by bank protocol, but eventually takes more initiative.

Sam Ritter

Street-smart NationsBank employee who provides help and guidance to Romaine while working for him. Sam is also very political and ambitious. Romaine suspects that he is attempting to play the right cards to maneuver into a position to eventually replace Romaine as project manager for the transaction engine project.

Larry Rogers

Senior Alltel manager assigned to the NationsBank engine project. He works with Andersen management in developing a request for information (RFI) response for the implementation phase of the engine project.

Steve Romaine

Independent consultant who leaves IBM when he sees opportunity for technology consulting business. Starts Informed Technology Decisions. After several years in a work-for-hire role, becomes senior vice president at NationsBank responsible for technology strategy within the Transaction Services business unit, a division of the NationsBank Services Company. Becomes entangled in conflict with corporate mercenaries.

Jim Schiller

IBM client marketing rep for NationsBank. Former marketing manager in Norfolk, Virginia, where he worked with Romaine.

Walt Shaw

Becomes senior manager at NationsBank responsible for running the Transaction Services division of the Services Company. Walt was with one of the acquired Texas banks, and although his background is in check processing, he brings a fresh perspective to the NationsBank Services Company.

Jack Tooms

A manager from Alltel Information Services who is brought on to the engine project to assume project management responsibilities for the implementation phase.

John Turner

NationsBank manager responsible for the Global Finance software-engineering organization. His high-tech group provides technical support to the Global Finance line of business, which handles major corporate accounts. Turner tells Romaine that he wants to submit a bid for building the new transaction engine.

Brad Wallace

Gartner Group large-systems consultant. Former IBMer who is the self-proclaimed "father of IBM architecture" for mainframes. Wallace is very respected by clients, including Newport News Shipbuilding. He advises clients on future IBM product announcements and recommends that clients "squeeze" vendors to get the best possible price.

Darlene Wittington

Manager responsible for Integration Services business unit within Transaction Services. Integration Services runs NationsBank's back-office systems for processing both checks and electronic financial transactions. While the strategy group for Transaction Services is engaged with consultants to create a "top-down" view, she contracts with another consulting organization to develop a "bottom-up" view.

Charlie Wright

Director of technology for Pitney Bowes. Gives Romaine and Logan their first big break by awarding a technology architecture contract to their new firm, Informed Technology Decisions.

Paul Young

Operations manager for Newport News Shipbuilding. He believes that before a technology solution is procured, one should ask the question "Who do you call if it breaks?" He enjoys hunting.

CHAPTER ONE

GLASTNOST
AT IBM

"Do you know what one of the first visible signs was of the fall of the Roman Empire?"

The question came from one of the sheep in a sea of blue suits and white button-down shirts. His dark brown eyes matched the coffee in his Big Blue mug. It was early morning and I wasn't about to come up with an answer anytime soon. My head felt like a big, heavy medicine ball.

The sheep smiled, and I realized from the sparkle in his eye that he liked straying from the flock. He didn't strike me as one of those typical IBMers who lived for staff meetings. He was a renegade, sporting a paisley tie. I decided I liked him even before he finished answering his own question.

"It was when they started hiring mercenaries to do their fighting for them."

People were still shuffling in as the meeting started. No doubt similar meetings were being held in the numerous IBM facilities spread across the rolling tree-filled hills of Westchester County, New York. My building, 1133 Westchester Avenue, was chock-full of marketing refugees who, like me, had fled from a branch office and the world of measurable objectives. We had retired our bags and were busy instead preparing internal presentations on a thousand ways to look at the same information.

In the early 1990s the search for a new company model to reshape what had become a sleeping elephant was in full swing. There were meetings upon meetings to discuss the need for remodeling IBM and discovering new ways of doing business. So who would we discuss cloning in today's meeting; Proctor and Gamble? Sears and Roebuck? Nah, forget about it, Sears was last time. It was hard keeping track. Some were a stretch, like the time we were told by a consultant that we needed to operate more like Harley Davidson. By now there was a daily parade of consulting firms coming through the doors to render opinions on the advantages and disadvantages of various model alternatives. What next? Unfortunately, there was always a next.

In spite of all the talk on a new model, little changed. The fire drills were beginning to ring hollow. Even the new advertising slogans were sounding out of touch. Senior executives had that slept-in-the-suit kind of look. Except for having to deal with an increasing number of mandates passed down from edgy executives, along with "new, improved" marketing slogans pasted against every inch of free wall space, and the exponential growth in meetings, it was business as usual for most of us. Suits stayed pressed. People left on time. We were oblivious to the seriousness of the problems and what lay ahead.

At one time almost two out of every three dollars spent in technology were spent with IBM.[1] Market share had been slipping for years, but financial measurement ratios, at least the ones important to Wall Street, had remained impressive. How could the company that had surpassed Exxon Corporation in the 1980s as the most profitable U.S. corporation come upon hard times? IBM performance issues had to be temporary. We always bounced back. One or two bad quarters back to back at most. So why all the fuss?

Suddenly my brain punched in. This meeting was different. We had been assembled for an announcement. A decision was being made. The executives were announcing plans to use a significant number of new business partners. Business partners had been used in the past as suppliers, and sometimes as resellers. Today IBM was announcing plans to "supplement" the traditional sales force with a legion of non-IBM salespeople. Was this the first phase of implementing a new model? Was the idea to eventually unload the in-house sales force and sell through dealers? Was it time to lose the suit for a biker jacket?

Potential business partners eager to sell for IBM were already lining up at the trough. They must have thought becoming an IBM sales partner could present tremendous opportunity. After all, Intel and Microsoft had become household names after partnering with IBM as suppliers. Then it hit me. The sheep had been trying to clue me in on an important history lesson about to be repeated.

Welcome to the world of big business. In the 1990s most American corporations went through a significant transition, leading to what many of the experts have called unparalleled economic growth and achievement. They say success always comes at a price. You always pay, sometimes now, sometimes later. This is my story of the 1990s based on experiences and observations working with several major U.S. corporations and the business partners they hired. As these corporations downsized and restructured, significant numbers of traditional employees were replaced with mercenaries. This is a story about paying later.

There have been numerous case studies on the problems IBM encountered in the early 1990s. Of course, most of the case studies were written by consultants. Plenty had weighed in on why IBM lost its shirt, but they missed one important factor—the role of consultants. Not surprisingly, few of the studies adequately described the critical role consultants played in upstaging IBM's leadership with customers. At the same time they were penetrating customers, recommending alternatives to IBM, they were telling IBM management that their problem was in the execution, and that meant employees. Nothing a new leaner, meaner model couldn't fix.

A few years before, it would have been unthinkable. The people running IBM claimed that full employment was there to stay. It was part of the very core of what made us IBM, the safest place in the world—almost as safe as a nuclear bomb shelter, or so we thought. As luck would have it, at about the same time it was announcing new partnerships, IBM was also announcing package deals for employees to leave. At first, employment policy was simply tweaked. In the employee guideline book where it used to state that IBM had a "full employment policy," it now read "full employment objective." Downsizing had to be just around the corner. At first it was called "voluntary separation."

Where do I sign? Not to sound ungrateful to IBM. It was a great training ground and some of my best and happiest working years were during my marketing rep days pedaling IBM gear. The field had changed. In the old days IBM reps called at the highest executive levels in corporate America and maintained strong account control with most major customers. There had been senior reps in my branch office who had degrees from Harvard, MIT, and Princeton. Others were just plain street smart and were successful by applying things like the art of tank warfare to selling computers.

In a sense, IBM senior reps were the original management consultants. They provided advice on business solutions coupled with IBM's comprehensive set of product offerings. At least they were up front about it. If you were surprised when the recommended business solution included an IBM system, you must have just dropped in from another planet. If for some reason something they sold didn't work, they had the power to flood the sky with IBM support teams who would descend on the customer like paratroopers, digging in until the problem was fixed. In those days there was a code of loyalty that permeated the renowned sales force and was reciprocated by IBM management. As noted by D. Quinn Mills and G. Bruce Friesen in *Broken Promises*:

Loyalty at IBM was two-sided: the company was loyal to the employee and the employee to the company. Going far beyond a no-layoff principle, management established a number of policies to encourage trust and pride in IBM. Trusting and proud, they made excellent representatives of the firm, and lifelong IBMers forged enduring bonds with customers. For the company, employee loyalty, much more than a feel-good objective, was the means to a greater end—the sustained competitiveness of IBM.[2]

I was fortunate that the branch manager who originally hired me understood the importance of team. He was an incredible motivator. Everyone within the branch was made to feel important in our success, which is probably why under his leadership we went from a sorry dead last in the Northeast region to number one. He also understood that while everyone was important, no one was more important than the senior sales reps. There was never any question who was in charge, but our branch manager was smart enough to give them slack and let them do their thing, their way.

In my branch office in Connecticut, there were three top-performing senior reps I'll never forget, Honest, Ice, and the General. They were all masters at driving IBM business year after year in the same overtilled territories. Managing sales reps and systems engineers, they orchestrated serialized soap operas in their territories that played out everyday. To be a part of it under their direction provided great training. While they were loyal to IBM and fiercely competitive, each came with a unique set of idiosyncrasies. Honest had been captain of Princeton's basketball team when he was a senior and Bill Bradley was a freshman. They had stayed friends. One day our branch manager met Bradley while he was still in the U.S. Senate, long after he had played out his career in the NBA. He said Bradley went on and on about Honest and how much Honest as team captain had helped him when he was just a frosh at Princeton. Bradley said they still talked all the time. Naturally, Honest had never told any of us. He probably figured we'd start bugging him for tickets to Knicks games. Like he was with Bradley as an underclassman, Honest was helpful to new IBM sales reps, as long as you asked. There was another catch. You had to ask at the right time of day.

One of the first things you were told as a new IBM sales rep was to get in early and park yourself close enough to observe Honest. We were instructed to act as if preoccupied with something else and discreetly watch his every move. "Don't say anything, just watch," we were told. "There's a lot you can learn from seniors." The Princeton Tiger would get in early every morning casting a gargantuan shadow from his six foot, six inch massive frame as he slumbered into the branch. Honest never liked making a grand entrance. It was a *Ripley's Believe It or Not*, for he somehow managed to squeeze his enormous body between two file cabinets, which looked as if they were touching, to get to his desk. In this way he always avoided walking the main thoroughfare that looped by the office of the branch manager, who also liked arriving early. Once seated, Honest would peer at the paper sprawled across his desk before leaving to meet with customers. It was a ritual. Every morning as he started to look through the piles, something would catch his attention; something he had presumably forgotten to do the prior day.

"Oh, . . . fuck me," he would bellow, as he spread his open, oversized hands over a pile, as if he was trying to levitate select pages from the mess. Ramming his fist onto the desk, Honest would make shattering thuds echo across the branch. The thuds would scare everyone in earshot who hadn't been sensitized by hearing it many times before. He would turn his attention to the next pile and repeat again, "Oh, . . . fuck me." Every once in a while his hands extended straight out well beyond the entire desk like a traffic cop facing the morning rush. Traffic stopped.

Honest would begin moving paper from one pile to another in between phone calls and scribbling ineligible notes that he would slam onto one of the piles in utter disgust. There was an unmistakable rhythm, like shooting meaningless foul shots into a basket when you were down by twenty and there was no time left on the clock. He would then get up and leave, still mumbling to himself as he slipped back through the file cabinets and bolted out the door. It was usually still early morning, and most employees were just beginning to arrive. You didn't want to get in his way.

There was not the slightest hint of deception in the man. Honest was honest. But there was something unnerving about him. His large, imposing stature, a mostly quiet presence, save occasional outbursts, bore a curious similarity to Chief in *One Flew Over the Cuckoo's Nest*. I always felt there were mornings when he was ready to snap. Something on that desk, or the wrong comment at the wrong time of day, especially from a sales trainee, and he probably would have lifted the entire desk, piles and all, and thrown it through a wall. If he came back to the office later in the day, it was like talking to a different person. He was calm, collected, and when asked, more than willing to provide advice and assistance. It was as if his desk, with all the piles, had been swallowed up by the Bermuda Triangle.

Ice rarely set foot in the office. He was a lone wolf who pioneered the original remote-worker concept. Eventually IBM would adopt remote working for most of what was left of the sales force in an effort to further reduce office costs. I doubt that had anything to do with Ice's motivation to minimize time in the branch. Every once in a while, Ice would make a cameo appearance at an IBM function, usually to collect a recognition award for helping the branch manager make his quarterly numbers. He would win lots of other awards, too, but apparently they didn't warrant a personal appearance. "I don't think he is here today. . . . At least, I haven't seen him . . . yet. . . . We'll have to mail it to him." Ice kept blowing his own numbers away, so no one really cared that he rarely showed up. Certainly, Ice didn't care what anyone at IBM thought. His focus was maximizing commissions and that meant customer face time, not hanging out with the suits. It was a good thing he didn't care about the suits. The feeling was mutual. More than once I heard his marketing manager say, "Ice is one hell of a rep, the best I have, but not the kind of guy I'd ever invite home for dinner with the wife and family."

And then there was the General. They say George S. Patton thought he was reincarnated. He was, as a sales rep for IBM. The General led the largest number of sales personnel and systems engineers in our office, supporting a defense contractor. Not because he had the largest account, but because the General even approached resource allocation like war. He was constantly maneuvering for advantage while keeping his superiors in check. Most seemed intimidated by his aggressive style for conducting business. Whereas Honest looked big, tough, and had his regular morning outbursts, he harbored a kind, gentle spirit buried underneath. The General, on the other hand, was a pit bull through and through.

The General was always in somebody's face demanding more of something for his territory. Whether it was systems engineers, sales trainees, or loaner equipment for "show and tell" pilots, the need was always immediate, before he and the rest of his team fell victim to a barrage of enemy incoming. Implicit in these scare tactics was an assumption that if anything happened to him, the rest of IBM would come to a screeching halt. Everybody was expendable, except the General. He held prebriefings and debriefings surrounding every sales call. New hires were often raked over the coals, but these meetings proved to be great training ground. They were instrumental for planning the next customer campaign, as well as building a team of stiff upper lips terrified of ever screwing up.

He irreverently called his customer "the Bible account." The General used to say he had a cast of characters from both the Old and the New Testament working with him. He had to deal with an extremely technical IBM support team straight from the Tower of Babel. There was a "Lazarus," an

IBM systems engineer who took long sick leaves and then would come back unexpectedly for a day or two before calling in sick again. You could place a bet in the office pool on what days you thought she might show up. There was the "Prodigal Son" who had left IBM to go to law school. He quit after a year and was uncharacteristically invited by our branch manager to return. "Here he comes," the General would say, "time to roast the fattest calf." The General would also complain that he had to spread around the loaves and fishes to "all those reps that keep eating off my plate." As a sales trainee or a systems engineer, you were safe because from the General's point of view, you were a "free" resource. When you became a qualified sales rep, you became a liability. The General didn't like splitting commission checks. It was best for a sales trainee to learn what he could while working with the General before qualifying, and then strike out for a different territory. That's what I did. Eating off the General's plate and putting up with all his grief required pretty thick skin.

A problem with the General, besides his insatiable need for additional free resources and incessant belligerence, was a case of self-induced hypertension. He would order two cups of coffee at a time, both for himself. In those days before a "no smoking" policy, he was constantly coughing up exhaust from his cigarettes, like an overheated diesel. There were rings of smoke in his trail. More than a few minutes in a stationary position and it appeared as if a bank of fog had settled around him. The years of bad vices resonated through his thick, raspy bark. He was always agitated. The rest of us knew it was just a matter of time.

One day he and one of the junior sales reps on the account had a meeting with the director of information services for the contractor. They were to meet at the customer location and planned to arrive separately. Calling in a few minutes after the meeting started, the General informed the customer that he had had a heart attack and was in the hospital. He told the customer not to worry. He was working on being released and would be there shortly, apologizing for being late. The junior rep said the customer sat as if in a trance for several minutes before he could speak. Old Blood and Guts eventually did show up for the meeting, against the advice of hospital personnel who wanted to admit him for further tests. It wasn't long before he was back in the office chugging coffee and lighting smokes as if nothing had happened.

Needless to say, the senior reps in the office where I was originally assigned had unique styles, and they were all very effective. They were making very good money while staying in one place, avoiding the relocation and corporate intrigue associated with a management career in IBM, the "I've Been Moved" company. While managers came and went, senior reps hung on to established relationships with top customer executives. These reps were real pros who would study the annual sales plan and pick it apart. In a good year they could make as much money as some of the senior executives running IBM divisions. I guess that stuck in some people's craw. Long before the officially announced voluntary separation programs, the sales plan changed with potential commissions substantially reduced. Many of the best and most seasoned salespeople began to strike out on new careers—many with consultant agencies and competitive vendor companies. Early downsizing efforts didn't pry loose the dead wood. It accelerated the attrition of the risk-taking, high-achiever types. Honest, Ice, and the General were among the first wave out the door.

You could argue the chicken or egg thing, but by the end of the 1980s, as consultants were becoming more prestigious and accepted, the reps that stuck it out in IBM often found themselves relegated to calling on purchasing agents and technicians. At the same time, relatively obscure IBM executives were now gaining a degree of celebrity status. Keynote speaking engagements at prestigious consultant conferences and IBM executive sound bites in the media were becoming the norm. Executives started "bouncing" strategy ideas off of industry analysts and soliciting their input on a more regular basis. The head of IBM's Networking Systems line of business formed an advisory committee of analysts. The analysts were "prebriefed" on future business plans. Contracts with consultants to assist with everything from corporate strategy to product announcements became more commonplace throughout the company.

Industry analysts had argued for years that IBM had become too entrenched and that more of an external focus was needed. They were absolutely right. There is a point, however, to maintaining a degree of confidentiality with regard to competitively sensitive information. The timing for discussing new products and strategies is critical. So is having the troops prepared in advance to maximize a concerted marketing blitz. Instead, consultants were considered a new, improved channel in providing IBM information to customers. A new spirit of openness prevailed— Glasnost at Big Blue. There was one small problem. Consultants were positioned to be first at spilling the beans on new product information through prebriefing sessions with executives. The IBM sales reps were finding themselves left in the dark, waiting for new product information to trickle down. This neutralized their effectiveness across IBM's major accounts.

As an IBM marketing manager, I could remember meeting with my customer to discuss the latest product announcements. They knew more about it than I did. Until the day of the official announcement, this information was to be treated by IBM personnel as confidential and restricted.

When I asked how they knew, the technology operations manager said, "Gartner told us about this weeks ago." He added, "Their assessment was mixed." He was being polite. Gartner Group was considered one of the most prestigious consulting research firms in the technology industry, and they were becoming increasingly harsher in their criticism of IBM.

While the focus was primarily research and writing reports, the Gartner Group often called themselves the undisputed leaders in technology. By the beginning of the 1990s, they had established an impressive list of followers. A *Barrons* report stated that forty-five of the fifty largest U.S. companies purchased Gartner Group reports on a regular basis.[3] Revenue was estimated at about $100 million. The firm was started in 1979 by an ex-IBMer named Gideon Gartner, with the help of $675,000 in venture capital. In 1988, with net income of approximately $15 million, Gideon sold his company to the advertising conglomerate Saatchi and Saatchi PLC for $90 million.[4] Gartner has been bought and sold several times since, eventually becoming Gartner Inc. In its earliest days, Gartner Group was primarily watching and reporting on IBM.

It was after leaving the field and taking a staff job in White Plains, New York, that I first learned about IBM "prebriefing" large numbers of consultants such as Gartner Group prior to making formal product announcements. It had been going on for years. Very often IBM would schedule briefings and conference calls for consultants to "Q and A" with development managers prior to making information on new products available to customers. Consultants were given all the goods.

The IBM marketing personnel, on the other hand, almost always had to rely on second-hand product information as it dribbled down through the complex bureaucratic structure of the marketing organization. It was estimated that in the late 1980s, there were as many as seventeen layers of management separating the sales rep from the chairman. This structure gave consultants a significant advantage over sales reps in communicating with IBM executives, understanding new product details, and relaying this information to customers in a timely manner. In many cases, consultants, not IBM, became the best source of new IBM product information for customers. IBM reps were increasingly left delivering yesterday's news.

At one time the IBM sales rep was highly respected, but not anymore. Conventional wisdom suggested that they had become complacent order takers. Reps became fodder for IBM internal jokes. Why do IBM sales reps look alike? They have to fit in the same size suit—empty. How do IBM sales reps make love? The same way they sell computers—they keep telling you how good it's gonna be, but never close the deal. As an IBM product manager, why waste energy on them? Yours was just one of the many products reps were responsible for hawking to customers. Wasn't it a better use of your time talking with consultant "experts" who specialized in technologies and products of mutual interest? If you could turn a consultant on to your product, wouldn't that have more credibility with customers than hearing it from a sales rep?

Unfortunately for IBM, consultants sometimes put a negative spin on the information they passed on from product managers to customers. At one point in the early 1990s, senior executives from the large-systems group became very upset about negative Gartner Group reports concerning IBM-flagship mainframe products. How could they do this after all those IBM briefings with the free lunch included? It was compounding problems for a division that had seen better days but still generated the lion's share of profit. The large-systems group tried to banish Gartner from IBM briefings. It was too little, too late.

Gartner hired many knowledgeable ex-IBMers. What they didn't know, they apparently knew how to find. Making matters worse, other consulting groups were also taking a more negative view of IBM. Thanks in large part to the consultants, IBM warts were immediately made visible to both customers and IBM competitors. The floodgates had been opened. There was no stopping Glasnost now. As IBM's dominant market position began eroding at an accelerating rate, consulting groups such as Gartner, which had originally made it as "IBM watchers," quickly adjusted. They became more generic, "market watchers." IBM was no longer separate from the rest of the "BUNCH."[5]

I decided to follow the flood and become one of the mercenaries. The 1990s were about cost cutting, and sales was a great place to get rid of fat. Especially with the Internet on the horizon, we were being told that products could practically sell themselves. It was a time to low key my IBM sales background and look for higher ground. At first I thought a desk job in White Plains was high enough. IBM's problems were supposed to be only temporary. Now even the staffers were at risk.

Single with no attachments and what most of my managers called insubordinate tendencies that I preferred to call an entrepreneurial spirit, I was ready to try something else. There was one obvious alternative. Initiating conversations with several friends, some in IBM and some in consulting firms, I talked up the idea of starting a new consulting company. Consulting was one of the fastest growing professions. My experiences convinced me that consulting was the best place to hide while corporate America was "restructuring" and "downsizing."

The nice thing about consulting is that anyone can become one. It took a year of intensive training to qualify as an IBM sales rep. To practice as a consultant, all I had to do was claim that I was one. No training, no experience, no bar exam required. The other major advantage was the lack of accountability. If, after all the bad advice they had given IBM, consultants continued to be solicited for more advice, there had to be little to no downside risk. It wasn't you who made the decision. If corporate managers got the credit when things went well, they also took the fall when things didn't go as planned. After all, the corporate manager made the decision to hire the consultant. Whether it was good advice or bad, the consultant adviser got paid.

Of course, everybody liked the idea of a new consulting company and said they would be interested in joining, as long as I could guarantee a reasonable income, benefits, and a piece of the company. Calling on lines I remembered from school, I tried in a polite way to point out things like: "Risk and return are positively correlated." "Security comes with employment." "Ownership brings different sets of obligations and rewards." In other words, if you want to partner with me, you've got to put your ass on the line, too.

With no early takers, I decided to absorb all the risk myself and start my own business, Informed Technology Decisions Inc., incorporated in September 1992. Shortly after starting the business, Will Logan, one of the consultants I knew from Gartner Group, claimed he was ready for a change and was interested in coming on board. We had been talking for some time about risk and return. While Will said he wanted to help share the risk, he had heavy financial obligations. He flirted with the idea of leaving Gartner Group, but seemed to get cold feet at the last minute. Logan probably wouldn't have done it if his employer didn't help by informing him that it was time for a new career. He and his boss had been at loggerheads for some time.

Due to his immediate need for cash, Logan and I made an agreement that I would start out by paying him a salary as an employee. If things worked out, he would eventually be given a piece of the business. At the present time that meant a part of my desk, and use of my PC and printer.

In my mind, Logan's Gartner Group background could be a real plus. There was much I could learn. He had a great brain, but was often difficult to comprehend. English was frequently discarded in favor of his first language—technospeak.

Logan had all the trappings of a professional consultant specializing in technology. He carried a beat-up brown leather bag over his shoulder that made him slump forward. He would dump most of the contents whenever he needed something. His bag was bloated by a heavy, early-generation "laptop" computer and all its peripherals. He also carried trade rags and crumpled up note paper, half detached from a thick spiral pad, with the spiral dangling away from the pad, placing anyone in his path in danger. His large brown eyes switched back and forth from a cool detachment to fiery resolve for no apparent reason. Like the General, he, too, was a caffeine and nicotine junkie. There was always a cup or a butt in Logan's grasp. In no smoking facilities, it was usually the cup, but not always. He had rusty brown hair covering most of his face and head. He talked in cipher more than he listened.

"How long you have the beard?" I asked.

"Since I started consulting. It gives you more credibility. Credibility can mean higher billing rates."

Logan added that he thought I should grow one as well. "If nothing else, it would be an ice breaker. They'll ask if we're the Smith Brothers," he said.

Our first official act was to evaluate other consulting firms to determine our best niche and ways we could differentiate our offerings. Based on Logan's knowledge and some additional research, we concluded there were four distinct types of firms. Little did I know that within the next few years I would become intimately familiar with the strengths and weaknesses of each type of consulting. I would also experience firsthand the curious dynamics between consultants and the corporate clients who hire them. As Logan explained, "customer" was a term used by vendors. For consultants, they were to be called "clients."

As I had already learned, consultants often talked about their experience based on previous engagements with major corporate clients. They never mentioned the names of the "clients." This was held confidentially, for the benefit of the clients, according to Logan.

"But as long as you do good work, wouldn't you want to use them as a reference?" I asked.

"It could impact their competitive advantage if you tell too much and no client wants to be barraged by lots of calls. You can always get by saying, 'a large New York retail bank . . .'" was Logan's reply.

Logan may have been right about the reason for keeping client names secret, but I couldn't help but wonder if there was more to it than protecting the client. Didn't it give the consultants a chance to fudge a bit on accomplishments? If projects with clients were a succession of failures, it didn't really matter—none of the new prospects would know. People tended not to check references anyway. Even if you wanted to, where did you start if all you knew was that the last job was with a "large retail bank"? I think Logan was having doubts about whether or not I would cut it as a consultant. He decided to take it slow and give me the "101" class on evaluating the field of consultancy.

The first and most prestigious were the *management consultants* who specialized in strategy and were a favorite with senior-level executives. McKinsey & Company was best known and most successful. I remembered how when I was an IBM sales rep my customers would shake in their boots when upper management hired the consultants from McKinsey. These were the high-level visionaries who dealt in macroconcepts. As a result, strategy projects were increasingly emphasizing analysis of internal operations, which always seemed to end up with recommended cutbacks. Heads usually rolled. Stocks went up.

There were also *process consultants* who created models that could be applied across various kinds of businesses. The Monitor Company, affiliated with Michael Porter of the Harvard Business School, was an example of a process-based consulting firm. Michael Porter was considered a leading authority on competitive differentiation. Helping clients develop competitive strategy was their primary differentiator from other consulting firms. Process consultants generally had a specific expertise they used as the hook. If it wasn't competitive differentiation, it might be "business process reengineering," which was a fancy way of saying "changing the way you do business"—the mechanics behind the work of creating a new product or distributing it to customers. Consultants could make changing a tire sound like a class in calculus.

Vertical-industry consultants were the third category. These firms provided consulting and integration services based on specific industry requirements. This was the Andersen Consulting approach. They provided expertise in industries such as retail, manufacturing, finance, and telecommunications. In addition to consulting advice, they built technology systems tailored for each industry. They partnered with technology integrators to build the systems and to tie all the component parts together. It was one-stop shopping, including everything from recommendation through implementation.

The fourth area fell into the *research analyst* category of consultants. They specialized in specific industries and watched for trends and developed projections. Gartner Group was a prime example, and Logan understood their approach from firsthand experience. He gave me an earful on his former employer. Given our small body count, analysis was probably an area where we could play best. We'd just have to figure out how to do it differently from the others, or at least make it sound that way.

Gartner's area of expertise was technology. Gartner published a series of monthly reports that evaluated new technologies and analyzed technology vendors, helping clients pick "strategic partners" from a crowded field. Reports were categorized by subject areas such as networking, large systems, midrange systems, and PC office-based systems. Research services were formed to cover these kinds of topics and the number of research services continued to grow as topic areas were sliced into smaller pieces.

The Gartner consultants responsible for managing each of these individual research service areas often had very distinct points of view regarding technology. According to Logan, they almost always had an exaggerated view of the importance for the particular area of technology they represented. "Not to mention an inflated opinion of themselves," he added. In the early 1990s, for a typical client trying to put it all together, it meant purchasing six or more services from Gartner Group, each for an annual fee of approximately $15,000. Like everything else, the rate would increase over time. Logan explained that while it might not sound like much, research became an important foot in the door for selling other programs and services.

An article in *Business Week* had once suggested that Gartner Group was "cashing in on the computer confusion."[6] The more complex computers became, the more services like those provided by Gartner were needed. After reading many of their reports and having conversations with Logan and others, I was convinced Gartner's approach to advising clients could actually help increase confusion. The reports were very specialized based on various technology topics and required someone with specific skills in these areas to understand them. In effect, this approach was helping to drive technology decision making further down in the organization. Gartner seemed to thrive on controversy. If there were recommended solutions, they were in granular pieces, carefully buried within the monthly reams of research documents. Synthesizing this fragmented approach to information dissemination and attempting to come up with a complete solution would mean getting technical specialists from different areas to communicate together and sorting through the various cause and effect issues. Sounded like more work for consultants to me. Logan agreed.

"They're using a classic divide-and-conquer strategy," I said.

"It's all a matter of driving more business. Consulting is about getting the next contract and increasing client dependence."

Gartner Group consultants also functioned like meteorologists. They would give probabilities as to the success of vendors in introducing new products and gaining market share. They were actually very good at it, or at least so they claimed. An internal audit estimated an 88 percent rate of accuracy in forecasted projections.[7] Sometimes when they missed, they missed big. When I asked Logan about this, he went into a dissertation.

"Let's say you're a corporate client who just installed a product from vendor X. I tell you that there is a 65 percent probability that vendor X will have only 30 percent market share in five years as opposed to vendor Y, which I project will have 50 percent. Let's even assume I'm right. Does this mean you rip out the vendor X product and replace with a product from vendor Y?"

Obviously my new associate still harbored strong feelings about his former employer. Prior to joining Gartner, Will Logan held an operations management position with a large insurance company. Unfortunately, he could never quite divorce himself from a real-world orientation. In spite of some of these kinds of issues, we both recognized that Gartner was one of the best when it came to technology research and vendor analysis. By now there were plenty of others trying to imitate their success. We would have to carve out a different niche. Logan insisted that he didn't want to compete head-on with his former employer. "That would be suicide," he believed. It was a growth industry, and there had to be a little room in there, in spite of all the middle managers leaving corporations and putting up their own shingles. "I think people are begging for practical, real-world solutions. They need to be educated so they can make more intelligent decisions about technology." Logan was getting worked up.

While I didn't spend much time thinking about it, a concern did arise briefly from some hidden abyss of my subconscious. Making this a successful business would require a different focus than launching a crusade. I would have to keep reminding Logan, who always seemed ready to suit up and charge.

With all the different kinds of consulting firms running around, the corporate technology organizations were under assault. In many companies there was a view that the technology group just wasn't getting it done. They were the mainframe bigots who were holding everybody back from new technology solutions. The new PC-based solutions would require a whole different set of skills. Employees were out, consultants in.

Now Logan had me going. "So why not focus on education and skills transfer?" Continuing after a pregnant pause, I asked, "What if we worked to help internal technology organizations regain credibility? Isn't it usually more effective in the long run to use your own people?"

At one point I remember Will suggesting half jokingly that if we were too successful at the skills transfer stuff, we could put ourselves out of business. I reminded him that first we had to get *into* business. This kind of logic was not atypical for a consultant. Educating the client could reduce dependency on consultants and impede the ability to secure future contracts. If, as Logan suggested, client dependency was a major goal, then skills transfer was to be avoided. From Logan's point of view, for the typical consultant, knowledge and expertise were to be carefully guarded. Information was to be shared very sparingly, and only one small nugget at a time when substantial fees were involved. Still, we both agreed that by offering skills transfer we could differentiate ourselves from other consulting firms.

"You know what's interesting?" I asked. "Lots of times there are different consultants working in the same company . . . all with a different mandate from a different group. I'll bet they rarely share information."

"Got that right," said Logan. "Different groups within the company are hiring them, and each group has its own agenda. So do each of the consultants. There is no incentive to share anything. The more divided a company is, the more consultants are needed."

What good is it spending all kinds of money on management consultants for strategy when the integrators who are going to build new solutions are on a different page? Lots of times they don't understand the business needs, only technology, and how do people responsible for the business needs and who don't understand technology make sure the integrators are doing the right thing?

We stumbled onto our own little niche, or at least so we thought: analysis that provided real-world results. Either I was completely misinformed, or there weren't too many people providing it. We would focus on specific companies and build a plan to convert business needs into technology solutions. At the same time, we would provide education on technology. Details still needed to be worked out, but we were ready to test the concept. Like all consultants, we'd refine it as we learned on the fly. And so we launched what we wanted to think was a noble cause.

One of my major roles was closing sales. Even consultants have to sell. I started by calling on companies where I had developed relationships over the years. There were several false starts. Many of my customers from my IBM-selling days seemed to have a problem getting comfortable with me in a new role as a consultant. I tried to make the argument that when I was a sales rep for IBM I was also a consultant, trying to understand their business and solve their business problems. Selling without a recognizable name like IBM behind you was a new experience and a little humbling. It also became obvious we needed to get much more specific in what we could offer and maybe not try and solve all the world's problems in one day.

The first real break came at Pitney Bowes late in 1992. They were the worldwide leader in mailing systems and had reported over $3.3 billion in revenue at the close of the previous year.[8] While they were moving into new markets and producing new, innovative software-based products that could exploit the "Web" for mail distribution, much of their revenue was still being generated from rental fees for postage meters that continued to be a thriving annuity stream. Pitney Bowes was faster to recognize the potential of the Internet, commonly called the Web, than most consultants and consultant wanna-bees, like me. At one time IBM enjoyed a similar advantage as the dominant leader in the computer business, with a high proportion of income generated from monthly customer payments. Products used by customers were still maintained as assets on IBM's books. Like Pitney Bowes, IBM had enjoyed years of a fairly predictable income stream. Reps could concentrate on generating new business while the old kept pumping.

It was another of those areas where the people running IBM miscalculated. IBM had encouraged customers to buy versus rent because management wanted a quick influx of cash. They wanted to fund an expansion program the likes of which the corporate world had never seen. Management was planning on hiring lots more people and building lots of new facilities. This expansion program was based on growth projections. Business as usual and breaking little sweat, IBM could expect compound double-digit revenue growth, year after year, with no end in sight.

IBM management was not alone in its optimistic projections, thinking that revenue generation was on accelerated autopilot. In 1979 Gideon Gartner had predicted that IBM would double in size by 1983.[9] Other consultants were equally optimistic. Why so bullish? It was all in the strategy. Now IBM was initiating another bold, strategic move. It was going to outspend the competition into submission with increased production capacity, faster speed to market, and more feet on the street. Not more senior rep types, just feet. Maybe if they had been a little more humble, a little more like Pitney Bowes. . . .

Nobody, not even the industry sages, anticipated the potential downside. As suggested in *Broken Promises*, when IBM rented to customers, its eyes and ears were inside the customer's business: "What almost no one saw at the time was that the switch from rentals to purchases damaged IBM's relationship with its customers."[10] Customers could now be more flexible in swapping out IBM for plug compatibles or other products from other vendors. As a former IBMer, you couldn't think about this stuff too much. It drove you crazy. To paraphrase Satchel Paige, one of the greatest pitchers of all time, it was time to stop looking back at my former employer and to concentrate on the opportunity at hand.[11]

As a new IBM marketing rep, I had worked briefly on the Pitney Bowes account. I contacted a financial guy I had known while working there who suggested that we call on one of the newer technology managers. The new technology manager had come out of the finance side of the business and, according to my contact, was considered a rising star in the company. With my new business colleague, I met with the tech manager at Pitney Bowes. His name was Charlie Wright, and he was a regular kind of guy. Charlie's office had a nautical atmosphere, one floor up from where the postage meter systems were manufactured. I remember him having the kind of piercingly dark, unblinking eyes that could shoot holes through sales reps, consultants, or anybody else who didn't know when to shut up and take notes. He sat politely for a while as we took turns discussing potential areas where we could help him in his new role, hoping to generate some interest.

Charlie finally cut in, "Do you guys know anything about architecture?" Of course we said we did. That was what our new business was all about, we told him. The great thing about a new company is that you can be flexible. Actually, technical architecture was about mapping a plan. This was not too far from turning business requirements into technology solutions.

It used to be a defacto thing that when you bought a system from Digital, Wang, or IBM, you also got architecture. Think of it as you would in the construction of a house. Before the builder can build, he needs a blueprint from the architect. Imagine building without a blueprint. You could have plumbing running through the middle of the living room or staircases poking through the roof. In the old computer days, everything usually worked pretty well together because it came from one vendor. All hardware and software was built to optimize the inherent capabilities of the underlying system. It was a prefab. This all changed with *open systems*, a great panacea for consultants.

Vendors complying with open-systems standards agreed to publish product specifications and to cooperate with other vendors in developing common industry standards. In theory, this would make products from different vendors compatible and interchangeable. Standards would be set by committee as opposed to the market-leading vendor. Consultants argued that open systems would expand options for customers and increase vendor competition, ultimately reducing costs. The reality was that most vendors didn't share things that they felt gave them competitive advantage. What it really did was force acceptance of the lowest common denominator, not the best or most advanced technology. It was the socialism of the technology business.

There was another major glitch to open systems—the inherent support issues associated with a multivendor environment. Publishing specs and meeting standards at only the most superficial of levels did not mean that products were now compatible, as many customers were finding out the hard way. It was up to the customer to figure out how to make it all work. When there was a problem, the network vendor might blame the software. The software vendor blames the hardware. The hardware vendor blames both the network and the software. As one of my IBM customers once said concerning multivendor open systems, "So who do I call when it breaks?" The same customer had also made another interesting point: "'Open' by definition is not secure," he said. "We need to be careful where we apply this stuff." He never would have made it as a consultant.

Consultants could play many roles in an open-systems environment. Confusion and complexity in technology were approaching a new crescendo. Lots of decisions needed to be made. Most customers concluded that they needed help sorting through the chaos and making things operational. Technology decision making became an industry of its own. "You could do this, but then again, you could do that. . . ." More and more customers were calling consultants—before, during, and after it broke. There was the initial needs assessment, vendor analysis, recommendations, implementation, integration, project management, and vendor coordination. Best of all, there was almost always a need for fix-it strategies with ongoing support requirements. Who better than an "independent" and "objective" third party to manage all these various activities and to keep everybody else honest?

As consultants, we could bill by the hour for each of these time-consuming activities. No wonder members of my new profession were recommending open-systems solutions for just about everything. It was the cost-saving alternative to the IBM-centralized mainframe. Now, how were open systems going to save money for the customer, I mean client, when all the decentralized support costs for all those distributed employee workstations, servers, and networks were added in? Not to mention consulting fees.

It should be pointed out that there were some very important benefits to open systems. There would not have been an Internet revolution without it, but even the Internet was not based on the best or most efficient technologies available at the time. The Internet standards, or rules of the road, that were eventually adopted were the ones most of the major vendors would agree to use, based on consensus. Almost all agreed, with a few exceptions, like IBM, which continued to fight it for years. They had the most market share to lose, and decided playing it safe meant resisting change. In spite of its acceptance, open systems in the corporate environment needed some controls to make sure all the parts would work together without breaking the bank. It was not as simple as mix and match, plug and play. There were only so many different vendor products, open or nonopen, that a support staff could handle. For business people, this was intuitively obvious. Unfortunately many of the business-manager types were overwhelmed by the new technology and decided to take a backseat to the geeks. Corporate America was becoming one big test lab for new products. For the geeks, it was great fun.

An architecture plan could be the answer for restoring some common sense. It could spell out corporate guidelines for technology: which products worked best together and which were merely high-tech toys to be avoided for business operations. It could also act as the translation dictionary, helping the business strategist and the technical integrator communicate. Architecture, however, didn't represent the large-dollar opportunities associated with either strategy consulting or integration work. Because many customers were now saying they needed it, many consultants claimed to provide it. In lots of cases, architecture was a prerequisite for getting the business. Most consulting firms did as little as possible in technical-architecture planning as they maneuvered themselves into areas where they had more experience and in what they believed would represent larger business opportunity. Both Logan and I saw this as an opportunity for us. It was a place where we could potentially build some unique expertise. First we'd have to figure out a way to cut through all the noise.

Architecture was fast becoming one of the most misused words in the technology industry. It was being applied to describe everything from the inside guts of a hardware product to a geographical map of technology facilities. William Safire could do a job on it in his weekly article in the Sunday *New York Times Magazine* section "On Language." There was no incentive to clear up the misunderstanding. Ignorance is bliss. Client ignorance for a consultant is blissful payola.

We told Charlie that we had both had experience in architecture, me at IBM and my partner at Gartner Group. For me it was a bit of a stretch, but you've got to start somewhere, I thought. Excusing himself, Charlie left the office to ask his secretary to get something. He returned with a document and suggested we both take a look. With a quick flip of the wrist, it spiraled across the table, landing directly in front of me. It was an architecture document created by my business associate's former employer, Gartner Group. In addition to the successful research subscription business, Gartner was also trying to get into the customized onsite-consulting business.

Charlie expressed his frustration with the document. "This was something we did in the past that fell short of expectations," he said. The document was in two sections. The first was written by his management team regarding the current business and technical environment at Pitney Bowes. The second part came exclusively from Gartner Group. Referring to the second part, he said, "We paid a lot of money and got a bunch of diagrams and writing that have nothing to do with our business. I don't think they ever read the first part we gave them." We left the meeting telling him we would prepare a proposal, taking a completely different approach.

When the elevator door closed behind us, I turned to Will and said, "Looked like boiler plate stuff to me."

"It was . . . and lots of it was taken from industry research and diagrams I created when I was with them . . . and I never set a foot in Pitney Bowes," he said.

Will pointed out that the bulk of the material was available within Gartner research notes. He added that this material focused on future technology trends and was obviously not business specific. Like me, he a had a hot-blooded Irish temperament that seemed to be busting out.

After several preliminary meetings with Charlie's key lieutenants, a final meeting was scheduled with a group that would comprise the "architecture committee." They came from different parts of the business, but were mostly technology folks. I thought this could be the deal closer. We were forewarned that some of the committee members had relationships with other consulting firms. It was sounding like each group had hired its own consultants for furthering its own cause. So much for all the talk about objectivity and the independent consultant view. If we won the contract, Charlie told us part of our role would be to resolve conflict between the various groups. Nothing like a little politics to keep the fire in the belly. One of Charlie's lieutenants suggested that we come prepared for lots of hard-hitting questions.

Things seemed to start out pretty well. There were introductory remarks from Charlie, and one of the guys who would have the day-to-day interface responsibility with us also talked about the recommended approach. They both said they liked the idea of working jointly with us to create one fluid report that discussed technology in a business framework. I talked about different aspects of the proposal. The floor was opened for questions. A couple fast balls were followed by a few curves, but we seemed to be holding our own.

During the question and answer period, Charlie expressed a personal view regarding his preference for one networking product over another. I noticed Will, who was sitting next to me, lunge forward in his chair. At one time he had mentioned that he was a Vietnam veteran and had received the purple heart. He started to get a crazed look in his eyes, similar to the Mel Gibson look in the *Lethal Weapon* series of movies. Gibson played a cop with a death wish that seemed to be a by-product of his Vietnam experience. He would occasionally whack out, scaring everybody, including his police partner, played by Danny Glover, who perpetually retorted, "I'm getting too old for this shit." Charlie was still talking when Will broke into the conversation with a loud, emotional outburst. "That would be a big mistake. It's a dead technology." There was a suspended moment of gut-wrenching silence.

So here we were trying to close the sale. The room had ten to fifteen managers who were either peers or worked for Charlie. The topic of discussion seemed to be only tangentially important, something we could have discussed later behind closed doors. Instead, we had just created a shoot out at the OK Corral with our executive sponsor. Needless to say, Charlie Wright wasn't about to back down. I found out later Charlie liked to hunt and was known as a pretty good marksman by some of the Pitney guys who belonged to his lodge. This was a showdown.

As Charlie began to raise his voice in response, I leaned across the table, making sweeping hand and facial gestures, attempting to discourage Will from continuing. He must have been the only person in the meeting who didn't notice. He interrupted again with further technology babble resonating through the room. I resorted to a swift kick under the table, landing my foot on what felt like the side of his shin. Not even a wince. We had stumbled onto one of those technology topics that he viewed as religious, and there was no turning back. The rest of the world would be suspended until his points were put completely across.

The barbs back and forth continued until I was finally able to get some airtime, suggesting that we take a ten-minute coffee break. My partner stormed out of the room. No one knew quite what to say. Charlie rose from his seat with a scowl, jolting the table as he pushed his chair flush against it. It was really important to grab Will alone, get him back on track, or at least to shut up. I was hoping that we had not already blown the sale. I walked through the meeting room doorway and strutted down the hall, attempting to look unshaken.

Naturally, I found him outside the building puffing his lungs away. I had to bite my tongue before I could speak. His fat, crooked fingers with splintered, yellow nails squeezed at the cigarette hanging from his bearded face. It was hard to comprehend how the mouth that was booming with sound a few minutes ago was hardly visible behind his dense crop of thick red facial hair. As I approached, he threw his cigarette butt to the ground and began grinding it with the tip of his shoe. A fresh butt was shoved through the beard till it stuck. It took several sweeps of the hand to ignite his match. Logan, who was lucky he didn't torch his beard, interrupted my first attempt to speak. Cracking emotion was still in his voice.

"He's dead wrong."

"Let me ask you this. . . . Would you rather make the sale or make your damn point?"

"Make my point."

Logan was definitely a computer research analyst. I realized for the first time that the odds of this business affiliation working long term were remote at best. Right now the important thing was damage control. I needed to calm him down and get both of us back to the meeting. It took a few minutes, but he eventually switched personalities again, reverting to the detached Will Logan. Later I asked him about the kick under the table. He claimed he never felt it. Hope I didn't kick somebody else.

Somehow, we still managed to get the contract. Maybe our bargain-based pricing strategy had something to do with it. It was easy for me to rationalize that a new business had to build references for future business, even if that reference was simply "a large manufacturer of postage meter systems." If it meant reducing charges on the first couple contracts, so be it. At this point I was just glad we had gotten the business. While it may not have been the case for Logan, for me the Pitney Bowes experience provided on-the-job training as a consultant. Not a bad deal from a consultant point of view. It was a great way to close out 1992 and begin the new year.

In the back of my mind I could no longer ignore that Will Logan for all his strengths as a technical consultant also came with some heavy baggage. In his previous life as a trusted Gartner Group consultant, he was considered a sage for the latest technical revolution. He was used to walking into a client location with instant credibility. He could speak extemporaneously while the client hung on every word, often taking copious notes and begging for more. Gartner guaranteed a regular paycheck every two weeks. For this compensation and additional bonuses, it was as if consultants were expected to perform on stage as opposed to providing advice. I suppose the more outrageous the act, the more brilliant the audience felt the consultant had to be.

If he wanted to be successful with our newly created Informed Technology Decisions, and believe me I badly wanted him to be for the sake of both of us, he would have to prove himself to clients all over again. Gartner had a one-size-fits-all approach with its research notes that could be sold like a retail product to most corporations with no alterations required. We didn't have a tangible product that could be reproduced— we were attempting to help companies tailor the technology plan to meet their specific business requirements. It would take time. This would be a tough sale in an environment where many technology organizations were being downsized and many company employees were busy looking over their shoulders. The new wave of technology was compounding problems from a support-and-maintenance standpoint. I was convinced the labor costs could be higher than the technology itself. Yet everyone seemed willing to accept the simple solution and jump on the new technology bandwagon with no reservations. Getting them to jump on ours was going to be a very big challenge, even if I could somehow program Logan to modify his behavior and refrain from untimely emotional outbursts.

We were facing another major obstacle. Few would be willing to stick their necks out for a brand new firm with no name recognition. The key was finding the few that would. We needed to identify and cultivate the ones that could recognize the advantages for building a unique plan that addressed their business needs and could offer competitive advantage. They would help us build our practice. Eventually the others would come around. It would make things a lot easier if Will did, too.

SUMMARY OF OBSERVATIONS

- There have been many case studies on what caused the problems with IBM in the early '90s. Few focus on the impact of consultants, but they played a role, upstaging IBM's leadership position with corporate customers. (More on the impact of consultants on IBM in chapter 3.)

- Consultants provide work for hire, which implies a different level of motivation than employees; the objectives of the consultants may conflict with corporate goals and objectives.

- Consultants gained more influence in the 1990s corresponding with corporate downsizing.

- Technology went through a major revolution in the '90s. It required a new set of skills that did not exist in most corporations. Companies relied on consultants to help them make critical decisions for implementing this new technology.

- Consultants used their influence in making recommendations to create increased client dependency and secure lucrative reengineering contracts.

- Few technology consultants offered skills transfer in spite of claims.

- Technical consultants sometimes let their enthusiasm for technology obstruct business considerations.

NOTES

1. Daniel Lyons, "IBM's Giant Gamble," *Forbes*, 4 October 1999, 3.

2. D. Quinn Mills and G. Bruce Friesen, *Broken Promises* (Boston: Harvard Business School Press, 1996), 65.

3. "Offerings in the Offing," *Barrons*, 27 September 1993, 44.

4. Todd Vogel, "Gideon Gartner Wants His Baby Back,"*Business Week*, 4 December 1989, 108, 110.

5. The "BUNCH" is a reference to the pack of competitors IBM left in the dust in the 1960s. Original BUNCH included, Burroughs, UNIVAC, NCR, Control Data Corporation, and Honeywell.

6. Catherine L. Harris, "Cashing in on Computer Confusion," *Business Week*, 20 April 1987, 85.

7. Mickey Williamson and Law McCreary, "Consulting Services: Making the Numbers," *CIO*, 15 November 1993, 48.

8. Pitney Bowes Annual Report 1991.

9. Robert Sobel, *IBM Colossus in Transition* (New York: Times Books, 1981), 321.

10. Mills and Friesen, *Broken Promises*, 183.

11. Satchel Paige is considered the greatest baseball pitcher of the 1930s. He played most of his career in what was called at the time "the Negro Leagues." In 1948, at forty-two years old, he broke into the previously segregated Major Leagues behind Jackie Robinson, becoming the first African American pitcher. His "don't look back" comment became legendary. In 1971, he was belatedly elected to the Hall of Fame.

CHAPTER TWO

TOOLS OF THE
TRADE

In all fairness, Will Logan was technically brilliant. He was good at both the micro and macro levels of technology. Although, he was probably a little stronger in the macro conceptual level, "the big picture stuff," versus the nuts and bolts. One day, while helping me install a burglar alarm for my car, Will shorted out the electrical system.

There was another problem. His technical brilliance was offset by his being socially challenged. When he had something to say, he didn't stand on ceremony. It didn't seem to bother him if others sometimes found him abrasive. I tried to not let it get to me, though I did worry about customer interaction. If they were willing to put up with the rough edges, there was a wealth of information that could be very useful. He was proving he could be patient in his dealings with me. He was willing to take great pains in helping me get over the habit of calling customers "customers." The least I could do was show the same level of patience with him.

"They're clients," he kept insisting whenever I slipped. "This is not about buying something off the shelves," Logan pointed out in an annoyed tone. "It's about providing a professional service."

"Sorry. I'll try and keep that in mind."

I didn't particularly like the term "client," which might have explained my unconscious tendency to stick with "customers." "Client" seemed presumptuous. Why not just call them "patients"? There was no telling how many operations it would take to make them well. Another valuable piece of information that I picked up from Will Logan helped provide a better understanding of the methods and tactics employed by consultants. It was a strategy to get business and keep it coming. It was called *FUD*.

The strategy FUD stood for "Fear, Uncertainty, and Doubt." I had heard of it before. It was a marketing ploy sometimes used in IBM after all else failed in a competitive-marketing situation. The idea was to create FUD in the mind of the customer, or for consultants, the client. It was more about preventing a loss than winning a sale. To both customers and clients, IBM was a known. "If you go with another vendor's product Mr. Customer, what happens if a part goes bad?" "What kind of inventory do they have for spare parts?" "How long before the replacement part gets to you?" "By the way, IBM has regional inventory centers worldwide, and we can get replacement parts to any one of your locations within hours." It was all in the delivery, so to speak. It was one of those things you had to be careful about. Given IBM's market dominance, you never wanted to give the slightest appearance of disparaging the competition or employing negative, predatory tactics. The antitrust division of the Justice Department was looking over our shoulders.

Logan was putting a different twist on it. "The key is to create FUD about the future," Logan explained. "There are lots of risks, lots of exposures. 'Wouldn't you, MR. CLIENT, be better off making decisions with the help of a consultant?'" He explained, "It's an effective technique to get them to keep coming back for more."

It was obviously working. More and more companies were making consultants a regular part of the decision-making process when it came to technology. Dress it up as much as you want, FUD was never about helping people make decisions. It was about preventing a decision from being made. If you were a vendor, this could be a customer decision to buy a product from a competitor. As a consultant, it could be applied to almost any business decision. New open-systems technology was a great arena, given all the inherent ambiguity, all the possible choices, and the exposure of making the wrong decision. Seeking assistance from the consultant became the prescribed antidote for overcoming the FUD. As new technology rolled out at a faster and faster pace, there would be even more opportunity for consultant involvement. The FUD strategy almost always went hand in hand with "analysis-paralysis." Before decision time when recommendations were due, some consultants would work to rack up the hours, interviewing "subject experts," researching, studying—all on the clients' nickle, of course. This is sometimes called "churning the business," when milking the project becomes the priority, versus finding the solution and moving on. Combining "fear" with "analysis-paralysis" may have been good for the consultants, but it had to create one big stalling process for companies measured day by day on the stock exchange, and by necessity, required to produce results. The only thing it didn't freeze was the decision by many of the IT guys to do nothing, save waiting to read the next research analysis report from the consultants. All decisions could be questioned, except the decision to hire the consultant. "Everybody does it."

One time while discussing Wall Street analysts, Logan said something I'd never forget. "Technology is moving so fast, as research analysts, none of us could really keep up. There's lots of pressure to be first out there with the sound byte on the latest products being released." Logan explained that sometimes an analyst will jump the gun, make a pronouncement on something without the proper due diligence. According to Logan, this was compounded when the Wall Street analysts call the technology analysts for an opinion. They, too, are trying to get out there first.

"Everybody starts cutting corners. The hype becomes the consensus opinion. I think we need to get back to the fundamentals, you know, 'punt, pass, kick.'" I would think about that often, as well as other nuggets of wisdom picked up from Logan that I would apply to future projects.

The Pitney Bowes document, which Will and I produced, received a very favorable response. This led to other contracts at Pitney Bowes and ongoing friendships with a few key managers. It really was a collaborative effort with the client and a great learning experience, at least for me. We now had a legitimate "client" that could help us open doors with others. Management didn't seem to have a problem with us using them as a reference, either. If there were concerns about us protecting them by keeping their name undercover as we pitched for new business, they didn't seem to mind.

To make our business successful, we needed to establish several client relationships. Given the limited amount of services we could provide as a start-up, there would always be downtime in this kind of work unless we could build a pipeline of clients.

I was able to develop an approach that proved successful in generating new leads. I would scour the trade press looking for articles and quotes from senior technology managers in major corporations or announcements of appointments of new executives. I would then draft letters, complimenting them on their success and accomplishments. There would be a brief description of Informed Technology Decisions (ITD) and how we could help in their efforts. I would also enclose a brochure on our business.

Sometimes a response would come without making a follow-up call, but this was rare. When it did happen, it was generally a sign that the executive's office sent the letter to a subordinate manager, probably with a buck slip saying something like "For Your Action." This was the case with Connecticut Mutual Life Insurance Company where the chief information officer sent our letter with a cover memo to a new manager responsible for distributed-systems development. We were engaged to help them select the right products for a major claims application.

Most of the time it took several follow-up calls to close a sale. The key for me was calling and immediately mentioning the letter I had previously sent. Of course they never remembered the letter, but it provided two important advantages. First, in my head, I was no longer making a cold call. I was following up to my letter. The second advantage was that it threw them a little off stride. It created a second or two of pause, dodging the immediate blow-off as they tried to think how best to get rid of me. This provided a little more time to pitch versus catch. Once they knew why I was calling, they sometimes decided to send me to someone who worked for them. Rarely did I get to meet with the person I had first contacted. A successful call meant a referral to a direct report—someone who reported directly to the manager I initially called. "I'm calling because your boss suggested you and I should meet." This was the case at Chase Manhattan, although it took multiple calls combined with some pretty good luck before I managed to get a face-to-face meeting.

In the early 1990s one could have easily suspected that the chief information officer (CIO) at Chase Manhattan Bank Corporation was on a public relations blitz. His name was plastered through many of the most widely read industry publications. Financial institutions were one of the first industries to begin using technology for competitive advantage, long before the days of open systems. They recognized early on that technology could have enormous potential for banking, trading, and other financial activities where transactions occur. Unfortunately, for banks, they started using technology in the 1960s. By the end of the 1980s they found themselves encumbered with old systems. *Legacy systems*, they were called, code for mainframe and usually IBM. Legacy was expensive to run, but also expensive to convert to something else. Chase, under the leadership of an aggressive CIO, was moving quickly to migrate from legacy to cutting-edge technology solutions. This was unusual at the time for banks that tended to be risk averse, particularly in the technology arena.

Chase could be the franchise. The bank had lost its position as the largest and most prestigious U.S. Bank to Citicorp in the 1970s, but it was still a major force in the industry with an international scope. David Rockefeller had stepped down as chief executive in 1979. Chase Manhattan had found it could no longer depend on blue chip personal relationships to sustain competitive advantage. The bank had become stodgy and paternalistic. As market share slipped and financial results declined, it was obvious changes needed to be made. They could no longer rely on a relationship with American barons or the royals in exotic countries to park a high percentage of personal assets while also opening bank doors with a big grin to family, friends, employees, and/or subjects.

In the early 1990s, the bank seemed to be reversing the negative results of its recent past. Under new management, it had implemented a strategy to reaffirm its market leadership in core business areas in retail (consumer banking) and wholesale (large corporate customer banking). Executives adopted a bold plan to exit from "nonstrategic" and "nonperforming" businesses. As a result, Chase's performance was significantly improving. Net losses in 1989 and 1990 were followed by net gains of $520 million in 1991 and $639 million in 1992.[1] Analysts were praising bank management for turning things around.

The CIO at Chase received a letter from me complimenting his quotes in a recent article. He had been calling for change and promising to make it happen at Chase. I would always call early in the morning or late in the evening, attempting to avoid the gatekeepers. The other key was to never leave a voice mail—it eliminates the element of surprise. After several attempts, I caught him answering his own phone early one morning. He had been expecting another call and quickly referred me to his vice president of strategy at the time, Michael Dellano. That was all I wanted. So far, so good.

Attempts to reach Dellano by phone proved unsuccessful, so I went to his secretary to try and get on his calendar. It took several attempts with Dellano's secretary to get an appointment. The secretary was a real pro at screening. She didn't seem so impressed with my mandate from the chief information officer to meet with her boss. Nothing I said did anything to heighten her sense of urgency. After repeated calls, an appointment was made. I speculated that perhaps she had either begun to wear down from all the calls, or she felt sorry for me. Maybe his calendar finally opened up.

It was about a two-hour commute either by car or train from my home in Connecticut to Chase Manhattan's new offices in the MetroTech Center in Brooklyn. It was one of several impressive steel structures in a high-rise complex that looked grossly out of place. It practically faced off with the old Brooklyn Navy Yard, just a few short blocks away. Stepping out of the MetroTech complex, crossing Flatbush Avenue, a nice guy from Connecticut could get himself hurt. It was early morning and MetroTech security was patrolling the area with German shepherds. One of the dogs sneered at me, displaying a serious case of overbite. The City of New York must have given an attractive tax break to the companies that agreed to move in, hoping to revitalize the area. I'm sure they didn't cross the East River for the local ambiance.

Being inside the Chase building was like being in a cocoon. You were totally oblivious to any of the external noise or potential hostilities. To get through security they needed a phone confirmation of my appointment from upstairs. I also had to fill out a form as if I were applying for a mortgage. I was told to go to the eleventh floor.

The secretary was very pleasant. Getting on the calendar made me legitimate. She escorted me into a conference room. It was a corner room on the northwest side of the building, overlooking the skyline of lower Manhattan. It was several minutes before my appointment entered the room.

Michael Dellano walked in as if very self-aware of the imposing presence he projected. He was well groomed, with a thick mustache and intelligent eyes. There was an innate toughness in the man that must have come from city living since his youth, or as they might say in Brooklyn, "yoot." The toughness wasn't the lease bit diminished by his polished appearance and self-contained manner that could have belonged to a high-profile prosecuting attorney. Dellano sized me up as we shook hands. He offered me a seat across the oval table that dwarfed everything in the room except him. A pack of cigarettes and a gold lighter from his pocket were placed on the table with a clunk. Dellano was another of those nicotine junkies in constant need of a fix. He was the poster boy for retro cool.

"So tell me . . . how did you get on my calendar?"

I told him I had been referred by the CIO.

"I usually don't meet with salesmen."

It must have been the wing tips. I explained that I was a consultant and went into a brief summation of why I thought it could be beneficial to talk. Dellano waited politely for me to finish and then told me that I needed to differentiate my sales pitch from all the other consultants saying similar things.

"Like what for example?" I asked.

"For example, providing skills transfer. Everybody says that . . . even though most never do."

Lighting a cigarette, he stood up and walked over to the window. I noticed he wore a silver ring with a miniature diamond on his pinky finger, similar to the one worn by my dad. It was one of those New York tough guy things. He asked me if I recognized the view. It was a beautiful day. Looking out, I could see the World Trade Center, still dominating the sky above lower Manhattan. The Brooklyn Bridge was a stone's throw away. "Most of the famous skyline shots of New York are from the Jersey side. This is the view from the beginning of the *Barney Miller Show*. I like this view better, myself," he said. He was right, it was very impressive, as long as you gazed straight out past the East River, and not down at the old, tired Brooklyn Streets surrounding the MetroTech Center.

Dellano asked me several questions, measuring my responses without any indication of concurrence or dissent. The questions centered around my views of technology. He asked me where I thought the industry was going and what the potential advantages and pitfalls might be. He then asked me how I would decide between a centralization strategy for technology versus decentralization. I told him about an experience when I first joined IBM. The heroes and demons of my past continued to haunt me.

At the time they were encouraging both new marketing representatives and system engineers to concentrate their first-year training on distributed, decentralized systems. That was back in the early 1980s. In looking at the senior reps who ran the large account territories, I noticed most had a large-systems background. There was one guy in the branch who had a beard and wore different colored shirts. He wore just about every color except white. I figured he must be a technology guru if IBM let's him look like that when everyone else dressed the same: white shirts, dark suits, and a clean recent shave. When I asked him for advice on which direction to go, he said, "If they tell you distributed, go centralized. When they tell you centralized, go distributed. That way they will always think you are ahead of the curve."

Dellano appeared only slightly amused. He filled me in on some of the activities recently initiated at the bank. Just about everyone else was decentralizing operations. Chase was going centralized. Dellano told me that he and his organization had played a critical role in building the case from the technology perspective. There was something about him that made you believe this wasn't just idle talk. It struck me that he was truly ahead of the curve. Out of the box in a commonsense kind of way. He displayed lots of pride whenever he talked about mother Chase.

"It's the best and only way to target our global customers. They don't want to deal with a lot of banks in different geographies that are Chase in name only. We need to build an infrastructure that can provide the same support all over the world . . . one global view."

Impressive. Lots of companies wanted to go global. This would make it important to provide consistent, comprehensive data to customers on all of their account information, wherever and whenever they needed it. At the same time, most consultants were recommending more distributed, decentralized systems. Go figure.

I shared with Dellano how we had developed a technology architecture plan for Pitney Bowes and handed him a copy to see. He politely glanced at it before passing it back. He then called to his secretary to get the Chase Architecture Document. In was in his hands in a flash. He must have asked for it often. "Take a look," he said.

Dellano, as I was about to learn, was one of the leading authorities in the business on technology architecture and a keynote speaker on the subject at industry conferences. After a couple minutes or so of turning pages, I told him I thought it was very impressive. This was not just respectful sales talk; it was obviously a top-notch piece of work. "Looks like it was written so any banker could pick it up and understand it. Not the typical technospeak."

"That's the point. I view my role as giving the decision making back to senior management. Technology in our business is too important to be left to technicians."

I couldn't, for the life of me, figure out why a senior manager who seemed as competent as Dellano would need consultants. This was a real puzzlement. He knew what he wanted to do, he knew how to get there, and he was not one of those managers afraid of making decisions. Nevertheless, Dellano indicated that he did use consultants from time to time. As we continued to chat, I kept looking for that hook to land a consulting contract. Chase would be a great account, and think of what I could learn just rubbing elbows with a guy like this. I was convinced from the start that working for him would be a blast. Not to mention, Dellano obviously had the clout to get things done. In the past when I thought of strategy, I thought of people who couldn't walk across the street by themselves. Dellano was a different breed of strategist. Not only was he an astute business executive, but clearly he understood technology beyond the buzz words. No FUD was gonna work here.

Before I knew it, my hour was up. The only commitment I was able to get from Dellano was an agreement to meet again. This was going to take time. Nothing worse for a consultant than spending time when you can't bill for it. Sometimes you need to know when to quit, but I was already determined to win Chase as a client, no matter how much time and effort it took. The free time would be easy to rationalize. I was earning my union card to work as a consultant at Chase.

I brought Will Logan along for a couple of the follow-up meetings Dellano set up with other managers. I knew there was risk, given the Pitney Bowes experience, but his presence could also prove important, particularly if anybody starting firing away to determine my technical credentials. In addition to his consulting knowledge, I wanted to demonstrate that this was more than a one-man firm. As if a two-man firm would make a difference.

From the platform waiting for Metro North in Fairfield, Connecticut, until we got off the subway at Jay Street, Borough Hall, I tried to coach Logan prior to each of these meetings. "Please, Will, think before you speak, let them do most of the talking, and don't get emotional about stuff." Not that it ever did any good. He would give me a condescending scowl, as if I were merely a facilitator and should remember my place, leaving all the thinking and serious talk up to him. Once we were in a meeting, I knew anything could happen. I tried my best to keep us away from any technology discussions that could become religious. Overall, I had to be honest with myself. Logan was at the top of his game. The best part was that nobody went storming out of the building.

My one-on-one meetings with Dellano also continued, between the "dog and pony" shows with Logan and various groups of Chase employees. There must have been three or four additional meetings with Dellano. As I got to know him, I realized we had things in common. Michael Dellano came from a family of New York City cops. My father had been a cop for twenty years, starting on a beat in Harlem and retiring as a lieutenant detective out of the District Attorney's office in Manhattan. In the old days, cops from both of our families rooted for the Dodgers, affectionately referred to as the "bums." This might have explained why they were quick to invoke this affectionate term whenever anyone got the least bit out of line. There were other similarities. We both had to work for people we respected. He was madly in love with his wife and liked to talk about her. A cashed-out Wall Streeter, she was now an entrepreneur in retail who made over double what she was making before. I was madly in love with whomever I was dating at the time. I envied him that he found one person where the passion had lasted.

I took him to lunch several weeks after our first meeting. As much as I enjoyed his company, it had finally come down to fish or cut bait. We needed to start getting some billable hours, and I had promised Logan that if I couldn't crack Chase this time, I would move on. I planned to full court press. Dellano's secretary had suggested I take him to a place he liked called Casey's, which was in the MetroTech complex. It was the perfect place, especially with it being a bitter cold day and the restaurant just a few hundred yards from the Chase building. Started by a couple of retired New York cops, it was a favorite lunch spot during the day and watering hole at night for many of those Chase people who had been banished from Manhattan and didn't want to fight rush hour when they could stop for a pop instead. It combined a rustic Irish pub with an upscale restaurant serving northern Italian cuisine. The best of both worlds, so to speak.

After we were escorted to the table, I extended my hand, offering the seat against the wall. "Think we're safe here," I said. "I usually never sit with my back to the door, but I'll make an exception today."

"OK," Dellano barked back. "You've already proved to me that your old man was a cop. Either that, or a wise guy."

"Don't I look like a wise guy?"

"More like IRA. So what kind of name is Romaine? Doesn't sound Irish."

"It's not. My dad was Lithuanian. The name was chopped when his parents got off the boat at Ellis Island. For some reason, more of the Celtic came out in my looks and temperament. You think maybe the milkman . . . ?"

"That's what I hate about this new DNA testing I've been reading about. . . . Can't get away with anything anymore. . . . So your dad was a New York cop? But he wasn't Irish. Hmmm . . . he married an Irish girl. Must have been a social climber."

I had established an early rapport. First objective in any sales call.

Lunch continued for the first few minutes with nonwork-related conversation. I'm not sure how we got on the subject, but we talked about some of our favorite books and movies. They shared a recurring theme— good guys fight bad guys. This common interest in similar entertainment could possibly have been a by-product from growing up around cops. At least for me, I'm sure it helped reinforce a binary view of life. From a cop's point of view, you're either a crook or you're not a crook. Sharing the same taste in entertainment also may have signaled a nostalgic craving for a simpler world when battle lines were more clearly defined and armies wore uniforms. A time before free agency, when teams had distinctive personalities that you could count on remaining virtually intact from season to season; some you loved, some you loved to hate. Of course, it's easy to sugarcoat the past.

"It's a shame the bad guys don't wear black hats anymore," Dellano said. "It so much easier when you can pick them out right away. You can never be too sure anymore."

"As Michael Corleone would say, keep you friends close and your enemies closer."

"But that was always true."

Conversation eventually turned to Chase Manhattan and some of the things Dellano was doing. It was time to try and bring this thing to closure. "I have one question. You know we have met with a bunch of folks. Have we been vetted to your satisfaction yet?"

Dellano smiled as he continued to talk about his work-related activities. Something called *client/server* was busting out all over Chase at just about all departmental levels.

There was the Internet lurking in the background, but most of the hype from consulting analysts was on this thing called *client/server*. Client/server was the next big breakthrough after open systems. Client/server went hand in hand with open systems. It was part of the revolution displacing mainframes. Mainframes connected "nonintelligent" terminals to large, centrally controlled systems. Client/server was a network connecting personal computers, usually in close proximity on the same campus. On a local network, the personal computer and the software that made it "intelligent" became the client. Clients generally shared one or more servers. Servers were stripped-down departmental systems where data, printing, and other services could be shared without requiring a large mainframe computer. Client/server wasn't exactly industrial strength yet, but the vendors and consultants kept promising. "Get rid of the IBM mainframe and save bucks with client/server, and we can help you do it."

It wasn't that I was against client/server. Will Logan and I had recommended client/server solutions at Pitney Bowes and Connecticut Mutual Life. I just didn't think it was the universal answer for everything. Certainly the cost advantages were overstated—for one thing, they were leaving out the ongoing consultant costs. Logan and I didn't spend the last five years building a bench with client/server specialists like so many other consulting firms had done. I liked to think that made us a little more open minded about using it. One of the few advantages of being small—we had no investments to protect, at least not yet.

Dellano explained that Chase was just getting started in a comprehensive effort to reengineer revenue reporting for the entire wholesale side of the bank. Then he finally answered my question: "I'm going to give you and Logan a chance to demonstrate what you can do." This was huge. I tried to be cool about it. Perhaps we could fit Chase in.

Chase was one of the market leaders in wholesale banking. The effort to develop a more comprehensive approach to reporting and analyzing financial results was driven by a question asked by the chief financial officer. He wanted to know how much money Chase had made in a previous quarter from one of its top corporate customers. It wasn't that the question couldn't be answered. The problem was that he got at least three different answers. Different groups were reporting revenue differently. There was no comprehensive system for tracking and reporting. I pictured back rooms with hundreds of different sized and shaped people, all wearing the exact same thick, horn-rimmed glasses and matching sneakers, working late through the night. They were taking numbers from different computer printouts and tabulating totals from an adding machine with rolls of paper spilling over desks to the floor.

Dellano wanted us to review the work to date and interview a bunch of people involved in revenue reporting and systems. There was a client/server solution currently in its pilot phase. It was called System 10, and it came from a relatively new high-flying database company called Sybase Inc. Unlike its previous solutions, which were geared for departmental users, System 10 was billed as a solution for the entire enterprise, the mainframe killer.

Chase had agreed to test a prerelease "beta" version, before it became generally available. Select customers could test a "beta," which meant it wasn't ready for prime time yet. Computer defects, called bugs, needed to be uncovered and fixed. The customer would test in a work environment for the vendor, helping to fix the problems prior to general availability. This was a great way for a vendor to hook a customer. The argument went that the customer would get a break on price. In addition, the customer would get up to speed on the new product faster than the competition. As part of the agreement, the customer ended up making people investments to help get the kinks out of the new beta version of the product. If the product was a no-go for the customer, the investments were wasted. Nobody wanted to waste investments. Often, during beta testing, the customer got lots of great publicity for itself while praising the new product, sometimes speaking at conferences. It became a partnership approach for making the product a success. For a vendor, it was a great way to shift some of the start-up risks and costs to the customer, as if you were doing them a favor. The refined product would hit the market after beta testing had been completed at a much lower cost for the vendor.

Chase executives were getting lots of press for their willingness to push the envelope on technology. Many at Chase believed System 10 could be rolled out to address the needs of the new revenue-reporting system. It was the prevailing view, according to Dellano. He wanted me and Logan to complete a thorough evaluation, make recommendations, and develop a plan for next steps.

"If I like the work you do, there's potential for follow-on work. If I don't, we can still chat now and then . . . your nickel."

We shook hands over a fixed price that would cover about a month's work for two consultants. It was a step up from what we charged Pitney, but still lower than market rates for the more established guys.

I paid the check, and we got up to leave. As we were waiting for the coat check lady to retrieve our things, he told me that he had started at Chase as a key punch operator and had worked his way up through the ranks. At one point he had left Chase to pursue a new career as a consultant. He built his own business before Chase made him an offer to come back in from the cold. As a former mercenary, it occurred to me that Dellano was in a unique position. He knew the other teams' playbook.

Dellano tapped me on the back as we slipped out the door, past the line of people waiting to get into the restaurant. "A few words of advice for the future. Don't buy lunch for potential clients without first getting the contract in hand."

At the beginning of 1993, Chase Manhattan Wholesale Bank was embroiled in a series of internal battles. My conversations with Dellano before getting the contract started to make sense. The big battle we were about to walk in on was between those who wanted to centralize all the customer-revenue data in one place and those who felt it should be distributed across a network of servers. The classic battle between the control freaks versus the "give them whatever they want and need" crowd. The appeal of System 10 was that it was billed as software that could satisfy both crowds. It was decentralized, but it performed and looked to the user like it was centralized.

The wholesale bank handled some of the largest and most prestigious international corporate customers. It was Who's Who of the Fortune 100, the envy of other banks. Great visibility if you did things right, and greater visibility if you did things wrong.

Michael Dellano said that for this project he did not want to tip the balance by sharing his own views with us. He was not one of the senior managers we were to interview. It didn't matter. After all the previous meetings, I already had a pretty good idea where he stood. Anyone who thinks consultants are hired for an objective view is fooling himself. If we were to win additional contracts, we knew Dellano, who hired us, was the guy to please. As Will Logan always said, every consultant comes with his own biases. We were fortunate. In this case our biases mapped pretty closely to Dellano's. If they didn't, he was the kind of guy who probably would have seen through it in about a New York minute and hired someone else.

We had just started interviews when Dellano told us that he had hired a program manager who would implement the new reporting system. "It would be a good idea for you to meet with him as soon as possible," we were told. I was getting the feeling that the train wasn't waiting for us to complete our work before leaving the station.

Tom Carter had a reputation in Chase of putting out fires and bringing high-risk projects in successfully and on time. His last assignment was international. He was short in stature, and his voice was a dead ringer for actor Joe Pesci. He had the same kind of larger-than-life demeanor that demanded your full attention. "You think I'm funny?" Like Dellano, he had strong opinions on just about everything. When I tried to initiate discussion, he wasted no time in clueing us in on his thinking. Carter wasn't much for small talk.

"I heard you have a pretty good track record in managing successful projects," I said, hoping to establish early rapport.

"Yeah? I hear yous guys are kinda new."

Before Logan or I could come back with an intelligent response, Carter had rambled on to his next point.

"You know the sad thing. Success doesn't seem to matter anymore. In the old days, when a project failed, everybody knew about it. People would walk around with their heads down and usually somebody would get fired. Today, the patient could be brain-dead and they still don't unplug the life support system. Money continues to get poured into it, and everybody talks as if it is a great success. I'm not about to let that happen here."

Before I started in, Will Logan quickly jumped into the conversation cutting me off, which was probably a good thing.

"Any suggestions for us on what we should look at?"

"Yeah," Carter replied with no hesitation. "Try to ballpark how big this monster's going to be and project how much it could grow. Just remember, once you give executives new information, they always want more. Tell them how much we made off of IBM and they'll want to know how much we made from IBM Europe versus IBM Far East. The key is to anticipate the follow-on questions before you get 'em. We're a lot bigger than just about everybody else. What might work for some, won't work for us. Sizing requirements will narrow the choices here real fast."

Here was another guy who didn't sound like he needed a consultant.

It took us almost the whole month to run people down and complete the interviews. We met with a cross section of Chase personnel, including financial executives, technology executives, and managers responsible for current revenue-reporting systems. We also interviewed some of the techies. Thank God that Logan was there to go toe to toe with them. You could tell some of them were the type who viewed ripping vendors apart as sport, a relaxing diversion from the more mundane aspects of their jobs. As a new, small start-up we could have been pulverized.

Logan's years of consulting experience came through. He was an expert at leading the witness. This came in handy when we met with the people running the System 10 pilot and the rest of the client/server bigots who came in all kinds. The System 10 pilot had been up and running before we came onto the scene. The people running it felt they had the answer, and it was just a matter of getting a green light to roll it out across the rest of Chase. The key for us was getting the discussion away from technology and onto business needs. A little FUD would also help. I let Logan take the lead. He would have anyway.

"So you say the vendor is pretty responsive when you have a problem?"

"Yeah, they're very responsive."

"Do you call them a lot?"

"Well, yes, but that's because this is the pilot. You've got to expect that with a pilot."

"If this is rolled out globally like you suggest, any idea how vendor support would be handled if you had a problem in Mozambique?"

We met with some very impressive senior managers. Most had a very different view of things from Dellano and Carter, particularly the manager originally responsible for initiating the pilot solution. We finally met with his boss, the key guy responsible for the System 10 pilot and a bunch of other client/server projects. The interesting thing was that he and the other senior managers acted as if they had already lost the fight. The people working for them were a different story, but the senior technology managers advocating client/server seemed resigned to defeat before our interviews even started.

So what was up with this? Chase had some of the best technology people in the business. There was a dream team of senior technology managers who could probably all be CIOs anywhere else. Whether it was intentional or not, Chase was based on a contention system where these high-powered managers with different points of view fought it out before important decisions were made.

Consultants weren't hired for objectivity or for expert knowledge. "What's the point?" I kept asking Will Logan when we were alone. He could not understand why this was so surprising to me.

"Don't you get it? I told you before . . . no consultants are completely objective. Nor does the client expect us to be."

I was starting to catch on. It was more important to keep the client happy. Objectivity could get in the way of lucrative follow-on contracts.

Logan could be a real chameleon, as long as we tiptoed lightly upon those areas where he held religious-like convictions. His background was in networking, and that was the area where he could really go off. If I mentioned a networking topic by mistake, Logan could spend half a day expounding. He could also sound like an expert on almost anything, whether he knew much about it or not. In these other areas, Logan could play it whichever way made the most sense, and most of the time, without getting long winded and emotional. Sounding the expert, whether he knew about it or not, helped make him a successful consultant. It was the amount of airtime that clued you in as to how much he really knew about something.

It didn't happen right away, but eventually I think I figured it out. Chase was a highly charged political environment. As consultants, we were merely providing cover for management. We were human shields, like the guys in trench coats who protect official heads of state. We would complete a report that could be pulled out and quoted if decisions were questioned. It was essentially an insurance policy to offset the risk of decision making.

There wasn't much more to it than that. Once the consultant was hired, the battle had already been won. Whoever did the hiring was the winner. As consultants, we helped carry forward the agenda of the winner who hired us. Consultants were playing parts in a ceremonial tribal dance with a predetermined outcome.

Still, Will and I had a report to produce. Future business would depend on it. We continued to research the various options. The more I learned, the more I was convinced Tom Carter was right. There was no client/server solution on the market at that time from Sybase or anyone else that could address the sizing requirements for the wholesale-reporting-and-analysis system. There were other issues as well. In spite of all the hype in the trade press, client/server was still, at best, a departmental solution for most large companies. It was very unstable and became increasingly more inefficient as it got bigger. It was bad enough the CFO had gotten three different answers to his question. What if he couldn't get any answer at all? "Sorry, the system crashed, we'll have to get back. Not sure when. It depends on what's wrong, and that will take some time to figure out."

If the system wasn't functioning properly, the answer was always to buy more client/server equipment and services. Studies were finding that over time the costs of client/server could dwarf the costs of the mainframe. What was saved on hardware was often lost on labor.[2] One study found that over 43 percent of the costs of client/server were consulting fees.[3] A definite pattern seemed to be emerging. If it was good for consultants, it was recommended to clients. But, how could corporate clients be so gullible?

Client/server required minimal investments on the front end. It always took time before the true cost and benefits could be properly evaluated. The problem was that once the client/server implementation began, who was going to call foul? It became almost impossible to turn back, even when the results were well below expectations. As Carter would say, "It's like a Ponzi Scheme. Everybody's too invested to call the bluff."

As I thought about it, I began to realize that in the minds of some, client/server could become a convenient excuse for implementing cutbacks. All those employees on the payroll costing an arm and a leg in accumulated salaries and benefits no longer had the right skill set. It didn't really matter what the right skill set was. Corporate success in the 1990s was measured by the stock value at the close of daily trading. Client/server could be used as the rationale to reduce technology investments and replace employees with contracted workers. That's where the big cost savings would come. An immediate impact on the bottom line was sure to send the stock up. Unload the traditional employees and hire more mercenaries. Luckily the people I was working for at Chase weren't in that camp. They knew better than to think of people like Logan and me as substitutes for Chase employees.

During the interviews, several people told us about the numerous articles on client/server success stories. By now you couldn't miss them. They were spilling onto the front pages of reputable business magazines and the major national newspapers. According to the articles, some of the most prestigious Wall Street firms had made the leap and were anticipating sizable financial benefits. They had readily embraced the new computer revolution being espoused by the technological consultants. Like corporate executives, I doubted they fully understood it, but I figured they must have loved the potential consequences to the balance sheet—less people, less costs.

Some of the big-name Wall Street firms were claiming in the press to be using client/server solutions such as System 10 as replacement for mainframes. I decided to check with some of these firms firsthand. It must have been that internalized cop thing acquired from dad. I had been raised not to take things at face value.

In every case, the client/server wasn't the full story. There was a mainframe computer, often many, in the back office doing most of the real work. "Over time, we will get rid of it," I was told whenever I asked. I doubted it would be any time soon in spite of their optimism. Mainframes may not have been very flexible, but they were stable, reliable, and could churn out an enormous amount of work when compared with the client/server world. No one talked about it because mainframes were yesterday's news. Everybody was reading about client/server. It was hot and everybody wanted to say they were doing it, too.

Logan and I recommended a politically incorrect mainframe solution with some client/server-like functionality. Will Logan joked that recommending mainframes could dovetail nicely with our going-out-of-business strategy. "Nobody will have to worry about skills transfer now," he said. This did not spoil my optimism. Our recommendations were a big hit with both Michael Dellano and Tom Carter. I knew they would be, and this was what was most important to me. Frankly, it was more of a surprise when they didn't say, "By the way, we already have it up and running."

At one point, I asked Tom Carter, "So why do you hire from the outside when you have the skills to do this yourselves?" A big, wide grin lit up his face. "Because you are the consultant," he said. His comment made me feel that in his mind as a consultant I was nothing more than a necessary evil, a prescribed medication he was being forced to administer. Consultants were all over Chase. The only way to fight off other groups hiring consultants was to hire your own. For an old-school guy like Carter, he must have felt there had to be lots of potential negative side effects with all those consultants running around recommending and implementing all kinds of different departmental solutions without much thought about how it could all work together across the rest of Chase. It must have made him nuts.

A new department was built around Tom Carter to support a new revenue-reporting system that everyone in wholesale banking could use. He employed other consulting organizations to assist in the development and roll-out. We were able to get follow-on contracts here and there, but the bulk of the work went to larger vertical-consulting and technology-integration firms focused on banking. These firms provided a combination of skills and lots of bodies. When I wasn't able to get any farther with Carter, I went to Michael Dellano. He explained to me that we were too small to compete against the bigger organizations and that he viewed us as having more of a strategic focus as opposed to the necessary "body shop" mentality of the integrators. "There's plenty of work for you and the others, provided no one gets too greedy," he said. "You can't expect all of it to happen overnight." But I did.

Of course, we all got greedy, too. If you want to grow business in an organization like Chase, it usually means taking it away from someone else. Several of the other firms approached us about coming to work for them. We decided to play hard to get. There was an attractive saleswoman who worked for one of the integrators. In addition to being lean with tight curves, she was also smart, and with a wicked sense of humor. I liked her. She seemed to like me. We went out a few times. While we tried to keep our jobs out of it, work-related topics invariably bubbled up. At one time after she mentioned something about her business, I asked her to explain how it worked. It sounded brutal. They threw bodies at jobs, all shapes and sizes. As long as the consultants could be sold as a billable commodity, they had a future in integration. The idea was to extend the billing as much as possible.

One night over a couple drinks after work, I said, "Don't think I could ever do what you do. You're a shark."

"And whom do you think you're foolin'? . . . You're a closet barracuda," she retorted without hesitation.

This was quite the compliment.

At one point, she set up a meeting between me and her boss.

"I don't want to work for anybody else right now," I declared.

"It can't hurt to listen . . . and this is not only to explore you becoming an employee," she suggested. "Maybe we can strike a 'partnering' agreement."

That was of more interest. Her boss was one of the principal owners. The conversation didn't go very well. It was all about employment, not partnership. After explaining that I could do both selling and consulting, he explained that he would want to start me out as "billable," and thought he could sell me into another project at Chase.

"But I'm capable of more than that. . . . I want to be more than 'billable meat.'"

"Billable meat? If that's what you think of consultants . . . then we have a problem. Consultants are the lifeblood of our business. I don't think of them as billable meat and no one who works for me should, either."

"Sorry, poor choice of words."

Discussion continued. He wanted to know about everything I was working on with all my clients to determine the proper "fit," based on my skill set and experience. He could call it or not call it what he wanted, but I couldn't help thinking that in his mind I was just another slab of marketable beef. As we talked, I had the feeling he was busy trying to kill two birds. First, figure out what business I was doing that he could move in on, and second, determine how much he could bill me out at. Feeling like I had better hold tight to the wallet in my pocket, I developed a quick case of amnesia. He was a little more than annoyed when I got fuzzy on the particulars regarding my work at Chase. You have to be wary of professional sharks.

Instead of forming a partnership, I continued efforts to outmaneuver my friend and her boss for future business opportunities. They kept trying to get more of the front-end business. I tried to get implementation work that could be subcontracted to less threatening integrators. They were a big firm compared to me, and at best, I was merely a slight annoyance. It didn't really matter. Carter kept defining the projects and, for the most part, he kept us swimming in separate tanks.

"You gotta decide what you want ta be," he told me. "If you want ta do strategy, fine, . . . stick with it. If you want ta manage projects, that's something else. I personally prefer projects. It's where the action is."

The money was better, too. Eventually my friend's company was bought out by Amdahl for several million dollars.

In spite of my best efforts to generate other business, we couldn't break out from getting the front-end architecture-related work. The integrators were cleaning up on the more lucrative implementation projects that came later in the cycle. Somehow it didn't seem fair. We were helping companies make the important up-front technology decisions, or at the very least, providing coverage to management as those decisions were made. Other consulting and integration firms were being commissioned to implement these plans for the really big bucks with engagements running over extended time periods.

We had been lucky with Chase. I was beginning to realize that Informed Technology Decisions, by itself, didn't have the scale or name recognition to provide the sufficient level of insurance to minimize the risk factor for new prospective clients. When we were hired, people seemed to like the work we were doing. It was just that the people they worked for had never heard of Informed Technology Decisions. That didn't seem to hurt us at Chase, but it could with other potential clients. Most senior managers had heard of the big consulting firms such as Andersen Consulting or Price Waterhouse. The decision to hire us could be questioned. In the risk averse '90s with everyone looking over their shoulders and waiting for the next corporate realignment, questionable decisions were to be avoided. Who would question hiring a reputable firm like Andersen, the consulting arm of the prestigious auditing firm Arthur Anderson? Skills and capability seemed less important than comfort level. If we were going to grow this business, we needed to smarten up.

I met with Tom Carter to plant the seeds for winning future business and get some of his street-smart advice. He, too, was a regular at Casey's. We met for lunch, sitting at his favorite table in the corner. Like Dellano, he told me to be patient. Additional business would come. I told him that patience wasn't one of my virtues.

"You can't expect to break into Chase in one fell swoop," he said. "You've done very well. Give it a little time."

The messages from Carter and Dellano were in sync.

What struck me most about Tom Carter were the apparent contradictions. There was a hint of the rebel, suggested by the cowboy boots he would wear underneath his dark blue and gray suits. People who worked for him described him as warm and caring, yet they seemed to be afraid of him. While he wasn't very tall, his presence somehow managed to overcompensate. He had all the necessary street smarts and controlled toughness of an urban individualist, but he was also very effective in communicating with top management and orchestrating meetings to gain their buy-in. At one point he told me that over the years he had helped bail out a lot of senior executives. "Hopefully, they won't forget," he said. "You never know when you might need to pull the card."

During our conversation, Carter mentioned that he had gone to Bishop Loughin Memorial High School with New York City Mayor Rudy Giuliani, in Brooklyn, New York. It must have been a breeding ground for maverick types. Some may have considered Tom Carter a little out of touch with the times, but that was fine by me. He was one of those guys who believed you "say what you mean and always think team."

Several months went by. I was starting to worry that Chase had forgotten about us. Logan and I worked on a few smaller contracts with other clients. On the tail end of another client's engagement, I received a call from Tom Carter. He wanted to see me as soon as possible to discuss a major contract opportunity. We met at a French gourmet cafe, somewhat out of place, deep in the heart of Brooklyn, not far from where my dad had grown up.

Like most corporations, Chase was under considerable pressure to improve profitability. The contract was to recommend a new profitability and portfolio-analysis system to be used throughout the Chase wholesale bank. Chase executive management had become highly focused on measuring profitability more effectively. This system could play a critical role in helping them make decisions related to this extremely important measurement. They liked what we did with revenue. Profit was the next logical step. This time it wouldn't just be recommending systems. More important, it would entail redefining a consistent measurement for profitability and how it should be reported across the wholesale bank. There were lots of different opinions on how it should be counted.

"So, you interested?"

"When can we start?"

Carter agreed to pay us big bucks on an hourly basis. "What you should know, is that this will be highly political," he said.

I guess when you're talking about "redefining" something as important as profitability in a bank, you've got to expect politics. But then, without politics, why would they need a consultant? I continued to be amazed at how Dellano and Carter continued to get control of these major strategic initiatives.

Carter was right again. I had thought the last Chase project was loaded with land mines. It was tame by comparison. The capital allocation department had its own view of what profitability was and how it should be measured. So did the credit policy people. Marketing thought both groups were out to screw them out of commissions by allocating net costs against sales. The new system would have to have the capability of measuring profitability of various products for each corporate customer. It would also be a tool for determining a method of paying customer relationship managers based on their ability to grow net income versus revenue. Everyone had her own view. There was also a group running the current profitability system based on current assumptions, and of course they felt nothing could be better than the status quo.

It took several months, but when we had concluded the first draft of the report, I met with Tom Carter to preview the findings. Like Dellano on our first Chase assignment, he didn't want to be officially interviewed as part of the project. Once again, as I started presenting the recommendations, I felt as if the report could have been written by Carter without any outside consulting help. He had all the arguments down cold. I'm convinced he knew what the recommendations would be before we did. Carter was already there. This whole thing could have been completed months ago. As the objective, independent consultants, we had finally arrived at the same conclusions as the manager who had hired us. Such was my introduction to the consulting business in the 1990s.

Our most important contribution wasn't so much what we did, but who we were. We were consultants. With all his strengths, Carter, as an employee, couldn't achieve the same objectives on his own. This didn't seem to bother him. He was the kind of guy who figured out how to deal with things as they were. Once you figured out how things worked, you could always figure out a way to succeed. After I had presented him with my recommendations, Carter set up a series of executive meetings. This was Carter at his best. He was the grand puppeteer, orchestrating all the meetings while maintaining a low profile. Letting me present the findings and recommendations, he would occasionally interject when it was needed to point out the "so what?" from the executive point of view, or to assist with a difficult objection. Carter got what he wanted. He would now control both revenue and profitability reporting for the wholesale bank.

One of our meetings was held in the board room at Chase Manhattan corporate headquarters on Wall Street. Arriving early, I had a chance to notice the display case just outside the room. It contained the pistols used by Aaron Burr and Alexander Hamilton in their famous duel where Hamilton was killed. American history typically vilified Burr for the death of Hamilton. Some accounts suggested that just prior to the duel, Hamilton had undergone a religious awakening and was slow to fire, attempting to give Burr time to reflect on this dastardly deed and back off on his challenge. That had always sounded a little suspect to me. According to the description on the display case, Burr was the father of the bank that eventually became Chase Manhattan. I knew that Hamilton was the father of Bank of New York, but Burr's connection to Chase was news to me. While political differences provoked the duel, animosity between the two men had been long standing. There had been a previous financial squabble. Hamilton wanted to maintain his early dominance in New York banking. The description on the display case suggested that Hamilton had attempted to prevent Burr from gaining a foothold in the lucrative New York market. The description also indicated that Hamilton had chosen rare pistols for the duel, imported from France. They had a secret quick-trigger release that only he knew about—in other words, Hamilton planned to cheat.

The secret trigger release jammed. Using the conventional release, Burr fired and his aim was true. Imagine, Hamilton, author of the *Federalist Papers* and a Founding Father carrying on like this, first attempting to maximize profitability by restricting free competition, and then, attempting to cheat in a duel. Assuming this was true, I wondered what kind of spin the Bank of New York would put on all this if it ever became public knowledge. Would Chase be more inclined to emphasize the Burr connection? Discussions of the duel, as described by their contemporaries, and later by historians, typically omitted the part about Hamilton cheating. He must have had a good public relations consultant. Today, both the Bank of New York and Chase Manhattan are highly respected bastions of conservative capitalism; dependable, but not exactly known as fast-paced institutions, encouraging employees to be entrepreneurial. I remembered how a friend of mine who worked for the Bank of New York once told me there was a standard joke in the firm about why things moved so slowly. Just before the duel, Hamilton had said, "Don't do anything until I get back."

The board room meeting was another Carter-engineered success, gaining buy-in from senior corporate executives. I was beginning to believe Chase would be a long-term client, and executive relationships could only deepen over time, setting me up for bigger and bigger contracts. This, I was convinced, was the threshold of a long-prosperous career in consulting.

Tom Carter knew I used to be a salesman. He often talked to me about consultants, and I never felt as if his comments were directed at me. I guessed, in spite of what I liked to think of as a successful transition to consulting, to Carter I would always be a sales guy. For him, that seemed to be fine, in fact better than the alternative. While Logan worked the technology folks, he wanted somebody who could help him sell up to his management. Nevertheless, it fed my occasional paranoid schizophrenic mood swings. Is he trying to tell me to stick to sales?

Carter had spent a good part of his career at Chase in assignments overseas. What I found most interesting were his stories about international consultants. He told me that while he was working international, Chase had hired a management-consulting firm to help cut costs. In Hong Kong, Chase had owned a junk boat that was used for shuttling executives between Hong Kong locations and neighboring islands. The consulting firm recommended selling the boat. After all, they argued, banks were not supposed to be in the boat-taxi business. As it turned out, meetings were delayed, appointments were missed, and business was lost. These problems occurred because of the inability to find alternate reliable transportation. According to Tom, it also turned out that Chase spent close to two times the cost of their own boat on annual junk boat rental fees.

Tom told me that in Germany a management-consulting firm had recommended firing the coffee lady in a major Chase facility as part of the cost-cutting efforts. This particular woman had been there for years, knew how everyone liked their coffee and what pastries they liked. She would go out of her way to provide high-quality customer service to employees at the facility. Her service had apparently become important and very much appreciated by the people who worked there. When she was fired, the employees went on strike. They refused to work until the woman was rehired.

"So, anyway, that's what I think about management consultants, and there's far too many of 'em around here."

"What do you say, . . . let's go back to the board room and get the guns."

I could live with Carter thinking of me as a salesman.

While I knew there would be periods of downtime working for Chase, I had managed to develop a good relationship with some key managers. When we did work, they paid well. After the initial contract, we were working on an hourly fee basis. What we delivered seemed to meet their needs. They were also fun to be around. We had somehow stumbled into a good thing. I just needed to work on that patience thing while I also worked on increasing revenue from all of my clients.

Consultants had become ingrained as part of the business model at Chase. Like anything else, there were trade-offs. Both Michael and Tom seemed to understand this. They also understood the importance of minding the store. They weren't about to give free reign to the consultants and let them run things their way—not on their watch. They had both been around long enough to see the abuses. They knew the risks in using consultants. Manage us, or we will manage you.

Given a choice, they probably would have sent all of us packing. For them, hiring consultants had two purposes. On the analysis side, it was purely a defensive move to neutralize all the other consultants hired by different groups at Chase with different agendas. As long as they had the clout to hire their own consultants for the cross-organizational analysis projects, they could maintain at least some level of control. For integration work, it was to offset the reduced number of employees, thanks to corporate downsizing. They both worked at keeping the "analysts," such as Logan and me, by default, separate from the integrators. They recognized the potential conflict of interest if the two were one. "We recommend you get rid of employees and hire us."

During one of our follow-on contracts, I dropped in on Mike Dellano.

He took me through a piece of work he had developed a while ago for Chase Manhattan on architecture. It was a mapping schema that tied every technology project back to a corporate goal. "This is how you put teeth in architecture," he said. "If a technology project does not relate to a corporate goal, I will not approve it." He went on to explain that this approach had proven to be a morale booster. It helped educate employees from senior executives to the programmer on how technology was being leveraged to help the business. "Even the programmers need to know that what they are doing is important for meeting our corporate goals," he said. For Dellano, Chase employees always came first.

When the right moment came, I asked Dellano a question that had been on my mind for some time: "Mike, how come you don't hire the big-name consultants for projects, you know, like Andersen?"

He paused before speaking. "A couple reasons. One, they're very expensive. The other reason is that Chemical Bank uses Andersen. Chemical is one of our major competitors. If our goal is to be a market leader, why would I want to use the same consultants advising my competitor?"

"There must be some groups in Chase using Andersen."

"Maybe, but not in my area. I know they are very good at what they do. . . ."

"So, are you telling me that if the opportunity presents itself, I shouldn't take any consulting work at Chemical?"

"I wouldn't stop you. It's your call."

He had said it with a devilish smile. Yeah, my call.

Being around guys like Carter and Dellano was truly a learning experience, sure to increase billing value. Carter provided the street smarts and Dellano the big-picture wisdom. One day Dellano took issue with one of the standard selling responses of the day. I don't remember how it came up, but it wasn't from anything I had said.

"You know, I don't buy that the customer is always right."

"What do you mean?"

"Sometimes the customer is wrong. For example, I want my consultants to tell me when they disagree or see something I might have missed. What good are they if they don't? Ever hear of Sy Syms?"

Of course I had. They were a New York–area clothing store.

"I think they have a terrific slogan: 'An educated consumer is our best customer.' Right now we need to better educate our people on the business and on this technology stuff. Unfortunately, we don't get education from most of our consultants. If they were smart, they'd educate us. And I'd probably hire them more."

Oh yeah? I wondered if he was playing with my head, or if he really meant this. In any case, Dellano was onto something, but an educated "client" didn't have the same ring as "customer." It was the last thing most in the consulting business wanted to provide. In a way, it was encouraging to know that one of the people I had grown to respect would never make the transition to client. He probably didn't care what we called him; the relationship would still be the same. Dellano would always be in charge.

He then asked me if I knew about the first known consultant. Here we go, I thought. Dellano explained that this was a legend passed down over the years through a tradition of oral folklore. It had somehow come to his recent attention. It happened thousands of years ago in a village near the cradle of civilization. A wise man from a distant land who was just passing through agreed to remain in the village when the elders promised him fabulous gifts if he stayed and shared his wisdom. While he was there, a terrible fire started and burned down the entire village. Fortunately, the villagers escaped in time. So did the wise man. When they returned, there was nothing that had escaped the flames. Even the livestock had been destroyed. The dead carcasses were still smoldering. The elders asked the wise man to walk through the burned remains of the village and assess the situation.

As he began to walk through the burned-out remnants of the former village, the smell of the charred livestock immediately caught his attention. He reached down and touched a burned pig with the tip of a finger. "Yeow," he screamed as he quickly stuck his finger in his mouth to relieve the pain. "Gee, that tastes pretty good," he said to himself. He walked back to the elders and suggested that they feast on the remains of the burned livestock. The people of the village had never tasted anything so good. It was far superior to the raw meat they had eaten in the past. The feast lasted for days. Several precious gifts were passed on to the wise man.

Eventually, they finished the last of the broiled livestock. As the feast ended, the elders gathered. They called for the wise man. They told him all the food was gone. They wanted more cooked meat, but from where? They asked him to go and think about their plight. He did. Several hours later he returned with an answer. As the wise man rose to speak, the elders could hardly contain themselves with their anticipation and great hopes for a solution to their problem. Finally, the wise man replied, "Go burn another village."

Naturally, I laughed. Why take it personally? I was a salesman.

Tom Carter's new department went on to be very successful. By the end of 1993 there were over fifty employees and consultants in his department dedicated to revenue reporting and analysis. Analysts on Wall Street and in technology continued to praise client/server solutions.

System 10 from Sybase was rolled out in lots of other companies to address "enterprisewide" requirements.

Early on many consultants had been enthusiastic about System 10. Several Gartner Group analysis reports, though somewhat guarded in typical fashion, talked about the potential benefits of the System 10 architecture. Gartner Group projected that Sybase with its new architecture would surpass all other vendors and fight it out with Oracle for the number one position in the database market.[4] They were right about the emergence of Sybase, but missed it with System 10. In *Datamation* magazine, Judith R. Davis, an industry analyst with the Patricia Seybold Group, said that System 10 had all the right pieces. "Sybase is looking at client/server at a higher level than a simple database tools and server vendor might. They are going after the client/server infrastructure," she said.[5]

Myke Miller, a manager of application development for Andersen Consulting, indicated that System 10 would allow Andersen for the first time to "replace mainframe systems with client/server equivalents." Miller was attempting to build a huge System 10 application for major airlines called "Passenger Revenue Accounting." According to the magazine, Andersen had sold it to Delta Air Lines and three other undisclosed carriers. "We are basically replacing a mainframe for each carrier with our PRA application," said Miller. A 1 percent revenue gain was estimated for each carrier. Miller went on to say that System 10 "is the only product that can meet the needs of this application."[6] For a product barely out of the gate, with no established track record for the roll-out of System 10, this was a high-risk proposition. The stock value of Sybase skyrocketed as many jumped on the System 10 bandwagon.

Shortly after it was rolled out, System 10 became a lightening rod for complaints. There was a combination of performance and support issues. Users were furious. Gartner Group issued a report critical of System 10's performance in large corporate environments.[7] Sybase's stock value tumbled. It was attributed in large part to problems with System 10.[8] Sybase eventually had to bite the bullet and move quickly to replace System 10 with a newly architected product. You got it: System 11. Sybase would regain credibility with future releases and other products, but even they had to admit that System 10 failed.

In a July 3, 1995, article in *Computerworld*, a Delta Airlines spokesperson said that they were dumping System 10 because it "doesn't meet vendor support requirements."[9] By then, Delta had purchased over $3 million in Sybase products and services. A senior technology officer resigned abruptly. There was no mention about Andersen Consulting's involvement in recommending the System 10 solution, or the implementation effort. I talked with a technology manager at Delta. He said that Andersen had become entrenched in the project and it took several years before they could be dislodged. Andersen managed to generate significant revenue from the project, and escaped without any negative publicity. As a consultant, you gotta love the lack of accountability. It sure beat sales.

SUMMARY OF OBSERVATIONS

- Technology needs to be viewed from a business context.

- Given that consultants most often want to secure the next contract, their ability to provide an objective view is questionable at best. They will attempt to steer things in a direction that best positions them for future work.

- A major role of consultants in the 1990s was to provide insurance for management, minimizing risks in decision making. This is often one of the most important reasons consultants are hired; it is not necessarily to provide unique expertise.

- There were hidden costs with client/server based on integration, support, and ongoing maintenance. Consulting fees represented a high percentage of client/server costs.

- Like in the construction industry, a technology architecture can provide a blueprint for meeting business needs with the right kind of technology working in concert. This requires a unique set of skills that are often missing from most integration-oriented consulting firms specializing in the roll-out of specific technologies.

- Manage consultants, or they will manage you.

- Consultants don't always lead you the best way to the solution. They may need "on-the-job training," provide misleading recommendations, and misread events and their consequences. Don't let them burn the village to cook a roast.

NOTES

1. David Rogers, *The Future of American Banking* (New York: McGraw-Hill, 1993), 126; "Digest of Earnings Reports," *Wall Street Journal*, 20 January 1993, 16.

2. Lynn Berg, "The Scoop on Client/Server Costs," *Computerworld*, 16 November 1992, 169.

3. Meghan O'Leary, "Work in Progress," *CIO*, 1 November 1992, 52–60.

4. Tom Davey, "Three Bay Area Companies Lead Pack in Database Race," *San Francisco Business Times*, 17 June 1994, 4A.

5. Mike Ricciuti, "Sybase Steps Up to the Enterprise," *Datamation*, 1 July 1993, 21.

6. Ibid, 21.

7. Kim S. Nash, "Sybase Disputes Report Slamming System 10," *Computerworld*, 11 July 1994, 7.

8. Katherine Bull, "Sybase off Base," *Informationweek*, 17 April 1995, 104.

9. Kim S. Nash, "Delta Ejects Sybase as Standard," *Computerworld*, 3 July 1995, 1, 103.

CHAPTER THREE

"ME, TOO,"

AND THEN CAME LOU

"**S**o you worked for IBM? . . . A real shame what happened to that company. They had the world by the balls. . . . Too bad those sales reps became so arrogant and complacent."

"Let me tell you about our consulting business . . ."

They call it cold calling for good reason. By the middle of 1994 things had dried up again with our new clients, and I was out again beating the bushes. I was starting to realize that our business was falling into a predictable cycle, and I didn't like it. Logan liked it less and was getting nervous. There were times when our clients all wanted us at once, but it never lasted more than two or three months. At all other times, we were shaking the trees to no avail. Efforts to expand the number of clients was time consuming and wasn't producing the desired results. If we didn't extend our offerings with our established base of clients from analysis into things like integration or selling products, as so many other consulting firms had done, we'd never get free from the cyclical pattern of work followed by no work.

During the busy times, we were limited by having only two people. The only way to get over the hump was to branch out into other areas where we could hire more help and multiply the billing. That's what we should have done. Instead, we kept up the crusade, looking for the next windmill.

We couldn't get the big jobs because we weren't big enough. We weren't big enough because we weren't getting the big jobs. Just when I was talking myself into biting the bullet and expanding, my company shrunk by half. It came to a final head between Will Logan and me. If things weren't happening fast enough for me, they were standing still for Logan. We decided to go our separate ways for a variety of reasons, not the least of which were financial considerations. We also realized we would always be fighting different crusades. And in the spirit of Danny Glover's character in *Lethal Weapon*, we were both getting "too old for this shit." In spite of the occasional broken glass in his wake, I knew I'd miss him. With Logan, you never knew what to expect. After finishing my IBM career surrounded by staffies, in a warped kind of way he was refreshing. I decided to continue on with Informed Technology Decisions. There were only two things I could do. One was to go back to letter writing and follow-up phone calls. The other was to grow a beard.

One of the opportunities I decided to chase was with my former employer. Why not head for the eye of the storm? With all the effort involved in managing my own business, I couldn't help but keep tabs on the changes taking place. Forgive me Satchel, I was still looking back. All the personal ups and downs with my former employer kept rattling around somewhere in the back of my head. In the meantime, IBM's competitive edge was continuing to erode faster than the beaches of the northern Jersey shore. The difference from just a few short years ago was jarring. By 1993 the stock had plummeted, and shareholders were up in arms.[1] Shockingly, IBM revenue had fallen from $64.5 billion in 1992 to $62.7 billion in 1993. The giant computer manufacturer was breaking the wrong kind of records. Back-to-back operating losses of $8.2 billion in 1992 and $8.6 billion in 1993 left little doubt that the company was in crisis. Consensus seemed to be that there wasn't much that could help now, short of selling off major assets. Some of the same consultants who talked incessantly in the past about IBM's strengths were now highlighting the weaknesses that caused the collapse.

This, I said to myself, could be the place where I as a consultant could find the right niche. It wasn't just that I had learned a lot while working for IBM. As a consultant, I now had credibility employees could only dream about. All I had to do was get to the right person within what was still a huge bureaucracy. That right person had to be someone who didn't know me when I was just an employee. The ones who knew me before rarely had the vision to see me as anything else, much less a valuable consultant worth shelling out bucks for getting me to share impressive nuggets of advice.

So what happened to IBM and its overwhelming dominance? It begged the question: What really did go wrong, and was it different than accepted opinion? I decided it was. Could it happen again to others? Maybe it had already started.

Competitiveness had always been a key differentiator for my former employer. So much so that the threat of IBM world supremacy had been on many people's minds for a long time, most notably federal judges, prosecutors, and competitors. Like Microsoft in the 1990s, IBM had been accused many times in the past of using its monopoly position to engage in predatory behavior. For IBM, it was a revolving door of cases for almost thirty years. Some of these suits were settled by "consent decrees" that increased competitive exposure and curbed a number of IBM's business practices. I remembered one of my college professors defining the term "consent decree" for the class. "It is when a company admits to doing nothing wrong and promises to never do it again," he said. In spite of the legal problems, IBM's financial results were off the charts, up through the beginning of the 1980s. Former McKinsey consultants Thomas J. Peters and Robert H. Waterman Jr., authors of the best selling novel, *In Search of Excellence*, had ranked IBM as "excellent" in all key financial performance measurements between 1961 and 1980.[2] If the government couldn't stop them, who could?

One of the great things about consultants was that in spite of all the times they had given bad advice, corporate managers continued to hire them. This was certainly true at IBM. It would be unfair to suggest that consultants, and IBM's handling of consultants, were to blame for the loss of revenue, the loss in the market share, and even worse, the loss in "mind" share, as customers looked elsewhere for technology solutions to meet their business needs. Yet, in several critical areas, consultants and analysts, from both Wall Street and the computer industry, helped fan the fire.

In the early 1980s, many were weighing in with opinions that IBM's success wasn't going to stop any time soon. Market share was expected to go no place but up. It's entry into the personal computer business, along with major capital investments, and reengineering its manufacturing facilities were applauded. From *Fortune* magazine in 1983: "Yet IBM's rewards have already been sumptuous and are likely to increase. Carol Muratose, an analyst for the brokerage house CJ. Lawrence, likens IBM's current situation to its position twenty years ago, when it bet $5 million on the System/360, revolutionizing its own prospects and the world of computing."[3] Gideon Gartner argued that IBM's strategies to reduce time to market by producing products faster and expanding plant capacity was putting tremendous pressure on competitors. "They [competitors] must greatly increase R&D and capital spending to keep up," he said.[4] The article suggested that IBM's competitors were feeling the ground "tremble."

Deregulation became the new battle cry as it blew into Washington, D.C., in the 1980s on the coattails of the Reagan revolution. The sentiment for antitrust went the way of the leisure suit. Now IBM could once again take off the gloves. There was more ground for trembling. With the changes taking place in the 1980s, consultants were saying that the "sleeping elephant" had risen from its government-imposed slumber and was dancing once again.

In the early 1980s, IBM began dancing with new business partners. Early on, the company misread the significance of the emerging personal computer revolution. So did many of the industry analysts. It wasn't until IBM observed the pioneering achievements of Xerox Corporation and Apple Computer that it decided to get serious. Plans were finalized to jump-start IBM's personal computer offerings through what was called an Independent Business Unit (IBU). By 1983 IBM was receiving rave reviews from analysts and the trade press for having the foresight to set up an "entrepreneurial" subsidiary for the personal computer business completely unencumbered by its large parent company. The IBU would be free to buy parts and outsource functions to non-IBM manufacturers.[5]

A stroke of genius, according to many, was the publishing of internal specifications for personal computer parts. This was the precursor to vendor sharing, or what became commonly called "open systems." But IBM did all the sharing. In general, industry experts considered it a good business decision. If more suppliers could make personal computer parts, it would potentially reduce IBM's purchasing costs and increase competitive advantage. Growth of the personal computer IBM-clone business was never anticipated. What, somebody buy a look-alike PC without the IBM logo? Somehow the strategists had missed that one, too.

If it was all in the strategy, then why not find cheaper help? IBM's senior management was led to believe that customers would continue to pay a premium for the IBM logo, whether it was on a product purchased from a sales rep, a business partner, or through a Sears and Roebuck catalogue. The logo sold itself. I remember seeing a commissioned study that supported these conclusions years later when it was no longer considered "confidential and restricted." The study argued that, based on the brand, an IBM personal computer could practically sell itself. There were those arguing that all IBM products should be treated as off-the-shelf retail stock, not just the personal computers. The IBM brand was everything.

Then there was the most colossal move of all. IBM had decided to outsource responsibility for personal computer major components to business partners. The most critical guts of the system would depend on third parties. The development of the personal computer operating software was outsourced to Microsoft Corporation, and the microchip business went to Intel Corporation. These moves were done in the pursuit of quicker turnaround and accelerating contribution to profit. Licensing agreements with Microsoft and Intel looked better on the spreadsheet than the alternative of building in-house. These licensing agreements were nonexclusive, paving the way for Microsoft and Intel to sell the same products to the clone makers. That they were nonexclusive contracts was reported early on in the press, but no one seemed concerned.[6] So where were those world-renowned IBM corporate lawyers who so often said no to the salespeople trying to structure customer deals? Where were the consultants and industry watchers? Didn't they see it coming? With all the IBM watching, how did they miss two little start-ups taking IBM to the cleaners without offering so much as a hint of caution?

I had heard an interesting rumor, the veracity of which I cannot vouch for, about how Microsoft got its first IBM contract—the contract that first put it on the map and launched one of the most incredible success stories in corporate America. Bill Gates's mother was on the board of directors for the United Way of America. So was John Opel, the chairman of IBM before John Akers. One day Gates's mother approached Opel, "John, my son Billy has a little software company. . . . Do you think possibly your company might be able to help him?" Help he did. Opel mentioned it to one of his administrative assistants, and before you knew it the entire staff was running around frantically trying to help Billy. It was a cultural thing. Everybody jumped when a request came down from the chairman. Helping Billy could help your career.

IBM outsourcing deals helped both Microsoft and Intel grow into giants in their own right. Both companies eventually surpassed IBM in leadership and influence in this important emerging market. They became the forces to reckon with in the PC market, while IBM fought it out in price wars with the PC hardware clones. Bill Gates became the richest man in the world. Yet, early on, many consultants thought the battle for PC mind share would be between IBM and Apple. They believed IBM's bold new steps with business partners would lead to unrivaled success. In the early days Microsoft and Intel received scarcely more than footnote attention from consultants and the trade press in the shadow of the accolades bestowed on IBM.[7] Microsoft and Intel were merely cogs in the IBM wheel. It was assumed they were all part of the same team, with Microsoft and Intel playing the supporting role to Big Blue. The new juggernauts flew by IBM and the analysts like stealth fighter jets.

I learned from a retired senior IBM executive a well-kept secret. Several years into the Microsoft partnership, Bill Gates paid a visit to IBM corporate headquarters in Armonk. He met with the top brass and offered to sell his company to them for approximately $72 million. According to this executive, Gates was laughed out of Armonk. Not only did they blow it on the front end, they had an opportunity to recap lost opportunity and still blew it. This is not to suggest that IBM could have been just as successful as Gates if they had bought him out and taken over Microsoft. Given IBM's track record with previous acquisitions, it is highly doubtful they could have equaled the entrepreneurial success of Microsoft under Gates's leadership. What is remarkable is that when Gates offered to sell, even he had no idea of the potential value of his company. A few short years later Microsoft would make Gates the richest individual on the planet.

By 1990 financial results for IBM were falling below expectations. IBM was spending money in all the wrong places. They were squandering one opportunity after another. Then IBM announced a series of reorganization plans along with new strategies to deflect concerns about declining margins. A common theme was that IBM needed to get closer to its customers. It was a back-to-basics strategy that was supposed to restore competitiveness. Ironically, more business partners were enlisted to assist here as well while IBM management continued placing primary focus on cutting costs. Business partners could help meet the new customer-focus objectives, while at the same time IBM reduced expenses.

In the beginning of 1991, IBM senior management was insisting that a new revamped "customer-driven" strategy would turn things around. Norton Paley, a strategic-marketing consultant who had previously done consulting work for IBM, praised the strategy that would help IBM get closer to the customer. If he wanted to get hired again, praising the strategy made good business sense. He also gave the executives responsible for strategy an escape clause if things didn't pan out. Paley asserted that execution could be the weak link in making the strategy successful. After outlining elements within the IBM plan for the industry publication *Marketing News*, Paley concluded his remarks by saying, "Maintain knowledgeable sales and customer service personnel and ally with other business partners to form mutually beneficial relationships to customize solutions for customers. Instill within each member of the team that excellence is the responsibility for every individual."[8] That execution was the problem became the accepted point of view of management, consultants, analysts, and just about everybody else. It's what all the mainstream press books were all about.

The decision to increase reliance on consultants and business partners for promoting IBM within customer accounts fit an ever increasing, quick-fix cost-cutting pattern. It also had some long-term negative consequences. In many cases it created a middle layer of people between IBM and its customers that flew in the face of the "get closer to the customer" strategy. Business partners were doing more of the selling. Consultants were debriefing customers on IBM announcements and strategies on a more regular basis, stealing the airtime that had previously been reserved for the IBM account manager. Loss of corporate account control to resellers and consultants further aggravated IBM's growing problems.

They had the direct contact with many customers. When things went bad, regardless of who was to blame, IBM was vulnerable for taking the hit. In lots of cases, they were no longer on-site to defend themselves.

For years IBM had played Wall Street analysts like a string section. It seemed as if overnight the street turned into a pack of hungry hounds. They were now telling IBM what it needed to do. To appease the pack, IBM had to slim down fast. Paley's argument crystallized. If the strategy was sound, and yet the business was not turning around as projected, IBM's weakness had to be in execution. Complacent employees became the convenient scapegoat for the erosion of IBM's market leadership. Only downsizing could address IBM's ongoing lackluster results and ballooning costs. The concept was all of a sudden less repugnant to a senior management team that had previously endorsed a full-employment policy along with rapid expansion. Aggressive efforts to downsize the IBM workforce were initiated. Affected employees became part of a "management initiated attrition" program. They were called MIAs. Reliance on business partners would continue to increase as more employees were MIAed.

No longer was there talk from consultants about IBM doubling, or even tripling sales within four to five years as there had been in the 1980s. By now they all seemed to have explanations as to what went wrong, and in most cases it was a problem related in some way to execution. In the midst of the turmoil caused by weakening business results, IBM Chairman John Akers criticized employees for not working hard enough, suggesting that sales reps should be told that if they missed a sale, their job was at risk. In a 1992 note to employees, he said, "I am convinced that some of our people do not understand that they have a deeply personal stake in declining market share, revenue, and profits." Wall Street analysts viewed the note as positive. It signaled future layoffs. Robert Djurdjevic, a market research consultant, said, "The only problem is that it is six years late."[9] As the lowest-level employees responsible for growing the business, sales reps were among the most vulnerable and least able to defend themselves. Low-level employees didn't hire consultants. In bad times they did what they were told and either waited for the next shoe to drop, or simply left.

By the end of 1991, it was estimated that there were 360,000 IBM employees, about 47,000 less than five years earlier. In the next five years, the number of employees would shrink to about 270,000. When downsizing wasn't improving results fast enough to please Wall Street, John Akers said in 1992 that his company would adopt a new model. He suggested that IBM would be decentralized into thirteen autonomous organizations. Todd Hixon, an electronics-industry specialist from the Boston Consulting Group, explained that IBM hoped to create leaner, more manageable lines of business. According to *Fortune* magazine, Hixon believed that, in general, IBM marketing and services lacked the kind of people needed for the new IBM "companies."[10] Here, too, IBM management was being served up an excuse. To make the new structure work, they would have to swap sales reps for a different breed of workers, business partners.

John Akers was finally dismissed as noted in the February 22, 1993, issue of *Fortune*.[11] In fairness to Akers, while the more fundamental problems were in flawed strategy, it was a strategy gone bad long before he took over the helm. With a shake-up starting at the top, the big question became, What should IBM do now? There was a chorus of analysts suggesting that IBM needed to be more like other companies. That's where I saw my opening. Preaching competitive differentiation as a solution could separate me from the pack.

When it starts to turn bad for a company, consultants smell lots of opportunity. That's not to say that all consultants try to benefit from the adversity of others. That would be the same as assuming that every lawyer chases ambulances or every prospective politician applauds economic downturns during the incumbent's term. Not every Wall Street broker starts thinking of what commodities will be needed and what stocks to buy up when disaster strikes. The thing that struck me about consultants was how easily they could transition from one point of view to another. One day they could be telling you the wrong things to do. The next they're telling you what went wrong, as if they had just stepped into your company for the first time and you had never laid eyes on them before. Of course management rarely calls them on this. Someone could question their judgment in hiring the consultant in the first place. Who else would they have to rely on? Employees?

With IBM in one hell of a mess, I knew there would be consultants knocking at every door offering their services. If I played my cards right, this could be a lucrative area for me, but how could I get myself heard? For me to stand any chance of cracking IBM, I would have to try something different to rise above the fray. I decided to go straight to the new chairman.

His name was Lou Gerstner. This was the first time IBM had hired from the outside to fill this role. He would be the highest paid IBM executive in history with a base salary of $2 million. There were also bonus kickers estimated at approximately $1.5 million if he hit certain financial performance goals.[12] Based on Lou Gerstner's previous experience at R. J. Reynolds (RJR) Nabisco, it seemed to me that after all those "what's the right model?" meetings and commissioned studies, IBM had opted for reengineering the company into a consumer-goods style business. Why else would they hire a cereal, cookies, and tobacco guy? This would probably mean lots of autonomy for separate business units. The buying and selling of different lines of business couldn't be too far behind. I assumed Gerstner would continue the recently announced plan of the previous chairman to break up Big Blue into many little blues.

Within his first year, Lou had set an unexpected tone. In his address to Wall Street analysts on March 24, 1994, Gerstner said that while he wasn't finished "draining the swamp," he would not break IBM up.[13] He was also going to get the house in order before worrying about the "vision" thing. Did this mean the hordes of "strategy" and "modeling" consultants were out? Not too many executives were talking this way at the time. Gerstner argued that the competitive strength of IBM was in its ability to put it all together. No other technology company had the same array of products, services, and people. He actually said it: "people." No other company had the breath, according to Lou, to put it all together and solve customer problems.

A liberal democrat couldn't have opened the door with China in the middle of the Cold War. It had to be Nixon. Similarly, it took a former consumer-goods executive to convince the board of directors that selling IBM wasn't like selling cereal. Gerstner was arguing that the sum of IBM's parts was greater than the whole. He immediately recognized that IBM's greatest strength was getting the parts working together. It took an executive from a different industry to see it. I was actually surprised to learn that in addition to working for RJR, Gerstner had also worked as a consultant with McKinsey & Company. He didn't get stuck on vision like so many consulting strategists, and he didn't need to commiserate for months with an army of like-minded advisers before announcing plans.

Gerstner wasn't opposed to using consultants. He brought McKinsey into IBM for specific tasks, just as he did at RJR. Like RJR, plenty of fat had accumulated, especially during those misguided expansion years, and McKinsey was renowned for its cost cutting. Nonetheless, Gerstner seemed to have figured out pretty quick what needed to be done. There would be more cuts, but he gave the distinct impression that his new strategy would go way beyond cost reduction. He didn't seem to mind if his conclusions were contrary to the pundits from Wall Street to Cambridge. You had a sense he was a different breed.

I worked on developing a rationale for why IBM should hire me, even though it was a stretch. As an "independent" consultant over the last few years, I had an opportunity to observe IBM in competitive situations, and it was not a pretty sight. They had fallen into an old football strategy, the "prevent" defense. I had observed IBM using this play firsthand at Chase, Pitney Bowes, and Connecticut Mutual. Much like the football plan, prevent defense was reactive. It really meant no offense. Lots of yardage was conceded with most players lined up downfield protecting the goal line. The problem was that it gave the other team a chance to get close enough to make scoring the goal easier. The only hope for the prevent defense was that the clock would run out of time before the other team could score. Exactly the same was true at IBM, where reps were protecting the mainframe data center, commonly called the "glass house." Circling the wagons didn't prevent the competition from taking business away. The only thing the prevent strategy was successful at preventing was IBM from taking initiative. Unfortunately, IBM's react mode played right into the competition's hands, and there was no clock to protect them.

Based on his comments to Wall Street, it was obvious Gerstner was a take-charge kind of executive looking to move on a different tack. I drafted a letter to him expressing my support of his new plan of action and how my company could help make IBM more successful in winning competitive bids. The letter said something like, "Tom Watson had once pledged to FDR the commitment of IBM to help win World War II. I think today IBM is at war and I am pledging the commitment of my company to help you." In other words, I would consult for IBM, not its competitors. Loyalty from a consultant, now that had to be a unique concept. You can try crazy things like that when you are your own boss.

Getting the letter in his hands would be the difficult part. If I got past the gatekeepers, I'd then have to explain how in the world a one-man operation with no track record could have any kind of a significant impact in helping IBM. That was something to worry about later. First I'd have to get through the organization that wrote the book on controlling the flow of information to the executive. Gerstner hadn't been there long enough to start trimming back the large administrative support organization he inherited. The swamp went all the way to headquarters.

With a new chairman from the outside coming in, there had to be lots of corporate angst. To be successful in the old IBM world, they used to say you needed a "rabbi." With the departure of one executive and the entrance of another, people scramble for safe haven. Whose rising career should I try and latch onto now? After all those years of sucking up, I'm back to ground zero? Maybe I should have taken one of those early retirement packages.

Plenty of IBM career staff people must have been hiding in trenches waiting for the smoke to clear. My only hope was for my letter to slip through the smoke. I sent the letter to Gerstner's attention, assuming that the odds of him ever seeing it were very low. Typically some administrative assistant would fire it off to some lower-level executive's office for a boilerplate response. "Thank you very much for your interest. At the present time, however, . . ."

Within a few days, I received an answer to my communication from the head of IBM Marketing for the United States. Unfortunately, it was exactly the kind of response I feared. He politely thanked me for my letter. He then indicated that there were already major efforts in place to market against competition, and at this time no additional help would be needed. "Not from you, anyway." That's not what was printed on the letterhead in my hand, but that's how it registered in my head. Oh well, I thought, it was worth the try. Some things never change.

A few days after receiving this rejection, I had a call from a staff assistant to the director responsible for IBM's worldwide marketing of client/server. By now even the mainframe-centric IBM had gotten into the exploding client/server market. The staff assistant told me that Lou Gerstner had recently met with his boss. Gerstner had handed him the letter. You had to love it. The chairman's office was operating as it did in the past. They were still trying to keep stuff from riffraff like me from getting in the gate. Apparently this was not the kind of executive you could simply handle. He was getting personally involved in the business. Imagine a CEO from one of the largest worldwide corporations actually reading his own mail and in some cases personally acting upon it. Everybody I met said, "Lou Gerstner really liked your letter." It had a way of making them like it, too.

The letter eventually led to a contract with the IBM Competitive Marketing Center in Copenhagen. This group was responsible for providing competitive analysis and education for the worldwide field force. My contract was to develop a one-day class to help IBM sales reps compete more successfully against Hewlett Packard. While it was a great opportunity, I didn't care much for the terms of the contract. That was because it was a very good contract for IBM, the client. The IBM Competitive Marketing Center would own whatever I produced. They would reserve the right to repackage it and use it as they saw fit. They also wanted to videotape my meetings with them to develop additional script material for marketing center presenters. "In case you say additional things during discussion that are not in the written material you provided," I was told.

I could see where this was going. Even if I could produce the greatest piece of competitive analysis ever done, my contribution would be buried, and they could take all the credit. If they didn't like it, I could just as easily be dismissed with no downside for them. They had fulfilled the request from the chairman to give me a shot. Informed Technology Decisions would still be an unknown within most of IBM. It was the equivalent of ghost writing and not exactly the break I was looking for. This was not going to establish more recognition and lead to an avalanche of business from my former employer as I had initially hoped. Unfortunately, I wasn't exactly in a position where I could pick up the phone and call big Lou about my concerns. They were still giving me a great opportunity.

A piece of the work was subcontracted to another consultant who had become a good friend. He was a little more low key than Logan. The bulk of the work was completed by me. I was beginning to build more confidence in my ability to play the role of consultant. The strategy we developed attempted to change the playing field to business requirements versus "speeds and feeds." It was becoming the Informed Technology Decisions mantra. Making this argument to competitive analysis people within IBM was an uphill battle. They were analysis specialists, not salespeople. Driving sales and preventing competitive losses was somebody else's problem. What was important was that they had a job to do. Analysis was king. It generally fit a prescribed format and this was "speeds and feeds" comparisons. Competitive Marketing Center was not the best of names given what they really did. The Center for Matrix Tables and In-depth Technical Comparison would have been more to the point: give us lots of boxes in a spreadsheet with IBM features and functions compared to somebody else's.

Staffs at IBM facilities such as the Competitive Marketing Center most often came from technical backgrounds and were responsible for supporting specific products and how they stacked up with the competition, technical spec to technical spec. Staff personnel sometimes had minimal to no customer marketing on their resumes. They went along with the accepted party line that was aped time and again by most industry analysts and splattered all over the press. For IBM to compete more effectively with a company like Hewlett-Packard (HP), it had to become more like HP.

At the time, HP had one of the hottest client/server hardware products in the market, the HP 9000. It was blowing away IBM's Risc/6000 and most of the other competitors in independent benchmarking measurement tests; or as they said in the industry, the "bake-off" wars. My suggested response was: so? I argued that people were caring too much about lab results and not enough about real-world performance. What mattered more than how a product tested by itself in a lab was how well it could work with other installed products at the customer site.

Few were starting with a clean slate. Few would throw everything out and start again with all new products. Even if the plan was to replace everything, there would be transition time, and it was almost always longer than projected. Why not go with a product that used the latest technology but could also integrate well with the current environment? There was still a lot of IBM gear out there, and IBM was still one of the best companies in both integration and minimizing disruption during technology transitions. Adding this to the equation could change the conclusion on what to buy. Don't drill down on the bells and whistles, I argued. Look at the big picture. "Hit 'em where they ain't."[14]

I also tried to point out that this was a highly competitive industry, and each of the major hardware vendors such as IBM, HP, and Sun Microsystems would continue to leapfrog each other in benchmarking tests. Product life cycles were collapsing faster than a speeding bullet as new generation products were introduced by all competitors at an accelerating pace. It didn't make sense to pick a vendor's product based solely on a single test in one isolated point in time. Instead, the criteria should be based on a combination of critical business factors. Of course, the factors I sighted were ones where IBM's product outperformed HP's.

At best, Copenhagen was luke warm about the work. They told me they were looking more for technical comparisons—exactly where HP wanted to drive the decision point. Most of the consultants they hired were technical specialists, kindred souls with the internal analysts. This time they had hired the wrong guy and only because an executive had sent them a copy of my letter to Gerstner. They got what I was absolutely convinced IBM needed to win more business. I was learning that on some subjects I could be as unbending as Will Logan, a scary thought. There were a few opportunities to present my work to IBM field personnel. They were much more enthusiastic. I received a letter after one of these presentations from a senior rep who helped coordinate things. This presentation was at IBM's old branch office on Maiden Lane in New York City. This was the branch serving the Wall Street financial district, and the sales reps who worked there were considered one of the toughest crowds in the company. In the letter, he indicated that they were under siege by HP in many of their major financial accounts. He said that, as a group, they felt they had finally gotten something "practical" they could use. According to the letter, they especially liked my suggested selling techniques based on *The Art of War.*

Here was a major advantage to being a consultant. In the old days at IBM, information flowed one way, and it was always downhill from corporate. You had to leave the company to be heard beyond the confines of your cubicle. Just as was the case with Chase Manhattan, there were probably lots of people still working for IBM who could have told them the same things. My views on IBM hadn't changed much from when I had left. Watching IBM on this side of the fence only reinforced my previous views. The nice thing about coming back as a consultant was that I was getting a lot more respect. Whether they agreed with me or not, people listened to the consultant. I liked that.

Shortly after finishing the work with Copenhagen, I was contacted by the IBM Networking Systems line of business to assist them in developing marketing education. The Copenhagen project may not have been the windfall I wanted, but having it under my belt did give me more credibility for winning additional IBM contracts.

The Internet was already starting to do to client/server what client/server had done to mainframes. Distributed departmental networks and individual users could hook up to a worldwide network with access for everybody. Why load up each client workstation with lots of software when most of what was needed could be accessed via the Web? The new buzzword was *thin client*, or in other words, a workstation with Web access, versus a souped-up personal computer fully loaded (*fat client*). Workstations could now be connected to Web-based networks at a fraction of the cost of traditional client/server workstations. Thin client wasn't very different from "dumb terminals" used with mainframes, except that it sounded more leading edge and politically correct. Better than admitting we were headed *Back to the Future*.

For vendors this fundamental shift meant an opportunity to reshuffle the deck. In IBM's 1994 annual report chairman, Lou Gerstner, stated that one of IBM's top priorities would be to establish leadership in network-centric computing.[15] This would be easier said than done, given IBM's rapidly declining position in this market. Gerstner's comments signaled that IBM as a company would finally fully embrace the Internet. Up until then there were still groups within the giant corporation trying to develop and promote competitive networking technologies.

There were those in IBM still saying things like: "Our networking solutions offer huge benefits. We can manage bandwidth and prioritize workload. You can't do that with the Internet."

Somehow they kept missing the obvious, "But the Internet is free." [16]

Cisco Systems was one of the early pioneers in the development and promotion of Internet technologies and had risen to become one of the top worldwide technology companies. Did IBM really think it could fend off Cisco and reclaim the top perch? This would be a huge challenge. A smart consultant with other sources of income would have surely passed it by.

I was hired to develop competitive marketing education for IBM reps to help them against Cisco. This included teaching classes in the United States, Europe, and Asia. In spite of the enormous challenge, I looked forward to the project, especially the chance to go to Asia. I had never been to that part of the world before. Asia was also one of the few bright spots for IBM networking in terms of business growth. A recent economic downturn in Japan didn't seem to be stopping IBM from winning networking business. It was a real contrast to the U.S. economy, which was beginning to boom while IBM Networking Systems was taking a bath.

Networking was still a multibillion-dollar business for IBM, but most of this revenue came from the networking requirements for the large number of already installed mainframe systems. In the past IBM didn't have to sell networking. When a customer bought a proprietary IBM computer, IBM communication hardware and software was a prerequisite.

By the middle '90s, IBM was under full-scale attack from the client/server internetworking vendors, led by Cisco Systems. Cisco sold routers, often called the "black boxes" behind the Internet. Routers passed data from one client/server network to another, across the corporate campus, or across the world. The mainframe, IBM's premier product, was no longer needed as the central brain of the network coordinating the flow of data traffic. As a new, commanding market leader, Cisco was proving to be highly flexible and was already attempting to reinvent itself. It was attempting to increase its dominance with an aggressive marketing strategy and some very astute acquisitions.[17]

At the same time that Cisco was expanding market leadership, many of IBM's newer products were late to market and were not selling as expected. The networking business for IBM had laid off an additional 300 people before the close of 1994, bringing the annual division total of eliminated jobs to over 1,000.[18] In early 1995 the head of this business unit resigned from the company at about the same time as the head of U.S. Marketing. She joined my brief pen pal, the head of U.S. Sales, who had replied "thanks, but no thanks" to my Gerstner letter. The new chairman was cleaning house in the executive ranks.

Networking in the 1990s was a great place to be, unless you were in the United States selling for IBM, where morale was below shoe-top level. Nothing much appeared to be working well for IBM Networking Systems on the domestic side in those days. These were a new breed of reps, and not just because they were now dressed "business casual," as opposed to wearing suits. Many of the new U.S. sales reps were "redeployed" from product development and other technical areas. It was not for any great love or expertise in selling. The only reason they were in marketing was that they were given two choices: start pedaling, or start walking. It was a subtle way of thinning the herd.

Imagine a sales force with a large number of people for whom selling was the last thing they ever wanted to do. They didn't have the benefit of a year of training before qualifying like I did. They didn't have senior people as mentors. No Honest, no Ice, no General. They didn't even have blue suits. So if there was no structured training program and no senior reps to teach them, what would they do? There could be only one solution: bring on the consultants.

I was one of many hired to help. Not surprisingly, most of the consultants participating in the education program were technical specialists who thought the sun rose and set because that's the way a great big computer program in the sky was written. Competitive marketing equals technojabber. How would reps learn to close a deal from technologists who never spent a day in sales? Making matters worse, most of the new reps were also techies and would rather hear talk on technology than talk on selling. There was a large number of technoconsultant wanna-bes within the new group of reps.

Before each Cisco lecture began, I would ask the IBM students to fill out a survey. The survey asked them to prioritize the factors they believed their customers used for making buy decisions. Prior to the class, I interviewed networking managers from large companies, eleven customers who recently bought from IBM, and eleven who bought from Cisco. I would then compare the answers from the reps and customers. While it was not a large enough customer sample to guarantee statistical accuracy, I felt it could at least turn some heads and help generate discussion during the classes.

There were significant differences in answers from attendees of the class and customers. In most cases, the students in the IBM classes felt that the price and performance of the specific product would be the most critical factors for their customer in making an IBM buy decision. If it was simply price and performance, why was a sales force needed at all? Management could put their price list and product stats up on the Web page and go play golf. According to the customers I interviewed, price and product performance were not top priorities. Surprisingly, the top categories were the same for non-IBM customers and IBM customers. It was support, service, and how it fit in their overall plan—that dreaded architecture thing again. Here was the problem: architecture required a little customer education backed up by good salesmanship.

In my admittedly biased view, the customer responses demonstrated that they recognized the importance of evaluating products based on their specific business needs. The client/server market was maturing, and it seemed that at least some decision makers were becoming more business savvy. A July 1995 article that had appeared in *Network World*, a leading IT publication dedicated to technology communications, pointed out that the highest cost item for networks was technical support staff, representing 35 to 45 percent of the total cost of ownership.[19] The cost of networking devices was often not much more than a rounding error compared to the people and usage costs.

Yet many corporations continued to install labor-intensive solutions.

This seemed to fly in the face of the corporate objectives of the 1990s to pair down to leaner organizations. Was it because the third-party knowledgeable experts and advisers continued to recommend these solutions? Didn't these experts consider the ongoing labor costs, or were they presenting misleading claims? Regardless of the reasons, I was convinced this represented an opportunity to reshuffle the deck and sell the importance of good support and service over product costs.

There were some differences in my survey between Cisco and IBM buyers. When the Cisco buyers talked about the networking environment, they were only talking about the client/server network. IBM buyers tended to look at client/server combined with all the other corporate networks, including telecommunications and non-client/server data networks. The IBM buyer was also more focused on fitting the product into an overall corporate infrastructure that went beyond networking, including other things like data storage, security, application development, and ongoing maintenance. If positioned properly, I was convinced this could increase IBM's ability to win against Cisco. I was also trying to deliver another subtle message for the IBM reps: Listen to the customer, not the industry analysts. The customer had to live with the decision.

Not all the students agreed with my conclusions. Some got emotional about it. "That's not what my customer needs." "I just lost a deal because our product sucks wind compared to Cisco's." "You got to sell at a lower price when your product isn't as good as the competition." Mission accomplished. My survey had caught their attention. Discussion about changing the playing field followed.

There was another big problem that became immediately obvious. Possibly the customers I interviewed were unique, but I doubted it. I gave the interviewed customers several choices as opposed to letting them throw out the first thing that came to their minds. The new IBM sales force for networking was relatively inexperienced. They didn't know that customers always complain about price to the rep. It's the usual customer-to-salesperson banter.

Bitching over price was a customer reflex action requiring no cognitive thought. It doesn't necessarily mean that the price of the product was the most important factor. Reps need to know how to blow through the smoke screens and identify the real decision factors. It can be a major problem when they take what is first said at face value without more probing, as experienced reps know how to do. If it wasn't a smoke screen, then the customer needed to be educated on the total costs of ownership. With an inexperienced sales force in networking, it seemed IBM was vulnerable to "the customer is always right" trap.

"We've got to lower our price even more, or we are going to lose the business." This was a downward spiral that could drive a vendor not only out of a market leadership position, but out of the business altogether. The scary part was how easy IBM had transitioned into an "also ran" in this area of the business, assuming they needed to conform to new business assumptions versus leading customers to better solutions.

Technology was moving so fast that even Cisco couldn't rest on its lead. Moving basic data through the network, the major strength of Cisco, was no longer enough. Customer demand for networks that could simultaneously handle different forms of media, such as voice and video, as well as larger chunks of data was expanding rapidly. There was a growing need for "broadband technology." Broadband was fast becoming the catchall phrase to describe the new, improved networking pipes that were needed—pipes that could transport multimedia while at the same time handle larger numbers of users. While Cisco seemed to bask in its glory, behind stage they were also frantically scrambling to solve a big problem beginning to unfold. Cisco's big black boxes running basic data networks were becoming obsolete. New technology, namely switching, from IBM and other companies could replace it, ushering in the next generation. Routers were good with data, but not with voice. Switching was a new breakthrough technology that could handle a combination of voice, data, and other forms of the new multimedia traffic customers wanted to push across their networks.

Cisco's routers were cash cows, representing high profit margins, just as the mainframe did for IBM. Switching was a real threat to Cisco's bottom line. It represented the next technology wave and a complete break from Cisco's area of expertise. Switching was also less expensive and easier for a support staff to administer.

Now IBM could do to Cisco what Cisco had done to them. This was my major argument presented in the classes. It was only a few years ago that Cisco had started convincing customers that they no longer needed mainframes to run networks. IBM could now argue that customers didn't need Cisco's black box. IBM had already built most of the technology while also reselling pieces of it from other vendors. It just hadn't been very successful at selling enough.

IBM could win by making the argument switching with IBM versus routing with Cisco. There was still a major hurdle to make this successful. Cisco's people were masters at leaving everybody else in react mode by framing the argument around their strengths.

Based on the overall feedback, the classes went well. As noted in a letter from the IBM program manager, I had "consistently received the highest ratings of the more than thirty instructors that participated in the week-long education program that was conducted worldwide." The entire letter was very positive and closed with him telling me that I could expect future contracts. While I appreciated the complimentary letter, I was disappointed that the classes didn't seem to light a fire with the reps. As one student said to me, "I don't need sales training, I already know how to do that." Many of the student-feedback forms suggested that "speeds and feeds" analysis would have been more valuable than emphasis on competitive marketing. They also took every opportunity to complain about IBM's weak products compared to those of Cisco.

The idea of emphasizing other areas where IBM had clear advantage, or trying a new approach, was apparently lost. It didn't matter that the purpose of the classes was to emphasize competitive marketing over product. I had failed to convince. The new breed of reps was still in search of the technical "silver bullets" that would blow the competition away. Too bad, but there were none. There usually aren't, except in gothic horror stories. By the look on their faces whenever the topic came up, Cisco was right out of a gothic novel—the invincible boogeyman. The classes did little to change this.

The other reason the feedback ratings were relatively high was that many students dropped out of the week-long U.S. class before it was over. The evaluation forms were passed out on the last day. The class also involved a case study that I worked on with another consultant. Students had been teamed up to play the part of an IBM competitor and apply things learned to developing a plan to beat IBM. It was sort of a *Top Gun* approach to training, designed to get the student into the other guy's head. The idea came from the other consultant, and I thought it was great. On the last day of the class, each team was required to present their winning strategy to the rest of the class, followed by class discussion. Instead of producing self-assured fighter pilot types sporting mirrored sunglasses, many participants dropped out before having to present. One who hung in until the end wrote in the comments section of the feedback form, "I didn't come hear to brush up on public speaking."

During the classes I had tried to get the IBM class managers to do something about the dropout problem. I was told that it would be impossible to make attendance mandatory. For one thing, in the United States, there was a fair number of business partners attending the classes. Like other areas of the business, IBM Networking Systems was utilizing independent business partners as a cost-effective way of expanding sales coverage. IBM class managers responsible for the training had little pull with business partners. "Sorry Steve, if they want to leave, there isn't much we can do." This was not the kind of environment where people wanted to stick their necks out. These managers would also be evaluated based on feedback from the students. Negative student feedback and the class manager could be redeployed somewhere worse. Better to let the negative ones go.

Reps and business partners were an uncomfortable mix. I could understand the level of frustration on the part of IBM reps. They had been through some bad times in the last few years and saw many of their friends get pushed out of the company. At the same time, IBM was becoming more dependent on business partners. How long, they may have wondered, before they, too, would be replaced? In spite of this, it struck me that if IBM really was at war, somebody needed to kick some butt. What would happen in the military if a soldier said, "No sergeant, I don't want to do my drills today"? God help him in the face of battle if the sergeant didn't kill him first. Unfortunately, there were no drill sergeants at IBM, and the army was comprised of too many separate militias with different codes and different objectives. Just as was the case with the handling of consultants, a combination of lack of discipline and management cave-ins deserved a good part of the blame. Business partners, like consultants, could provide real value if they were properly managed and conformed to your business approaches and tactics. The problem was that IBM Networking reps were becoming more like business partners, versus the other way around. I couldn't help but think back about the comment I heard while still working for IBM. The one about Rome, when they started to let the mercenaries take over. As noted by Arthur Ferril in *Fall of the Roman Empire*:

> "Barbarization," the use of Germans on such a large scale that the army became German rather than the Germans becoming Roman soldiers, begins with Theodosius the Great. The emperor won the battle with his Gothic allies, but they began immediately to demand great rewards for their service and to show an independence that in drill, discipline and organization meant catastrophe. They fought under their own native commanders, and the barbaric system of discipline was in no way as severe as the Roman. Eventually Roman soldiers saw no reason to do what barbarian troops in Roman service were rewarded so heavily for not doing.[20]

As major educational activities were "outsourced" to consultants, primarily technology consultants, motivational efforts appeared to have slipped through the cracks. They were replaced with dispassionate analysis. Feedback surveys were used to modify education and give reps more of what they wanted. It wasn't necessarily what they needed. More competitive marketing education for next year? Forget about it. "Survey results say: more emphasis on technology. Then, more technology it will be." Competitive-marketing education was short lived. No question it was a technical business, and sales reps needed to have a strong background in this area, but technical knowledge alone wasn't going to close a competitive sale.

Products change. Selling stays pretty much the same, although it does require a type of learning students can't get from consultant lectures, research notes, or even books. This new breed of sales rep would have to learn things the hard way. I knew some of them would rise to the occasion. IBM still had lots of smart, hard-working people. They were the important part, not the logo. In the meantime, Cisco and others were grabbing up more market share.

There was a marked contrast in the classes conducted overseas, particularly Japan. It was Japan that really opened my eyes, and it started before my plane touched down in Tokyo's Narita International Airport. I had completed classes in the United States, Belgium, and Thailand. I had only one left. Japan was the last leg before finishing the training and heading home. I was flying there from Thailand after a week of intense sessions, and I appeared to be the only non-Japanese passenger, or *gaikokujin* as they say, on the flight. It was in April, and we were bouncing along through jet streams and air pockets. I couldn't wait to land. There was a heavy-set Japanese man sitting next to me who started nudging with his elbow.

"You no like to fly?" he asked.

"I'm just tired."

"I like to fly. My father, kamikaze pilot, World War II."

"My father used to shoot them down."

The man smiled and nodded his head. I couldn't tell if he did not understand or was just being polite. In any case, I was unsuccessful in discouraging further conversation. He pulled out pictures of his family and his places of residence in Thailand and Japan. He then asked me if I liked military history. I decided he must have understood my earlier response. While his pronunciation of English could use work, his comprehension was apparently quite good. His outgoing, friendly manner was actually very likable. I told him that I was teaching competitive marketing based on some military tactics and concepts. He then told me about a military museum in Tokyo. He wrote the name on the back page of my travel guide, *Yasukuni-Jinja*. I later learned that the translation was "Shrine of Peace for the Nation." He told me I could get there by train, and it was relatively easy to find, close to the Imperial Palace. It was early afternoon when I arrived at my hotel in downtown Tokyo. My room would be unavailable for least a few hours. I decided to leave my bags with the concierge and go see some of the sites, including the museum. First, I grabbed my tour book and a map.

Tokyo was sprawling with rows of bland oval towers intermixed with nondescript block-shaped buildings, squeezed tightly together. It was a modern art mosaic of orderly confusion. There were secretly hidden pockets of lush gardens, ponds filled with lily pads and carp, ominous ancient walls, and forbidden temples. Unearthing these exotic gems within Tokyo's urban jungle required careful attention to a good map. Mine worked fine. It was still a hit-or-miss search for some of the hidden treasures in an immense fortressed city. It was as if Tokyo was intentionally designed with a countless maze of tunnels to baffle unwanted intruders. It was a beautiful day, and the man in the plane had provided good directions for my final destination. I found the Imperial Palace with no problem. The massive castle fortification surrounded by impeccably coiffed gardens was awe-inspiring. I had been told the museum was close by.

There was a festival across from the palace. The cherry blossoms were in full bloom, gracing the landscape with their snowlike petals. I had stumbled into the annual and probably most original cherry blossom festival in the world. Young women were dressed as traditional geisha girls. Elderly Japanese men who appeared very friendly passed flyers to people walking by. As I approached, they would turn away, apparently to avoid handing one of the flyers to me. Now how did they know I didn't speak Japanese? Either they thought I didn't speak the language and were trying to avoid any embarrassment, or the flyer was an invitation to some kind of place with a "No *Gaikokujin* Allowed" policy.

From the outside, Yasukuni-Jinja could have passed for a shrine of peace. On the inside, it provided an incredible tribute that glorified the accomplishments of the Japanese military, both before and during World War II. Although there were no English translations for the museum pieces, one couldn't help but appreciate the high level of honor and respect in which these artifacts, paintings, and photographs were displayed. A kamikaze plane caught my immediate attention when entering the museum. There were encasements paying tribute to great Japanese warriors of the past such as Masujiro Omura, founder of the modern Japanese army over a hundred years ago. There was a display of personal items, including the uniform that belonged to Yamamoto, the Japanese admiral who led the attack of Pearl Harbor and eventually lost the Battle of Midway. It looked like an altar. I watched people much younger than me bow before the area dedicated to Admiral Yamamoto. I found out later that the Japanese believed that Yasukuni-Jinja enshrined the souls of those who fought for the country. They were considered deities. Some, like Yamamoto, were celebrated more than others.

Japan was a great educational experience, for me if not for the students in my classes. I learned to modify my teaching style to address language barriers and cultural issues. Even though all of the participants in the class could speak English, there were very few questions. As the class progressed, I started to write more on the board as someone tipped me off that the participants could probably read English better than understanding the spoken words, particularly with my rapid-fire style of delivery. I was also told that in the Japanese culture asking questions to the instructor could be viewed as insulting. It implied that the instructor did not do a very good job of teaching. For the class to be successful, I had to get them raising hands and participating.

If I were successful in getting them to speak, I would also have to make sure that when they answered "yes" it didn't just mean that they understood my point of view but the answer was really "no." I had heard about contract negotiations with the Japanese from friends who had worked in Japan. "The Japanese have a hundred ways of saying no and ninety-nine of them sound like yes," I had been told. It was a cultural thing, they said, where it was more important to be polite and agreeable, even when the answer was no. A handshake followed by a "Yes, we are very appreciative" was often misinterpreted as an unqualified yes to the deal.

I used a little Yankee ingenuity to get class participation. I offered a prize for the best-asked question during an early lecture. A woman attending the class asked the first question. This was followed by lots of hands shaking wildly in the air and lots of good questions. The class voted unanimously to give the prize to the most senior man in the group. In my opinion, he did not have one of the better questions. Must have been that cultural thing again. I gave him an elephant statue I had purchased during the last class in Thailand. I had had to haggle for a good price. The winner in my class now was getting an even better deal, and with no haggling. After I gave him the elephant, the older man smiled and shook his head approvingly to the other students. Participation was good for the rest of the class. I tried to stay away from yes or no questions, soliciting more open-ended responses.

Whereas in the United States many students left before the last day of class when they would have been expected to present their competitive strategy, in Japan everyone stuck it out. They, too, were not thrilled with having to present a marketing strategy to the rest of the class, but it was made clear by the Japanese class manager that skipping the final session was not an option. God knows what else he said because many of the students in Japan stayed up all night preparing for the final presentation. When it was over, the students expressed what at least appeared to be a high level of satisfaction. The opinion surveys were very positive.

I couldn't help but contrast this experience with the U.S. classes where many left before the surveys were returned. If nothing else, being a consultant from another place probably added to the credibility factor. It was also possible that students from the international classes were starved for any information they could get. They most certainly did not have all the resources available to them that reps would have in the United States. Maybe they were just being polite in giving the classes a good rating and being so positive. I was convinced there was something more to it. The students from Japan worked harder and seemed more open to different ideas then their counterparts in the United States. They didn't act like they already had the answers. If they had, Japanese management probably would have reprimanded them. In the end, they seemed pleased with themselves after presenting and successfully completing the class.

After all, IBM Japan was operating from a more traditional Japanese model, according to an IBM manager supporting the networking business for IBM Asia Pacific. He explained that in Japan long-term customer relationships were more important than short-term profits. I was told that management and employees shared common goals. Mutual respect and loyalty prevailed. It was an ancient custom that could be traced back to the Samurai, a warrior class dating from the Middle Ages in Japan who upheld virtues such as loyalty, righteousness, and proprietary.[21] IBM Japan may have been patterned after a uniquely Japanese tradition, but it also sounded a lot like the way I remembered the old IBM in the United States. The IBM manager then jarred me with an off-the-cuff comment.

"Too bad. Looks like before long they'll be forced to go with the new business model, same as in the United States."

"What's that?" I asked.

"Business partners. It'll be interesting to see how well it works here."

Of course. These participants had been bred as IBM salespeople. There were no business partners in the Japanese classes. The IBM Networking Systems organization in Japan was still relying almost exclusively on employees with an IBM-selling background to push products. In the United States, IBM Networking was relying on a combination of new sales reps redeployed from other parts of the business and resellers. Many of the U.S. business partners not only sold IBM products, but products from IBM competitors as well. Given that IBM was no longer perceived as the leader in this market, I wondered how many of those business partners would go to the wall to sell IBM to a customer with a preference for another vendor's product. IBM seemed to think it could fix this by offering higher margins than resellers could get from the competition.

I asked a consultant who had done quite a bit of work for IBM Networking Systems about the rationale in using business partners. "This has become a highly technical business and IBM needed a quick jump start," he said. He went on to tell me that IBM had used business partners successfully in the past, such as with a product called the AS/400, a highly successful family of computers for small to midsize companies, as well as corporate departments. He was right, but this was an area where the relationships had been well managed from the beginning of product launch. The AS/400 was highly differentiated from other products on the market and had developed a cultlike following of committed IBMers, resellers, and customers. It came from one of IBM's most entrepreneurial development groups, established in Rochester, Minnesota, close to thirty years ago.[22] No one waited for the consultants to tell them how to sell it. It also outlived all the analyst predictions of its demise.

While IBM was new in using business partners for pedaling networking products, many of IBM's competitors had worked with partners for years. In many cases, they were the same business partners IBM was now attempting to use. These business partners had developed strong relationships with IBM's competitors. They had established ways of doing business. If IBM was to work with the same partners, they would need to conform to the established selling approach. IBM would be a "Me, too."

Changing customer preferences and displacing competition took time, and people's time was a particularly expensive resource in the cost-conscious, service-based economy of the '90s. There was an opportunity cost. It was tough enough trying to convince customers to switch to the IBM brand for networking. IBM also had to convince its partners to sell more of its products as opposed to competitors' products. "Now IBM, you want us to do what? Change our approach to selling? Change the playing field? We've been selling this way for years, and it works just fine for us. Thank you very much." It then hit me. My suggestions for changing the playing field to sell IBM Networking Systems products differently than the competition was doomed from the beginning to falling on deaf ears.

In spite of everything IBM attempted to do, Cisco continued to increase market share, and IBM continued to have disappointing years. Cisco was a great company. Not to take anything away from Cisco, but IBM helped them along with a series of blunders. IBM had adopted a profit-center mentality. This led to the mainframe line of business selling technology to Cisco, undermining a potential exclusive competitive advantage for IBM Networking Systems. Client/server was supposed to make mainframes go away. When they didn't, it became clear client/server vendors would have to coexist with the "big iron." Mainframes were given a new identity: they became "big servers" that needed to be connected with the new client/server networks.

As it became obvious that some mainframes were here to stay, vendors such as Cisco started scrambling for mainframe integration technology. They didn't have to scramble much as the IBM mainframe group was eager to sell it. The mainframe group didn't seem to care that Cisco, who was already eating IBM's lunch, could now eat bigger chunks faster. "We're measured on profit for large-systems products, not networking." Sales reps representing other IBM business units were bidding on large proposals, as if they were "general contractors" in the building industry, subcontracting networking business to Cisco, versus including IBM Networking Systems products in the bid. It was an easier sell with Cisco in the mix. They were the new networking leader. Who would question Cisco?

The other major problem that was ignored was the bad advice from consultants. Most of the executives running IBM divisions had skated through their careers in the days when IBM was experiencing unprecedented growth. By the early 1990s, they were faced with problems they had never experienced in the past. They must have felt reluctant to ask subordinates for advice, even though there were still plenty of highly skilled and intelligent employees with their fingers on the pulse of the market. From what I had been told, the older executives didn't seem to have this problem. In their day, there was less of a gap in salaries, attitudes, and work ethic. A more palatable alternative for the new executive was to turn to outside consultants for help. They could not only ask for advice, but could drop their guard and admit what they didn't know. IBM executives could use consultants as a sounding board, sharing problems that they didn't feel comfortable discussing with subordinates. Besides, conventional wisdom shared by executives and consultants was that the employees were a big part of the problem.

In the early 1990s executives from IBM's Networking Systems line of business began to rely on the advice of an elite group of consultants and industry analysts from several different firms. They were eventually used as an informal advisory committee. It may have started as part of an effort to get a more "objective" outside opinion. As things in the marketplace heated up, so did the extent of consulting reviews. With the blessing of its new consultant advisers, the line of business made a series of strategy announcements in the trade press in the early 1990s. These announcements implied that there would be sweeping changes in IBM products. It would take years before these changes could be implemented, giving the competition plenty of time to respond. The intent may have been to freeze the market until the new IBM products were ready. All it really did was freeze IBM. They were actually suggesting that customers make initial investments in wiring to support the coming new line of IBM products before they were market ready. The strategy failed miserably.

When things didn't quite turn out as planned, IBM moved from a focus on high-level strategy to a more tactical focus. "Seed" money was spread around to various development projects to help them get started. An assortment of technology was acquired from other firms. Throw it on the wall and see what sticks. As things got even worse, downsizing reared its ugly head. Employees would go, but the consultants stayed. Old habits of full employment no longer held. Newer habits of relying on a select group of consultants became tough to break.

Among other things, in the early '90s IBM executives had decided to change the dynamics of the sales force for selling networking products. Redeployment of technical people to selling jobs became the answer. Whether consultants first provided the idea, or merely validated it, they weighed into the process and helped promote the sales force changes at industry conferences and in internal IBM planning sessions. The argument was simple. IBM needed highly technical specialists who focused exclusively on networking to improve business results. The head of this IBM business unit was a networking technologist, so were the consultants she and her direct reports were using as advisors. They say people like to surround themselves with others in their own likeness. Pretty soon some of the new sales reps were becoming chummy with the consultant advisers. The only thing missing in the new sales reps was the same level of arrogance. If the consultants were advising executives, it could be a good career move for a new sales rep to look up, learn, and emulate.

One of those trusted consultants retained by senior management for Networking Systems had been Jerry Guston. It really was a small world. Guston was Will Logan's former boss at Gartner Group. They got along as well as President Clinton and the Republican-controlled Congress.

Guston was considered one of the top networking consultants in the business, long before joining Gartner. In the early '90s, while still working for IBM, I had worked with individuals from IBM Networking Systems on a major product announcement. This information was considered highly confidential at the time, and sharing it outside of IBM could have cost us our jobs. Yet Jerry Guston was busy sharing this same information with the trade press and getting lots of exposure for himself. Several of his quotes regarding the planned IBM announcement sounded rather disparaging, and I wasn't the only one to notice. Several of the people working for IBM Networking Systems shared similar concerns: "Why do we let him get away with this? If he was sharing it with the press, don't you think he might also be sharing sensitive information with the competition?"

There had been situations in the past that one might have considered cause for concern. Back in 1983 Gartner Group had settled a lawsuit brought by IBM. The suit alleged that a Gartner consultant who was a former IBM employee had shared competitively sensitive IBM information with Hitachi Ltd. of Japan. This was at the time when there was much concern about Japanese companies as an emerging competitive threat to the United States in technology. While Gartner admitted to no wrongdoing, as part of the settlement it agreed that it would return all information IBM considered trade secrets.[23]

Nevertheless, Guston's consulting services continued to be used after the obvious leaks. No one ever seemed to go back and question decisions already made. It was as if management never made mistakes. If their predications regarding the market didn't pan out, it was because the market was wrong. Firing a consultant who had been given privileged access could have been detrimental to the "no mistakes" image. Apparently no one within the networking organization would dare suggest that there was anything wrong. No one to my knowledge ever asked senior management, "Whose side is Guston on?" If IBM executives were still briefing Guston and getting his advice, there had to be a good reason behind it. Certainly, no one within the ranks was going to tell a senior IBM executive that she needed to rethink a decision.

By 1994 IBM was just beginning to sell networking products under a new label, called "AnyNet." Guston was quoted in a communications publications as stating, "Unless IBM can garner wider industry support, it looks like AnyNet is not going anywhere."[24] Nothing like self-fulfilling prophesy from a recognized industry expert who was advising clients on networking decisions. In a subsequent issue of the same magazine, entitled "IBM Customers Face Tough Networking Choices," Jerry Guston suggested that there was much confusion with IBM's networking products and strategies.[25] I didn't understand. I had thought Guston was involved in providing advice and counsel to IBM over the last few years as Big Blue attempted to map out its new networking strategy.

In 1995, at the same time I was involved in IBM marketing education, Jerry Guston was the keynote speaker in a Cisco-sponsored road show that talked to customers and consultants in various cities about the benefits of Cisco strategies and products that competed directly with IBM. I knew about it because I was one of the consultants invited. Unfortunately, I was overseas at the time. Although I wasn't able to attend, I'm sure it would have been very interesting. With IBM management relying on the same consultants who were also advising the competition, was it any wonder why differentiation in this market was becoming a thing of the past? If Guston could so easily transition from an IBM adviser to a Cisco adviser, what would prevent him from transitioning again to the next up-start company challenging Cisco? It didn't really matter who was gaining or losing market share, it seemed there was always work for consultants.

Guston and the other consultants surrounding IBM senior management had somehow convinced them that being a technologist equated with the ability to sell to technical customers. Apparently this was the only litmus test necessary. The traditional marketing reps were out. A new breed of networking specialists was in. What the consultants advising IBM management had failed to mention, or somehow never recognized as a fundamental strength of Cisco, was selling. As the most successful of the new breed of competitors, Cisco created a perception of being a pure technology company, but it was actually one of the shrewdest and most aggressive marketing companies to come along in years. By 1995, Cisco had acquired various companies with very different technologies. It would take years to make it all work together. This didn't stop Cisco from selling an overall architecture as if it all fit together seamlessly. My consulting partner for the IBM education program called it "marketecture." They may have looked like technologists, but they were really top-notch marketeers.

Cisco appeared to be a master at controlling the playing field. It was uncanny in predicting moves by its major competitors and consistently cut IBM off at the pass. An example was in the end of 1994. IBM at the time was reselling products manufactured by a switching vendor, Kalpana Inc. My sources within IBM told me that they were just beginning to explore a potential acquisition with Kalpana when "Cisco rips the plum from IBM's hand."[26] It was an out-of-the-blue preemptive strike. Cisco made all the right moves at the right times. Was it simply a combination of good marketing instinct and intuitive genius? Cisco didn't stop with Kalpana. As things changed, so did Cisco. I couldn't remember seeing a technology company change course so quickly in response to new market conditions or competitive threats. It went on a buying spree, snatching up companies selling the new networking solutions that posed the greatest threat to its flagship routers. Within two years, Cisco had not only revamped its entire product line, but also repositioned itself with a powerful marketing blitz.

Cisco was now in a position to argue that switching should not replace routing, but rather be "integrated" with it. Many research analysts quickly jumped on the bandwagon agreeing with Cisco. With an aggressive and highly effective marketing campaign, Cisco was able to save its cash cow routers from early obsolescence. Winning over research analysts was only part of the campaign. It also took old-fashioned selling with customers. Routers were carried along with the next wave of technology, as part of an "integrated" solution. Customers may have no longer needed expensive high-end routers as the backbone workhorse of their networks, but they were going to get them anyway. Cisco successfully avoided the threat of obsolescence through a series of very smart acquisitions. IBM's window was quickly disappearing.

Prior to the Cisco acquisition, Kalpana had been just one example of IBM selling products manufactured by another vendor. Consultants had also played a role in many of these decisions, recommending that IBM acquire many of its networking products from other equipment manufactures (OEMs) and scrap many of the internal development efforts. For example, back in 1992, about the time I was leaving IBM, Forrester Research had been hired by Networking Systems. Forrester convinced senior management to acquire and market internetworking hardware products from Chipcom Corporation as opposed to building their own.

Forrester Research was a fast-growing technology research firm at the time, offering technology research services for a subscription fee, similar to Gartner Group. Chipcom was one of IBM's first major OEM alliances in the emerging internetworking business.

The arrangement was announced as a partnership between IBM and Chipcom where technologies would be exchanged.[27] I believe what Chipcom was probably most interested in, even more than IBM technology, was the ability to rely on IBM to expand its market share. It would not be the first time that an alliance with IBM helped a smaller company gain more name recognition and improve market penetration. You'll recall that Microsoft Corporation was just such a company.

While Chipcom did produce high-quality products, placing an IBM logo on the box was no longer a guarantee of increased market acceptance, particularly in the highly competitive networking market. Without a strong marketing campaign and competent, aggressive selling to differentiate offerings from its competition, this approach could be very disappointing. This was the case here.

The book *Waves of Power* related a common industry joke concerning IBM's competitors from Japan. It suggested that Japanese technology companies such as Fujitsu Ltd. and Hitachi Ltd. admired and tried to imitate IBM. When pain, losses, and self-doubt began to intensify, it was concluded that they had succeeded in becoming more like IBM.[28]

In reality, in the 1980s American companies, including IBM, were trying to copy different aspects of the Japanese model. As the Japanese miracle economy started to skid in the 1990s, Japanese companies were criticized for not being more like American companies. What a difference a decade makes.

It was argued that the emerging problems with the Japanese economy were related to a defective model. The Japanese model combined cozy "good old boy" business relationships with poor banking practices. The argument generally assumed that Japanese relationships among various large corporate conglomerates and government protection were a uniquely Japanese phenomena. There were hidden agendas and hidden liabilities, inconsistent with a free market economy. The arguments also assumed that the current American model, based on open-market competitive forces, had proved to be superior and sustainable long into the future.

While they might not have anything as dominant and restrictive as the Japanese interlocking financial interests, called *keiretsu*, corporations from countries such as the United States most certainly had their own variations of crony-based business relationships, both formal and informal. I had become convinced there were still lessons to be learned from Japan. If their miracle economy could tank, so could ours.

Could we not make similar mistakes if we kept collectively pounding our chest, remaining blind to problems? In addition to learning that yes doesn't always mean yes and that like the Shrine of Peace, things are not always what they appear to be, I also learned an important Japanese proverb. In translation, it went something like this: "When a fish goes bad, it stinks first in the head."

In the 1980s the Japanese competitive threat became a rallying cry for new business alliances and industry deregulation. New business alliances were being established in the United States that extended across various industries. Mega-acquisitions were becoming commonplace with little to no government intervention. Arguments suggested that competitive pressures, particularly from Japan, demanded that companies achieve market diversification and greater economies of scale. Bigger was better. Realized benefits would be passed to consumers, stockholders, and employees. It was good for America. Many of the corporate giants began to rely more heavily on the advice of consultants on how to diversify and who to buy. Extensive use of American consultants was a practice adopted by Japanese companies after World War II in its effort to rebuild its industry. Who was copying whom?

By the middle 1990s American business leaders were becoming increasingly more arrogant, asserting that the U.S. economic model was beyond reproach—even though American business was now part of a larger global market with a growing complex set of interdependencies. No one was terribly concerned about overinflated stocks for many companies that had never turned a profit, or the accelerating imbalance of consumer debt over income fueling much of the economic boom. The Japanese had held a similar sense of invincibility back in the 1980s. There must be one hell of a blind spot when you're sitting way up on top.

With Cisco now on top in networking, I wondered how long it would take before it built the same level of arrogance that had helped cripple IBM. Cisco was already listening to the same consultants. It was continuing to promote the Internet as the solution for everything, exchanging stock versus cash to form business partnerships with the new wave of .com start-ups. The market was exploding with stock values of the new high-tech start-ups soaring astronomically in optimistic anticipation of future earnings, not actual performance. The Internet companies claimed they were driving increased productivity for customers and themselves. Partnering with Cisco, which seemed to be leading the charge, could only accelerate success. Industry analysts were bullish. Stocks continued to soar.

But IBM continued to lose market share in networking products and eventually threw in the towel in its battle against Cisco. Instead, IBM decided to sell networking chips and patents to its former bitter enemy and now the unquestioned market leader.[29] IBM reps may have thought their company's technology was poor and an impossible sell. Apparently Cisco felt it was worth buying. Patents were one of the few remaining areas where IBM had no serious rivals. It was consistently awarded more patents than any other U.S. company for switching and other networking technologies. A hardly noticed aspect of the deal was that in return for IBM selling what was estimated to be worth approximately $2 billion in chips and patents over five years, Cisco would pay IBM $300 million in cash and would recommend IBM Professional Services Group for networking installations and consulting.[30]

IBM had endorsed a new strategy of selling its technology and products to other companies and planned to step it up. IBM wanted to do to others what had been done so successfully to it. This was a major epiphany. IBM was no longer blinded by its own logo. Under Gerstner's leadership, IBM would embark on an aggressive strategy to wholesale its technology to *other equipment manufacturers* (OEMs).

Many computer analysts had promoted this kind of approach in technology for years, calling it "co-opetition"—when other competitors in the same market agree to cooperate. They were quick to point out that it worked incredibly well for Microsoft and Intel, as if they knew that it would the whole time. There were some dissenters in the case of IBM's decision to adopt this strategy across its varied product lines. In discussing the new OEM strategy, William F. Zachmann of Canopus Research said: "It's what every dying company does in its final moments. Once your businesses start to fail, you try to make money selling pieces."[31]

Zachmann probably wouldn't be getting a consulting contract from IBM any time soon. Dying company? I didn't think so. It was more a question of reversing mistakes of the recent past. Before Gerstner took over, IBM's share in many of its markets had been running flat or slipping. Profits were falling through the floor. IBM had also fallen in stature, dropping from the most admired company in America to number seventeen on the list, behind Intel and Microsoft.[32] Profits on Gerstner's watch began to climb again, and IBM stock approached new record highs.

There was one market where IBM was dramatically growing. This was IBM Global Services. IBM, which had still maintained unparalleled strength in a wider range of technologies than anybody else, was combining this with its large economies of scale and teamwork culture, differentiating itself from the rest of the services market. The man most responsible for the success of IBM Global Services was Sam Palmisano. He was a stand-up guy who, unlike Gerstner, came up through the ranks from IBM sales. While he had a reputation of being fiercely competitive, he was also considered a people person who didn't stand on ceremony. He was slated to be Gerstner's replacement, and for good reason.

The OEM business could make IBM even stronger. This was the reverse of IBM putting its logo on someone else's product. This was a strategy where others would be OEMing IBM products and services from IBM. It complemented the overall strategy for growth in services as technology products became low-margin commodities.

"Today IBM is Cisco's biggest installer, with sales of services at Cisco installations up eleven-fold last year. The Cisco agreement (IBM selling technology and patents to Cisco) paved the way for similar pacts with telecom giants Alcatel SA, Lucent Technologies Inc., and Nortel Networks Inc.—vaulting IBM to the No. 1 spot in networking services, with more than $3 billion in sales last year (2000)."[33] Gerstner, in spite of inheriting an impossible situation, had achieved his goal of making IBM a network-centric leader.

Following the Enron scandal, several major companies would be accused of "cooking the books" to inflate profits and hide losses. There were some who would imply that IBM's unexpected rebound at the end of the 1990s was merely based on financial manipulation, but looking closer at the strategic IBM success stories—professional services and OEM—suggests otherwise. Once again, many analysts had bet on the wrong horse.

I now realized the classes I taught were flawed. I should have made adjustments to accommodate the new IBM. My advice had been based on the old model with a window of opportunity that was already shut.

Luckily, I was in a profession where as long as you played by the rules there was a good chance of an afterlife, whether you were wrong or right in the last one. OK, I was finally getting it.

The client who gives you work is always right. Keep that in mind and always try to be politically correct. I still had to work on the politically correct part.

Speaking of politically correct, by the time I left Japan in spring 1995 and arrived back in the States, the controversy about displaying the B-52 bomber *Enola Gay* at the Smithsonian was at its height. The *Enola Gay* was the plane that dropped the atomic bomb on Hiroshima. An editorial in the *Washington Post* noted, "The museum will open its much-abridged version of the *Enola Gay* exhibit in June, and, though mum on specifics, official [sic] say that the presentation will be 'commemorative rather than interpretive' and will not address the historical questions that got the original exhibit plans in such trouble."[34]

SUMMARY OF OBSERVATIONS

- Positioned as independent experts, consultants tend to have more credibility than employees in the minds of senior management.

- Focusing on short-term profitability plays to the interests of consultants and business partners and can increase their leverage within client organizations. Rather than investing in training, companies hire third parties with specific skills, under the assumption they can provide a quick fix. However, this can create long-term increased client dependency on consultants and business partners.

- Risk-averse companies can become preoccupied in running with the pack and playing "me, too." Consultants often help to promote this point of view. It gives them an opportunity to use similar approaches with multiple clients and "reuse" work from one client with the next.

- Both consultants and business partners need to be carefully managed and contracts must explicitly prohibit the use of confidential information. A good example of a confidentiality agreement for consultants and other third parties is available from Donphin.com at www.inc.com/law_and_taxation/Freetools/21532.html (see appendix E).

- Evidence or suggestions of potential conflict of interest on the part of a consultant needs to be addressed immediately. If, for example, they do not meet terms of the confidentiality agreement, that is, you become aware that they have shared sensitive company information with another client, they need to know they have put all future business at risk. Contact your management, their management, notify your Contracts and Standards personnel, and other personnel you believe to be appropriate, so that in future others within your company who may consider engagement with this (these) consultant can be alerted to potential risks. Consultants and their companies need to be told (in writing) that there will be consequences for noncompliance, for example, abuses will be penalized with the consulting firm forfeiting current and future contracts.

NOTES

1. Leslie Cauley, "Shareholders Demand IBM Make Changes," *USA Today*, 25 January 1993, B1.
2. Thomas J. Peters and Robert H. Waterman Jr., *In Search of Excellence: Lessons from America's Best-Run Companies* (New York: Harper and Row, 1982), 20–23.
3. Peter D. Petre, "Meet the Lean, Mean New IBM," *Fortune*, 13 June 1983, 82.
4. Ibid., 74.
5. Thomas Moore and Michael Rogers, "Apple vs. IBM," *Fortune*, 18 February 1985, 8; "IBM Forecast: Market Dominance (IBM PC Line)" *Byte*, fall 1984, 8; "Personal Computers: And the Winner Is IBM," *Business Week*, 3 October 1983, 76–80; "IBM's Personal Computer Spawns an Industry,"*Business Week*, 15 August 1983, 88–90.
6. Petre "Meet the Lean, Mean New IBM," 82.
7. Norton Paley, "When Everyone Is Good, You Need a New Strategy," *Marketing News*, 29 April 1991, 12.
8. John Markoff, "IBM's Chief Criticizes Staff Again," *New York Times*, 19 June 1991, D1.
9. David Kirkpatrick, "Breaking Up IBM," *Fortune*, 27 July 1992, 44–58.
10. Lawrence Hooper, "IBM Grants Gerstner Pay Package Valued at Up to $3.5 Million," *Wall Street Journal*, 31 March 1993, A3.
11. Carol J. Loomis and David Kirkpatrick, "The Hunt for Mr. X: Who Can Run IBM?" *Fortune*, 22 February 1993, 68.
12. John Burgess, "IBM Chief Outlines Vision for the Future: Aim Is to Create 'Sense of Urgency,'" *Washington Post*, 25 March 1994, B1.
13. Ibid.
14. William Manchester, *American Caesar, Douglas MacArthur, 1880–1964* (Boston: Little, Brown and Company, 1978), 336.

15. IBM Annual Report 1994, 5.

16. The Internet Protocol (IP) is free. Internet services might not be, but the total computing costs provided significant savings over other alternatives. Protocol represents the characteristics of a network that determines how hardware and software will interoperate. In comparison, proprietary protocols, such as IBM's Advanced Peer to Peer Networking (APPN), were often very expensive.

17. Noel Lindsay, "A Look at the New Networking Paradigm," *Communicationsweek*, 31 October 1994, 72.

18. John T. Mulgqueen, "Net Unit Sundered in Big Blue Reorg," *CommunicationsWeek*, 16 January 1995, 1.

19. John Morency, Nick Lippis, and Eric Hirdin, "The Cost of Network Complexity," *Network World*, 31 July 1995, 44–46.

20. Arthur Ferril, *Fall of the Roman Empire* (London: Thames and Hudson, Ltd., 1986), 84–85.

21. Stephen D. Cohen, *Cowboys and Samurai: Why the United States Is Losing the Industrial Battle and Why It Matters* (New York: HarperBusiness, 1991), 71.

22. Roy A. Bauer, Emilio Collar, and Victor Tang, *The Silverlake Project: Transformation at IBM* (Oxford: Oxford University Press, 1992), 17.

23. "IBM Reaches Accord with Gartner Group over Trade Secrets," *Wall Street Journal*, 2 December 1983, 39.

24. "Is AnyNet Going Anywhere?" *Business Communications Review* (October 1994): 22.

25. "IBM Customers Face Tough Networking Choices," *Business Communications Review* (November 1994): 22–24.

26. Jim Duffy "Cisco Rips Plum from IBM's Hand," *Network World*, 31 October 1994, 1.

27. "IBM, Chipcom Form Superhub Partnership," *Computerworld*, 27 July 1992, 49.

28. David C. Moschella,*Waves of Power: Dynamics of Global Technology Leadership 1964–2010* (New York: American Management Association, 1997), 51–52.

29. Daniel Lyons, "IBM's Giant Gamble," *Forbes*, 4 October 1999, 92.

30. William Bulkeley, "These Days, Big Blue Is about Big Services Not Just Big Boxes, *Wall Street Journal*, 11 June 2001, A1.

31. "IBM's Giant Gamble."

32. Ronald Alsop, "The Best Corporations in America," *The Wall Street Journal*, 23 September 1999, B1, B6. Based on Reputation Quotient (RQ) measuring public perception of twenty different attributes. IBM ranked seventeenth, behind Intel at four and Microsoft at fifteen. Adverse publicity resulting from recent antitrust litigation may have pulled Microsoft down from a higher rating. In the past, IBM had ranked as the most admired U.S. compan in various surveys.

33. Bulkeley, "These Days, Big Blue Is about Big Services Not Just Big Boxes."

34. "Smithsonian: After the Shouting," *Washington Post* (May 7, 1995), C6.

CHAPTER FOUR

FEEDING
AT THE TROUGH

While still in Japan working on the IBM contract, I had noticed in an international newspaper published in English that Chase Manhattan Bank was under attack. An activist investor had acquired enough shares to make him the bank's largest shareholder. It was only 6 percent of outstanding shares, but it bought enough clout to make his criticism heard all the way to Tokyo. He was outraged by declining profitability at Chase. The successful turnaround in the early '90s could not be sustained. What a difference a couple bad quarters make. There was speculation about a hostile takeover. I couldn't imagine Chase being bought out. Maybe it was a translation problem.

I called on Chase the day after returning home in early May 1995, still feeling a little jet-lagged but wanting to get a reading on what was going on and its potential impact on my business. Chase was by far my largest client. While Chase had reported a decline in annual net profit for 1994, the $1.2 million was still almost double what had been reported in 1992. I learned that while I was overseas Chase Manhattan had announced a 28 percent slide in 1995 first-quarter profits, attributed to losses in Latin American markets.[1] It started with one investor. Now it seemed all of Wall Street was demanding action. Executive management from the bank appeared to be on the ropes. There was only one thing to do. They promised an aggressive cost-cutting campaign. That usually meant employee heads would roll. It didn't occur to me that it wouldn't be only employees.

Michael Dellano's secretary had scheduled a meeting on my first call. Familiarity might breed contempt, but it still makes it easier getting past the gatekeeper. It was in his new office on the twenty-third floor. Dellano did not look like he was in a good mood. It might have been the new "no smoking" policy. Even in your own office with the door shut, smoking was now prohibited.

"Nice beard."

"Thanks. You think it makes me look wiser?"

"Makes you look older."

We walked down the hall to a minikitchen where we both nursed cups of high octane coffee while parked around a table designed for intimate gatherings. As usual, it was my back to the door. Conversation began with some small talk regarding his new office on executive row, followed by my giving a quick rundown on my trip to the Far East. In spite of my best efforts to lighten things up, Dellano was still not looking happy. When I finally got around to asking about the current business climate, he shook his head with obvious displeasure. Big mistake, I should have never ventured there.

"We hire executives from some of the top MBA schools in the country for big bucks. So why do they have to hire consultants every time they have to make a decision? They've made it bad for all of us."

Dellano went on to explain that some of the upper-level executives didn't want to look at recommendations from anybody at Chase unless they had first been vetted by a consultant.

"Before long, consultants were involved in everything. It kind of snowballed," he said.

Now I understood. For years, consultants of all varieties had become fixtures, completely ingrained at Chase. Everybody used them, even the guys like Dellano and Tom Carter who had no problems making decisions. Dellano told me that there were now over thirty different consulting firms working at Chase. That's a lot of political capital for pushing agendas and covering butts. He said they now needed to get the list down to about five consulting organizations in the technology area. For me to continue on at Chase, he told me, I would have to find a way to partner with one of the larger firms. Suddenly Dellano looked down at his watch. He had another meeting and was giving me the cue to pack up and leave.

Shortly after, I found Tom Carter on his way back to his office. He was now running a very successful department, responsible for producing comprehensive financial analysis reports for the entire wholesale bank. We walked through the bullpen where his people sat. It made me feel pretty good to think that I had helped him create his little empire, not that he couldn't have done it without me. My part, which in this environment was key, was providing the necessary "independent" blessing. I would have preferred thinking it was my valuable advice, but this would have been delusional. And yeah, Logan had helped, too, not only with Chase, but in getting my head straight on what this was all about. Too bad he and I had a falling out. Carter invited me into his cubicle. He also didn't have much time, and his mood wasn't much better than Dellano's.

He told me that Chase had hired a consulting firm called Tandon Capital Associates to help cut costs by $400 million. I couldn't help but wonder if Chase executive management had felt they were out of the woods a little too soon after posting good results in the early '90s. What if they had spent less time fighting over how to measure profitability and more on improving it? For one thing, I never would have gotten that nice little project.

The president of Tandon, Chandrika K. Tandon, was a former McKinsey & Company associate. Like McKinsey, Tandon's primary focus was management consulting. This meant that Tandon and her firm would work with senior executives in developing and implementing corporate strategies. Tandon specialized in the banking industry. As part of the arrangement with Chase, Tandon would find ways to cut expenses, getting a percentage of the money they "saved." "Strategy" in the '90s was usually cipher code for cutting costs. It seemed to work for McKinsey. It was apparently also working for Tandon. As noted by the *New York Times*, "The banking industry's toughest cost-cutter is coming to Chase Manhattan Corporation. That means the sun may soon set on the potted palms at Chase Manhattan Plaza near Wall Street—and on the careers of thousands of the bankers whose offices they adorn."[2] Tom Carter told me it was Tandon who had recommended getting rid of the little consulting fiefdoms spread all over Chase. The big fish had first gone after all the little fish. Pretty smart move, I thought.

Tom asked me, "What do you think this sounds like?"

He explained that after setting up operations in a project office close to the chairman of Chase, Tandon Associates had sent a letter to employees, suggesting that if they had any ideas for reducing costs, they should send a memo to the new Tandon office at Chase. Upon receiving the employee suggestion, Tandon would send a letter to the manager responsible for the department that would be impacted by the suggestion. The Chase manager would be given a limited period of time to respond to Tandon with a financial analysis of the impact of implementing the suggestion. Tandon would review the analysis and then pass recommendations up to senior management. In effect, they were creating a buffer between senior management and everybody else. According to Carter, this was intensifying a general climate of distrust and turning one group against another.

"It sounds like the standard definition of a consultant," I said. "Let me borrow your watch and I'll tell you what time it is."

"It's worse than borrowing," Carter replied. "We won't ever get it back."

As I was leaving the bank, I ran into one of the guys who worked for Carter.

"Romaine, did you hear about us hiring Tandon? Rumor has it their first piece of advice was to recommend a salary increase for Labrecque." (Labrecque was the chairman and CEO of Chase.)

This comment was unexpected and completely uncharacteristic. This was from one of those employees who punched in, punched out, and never spoke unless spoken to. He must have felt that he could safely let off his built-up steam with me, a non-Chase worker. No risk of jeopardizing his status as part of the loyal, dependable fold. Especially now that I was one of the "expenses" about to be amputated.

Both Dellano and Carter had always talked favorably about Labrecque, but then they were good company men. As I started mulling it over, it occurred to me that nobody thinks he is paid enough, no matter how much he makes. What a great way to start your consulting engagement: "After an initial review of the landscape, and comparing your personal income with that of executives running comparable companies, we have concluded that you're underpaid. We plan to address this in our report to your board of directors."

It did beg the question: When senior executives hired consultants, were they hired for the best *long-term* interest of the company? Sure, their recommendations could reduce costs and increase shareholder wealth. That meant executive wealth, too. Of course, if the executive didn't focus on stock price, she wouldn't be around for the long term. This was certainly the case at Chase where Wall Street was demanding a quick fix to the profitability ratio. So what have you done for me lately? The whole system was based on demonstrating immediate results.

Everybody knew that the cost-cutting aspect of Tandon's contract could get ugly, leading to nasty things like layoffs. In my short tenure in the consulting profession, I had learned that most consulting firms act as if business is a zero-sum game. There was a limited amount of money in the bucket. To get paid, they had to take it away from somebody else. That could mean replacing employees with consultants, or replacing consultants of another firm. To help your particular client increase the ratio of revenue to expenses, the same logic applied. You had to get it from current corporate assets, or some other company's assets. The whole world was one big balance sheet where the aggregate gross value of assets could never change.

Viewing it as a balance sheet may have been the reason so many of the major accounting firms had easily made the leap to offering consulting in addition to auditing. Rarely during the client/server cost-cutting days of the early to mid-1990s did consultants consider increasing revenue by multiplying new and additional sales as part of the equation. Most of the consulting work in the early 1990s was in reengineering back-office systems. By the end of the decade, efforts to automate and integrate sales and customer service would become the new frontier, something called customer relationship management (CRM). But this was only after the back-office well was starting to dry up. Even so, engagements in the sales area were usually about finding more cost-effective alternatives. "By leveraging the Internet as your primary sales channel, you can get rid of those expensive order takers." One could argue that there was little consultants could do in the short run to improve sales. But if new sales were successfully executed and expanded, why couldn't the company grow the business and break out of zero-sum gridlock? Wouldn't almost all the problems looking for solutions go away, including the consultants?

Sometimes it seemed as if nobody in the 1990s running the top established U.S. corporations was thinking much beyond cutting costs. So instead of looking for creative alternatives to drive additional business, consultants were hired to evaluate and recommend on downsizing and consolidation initiatives. This was a great business opportunity for us consultants. It was best for management consultants who were hired by senior executives for substantial fees, sometimes a percentage of what they recommend cutting, as was the case with Tandon at Chase. These management consultants could improve their numbers by helping to surgically remove the fat.

These consultants would start with the assumption that profitability was a matter of manipulating assets. There were a number of ways to improve profitability. Acquiring another company was one way, sometimes with the management consultant brokering the deal. An acquisition would provide a quick infusion of revenue for the income statement by showing increased assets and combined sales of both companies. More important, the consolidation could reduce costs as duplicate resources of combined operations were eliminated. Increased economies of scale were always promised. The cost of buying the other company was hardly ever a major issue. It could be argued away as a one-time expense, or spread over a couple years to ease the pain. In these heady days, corporate acquisitions generally made Wall Street very happy, regardless of the purchase price.

Pure cost cutting could also improve profitability. Many consulting engagements were about trimming back on current facilities and operations. Property and equipment could be sold. Employees could be let go. It was a quick and easy way to impact the bottom line without having to break a sweat selling more product or services. Significant cost cutting, say thousands of layoffs, would definitely improve profitability. The chairman would receive credit for improving profitability and would be compensated accordingly.

Sometimes all it took was the good sense to hire the right consultant.

The bulk of the savings from layoffs could be passed on to stockholders as earnings. In comparison, the jump in executive pay and consulting fees were rounding errors compared to the savings from downsizing. Between 1995 and 1996, CEO pay rose 54 percent, and almost 500 percent since 1980. While this did reflect rising returns to stockholders, it did not, according to the *Multinational Monitor*, represent expansion of the economic pie. Employees were taking the hit. The gap between CEO pay and that of the average worker has ballooned to a ratio of 200-to-1.[3] If they were doing the right thing for the company, and no doubt many executives were, that was one thing. In some cases, especially in light of problems uncovered at Enron, you had to wonder. Executives were not the only big winners. Consultants, who were helping to redistribute corporate wealth, were also building their own coffers. There were at least some CEOs and consultants who appeared to be on the same page, more concerned about sharing in this new windfall than meeting stated corporate objectives. "We'll recommend downsizing, which will immediately impact your stock options. You can then hire us to pick up the slack from your reduced workforce."

Who would question an increase for the executive if she was helping to increase the value of shareholders' wealth? That was what they were paid to do. Layoffs were a telltale sign of better quarters to come. Wall Street seemed to be clamoring for more and more employees to be axed. The more axing, the more macho the management team was viewed as being in the eyes of the business community. Within the confines of the company being pared, consultants provided a buffer for management. "My decision was a tough decision, but it was based on an independent and objective recommendation from the consultants." Not all operated this way, but no question some did.

What happens if, after all the cutbacks, there are not the proper resources to build, sell, and distribute products? Consultants had an answer for this as well, "outsource." Outsourcing was another of those 1990s solutions for just about everything. Why build, sell, and distribute when you could get someone else to do it for you? It was cheaper, better, faster, and, most important, it seemed to minimize the risks to management. The outsourcer could do the day-to-day operational management, allowing the executive team to focus on more strategic pursuits—so went the logic. For a while things might look pretty good, but what happened when you needed to make new strategic changes based on new market forces, technological advancements, or changing environmental conditions? Not a problem. Let the outsourcers take care of it.

But there was a potential problem with outsourcing. It wasn't always the right answer, especially if it was a critical business function recommended for outsourcing. Outsourcing contracts were most often for several years based on a fixed pricing schedule. They assumed business conditions would remain relatively constant. I guess nobody worried about the potential of a greedy outsourcer holding the corporate customer hostage if conditions changed. "This requires additional charges, or a brand new contract." What other choice have you got? Think of the cost and embarrassment of bringing it back in-house once all the skilled resources and facilities had been stripped out, or "redeployed." By the time changes are made additional budgets are approves, and new outsourcing contracts are signed, the business could be in free fall.

It was becoming obvious that Tandon, with its unfettered access to the chairman's office, had a decided advantage over the rest of us—consultants and employees alike. It started to sink in. I was at best a "Double A" ballplayer facing big-league pitching for the first time. It may take several smacks against the head, but after a while, I usually do catch on. To be successful in this business, and not only at Chase, I would need to align myself with a consulting organization that had more clout. Wasn't that what Dellano and Carter had been telling me from the beginning? I loved my independence and doing things my own way, but I also wanted to make a decent living. As Tom Carter had said, "You'll never make the big bucks in your own business unless you're in a position to multiply yourself." In other words, having more bodies to bill. If I didn't want to run this kind of operation myself, then I needed to either partner with someone who did, or become an employee for one of those bigger firms.

Efforts to find the right partner or employer became a full-time endeavor. I was getting tired of hearing the same kind of things from various clients. "The work you do is very high quality but you just don't have the name recognition," or "Our senior executives never heard of Informed Technology Decisions." I was talking to myself on a more regular basis. "Well, there's a simple answer to this. Why don't you set up a meeting with your boss and me?" If it wasn't the lack of name recognition, it was the lack of scale. "We need to team with a company that has the resources to throw at big projects." It struck me that as businesses continued to downsize and consolidate, the boutique consulting firms such as mine would go the way of the punch-card machine. In a world increasingly more obsessed with downsizing, a small consulting firm peddling things like "skills transfer" could become totally irrelevant. Now I was also hearing Logan's voice in the back of my head. "Told you so." At this rate, pretty soon there would be nobody left for transferring skills, just "work for hires" passing through. Unfortunately, I was not having much luck finding the right partner. The ones I looked at were too much into "how many bodies can we throw at the job," or they were self-proclaimed gurus who I couldn't understand without a technical dictionary.

There was another option that could help me increase revenue, provide some additional stability, and yet allow me to remain in business as an independent. I could become a product reseller. There were plenty of consultants who had stepped beyond making recommendations in order to sell and install products. The beauty of reselling was that I could get a percentage of gross sales without having to own or inventory products. It could be a high-opportunity, low-risk proposition. Using some of my new IBM contacts, I was approved as an IBM partner for database products. I could now get paid a percentage on sales. Fortunately, there was little holding me back from signing similar agreements with other IBM lines of business, or IBM competitors.

Nonetheless, I did worry about a potential conflict of interest by moving in this new direction. I really like the front-end strategy and vendor analysis stuff. Wouldn't clients question my ability to be an objective evaluator if I was also selling products for a vendor? Was there potential liability? Yet there were other companies that did this. They called themselves consultants, but they were also vendors, selling products and installing products that they themselves had recommended. In many cases, most of their revenue flowed from doing the vendor implementation stuff. Somehow they were still getting hired to provide an "objective view," but the front-end advising was simply a foot in the door for more lucrative work. Nevertheless, the idea of doing "consulting" and selling at the same time made me uncomfortable. I decided to ask a friend. His name was Joe Levy. Joe had been an executive with IBM in the World Trade organization. He had gotten to know Gideon Gartner, the founder of Gartner Group, while they were both students at MIT. Both Joe and Gideon ended up working at IBM and eventually the Gartner Group. In spite of a small, skinny frame, thinning hair, and a high-pitched voice, he had a strong, dominant personality that usually crowded the room.

According to Joe, when Gideon first started Gartner Group, he tried to persuade him to throw in the towel at IBM and join his start-up firm. "I stuck it out with IBM longer than I should have," Joe said. Joe finally did join Gartner Group, several years later to develop the on-site consulting practice. This was a different side of the business than the research practice where Will Logan had worked way back in 1984. An article in *Hi-Tech Marketing* magazine pointed out that it was Gideon Gartner's background and knowledge gained in IBM, combined with his experience on Wall Street, that contributed to building the necessary skills and talent that helped him create one of the most successful consulting firms in the technology business.[4]

It made sense. He had all the necessary skills and contacts to make IBM voyeurism a moneymaking operation. He could also show his technology consultants how to take on the persona of Wall Street analysts, talking megabytes instead of stock price. There was a major distinction from Wall Street analysts. Their wardrobe wasn't quite as flashy. Looking the part of the eccentric seemed to play better with the corporate technologists.

Like his friend Gideon, Joe Levy also credited IBM for honing his skills and developing his credibility. Both had left Gartner Group, although Joe once again waited too long and left several years after Gideon, missing an opportunity to maximize his exit package. When he did finally leave, he was more than ready. "I couldn't take another day with all the backstabbing," said Levy. He had started his own consulting practice and was also involved in another new business venture with Gideon. I valued his advice and met with him fairly regularly to exchange war stories and discuss potential opportunities. Both of us were still trying to bag the really big one and promised to share the payload if we finally cashed in. Consultants always talk about landing the big one, just like everybody else.

One day we met at Joe Levy's home in Westport, Connecticut. He had a beautiful house, set back from the road, surrounded by acres of lush woods and a private tennis court in mint condition. IBM couldn't have been that bad.

Over a few deli-style sandwiches in the kitchen, I asked his opinion on the conflict of interest issue which I could potentially face playing a dual role as advisor on technology decisions and technology salesman.

"Everybody does it, although I would personally have a problem with it. Before you advise on purchase decisions, I think you have an obligation to lay your cards on the table. Better to be up front regarding affiliations with integrators, vendors . . . your interest to compete for follow-on business. If you do that, I don't see too much of a problem. No one is completely objective. It's the ones who claim that they are you need to watch."

"How do they get away with it?" I asked.

"Weak corporate management, that's how. These guys are too eager to bring consultants in. They rarely consider the potential downside."

"Are there liability issues for the consultants?"

"There could be, but not usually. Most corporate contracts are pretty standard, and consultants are rarely asked to disclose affiliations or potential areas of conflict."

He then turned the tables. He said, "Let me ask you something, you know a lot about IBM . . . ever think about doing consulting for IBM's competitors?"

"I've thought about it," I said. In fact, IBM contracts did have strict confidentiality agreements that would stay in effect for several years after completing a consulting assignment. Apparently it was rarely enforced.

If I did lay my cards on the table, who would hire me to do evaluation? I decided to bounce my concerns off Dellano. His comments seemed to confirm Levy's point of view. Dellano seemed surprised, as if to say "you mean, you still don't get it?" He explained that it was not objectivity that he wanted from his consultants. "It's solutions that work," he said, adding, "I don't have time for games. Just help me get it done."

Dellano thought that my selling products from IBM would be a good move. Nonetheless, my concerns about the long-term viability of my company were intensifying. Let's say the objectivity thing wasn't a problem. Still, my recommendations weren't exactly mainstream. Dellano wasn't mainstream either, and I had simply lucked out finding someone who shared similar views. He was a few points off the standard deviation curve based on my encounters with other clients. Dellano wasn't trying to fool anybody, not even himself. This was the big difference between him and me.

I continued to give some thought to a lot of different options. Combining consulting with selling was becoming less desirable as an option. I liked doing technology evaluation work for clients, but I didn't see how I could feel comfortable doing both. There were all kinds of concessions I found myself willing to make as a consultant that I at one time never would have thought possible. This, however, was the Rubicon I didn't know how to cross. If I couldn't feel comfortable doing it, I couldn't do it.

"After careful evaluation, I think you should buy 'X.' By the way, if you buy it from me, I can get you a great deal."

I'd feel exposed. My inability to project the right poker face had always been a shortcoming. I remembered one of the more experienced IBM reps telling me when I started out in selling, "Man when you don't like somebody it's all over your face." Needless to say, this could be a big problem for a salesman. "Find something positive about 'em," he suggested. "Maybe the tie, or the picture of the family behind the desk. . . .' "

It never really worked. Luckily, I had always been assigned to big accounts where I could usually find someone I liked. In my own business, I figured it would be even easier to cherry-pick, but finding the Dellanos in this new corporate arena, where the yes-men incessantly droned the party line and seemed to be calling more and more of the shots, had proven very difficult.

Finding somebody I liked to sell to was only part of the problem. I also had to believe in what I was doing. These personality quirks could surely do me in. Not to mention, I would be reentering the world of quotas and forecasts—a far cry from the consulting world of limited accountability. The salesman and consultant in me would have been at constant war. "This is a good deal. . . . I think we need to evaluate further."

I decided to keep looking. Through another friend, a meeting was scheduled with McKinsey & Company to discuss potential employment. McKinsey was considered the premier management consulting firm with over sixty offices in more than thirty countries. A 1994 cover story, "The Craze for Consultants," in *Business Week* estimated that McKinsey & Company was doing over $1.3 billion in revenue and were hands down, "The pricey high priests of strategic consulting."[5] By *Hoover's Online* estimates, this would grow to an approximate $3.4 billion by 2000.[6]

My friend set up a meeting with one of the principals of the firm in the New York City office. I went into the meeting knowing that McKinsey preferred hiring kids straight out of school, and the schools tended to be the cream of the crop. The office smacked of elitism. Tastefully understated pastel blue and brown carpet strips ran across the center of the reception area, spilling out over hardwood parquet floors, so polished you could glance down and see a mirror image of the people and objects in front of you. Strategically positioned pieces of office furniture complemented the décor, or was it the other way around? The bulk of the richly finished furniture appeared to be deep cherry. There was a Japanese mural on the center wall. I wondered if the décor was seasonal. Even the secretaries had an elitist demeanor. I was escorted down the hall to meet the principal. After shaking hands, we sat down in his office, faced off across a huge desk where everything was neatly stacked in small, discernible piles.

His expensive threads were custom tailored. He wore his dark, graying hair slicked back.

His oversized thick glasses distorted the countenance of his face. I was reminded of an old commercial where after swallowing a spoonful of cereal, adults are transformed into little kids. After glancing at my résumé, he told me in a slightly condescending, high-pitched tone that he felt I had an impressive background.

"You have obviously held various positions. Tell me, what do you believe are your defining characteristics?"

"I produce results," I said proudly.

"Oh . . . here at McKinsey we do not produce results. We problem solve."

How naive of me to talk about results. Results imply getting your hands dirty with implementation. Results also represent minimal billable hours to a management consultant. Now problem solving is quite different. It can be repositioned and packaged as an extended Socratic process with lots of layers. Each layer of process translates to lots of billable hours and potential follow-on contracts with any client expectation of tangible results blurred and redirected.

For example, assume a consulting firm is engaged to help make a decision regarding the best market channel for selling a new product, either using the current sales force or selling over the Internet. There are two distinct points of view within the client organization regarding which approach would be most effective. One group subscribes to the importance of personalized-relationship selling that can only come from direct customer contact. The other supports the Internet as more cost effective. The consultants will want to study the decision-making processes currently used by proponents of both points of view that led them to their current conclusions. This would most probably require meetings with other groups within the company. The consultants will also want to better understand the client's "thinking" as it related to various topics. They will argue that only after understanding the information selected by various groups that led to their divergent points of view can they understand the issues and help resolve the problem.

While the consultants are interviewing company personnel and gathering historical perspective, they are also in education mode and billing the client for the time in learning the background information employees already know. Additional hours will also have to be billed to assess external marketing factors that may alter the current points of view, review a potential hybrid solution, or consider additional alternatives. These, of course, will extend the problem-solving exercise. The consultants may suggest meetings with customers. Benchmarking the competition might be an additional component added to the engagement. This could take a month. Depending on the scope and complexity of the project, perhaps several months.

During this whole process, there is no telling what additional problems might be uncovered that will require more in-depth analysis before final conclusions can be made. Achieving immediate, tangible results may be a desirable outcome for the client. They are not necessarily part of the consultant model. While the consultant continues to dabble away absorbing significant client resources, the competition may have already prototyped a creative new selling approach, well on their way to snatching up the lion's share of the market. Luckily, most of the other established companies in the 1990s were also opting for the consulting approach.

A good guess is that the best alternative, as recommended by the consultants, would most probably turn out to be the cheapest. Recommendations to reduce expenditures were well received by executives whose compensation was often tied to stock. It didn't take years of industry experience and proficiency to recommend a cost-cutting solution. Costs go down, profit goes up. So does the stock. Was it really necessary to go through all of the process to figure this out? For political reasons, many corporate-savvy executives would probably say yes. The executives can point out that the decision was made after an in-depth independent review. If the answer was late in coming, it was because these important business decisions require careful consideration. Translation: lots of billable hours for the consultant.

My interview with McKinsey continued. After mentioning the problem-solving orientation, the principal partner went on to tell me more about McKinsey. If I did want to work for them, he explained how I would have to start at the bottom of the ladder, "just like everyone else." He shared an example of a first-year assignment where new hires stand in airports, soliciting volunteers to fill out questionnaires. Obviously, he was trying to paint a most unappetizing picture for me. Referring to my experience in working at Chase, he handed me a book written by several McKinsey partners on technology in banking, pointing out that it included Chase as a case study example and that "this could be quite educational for you."

As the brief discussion began winding down, he asked me if I had any remaining questions for him. I told him just one. "Who do you view as the major competitors of McKinsey?" He gave me one of those "what, are you kidding?" kind of looks. "We have no competitors," he said following a brief pause.

It intrigued me to think that these types of people were advising CEOs in corporate America, as well as around the world. I didn't expect to get a job offer any time soon. I managed to read only about one-third of the book I was given. It had been fairly recently published, but the material was as dry as the Mojave. The most interesting part for me was the section on Chase and the technology systems they were using to gain competitive advantage. The systems to which they referred were systems that Dellano and Carter would have called "legacy." They were systems up for replacement or major rework. Maybe those same McKinsey guys in the airport had collected the technology information for the book.

There was something else about the problem-solving orientation versus results that left me puzzled. Wasn't all the emphasis in business these days concerning improving results? Wasn't it the inability to produce a quick fix in net profits that had gotten Chase in trouble? Could it be possible that the objectives of the consultants to cut down on problem solving were not always consistent with the objectives of management? Weren't there more effective ways to impact the bottom line than hiring an "objective" third party to launch an expedition in analysis? It all came back to management. If they weren't careful, they could end up with a series of expensive exer-

cises with minimal, tangible benefits. That is, until the startling recommendation came that they needed to downsize. The unwary executive might
think that given all the new competitive pressures on business, all these
efforts were in the best interest of the company stockholders, including
him—a "win-win" situation. Why? "The consultants told me so."

It looked like finding a workable partnership or employer to continue
in the consulting just wasn't going to work. Either they weren't interested
in me, or I wasn't interested in them. Sometimes both. The timing was bad.
While many consultants thrived on the "downsizing business," it wasn't
for me. After responding to the *Wall Street Journal* ad regarding a technology strategist position, I received a call from NationsBank. This was
before they gobbled up Bank of America, assuming the prestigious and
more familiar Bank of America name. I turned down their first offer. In the
meantime, I was in the process of completing another contract with IBM.

Life was now good, in spite of long work days. My income had more
than doubled from my best earning years with IBM. It almost made the
long hours bearable. One morning I read in the paper that Chemical
Banking Corporation was going to acquire Chase Manhattan. This would
create the biggest banking company in the United States, at least until the
next megamerger.[7] The new entity would be bigger than Citibank. While
it was called a merger of equals, the fine print made it clear that Chemical
as the buyer would be the more equal. The unthinkable was happening.
This was followed by changes with my other clients. Massachusetts
Mutual Life Insurance was making a play to acquire Connecticut Mutual.
And IBM was reorganizing once again to make room for newly acquired
Lotus Development Corporation within the Networking systems line of
business. The acquisition of this software powerhouse had been
announced in June 1995 as part of Lou Gerstner's attempt to solidify IBM
as a network-centric leader.

I learned that IBM was acquiring Lotus for a specific client/server
network product for calendaring, mail, and team collaboration. It was
called Lotus Notes and was often referred to as the prototype for a new
breed of networking, called *groupware*. This was the next generation of
client/server, more efficient and powerful than the previous attempts at
it. Groupware had the potential to make Web-based computing more
user friendly. Like IBM, Lotus had acquired another company to first get
this technology and had great success in selling it. Business 101: it doesn't
matter who built it; what matters is who has the rights and how well they
sell it, or get someone else to sell it. It doesn't even matter if it is a look-
alike, if you can sell and distribute it better then the other guy. One could
argue that even Microsoft had initially bought its way to success.

Microsoft purchased the software IBM needed for the original PC, Disk Operating System (DOS), from somebody else to position itself for its IBM contract.[8] Since then, some critics have argued that Microsoft never invented, but simply continued to buy or emulate other companies' products, backed up with aggressive marketing maneuvers. Even the critics had to admit the strategy had worked.

Unlike the spreadsheet product 1-2-3, which helped put Lotus on the map, Notes would be more difficult for others to clone, or as they say in the business, *reverse engineer*. Using its dominance in the marketplace, Microsoft had by now made Excel the spreadsheet standard, surpassing Lotus 1-2-3. It could be done again. Microsoft had bits and pieces of products that could eventually catch up to Notes in functionality. They were in products called "Outlook," "Exchange," and "Access." They could also package it with other popular Microsoft products, like Windows, giving them a huge competitive advantage, as they did with their Web browser in the competitive battle against Netscape, which would before long land them in court.

The key for IBM was to exploit the temporary uniqueness and popularity of Notes. The key for Lotus was to take it from client/server and make it Web enabled. Combined with IBM, it had the potential to become part of a new defacto standard for networking solutions. But IBM needed to act swiftly and decisively if it was serious about this market.

Microsoft was already nipping at its heels.

From my perspective, the acquisition of Lotus would mean an additional shake-up within the management ranks of IBM Networking Systems. It was announced that a more aggressive management team would be taking charge. This was good for IBM, but not so good for my business. I was losing the contacts I had invested time in cultivating. All at once I was about to lose my little nest egg of clients who were always willing to give me repeat business.

Just before the end of 1995, I was offered a two-year international consulting contract with Colgate-Palmolive Co. It was to provide technical assistance and education for implementation of a major client/server solution they were interested in making available at company locations worldwide. The solution was to reengineer back-office business processes with software from a company called SAP AG. As noted by the *Wall Street Journal*, "Colgate is making a huge bet on controversial new software; if it works, no corner of its business will go untouched."[9] The software company was started by five ex-IBM system engineers from Germany. They had become one of the most successful software companies in the world.

Revenue at SAP in 1995 was 2.7 billion in German marks, or about 1.8

billion in American dollars, representing 49 percent growth over the previous year.[10] While SAP was marketed as providing a "rapid-implementation" method, it had developed a reputation for being complex and difficult to install. Implementations often took many years because the old business had to be converted and there was a steep learning curve for users. The standard joke was that if your company was planning to implement SAP modules, you better have programmers who could read technical manuals in German. For a consultant it could mean years of gainful employment. According to *Computerworld*, for every one dollar spent on SAP AG's flagship R/3 product, companies could expect to pay ten dollars in consulting fees.[11]

In spite of some obvious issues, SAP had become the New Age religion for techies. Every once in a while a customer would be quoted in one of the computer trade rags complaining that SAP was inflexible and forced changes to the business to conform with the SAP model, instead of the other way around. This, however, was rare up through the middle 1990s. Most of the hype made it sound like SAP was more than a product; it was the fully automated and interconnected company-wide solution of the future. Top computer analysts and integrators were leading the charge. There was one major issue: like Lotus Notes, SAP was not built in anticipation of the Web. It would have to undergo a major rewrite to become "Web enabled."

I would be one of six or seven consultants hired individually by Colgate-Palmolive. My main responsibility would be to manage the training, but I would also have other tasks. When you're in a foreign country with a limited staff and something needs to get done, it doesn't take a McKinsey analyst to figure out you'll be doing a little of everything. On the plus side, in addition to a guaranteed sizable income for two years, they would pay all of my travel and living expenses. Colgate was committed to training me on SAP so I could then train Colgate International employees. It was a chance to keep the business going as an independent consultant and gain some great experience for my résumé. What was not to like?

I learned that Andersen Consulting had completed the SAP installation for Colgate in the United States. Andersen was a strategic partner with SAP, and the alliance had helped both companies win major contracts with Fortune 500s, Colgate being just one. The chief information officer for Colgate-Palmolive had decided to solicit a different kind of help for its overseas locations. He was not very explicit about the reasons for dropping Andersen, but he did hint that his company felt Andersen's billing rates were very high. He also said, "I want to create my own team of handpicked, experienced consultants. I don't want them picked for me from some large pool of people sitting on the bench."

Colgate-Palmolive gave me some time around the holidays to consider the offer. This prompted friends to give me a book for Christmas, *The World's Most Dangerous Places*. It was billed as "the hard core adventurer's guide to getting in, getting around, and getting out of . . . hot spots, war zones, and lethal lands." Scanning the book, I learned that in some of the locations Colgate planned to send me I might have to hire a bodyguard if I merely wanted to go for a stroll, and this was no joke. It was open season for foreigners in many of these countries, especially foreigners from the United States. The following excerpt talked about Russia, one of my first stops:

> How tough is it? In August 1994, in the grubby town of Nizhini Tagil in the Ural Mountains, Russian criminals hijacked (or rented) a T-90 tank from the local military base, drove it back to town and shot it out with Muslims who had tried to strongarm control of the market stalls. Makes our Wild West look like a sorority pillow fight.[12]

From a business perspective, it would have been a high-risk client/server project with a very tight implementation schedule. In addition, in spite of my turned-down request, I wouldn't have any say on the other consultants being hired. They wanted me to accept the position without even an introductory meeting. What if the team didn't get along?

Imagine, two years abroad in remote, desolate places with a group of potential miscreants. By the start of the new millennium, the major television networks would be killing the rating charts with situational "reality TV" shows scripted like this. I would also be moving from the technical and marketing strategy business, which I enjoyed, to "hands-on" implementation work. To be perfectly honest, just loading new software onto my own personal computer had always been a challenge. I wasn't up for the challenge in an area where I had no skills and no track record. It didn't seem to matter in consulting with all the on-the-job training available, but I was of the old school. As Tom Carter had once quipped, "If at first you don't succeed, don't try skydiving."

Getting vendor support if there was a problem with products in some of these remote locations could be extremely difficult—even for a prestigious customer such as Colgate-Palmolive. If there was a software problem in my little outpost in Tanzania, how could I hope to get adequate help from the vendor when SAP was struggling to build a support structure for its new customers from all over the world? I couldn't see getting a lot of attention from a remote Third World country. SAP was still steadily increasing. No one, not even the research analysts, anticipated the huge windfall of customers choosing SAP. Demand was being created by the hands-on consultants and integrators who loved those long-term implementation projects. I have to admit, whenever the techies started sounding religious about a new technology, it made me suspicious. In spite of what the market would pay for an experienced SAP consultant, it didn't really thrill me to exile myself to remote lands for a couple years to become one. On top of all this, I didn't speak German.

It wasn't until 1999 that problems regarding SAP had emerged. After years of phenomenal growth, often as much as 50 percent a year, it appeared SAP was losing traction, and revenues were slipping. Profits were down over 24 percent for the first three quarters of 1999. Profits would rebound in the fourth quarter, but still fall "below expectations." For the first quarter of 2000, SAP would post a 43 percent drop in net income. Senior executives at SAP were jumping ship. As noted by the *Wall Street Journal*, "Much of SAP's problem, say current and former employees, stems from the dominance of its headquarters. Ensconced in Walldorf, a sleepy village an hour south of Frankfurt and nine time zones from the Internet revolution's front lines, the headquarters team brushed off warnings that e-commerce was changing the rules."[13] By now e-commerce was generally known and accepted as the buying and selling of goods and services over the Internet. Once again, the consultants who had recommended SAP and aggressively promoted it with clients seemed to get a free pass when it came to the blame game. In fact, SAP problems represented a new consulting opportunity. Those who installed SAP would now need help figuring out how to integrate back-office SAP with front-end solutions that could provide e-commerce capability and customer relationship management functionality. It was either that or wait for SAP to play catch up.

Before making my decision about Colgate, I also talked with some business friends who had considerable international experience. Several told me that there was the potential for a backlash against U.S. consultants in Russia as well as some of the Third World countries where I would be working. Brought in to help Russia privatize industries and develop a free market economy, there were consultants who exploited the situation.

Reports in the *Wall Street Journal* substantiated some of this. One article pointed out that Russians were appalled that American consulting firms were major beneficiaries for a $5.8 billion aid package allocated by the U.S. government to the former Soviet Union: "This may work in the long run. But short-term, it is galling to many Russians, who find the U.S. attitude both patronizing and stingy—while enriching scores of U.S. consultants who are pocketing between 50 percent and 90 percent of the money in a given contract. With cash starved Russians trying to jump-start their fledging businesses and economy—and antireform politicians gaining ground—'we don't need 90 percent of technical-assistance money going to American experts,' says Alexsandr A. Jitnikov, head of a Russian commission coordinating foreign aid."[14] Similarly, when the Palestine Liberation Organization signed the peace accord with Israel on September 13, 1993, consulting firms lined up in hopes of helping the Palestinians spend the expected windfall in financial support pledged by Western nations.[15]

Eventually consultants would also become embedded in the Israeli political process, a sure sign that they were turning up everywhere. In the past, Israelis were highly critical of American dependency on consultants. It was obvious to most that there was no love or affection between President Bill Clinton and Prime Minister Benjamin Netanyahu. James Carville, the attack dog consultant who helped get Bill Clinton elected, turned his consulting talents to the Labor Party candidate Ehud Barak, helping him unseat Netanyahu in 1999. In a vain effort to defend himself, Netanyahu also hired consultants. While many in the Israeli press pulled for Barak, they also bemoaned the increased influence of American political consultants. The consultants helped Barak get elected, but he wasn't there for long.

Also in 1999, a Russian money-laundering scandal of huge dimensions was exposed. Billions of dollars in U.S. aid was being siphoned off, diverted to purposes for which they were not intended. In an editorial in the *Wall Street Journal*, the former national security adviser for the Carter administration, Zbigniew Brzezinski, suggested that this had a tragic political consequence. He pointed out that millions of Russians have come to view democracy and the free market as "synonymous with theft and criminal self-enrichment." Consequently, this massive flow of illicit money from Russia conflicted with the intended goal Washington was attempting to achieve. Brzezinski pointed out that this didn't happen without help from the West. He asked the following:

> Who from abroad helped the self-enriching Russian elite master the arcana of international financial transactions? It is unlikely that the cluster of official and unofficial Russians who a mere five years ago were poor but are now billionaires could have maneuvered with such skill in the Western financial markets without expert Western advice. Who might have been the "consultants" helping their Russian clients operate so smoothly on the world scene? Were any Western officials involved? Given the billions of dollars at stake, it is not very likely that the beneficiaries were exclusively Russian émigrés in the Moscow-Tel Aviv-Brooklyn triangle.[16]

This was not to suggest that consultants only focused on lining their own pockets at the expense of clients. Not all consultants were carpetbaggers. What this does suggest is that without the oversight of responsible and ethical management, consultants may not operate in the best interests of the corporate or government organization. This was more than a Russian problem, although there was definitely more of a backlash in the former USSR where the stakes were incredibly high as they tried to transition to capitalism. In any case, I was glad that back in 1995 my final decision was to pass up two years of traveling the globe and touching down in some potentially dangerous places, growing more hostile to American consultants all the time. Bottom line, I wimped out.

Consulting didn't leave much time for a personal life. If I wasn't working on a contract, I was working to get one. In addition to the potential loss of my established clients, I was getting tired of filling out government tax forms and chasing receivables. It was a rootless kind of life. Moving from job to job and working long hours was taking a toll. It didn't leave much time for personal relationships or getting involved in the community. My situation was not unique. Consulting represented a fast-growing new breed of corporate worker, the contractor for hire. You were a rentable product, and personal time meant the meter was running idle.

In spite of the drawback in carving out time for myself, I had hooked up with a new girlfriend who was also a consultant. She did health and fitness consulting for Reebok. It amused me when she complained about my working too hard. She was the classic overachiever who grew up on a farm in Indiana, was magnum cum laude in college, and had worked as a singer-dancer on Broadway. She once said, "When you're on your death bed, you're not going to be saying to yourself, 'gee, I wish I billed a few more hours.'" Not that she herself didn't work 'round the clock as a fitness consultant and aerobics instructor. At least her work was fun and relieved stress as opposed to increasing it. Trying to keep up with her on marathon bike rides helped convince me that I needed to reset my priorities.

When NationsBank called again with a higher-level position, as a senior vice president, and a better financial package, I decided to take it. More and more people were leaving corporations to become contracted workers. I was bucking the trend and moving in the opposite direction. Rejoining the ranks as a corporate employee was sounding better all the time. Working in my own business as a consultant had provided an incredible education, but it did have its downside. In many ways it was an extremely frustrating experience. I also concluded that the NationsBank position would be much less risk averse than the Colgate-Palmolive consulting assignment, or so I thought.

NationsBank was a big consumer of consultant services, particularly with Andersen Consulting. Sure I had heard negative things about Andersen. While everybody liked to take pot shots at number one, there was no question that Andersen Consulting was the best in the business as measured by their revenue growth. Andersen had to be doing something right with reported revenues from consulting fees and services for 1995 of over $4.2 billion.[17] By 1998 it would be $8.3 billion. As opposed to trying to follow their footsteps in Colgate-Palmolive, I would have an opportunity to work with them at NationsBank. If I ever decided to go back to my own business, I would have had a chance to learn from the best. In the meantime, like Dellano at Chase, I would have the benefit of using my former consulting background to help my new employer manage the work-for-hires.

In early January 1996, I made one last trip to Chase to say good-bye to the friends I had made, stopping first at Michael Dellano's office. He congratulated me on my new job and reminded me that NationsBank had attempted to negotiate a takeover of Chase prior to Chemical. "That would have been a market-expansion strategy and probably good for both banks," he said. "Instead, we are about to implement a cost-cutting strategy with two banks in the same market. Branches will have to close. Technology will be outsourced. Lots of people will go."

Dellano referred to a recent article where the newly named chief information officer discussed his plans for the consolidation of technology operations. Formerly from Chemical, the CIO said that he planned to outsource application development for the combined bank.[18]

There didn't seem to be any silver lining if you accepted Dellano's point of view. He looked like someone had kicked his teeth out. The decision to keep the Chase name seemed to be just another source of irritation. Michael Dellano had spent too many years competing against Chemical. They were the enemy. He would leave shortly after our last meeting, following several senior executives from the old Chase to the new Prudential, Prudential Insurance Company of America. They would wrestle lots of alligators, but eventually take Prudential from a Mutual Company owned exclusively by policyholders to a corporate-traded company with stockholders. Dellano would be on point to create the technology architecture for the new Prudential Financial, a one-stop shopping opportunity for meeting insurance, banking, and investment needs for customers under one safe and secure umbrella. Insurance, safe and secure investments, privacy of customer information; they would take on new meaning after September 11, 2001. Want to minimize risk? Don't think consultants. Think insurance.

This group of ex-Chase refugees had been tight-knit. They were often called the "blue-collar executives," as so many of them had come up through the ranks. Prudential was about to be infused with a lot more rock.

I also went to see Tom Carter, but he had called in sick that day. I learned that Carter's health was not good. I said so long to some of the people who worked for him. Anxiety combined with anger seemed to be the crippling sentiment of the day for most of the people.

"Why do you think they went with Chemical over everybody else?" I was asked by a woman I had worked with on my last project at Chase. "Our chairman got a better package for himself, that's why."

It was another nasty rumor, and I remember thinking at the time that it was a cheap shot. As reported by the *Wall Street Journal* a few years later, the chairman "was shocked by the ferocity of written comments he had solicited from workers at the old Chase after the deal was announced. One asked if he had gotten '30 pieces of silver' for the deal, insiders say."[19] In the same article it was noted that the former Chase chairman had become president at the new Chase, reporting to the new chairman for a compensation package, worth close to $10 million. It may have been shocking for some employees, but all they needed to do was look at what other executives were now making across the new corporate environment. I'm sure Tandon could have explained why he deserved it, with some very compelling arguments.

Was it possible that the high-priority effort to cut costs was part of a bigger plan to set Chase up as a more attractive candidate for acquisition? As I thought about it, I couldn't help but wonder if that was what was really behind the Tandon quest to improve profitability. Later, I would learn that even though most consultants familiar with both banks believed that Chase was ahead of Chemical in technology, many of the Chase technology systems would be shut down, including the financial systems run by Carter's department. To the victor goes the spoils. It wasn't a question of who had the best systems. The systems of the acquiring company were generally the ones that would prevail. The consultants working for the acquiring company would also come into a nice windfall. Like NationsBank, Chemical had been considered a premier Andersen Consulting financial-industry account. Consultants were slated to play a major role in the consolidation effort. Not long after the dust settled, there would be another merger with the brokerage house J.P. Morgan, creating even more integration work for armies of consultants.

I was told by friends within the systems area that before Tom Carter left to accept a position in a different part of the new Chase Manhattan Bank, he placed all the people who had worked for him in other jobs. He was one of those old-fashioned guys with a lot of character who cared about his subordinates. A few months later, Tom Carter would be diagnosed with an inoperable brain tumor. He told me he planned to continue working for as long as he could. He worked until the end. About three years later, the former chairman and now president of the new Chase, Thomas Labrecque, would retire. Several months later he, too, would pass away. Labrecque was only sixty-two years old. He was recognized as a successful executive with a strong overall track record. He had been popular with employees prior to the takeover, and he regained popularity as he stuck it out in the new combined bank. In hindsight, in the new world where the stock market is the supreme measuring stick, I reached to the conclusion that Labrecque's options were limited once profitability unexpectedly dropped. I think he had done the best he could for Chase. Apparently, most employees came around to thinking this as well. If it's true that, as Billy Joel sang, "Only the Good Die Young," I figured I'd live to be a hundred.

From these experiences, I concluded that consultants come in waves. First on the scene are the strategists who circle the executives and provide analysis. They may recommend sweeping new directions, but more likely, they'll recommend cutbacks and consolidation. Next come the integrators, taking small chunks of business, charging whatever the market will bear. As was often the case with the recommended multivendor client/server-based solutions, costs continue to spiral and competitive pressures mount. These are followed by the reengineering consultants and outsourcers, snatching larger pieces of the business based on longer-term contractual arrangements to "downsize and realign infrastructure to increase productivity and reduce costs." The barracudas are displaced by sharks. By now the company was completely gutted and a prime target for acquisition. The strategists may help in final preparation to put the company up on the auction block. The company sells. Executive management is rewarded. Consultants of all varieties continue to feed off of the consolidation efforts and eventually move on for the next opportunity. This eminded me of Jacques Cousteau:

> The attitude of the sharks in their first approach was perfectly clear-cut. Carrying prudence to its extremes, they circled around the still-warm carcass of the baby whale, maintaining a constant, almost lazy, speed. But even so, they seemed very sure of themselves. They quite obviously had no fear of us. If we chased one of them away with boat hooks, he returned a moment later. Time was working for them, and they knew it. The prey could not escape them.
>
> For an entire hour these maneuvers continued, and still not a single shark had ventured too close to the little whale. Then they began to

touch him with their snouts, barely grazing him, one by one and hundreds of times, but making no attempt to bite. They behaved the same way with our protective cage.

Suddenly, the blue shark lunged and bit. With a single blow, as if from some giant razor, pounds of skin, of flesh, and of fat were sliced away. It was the signal; the orgy was about to begin.

With no apparent transition, the calm of the preliminary round gave way to the frenzy of sharing in the spoils. Each mouthful snatched by each passing shark dug a hole the size of a bucket in the body of the dead whale. I could not believe my eyes. Instinctively, and horrified, I thought of similar scenes which must have taken place after a shipwreck or the crash of a plane into the sea.[20]

It wasn't the time to be getting cynical. Besides, I had swum with the sharks, albeit, as a small pilot fish, undetected until now. I had learned from observing. Truthfully, though, more skills had been transferred to me from watching and listening to clients like Michael Dellano and Tom Carter than anything I could have learned from the consultants. They had done most of the skills transfer, helping to make me successful. This was also part of the consulting game. Learn as much as you can while working for a client. It makes you more valuable for the next one.

Probably most important, I had discovered that as much as I liked it, being out there on your own in this new emerging business world was dangerous. Independents were becoming as vulnerable as the spotted owl. Accepting a new position as a bank employee, it was time to go undercover once again. It had to be safer than independent consulting, whether that was in the Third World, or in those fancy New York highrises. Me, a banker. Who would have guessed?

All I had to do was remember to play the part of the good corporate citizen and always say yes, or at least sound like you mean something close to yes. At the time, this seemed perfectly acceptable, given that I would be getting a regular paycheck that would help ease the adjustment. You don't know how nice getting paid regularly really is until the checks stop coming.

SUMMARY OF OBSERVATIONS

- In some companies, high-paid senior executives hire high-paid consultants to help them make decisions. Essentially the company is paying twice for the decision-making function. The best executives may engage consultants with specific expertise for advising or other services, but they make the decisions and control the problem.

- Management consulting firms often offer "problem solving" over results. This increases the time frame and cost of their engagements.

- Consultants are not always objective. They sometimes benefit from their own recommendations, which can drive fees higher for services and create increased client dependency. Understanding their background and the type of firm you are working with can help you determine where their recommendations might lead. For example, if a vertical-industry consultant is brought in to evaluate SAP against PeopleSoft, and he is a trained SAP integration specialist, most likely he will recommend SAP—even if PeopleSoft might be a better fit for your company. If she is a management consultant, she might recommend more "problem-solving analysis" as this is her comfort area and where she has the most expertise. Today many consulting firms claim to be "comprehensive service providers," but few are. Understanding who they really are (management consultant, process consultant, vertical integrator, research analyst) and the skills they really have (analysis, project management, programming, integration, etc.) will improve your ability to manage and achieve your objectives (versus theirs).

- The downsizing environment of the '90s proved to be fertile ground for consultants. With less-skilled internal resources, clients became more dependent on consultant relationships.

- Consultants seem to come in waves, first the strategists, followed next by integrators, then the reengineering experts, the outsourcers, and, finally, the cost-cutting-for-a-fee-sharks.

NOTES

1. "Chase Reports Profit Dip in First Quarter," *New York Times*, 18 April 1995, D4.
2. "Chase Is Turning to a Specialist to Help Sharpen Its Budget Ax," *New York Times*, 6 May 1995, A35.
3. "Executive Decisions," *Multinational Monitor* (March 1998): 5.
4. "Gideon Gartner: Building an Empire," *High-Tech Marketing* (May 1987): 10–15.
5. "The Craze for Consultants," *Business Week*, 25 July 1994, 65.
6. www.hoovers.com.
7. Steven Lipin, "Chemical and Chase Set $10 Billion Merger, Forming Biggest Bank," *Wall Street Journal*, 28 August 1995, A1.

8. Paul Carroll, *Big Blues: The Unmaking of IBM* (New York: Crown Publishers, 1993), 24.

9. "Overhaul; Colgate Is Making a Huge Bet on Controversial New Software; If It Works, No Corner of Its Business Will Go Untouched," *Wall Street Journal*, 18 November 1996, R12.

10. "Digest of Earnings Report," *Wall Street Journal*, 1 February 1996, 20.

11. Julia King "Consulting Conundrum," *Computerworld*, 27 May 1996, 45.

12. Robert Young Pelton, Coskun Aral, and Wink Dulles, *Fielding's the World's Most Dangerous Places* (Redondo Beach, Calif.: Fielding Worldwide, 1995), 540.

13. "How a Software Giant Missed the Internet Revolution," *Wall Street Journal*, 18 January 2000, B1.

14. John J. Fialka, "Helping Ourselves: U.S. Aid to Russia Is Quite a Windfall—For U.S. Consultants," *Wall Street Journal*, 24 February 1994, A1.

15. "Consultants Vie for Slice of Aid for Palestinians," *Wall Street Journal*, 25 January 1994, A9.

16. Zrbigniew Brzezinski, "Bombshells Lurk in the Russian Scandal," *Wall Street Journal*, 3 September 1999, A10.

17. "Earnings, Andersen Consulting L.L.P.," *Chicago Tribune*, 27 February 1996, 3.

18. "Retraining, Outsourcing Rule the Roost at Chase," *Computerworld*, 2 October 1995, 93.

19 "Tom Labrecque, Left for Dead in a Merger, Found Alive and Well," *Wall Street Journal*, 25 November 1998, A6.

20. Jacques-Yves Cousteau and Philippe Cousteau, *The Shark: Splendid Savage of the Sea* (Garden City: Doubleday & Company, 1970), 36–37.

CHAPTER FIVE

BUILDING A BANK
WITH BAYONETS

By the beginning of the new millennium, Bank of America, the largest U.S. bank based on branches and deposits, had problems. The stock had plummeted, and bank executives were warning that results would not improve for at least two years. Employees at all levels were losing their jobs. How was this possible? Here, too, consultants played a critical role.

Just as Chase Manhattan was no longer Chase Manhattan, Bank of America wasn't really Bank of America. Corporate offices had migrated from that trendy left coast "city by the bay" to Dixie. Changing headquarters from San Francisco to Charlotte was only part of the story. Under the cover of the new Bank of America logo, it was really a very different bank—NationsBank. Like Chemical-Chase, it was initially billed as a merger of equals, but analysis of the fine print made it clear that Nations-Bank, at one time a small regional North Carolina bank, was the acquirer of Bank of America, one of the prestigious financial icons of the United States. Chemical had decided on using the more prestigious name of Chase Manhattan. For similar reasons, NationsBank morphed into Bank of America in name only. The culture was still very much NationsBank.

A relatively new upstart, NationsBank was first created in 1991 when two southeastern North Carolina banks merged. At the time no one would have guessed it would become the largest U.S. bank. No one would have guessed the long-term consequences, either.

As a result of the acquisition, the new Bank of America immediately doubled in its number of brick-and-mortar structures. Like lots of victims of the corporate takeover frenzy that swept the United States in the 1990s, the old Bank of America was long on tradition, but had recently become short on profitability—at least according to industry analysts, who supported the NationsBank takeover, assuming the downsizing that was expected to follow would create a stronger and more efficient national megabank. The new economies of scale would make the combined bank stronger than the sum of its parts; or so went the worn logic spewed from the mouths of the Wall Street talking heads. The heads seemed to swirl around all the wounded structures as executives searched frantically for a way to carry some cash as they bailed the sinking ship. Of course the public relations surrounding the acquisition of Bank of America was different than the reality. As is the case with most mergers, there was lots of head butting as two very different cultures clashed. The former Bank of America chairman didn't bail right away, although most knew it was inevitable. Within a few months he was gone.

In a word, NationsBank was Hugh McColl. Never heard of him myself until I began the interview process for a job at NationsBank. Whoever coined the phrase "North Carolina is a valley of humility between two mountains of conceit," never met Hugh McColl. McColl was a former marine. As chairman of NationsBank, McColl quickly assumed a "take no prisoners" reputation as he transitioned from enlisted man to banker. He was a little man who didn't hide his larger-than-life aspirations. He appeared on the cover of the August 21, 1995, issue of *Fortune* magazine in a patch of high grass striking a stalker pose while clutching a hunting rifle and wearing a wide-brim hat with matching hunting fatigues.[1]

McColl was a far cry from your friendly town banker. Back in the 1980s, as an executive with a small North Carolina bank, he had shocked some when he shared his belief that this was a dog-eat-dog competitive world and he wanted to be the dog doing the eating. He later nicknamed his first major acquisition effort "Operation Overlord," the former code name for the Allied invasion of France in World War II. Comparing a bank acquisition to the storming of the beaches of Normandy was a little beyond the pale, but it was quintessential Hugh McColl. During a more recent hostile takeover bid, he reportedly told another bank president he was sending his missiles. He kept a hand grenade on his desk, which was amusing to many and the source of speculation.[2]

The NationsBank chairman had quickly established that he was more than just bark. He developed a well-deserved reputation as a highly successful dealmaker. In 1989, long before making the cover, *Fortune* pronounced McColl as one of the "25 most fascinating business people."[3]

He was both fascinating and street smart. McColl was credited for having the foresight to move into Texas when the oil-based economy was struggling and others were selling off assets and bailing out. The *Fortune* write-up on McColl pointed out that he had made friends with the ex-IBM billionaire, H. Ross Perot, who agreed to guarantee standby capital for the acquisition of First RepublicBank Corp. Rumor had it that Perot also put in a few kind words with the Texas legislature. This and another back-to-back

Texas bank acquisition doubled the size of NationsBank and cost next to nothing after tax breaks.* It was the kind of sweet deal consumer advocates would label "corporate welfare" because, they argued, it made it possible for big companies to privatize profits while socializing the risk to taxpayers.

A short time later, in 1991, McColl signed a five-year outsourcing agreement with H. Ross Perot's business, Perot Systems Corp. The contract for running NationsBank data centers in Dallas, Texas, and Charlotte, North Carolina, was estimated to be worth over $50 million a year. When the agreement was prematurely terminated after a series of financial transaction–processing issues, including a serious glitch that went unresolved for four days, NationsBank management concluded that the problem was the integrators and consultants at Perot Systems who didn't understand enough about banking. Unfortunately, it took a catastrophe before questions in this regard were raised. M. Arthur Gillis, a consultant and president of Computer Based Solutions Inc., said he was not surprised. He called the original agreement a "clublike arrangement based on camaraderie," suggesting that the ability to do the work was a less important consideration.[4] At considerable expense, NationsBank had to bring the business back in-house.

There had been talk of a Bank of America merger long before it happened. The first round of talks broke down in 1995. At the time it was reported that Hugh McColl and the chief executive for Bank of America could not come to agreement as to who would run a combined operation. Hugh was not the kind of guy to take a backseat to anyone. The experts speculated that at some point in the future discussions would reopen.[5] It wasn't exactly rocket science to figure out. The chairman of Bank of America was scheduled to retire in a few years. McColl wasn't going to retire until he was number one. Instead, he would most certainly keep stalking until the time was right. Everybody knew he wanted it badly, and McColl usually got what he wanted.

NationsBank Corporation was already one of the top five banks in the country, experiencing a torrid growth rate through a series of pre–Bank of America acquisitions. These were warm-ups, setting the necessary groundwork for grabbing the big prize. By the time I started interviewing, NationsBank was well on its way. By the beginning of 1996, NationsBank ranked as the twenty-fourth most profitable company in the Fortune 500. They were over $180 billion in assets, with earnings of $1.95 billion and over 50,000 employees.[6] NationsBank was capitalizing on the phenomenal 1990s spread between lending rates and the cost of funds.

---

*Government incentives to corporations "investing" in expansion.

Unlike many of the other large U.S. banks that were running into debt problems from international loans, NationsBank had been primarily focused on the New South where plantations had been replaced by the migration of U.S. companies from the North. These companies, formerly associated with colder parts of the country, were looking for lower costs, less organized labor, and a little more warmth.

Southern hospitality might be only skin deep, but it can be very enticing, especially when you come down out of the snow offering a large contribution to the tax base, more jobs for locals, and a stream of investments to help the community. "Howdy? . . . Come right in and make yourselves at home."

None of NationsBank's tremendous growth would have been possible without changing banking rules and regulations. Not since the Great Depression had the rules become so relaxed. As we will see, Hugh McColl played one of the most critical roles in relaxing them. Back in 1992 he was quoted as saying, "It should not be lost on us—or on the White House or on Capital Hill—that our major trade competitors, specifically, Japan and Germany, have instituted nationwide banking and, in turn, have the financial muscle to foster their export sales and sustain their domestic economies. We must allow our banking industry to grow and prosper. We must update regulations left virtually untouched since the FDR administration. We must allow market forces to work—for the soundness of the banking industry and for the good of the country, its taxpayers, and businesses."[7]

This, of course, was a few years before the Japanese economy tanked with the big banks facing unanticipated serious trouble. Critics would blame it on overconfidence and a concentration of bloated companies. They also charged that Japanese companies were dependent on sweet deals predicated on corporate cronyism and government patronage. A subtle form of Japan bashing was implied. The Japanese system of *keiretsu* (corporate "Sonyism"), was somehow viewed as more Machiavellian than the American "good ol' boy network." The experts were constantly reassuring us that "American companies have grown successful based on competitiveness. Unlike Japan Inc., they are forced to operate in a free, open market." No *keiretsu* here, in the good ol' U.S. of A.

In another press quote, McColl cited a McKinsey & Company study concluding that multistate bank holding companies could save "$5 to $10 billion a year and generate up to $100 billion in new loans."[8] He argued that the regulators should back off for the common good.

In 1994 McColl's compensation included a $10.7 million restricted stock award from his board of directors for his role in helping to shepherd legislation through Congress to deregulate interstate banking.[9] He was, not by coincidence, one of the first to successfully cross over state lines without garnering a rash of restraining legal action from the Feds.

McColl had not only made fast friends with Congress, but according to the *Washington Post*, he was a "social companion and informal advisor to President Clinton." Columnist Jack Anderson reported that Clinton hailed McColl as the "most enlightened banker in America."[10] Well, somebody needed to replace that renowned financier icon Walter Wriston, who seemed to tower over the others when he ran CitiGroup in the '70s and became the major industry spokesperson. Why not McColl for the '90s?

McColl knew how to trade horses, too. As noted by the *Charlotte Observer*, McColl endorsed Clinton over George Herbert Walker Bush and his other buddy, H. Ross Perot, for president in 1992. He became a welcomed guest at the Clinton White House. The relationship deepened over the years. By 1996, NationsBank, with McColl at the helm, had become an important backer of President Clinton and the Democratic National Committee.[11]

It was winter 1996 when I interviewed with NationsBank, two years before NationsBank would assume its new name. I surmised that NationsBank could not possibly have gotten to where it was by playing it safe. If nothing else, it could be an interesting ride. Where else would I find a CEO who thought he was in the "Big One," and not only gets away with it, but is respected as a new, bolder breed of banker? It was sure to be interesting. Things were really changing, and NationsBank was a driving force in making change possible.

A month or so after I turned down their first offer, they called back and asked me to interview for a higher level position with a better compensation package. Why not? The first set of interviews were in Charlotte. This time it would be Dallas. There was a bad snowstorm in New York, and I felt lucky to get out just before LaGuardia Airport officially closed. By now I did hate flying, but the last thing I wanted was for anyone to think I was some kind of wimp, afraid to fly through a blizzard. We deiced a couple times and finally took off. It was a roller coaster ride, and I wasn't the only passenger relieved when we finally touched down.

I met with Barbara Albrecht who had been recently named head of the strategy group for the Transaction Services line of business. Transaction Services was a major business unit that processed almost all of NationsBank's financial transactions for customers, both paper-based checks and electronic payments. This included individual retail and small commercial business, which was considered the General Bank Division, as well as transactions for the major corporate customers in what was called the "Global Finance" Division. They weren't exactly global, unless you counted the American corporate customers with satellite offices in international cities ranging from Toronto to Beirut.

Barbara Albrecht looked very professional, dressed in an expensive business suit and jewelry one couldn't miss, although it was tasteful and not overly extravagant. She had short blonde hair, a roundish comely face, and an engaging smile. An intense, serious expression quickly swept over her when she switched from small talk to business. Her big brown eyes turned darker. Her eyebrows tightened, and a slight trace of scowl seeped over her slightly powdered face. The first thing she did was pull out an organizational chart representing her new area of responsibility. Barbara said Andersen Consulting had helped her in developing it. "Nice chart," I said, trying my best to sound both agreeable and impressed.

"This represents a whole new beginning for us," she said.

There was a series of connected boxes, straddling symmetrically across multiple rows of other lines of boxes—the typical corporate organizational chart. The largest box sitting on top of all the others represented Barbara Albrecht. There was one box representing a person responsible for "electronic banking" strategy, which would include the hot new Internet banking that was picking up lots of Wall Street buzz, one box for the more traditional "check processing," and another for "account services." Other boxes included "business planning," "competitive analysis," and "technology strategy."

Technology strategy? An oxymoron if there ever was one. Technology was all about laying the plumbing. Strategy was about not getting your hands dirty. What strategist wanted to delve into the optimal process for storage and retrieval of exciting bits of computer information like customer numbers, product types, and account totals? As I had guessed, the technology strategy box was mine if I impressed enough people during the interviews. Then I could spend long hours converting concepts into computer design, or as they say in the business, "creating the systems architecture." In other words, creating the blueprint design for bringing all the technology systems together. Not too different from what I was doing in my own business, or so I thought.

In addition to building technology architecture plans, responsibilities of the job would include advising on new technology directions and working as a liaison with another strategy group out of NationsBank Corporate. I had interviewed with them last time, and I was already beginning to realize that for a bank with a reputation for people slugging it out the hard way to get the checks out on time, there were also a whole lot of groups trying to do strategy. Some bigwig must have said something like,

NationsBank Services Company

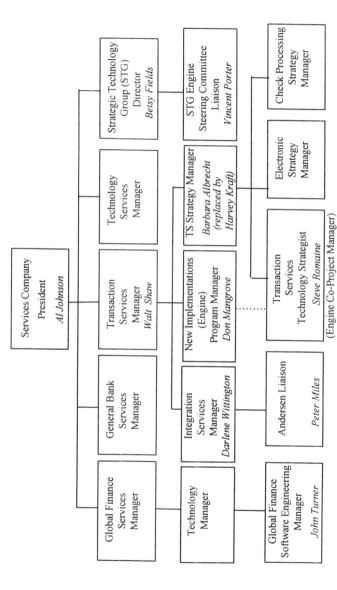

The above organization chart reflects only those positions within the Services Company of NationsBank relevant from the topics discussed in this book. It does not reflect the complexity of the entire organization which consist of various service functions established to support NationsBank business units. This is based on recollections of the author and provided to assist the reader. It is not intended to represent the actual NationsBank organizational chart at the time, which was significantly more complex.

"We need to be more strategic." Then the banking strategists quickly popped up all over. I figured banking strategists would stay hot until the next executive pronouncement. At least banking strategist sounded as if it was one or two steps up in the floor planning from technology strategist.

After a few minutes of explanation on the organizational chart, Barbara switched to a new train of thought. She explained how it infuriated her when Microsoft Chairman Bill Gates said that banks were dinosaurs and incapable of making the necessary changes to compete in the emerging electronic market for commerce. "I want to prove him wrong," she said. Gates must have eventually realized the mere suggestion of his drawing prehistoric allusions to banks could have some damaging repercussions for his company. He claimed in his book, *The Road Ahead*, that the dinosaur reference was misquoted by a reporter.[12]

Nevertheless, Gates's comments with respect to the need to modernize banking via technology, both in his books, as well as during speaking engagements at conferences, continued to have a stinging effect. It seemed to me that Gates was making a good point. When it came to assessing business opportunities, he usually did. Banks with heavy emphases on labor-intensive check processing and lots of branch offices were expensive to run. With the rise of cheaper, more convenient, and easier ways to manage alternatives for customers, such as credit cards, debit cards, and home banking on the "Net," banks overly burdened with checks could be as vulnerable as the brontosaurus. Like ATMs when they first appeared, Net banking was catching on slowly with the general public, but everyone expected that it eventually would. There was lots of speculation about a future with branchless "virtual" banks relying on the Internet to provide products and services to customers. People could bank anytime, twenty-four hours a day, at their own convenience. It was argued that as Internet banking caught on, the new virtual banks could eventually finish off the traditional banks who failed to embrace new methods of online banking. No doubt there would be false starts, but it was coming.

It didn't get anywhere near the same media hype, but legal problems for Microsoft didn't start with the controversy surrounding the bundling of a Web browser with the market-dominant Windows operating system. Several years before Netscape and other technology vendors started crying foul, some of the nation's leading bankers were arguing that Microsoft was preparing to use its unfair competitive advantages to enter their turf. In 1995 Gates had aggressively pursued the acquisition of Intuit Inc., a leader in personal finance software. In addition to electronic bill paying, Intuit was developing the capability for PC home banking.

Home banking was already being touted as the wave of the future. Gates's interest in Intuit sent shock waves through the central nervous system of banking. This could help Microsoft become one of those dreaded "virtual" banks, using the Internet as its primary channel, significantly undercutting banks on price, while at the same time providing better accessibility and convenience in service. The traditional bank could become just one more Microsoft icon sitting on the customer's computer screen. Freedom from long lines at the branch office would be only a mouse click away. The whole industry seemed to go on red alert. Microsoft's efforts to acquire Intuit were abruptly curtailed when U.S. District Court of Columbia Judge Stanley Sporkin stepped in, threatening potential antitrust litigation.[13] Banking executives were not so displeased when federal judges began raising the gavel against Microsoft.

Unlike banks, which had traditionally placed great emphasis on watchdogging and lobbying government, Microsoft had for the most part ignored the Feds during its meteoric rise out of nowhere. Microsoft helped forge a new software industry, one in which the rules were still being written. Regulatory concerns were not a chief priority of the new high-tech entrepreneurs. Pay your taxes, live, and let live. Banks, on the other hand, appeared to be obsessed with regulation and all of its terrible consequences. The banking trade press and speakers at banking conferences continued to argue nonstop for deregulation, echoing McColl's early cries.

The cry for deregulation wasn't only about ridding banks of antiquated laws left over from the postdepression era. Having the ability to expand across state lines was only part of what bankers wanted. Deregulation could allow them to concentrate on high-income potential customers living in the right communities. Less profitable branches in lower-class neighborhoods could be abandoned. They also wanted to take advantage of higher margin opportunities provided by the brokerage business traditionally open only to nonbanks. Yet their definition of deregulation didn't allow for new market entrants into banking from other industries. Banks had a time-tested argument whenever they found themselves under assault. "Who else will protect the money for widows and orphans?" They wanted deregulation for banks and regulation for anyone else trying to get into banking. Who knew better than bankers about the power of regulation as a tool for resetting the tables while keeping the invitees at a minimum? Bankers, with the help of their lobbyists, usually got what they wanted.

Now Microsoft was being challenged by the courts in much the same way IBM was challenged thirty years ago when it was the dominant force in computing. Like IBM, Microsoft would be accused of predatory marketing tactics. There was one major difference between Microsoft and IBM. A series of questionable management decisions had helped make antitrust considerations concerning IBM irrelevant.

So far, Microsoft, which had benefited greatly from IBM's mistakes, had not fallen victim to the same kinds of major gaffes. When government regulators started challenging Microsoft's alleged predatory tactics, there was no escape hatch. Continued success made them incredibly powerful and an easy target, starting when they made noises about buying Intuit and expanding into sacred markets like banking. The Intuit fiasco was just the beginning. It established some powerful enemies in the banking lobby with lots of political influence. Perhaps Gates should have been contributing to politicos instead of schools.

Barbara Albrecht suggested that even if it weren't Microsoft, surely somebody else would eventually challenge the traditional financial institutions. "We can't be caught sleeping on this one," she said.

This was her biggest concern. Her competitive nature and sense of urgency captured my interest. This combined with her hard-hitting comments about my potential role and responsibilities made the position sound very promising.

"You know," she said, "between you an me, I think we still have people walking around here that have never heard of electronic commerce."

When I explained to her that I tended to be entrepreneurial in style, Barbara said that was exactly what was needed. She didn't need to know what I called entrepreneurial some of my previous managers had labeled insubordinate. Barbara said she wanted someone who could build a technology strategy in an area where it had never really been done. She explained that the rapid expansion through acquisitions had led to a very tactical approach in implementing technology solutions. Barbara was looking for someone who could help her in breaking down the status quo.

"So how much is it going to cost me to hire you?"

I liked the way she talked. I also liked her. No way I was ever going to work again for someone I didn't like. Not if I could help it. We agreed on a price.

"It doesn't really matter to me if you work out of Charlotte or Atlanta. Based on the job, an argument could be made for you being in either."

"I'd prefer Atlanta."

As a single guy, that was an easy choice. On the business side, Atlanta had major NationsBank operations supporting Transaction Services. In

Charlotte I would be too close to all the high-level muckety-mucks playing soldiers. I subscribed to the Boris Yeltsin theory, "You can build a throne with bayonets, but you can't sit on it for long."[14] The farther from the throne, the better. I also had another concern, albeit somewhat irrational. I knew my former IBM branch manager from the days when I worked in Norfolk, Virginia, now lived in Charlotte. If I never saw or heard of him again, it would be too soon. I had worked for some great people in IBM and had learned a lot. I had nine managers in nine years. Working for that guy had been a very painful experience. One bad apple after all those managers wasn't a bad ratio. I had actually learned more from him than all the rest, but it was painful. Once was enough. Every so often I could still hear his voice in the back of my head.

"You know Steve, . . . if you wanna run with the big dags, you gotta get off of the porch."

It was eerily similar to the kinds of things attributed to McColl in articles I had read while researching NationsBank, and it gave me pause, but not enough to renege on the deal. I passed it off as my own self-induced personal brand of paranoia, residual psychological damage from a few old battle scars. Not enough to skunk a good deal like this. I wasn't going to let completely irrational misgivings based on my past influence my behavior now.

Atlanta was a long way, physically and organizationally, from McColl and the upper brass. Somehow, I was naïve enough to think Atlanta would be a safe place.

Atlanta, I was told, had a lot going for it, especially for singles. On the other hand, I was warned in advance about a few things. Atlanta could be confusing for getting around. There were over thirty streets with "Peachtree" somewhere in the name. I also heard that they still celebrated Confederate Memorial Day in the Stone Mountain area. Stone Mountain was a huge piece of granite, the largest on the planet, rising about 650 feet, just due east of the city, only about fifteen miles or so from downtown. In an area almost as big as a football field stood an engraving of Robert E. Lee, Stonewall Jackson, and Jefferson Davis gracing the face of the mountain. Stone Mountain played backdrop for year-round fireworks accompanied with a fusion of disco, Dixie, and *God Bless America*. It was the Confederate Mount Rushmore.

The myth of the noble cause may have been low-keyed in Atlanta proper, but it was still very much alive and more audaciously conspicuous than any of those clumped together corporate domes in downtown Atlanta attempting to paint a more sophisticated and cosmopolitan image. Not even the prominent NationsBank Plaza building, a 1,000 foot renowned Atlanta landmark, could compete with the Confederate men of granite. No larger-than-life image of Hugh McColl was engraved on the building, at least, not yet.

The peach-obsessed megalopolis was limited on the creativity scale when it came to naming streets, but was an emerging center of business, education, and some said, the arts. There was a new blatant "in your face" form of tackiness that conflicted with efforts to combine culture with home-baked Southern tradition. Atlanta had become a booming Sun Belt phenomenon with hordes of Northern transplants, a lower cost of living when compared with the New York area where I was living at the time, and plenty of other amenities. It may have been land-locked, but for the most part it was a good-looking stretch of land, with rolling hills and dense forest areas within the city limits. They had managed to keep concrete to a minimum, but they couldn't keep Margaret Mitchell's home and all of its subsequent and unending reconstructed versions from burning down. And, of course, snowstorms would be rare.

On balance, things were sounding great. That's why I accepted the position, in spite of a few minor misgivings, as a senior vice president in Barbara Albrecht's strategy organization, starting shortly after the beginning of the year in 1996. I found a nice apartment in an upscale neighborhood close to downtown Atlanta with no streets, avenues, places, or courts with "Peachtree" anywhere in the name.

To say Barbara had a competitive spirit was like saying Michael Jordan could shoot hoops. Her game face was outright scary. She reigned down terror when she wanted something. I was one of the last hires into the new strategy group and one of the few hired from outside the bank. A few more internal transfers followed me, rounding out her new organization. They did not come quietly. There was a series of senior management brawls before Barbara successfully culled them from current assignments. Barbara used a scorched-earth campaign to steal away the best that she could get from other NationsBank organizations. One altercation took place in a meeting I attended. Barbara duked it out with another senior manager over a popular employee. Like most companies, at NationsBank it appeared if one manager thought an employee was worth recruiting, he immediately became a valuable commodity that all the other managers wanted. Whether or not he had any skills or talent seemed to be completely irrelevant and extraneous to the inevitable fight to claim or retain him.

Barbara Albrecht took no prisoners. She had a hot temper and hated to lose. It was great having a manager who usually won, but with conflicts often escalating to nuclear winter, it made the rest of us within her group uncomfortable. She had a way of stripping down the manager she was arguing with, making the person look powerless in front of everybody else. As a result, there were some very angry people. The rest of us in Barbara's department would be left to pick up the broken glass. From the beginning, we were hated by many of other groups, simply because we belonged to "that woman."

The meeting I attended to discuss possible personnel changes went like this:

"Strategy is now a priority for this organization. That's why my department was created and that's why *I need Willard.*"

"I understand that strategy is important. That's fine, but we still have to get the checks out tomorrow. Willard is one of the few senior people I have left in my organization. We still have a business to run. What am I supposed to do?"

"Find somebody else. *I'm taking Willard.*"

"You can't do this. I'm not gonna let you. I'm goin' to talk with . . ."

"Don't bother. I already did."

It didn't stop there, although it should have. Barbara had pummeled the other manager who was left hanging precariously against the ropes. She had won. She had what she wanted. There was no need to keep up the attack, but she did.

"Let's see, what's the day after tomorrow? Thursday. I need Willard to report to me first thing Thursday." Glancing at her calendar, she added, "Oh, no. I can't do it Thursday. Gotta conflict. Have him come see me tomorrow afternoon. Tell him to be there 2:00 P.M."

"I need him to finish up what he's working on before he can go."

"Sorry, but we need to hit the ground running, and I'll be out of town after tomorrow. Call him when we're done here. Have him start to turn it over to somebody else today."

It was embarrassing. Something I didn't anticipate during my interview.

Willard had been a popular project manager. From Barbara's perspective, this made him a perfect candidate for strategy. Most of my new peer managers were former project managers within Transaction Services. Barbara, as the new head of the strategy group, was also a former project manager. Project management was considered the primary set of skills for enjoying a successful management career at NationsBank.

In most of the corporate clients I had worked with, strategy groups tended to be relatively small organizations infused with cerebral types. The Transaction Services strategy group had twenty-six people, mostly former project managers, with a few techies and operational "gofers" thrown into the mix. I had never been a big fan of project management and had tried to avoid this kind of work when I had my own consulting business. Project management had always been a matter of building linear, incremental timelines and managing phased implementation plans. First Step A, then Step B, followed by Step C. Not very appealing for the attention deficit set like me, but it was the area where the big-name consulting firms were making all the big bucks. If they decided to leave, for a career in the field I just left, NationsBank project managers would have all the right skills.

There was one former project manager who I inherited. His name was Dan Price. He had worked on systems architecture for the past year as "acting" liaison with a very important organization, the Corporate Strategic Technology Group, known in NationsBank as the STG. We strategized for a division; they were charged with doing it for the entire company. No doubt, this meant more opportunity for battles over turf. Lucky for me, the fact that I had turned down the original job offer from the STG before accepting the job with Barbara didn't seem to be a problem.

Dan Price would now report to me. Dan was a nice guy, but every time I asked him to do something, he would explain bank protocol and how, before he could do it, I was supposed to call the manager in this or that department and give them a "heads up" that a request was coming. Hmm, might as well just ask for it myself. He probably figured after a while I'd stop asking. If not the "you have to get approval first" routine, he would tell me that there was another group that had recently done something along similar lines that could potentially satisfy my request and that he would be happy to check into it for me. After one or two of these incidents, I snapped. This was a guy who was obviously very smart and had been around the bank for a long time, but how did he ever manage projects? How would he ever get things done? How could I make this work?

"Dan, do me a favor. Please don't give me excuses why you can't do something. Here is what I need and I need you to help me by getting it. You know this place, I don't. Would you just go do it, please?"

"Yes, Sir, . . . I'd be happy to . . . , but first you have to understand, . . ."

"Look, I don't have anymore time for this. Why can't you just do it? If anybody gives you a hard time, I'll take the heat. One other thing, you don't have to call me 'Sir.' Just Steve will be fine."

When I had worked in Virginia for IBM, it had taken me over a year to get some of my team members to drop the "Sir" stuff. It always sounded so patronizing to my unrefined Northeastern ears. They say in the South it was a sign of respect, but it made me uncomfortable.

"OK, OK. You are new here, but you should know, we do things a little differently. There's a process for getting things done. We've been told to always go through the process."

He seemed reluctant to tackle the NationsBank organization, but he wasn't afraid to come back at me. He probably decided I hadn't been around long enough to hold any clout.

Perhaps he was investing short on my ability to survive. Dan Price was politically astute. What was it that made him so tentative about doing anything that could upset "banking protocol"? When I asked Barbara about this, she said it was more of a Dan problem than anything else.

In spite of her assurances that it wasn't endemic to NationsBank in general, I wasn't so convinced. She suggested that eventually I could pick the rest of my team by combing other organizations within the bank, "just like I did." In this way I could round out my team with some "Type As" who would get things done. A few interviews made me worry that there were a lot more Dans than "As." Barbara repeated a familiar refrain: "What we're doing is very important. Senior management knows this. It won't be any problem getting the right people we need. They'll know the spotlight is on them."

Spotlight didn't sound like a selling point to me. I decided as the new guy I would try a different approach as opposed to spotlights, or Barbara's patented scorched-earth campaigns. First, I wanted to understand more about the bank. Then I'd figure out the kind of people I needed. At this point just finding someone who followed through on requests would have been a major leap forward.

In my usual fashion, I immersed myself in the new job. There were positives and negatives. One of the top negatives was having to wear a pager. Pagers, cell phones, beepers, they were merely electronic leashes to me. I couldn't believe as a senior vice president that I was subjected to this kind of continuing harassment. I could be jerked around by almost anybody at the bank who held my pager number whenever one of them had an urge to beam me up—anytime, anyplace. I was told it was only for emergencies. "As a technology strategist you shouldn't get too many calls." They were wrong. NationsBank was the kind of place where there were always emergencies, particularly when it came to technology. With a new technology strategist in position, there was a new name on the Rolodex to call.

On the positive side, I got to ride the corporate jet in my many travels between Atlanta and the corporate headquarters in Charlotte. This was very cool, in spite of my phobia about flying that remained ever since that trip to Japan. It was the only place where I could let the illusion that I was an executive settle over me for a while. Those short spins through the air were the only guaranteed relief from getting paged. It rarely bothered me when we were forced to circle a few times before landing, due to air traffic; only when it was bad weather. That was when being firmly on the ground and susceptible to pages wasn't so bad after all.

Thanks to NationsBank, its rival First Union, and a few other distinguished corporate entities, Charlotte had assembled an impressive new downtown. There was a clump of silver and gold towers of various proportions reaching high up through the sky, but there was not much else as far as the eye could see. Of course, as in Atlanta, the NationsBank Tower was the highest. It boasted sixty stories. There was also a brand-new stadium that would house the Carolina Panthers. Hugh McColl had been instrumental in bringing professional football to Charlotte. They were proclaiming that Charlotte, thanks in large part to McColl and his archenemy, Edward Crutchfield, from First Union, was the new financial capital of the South. Some said it would one day challenge New York City's position of global dominance. No doubt many of the scattered homes and farms across the rest of the landscape owed mortgages to either NationsBank or First Union. With all the growth expected in Charlotte, I wondered how many years it would take before the outlying countryside would start to resemble Queens.

I also quickly learned that while "Senior Vice President" looked good on the business card and could potentially impress some of those great-looking Southern belles I was destined to meet, it was no big deal within the confines of NationsBank. There were many of us. NationsBank gave out titles versus money as it grew through acquisition. The SVPs often reported to other SVPs, as was the case with me reporting to Barbara. I had to get Barbara to sign off on all expenses—everything from coffee for a business meeting to paperclips. In effect, I was a glorified middle manager with a misleading title that only came in handy when barhopping.

During my first week on the job, I ended up working late into the night, soaking up as much information about my new employer as I could. Most of these nights were spent in my new office on the seventeenth floor of the Plaza building. Up close it was equally impressive, becoming a towering prism for the afternoon sun and a beacon projecting its own powerful light high and wide against the night. I had by now figured out that tall buildings were an important part of the NationsBank image. From my office I could look out beyond the city into that great expanse of green, flat Georgia landscape, which extended well beyond the horizon on one side and to the base of the Blue Ridge Mountains on the other.

One day I had been to a late afternoon meeting in one of the old

Atlanta downtown fixtures owned by NationsBank and decided to work there a little longer before heading home. It was old and drab, tucked away in a bad neighborhood. It contrasted with the NationsBank Plaza building the way an old, tired workhorse would stack up when compared with a prized thoroughbred. NationsBank had lots of buildings like this. They just weren't as visible as the Plaza, and they didn't enjoy the celebrity tour extended to customers and distinguished visitors. The old operations building I was in may have been where most of the important work was done, but it made me feel lucky that my new office was in the Plaza. It was very late when I finally finished up. Most everyone else had already left the building, but you could still feel their sweat.

When I left the building with my newly issued lap top computer hanging from my shoulder, it was as if I had a bull's-eye stitched across my shoulder and a big sign over my head saying "look what we have here." The neighborhood didn't seem this bad when I had arrived in the middle of the day. I thought about hailing a taxi, but there were no cabs in sight. In fact, there were only a very few cars moving through the neighborhood. It could have been my imagination, but one or two were moving slowly, as if they were prowling. There were people hanging out at the corner. They didn't look too friendly. The door behind me had shut and was now locked. There was no other way to go but the way I had arrived.

I walked toward the entrance to the Atlanta subway, called "MARTA," sounded like Atlanta-ese for murder or martyr. I had fears of becoming one myself. If anybody wanted my laptop, it was his. This made leaving late from the MetroTech Center in Brooklyn during my Chase Manhattan consulting days look like a trip through candyland. As I approached the Four Points train stop, I noticed a large group of street people blocking the entrance. Forget the computer. By now I was worried about losing some important body part. People were yelling. They seemed to be purposely blocking my entry to the train stop. A car pulled up behind me, and several guys in hoods got out and started to taunt. I wasn't sure if it was directed to me or other hoods. This could be it. I kept my eyes pointed downward and maneuvered my way around the human obstacle course in my path, walking at a brisk pace as if I did this everyday. People were now moving. They seemed to be crossing slowly in front of me. With my best effort, I tried not to brush against any of the moving masses. My feeling was that this was the kind of instigation they wanted. Thank God I made it down to the platform and onto a train. This was the first time I realized that working for NationsBank could be dangerous. It would not be the last. When I mentioned something about it to Dan, he got very upset. Apparently my concerns were grounded.

"You did what? Nobody goes there at night unless they're looking for trouble. Somebody from NationsBank was killed in that area just a few months ago. You'd never catch me there at night."

This was saying something. Dan was a case in point on how looks could be deceiving. He had a "don't mess with me" appearance. Dan could have passed as a football lineman, a gang leader, or maybe even a hit man. He was big, thick, and had a squared-off chin with no neck. Like McColl, he joined the bank after the marines, but the similarity with our chairman stopped there. For one thing, Dan never used military jargon in the course of conversation. While he presented an imposing figure, Dan was always deferential and very reserved. He was consistently proving to be very tentative about taking any kind of business-related initiative. This I found incredibly frustrating. One day I made the mistake of calling Dan an "ex-marine."

"There are no ex-marines," he insisted in an explosive tone. He was glaring at me like I was Charlie. "Unless of course you are dishonorably discharged. Otherwise, once a marine, always a marine."

He had my attention. I had a mental picture of him in uniform patrolling the DMZ or some other god-awful place. There was still some fight left in the man. So why did he operate in NationsBank like a tentative choirboy? I wondered what kinds of things might have happened to shrink his spirit into remission. As I was learning, NationsBank had lots of employees who fell into a similar mode. It wasn't just a Dan problem as Barbara had suggested.

It didn't take long before I started getting the feeling that I had stepped into a time warp.

My new strategy organization was a microcosm within a huge bureaucracy. We were responsible for strategy for Transaction Services, which was a business unit within a larger organization called the Services Company. The Service Company provided support to all of Nations-Bank's operational divisions. There were mirror image service groups supporting each of the lines of business. In other words, there was a General Bank Division that was supported by a General Bank support organization within the Services Company. It was as clear as mud, and no one else was ever able to explain it well enough for me to completely get it. Why create all these separate support groups where duplication and conflicting reporting structures from the line of business were sure to exist? I was told not to worry or spend too much time trying to understand. With the assistance of consultants, the bank reorganized almost every year. All it took was a few new charts.

One of the major responsibilities of my group, Transaction Services, was supporting the back-office functions for "routing and settlement" of payments. This was a critical element in processing, crediting, and disbursing financial transactions for all lines of the business. Our major role was to support other support groups within the Services Company, which in turn provided the direct contact with the lines of business. These other support groups were our "clients." In turn, their clients were the lines of business. It wasn't until you got out to the business units that there was any direct customer contact. Customers to the bank, the ones who paid the bills, were as remote to Transaction Services as urban fruit stands were to farms. If they had a complaint, it wasn't our problem.

The back-office systems supporting Transaction Services were as old as the Georgia hills. It was a jackpot for Y2K consultants who were arriving in herds. We were running hard-coded mainframe software, older than Nehru jackets. It consisted of IBM Assembler programs. I hadn't heard anyone talk about Assembler since my early days in IBM, and by then, it was already considered ancient.

As noted in a 1984 edition of *Introduction to Computers and Information Processing*, "Prior to 1970, machine- and assembler-level languages were used for application program development and exclusively for systems software development. Even though it took longer, many programmers felt it used the computer system more efficiently. Since then, the power and flexibility of high-level languages surpassed low-level languages in terms of both human and computer system efficiency. Consequently, most programming is now done in high-level languages."[15] It might be, but not in Transaction Services at NationsBank, where thirty-year-old vintage technology was the core of financial transaction processing.

Programmers skilled in low-level machine languages still reigned in the NationsBank back offices. If the technology we were using in 1996 was considered old in the 1980s, how did we garner our reputation on the street as a high-tech, innovative bank? We were still operating in the bowels of archaic systems.

The network design looked like a plate of linguini. NationsBank was a large retail business, close to 90 percent of the operation was labor-intensive check processing. Little was being done in electronic banking, except for studies. It just wasn't adding up.

The worse part about it was that almost all of the check processing was handled by Transaction Services and fell within my realm of responsibility. As the new guy responsible for technical strategy for my business unit, I would have to report in corporate meetings on our strategic progress in check processing. It was the equivalent of being the spokesman for the Jamaican bobsled team. I could hardly wait. In the meantime, people within the Transaction Services organization kept saying things like "Checks are the most important part of our business. They were here when I started, and they will be around long after I'm gone."

The continued emphasis on check processing seemed a little inconsistent with published comments from the chairman. Hugh McColl was always talking about the importance of electronic online banking and exploiting new technology. It was also inconsistent with trade press speculation on the expected explosive growth of electronic commerce via the Internet. If not completely branchless, a combination of "clicks and bricks" would certainly provide more options for round-the-clock convenience and service for customers, while also reducing costs. In a fair fight, they could kick butt against the check-processing goliaths. Nobody seemed to question that electronic methods of payment would eventually eat away the more traditional method of check payment. The question was when. In spite of the big danger sign staring out at me, I was upbeat about future prospects. I saw this as a great opportunity to implement change and demonstrate results. Yeah, in spite of my years as a consultant, I was still thinking results.

A few weeks into the job, I was asked to present to a group within the bank responsible for operations and systems. They were interested in hearing from the new technology strategist. I made the mistake of talking about the Internet revolution and the need to convert checks to electronic payment systems. This, after all, was Barbara's big reason for hiring me and what my new job was supposed to be all about. I talked for several minutes. It was a videoconference, broadcast to several different sites, which may have explained at least part of my delayed reaction in reading the crowd.

"It's not just a matter of building a Web site. It means changing the way we do business. That means new interfaces to back-office systems, and it may mean replacing some of them. It also means changing the culture and the way people work and think."

A remote listener chimed in. I was reminded that check processing was very important to NationsBank and we did it better than anybody else. "You need to keep this in perspective when you talk about banking around here."

"No question," I said. Borrowing a throwaway line used often in the technology business, I added, "but sometimes you have to eat your own children before somebody else does." I continued with my presentation.

The next day I saw Dan Price.

"I'm hearing you created quite a stir talking about cannibalism."

"Cannibalism? A stir? You mean about eating your children?"

"Yeah, that's exactly what I mean."

"You know I was speaking figuratively. I was talking about becoming less dependent on payment by checks, before we lose our customers to someone else who offers a better alternative."

"I know," said Dan, "but you have to be careful how you say it. At least, that's what I would suggest. These check guys still run the place."

I had made a big goof and my benefits hadn't even kicked in yet. I should never have talked about changing systems and the culture, and then adding that line about eating children . . . what was I thinking?

Who the hell was I to come in and preach change? I was acting like I was still a consultant. These people had been doing things the same way for years, and nobody else understood what they did, least of all a new employee from Barbara Albrecht's infamous strategy group. Who was I to come riding in on a high horse? This was not exactly an auspicious start. I wasn't going to be winning many friends or influencing people at this rate—forget changing the culture. The good news was that if Barbara had heard anything, it didn't seem to bother her. She was the kind of manager who would have said something if it did. Thankfully, she was more focused on kissing up to the big bosses.

During my first staff meeting, Barbara Albrecht informed us that she had sent a request for proposal (RFP) to both Andersen Consulting and Gemini Consulting. She had made a presentation to upper management, and it had gone well. She was given the green light to hire a consulting firm. The firm that won the bid would work with us in creating the new strategic vision for Transaction Services. Barbara was planning to buy outside help to fill in the details on her new "strategic vision" for the business. While I was very aware of Andersen Consulting, Gemini Consulting was a firm I knew little about.

Barbara explained that the advantage of Andersen Consulting was its involvement and familiarity with NationsBank. It was hard for me to believe, but we were spending close to $100 million a year on Andersen Consulting services. Most of its work was related to check processing. This made sense for consultants trying to maximize revenue from a client whose business was primarily checks.

Gemini Consulting was part of Gemini Sogeti, a Paris-based firm. She said that Gemini could assist us in understanding the European market where electronic-transaction processing had grown faster than in the United States. It was growing rapidly, replacing checks. "They also have a lot of expertise in developing technology infrastructures," she explained as she looked directly at me. It finally dawned on me. The consultants were not only going to create "a vision" for Transaction Services.

They would be building the technology plan as well. I had been hired to assist whomever got the contract.

During one of our meetings, Barbara mentioned that Gemini had experience building system architectures for large financial institutions. "They did the technology architecture for Chase Manhattan," she said.

That was interesting. Not only did they actually reference a client, it was one I knew very well. Architecture was the area where I had worked, and I didn't remember Gemini being involved at all, but then, Chase was a big place. I called my old friend Michael Dellano. He would know about their work. It was prior to his leaving Chase for Prudential. He had submitted his resignation, but was still the chief architect. No major architecture projects would be approved until the new organization was introduced.

Dellano sounded no more upbeat than the last time. I wondered if Prudential had a "no smoking" policy within its corporate facilities across the river and a few miles over in Roseland, New Jersey. I would later learn that they did. The blue-collar executives moving over from Chase would put up heated tents situated near all strategic building exits. It would eventually look like a group of nomads had set up camp. There would be lots of smoke spilling out from those tents.

"Gemini did some work for us, but I believe it was on an implementation project, not architecture. You know Steve, if it was architecture, not only would I have known about it, I would have been the guy who approved it."

He gave me the name of someone else still working for Chase who he thought had contracted with Gemini. I checked with this other manager. It was an integration project, and he had been pleased with their work. It had been done by Cap Gemini, a subsidiary specializing in the nuts-and-bolts work of integration.

I did some additional research on Gemini Consulting. They were the fifth largest consulting firm in the world, but had been experiencing some internal problems, according to a June 1995 article in *Business Week*. Problems were attributed to management infighting, trouble in differentiating their offerings, and an inability to gain a strong foothold in the U.S. market. The article presented a question, "Has the consultant ignored its own advice?" It mentioned how the cochairman of the firm was touring the United States to promote a new book on how to run your company more effectively. It was selling consulting services to help companies develop strategies, yet "Gemini's failure to develop a viable strategy to attract new clients is causing earnings and revenues to fall." The article also noted that sources believed revenue for Gemini could fall as much as

$100 million by the close of 1995, off from $551 million in 1994.[16] No wonder Gemini was talking to us more about their expertise in European banking and little on their experience in the United States. Eventually it would take their acquisition of Ernst and Young Consulting before they would gain a more solid foothold in the United States.

I shared some concerns about Gemini with Barbara, but her mind was already made up. Her decision was to go with Gemini, and she appeared elated about her good choice. I was really surprised. Where Gemini's business was having trouble, Andersen's business was going through the roof. I found out that the contract with Gemini was based on a fixed rate of $1 million for eight weeks of work, beginning in April 1996. Fixed-rate deals were a typical consulting ploy to gain a foothold. Follow-on contracts were time and materials where they would rack up the billable hours, more than making up for the initial "investment." As competition in consulting stiffened, fixed-rate contracts became more prevalent. In this case, we were going to pay them handsomely for this foot in the door. The Gemini contract represented their largest U.S. contract to date. Travel, meals, and lodging expenses were to be billed separately. What, I wondered, could we possibly get in eight weeks that would be worth $1 million? I wondered why Barbara was so eager to hire them.

Barbara would later point out that this was one of the most important initiatives for NationsBank, and one of the most visible. Others might not want the spotlight, but Barbara was eager to grasp as much as possible. This project would do the trick.

There were several reasons why I think Barbara went with Gemini. One was their international experience. It made them sound somewhat exotic. Part of the proposal was for Gemini to research the European banking market. The other important component was that Gemini would act as broker in setting up a junket trip to Europe. They would facilitate meetings with executives from European banks and initiate discussion about potential partnerships. These partnerships could prove beneficial. There might be a potential acquisition candidate, should we decide to aggressively pursue international banking. Barbara could be the hero in initiating the relationship—with Gemini's help. I also think Barbara was determined to do something different. Barbara wanted to emphasize electronic alternatives to check processing. She was also political, and the senior partner for Gemini, Ben Elders, was a former business partner of a NationsBank executive.

There was another reason, and probably the most important reason Gemini won and Andersen lost. Barbara's confrontational style had made enemies out of several of her peer managers. Like me, she was from the

Northeast and hadn't cultivated the more refined aspects of Southern grace and subtly. Her most bitter rivalry was with a manager who ran Integration Services within our same business unit. This was Darlene Wittington. Her organization was responsible for keeping the check-processing machines up and running while we in strategy got esoteric. Everyone knew there was no love lost between the two. Darlene had endured the brunt of Barbara's raid to recruit people for strategy. She had a close working relationship with Andersen Consulting. In fact, Andersen consultants worked side by side with Darlene's people. They were indistinguishable from bank employees. Barbara was the kind of manager who demanded complete loyalty from her employees. It was only natural that she would also want her own consultant who would be beholden only to her. Darlene had Andersen. We now had Gemini.

NationsBank was good for the restaurant business. It seemed whenever a senior manager wanted to have a serious talk with another senior manager, it was over a late-night meal and a few drinks. My new boss fit the mold. When I told her I wanted to talk about some ideas concerning my new position, Barbara Albrecht said, "Good, let's do dinner." We were both in Charlotte. I suggested a restaurant close to where I was staying. It was a nondescript steak house that could have been part of a chain, but it wasn't. This must have been a real step-down for Barbara who liked to dine at hot spots like Veni Vidi Vici or City Grill when in Atlanta, or real steak houses like the kind so prevalent in her hometown of Dallas. This, however, was Charlotte and the options were more limited. Barbara didn't appear very pleased with my choice. She entered the restaurant and gave it a disapproving once-over. She looked at me as if I had tricked her into attending a cheesy fund-raising event.

"If you'd prefer, we could try someplace else," I said.

"No. This is fine."

She didn't look like it was fine.

By halfway through our steaks, we had dispensed of the small talk surrounding my first impressions of NationsBank. Barbara looked tired and frustrated from cutting. I assured her everything with the job was cool so far.

"I put some things together based on my assessment of where we are. I've also attempted to identify some work areas based on some of our previous discussions, would like to make sure you agree, and then I wanted to see if you could help by prioritizing." Once again I was blabbering. At least it seemed to get her mind off the steak.

Rearranging a few things on the table, I moved a stack of papers close to Barbara. She looked down at them for a few minutes as she turned the pages between bites and an occasional sip.

"This looks good. I think it looks pretty good. You're on the right track. A good first effort," she added. Barbara was not a technologist. She then said, "I think we need to have a planning session for validating some of these assumptions."

Validating, . . . assumptions, . . . great corporate buzzwords, and Barbara was highly prolific in corporate buzz.

We ate dessert with coffee. I had what was called on the menu "New York cheesecake." It was more like pudding. Before leaving to go our separate ways, Barbara told me that I was behind the other technology strategists from other lines of business. She explained that they had already knocked out new architecture plans for building systems. From what I had seen, there were lots of nice-looking charts, but not much else. They had that "made by a consultant" boilerplate look about them. I decided not to press it. Coming up with a chart shouldn't take too long and could get me a reprieve.

"Hopefully this planning session will help you jump-start and get us closer to where we need to be. Good night, Steve."

She obviously didn't want me walking her to her rental car. As I turned to walk away, she called out to me. "By the way, next time, I'll pick where we eat."

Barbara wanted me to moderate what she was now calling the "infrastructure planning session." She said it was very important to do this prior to the kickoff of the Gemini project. The plan was to invite her entire staff and special guests from other areas of the bank, including some of the Strategic Technology Group people from corporate headquarters.

The session was held in a hotel within the Dallas/Fort Worth Airport. Every so often during the meeting it would sound as if a 747 was about to fly through the room. Gemini had a representative in the meeting who was billed as a technical architect. Barbara told me to observe the Gemini representative during the session and make a judgment as to his capabilities. "We're paying a lot of money for Gemini, and I want to make sure that we have the right people involved," she said.

There was more than one Gemini consultant staying in the hotel. Gemini created a "war room" down the hall from our meeting room. They filled it with nine or ten consultants. The Gemini consultant attending our session was hard to corner. He kept slipping out the door during breaks. I concluded after my initial observations that his main role was to supply the Gemini war room with whatever handouts he could grab. He was the designated runner between us and them. In this way, the consultants in the Gemini war room could monitor our session, sifting and plucking through materials.

The planning session went well. Everyone agreed that we needed to build a new payments system for handling online financial transactions. It was called the "Transaction Engine."

It would perform routing and settlement, a function important to us, and arguably one of the most critical processes in banking. It could replace a bunch of inconsistent and inefficient processes that sent credits and debits to posting systems. It would use new technology as opposed to the back-office sneaker brigade working hard against serious odds to keep all those old systems humming year after year. With all the bank acquisitions that had taken place, these systems developed for much smaller banks were quickly running out of gas.

Everybody seemed to agree, as NationsBank continued to grow, the big risk was doing nothing.

After the session ended, we got to meet with the Gemini consultants in the war room. Presentations used in our planning session were pulled apart and scattered on a long table. Flip chart paper covered most of the available wall space. The charts contained bullet points regurgitating information from our planning session. There were also several sketches of what appeared to be different variations attempting to depict a trans-action engine. The Gemini consultants told us that the idea of building a new engine would dovetail nicely with what they planned to propose. What a coincidence.

Over the course of the planning session, I became more successful in engaging the Gemini "runner" in discussion to determine his capabilities and experience. He had been billed as a technical giant. After a few exchanges, he confided in me that his technical experience was "minimal." At the end of the session, I informed Barbara that I didn't think he was up to the tasks at hand. I was assured, both by her and by Ben Elders, the Gemini senior partner working the project, that they would assign someone else with top credentials. In spite of his early campaign to promote this con-sultant as an experienced technologist, followed by a feeble attempt to finesse it, Elders now turned on him, as if he had somehow gotten past the bouncer by flashing a fake ID. The technical giant quickly disappeared.

Ben Elders was a curiously aloof man, at least when surrounded by the rest of us from NationsBank. He wore monogrammed cufflinks and Brooks Brothers sports jackets. Elders loved to talk about yachting. I doubted there were many working for NationsBank who could relate, particularly when most came from Atlanta, Charlotte, or Dallas. Elders had the thickest pair of glasses I had ever seen.

An army of Gemini consultants descended on Atlanta from all over the country. The project office would be in the NationsBank Plaza building where I worked. No small coincidence, I'm sure, that this was also the location of Al Johnson's office, president of the Services Company. It was a combination of Gemini and Cap Gemini consultants. It was explained to me that Gemini's role was to provide management consulting with an emphasis on strategy. Cap Gemini would provide the technical consulting and provide the arms and legs if there was follow-on implementation work.

Many consulting firms were now attempting to combine management consulting with technology implementation, running activities for both concurrently. It was an effort to provide a more comprehensive, seamless offering for the client, while accelerating "time to market." I liked the idea of strategy working collaboratively with technology, versus the long, drawn-out project plan where technology sits on its butt until strategy passes its work forward. It seemed to me that sometimes strategy needed to better understand the changes in technology so it could be more fully exploited in their planning. But to do it all simultaneously in eight weeks? This would require strong management and lots of cross-team buy-in.

Gemini consultants told us that there was an incredible amount of work to be done as part of the first phase, before we got to implementation. It would all have to happen within eight weeks if the contract was to be completed on schedule. They were already assuming that the eight-week million-dollar contract was only the beginning and that they would cruise into the implementation.

Each of us within the strategy group was assigned to work with specific Gemini team members. There were teams to look at organizational effectiveness, analyzing the U.S. competitive market and international country profiles, developing a business case, creating the new vision for Transaction Services, and infrastructure planning and "transaction mapping," whatever that was. It would be interesting watching how the teams were to kick off at the same time and run in parallel.

From the beginning, I noticed how different Gemini consultants contrasted with other consulting groups more familiar to me. They dressed better with expensive suits, gold rings, watches, and bracelets. Only the women wore earrings. Several men wore cufflinks, but only Elders's were monogrammed. They talked business jargon, not technology. They were actually pretty good listeners. Instead of inspirational outbursts on the technology revolution, they clung to process methodology and the importance of business reengineering.

Gemini consultants had their own language. For example, they would substitute the word "streams" for "teams." Changes to presentation material were called "builds" versus "edits." Gemini also planned on evaluating key business indicators for NationsBank. This would be presented with the help of software packages used by Gemini to create "management dashboards" and "balanced scorecards," where key performance indicators for various activities could be easily observed and measured. The "reengineering process" that needed to occur was called "transformation." Just as the technology vendors and consultants had created new, complex-sounding jargon, making customer feel "out of touch" and unable to address new requirements without outside assistance, Gemini had created its own language, attempting to develop a mystique around its process.

There was another major activity that Gemini had agreed to provide, although reluctantly from what I understood at the time. Gemini wanted to interview real, live bank customers. It seemed like a reasonable request given the assignment. Senior management decided that they had already invested considerable dollars on similar consulting engagements in the past. Instead of initiating additional interview processes with customers, management suggested that Gemini review all the other consulting material that had been accumulating over the years. Trying to understand customer preferences and not talking with customers? I didn't get it. There were more choices. New competition. Technology was changing rapidly. This was like trying to learn golf by reading a book—a very old book.

Material from previous consulting projects was stored in a huge file drawer of a bank executive office on the fifty-fourth floor of NationsBank Plaza. This part of the review became known as the "file drawer process." If these reports were so valuable, why had they not been implemented in the past? One couldn't help but question the relevance of these dated reports, given the dramatic changes taking place in banking. I doubted Gemini would find much on the Internet in the file drawer. Gemini's conclusions concerning customer needs and wants would be based on surveys and data accumulated by other consultants during previous engagements. So how were we going to be responsive to new customer needs and wants? Sounded like we were about to take yesterday's needs and tailor them to fit the new solution du jour.

Bob Betts, a new technology giant, had been assigned to the project. I was told he had stronger credentials and would work closely with me. "I want you to know you have one of our best with Bob," I was told by Ben Elders, the Gemini partner. The first thing Bob told me was that he was not a technologist either. Here we go again. He also indicated that he had no previous experience in banking. This hardly dampened his arrogance. He expected me to provide the knowledge. "That's your role," I was told. "I will use my consulting expertise to determine what we can use and how to build it into the right solution." Me provide the knowledge? Boy, were we in trouble.

I'm not sure which irritated me more, his lack of skills and background for the project or his attitude. Probably the attitude. I hated doing it, but I went back to Barbara and expressed my concerns, thinking it was better to do it now than later. I could tell she was losing patience.

"Ben Elders tells me he is the right guy and will do an outstanding job. Ben worked with Betts on similar projects and can personally vouch for his capabilities."

"Technical capabilities?" I asked.

"Yes. Of course."

One million dollars. You'd think you'd get the cream of the crop. Call it sour grapes on my part, but both Bob Betts and his boss, Ben Elders, were losing credibility with me at warp speed, and we had hardly kicked things off. Nonetheless, it was time for me to shut up and back off or risk alienating my new management.

Barbara told us she wanted the "technology stream" to build a graphic sketch for an overhead slide presentation. She wanted to show the executives a picture that could demonstrate how we planned to map our new strategic vision for a technology solution. She showed me some examples of older charts and a few new ones from other lines of business. Never mind that the vision creation was also just getting off the ground, she wanted a picture displaying the new Transaction Engine and she wanted it right away. Barbara called it the *kodachrome slide*.[18] Barbara, sensing my surprise, invited me to dinner once again to discuss the project further. She wanted to eat something fast, so we went to an eclectic, mostly American cuisine place across from NationsBank Plaza. We weren't through the appetizers when she said, "We can worry about the details later, but I need the kodachrome slide right away."

Kodachrome it would be. Betts and I produced a first draft. Barbara made some changes. Along with slides from other streams, she and the consultants presented it to upper management. I then scheduled some meetings to fill in the details.

My heritage was with a company where overhead slides were the primary communications vehicle. I still had several close friends working for IBM. Overhead slides, referred to internally at IBM as "foils," were the standard presentation format for years. The story I heard from several sources was that shortly after accepting the chairmanship, former RJR Nabisco executive Lou Gerstner had essentially banned foils from the corporate office. He informed his senior executives that if they wanted to meet with him, they needed to deliver the detailed information pertaining to the subject matter in advance of the meeting. Gerstner was a workaholic who would read all the material prior to the meeting. He told his senior executives that they should come prepared to answer his questions concerning the material. My friends said he also indicated that if they needed someone from their support staff to attend the meeting, it wasn't necessary for the senior executive to attend. They should just send the assistant. It was just one of the little ways Gerstner helped get some focus and stop the hemorrhaging at Big Blue.

This must have caused a huge shock wave through Westchester County. Careers had catapulted based on the slide presentation format. Executives would march into a meeting room with an entourage of assistants to adjust the slides, lights, room temperature, and so forth, and most important, provide answers to unexpected questions. It is easy to assume that there is the right kind of detail behind the bullet points on a slide. It was rare that anyone had the time or the inclination to check. Where the rest of the world seemed to be accelerating the use of sound byte news as the best means of communication, Gerstner's IBM was stripping itself of bullet talk.

It was not the time for getting into a deep funk, but I couldn't understand why NationsBank had hired me at a senior vice president level to assist an outside consulting firm in making overhead charts. Needless to say, when a company agrees to pay significant dollars for a consulting contract, there is serious pressure to demonstrate that the money was well spent. This, combined with the high-level access granted to the consulting group, meant internal staffs could become absorbed working "for" as opposed to "with" the consultant.

I was amazed, watching my peer managers within NationsBank actually cleaning up after the consultants, fixing Gemini presentations, teaching them banking business, and giving them access to whatever information they requested. I wondered if these managers thought that this would improve their own status within NationsBank. Apparently it did. NationsBank managers were allowing Gemini consultants to suck their brains.

One night I went to dinner with my peer managers in the strategy group. We ate in the Savannah Fish House in downtown Atlanta. During the meal, most of my peers voiced concerns about the project, particularly regarding the lack of linkage between the stream-teams. Everyone agreed that it was too ambitious attempting to handle all of the different components of the project concurrently. Some of the tasks running concurrently were dependent on successful completion of other tasks.

In short, the group felt that nothing could be done to fix current problems. I mentioned that under the current schedule the infrastructure stream could not finish in time. This was getting bad. I had slipped up and used the word "stream" instead of "team" without even thinking about it. Not finishing in time would prevent "handoff" of the technology cost information needed for the business case team to complete its work. Expressing some of my frustration in my new position, I called it a classic example of "responsibility with no authority."

"But we all have jobs like that," was the reply.

After the first few weeks, Gemini decided they needed to bring in additional talent to assist in developing the technology architecture. Elders finally admitted that Gemini didn't have any technology heavy hitters on the project, but this was only after Barbara had finally recognized the problem herself and started to complain. Elders seemed to be having difficulty finding the right kind of skills. I empathized with his position. There must have been good technical people working for Gemini. They just weren't sitting around on the bench—they were immersed in other client engagements and hard to pull out on short notice. That must have led to his strategy to try and pass off less-qualified consultants as heavy hitters. Perhaps he felt bankers wouldn't create a fuss. He must have thought that if we were intimidated into thinking they were gurus, we wouldn't ask as many questions. I convinced Elders to subcontract some of the work to another consultant I had worked with in the past who I knew could do the job. This was disastrous and lasted for less than two weeks. The subcontractor could never quite pick up the Gemini consultant language and didn't operate from a "model" approach. He was perceived as a loose cannon working his own agenda.

Process consultants such as Gemini had a model, in Gemini's case, a "transformation model." The model became a blueprint for our engagement. It provided a step-by-step cookbook approach of adding input obtained from the client and producing a formula-like deliverable. Instead of tailoring a solution for the client, I felt like we, the client, were being tailored to fit the solution. To the process consultant, the model is truth. Any suggestions or recommendations that might require change to the model are considered heresy. My friend the subcontractor was lucky to get out when he did.

Gemini brought in a British consultant from its Hoskins subsidiary across the pond. He was the fourth recruit brought in during the project to get a handle on the technology consulting required for the transaction engine design. His name was Richard Edmonds, a technologist. At least he could talk on various technology topics. Most interesting to me, he seemed to garner instant credibility by the virtue of his accent. This appeared to be another consulting technique: dazzle with consultants who speak with exotic accents, playing to the theory that you can't be a prophet in your own town.

He was easily excited and loved to draw sketches to illustrate his lightning bolt thoughts whenever they struck. "Look, this is what I mean," he proclaimed as he jumped up from his chair and walked to the front of the room. He drew a circle on the middle of the white board and began sketching what looked like tentacles snaring each of the boxes he scribbled up and down in stacked columns on both the left and right of the circle. He labeled the center circle "Transaction Engine." Boxes on the left were labeled "Upstream Systems," boxes on the right, "Downstream Systems."

"This is how we do it in Europe," he said. "We've eliminated all the intermediary steps and redundant processes."

Elders added, "NationsBank has a real opportunity here to be the first in this market to build a comprehensive, highly efficient electronic payments engine. It will be key for achieving your goals for future growth. It will provide unique competitive advantage."

Unlike Elders, who always appeared professionally manicured and well pressed, Edmond's rusty, disheveled hair was unknown to a comb and badly in need of a trim. His round, wire-rimmed glasses were smeared with smudge marks and hung crookedly off his Roman nose. His shirttails were always hanging out. Even the other Gemini consultants viewed him as a rogue eccentric.

Bob Betts stayed on the project as the Gemini stream leader for infrastructure. He and Edmonds did not get along. Edmonds took over the heavy lifting, putting up with Betts and his constant badgering. Team was a forgotten concept. No wonder they called it "stream."

The Brit worked at a furious pace through the back end of the project, collecting data on the current business applications and the technology they employed. He even worked weekends as opposed to going home to England. A noble effort to reduce travel expenses, I thought. Wrong again. Like other Gemini consultants, when Edmonds was in town, he stayed in the Atlanta Ritz Carlton, one of the city's more exclusive hotels. Later Edmonds confided that as a chain smoker he wanted to minimize the flying back and forth. He would rather stay with the colonists than deal with the long, smoke-free flights to Brittain. Eventually he would become a regular on Air India based solely on their relaxed smoking policy. His travel adventures made for entertaining discussion, particularly when he kept the inside jokes to a minimum.

Edmonds eventually produced a large, brown-paper diagram of the "as is" technology environment that hung across a long stretch of wall on the sixteenth floor of the NationsBank Plaza building. This was a standard Gemini "deliverable" for projects. It actually made transaction mapping understandable and useful. After several revisions, Edmonds's "as is" diagram would highlight all of the redundant, labor-intensive steps involved in the way we handled check-based transactions. Edmonds then created what he called the "to be" infrastructure picture on the opposite wall. In the middle of the "to be" diagram was what was now becoming a household name, the "Transaction Engine." He talked about it in his thick British accent as if it were the Holy Grail and his knightly responsibilities were to fight to the death to turn it from fairy tale to reality for NationsBank. "We've done these before in Europe," Edmonds pointed out. "We have the expertise to do it for you as well."

It was not the first time the term "transaction engine" had been used, but it took outside consultants to give it official blessing. Edmonds's diagrams were actually an impressive piece of work, as far as diagrams go, becoming known as the "brown paper" exercise. As a work-in-progress activity, visitors to the sixteenth floor from various parts of the business were encouraged to add their "builds" to the diagram, slapping yellow stickum notes to the area of the wall in question. "You need to add this," or, "What about that?" While no detailed documentation was being produced, it was a great quick-and-dirty way of picking the brains of employees. The picture would be modified at the end of each day reflecting the new "builds."

After numerous revisions, the brown-paper illustration was reproduced on an overhead chart. It was the closest we ever came to the kodachrome slide, thanks mostly to Edmonds. His picture was still not a complete architecture, but it was more based in reality than all previous efforts to sketch without the details. It goes to show that the manager who owns the contract needs to scream and yell to make sure the right people are assigned—from the beginning. Perhaps I should have been more convincing and forceful in my early questions and objections. I filed away for future use the suggestion that we get resumes of all potential participants well in advance and interview the potential candidates before kicking things off, especially a project of this magnitude.

It would have been a lot better to have spent more time doing the work versus covering up weaknesses, sugarcoating issues, and searching for the right talent to add to a project already in progress. I was more convinced than ever that when consultants are granted too much control over a project, and too much executive access for marketing versus demonstrating tangible results, these kinds of concerns become a nuisance that get in the way of the number one objective—the consultant securing the follow-on contract.

With the assistance of NationsBank associates, Gemini produced slides on the overall strategy, or as they were saying, the "vision" for Transaction Services. They illustrated how the business needed to move from a tactical product orientation to a more proactive service provider. Unfortunately, it never got much deeper than the illustrations on the slides.

There was another important slide of note. It consisted of an impressively configured diagram showing new objectives that looked like a spinning wheel on fire with each objective hanging off a spoke. The idea was to get us out of transaction-only thinking and begin to use the wealth of information we accumulated about customers to sell more products and services, and develop stronger relationships. Gemini, with the help of NationsBank employees, came up with these objectives. What seemed important to Barbara, as well as upper management, were the charts that Gemini created. They were more important than the words. The important thing was that Barbara Albrecht had come to love the charts.

Privately, many at NationsBank questioned the new objectives. "Facilitate the transfer of value? Preserve and enhance value through solutions? Provide access to useful information? What the hell are they talking about?"

Darlene Wittington was most vocal in her criticism: "This doesn't make any sense. Our business isn't about vision. It's like *All the President's Men*, 'Follow the money.'" Her outrage didn't stop there. "How would we ever implement a vision? I can't believe what we're spending for this." These comments were never in meetings, only in informal conversation. Publicly, almost everyone seemed to embrace the Gemini "builds."

There was an interesting progression in the charts. Our new objectives could only be realized if we had a different transaction engine. From a fireball with spokes—or was it a spinning wheel on fire?—this was an enormous leap. If we as employees didn't understand, it didn't really matter. The consultants did, or at least acted as if they did. Barbara Albrecht gave them numerous opportunities to present the charts to our senior executives. From all accounts, the presentations continued to be smashing successes, one after another. Senior management loved the kodachrome slides. NationsBank had a new "vision." In the meantime, we could keep processing all those checks.

SUMMARY OF OBSERVATIONS

• Process consultants operate from a model that is often inflexible and difficult to implement. Consultants may attempt to fit the client's business into the model versus the model being adapted to fit the business.

- Companies do not want to admit that they made a mistake in hiring consultants. Employees will often work to help prop them up.

- Management must be vigilant in its negotiation of consulting contracts to ensure that the right people are assigned from the beginning. Do not take the consulting partner's word on the skills of the consultants assigned to the project, or allow them to "bait and switch," arguing they will find "comparable" talent as originally proposed because of recent changes in availability. Partners are often measured on their ability to "clear the bench" of consultants, in other words, find a project for consultants not currently billed out to clients. Good consultants in major firms are not difficult to place, and rarely idle on the bench. Consulting firms may pitch a proposal with the "A team," and try to fill project teams with those sitting on the bench, unless pressed by the client to provide specific people with specific skills.

- Company employees were less willing to stick their necks out in the downsizing and acquisition environment created in the '90s. This provided considerable advantage to consulting firms attempting to expand their presence in corporations.

- There are few consultants capable of developing a technology architecture that marries business requirements and technology implementation plans.

- If you as a consultant use references, make sure they check out.

NOTES

1. "Open Season on Banks," *Fortune*, 21 August 1995.

2. Mark Calvey, "Executive of the Year: No Matter What You Think of Hugh McColl Jr., the Carolina Banker Rocked the Bay in 1998," *San Francisco Business Times*, 25 December 1998, available at http://www.bizjournals.com/SanFrancisco/stories/1998/12/28/story2.html.

3. John Huey, "The Year's 25 Most Fascinating Business People," *Fortune*, 2 January 1989, 63.

4. Karen Epper, "NationsBank Sidelines Perot as Its Outsourcer," *American Banker*, 11 April 1995, 1.

5. "BankAmerica and NationsBank: No White Smoke Yet," *Business Week*, 6 November 1995, 42.

6. *Moody's Bank and Financial Manual 1996* (New York: Moody Investor Services, 1996), 1824–29.

7. "McColl: Approval of Interstate Banking Could Spark Greater Economic Activity Across the Country," NationsBank Release, 24 November 1992, www.nationsbank.com.

8. "NationsBank Chairman Hugh McColl Says Deregulation of the Banking Industry Could Provide Powerful Nationwide Economic Stimulus," NationsBank Release, 24 February 1993, www.nationsbank.com.

9. "NationsBank Merger," *Atlanta Journal Constitution,* 31 August 1996, D4.

10. Jack Anderson and Michael Binstein, "Special Treatment or Great Deal," *Washington Post*, 1 August 1994, B8.

11. Pamela L. Moore, "Bottom Line on the Line for Bank NationsBank Could Lose Contracts If Bias Proved," *Charlotte Observer,* 10 August 1997, www.charlotte. com/services/reprints/nbank.html.

12. Bill Gates, *The Road Ahead* (New York: Viking Penguin Books, 1995), 180–82.

13. Deborah Gage and Darryl K. Tuft, "Justice Says, 'No!'" *Computer Reseller News*, 20 February 1995, 1.

14. Quote attributed to Boris Yeltsin available at http://www.sccs.swarthmore.edu/users/01/Kyla/quotations/y.html.

15. Larry Long, *Introduction to Computers and Information Processing* (Englewood Cliffs, N.J.: Prentice-Hall, 1984), 246.

16. Willy Sterr and Gail Edmondson, "Memo to Gemini: Read This Book," *Business Week*, 26 June 1995, 40.

17. Kodachrome is a trademarked product of Kodak Imaging Services, Inc.

CHAPTER SIX

THE EUROPEAN
THEATER

The most interesting part of the Gemini Consulting project was "country profiling." Given that electronic payment systems were becoming increasingly more important in the United States as a replacement for checks, it made sense to evaluate the European market. European banks had experienced early success with electronic payments, which far outpaced checks. Why were they successful when the United States was not, especially when we were considered the innovators and leaders in technology? Country profiling, we were told, would answer this. Gemini had sold "country profiling" as part of their contract. It helped provide competitive advantage over Andersen Consulting. At least, that was the accepted party line.

I was assigned to assist on this activity in addition to my responsibilities in technology. Overseas offices of Gemini supplied stacks of data I was told to review on the financial industry markets in Europe and the expected impact of the European Common Market. Most of it was generally available to anybody, not just consultants. Some of it could have been found on the Internet if anyone was willing to take the time to look. Pouring through hundreds of pages of data, I attempted to better understand the growth of electronic payments overseas.

According to the information received from Gemini, the electronic processing and financial transactions represented close to 50 percent of payments in France and the United Kingdom. Electronic processing represented over 90 percent of payments in Germany. The movement to replace checks with electronic methods of payment was moving much faster than in the United States where only about 20 percent of payments were handled electronically, with checks still the primary method. At NationsBank, electronic processing was only 10 percent of our payments. How European banks had achieved so much success in moving customers off of checks was only part of the equation. The other even more important piece of the puzzle was how they had managed to keep the competition out and retain their customer base during the transition. The risk of losing customers was one of the arguments most often used by bankers for doing nothing. These critical areas needed to be studied and their lessons learned—then applied to help NationsBank. If the attempt was to overwhelm me with information, Gemini succeeded.

Gemini was also playing the FUD (Fear, Uncertainty, and Doubt) card. "There are lots of scary things going on out there, tons of information that needs to be sorted through before making an intelligent decision." They were right about that. Whether they could scare those senior executives still partial to checks remained to be seen. It also remained to be seen if Gemini could help us develop an effective competitive response. In any case, Gemini kept reminding us that technology companies and other banks could come out of nowhere, creating easier to use, faster support and service with new electronic banking offerings—just like those offerings available today in Europe. Ben Elders suggested that we had better understand the European electronic marketplace "in depth." This tied nicely to Barbara Albrecht's fears about Microsoft or somebody else helping to accelerate the extinction of U.S. banks like ours. Gemini added a few charts to the vision presentation on the threat of competition from other banks and new market entrants. There would also be a few charts on European banking. My job was to help fill in some of the blanks.

What if we didn't wait but jumped in ourselves, becoming an early pioneer in the U.S. electronic payments business? Could NationsBank develop an effective electronic system for replacing checks? Was it possible for us to become the new de facto standard? All these questions needed to be answered. Ben Elders suggested that we check out Europe firsthand and see what this electronic banking was all about. Elders told us that Gemini had helped contribute to the solutions used in Germany and France. "Only after seeing it will you understand why electronic payments are so popular in Europe," he said. Barbara agreed. I was going to Europe.

A group trip was also planned, but first I was selected to go on a preliminary reconnaissance mission. My job was to do some initial fact finding. I was also to make the call as to whether a group trip was a good use of additional NationsBank time and resources. Already I was feeling the pressure. Nobody in the group wanted me to squash their opportunity for an expenses paid trip to Europe. Once again, Barbara said she wanted to make sure we were "getting what we are paying for." After Barbara had begun to realize that my concerns over the competence of the technology consultants were justified, her confidence in me seemed to rekindle.

In addition to checking out what Gemini had in store for the group trip, this was an opportunity for me to get an early peek at a European transaction engine. As Elders continued to remind us, "If NationsBank does the transaction engine we are recommending, you can be way ahead of everybody else in the U.S. market." All we had to do was mimic what had already been done in Europe. Few bank executives liked risk. Elders was arguing that we could gain advantage with a unique solution for our market, but a solution already proven to work someplace else. That it was done before in Europe was reassuring to Barbara and the higher-ups. It sounded too good to be true. I was off to Europe to see it firsthand and report back to management.

Bob Betts, the Gemini leader of the technology team, would meet me there. There was no question in my mind that he was being sent to work me on how Gemini had the solution we needed, and what a wonderful opportunity this whole thing would be. All that was required was for me to play along. His other mission was to advise Gemini's Paris office on how to handle us American banker types and to get any kinks out during the trial run. I thought it was interesting that Edmonds, who was from Europe and supposedly involved in some of Gemini's pioneering work on the Continent, was not slated to go. His time must have been considered too valuable working the kodachrome. It was also interesting that the people I met "over there" didn't seem to know Edmonds. Betts and I had something in common. We were both expendable. Edmonds could benefit greatly from working without us.

The City of Light will bring out the continental in almost anybody, even a kid originally from Bayside, Queens. The Hotel Majestic, where I was staying, was just a few streets north from the Paris office of Gemini. It was a typical European hotel, small accommodations, but very elegant. This was a favorite place to stay in the twenties for larger-than-life expatriates like Gerald and Sara Murphy, when they could pull themselves away from their famous parties on the Riviera, as well as Dorothy Parker during some of her occasional jaunts to Paris. During World War II, the Hotel Majestic had been a German occupation headquarters and was later used by the Allies as a temporary POW facility. I would be sleeping in history, but first I felt compelled to explore. In the opposite direction of the hotel, a few short blocks away, the Arch of Triumph crowned the top of the Champs Elysees. It was as good a place as any to start. I had almost a full day to enjoy the splendor of Paris before meeting with my Gemini contacts the next morning.

It was late winter but, unseasonably warm, and I wore down my soles on the walk from the Arch to the Left Bank. I stopped along the way at Harry's Bar, made famous by the Lost Generation. I half expected to run into Jake Barnes with Lady Brett Ashley from Hemingway's *The Sun*

Also Rises. In spite of the infiltration of a few American franchised establishments from the new generation you would expect to see at Baltimore Harbor or Boston's Quincy Market, Paris with its sidewalk cafes, fountains, and tree-lined boulevards still had a rich authenticity that could not be duplicated, not even by Disney. Playing the shameless tourist, I thoroughly enjoyed taking it all in, everything from the Notre Dame Cathedral to the tomb of Napoleon. I had just finished reading the first volume of William Manchester's biography of Winston Churchill. In it he quipped how many believed this was the place where the last competent French general was entombed.[1] Napoleon, by necessity, was close to his troops. He lived in an era when military leaders couldn't rely on technology and behind-the-lines communication for fighting wars. He wasn't too big on mercenaries either.

My internal clock was six hours too slow, and I stayed awake through most of the night. I dressed early and decided to go look for coffee. I was to meet with Bob Betts and a Gemini consultant from Paris in the lobby of my hotel around nine. I figured I had some time. As I remembered from trips to Europe in my previous life as a consultant, no one is in any great hurry to get to work early. There is something to be said about the European approach to life with its pronounced emphasis placed on smelling the roses and everyday meals. Many of those meals last late into the night, which could possibly explain the slow start to the European workday. As a French woman I dated for several years often said: "In America people live to work, in Europe they work to live." She would also say, "Ask an American what he does, and he will tell you about his job. Ask a Frenchman, and he will tell you what he likes to do, not what he has to do."

Morning raced up on me abruptly, after a brief hour or two of sleep. Thoughts of a steaming brew of French roasted java filled my head, and I needed it—badly. There was a slight drizzle as I walked along the cobblestoned avenue that snaked away from the hotel. All of the cafes I passed were closed. It was still too early for the French. I finally spotted a place. It was a few blocks away, on the other side of the narrow, uneven street. Inside, there were several men and a woman standing around a counter. There were no chairs in sight. They were sipping what I was craving out of espresso-sized cups. There was an older man with a mustache on the other side of the counter. They seemed to be engaged in light-hearted small talk.

"*Bonjour,*" I said, using what little French I knew. They all responded "*bonjour*" with what appeared to be genuine smiles of good will. I had been told that attempting to speak the local language, even with a few words, went a long way. I continued, "*Parlez-vous anglais?*" They shook their heads as if to say, "Not very much."

I continued, "*Excusez- moi, . . . café to go? . . . s'il vous plaît.*"

They looked confused. "*Je ne comprends pas,*" the man with the mustache said. They started speaking to each other in a rapid succession of unintelligible words. They occasionally looked back at me. Finally, I heard "Ahh" from the woman. She smiled at me and nodded affirmatively. She turned and pointed to a back room, motioning for the man across the counter to fetch something. He returned with a plastic cup in which he poured a shot of piping hot black coffee. I pulled out a handful of francs and pushed them across the counter. "*Merci, merci,*" I said. The man with the mustache looked annoyed as he slid most of the francs back. "*Merci,*" I said again and left.

Imagine, they must have been saying to themselves, first the doggie bag, now the coffee to go, what will those crass Americans think of next? I could smell the plastic melting in my hand as I walked back to the hotel, just in time to meet Betts and his Gemini consultant from France. Bob Betts had also flown in the day before. "Oh, where'd you get the coffee?" said Betts. "I could use some myself." He apparently couldn't smell the melting plastic. I had to restrain myself from giving him what was left. The French consultant looked disapprovingly at both of us. Ignoring the last comment, he motioned for us to follow him in his Peugeot. They all had Peugeots.

When we arrived at the corporate headquarters of Gemini, the Frenchman escorted us to a back-office conference room. As ridiculous as it might sound, my impressions of Paris were based on Hollywood-made movies from the '40s. Unlike these movies filled with international intrigue, I was disappointed that we had been relegated to a nondescript room with a simple table and chairs. Forget intrigue, this room was lacking even the slightest usual American business meeting amenities. No windows overlooking the street life in Paris, no impressionist art gracing the walls, and definitely no interesting characters of questionable intent. Worse of all—no coffee. As a former consultant, I already knew what Gemini wanted—the next contract. They had sketched out the kodachrome engine. Now they wanted to build it. If the cost was one million to draw conceptual diagrams, we were talking big bucks. The least they could have provided was some coffee in a cup that didn't melt. I would have been so much more agreeable.

There were just the three of us in the room. Betts, the Frenchman, and me. Bob Betts had arrived the day before from his home in Dallas and looked worn out before the day had started, the same way I felt. The other consultant would have fit the classic description of a Parisian. He loved to talk, was dressed in a crumbled-up, but expensive, custom-tailored suit, wore a fashionable silk tie, and smoked continuously. He launched into an extemporaneous presentation with the assistance of flip chart paper on the French banking industry. Thank God his command of English was relatively good. He acted as if he had been through the drill a few times before. I was one of the usual suspects.

The regulatory organization in France was extremely supportive of banks. This was very different than in America, where from the point of view of many bankers there still existed an adversarial relationship, in spite of the recent relaxation in some of the government's policies. The banks in France worked through and with the regulatory organization to create entry barriers for nonbanks. I also learned that until recently one of the major banks, Credit Lyonnais, was partially owned by the French government. Consequently, electronic payment based on strict bank control could be mandated through government legislation. The consultant felt the jury was still out with regard to how the Common Market and the movement to a Euro currency would impact banking in his country.*

From a technology perspective, the French regulatory group had formed one big clearinghouse for the routing and settlement of payments shared by all banks. Essentially there was one nationwide transaction engine that handled electronic payments for the entire banking industry. The regulatory group, in conjunction with the French banks, had set compliance standards that required the use of specific hardware and software platforms to participate in the banking industry in France. This helped reduce complexities associated with the integration of banking activities. Nevertheless, it was supported by old mainframe-based legacy systems, not new technology. Several experiments were in progress to determine the potential of leveraging new technology, but not much had been implemented. Gemini, which had strong ties to the French regulatory organization as well as Credit Lyonnais, was participating in several of those experiments. I found out later that this was what Elders was referring to when he said Gemini had helped develop a "breakthrough answer" for handling electronic payments.

The more I learned, the more I became concerned. The French were successful because banks still enjoyed the advantages of a monopoly market and favorable probank regulation to keep it that way. There was a long-standing cooperative spirit and considerable trust among the

---

*France has experienced increased foreign investment, attributed in large part to acceptance of the European Common Market. Credit Lyonnais has recently privatized. France has also experienced the strongest growth of GDP of the major economies in the Euro area (2.7 percent in 1999 compared to 1.4 percent for Germany; for 2000, forecasts are around 3.6 percent (dp) for France versus around 3.0 percent for Germany. Source: "France's Economy: Facts and Figures," Embassy of France, 10 April 2000, http://www.info-france-usa.org/news/statmnts/2000/be100400.asp.

banks. There were no clear technology breakthroughs that could be simulated and transplanted to U.S. soil. Add to this the differences in marketing to a homogenous population sharing common demographics as in France, versus marketing to a diverse and geographically dispersed U.S. population. This was disappointing, but not only because there didn't seem to be a solution we could borrow. Somehow, I needed to return with at least some recommendations or astute observations. I felt I was on thin ice. What would I say to my boss? I could be back in the doghouse. "Fun trip had a blast. Sorry, but we didn't find the engine. Not much there we can put to good use, either. Don't bother to set up a major trip."

I felt that if we didn't get what we were paying for, at least some of the burden of guilt would fall on me. There had to be some kind of benefit I could find to justify the trip. If the trip couldn't be justified, then the whole project could also be questioned.

As it turned out, I didn't have to say anything. By the time I arrived back to the project headquarters in Atlanta, the group trip had already been approved. Barbara wanted to do it, and her mind had already been made up. Arrangements were made for a large combined group of NationsBank associates and Gemini consultants to descend on Europe. There were about twenty people involved, including five from Barbara's organization and another five from other NationsBank organizations. Others attending from NationsBank would include a cross section of managers from different parts of the business, including check processing. The team would also include an equal compliment of consultants. Five Gemini consultants from the project would fly over with us, joined by five additional consultants from Europe. Each of us from NationsBank would have a consultant shadowing us as a chaperone. As expected, my shadow would be Bob Betts.

One manager, whose absence was obvious, was the NationsBank manager responsible for electronic processing. He declined to participate. You would have thought he would be the guy most interested in taking a look at "models" where electronics had replaced most of the manual check processing. Possibly, he already knew what we would find, or not find. There was another potential reason. He was another of those senior managers who was supposedly no big fan of Barbara. Was this corporate politics rearing its ugly head? Perhaps it was simply that he didn't like the idea of making Barbara a hero. The potential impact on the business always seemed to be a secondary consideration. In any case, he said he had other things he needed to do.

We would not be confined to Paris on the group trip. The game plan was for us to split up, spending a few days in separate countries, including

Great Britain, Germany, and France. Gemini had prearranged meetings with bank executives from each of the respective countries. We would then meet in Paris for a series of planning meetings to share information and begin to develop what Gemini called "the path forward." This was more of Gemini's unique language. It loosely translated to "the next contract," and made the journey sound less self-serving. While it may have been less costly to do the planning back in Atlanta, everybody seemed to like the idea of doing it in Paris. Now that the pressure was off, I was all for a second trip.

There were some good ideas circulated by the European bankers in some of our meetings. I was amazed at how free they were in sharing information. Was it to impress us with their competence? If so, it did little to change our views, much less impress us. We were Americans, and there was always that underlying arrogance. We bailed them out of two world wars.

Americans were the new force to be reckoned with now that we had won the Cold War. We would rule in the emerging global market. Most important, NationsBank represented the brash new player in U.S. banking. We were on a mission to become number one. If we saw or heard something we liked, it was always an acquisition away. Dole out some cash; put together a team of business partners to help with the acquisition; send the missiles; name the campaign something like "Blitzkrieg"; and NationsBank could wage a campaign to become the bank of nations.

Although I was able to go to Germany for the first time, my second European trip was packed with meetings, tight agendas, and planned meals. There is less personal flexibility when you are part of a school trip, complete with monitors. Everyone seemed to enjoy the international travel, but in spite of the hype from the Gemini duo of Ben Elders and Bob Betts, the search for a European holy grail ended with no grail. We did manage to develop a list of recommendations, although none of them would jump out at anyone familiar with banking as creative, innovative "out of the box" thinking. To gloss over the wasted time and money, Gemini threw a dinner soirée the last night we were together in one of the finest five star restaurants in Paris. As far as I was concerned at the time, it was a great consolation prize. Spirits ran high. We would somehow find what we were looking for at some later date. No one, including me, wanted to rain on the parade, at least not while we had the backdrop of Paris to enjoy.

Returning to the United States, the combined Gemini and Nations-Bank team worked for the remainder of the project on refining our recommendations and developing the final presentations. It became difficult to distinguish one meeting from the next. They started running together as if it was just one big convention of extreme importance with the future of international banking weighing in the balance.

Somebody from the NationsBank team joked, "If we could only win our regulators over to our side like they are in France, we wouldn't have to worry about all the nonsense we do in the States."

"What do you mean?" asked one of the junior Gemini consultants.

"The governments in Europe are probanking," he responded. "They help facilitate banking. They don't get in the way."

That was one way to look at it: make the watchdogs more banker-friendly, no threat of outside competition, limited customer choices, no driving competitive necessity for breaking from the pack.

During the Gemini meetings following our trip to Europe, I noticed that Ben Elders, the Gemini Consulting partner, had a habit of slouching in his chair with his head hanging down. I wasn't the only one to notice. There was a meeting I remember when two senior NationsBank executives, several levels higher than me in the organizational structure, were discussing Ben Elders and his penchant for falling asleep. They apparently found it amusing. In William Manchester's *The Last Lion*, it is noted that Winston Churchill had a similar habit while sitting through long-winded meetings. Once, when an opposition speaker was addressing the House of Commons, he noticed Churchill sitting in his customary reclined position below the gangway. His size alone must have made him hard to not notice. The speaker asked the great statesman if he was asleep. Churchill replied, "I wish to God I were."[2]

The difference was that Churchill assumed this position when he was thinking. Ben Elders, Gemini's crack lead partner on the engagement, was actually sleeping. Every once in a while someone would have to give him a nudge. When he was awake and participating in the discussion, he usually had some intelligent things to contribute. Like most consulting partners in client engagements, I surmised that his primary role was cultivating executive relationships and working to secure the next contract. Mundane topics concerning banking barriers to entry, technology infrastructure planning, or management of payment disbursements apparently didn't hold his interest for very long. Not that these were the most interesting of subjects, but we were all getting paid, consultants and employees alike, to focus on them. You could bet Elders was getting paid a lot more than anybody else.

I learned later that his main residence was on the island of Saint Thomas in the Caribbean. It must have been a great place for yachting, but a long way from the NationsBank Plaza building in downtown Atlanta. No wonder he was always tired. Apparently we were also paying for his weekly commuting expenses as part of the contract, just as we were for all the Gemini consultants. Ben, in particular, didn't look like the kind of guy who flew coach.

SUMMARY OF OBSERVATIONS

- Management needs to assess progress on consulting contracts on an ongoing basis to ensure that the project is meeting requirements. Projects should be segmented into milestone dates, with tangible deliverables due at each milestone. Deliverables should be very specific. Examples of deliverables for a vendor-analysis project might include, documents, or sections of a document, with specific sections due on specific dates. These might include criteria and method of analysis, a request for information for vendor distribution, a scorecard, a review of each vendor response, or a recommendation paper or document. In addition to milestones, there needs to be ongoing periodic review.

- Many consulting organizations merely pass information they have learned from one client to another. "Out of the box" thinking is rare and infrequently encouraged.

- Travel expenses can become a very large additional cost item in consulting engagements, which is often underestimated. Are there qualified local resources that can be used? This is another factor to consider in evaluating consulting alternatives. Ask consultants to itemize projected travel and living expense in advance of final project approval and make responsible budget management of these items part of total project requirements.

- In many consulting firms, the primary function of the partner is to cultivate executive relationships and to secure the next contract. Make it clear that there will be no follow-on commitments until the current project is completed satisfactorily.

NOTES

1. William Manchester, *The Last Lion: Visions of Glory 1874–1932* (Boston: Little, Brown & Company, 1983), 491.
2. William Manchester, *The Last Lion: Alone 1932–1940* (Boston: Little, Brown & Company, 1988), 108.

CHAPTER SEVEN

THE PREEMINENT
STRIKE

Eventually the Gemini project began to wind down. The final recommendations would include adopting the new "vision," implementing a transaction engine, and building new strategic partnerships. Partnerships with other banks had been a major focus of my employer long before the recommendations from Gemini were presented. Other consultants hired by NationsBank in the past had recommended bank partnerships to address new competitive threats. Circling the wagons was the perfect answer for the risk averse. Gemini was more than happy to play the "go-between" in setting all this up. Gemini, like other consultants before it, was suggesting that, in addition to creating alliances with other banks, we form a long-term special partnership with it.

Partnerships didn't strike me as an adequate solution, particularly when we continued to partner with banks having the same structural and business-related issues that we did. Surround mediocrity with mediocrity and you get more mediocrity. Working together, one could expect a lethargic pace for creating change. Too many risk-averse bankers in the mix. I felt it would be the banks with the vision and competitive fortitude to break from the pack that would ultimately win. It wasn't the time to be circling the wagons, no matter how comfortable it made us feel. That was my opinion, but I knew it didn't count for much.

We had time for only a few more meetings to complete the final deliverables. The deliverables were overhead presentation materials with heavy emphasis on the "vision thing." There was no backup documentation on how any of these sweeping conceptual ideas could be implemented. It was now becoming painfully obvious to all of us participating in the "stream-teams" that the infrastructure presentation was the weak link. This was not because we had the weakest set of overheads. Thanks to Edmonds, some of the charts were among the best, and in NationsBank, this was no small matter.

The problem was that, while partnerships would solve the external threat problems, the transaction engine had been oversold as the solution for all of our internal problems. It would improve efficiencies, eliminate bottlenecks, and reduce costly errors requiring labor-intensive "exception processing." It would also position us for offering new high-tech methods of banking. It would "transform" us from a basic savings, loaning, and collecting institution into a grand new entity, a company highly adept at "financial-knowledge management." In other words, we could use the collected financial information from our customers to sell them more and more products and services. The engine wasn't just going to help us handle electronic payments. It was now going to help us spend less time processing the payments and more time analyzing the information the payments could provide. It would not only help us know more about the customer, it would help us know who the right customers were. We could customize financial advice to high-end potential targets. "Hello, Mr. Brown, based on your excellent payment records, we have an exclusive offer, just for you."

Unlike the other concept charts, this transaction engine couldn't stand forever as a concept. People wanted to touch, feel, and see it. Trouble was sure to follow. It was similar to the way a little-known politician gains mass appeal until he is forced to state positions on specific issues. The consultants were talking about radical changes, invoking popular images, and speaking in generalizations. "Oh yes, it will do that, too." It was goodness for everybody. For electronic advocates it was the final solution for the conversion of checks to automated transaction processing. Internet enthusiasts would have a routing solution for home banking. Data analysts were now expecting a data-mining engine for conducting "what if" analysis. It was even billed as a better alternative for processing checks. Mainframe bigots saw it as another large system that extended their empire. Distributed-processing enthusiasts saw it as client/server. It had become all things to all people.

There was another problem. As it turned out, the business case "stream" had been relying on the engine group to provide financial data on the costs for rebuilding the infrastructure to support new technology requirements. "So where is it?" they asked. It was as if all of a sudden everyone within the other groups began to realize that the emperor had been parading around all this time stark naked. We in the technology stream had failed to provide the clothes. Little progress had been made in developing anything on the engine more than the brown-paper material stuck on the wall.

That's when the most bizarre thing happened. Bob Betts said matter-of-factly that it would cost $100 million over five years to build the engine. This must have been a magic number for Gemini. It was the same amount *Business Week* had estimated they had lost in American operations in the previous year.[1] I couldn't help but ask.

"How did we arrive at this number?"

Betts responded, "At this point it is still a rough estimate, but we believe, based on our experience on similar projects, the actual number will be close to that."

I looked around the table at the NationsBank people. Nobody blinked. Partner in charge Ben Elders, recently back from his home commute from Saint Thomas, was sporting a deeper olive tan and was awake enough to concur. "I've already shared this with Al Johnson," Elders said.

This was a great way to cut off conversation with the underlings. The inference was that the president of the Services Company had bought in. It was never made clear how this number was derived. It didn't matter. We needed a planning number for the business case, and our consultants told us what it would be. Everyone seemed happy again. We could get back to developing charts for the final presentation.

The $100 million figure became the definitive planning number for building the engine. I wondered how bankers, who could be so tough when it came to approving loans to customers, could let consultants get away with pulling numbers down out of the air with no business justification behind them. Gemini must have felt it had dodged the bullet. We were too far along with what it called the "path forward" to raise troubling questions. As long as corporate managers accepted information at face value, consultants were safe.

To say the least, I was disturbed. We had not even checked to see if there were off-the-shelf solutions available, and yet we were getting ready to commit to a long-term construction project. This raised a troubling question in my head: "What business are we in, building technology platforms or banking?" This was a competitive market, and in the five years projected to build the engine, it could be game over. There was no assurance we'd have it completely done in five years either, and by then, it could be out of date.

Enough was enough. I didn't see how I could continue to sit back idly as we added conceptual numbers to conceptual kodachrome and called it a "path forward" for "transforming" the bank. As the technology strategist for our group, sooner or later it could come back to bite me. What happened if we actually tried to implement it and the whole thing exploded all around us? My ass would be one of the first to go. I knew enough about consulting at this point to know how well the game could be played by the contractors, skating away from any semblance of accountability. The engine was in my area of responsibility. I was an employee. Upper management would plead ignorance on the technology. "That's why we hired you." If things went bad, I was expendable. At least from my perspective, nobody had more to lose than me, and I didn't like it.

I had to try at least one more time to get through to Barbara. In spite of our recently improved relationship, it wasn't easy setting up a one-on-one meeting. Gemini consultants were always around her. It was as if they had moved into her office. They helped her prepare for meetings with senior executives. They sat through most of her meetings with the rest of us. From Barbara's perspective, the Gemini project was the priority. Her reputation hung on its success. Criticizing Gemini was equivalent to criticizing her. Everything we were doing in her strategy group could be traced to an overhead chart in a Gemini presentation. Finally, after several attempts, I got my chance for a private meeting.

I told her that the infrastructure work was conceptual only and there was still considerable work involved in attempting to "operationalize" this plan. "As it stands right now, this is a high-risk venture and I have serious concerns that we could be headed off a cliff," I said. This got her attention. With the project winding down, Barbara had concerns of her own. Where's the beef? Senior management would eventually need to see more than charts. She, too, could be exposed.

"You know, Steve, I see what you are saying. So, how do we fix it?"

I gave her a couple suggestions that I thought could get us more of what was needed, while at the same time saving face. It required holding Gemini's feet to the fire. We would demand the deliverables they had promised from the beginning, namely, a workable plan for the engine, a plan that provided functional details, not just good-looking, charts. Who better than Barbara? All she had to do was go after them as if they were a rival bank executive fighting her over resources.

At the next progress review meeting, she challenged Gemini management and said that we needed a more detailed level of information. Barbara said they had committed to providing this as part of the contract. Gemini appeared to be on the ropes. One of the Gemini project managers agreed that they had promised more, but he also appeared perplexed as he looked back and forth from Barbara to Ben Elders. His head was bobbing from side to side, like a spectator at a tennis match. They all acted as if they were surprised that anyone at NationsBank would want anything more than charts, especially Barbara.

After she hounded them for a while on not delivering on all of the goods, there were several uncomfortable moments of silence. Both the project manager and senior partner Ben Elders had their eyes cast downward. While Richard Edmonds tried to talk his way around it, Bob Betts, my *compadre* on the technology stream, was looking for someplace to crawl. As conversation resumed, I noticed Ben Elders slip out of the meeting. He had a funny look in his eyes. Ben Elders wasn't running to get away. He was up to something. I was sure of it.

Later that afternoon I ran into Elders, who looked like somebody had just pulled his lottery ticket, not like a consultant responsible for a failing project. He told me he had met with Barbara's manager who ran Transaction Services. An agreement had been reached that Gemini would assist the bank in a subsequent phase of the project focused on the "transaction engine." His comments made the hair on the nape of my neck stand up.

Needless to say, his preemptive strike had put a very positive Gemini spin on what had been done and where NationsBank needed to go. Elders seemed very confident that his efforts at damage control had not only been most successful, but were also the final word. He was gloating. It occurred to me that my immediate manager's hands were tied. Barbara wasn't as important to Gemini anymore. She had simply opened the door. The contract had given them exposure to higher-level executives. While we worked on completing the deliverables for the current project, Elders was busy working, too, solidifying relationships he would need for approval of the next phase. Barbara may have given them the entrée, but she was now becoming a threat. Criticizing their work could jeopardize the next contract. Consultants neutralize potential threats by getting higher in the organization, where they can provide upper management a "filtered" view from "objective" advisors. If there was a problem with the project, it wasn't a Gemini problem. The consulting firm could easily slip the word that it was lack of management direction. Coming from an independent consultant who was able to observe firsthand this could be deadly.

Not only had Gemini gotten to Barbara's immediate boss, it had also gotten to his boss, the division president. Gemini had already previewed with Al Johnson most of the work in progress during the engagement. There had been several Gemini meetings with Johnson. Gemini management had said that this series of meetings went "extremely well." So did Barbara. At one point during the project Johnson had come down to the sixteenth floor to see the brown-paper diagrams of the "as is" and the "to be." Gemini had also gained access to other executives who had paraded through their process and seen the "transformation" output. It occurred to me that none of them knew there was nothing behind the nice-looking charts. Everyone played along as if significant amounts of work had been done to get to where we were. To question Gemini's performance now was risky. Get on the train, or get run over.

I count myself as very fortunate that there have been different people at critical periods of my life who have provided me with very important advice. One of them was a retail industry consultant who co-owned his own business and had moved to Atlanta a year or so before me. I had worked with him while we were both at IBM. During those years he provided invaluable advice in helping me get around some of the internal IBM politics. He had a private pilot's license, and he loved to fly. When he wasn't working or flying, he loved to hang out in a place called the 57th Fighter Group Restaurant, adjacent to the Dekalb Peachtree Airport, something else in Atlanta named Peachtree. The grounds surrounding the restaurant looked like the movie set for *Twelve O'clock High* with a burned out DC-3, World War II army jeeps, and other appropriate military paraphernalia scattered across the yard that separated the restaurant from the airfield. One night we met at his favorite watering hole to grab a bite to eat and slug a few beers. We sat outside, close to the military props, as dusk disappeared along with our drinks. The emerging pool of bright light that began spilling from the sky reminded me that I was hundreds of miles from New York. In New York there were a lot fewer stars, at least in the sky. I drank some more.

After getting caught up with one another, I shared with him some of my frustrations with the engine project. I told him that I felt Gemini was about to propose a prototype for building a new transaction engine that (a) would take too long and cost too much before it would be production ready and (b) would utilize unproven technology that would not have the industrial strength needed for the NationsBank environment. I related how others in NationsBank also had concerns, but none of them seemed willing to make any noise. My boss had given it a shot, but her efforts were defused when the Gemini partner went over her head. I shared with him some background on the recent meeting where it all seemed to unravel only to be quickly boxed up once again. In general, NationsBank managers and associates continued to express support during Gemini meetings. It was only in sidebar conversations that they would talk about misgivings.

"Well, for one thing, Steve, you now work for a bank. Bankers don't make waves. Consultants have more clout with the executives than employees do. That's a fact of life, but I'm sure you already know that."

"So how can we pin them down to finish the work on this contract before they get the next one?"

"You've got to get as high up as they have. Higher if you can."

My friend had a point, but it was fraught with all kinds of personal risk. Trying to get airtime with someone higher up in the organization, regardless of the reason, would most certainly be viewed as insubordination.

My feeling was that Gemini Consulting had been very good on the conceptual level. They had a fairly good process methodology. Whether they could have done a better job of gathering content information for our engine project, or simply didn't have the skills to collect it, I wasn't sure. There had been little effort in this area. All focus was on the charts. They also suffered from a typical consulting problem. There was a gaping void in effective communication between the strategy people and the technology consultants.

In addition, the stream-teams didn't appear to join in an integrated fashion, in spite of the weekly status meetings. Someone said this was one of Gemini's biggest projects. Maybe the Gemini people had tried to do too much in too short a time, but my feeling was that there was considerable architecture design and product research work that still needed to be done before committing to build a high-priced prototype. This was a high-risk venture, and we needed to get it right. NationsBank would be the loser if we didn't.

I told my pilot friend that most of my concerns continued to get drowned out and there didn't seem to be much I could do to change the momentum, particularly after Elders had gone over Barbara's head. He asked me when the contract would be over. There was about another week or so for the current project, which had been extended for an additional two weeks, through the end of May. He suggested that I lay low for the time being. A day or so before the final presentation to the division president would be the time to strike.

"From what you tell me," he said, "your only chance of winning here is to get to the president; and that's a high-stakes gamble. You probably want to think it over and then decide if it's worth it."

"I've already decided."

We both knew the Gemini final presentation would be structured as a sales call to get a commitment for the next contract. It was part of the consultant's modus operandi.

"The key is to move swiftly, right before they present, and not give them a chance to recover. If they are able to recover, you must realize, you lose big time."

"Yeah, thanks. You're right. I need to get to Al Johnson."

I knew that even if I were successful in getting to the president of NationsBank's Services Company and putting my points across, the political fallout could be fatal.

I was assuming that Ben Elders's boasting about the next contract was based more on brag than fact. I guessed that he had at best a tentative verbal commitment from senior management. While I was fairly certain no contracts had been signed, I realized there was a chance that a more formal arrangement was at least assumed. After all, this was the South and handshakes seemed to mean more than they did in other places. The flip side, however, was to do nothing and watch NationsBank invest considerable dollars going down a path that appeared to be questionable at best. The market wasn't very forgiving. On top of this, I knew that senior management was not in a position to understand the new technology being proposed. As the technology strategist responsible for architecture-related decisions in this area of the business, I felt I had to act. I also think I liked the idea of the challenge of trying to beat Elders at his own game. If possible, it would be important to do it in a way that wasn't construed as insubordinate.

As an outside consultant, Elders had access that I didn't. Elders had plenty of opportunities for backup plans. I would have one shot. He didn't have to worry about organizational protocol. As Dan Price constantly reminded me, employees at NationsBank always needed to consider protocol before acting. My one shot could be suicidal.

Several years ago, as an IBM marketing rep in Connecticut, I was one deal away from making my quota in a territory where all the bets had been off for winning any IBM business at all. The year was winding down, and I couldn't get my new marketing manager's attention. I needed his approval on one aspect of the deal. He was also responsible for other reps with territories much larger than mine. In his mind, I was small potatoes. He once showed me on a computer printout how my territory was only a fraction of a percent of his total area of responsibility. It was his unique style of motivating reps.

There was a more seasoned salesman who picked up on my frustration. He was one of only a few former IBM typewriter salespersons who had survived the transition to large-systems marketing. People used to say that the typewriter guys were the true salespeople within the company. Most of them never made it through mandatory systems training when IBM reorganized for probably the hundredth or so time. Training was sometimes used back then in the days of IBM's full-employment policy as a subtle way of weeding people out. The typewriter salespeople began leaving in droves, some voluntarily, others not so voluntarily. Ironically, they were probably closer to the kind of salespeople required for the *Brave New World* of end-user computing.

This particular typewriter peddler was a marine who fought in Korea; his nickname in the branch was "Chainsaw." They could phase out the entire typewriter sales group, but Chainsaw would be the last to go, fighting every inch of the way. I explained my problem to Chainsaw and how I felt the only chance I had was to talk with the branch manager. He might be more sensitive to the situation, I explained. I knew, however, that my marketing manager would get pretty upset if I went over his head. There could be hell to pay. Worse than not making your numbers in the old IBM was the appearance of insubordination.

The seasoned salesman said, "That's easy." He told me that the branch manager got to work between 7:30 and 8:00 A.M. By 9:15 to 9:30, he would have had three cups of coffee and would be on his way to the men's room. He said I should make sure I ran into him there.

"When he asks you how it's going, that's your chance to open up. Later you can say you ran into him unexpectedly and it came up in the course of conversation. If your manager wants to know the details, tell him where you were at the time. It will shorten the conversation."

It worked like a charm back then. I decided to take a similar tack, except for the location. I had met Al Johnson several times, so that I was reasonably confident that he would recognize me. I got to the Nations-Bank Plaza building by 6:00 A.M. I remembered how Chase Manhattan executives always got in very early. It was two days before the final Gemini presentation to Johnson was scheduled to take place. Positioning myself on the ground floor, between the elevators to the parking garage and the elevators to the executive offices, I felt I couldn't miss Johnson as he made his early morning trek to the office. I would later argue that we had simply run into each other, just like Chainsaw had taught me. As I waited, I remembered what I had been told about Johnson: "He's a tough son of a bitch who doesn't suffer fools."

Hundreds of people must have passed through the elevator doors while I stood waiting, occasionally pacing back and forth, as if my scheduled appointment was running late. I worried that he might have had business out of town. At a quarter before 9:00, Johnson stepped off the elevator. So did several other people.

He seemed to be engaged in light conversation with a group of four or five people surrounding him. The group approached as if they were bodyguards with Johnson safely protected in the center. I stepped out in front and tried my best to offer a pleasant but firm "good morning" to Johnson, who was behind somebody else. I was hoping to distract him just enough to get his attention and secure a few seconds of hang time. The guy in front stepped aside, allowing Johnson and I to establish direct eye contact for the first time. He looked me over and finally said, "Yes it is, good morning." It wasn't much of an opening, but it was the best I was going to get.

I nodded affirmatively. "I'm not sure you remember me, but I've been working on the Gemini project."

"Yes, I remember," Johnson said. He looked puzzled, as if saying to himself, "What the hell is this all about?"

"If there is any chance to speak with you for just a few minutes, I think what I have to say is very important."

Al Johnson stopped in his tracks. He turned away from me and started nodding his head in a slow, deliberate motion. While the guy who had been in front of me stayed firmly planted at my side, the rest of the group began to move, passing around the corner to the elevators. Johnson was holding his ground. With his head tilted upward, he seemed to be thinking. I asked if it would be possible to meet prior to the Gemini presentation. He finally turned back and this time nodded his head in my direction, as his penetrating stare caught my eyes, but for only a brief moment. As he began to move away, he suggested that I stop by his office around 9:00. By now it was ten minutes before the hour.

I briefly sat outside his office on the fifty-fifth floor before I was told to go in. He was very cordial as I entered, offering me a seat with a sweep of his arm. I thanked him for his time and immediately plunged into a few preliminary positive remarks in an effort to put him at ease.

"I'm very appreciative of the opportunity to be working here at NationsBank."

Sales training 101. I was trying to establish that rapport thing again, but he was still looking at me as if he suspected that I was some kind of wacko. I threw out another.

"As a relatively new hire, I have to say I am very impressed with the caliber of people working for NationsBank."

I told him that I was particularly impressed with the leadership of my manager Barbara Albrecht and her efforts in developing the strategic direction for Transaction Services. His mood didn't seem to change. Might as well just go for it. I mentioned that in my opinion Gemini had done a commendable job assisting in the development of the vision and the conceptual view of the "transaction engine." I may have laid it on a little too thick.

"I do have a concern with Gemini. They haven't convinced us that they are capable of building the engine, or that we need to build it. There may be other options, like an off-the-shelf product we could use. One thing I do know, if we continue to sole source the engine project as currently proposed, we could be exposed."

As my pilot friend indicated, words like "sole source" and "exposed" can be very powerful when talking with an executive. I went on to tell the president of NationsBank Services Company that I knew I was taking a risk coming to meet with him like this but that I felt the engine was important for our future. I really believed this. When he asked me what I would recommend as an alternative, I suggested that we send out a request for proposal to several consulting firms, asking them to bid on the design of the engine. I told him that sending bids to firms like Andersen and KPMG Consulting, as well as Gemini, would help ensure that we got the best deal for the bank—even if we ultimately decided to give the follow-on business to Gemini. A competitive bid process could make the cost numbers more realistic and give us a chance to compare different alternatives. It would also force the consultants to do some of the thinking on their time as opposed to ours.

Al Johnson asked me a little about my background and thanked me for the information. He gave no indication what he would do with it or what would happen next. I felt good that if nothing else I might have planted a few seeds of doubt before the big extravaganza. I had taken my one shot. All I could do now was wait.

I heard nothing before the final Gemini presentation. We learned that after the Gemini meeting took place, my manager, Barbara Albrecht, was behind closed doors with Al Johnson for over an hour. Based on previous experience, I prepared myself for the worst.

It was not like I was unaware of the potential fallout. I knew consultants could make high-level calls while working on projects. When an employee attempted to do the same, he was assuming a high level of risk. It wasn't the first time I had engineered a high-level executive meeting. I knew about the potential consequences. The ghosts of my past were calling again. Some people never learn. As I waited to hear about the outcome, I remembered a firsthand experience involving a botched meeting with my customer and the chairman at IBM.

IBM TIME CAPSULE: EXECUTIVE MARKETING

It was the beginning of 1990, one year since I started as the IBM marketing manager for Newport News Shipbuilding. Newport News was the largest employer in the state of Virginia and for a long time one of IBM's top manufacturing customers in the Southeast. I thought I was taking over one of the best territories in the branch, but with my usual good sense in timing, I took over the account in one of the worst possible years. Newport News depended on the U.S. Navy for business. They had just lost the Seawolf contract to their major competitor for submarine construction, Electric Boat in Groton, Connecticut—the state I had just left. Making matters worse, the previous year Newport News completed a five-year migration from Honeywell to IBM systems, and there was no plan for any significant additional IBM business for some time to come. During the migration, IBM had a nice annuity stream of revenue it could depend on with minimal selling required. It was the kind of thing that made sales reps a little cocky and complacent. Almost overnight, the stream had dried up. A few years before, IBM executives blanketed the landscape, posing with customers for one photo op after another. Now they were gone.

Newport News Shipbuilding had also become a major client of Gartner Group. Gartner was writing some very negative IBM reports back then. They were recommending that clients mix things up by installing computer products and peripherals from IBM competitors, creating more of a multivendor environment. According to customers, Gartner was suggesting that this would reduce control of IBM within their business and keep Big Blue more on its toes. Brad Wallace, a vice president with Gartner Group, had become a household name with employees at the shipyard. Another ex-IBMer turned consultant, Wallace was providing detailed information to clients on a new mainframe product that his former employer had not yet publicly announced. In the early 1990s, according to both my customer and the trade press, he and other consultants were advising clients to "squeeze" vendors to get good deals on new computer purchases. As a result, we as IBMers found ourselves engaged in discount-pricing wars with significant impact on profits.

I did some checking on the background of Wallace. I talked to one of the top development managers for IBM mainframes. Given IBM's bureaucratic structure, a guy like me rarely talked to a guy like him. We got to know each other working on a United Way project and had stayed in touch. The development manager told me that Wallace had been a "chart maker in Poughkeepsie." Yet Wallace was proclaiming to clients that he was the "father of IBM architecture" for mainframe computers. He had developed significant influence with companies like Newport News Shipbuilding.

Digital Equipment Corporation (DEC), a formidable competitor in those days, had started making inroads at Newport News. For the last few years, Gartner Group analysts were advising technology customers that DEC was becoming the new "pacesetter" for departmental computing. The president of Newport News had just signed a deal with the chairman of DEC to work together on navy integration business. Digital Equipment appeared to be winning over the hearts and minds of most of the key decision makers— amazing how that happens. During one of my first meetings with the director of information services, Frank Nichols, I was handed a document entitled "Major NNS Issues with IBM." It was a manifesto that listed grievances from his staff and presented a justification for reducing reliance on IBM and developing a closer relationship with other vendors. The document was filled with price and performance issues related to IBM products and services. The issues paper contained all the standard Gartner Group criticisms. It also talked about the lack of IBM executive attention. Nichols was still an IBM friend, but he was caught in the middle of a bad situation. He warned me that the recent lack of IBM executive focus on his upper management was damaging the relationship between our companies. Unless things changed dramatically, future business was at risk. "You'll still get some data center business now and then, but not much else." He went on to tell me that there were a few people working for him who also saw opportunity promoting DEC over IBM. "They think it will enhance their careers . . . maybe thinking they can replace yours truly."

It felt as if I had been hurled into a snake pit. While we had somehow managed to grow IBM revenue during my first year assigned to Newport News, we could not meet a quota that had been set significantly higher than the last and best year of the migration from Honeywell to IBM. I was a new marketing manager living a block from the ocean in Virginia Beach. What was not to like? I had been in tough spots before and had always figured out a way to make my quota. I'd do it again. But this time I didn't. Screw character-building experiences. It was the first time I had missed the numbers and I was a wreck, the only manager in the branch not to make it. Meeting the plan for reaching quota the next year looked equally grim and my branch manager, Toby Hobson, had set the early tone.

"Hey Steve, ya know, socialism is now officially dead in IBM. When you don't make your numbers, there's nuthin'I can do to help ya, bud."

In the beginning of 1990, I was on the ropes. Unlike my reps, I had not been there during the good years and couldn't afford to wait it out like they could until things changed—like a new manager being named, someone more agreeable who would leave them alone like in the old days. Without some unforeseen windfall, we were going to miss again, and I would be taken off of the job. I couldn't think of anything more humiliating. Toby Hobson called a meeting with my sales reps and me to discuss the territory and our plans for turning things around. Sales quotas had once again been set very aggressively. The reps presented the territory outlook for 1990. They indicated that even after a considerable stretch to make the forecast we were projecting, and even if we won all the anticipated competitive bids, we would still miss the revenue objectives. After they had concluded the presentation, Hobson said it wasn't good enough. He turned to me and asked if I had any suggestions on how we could generate more business. I pointed out that the highest level we were calling on was the director of information services, and I felt we needed to initiate an aggressive marketing campaign targeted at the executives.

"Well, Steve, you know John Akers, why don't you set up a meeting with him and the president of the shipyard?"

He immediately turned back to the reps and winked. He may have thought this was some kind of joke, but I didn't. I would figure out a way to do just that. It was true that I knew John Akers, but only because of a previous assignment. It was the United Way project, and it was run out of his office. It was an insignificant role at best, and it was not as if I was on speaking terms with Akers or any of his current administrative assistants.

After numerous calls to the IBM chairman's office, using every possible argument I could think of, his executive assistant agreed to set up a briefing. I'm not sure if any of the arguments I used were compelling enough to obtain approval, but I tried everything.

"You know, John Akers was a navy fighter pilot. He flew off of aircraft carriers built by Newport News Shipbuilding."

"I know IBM has been having problems lately in winning government contracts. The president of Newport News is friends with President Bush."

More then likely, he gave in to my request because I was relentless.

There were other conditions. I needed a direct personal commitment, which implied a meeting between me and the president of Newport News. I was also instructed to make the invitation tentative using the phrase "schedule permitting." Maybe those in the IBM chairman's office thought I would have great difficulty gaining access to the president of my customer, and they would never hear from me again. After all, I was only a marketing manager and that didn't count for much in the large bureaucratic structure of IBM. Being honest with myself, I felt they were probably right. I called the Newport News president's office asking for an appointment. To my surprise, an appointment was made.

By the time I arrived at the shipyard, the butterflies in my stomach had turned into a squad of kamikazes crashing against my intestinal walls. If any of the people I generally called on at Newport News caught wind of this, there would be hell to pay. According to his secretary, the president of Newport News liked to get in early in the morning, and I was his first appointment that day. When I entered the president's office, he greeted me with a firm handshake and a subdued yet friendly smile that helped reduce the tension I was feeling. I thanked him for his time as well as the business IBM had received over the years.

He said he appreciated my coming to meet him and asked me about my background. It was obvious he came from Boston. We talked a little about his team, the Red Sox, and also about my team, the Mets. Poor Bill

Buckner, people from Bean Town would never forget the infamous ground ball through his legs during the 1986 World Series. He had been a terrific ballplayer, forced to play while injured. Most guys probably couldn't have gotten out of bed. We agreed it really wasn't his fault. It was the curse of the Red Sox that went back to the days when they traded Babe Ruth to the New York Yankees. After I discussed the briefing and presented a tentative agenda, I told him that, schedule permitting, the chairman of IBM would join him for lunch.

"He would do that for me?" he asked.

"Absolutely. You are an important customer."

He indicated that he would be delighted to accept the invitation. As the meeting concluded, I mentioned that I had one other request. I told him that I had noticed a book on a credenza in the waiting room. The subject was one hundred years of shipbuilding. I asked him if I could have a copy to give to my chairman. He asked me to wait in his office. When he returned, the president of the shipyard said, "Here is a copy for your chairman and here is a copy for you." I thanked him for the generosity and said I would be in touch regarding tentative dates. As I left his office, I felt as if I had hit a grand slam.

A date was confirmed on Aker's calendar. A different assistant was assigned to work with me. She seemed excited that she had been able to help set this up and instructed me to contact the president of Newport News Shipbuilding to confirm with him as well. It seemed to be a lock, schedules permitting. In spite of my feelings of accomplishment, there were no commendations, not even a slap on the back for my efforts. Instead, the news of the briefing set off the smoke alarms and fire detectors from my branch in Norfolk, Virginia, all the way up the coast to IBM headquarters in New York. I had been worried about chain of command issues with my customer. It never occurred to me there would be problems within my own company.

The briefing was canceled. My instructions were to call the office for the president of the shipyard and say that the meeting had to be "postponed." I was informed that the IBM area manager, three levels up in the organizational hierarchy, was very upset. "He gets real nervous about things like this." Going back to the IBM chairman's office, I asked if under the circumstances they could send a letter I drafted, explaining that it was unfortunate that the meeting needed to be postponed and also thanking the president of the shipyard for the book. I was told by one of the assistants to the chairman "that would be inappropriate at this time." As if it might be appropriate at some later date. Subsequently, Hobson clued me in that the area manager was even more furious about my latest call to Aker's office. I was instructed not to contact the chairman's office "ever again."

Shortly after, the area manager came to the branch for a "roundtable meeting" with the marketing managers. He was an IBM celebrity. The management committee had decided he had the best "customer-driven" strategy when compared with all the other area managers. I was told they loved his presentation. It didn't seem to matter that his area had missed last year's quota and ranked lowest in customer-feedback surveys. The sales slogan that year was "make it your business." By that time, IBM's gravy train days were obviously over. A video had been released in which John Akers was desperately asking marketing reps and managers to get aggressive and take more risks. When Hobson had asked for an explanation as to why I had gone to Aker's office "with no authority to do so," I had referenced the Akers video in my defense. As the meeting started, the area manager looked directly at me with a skin-piercing stare. He came from the Southeast and spoke with a pronounced drawl. He said that the chairman didn't do many customer briefings. When he did, I was told, it was only with select, high-potential customers, "certainly not a Newport News Shipbuilding." Others laughed.

"When we say 'make it your business,' we really mean, make it 'my business.' When we say 'take risk,' we mean 'controlled risk.'"

As I glanced around the room, it appeared that the other managers were getting quite a charge out of all of this. At the time, I couldn't figure out why this had generated such a negative response. Obviously, IBM senior management did not see large business potential in my territory. No one else did either. In their minds, I had skirted the organizational hierarchy.

Maybe it was also because IBM was a "no surprises" culture. No one was quite sure what the president of Newport News might say. If Akers asked which IBM people the president of Newport News knew, it could be an embarrassment. Select customers were prescreened: relationships had been developed, and they could be counted on to say only the right thing. Possibly, if given this kind of exposure, they would compliment the right senior manager in front of the chairman. After all those spectacular years of considerable business coming from Newport News Shipbuilding, no one in the marketing chain of command had met the president, except for a low-level marketing manager who flaunted his irreverence to protocol and took uncontrolled risks. Upper management had given up on my account. While our time was sucked up even more by internal meetings, processes, protocols, and manipulating numbers, Newport News Shipbuilding was being left for the consultants and other vendors to exploit.

There had been considerable emphasis to make our first-quarter quota. IBM had posted a dismal earnings report for the end of 1989, which rattled Wall Street. The pressure was on. Forget year-end, I was now being told that if my team didn't meet the revenue quota objectives for the first quarter, I would be taken off of the job. There was no early-year business on the table. As a defense contractor, business was awarded only after an extended competitive bid process. In fear of more antitrust litigation, IBM had imposed strict business guidelines that went well beyond the letter of the law when conducting business with government suppliers. And IBM sales personnel were held to high ethical standards to avoid even the appearance of impropriety. Doing anything out of the ordinary could put all future business with the government at risk. It could also cost you your job.

With, my manager Toby Hobson's approval, I credited a business that would go out for competitive bid later that year, mortgaging our immediate future on a high-risk gamble. "Do what you gotta do," I was told by Hobson. As it turned out, we weren't the only team crediting future business.

First-quarter earnings for IBM in 1990 were very positive. John Akers was quoted as saying, "Our strategy of listening to our customers and improving the competitiveness of our products and services is working." Wall Street apparently agreed. It was the best first quarter in years, helping to drive up the Dow Jones Industrials. Analysts were suggesting that IBM had turned the battleship around, and they were optimistic in their future projections.

Luckily, we were able to make the credited first-quarter business at Newport News Shipbuilding good, but we were still a long way from making our quota. It was not all I had to worry about. A month or so later Toby came to see me.

"You know, Steve, considering everything, you are lucky you were able to make first-quarter numbers. But, you did credit the business before it was good. I'm afraid you need to get approval for this from IBM Marketing Practices. They are very concerned about this."

Apparently a "do what you gotta do" from Toby didn't count as management sign-off. And how did Marketing Practices know anything about it if Toby hadn't told them? I certainly didn't.

Marketing Practices Group out of Washington, D.C., reported to the area manager. The group had a reputation of ripping apart sales reps for the slightest of infractions. In my case, I figured they'd really be loaded for bear. "What part of the warning directly from your own area manager about 'controlled risk' didn't you understand?"

I decided to take it straight to Corporate Marketing Practices where my chances of getting an approval had to be at least slightly better to even. Toby said Marketing Practices; he didn't say Area Marketing Practices. Nobody had ever indicated that chain of command protocol applied here. It also didn't hurt that a sales rep from my old branch was now working at Corporate Marketing Practices. He helped walk it through the process and got it approved. I would owe him big time.

At our next meeting, Toby asked, "So, didn't I tell you that you needed to go to Marketing Practices?"

"I did." I reached into my briefcase and pulled out the approval letter.

Toby put on his granny-like reading spectacles, which hung low off his hawk nose, and stared at the paper for a few moments.

"You went to Corporate. . . ."

I jumped in before he could get off any rounds. "Remember I took a few personal days last week? Well, I was in New York and thought I'd get it taken care of while there."

Toby looked pissed. There wasn't much he could do. I had stepped around the bear trap this time. Next time, I might not be so lucky.

I decided for the rest of the year to focus exclusively on generating sales, keeping a low profile, and maintaining a "team player" attitude. It would be my only chance at surviving. That is, until the year-end numbers were in. Then I was certain I'd be toast.

❊ ❊ ❊ ❊ ❊

Keeping a low profile and demonstrating that I was a good team player would be important at NationsBank as well. No one within my management reporting structure directly confronted me regarding the meeting that I had with the president of the Services Company. That seemed to be one of the nuances of NationsBank culture. Senior managers avoided discussing the unpleasant things with subordinates. Decisions were made behind closed doors. Sometimes major changes were implemented without being announced, not even to the individuals or groups who would be affected. These changes could result in the shifting or trading of employees from one manager to another. Because the organizational structure employed a matrix style of management where an associate could be on "loan" to another manager for an extended period of time, changes were often not clearly defined. One of the standard lines I used to hear was "If my manager calls, please get the name."

Staying within the chain of command was very important for employees at NationsBank. Process, protocol, and your place in the pecking order were not to be ignored. While nothing was said to me directly, for a period of time my relationship with Barbara Albrecht had turned to glacial ice. Her immediate manager let it be known through the corporate grapevine that he wasn't thrilled with me operating like a loose scud. It wasn't that I was craving the visibility. I had been well aware of the potential repercussions, but had talked myself into doing it anyway.

Barbara Albrecht put a tighter chain on me for a while, asking me to report to her on a weekly basis so I could share *all* of my activities. I was also assigned to several additional project-management activities. Did they really think making me busier would keep from getting in more trouble?

For a while it seemed that all my call on Al Johnson had done was to confirm my burgeoning pariah status in the Services Company. The only fallout seemed to be that I wasn't getting invited to as many planning sessions. Not that this was so terribly disappointing. Then one day Barbara told me that an executive vice president had been assigned to "validate Gemini's assumptions" and make recommendations to Al Johnson on what we needed to do. It seemed like we were never going to get past this validation of assumptions stuff. "Al's lost confidence in the Gemini work," she said with her eyes in missile lock.

This particular executive vice president was Denny Billings. He was point man for bank president Ken Lewis on one of NationsBank's most important efforts in consolidating new banking acquisitions. It was called "Model Bank," and Ken Lewis, who was "widely considered the likely successor to Chief Executive Hugh McColl Jr., is the architect of Model Banking."[2] Denny Billings was the program manager. He worked for Services Company president Al Johnson, with dotted line—a matrix management convention implying an informal, direct connection—to Lewis on Model Bank. Denny Billings was a NationsBank heavy hitter.

Model Bank was a collaborative effort between NationsBank, Andersen Consulting, and another vendor called Alltel Information Systems. McColl, Lewis, and their lieutenants were always quoted as saying that Model Bank was critical to NationsBank's growth strategy. Andersen and Alltel were critical in making this possible. I didn't pick up on it right away, but I was about to get a crash course on Andersen Consulting and its powerful relationship with NationsBank.

Model Bank was a major project to standardize the branch offices as well as back-office systems. As far back as February 1994, an article in *Bank Marketing* noted that the Model Bank program was a major reengineering effort, "where standards for quality service and products are being examined and implemented from the customers' perspective." Rusty Rainey, a NationsBank executive, was quoted as saying: "We're looking at everything and considering its overall return to the company. You have to spend money to make this happen, but there are some savings as common systems are consolidated to eliminate some costs."[3] In the same article, Joel Friedman, a managing partner for Andersen Consulting, said, "You have to keep an open mind and be willing to shoot a few sacred cows. Retail banks are competing with nonbanks that have a 10-to-1 cost advantage."[4] There was that FUD thing again.

Model Bank had become the new "sacred cow" at NationsBank and was still going strong. Andersen and Alltel were silent partners. With all the press regarding Model Bank, NationsBank executives rarely mentioned Andersen or Alltel in their public statements—even though they played critical roles in both the implementation and ongoing day-to-day operations. In effect, Model Bank, though operating in NationsBank facilities, had been outsourced to Andersen and Alltel personnel. Perhaps it was thought that continuing to run within our own facilities could avoid some of the problems of the past. NationsBank management was still involved in running project-planning meetings. According to the organization charts, NationsBank management still held ultimate accountability—and why shouldn't it? If it went into the ditch, it would be management at the bank who had been taking the bows who would also take the fall. So much for the theory that consultants eliminated the risk of decision making.

Andersen had skyrocketed as one of the most successful consulting firms in the world. The consulting business had started to significantly outpace the traditional accounting practice of its parent, Arthur Andersen LLP, in revenue generation. It had more than doubled in consulting revenue since the operations were separated in 1989.[5] At the time, they were still skirmishing in the courts to make the separate operations separate companies. While the accounting business had provided the credibility that made it possible to build a successful consulting practice, now that consulting was more successful, they didn't want to share the success with the parent. They would fight it out for a few more years before Andersen consulting would split, becoming Accenture Ltd., on July 19, 2001.[6] Andersen would continue to provide consulting related primarily to accounting and auditing services, but the lucrative vertical-industry consulting and integration business would go to Accenture. Luckily, this major division of the firm broke away before the Enron scandel broke.

Alltel, a firm from Little Rock, Arkansas, provided technical products and services, had entered the telecommunications business, and had established a successful outsourcing business—a business Andersen was attempting to exploit more and more with clients. I had been told that just like Hugh McColl at NationsBank, the senior executives at Alltel were major supporters of another Arkansas native, President Bill Clinton. The chairman of Alltel, Joe Ford, a former Arkansas state senator, and his wife, Jo Ellen Ford, were listed as Arkansas FOBs (Friends of Bill) who were part of the controversial "White House Sleepover List," where it was alleged that the Lincoln Bedroom and other presidential facilities were provided in return for campaign contributions and other favors.[7] At one time the information services core company of Alltel had been called Systematics and was represented by Hillary Rodham Clinton and Webster Hubbell, attorneys of record from the Rose Law Firm.[8]

Andersen provided project-management assistance for Model Bank while the ongoing system support was run by Alltel. I did some checking and found out that Andersen Consulting and Alltel had originally joined forces in 1991 to jointly market software, systems integration, and data-processing services to the banking industry. In making the announcement, William E. Storts, Andersen's managing partner for Retail Financial Services had said at the time, "We felt we needed hooks to good application software for banking."[9] So much for maintaining the independent and objective consulting view. Bankers wanted to reduce the risk in decision making. Andersen Consulting wanted "hooks." Together, think of the possibilities.

Model Bank had become a huge NationsBank initiative for Andersen and Alltel. It was credited for providing the necessary technology for NationsBank to standardize bank services and increase productivity.[10] We were told Model Bank was a major competitive advantage by making it possible to accelerate acquisition activities.

There was one small problem with the Model Bank solution. It was the middle of 1996, almost two years later, and it was still not fully implemented. Major states in the NationsBank franchise, such as North Carolina, South Carolina, and Texas, were not yet converted over to Model Bank. NationsBank was still operating like a federation of separate organizations.

When I first started at NationsBank, I had opened an account in a branch downstairs from company headquarters in Charlotte. Barbara had asked me to work from corporate for a few months so I could get to know some of the important people there, including personnel from the Corporate Strategic Technology Group (STG). When I finally arrived in Atlanta, I walked into the downtown branch and tried to take care of some business. I was told, "Sorry, you'll have to contact your bank in Charlotte"—as if it was a completely separate bank. The explanation was that they were on separate computing systems. They didn't even offer to let me use their phones. Not exactly what I'd call responsive customer service. I showed them my SVP business card, but that didn't help either. They worked for a separate NationsBank organization. If I didn't work for them, I would have taken my money elsewhere. Anyway, Model Bank was supposed to fix all this. From reading the trade press, it sounded like everything had already been done.

My manager, Barbara Albrecht, said that Gemini was being given another thirty days to complete the technology design work. Barbara said she would hold off on paying Gemini until they completed the work they had committed to in the contract. Almost immediately, three technical consultants billed as architects from Cap Gemini appeared on the scene to sprint the last lap and help collect the dough. These people were pretty good. Too bad we didn't get them earlier in the project.

I was told that Denny Billings, the executive vice president for Model Bank, liked to use Andersen Consulting for just about everything. He was a low-key banker who often spoke with slow, thoughtful pauses interspersed in the middle of his sentences. If the literary wit Dorothy Parker and Billings ever met, she might have called him "a rhinestone in the rough, who spoke at glacier speed."[11] He was tall and lanky with a high squeaky voice, which sounded a bit whiney when he wanted to make a point. Denny and I went out to dinner one evening in August 1996 when our paths crossed while working on separate bank activities in Dallas. He told me that NationsBank was a difficult place for someone new to gain acceptance. He said that he would work with me in getting to know the right people and attempting to move my career in the right direction.

"You could have a good future here," he said.

When I asked him for advice on how I could pick up the broken glass I had shattered within my current reporting structure and get back in good graces, Denny said, "I wouldn't worry about it. No, don't worry about it. We need to get on with this engine."

Ben Elders's end run begot my end run, which begot one more end run. By slamming Gemini, I had opened the door for Andersen. They had executed a successful "preeminent" strike. I wasn't ecstatic about how it played out, but at least now I'd have a chance to work with the best.

SUMMARY OF OBSERVATIONS

- Within corporations, consultants will leverage their access to senior management to put their own spin on things, dodge bullets, and neutralize potential threats.

- Employees do not have the same level of access to senior management, as the consultants do. Employees take great personal risk when attempting to present a different point of view than what highly paid consultants have already presented and carefully packaged. Companies need to consider building a communications program for employees so that consultants can't pit one employee, or group of employees, against others.

- Companies sometimes attempt to create a public relations perception for stockholders, customers, and the general public that can be inconsistent with operational objectives.

- Background and references of consultants should be verified, just like employees. Too often consultants hide behind the argument they can't disclose previous clients because of confidentiality agreements. It helps them more than their clients. Make reference verification a prerequisite for engagement. Surely they can identify previous clients who could talk about their skills and capabilities without disclosing confidential information about their companies. Let previous clients decide versus the consultant what can be said or not said.

- Competitive bid processes can help keep consultants more honest.

- Matrix management can add mixed signals, uncertainty, and complexity to the manager/employee relationships in business operations.

NOTES

1. Willy Stern and Gail Edmondson, "Memo to Gemini: Read This Book," *Business Week*, 26 June 1995, 40.

2. David Mildonberg, "New NB Fees a Bottom Line," *Business Journal*, 21 February 1997, http://charlotte.bcentral.com/charlotte/stories/1997/02/24/story4.html.

3. Katherine Morrall, "Re-engineering the Bank," *Bank Marketing* (February 1994): 68.

4. Ibid., 67.

5. Alex Markels, "Consulting Giant's Hot Offer: Jobs, Jobs, Jobs," *Wall Street Journal*, 6 March 1996, B1.

6. "Briefing.com Story: Accenture," *Cnet.com*, 19 July 2001, http://investor.cnet.com/ investor/news/newsitem/0-9900-1028-661330-0.html.

7. "White House Sleepover List," 23 September 2000, http://detnews.com/2000/nation/0009/23/nation-124065.htm.

8. Bill Frezza, "Conspiracies Afloat: Keeping Tabs on the Inslaw Affair," *CommunicationsWeek*, 11 August 1997, 28.

9. Karen Gullo, "Andersen, Systematics Join to Offer Technology Services," *American Banker*, 18 September 1991, 2.

10. Mary Jo Foley, "Service with Smiles, Thanks to OS/2," *PC Week*, 19 June 1995, 25.

11. http://users.rcn.com/lyndanyc/dorothy.html, Marion Meade, *Dorothy Parker What Fresh Hell Is This* (New York: Penguin Books, 1989), 171.

CHAPTER EIGHT

SINK, SWIM, OR FLOAT

Gemini's work was labeled a "top-down" view. Not that it started at the top. And it didn't go very far down. It was the "vision" thing, immersed in eye-catching graphics that gave it the perception of possessing high-level strategic merit. Amazing what a few good-looking charts can do.

We were now learning that at the same time we were working with Gemini on the top-down view, Andersen Consulting was contracted by another group in NationsBank to provide a "bottom-up" review. As coincidence would have it, they were both looking at ways to replace the current routing and settlement systems as the tangible solution for their respective visions. In other words, what we were calling a transaction engine. Of course if NationsBank wanted to implement either engine solution, it would require purchasing additional consulting, along with a significant outlay of funds for hardware and software. I was painfully aware that by going to Division President Al Johnson I had played right into the hands of Andersen and they were now driving.

Piecing it together, when Andersen originally lost the contract awarded to Gemini, they didn't exactly pack their bags and go home. Instead, they had found another group within Transaction Services to hire them—a group where they were already doing work. It was for a lot less money, but it kept them in the game. This was a very astute move. Gemini couldn't say that only they understood the Transaction Services environment after weeks of careful review and assessment. It diffused the typical arguments from the incumbent vendor assigned to a project. "Time to market is everything. We hit the ground running. Anyone else, you'd have to first bring up to speed." Andersen had been studying it as well. No need to train them either.

The group that hired Andersen was called Integration Services. Like Barbara Albrecht's strategy group, Integration Services was part of Transaction Services, but where we were charged with strategy, they were responsible for the "hands-on" processing of payments, both checks and electronic.[1]

Integration Services was the group responsible for running the current transaction systems. The senior manager of this group was Darlene Wittington. Darlene was a tall, striking African American lady with a quick smile and a wonderful sense of humor—except when she was around Barbara. Where Barbara worked on creating the image of a corporate sophisticate, perfectly coiffed, dressed in the latest fashion from the catwalks of Rome or Paris, Darlene was homespun, almost always "business casual" in her attire. She was family oriented, often sharing the latest updates on her kids at school, before, after, and sometimes in the middle of business discussions. Darlene was well liked, but everyone knew how she felt about Barbara. You didn't have to be Inspector Clouseau. Her tall body stiffened and her voice dropped a few octaves whenever Barbara entered the room.

Darlene was the one of those senior managers who had lost some of her best people to Barbara Albrecht when the new strategy group was formed in Transaction Services. She was obviously not pleased with Gemini's work. She was less pleased with Barbara. Darlene didn't want anyone, especially Barbara and her consultants, interfering with her part of the business anymore than they already had. They would be most effected be a new transaction engine.

Between top-downs and bottom-ups, surely one of these consulting groups would stumble on good information we could use to improve the business. If bank management didn't like their work, there could be only one other alternative: hire another consulting firm. That's how we at NationsBank did business. By now it had become pretty clear that hardly anything was done at NationsBank without hiring consultants. If you wanted to put an idea across to upper management, you needed to get a consultant to take it forward for you. If you didn't like what a consultant was saying, hire another one.

Unlike Gemini, with emphasis on analysis and a "model" approach for creating a "vision," Andersen Consulting had a reputation of focusing on execution. I remembered thinking to myself at the time, "At least now we have a shot at a down-to-earth, feet-on-the-street approach." According to a 1993 article in *Fortune*, "Andersen leads the world in system integration."[2] This was the business of configuring hardware and software for systems to work together, as well as managing the implementation. As noted by *Fortune*, "Despite its name, Andersen Consulting is not exactly a classic management consulting firm in the mahogany-paneled mode of a McKinsey & Company or a Boston Consulting Group. Andersen is not the place you're likely to turn to first if your paradigm needs a shift, your shareholder value needs enhancement, or your core needs competency."[3] If nothing else, Andersen was sure to serve as an interesting contrast from Gemini. Even with all the high marks afforded Andersen, I wasn't going into the next round with blinders. Integrators were the plumbers, and they sometimes forgot to start with the blueprint.

In the last ten years with the advent of open systems, technical integration had become a huge moneymaker for consultants, and nobody had done better at it than Andersen. Consultants were still arguing that the sharing of technical specifications among vendors, along with creating open-systems standard bodies, would help customers save money by pitting vendors against each other.

What customers were now learning the hard way was that it also added significant complexity. No matter how "open" they claimed to be, there was no such thing as plug and play for corporate installations. Considerable integration was required to get different vendor products to work together, and it wasn't a one-time effort. Trying to capitalize on new technological advances became much more precarious. A new upgrade or software release from one vendor in the mix could send compatibility ripples through the entire open-systems configuration. Other vendors would often need to upgrade their product, or add fixes, to maintain compatibility and avoid failures. There were more points for potential failure, and they were more difficult to trace. Who do I call if something breaks? Combine this with the cost of consultants to help integrate and manage vendors. Costs did anything but go down. More and more information technology projects were missing deadlines. More than ever before they were coming in overbudget. It was usually blamed on the technology being so new. It was rarely blamed on the consultants who had quickly moved from advising to cashing in on the lucrative integration business.

About two-thirds of Andersen's revenue was coming from this area, "a market where strategy firms have either limited presence or none at all."[4] By 1996 other firms were beginning to give Andersen a run for its money. These included the other Big Five accounting firms now in consulting (and still counting downward). The Big Five included Andersen, Price Waterhouse, Ernst and Young, KPMG, and Deloitte & Touche. At one time it had been the Big Eight. As far as consulting was concerned, for a long time it was Andersen and the Seven Dwarfs. Then through a series of mergers, the Big Six, Five. Perhaps one day the Big One. Missing deadlines and budgets wasn't as bad for them. It meant more billable hours.

Other successful integrators included technology vendors such as Hewlett Packard and IBM, as well as some of the traditional strategy firms. Everyone was looking to cash in on this lucrative opportunity area that Andersen had helped pioneer. Andersen complimented integration with additional services including software development, project management, and management consulting. Andersen Consulting had been working closely with the NationsBank Integration Services organization for several years providing an assortment of these services. They had penetrated organizations all over the bank. The most notable exception was Barbara's group where Gemini had taken over. Until now.

After putting my career on the line with that impromptu meeting with Al Johnson, people within Transaction Services started coming out of the woodwork criticizing Gemini. All of a sudden I was popular. I was invited to planning sessions again, and even an occasional lunch or dinner. Gemini was now openly demonized. Darlene Wittington said that the Gemini work was abstract and couldn't be implemented. "Great fiction," she said. "Not much good for us down here living in the real world." Denny Billings, who was now reviewing the work and meeting regularly with Gemini, said he could never understand what the Gemini consultants were talking about. Harvey Kraft, the operations manager responsible for electronic payments, said that the Gemini work lacked relevance to the business. I knew that Denny Billings and Darlene Wittington had close ties to Andersen. So did Harvey Kraft, as I would soon discover.

Then something strange happened. A series of meetings were scheduled by Denny Billings. He asked me to present Gemini's findings to managers from various areas within the bank. Apparently his way of evaluating the work done by Gemini was to get other opinions. Why me? I was the guy who nailed them in front of Al Johnson.

After mulling it over, I somehow managed to talk myself into thinking that there were some good things Gemini had captured in their presentation charts. As one of the other managers from Barbara Albrecht's strategy group said, "You have to give Gemini credit, the charts they produce look really sharp." While there may not have been much behind the charts, my feeling was that they had clearly identified a major problem. Gemini was right about NationsBank needing to move aggressively from physical checks to electronic transactions. It was the lack of documented requirements combined with no real tangible plans that I found most bothersome. I would try to focus on the Gemini charts that made the case for change. This was still the direction we needed to go. If this was a rationalization, I didn't spend a lot of time worrying about it.

Ironically, I became the Gemini pitchman. Gemini representatives were invited to the review meetings. It was only fair as the meetings were all about reviewing their work.

When I suggested that they get involved in the presentation, they declined. For most of the meetings, the Gemini consultants sat and watched. They told me that having someone from the bank present added credibility. Somehow they didn't realize I was the guy who had put them under the microscope in the first place. With me in this role, they were flirting with danger because I rarely followed the script. Apparently there was no one else, either on our side or theirs, who could do it, or was willing to do it—except for maybe Richard Edmonds, the British chap.

Unfortunately, Edmonds was not part of the reduced Gemini team still on the ground. He had been reassigned to a new client in some other far-off land where the Union Jack flew no more. He was getting there via Air India, no doubt. With me taking his place as the presenter, I'm sure the Gemini project manager found my regular deviations from the overhead slide material cause for grief. In spite of swelling criticism of their work, they were still hoping to snag a follow-on contract. Eternal optimists, I suspect. They certainly had the wrong closer with me.

In spite of some obvious drawbacks, the meetings went well. I talked about the importance of embracing a consistent electronic-banking solution for all applications. Trying to make the point that whether it was an automated teller machine (ATM) transaction, a wire transfer, or a PC-based home-banking payment, it didn't make sense to maintain or create new separate transaction engines for posting and settlement—not for customer convenience, and not from a banking-efficiency view. A comprehensive one-size-fits-all electronic-payments solution was the way to go. We needed a standard transaction engine that could catch and pitch payments for everybody.

Judging from the discussion that followed the presentations, there was agreement that NationsBank needed to address new transactional requirements with a standardized brand-new approach. At least publicly there was consensus. I was feeling pumped. The turf wars for the engine either stopped or went underground. In either case, it worked to our advantage in promoting a unified transaction engine initiative to executive management. Everything seemed to be pointing to electronic payments over checks and a green light for moving forward.

The most reassuring part for me was that the arguments used in the Gemini presentations seemed to be consistent with public statements from NationsBank Chairman Hugh McColl. If they didn't like it, they could talk to the big guy. Hugh had been arguing for some time that electronic banking had the potential of reducing the costs of doing business and making physical location immaterial. In his public statements, he consistently embraced change. Market trends would create the impetus for a mass exodus of customers from traditional banking services and NationsBank needed to be ready. Sifting through his published speeches and press quotes, Hugh McColl seemed to understand the potential benefits, as well as the threats. It was less than a year earlier, at a retail banking conference, that he had told bankers that technology companies with control of the electronic medium could ultimately gain control of the customer relationship. Banks needed to act sooner rather than later, he said, and NationsBank planned to lead in this area. Taking it literally, it sure seemed we were on the right track. I was always hunting for McColl quotes to help justify the effort.

Looking through NationsBank press releases and the text of executive speeches at conferences, I was beginning to realize why Barbara was obsessed with proving Bill Gates wrong. It was because the top dog was obsessed himself. The NationsBank chairman referenced the Bill Gates "dinosaur" comment in more than one speech. Addressing a retail banking conference, he suggested that Gates had it wrong. McColl said, "Unlike the dinosaur, bankers can see changes ahead. We have a choice in the matter the dinosaur never did." Hugh McColl also pointed out that industry mergers and acquisitions represented the old "paradigm."[5] Banks needed to grow by using new technology wisely, not by buying other banks with archaic infrastructures. Did this mean that the man who helped pioneer interstate banking acquisitions and was responsible for over fifty in the last thirteen years had adopted a new strategy for growth? It sure sounded like it.

As a keynote speaker at another industry conference, McColl warned banks of the need to fundamentally change the way they did business. The real fear was not as much Bill Gates and Microsoft, but inertia within banking, he said. McColl recommended new emphasis on electronic commerce and strategic partnerships. This could have been lifted right out of the Gemini charts. In many of his comments in the press, McColl emphasized these same points over and over again. He stressed the importance of spending on strategic technology over traditional banking and cost cutting. Hanging on to the old ways of doing business would hurt banks in the long run, according to McColl.

Speeches by the NationsBank chairman were highly praised. In addition to being picked up in the trade press, excerpts were often distributed throughout NationsBank. He had become somewhat of a celebrity with Wall Street. His southern drawl and wise cracking, humorous responses blended well with his larger-than-life persona and his unquenchable ambition to pull out all the stops to get his way.

It sounded like we were on the right track with the focus on electronic payments. It was consistent with McColl's directives. Yet senior management within the NationsBank Services Company continued the old refrain, "checks will always be around." They argued that with our latest acquisition of Bank South Corp., just before I was hired, in January 1996, the check-processing base was actually increasing in size and would become an even more important part of the business, at least for the next few years to come. They had a point. In the past we had acquired banks that looked just like us. They also pointed out that industry analysts had been predicting the conversion from paper checks to electronic transactions for some time, but there was no hard evidence to support any dramatic shifts in the United States. My concern was that while we waited for approaching signs from the sky, astute competitors were working on ways of controlling the floodgates. Wasn't this precisely what the chairman of the bank was trying to warn us about? We were facing a limited window that demanded aggressive action.

Published reports supported McColl's conclusions that there wasn't a lot of time left. Several consultants from McKinsey were quoted in *American Banker* suggesting that in the payments sector banks were losing significant ground to nonbanks. These nonbank competitors such as mutual funds and brokerage houses were skimming the cream, targeting the highly profitable electronic transactions and leaving the more costly cash-and check-processing burdens to banks. "Because the banking business is 'fairly fragmented,' bankers don't even notice," said Jack Stephenson, a principal from McKinsey.[6] Studies showed that intermediary assets held by insured depository institutions had shrunk from 75 percent in 1950 to less than 30 percent by 1995.[7]

All indications were that this trend would continue as money market and mutual funds cut deeper into traditional-banking market share. Bank advisory organizations such as the Bank Administration Institute (BAI) were recommending increased emphasis on electronic payment systems as a way of fighting back.[8] The answer was not merely sitting on committees or commissioning additional studies. It wasn't conducting business as usual, either.

After the round of meetings with various NationsBank groups discussing the Gemini vision and the transaction engine, Denny Billings and I met with Andersen. We were given a chance to review the work they were doing on the "bottom-up" initiative. Several representatives from the Andersen project team attended the meeting. One of the Andersen consultants attending was named Peter Miles. He held what I thought must have been a unique position at NationsBank for a nonemployee. He worked in the role of a manager with the NationsBank Integration Services organization, reporting to Darlene Wittington. He actually appeared on the Integration Services organization chart as a direct report to Darlene. In fact, since joining the bank, I had assumed he was an employee. Miles functioned as if he worked for the bank on a full-time basis, managing both employees and other consultants.[9] He blended well. The talk was that he had been in Andersen for a while and was desperate to become a partner.

Whereas Gemini was focused primarily on developing electronic-banking capability, the Andersen work focused almost exclusively on check processing. The bottom-up was nothing more than a back-office operational view, offering some basic improvements to the current system. Their version of the transaction engine was nothing more than a bigger, better, faster system for routing and posting checks. Up until this point, my assumption was that we were all talking about electronic routing as the number one priority for meeting current and future demands. At least, that was what I was talking about in the meetings in which I presented. It was the reason I was hired. It was the reason the engine project was launched. It was all the buzz in the banking industry. More important, if the press reports were accurate, it was also an important obsession with Hugh McColl.

Besides, almost everyone agreed that NationsBank had check processing down cold. There were plans moving forward to make it Y2K compliant. Needed changes could be made and new mainframes could be added to handle additional workload. There didn't appear to be any burning need to reengineer the process. It was the electronic side that was wanting. There were pressing needs for electronic capability in this changing market that required immediate attention. These needs also hit close to home. Several of the business units we supported were developing new applications based on Internet technology. We needed a new transaction engine that could handle these new routing requirements, or each of these units would be forced to go off and build or buy their own. We didn't need a whole new generation of silos.

Andersen was also recommending that we rebuild our float-management system as a major component of the transaction engine. Float management was one of the critical elements in check processing, a repository for warehoused check information that runs interest calculations. Individuals and businesses deposit millions of checks every day. Banks could make interest income from those combined check payments before they were cleared to the depositor. Essentially the uncollected payment became an available asset on the books of the bank, before the customer was given access to her own deposited check. Rather than sort all the collected checks and send each one back to the bank it was drawn upon for settlement, banks transfer checks to Federal Reserve banks for collection.

Float occurred as these funds are double counted for a period of time before collection and settlement. The reserve banks paid interest to the depositing banks for the total amount of checks transferred. Based on volume, this could represent a substantial sum. Banks earn interest from the Fed, sometimes for two to three days, working the float. The case could be made that banks were freezing the customers' money while they themselves used it for their own gain.

In a 1996 published report, Kirstin E. Wells, a senior analyst with the Federal Reserve, had calculated the float value of an average check to be approximately $0.09[10] I had been told that NationsBank processed close to 90 million checks a day, 365 days a year. Based on these assumptions, float for NationsBank could represent more than $8 million of daily income, or an astounding $2.9 billion a year. Although float was a very profitable source of income for banks, it's contribution to the bottom line was hardly ever publicly discussed. The income statements made available by banks rarely broke it out. I guess most bankers felt the less said about this topic the better.

There had been much research commissioned by banks, including the work we had just completed with Gemini Consulting, to evaluate why U.S. consumers were not more eagerly adopting electronic-payment alternatives to writing checks. Some of them actually interviewed customers. Electronic payment would be easier to use and more cost efficient for both the customer and the bank. Theoretically, electronic-transaction capabilities would spell doom for checks. Instant transactions via electronic systems would also eliminate float.

Mary L. King, in her book *The Great American Banking Snafu*, pointed out the problem was not with the banking customer. "Hence, it is not consumers who have blocked EFTS (Electronic Funds Transfer Systems), because they are the winners; it is the large check issuers, including the bankers who created the system. Banks that issue payrolls, dividends, and trust account payments have not used EFT because the float value of the checks they issue far exceeds the cost of issuing them."[11] Banks couldn't depend on float forever. Electronic capabilities would allow for more customer convenience, ease of use, immediate account updates, and reduced banking costs, which could be passed back to the customer. Now that the technology was here, if banks didn't provide it, someone else would.

A sinister thought flashed through my brain. We had commissioned Gemini to study customers' reluctance to switch from checks to electronic banking under the stipulation that they not talk to our customers. Was it only because we did not want to bother our consumers with another study, or was it also to avoid putting the idea of switching from checks to more convenient methods into any more heads? Like most banks facing competitive pressures, NationsBank did have a home-banking program for interested customers, but this was still a relatively small number of customers with PC equipment, PC knowledge, and a willingness to pioneer the concept in spite of potential start-up problems. Our home-banking software offered only limited function and could not provide a complete solution for replacing checks for all customers. Like other institutions, we were counting hits on our Web site as proof that we had made a successful transition to the Internet. Web hits and doing real e-business are very separate things. If all our customers decided to switch to electronic banking, we would have been incapable of accommodating them. We just didn't have the electronic capability or capacity to support the volume. It would take a considerable all-out effort to transition from checks to electronic. It would take a powerful new transaction engine. More important, it would take seriously committed management, and I was concerned that there were still a whole lot of check bigots running the Services Company.

Float had become a major controversy in the 1980s, when consumer groups began an extensive campaign to change bank policies.[12] Even the nation's most powerful banks couldn't escape the consumer revolution launched by concerned advocates like Ralph Nader. Corporate executive types often dismissed the champion of consumer causes as if he were nothing more than a crazed fanatic, out of touch with reality. They would say things like: "If Nader went to an X-rated movie, he would come out complaining that the mattresses were flammable." Some might call it fanaticism. Perhaps it was more a question of vigilance and integrity. Safer cars, improved food packaging, regulations controlling the use of cyclamates and DTT, along with countless other examples, could be attributed to Nader's leadership. He had made all of our lives safer, including his critics. The fight over float was about getting bank executives to recognize that they were playing with customers' money and not their own. Even if they could drown out all the consumer advocates of the world, sooner or later someone would make better solutions available that didn't rely on float. It was about putting the customer first in more than advertising slogans.

While consumer advocates achieved some success in curbing abuses associated with float, electronic banking would provide the knockout punch. There would be no float with real-time electronic payments. In the meantime, some banks like NationsBank still managed to exploit it in varying degrees. As customers became more sophisticated in managing their money and using alternative electronic-payment instruments, float was expected to nose-dive. Float was also considered one of the most complex systems inside a bank and would take years to rebuild. More to the point, NationsBank was considered to have one of the best float systems in the industry. It had been acquired during the purchase of another bank. I would never forget the advice I had once received from a client at Chase Manhattan who spent years managing back-office processing: "Whatever you do, stay away from float. You're talking years of nothing but headaches." One of the guys I worked with at NationsBank provided similar advice, laced with a slow, deliberate Dixie delivery: "If it ain't broke, don't fix it."

Given industry projections and the current business situation, I didn't understand why Andersen was placing so much emphasis on the need for a new float-management system. With their industry expertise and knowledge of future trends, why were they not promoting electronic banking like the rest of us? Float may still have been a profitable source of revenue, but with electronic commerce and other market changes taking hold, why would we rebuild something we already had that was by all reports doing just fine? Wouldn't it make more sense to build electronic capability and then gradually phase out of the old check-processing stuff? We could provide some leadership here, instead of sitting back and waiting for it to go away—a certain way to be caught in total react mode.

During the meeting with Andersen, I asked for explanation on why they were proposing to build a new float system. It was as if I had just asked the dumbest possible question ever presented on the face of this planet. Even Denny Billings gave me a look of annoyed disbelief. Peter Miles said, "Check processing is the largest part of the business. Any transaction-routing system would have to include this critical component." The presentation continued. I didn't get it. We were on the dawn of the new millennium. All the articles in the press said that we at NationsBank were leaders in implementing the latest and greatest technology of banking. They also said that embracing new technology was critical for the survival of banks. Yet, our consulting partners were advising us to build bigger, better, faster check-processing systems.

A possible explanation for Andersen's keen interest in NationsBank checks did occur to me as they droned away from one check-processing chart to the next. Even though it might not be quite as important to the future of the bank as the market changed, rebuilding check processing could represent years of lucrative consulting fees. I hoped I was wrong. Surely, even if this was the case, wouldn't NationsBank senior management see right through it?

At the conclusion of the meeting, Denny Billings asked Peter Miles from Andersen to give him a proposal for the detailed design of the new transaction engine, as well as the implementation project. "We need to get on with this," he said. So much for opening things up to a bidding process.

Several key decisions were made during fall of 1996. Denny Billings told our Gemini/Cap Gemini partners that their services would no longer be needed. The party line was that Gemini was too expensive. There were efforts in the bank to reduce budget expenses prior to year-end. Ironically, the bulk of the Gemini work would join the other consulting reports in the file drawer on the fifty-fourth floor of NationsBank Plaza in Atlanta. It wouldn't see the light of day until the next consultant commissioned to write a report was given a peak. Barbara Albrecht, who in the beginning had been so positive about Gemini, now refused to make final payment. This was in spite of Gemini's substantial effort to finish things up and my signing off on the technology piece. Apparently the overall work still wasn't to her satisfaction.

We may have been lucky ending our Gemini/Cap Gemini partnership on the engine before it was turned over to development. A front page article in the December 13, 1999, issue of *Computerworld* reported that the United Way of America terminated a $12 million contract with Cap Gemini America Inc. after a third party found more than four hundred problems with a newly developed donation-processing system. The system, which took almost two years to develop before being scrapped, was designed to streamline processing to boost the percentage of donations going through the United Way to various philanthropic causes.[13] In the same article it was also noted that the U.S. Chamber of Commerce had filed suit against the company in October 1999, alleging that Cap Gemini had failed to upgrade the organization's legacy systems, according to a senior Chamber of Commerce official. That charge came after the Washington-based organization ended a ten-year, $75 million outsourcing deal with Cap Gemini. Eventually Cap Gemini and its parent, Gemini Consulting, the largest consulting firm in Europe, would enter talks to acquire Ernst & Young, one of the most successful American consulting firms, a prestigious member of the Big Five.[14] A newer, improved consulting firm was expected to emerge.

Surely problems with consultants on fulfilling technology contracts was not exclusively a not-for-profit problem. Yet, something was different on the profit side. The press was overwhelmingly positive about corporate technology projects. The success stories were all over the place. The project failures were rarely discussed, and when they were, rarely was the blame placed on the consultants. Was it less publicized when consulting-induced problems hit the corporate clients? Was it easier to keep consultant mistakes under wraps, or was it simply a question of accountability? Was it possible that volunteer boards of directors took their fiduciary responsibility role more seriously and were less tolerant of consulting failures, less afraid to challenge? Perhaps it was because volunteers had no worry about someone docking their pay or devaluing of their share of company equity when they admitted that a major undertaking they had approved actually failed. Perhaps there were fewer employees around who could be blamed.

My friend the private pilot called.

"Hey Steve, remember you said you'd like to go for a little plane ride one of these days?"

"Yeah, I remember."

"So, Steve, how is it going with your project?"my friend asked when we got together that Saturday.

"Looks like Gemini is out and Andersen is in. It never went out to bid."

"Well, that's OK. Andersen is one of the best, and they have more experience at this kind of consulting than anybody else. I think you should be fine with them. They should be able to give NationsBank the kind of help it really needs."

"There are a lot of people who think they already do."

After my last meeting with Andersen, I wasn't so confident anymore.

Then things at NationsBank really hit the fan. A decision had been made to acquire Boatmen's Bancshares Inc., a large St. Louis–based establishment. We paid $8.7 billion, estimated at about 2.6 times Boatmen's book value, and about 15 times anticipated 1997 earnings.[15] Not exactly a bargain-basement price, but it would make NationsBank the fourth largest bank in the country—helping McColl get closer to his goal of becoming number one. But, weren't we worried about credibility? Boatmen's was a mirror image of NationsBank in a different geographic area. It was a check-processing monster. We had dismissed consolidation deals as the old banking paradigm and suggested that we were following a more strategic direction. Somehow all this was buried in the merger-mania hype hitting the press.

Given all the talk about moving away from checks, the Boatmen's deal astounded me.

Wouldn't somebody call us on it? I asked one of the other senior vice presidents I worked with about the deal. He and I had talked several times in the past about the importance of implementing an electronic commerce (e-commerce) strategy.

"Why," I asked, "do we acquire another bank that is so immersed in check processing when our goal is to emphasize electronic banking? It sounds counter to our strategy."

"It was a defensive move," he said. "We needed to prevent Banc One or somebody else from buying them."

"So, let me ask you this. If we block them by doing it first, aren't we discarding our own strategy and now chasing theirs?"

"We've always had an acquisition strategy. Boatmen's is just a warm-up. Hugh's real goal is Bank of America. You'll see. . . ."

There was something very confusing about all this, but I decided not to press it.

Boatmen's was a done deal. It was get-with-the-program time. The conversation shifted to lighter subject material. I tried to take the edge off. This was a very different corporate culture, and I wanted to do my best to blend in. My peers kept reminding me that I was no longer in New York.

If there was a man who was preoccupied with North versus South, it was Hugh McColl. In speeches and in published comments in the North Carolina press, McColl often equated his quest to expand his bank as the new offensive for the South. It was a quest to reclaim the former stature of the South, lost in the Civil War. The Civil War was still called by some folks below the Mason Dixon, "The War of Northern Aggression," and Hugh often referenced the struggle and the unfair effect it had on his beloved South.

In a speech to a Japan conference in Charlotte, McColl pointed out similarities between the southern United States and Japan, both having to rebuild after defeat. He alluded to NationsBank, which had grown through acquisition, as doing its part to help the rebuilding process.

Based on comments in a speech, McColl had his dander up about a story in the *New York Times* about the phenomenal growth of the South. The *Times* article had been fairly positive in general. McColl took issue with a statement that twenty-five years ago the thought of the tremendous growth the South had experienced would have seemed "preposterous." In his speech, McColl griped, "But most southerners I know would take issue with the conclusion that these achievements were 'preposterous.' Where I grew up, we would say that the *Times* misjudged 'the size of the fight in the dog.' He also said, "My great-grandfather did what he could. He returned from the war, built a mill that provided jobs, a bank that provided capital, and a railroad to connect the country to other railroads—most of which were being rebuilt after the Union General Sherman had literally tied them in knots."[16]

As noted by the *News and Observer* of Raleigh, "But if there is one more thing that can be said about McColl, if there is one largely overlooked aspect of NationsBank Corp.'s rise, it's this: He has created, singlehandedly and with forethought, a new metaphor for re-fighting the Civil War. We're licking the Yankees these days in a new and wholly satisfying manner. What better reason to make him Mover and Shaker of the Year?" It added,

"He has, by most accounts, relished the fact that he's kept the New York finance community back on its heels for most of the past decade. In fact, in an interview with the *News and Observer* of Raleigh a year ago, McColl flat out said it: 'Do I think Northerners are evil? Absolutely not. Do they think less of us because we're Southern? Yes, I think so. Do I take pleasure in demonstrably being successful against all corners? Absolutely.'"[17]

This, however, did not stand in the way of his working closely with some of the best Yankees on Wall Street. Yankees often assisted as advisers on acquisitions. In the case of structuring the Boatmen's deal, McColl worked with Goldman Sachs & Co.[18] These highly regarded investment advisers had essentially become Boatmen's merger consultants. McColl would work with them on future deals as well.

Behind the media splash, there were some naysayers concerning the Boatmen's takeover. Some complained about the acquisition price, 2.6 times the value on the books. These were for the most part drowned out by voices of authority that were bullish on the merger. Leading the charge, as one might expect, were analysts from the same company advising McColl on the merger, Goldman Sachs. J. Christopher Flowers, managing director and head of the financial institutions group at Goldman Sachs, suggested in the *American Banker* that the future of banking would belong to well-capitalized institutions such as NationsBank with the ability to acquire other banks and offer a broad portfolio of financial services. "At the same time, he believes there is ample reason for more huge deals like the NationsBank-Boatmen's merger. A merger between NationsBank Corp. and BankAmerica Corp. would create a company that could serve 63 percent of the population, he said."[19] Many believed Boatmen's was a stepping-stone to help position NationsBank for seizing the bigger prize.

In a separate article in *Banking Strategies* discussing NationsBank's acquisition of Boatmen's along with other mergers, Flowers pointed out, "The higher the market, the easier it is for these deals to be done. Acquirers have more currency, so they're more willing to part with their stock, and sellers are getting higher prices. It works better for both sides."[20] It worked nicely for the investment advisers, too. Goldman Sachs led all other investment firms as financial advisers on bank mergers in 1996, totaling $25,585,800,000.[21] Nevertheless, it sounded as if they were still chomping at the bit for a NationsBank-BankAmerica face-off, which seemed sure to come, pending any unforeseen negative changes to the run-up market.

There were others of influence who came out in support. Nicholas Krasno, a vice president and senior analyst at Moody's Investors Service Inc., said, concerning NationsBank and its proposed acquisition of

Boatmen's, "The market will increasingly favor large institutions which can make major investments in new technology, which is an area in which they excel."[22] He must have gotten a heavy dose of kodachrome.

After the acquisition, retail would still make up about 80 percent of our business. It struck me that given everything I knew and heard about him, McColl and his generals must have had a war room with a map of the United States. The acquisition of Boatmen's helped add a slew of western and midwestern states to the empire. A few more pins on the map, say BankAmerica's West Coast holdings, and we would truly be a national bank. Granted, through each acquisition we were buying a larger customer base. With those new customers, there was also coming more bricks, more mortar, and a boatload of checks.

To make the acquisition successful and quiet some of the lingering critics on Wall Street, we would have to consolidate operations and absorb Boatmen's at near lightning speed. This had been done in the past with other acquisitions, but none were as big as Boatmen's. This represented the third largest bank acquisition in U.S. history. NationsBank had gone on record that we had advanced technology in place to facilitate major transitions. "Transition" was the more politically correct terminology used at NationsBank for "consolidation." Now we were reporting that the transition of Boatmen's into the NationsBank franchise would save $335 million through combined-expense reductions. Analysts were quick to agree, helping to sway market acceptance.[23]

Old paradigm or not, as noted in the Associated Press article: "The savings would come from consolidating operations and business lines and from exercising more leverage with vendors, the company said. There was nothing said in the announcement about job cuts, but analysts said they were inevitable."[24] Job cuts didn't have to be stated. Simply implying them was enough. Downsizing was good news on Wall Street. Attributing the expected improvement in profitability ratios to advanced technology, the consolidation of operations, and leveraging vendors was a far more positive spin than "job cuts," "shutting operations," and "outsourcing." This kind of language didn't offend sensibilities, but the consequences could not be ignored. Out go more employees and in come the vendors. Andersen Consulting and Alltel were sure to be big winners. These were the new breed of workers.

Compounding the problem, there was already talk of additional acquisitions soon to follow.

There were rumors circulating in the bank about a possible play for Bank of Boston or Barnett. Bank of America was almost always discussed as the ultimate prize McColl wanted more than anything else. Some said he simply liked the name.

Boatmen's made everybody working in Transaction Services think more about checks. Transition was about making Boatmen's checks NationsBank checks, and as soon as possible. Electronic banking quickly became a secondary concern, at least internally. In public announcements and interviews, senior executives continued to harp on the importance of electronic technologies and our continued investments in these areas. Behind the walls of NationsBank, people continued to run as fast as they could to get the checks out on time and to make room for more.

All key indicators seemed to demonstrate that we were driving the business forward. NationsBank had posted an 18 percent increase in third-quarter profit over the previous year, representing $6.07 per share and a 26.4 percent change over the first nine months of the year.[25] Still, the new NationsBank strategic vision was dropping off someplace between the view over the "dashboard," to steal a Gemini expression, and the next intersection. Tactical took place over strategic. I was told tactical emphasis was always standard procedure following acquisitions.

Like NationsBank, Boatmen's was a large retail bank with heavy check-processing requirements and a decentralized infrastructure. They had a reputation of being a well-managed bank with a strong commitment to supporting community services. Their technology infrastructure, however, was antiquated. A major reason for putting themselves up on the block was that they had evaluated the costs in reengineering their current infrastructure and found them to be staggering. The chairman of Boatmen's was quoted as saying, "We would have had to invest hundreds of millions of dollars in technology to remain competitive. That would have affected our future earnings."[26]

In a subsequent NationsBank newsletter, the Boatmen's chair would point out that one of the major advantages he saw with NationsBank was its commitment to new technology. "To be successful in the future, and particularly to compete effectively against the nonbanking industry, you have to have hundreds of millions of dollars invested in new technology. NationsBank is the company that has done that and is continuing to do that."[27] Already done that, continuing to do that? Not in Transaction Services where the bulk of financial transactions were handled. Everybody accepted that we were a leader in technology without looking very closely.

Model Bank had always received the lion's share of credit for providing the technology that helped us consolidate new acquisitions so rapidly. Never mind that most of NationsBank was still not fully converted to the Model Bank platform. The September 25, 1996, issue of *American Banker* included an interview with Ken Lewis, president of NationsBank, who was often credited as the "father" of Model Bank. The article noted that making the acquisition work "depends on integrating the Boatmen's branches into the 'model banking' program, a mammoth effort to convert all the company branches to a common sales culture and technology platform." After discussing the benefits of the Boatmen's acquisition and NationsBank's capabilities for consolidation, Ken Lewis, who was Al Johnson's boss and had become Denny Billings's mentor, concluded his interview by stating, "As far as I can see, we have a few more years of nice sailing."[28]

Model Bank was also about checks. "Damn the torpedoes, full speed ahead."

Ken Guenther, a Washington lobbyist and a critic of interstate banking, said in an article in the *Wichita Business Journal* that he believed it was McColl's connections that had made the Boatmen's acquisition possible.

> I think it's bad public policy because I don't think the interests of McColl are the same as those of citizens of Iowa or other markets where Boatmen's operates. . . . But I'm philosophical because we fought this battle for fifteen years and we lost it because of Hugh McColl's friendship with Bill Clinton and because no Republican leader in Congress was concerned enough to fight it. [29]

SUMMARY OF OBSERVATIONS

- Consultants provide work for hire, which implies a different level of motivation than employees; objectives of the consultants may conflict with corporate goals and objectives.

- Fragmented organizations with internal focus have limited capability to recognize and respond to change.

- In the last ten years, banks were losing significant ground to nonbanks that were skimming the cream, targeting the highly profitable electronic transactions, and leaving the more costly cash- and check-processing burdens to banks.

- Companies often pay fees for consulting services from individuals with little to no industry background. Essentially, the client is absorbing the costs of training while the consulting firm is billing time for services.

- People sell what they know. Consultants very often recommend what they sell.

NOTES

1. See figure 1, chapter 5, page 151.

2. Ronald Henkoff, "Inside Andersen's Army of Advice," *Fortune*, 4 October 1993, 78.

3. Ibid., 78.

4. Ibid., 79.

5. "Bridging Today and Tomorrow: A Call for Evolution and Partnerships in the Banking Industry," NationsBank Chairman Speech, Bank Administration Retail Delivery Conference, 4 December 1995, http://www.nationsbank.com/newsroom/.

6. Steven Marjanovic, "Payments Inroads by Non-Banks Worry Bankers," *American Banker*, 16 October 1996, 13.

7. Richard Crone, "Banking Without Banks," *Bankers Magazine* (January/February 1996): 41.

8. "BAI Study Calls Banks to Action on the Electronic Frontier," *Bank Systems & Technology* (October 1995): 18–20.

9. See figure 1, chapter 5, page 151.

10. Kirstin E. Wells, "Are Checks Overused?" *Federal Reserve Bank of Minneapolis Quarterly Review* (fall 1996): 4.

11. Mary L. King, *The Great American Banking Snafu* (Lexington: Lexington Books, 1985), 107.

12. David H. Friedman, *Money & Banking* (Washington D.C.: American Bankers Association, 1985), 134.

13. Dash Julekha, "Two Big Failures Cite Cap Gemini," *Computerworld*, 13 December 1999, 1.

14. "Cap Gemini Is in Talks with Ernst & Young," *New York Times*, 7 December 1999, C14.

15. Daniel Dunaief and Kenneth Cline, "NationsBank's Midwestern Deal: 7 New States, But Questions on Price," *American Banker*, 3 September 1996, 1.

16. Hugh McColl, "Of Common Ground and New Identities," keynote address to Japan Conference, Charlotte, N.C., 26 September 1994, http://bankamerica.com/newsroom/.

17. G. D. Garino, "Rebel Yell," *News and Observer of Raleigh* (January 1999): 36.

18. Gordon Matthews, "Goldman Sachs No. 1 Last Year in Bank Merger Advice," *American Banker*, 31 January 1997, 18A.

19. Aaron Elstein, "Goldman Director Says Banks Have Edge in Consolidation Endgame," *American Banker*, 11 February 1997, 18.

20. "Momentum Builds," *Banking Strategies*, 1 March 1997, 46.

21. Matthews, "Goldman Sachs No. 1."

22. Dunaief and Cline, "NationsBank's Midwestern Deal," 9.

23. "Cost Savings Pegged at $335 Million a Year by '99," *American Banker*, 3 September 1996, 21.

24. "Merger to Make NationsBank a Giant," Associated Press, 31 August 1996.

25. Laurie Hays, "Big Banks Post Healthy Earnings for the Third Quarter," *Wall Street Journal*, 16 October 1996, B4.

26. Stephen Kleege, "Millions in Technology Needs Changed Craig's Mind," *American Banker*, 3 September 1996, 8.

27. "We're on the Same Team . . . and the Customer Benefits!" *NationsBank Times*, January 1997, 2.

28. Kenneth Cline, "NationsBank Sees Boatmen's Revenue Potential," *American Banker*, 25 September 1996, 4.

29. David Mildenberg, "NationsBank's Bid for Boatmen's Has Nationwide Implications," *Wichita Business Journal*, 30 September 1996, http://wichita.bcentral. com/wichita/stories/1996/09/30/focus2.html.

CHAPTER NINE

BILLABLE
MEAT

It was one of those bad karma days when you feel nothing else could possibly go wrong until it does. I was informed that senior management had placed the new transaction engine on the critical path for the Boatmen's transition. They had decided that the new payments engine would help with the integration. I told Barbara Albrecht that in my judgment we could potentially build something in time to handle the requirements of electronic processing. I tried to make the point that if we started building the check-processing float-management component today, we might be done by sometime in the new millennium, certainly not in the timetable for Boatmen's. That wasn't the answer she wanted to hear. It was all too familiar. I was running late and we hadn't even started. Call me paranoid, but I couldn't help wonder, Am I being set up? How could we meet the Boatmen's deadline? Douglas Adams, author of *Hitchhiker's Guide to the Galaxy*, once said, "I love deadlines. I like the whooshing sound they make as they fly by."[1] I wasn't loving this.

Senior executives were already saying that the transaction engine would have to handle all of Boatmen's transactions—both checks and electronic. Never mind that contrary to public posturing, the highly acclaimed Model Bank program was still converting current NationsBank branches and was no where near ready to absorb the new workload from Boatmen's. The engine was supposed to be ready, even if Model Bank wasn't. Nothing like a little incentive to accelerate the work effort and create some motivation.

Consultants from both Gemini and Andersen had told them that one system could do both checks and electronic transactions. It was often drawn that way on the overhead charts. Never mind that checks and electronic payments required completely different processes. I was now convinced I had figured out a major flaw in the projects and why so many of them failed to deliver as initially billed. Consultants and vendors were setting the expectations in the pre-engagement selling phase. The cost savings, potential revenue returns, and new functional capabilities were all hyped to win the business. Once it was won, no one wanted to appear inconsistent or unreliable by suggesting that they revisit these claims. I decided to not press the issue for the time being. As an employee, contradicting high-paid consultants was suicidal. I had dodged a few bullets already and didn't want to press my luck.

Boatmen's represented manna from heaven. The transition budget could potentially fund the transaction engine as well as other projects that were not part of the approved annual plan. There was only one catch—to justify the engine costs, it had to play a critical part in the migration from Boatmen's systems to our systems.

I had tried several times to get Denny Billings to meet with other consultants before a final decision had been made on the engine proposal. As I had suggested to Al Johnson in my impromptu meeting with him, I thought it was important to understand and compare what different organizations could bring to the table. Based on my request, meetings with other consulting firms had been scheduled by Billings, but they were each subsequently postponed—some were canceled the day of the meeting. I remember one group flying in the morning they expected to meet with Billings, and it was my unpleasant task to meet them in the lobby and tell them the meeting had been postponed.

Billings finally agreed to attend an introductory meeting with KPMG Consulting. It was a day or so after the meeting in which the Andersen proposal had been tentatively approved by the senior management team. The meeting with KPMG had been juggled on and off Billings's calendar several times. I didn't see the point of meeting with them now, given that it was fairly obvious at this point that we were going to give the business to Andersen.

I attended the meeting and was frankly impressed with the consultants from KPMG. Both of the KPMG guys at the meeting had worked in banking for several years prior to consulting. They seemed to have considerable knowledge related to routing and settlement. The KPMG consultants talked about "execution" and "time to market," things I wasn't hearing from any of the consultants we were using. During the meeting with KPMG, Billings announced that a contract had already been signed with Andersen Consulting to design a new transaction engine. Billings suggested that they could schedule another meeting. "Why don't you fellas give me a call... say... three or four months out? We can see where we are and chat a little more then," he said. The KPMG guys were a lot more cordial than I would have been as they left.

There was a follow-up meeting Billings invited me to attend to finalize acceptance of the Andersen proposal. There were several senior managers present and ready to discuss the Andersen contract. Billings, who had set up the meeting, proudly provided a brief overview of the Andersen proposal. "This is what I got them to agree to," he said.

When I started to ask a few questions about the contract, Billings looked annoyed. I was interrupted by one of the most senior executives in the meeting. "I'm not worried about this. I'm confident Denny Billings will provide the necessary management on this," he said. It had become fairly obvious that these people really didn't like it when the new guy inserted myself into the dialogue. I guess I had not been around long enough to have paid my dues. I had been spoiled as a consultant. I needed to continue to remind myself that back in the role of "employee," all that objective, third-party credibility was gone.

At the conclusion of the meeting, I asked for a copy of the proposal from Andersen. The proposal merely called for interviewing clients and subject experts. Any plan for resolving issues or establishing priorities was not defined. There was also no mention of the qualifications of the people from Andersen who would be assigned to the project. I decided not to press it. The proposal had just been approved, and contracts were to be immediately signed. I knew my focus would need to be making the project successful. I was going to need all of the bodies I could get if there was any hope at all of pulling the engine off in time for Boatmen's.

The original Andersen proposal was to develop a "detailed" design for a new transaction engine. According to Billings, the cost would have been $700,000. Based on his suggestion, a revised proposal for doing a more high-level, less-detailed design was presented with a price tag of $580,000 for three months of work.

High-level design? I thought we already went through that. Who's got the time to do this all over again? Those were my concerns as we got ready for welcoming the next army of consultants about to descend. That we were swapping one sole-source arrangement for another was not so important anymore. Not only that, but wasn't the big issue with Gemini that it was too high level? Were we not about to cover the same ground? It sure sounded that way. While Gemini had talked about a payments engine that could handle both electronic processing and checks, they emphasized the electronic component. Andersen was also assuming that the transaction engine would handle both electronic payments and checks, but they talked mostly about checks. If they could pull this off, then they deserved all the cudos they got.

Billings was proud of his successful effort to reduce Andersen's initial proposal costs. It had been scaled back in scope, but as he told the rest of us, it was still an ambitious work plan. Billings pointed out that if all went well we could expect a follow-on contract with Andersen and Alltel for building the engine. The fixed front-end deal was sure to be followed by either bill by the hour for lots of bodies or a megabuck fixed contract for an extended period of time. That was the nature of this business. Set the table for the next one. At this point, I didn't think it could happen fast enough.

Like it or not, for consulting firms, consultant bodies were products. Even the prestigious firms could be viewed as glorified body shops, hawking as many consulting bodies as they could squeeze on client payrolls and getting them "off of the bench," or as sometimes called in the business, "off of the beach." The $120,000 reduction would be pocket change compared to all the resources Andersen could pile in the door to support the follow-on implementation on a project like this.

Andersen proposed identifying functional requirements from a new, improved, expanded list of users. A few of the people interviewed by Gemini would be interviewed one more time. Consultants rarely want to accept the work of other consultants at face value. The same is true when it comes to the previous work of employees. While they form "teaming arrangements" with employees, consultants most often work from the premise that all client business information related to the project needs to be transferred from the employee to the consultant. This is why so many engagements are front-end loaded with analysis. Rarely does it work the other way around, where consultant skills are transferred back to the client. They often insist on plowing the same turf—doing it their way, which is always superior. The only way to prevent this is if the client insists that the consultants accept the work of others. That wasn't about to happen here.

Once again, the users to be interviewed were not customers, but bank employees who would tell us what they thought customers wanted—not only NationsBank customers now, but Boatmen's, too. In addition to completing the high-level design, the proposal called for selecting the best vendor solutions to help build the new transaction engine.

The new assumption was that it would be a combination of build and buy. Determining the right parts to build and the right vendors to buy from could be an enormous effort that would require digging well below a high-level design. This needed to be accomplished in an environment where nothing was approved without consensus. The consultants made recommendations, a committee would approve them, and only then would it get passed on to the appropriate executive for a final decision. Everyone else seemed happy with the Andersen proposal. Was I the only one on the line if we didn't make it in time for Boatmen's accounts to be handled by NationsBank? "I'm not taking anymore personal risks," I said to myself. "Keep it cool. Be a team player."

Andersen Consulting was not only a favorite with NationsBank, but in the banking industry in general. As noted in *American Banker*, "To a certain extent Andersen and other consulting firms have stepped into the void left by diminished influence of International Business Machines in today's computing environment. With Big Blue no longer providing the blueprint, bankers are looking elsewhere for big-picture strategizing."[2] While Andersen might "sell" strategy to get a foot in the door, it was pretty obvious the company was highly focused on implementation. Andersen had become the new safety net for many banking institutions faced with operational and technological decisions, whether they were considered strategic or tactical. Many bankers tended to be risk averse. Any decision could be viewed as a risk. As I had previously learned, consultants were used to make recommendations and "validate" management decisions. If things didn't work out, the manager felt covered—"it was the consultants who recommended this . . ." Consulting bodies were a small price to pay for helping to reduce the risk of decision making.

A decade ago many would say that no one was ever fired for making an IBM decision because IBM had developed name recognition and a positive reputation. It didn't matter if IBM was best. In the era of downsizing and increased consulting influence, Andersen had become a decision no one seemed to question, particularly in banking.

As part of the proposal, Andersen had recommended an elaborate organizational structure that it mapped out with a pyramid of attached boxes. The top box, "Program Leadership" included Denny Billings and an Andersen partner. This was another great ploy also used by Gemini. Clients were less likely to point fingers at mistakes if the leadership responsibility of the project was shared with a client executive.

Underneath was a box for two project managers, one from Andersen and one from NationsBank. Each subgroup had a NationsBank employee shadowed by an Andersen consultant. A classic "cover your butt" organizational structure had been created in much the same way that Gemini had done.

There were teams proposed to handle various activities. Activities would include identifying business requirements, technology design, and evaluating viable vendor solutions. There was also an implementation team with representatives from all facets of the bank. Obviously, this team had nothing to implement until the other groups had completed their work and recommendations were approved, but it helped round out the chart. It was also a great bridge to get started on the more lucrative implementation project and attempt to tightly couple follow-on activities with the design work Andersen was about to do.

NationsBank & Andersen Consulting
Transaction Engine Project Team

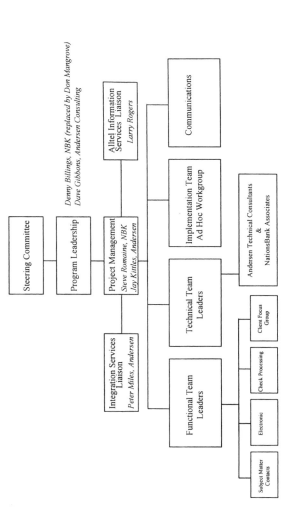

The engine project team consisted of both NationsBank Associates and Andersen Consultants. Program leadership representing a senior manager from the bank and a partner from Andersen. Project Management was split with a manager from NationsBank and a manager from Andersen. The Liaison to the Integration Services Organization at NationsBank was an Andersen Consultant who also reported to the Senior Manager running Integration Services.

Andersen also recommended an executive steering committee with key influencers from different organizations within NationsBank. The committee would be comprised of senior executives representing different lines of business. Additional personnel from Andersen Consulting and Alltel Information Systems were also slated to play supporting roles as "liaisons."

No one seemed concerned about using vendors like Alltel with potential vested interests in a particular solution, even though as part of the project, both Andersen and Alltel would be reviewing all vendor choices. How could Alltel possibly be an "objective" participant when evaluating a potential competitor? Were we opening ourselves to criticism and a lack of cooperation from "nonpartner" vendors? I decided to ask Billings about this privately when the right moment presented itself. Billings said, "I'm not worried. They know we expect them to be objective about this." My instincts told me that from Billings's perspective, his statement on the subject had put the matter to bed. Further discussion was pointless.

As I already expected, and feared, I was officially named as the project manager to represent NationsBank, one level down on the chart from Billings. I would have preferred being a liaison with less tangible responsibilities, but these roles were reserved for consultants only. Project management was never a career aspiration. Privately, I wondered if this assignment was payback for breaking the chain of command when I had met with Al Johnson. In separate conversations, Barbara Albrecht and Denny Billings told me that they were personally responsible for placing me in this great plum of a job, as if they were doing me a favor. Both of my managers pointed out that it would be a high-visibility position. Visibility, as I had learned, was not always a good thing. Both Albrecht and Billings had made careers out of project management and couldn't understand why anyone would want to do anything else. As Barbara Albrecht said, "When the ship leaves the dock, you want to make sure that it's course is consistent with our strategic vision." She was talking about the "vision thing" chart, but she was also talking about pushing for an engine that would handle new electronic-payment requirements.

Never having an opportunity to work with Andersen, I was still, to a certain degree, looking forward to the experience. They were by far the most successful consulting firm based on revenue and had been growing at over 20 percent a year since 1993. Andersen Consulting was not only the recognized industry leader in consulting. They were a major trendsetter across various industries, forcing companies to rethink the fundamental ways they did business. For me to be successful, they needed to be successful, too.

From the beginning, there were problems in recruiting bank associates to participate on the new engine project team. I was told there was still a lot of bad blood over the Model project. Bank personnel had helped Andersen and Alltel in learning the business and developing the new systems that became Model Bank. Many found their jobs lost when the systems were eventually outsourced to Andersen and Alltel personnel. Andersen took over the project management, and Alltel began running and maintaining ongoing operations.

Andersen filled most of the engine project positions with inexperienced personnel. It appeared to be the classic "bait and switch." The group of consultants assigned to the project were a far cry from the more knowledgeable consultants who had initially reviewed the "bottom-up" project with Billings and me. In fact, there was only one consultant from the previous "bottom-up" project who was assigned to the next phase. Most of the others were relatively young, with minimal to no previous banking experience.

A few years before, *Fortune* had contrasted Andersen Consulting with the highbrow management strategy consultants as "Chicago versus Cambridge." The magazine went on to say, "Andersen, by contrast, blitzes jobs with people power—masses of junior and mid-level consultants commanded by a small cadre of partners, an approach known in consulting as leverage."[3] They were the largest army of advice merchants, according to *Fortune*.

Back then Andersen was still hiring most of their consultants straight out of school. While Andersen was billing us for an army of consultants, we would be training them in banking and technology. In hindsight, Andersen should have been paying us for the time and effort in training these "consultants" who were still wet behind the ears. We never should have allowed them to train their personnel on our nickel.

The project was kicked off with no technology team leader from Andersen. Dave Gibbons, the partner in charge of the engine project, assured me he was working aggressively in finding the right person. That sounded vaguely familiar. Just as was the case with Gemini, finding warm bodies was not a problem. Bringing in qualified technical consultants seemed to be a major challenge. One day early in the project, Dave Gibbons confided in me that most of the good people at Andersen had moved into client/server distributed systems. He told me that he was trying to find someone with check-processing and mainframe experience who understood systems similar to the ones being used for Model Bank.

"You sure that's what we need?" I asked.

"Of course. This is definitely a mainframe solution."

Let it go. Say nuttin' about nuttin' Romaine. What possible good could it do?

Many of the NationsBank employees who were asked to participate in the project declined. Additional Andersen and Alltel representatives came on board to fill the gaps. I didn't give the people who reported directly to me an opportunity to decline. While working on Gemini, I also added some people to my team. There were now six of them, reporting directly to me as part of the strategy group for Transaction Services. The good news was that they all had a wealth of experience in banking. The best part about it was that I didn't have to put up too much of a fight to get them. In other words, I didn't alienate too many other senior managers in building my team, at least not yet. These were the few and far between risk takers, and they came looking for this kind of work. When I asked one of them why, she simply said, "This is different, and you seem to be getting into some interesting things." I think there might have been a compliment buried somewhere in that response. Perhaps she was fascinated by the bizarre, or was some kind of masochist.

I assigned three of them to work full time with me on the engine project. The remaining three were given other assignments, including some additional research on the U.S. banking market. My plan was to hold them in reserve on the engine project for the time being. I told them that they could be called at anytime to jump in and serve in a swat team role. They seemed to like the idea of acting like special forces when the right time came.

All the people reporting to me were professionals, including Dan Price, who seemed to be coming out of his self-imposed shell. In each case, they indicated a strong willingness to help, even though for most it would mean traveling from their homes in Dallas or Charlotte to the Atlanta project office on a weekly basis. Andersen, like Gemini, saw value in being close to the executive sponsors and that meant working in Atlanta.

We worked aggressively and eventually recruited several subject experts from Darlene Wittington's Integration Services organization. We went through great pains to do it without breaking any more glass. This time around, Darlene was more cooperative about lending resources. It was an Andersen project where she could exert more influence.

Looking for additional help, I approached the Corporate Strategic Technology Group (STG) out of Charlotte. After all, they held overall corporate responsibility for technology strategy, and the transaction engine was now a full-fledged cross-organizational project. Although I knew we were "reaching" asking a strategy organization outside of Transaction Services to participate in the effort, I felt it was an important enough project to try. The engine could impact the entire bank. The STG had the clout to keep the focus on future needs as opposed to remodeling old systems to satisfy a specific division.

The STG people said that they could help but that it would be inappropriate for them to have hands-on responsibility. They told us that this was because the STG was only an advisory group. Getting involved in a business unit project, even with corporate sponsorship, would be "out of scope." It was OK for them to test new solutions in a lab they had created with the latest high-tech products, review consultant research notes, and pontificate, but rolling up their sleeves for an actual business unit project was out of the question. We decided to take them up on providing advice. It was better than no help at all. Given all their other activities, getting the STG involved was a coup d'état. They usually spent most of their time pontificating.

I attended a presentation from the STG on NationsBank's early plan to partner with other banks to use a common Internet banking program. When the speaker opened the floor to audience participation, I asked how NationsBank planned to differentiate itself in this commodity-based market where we were sharing ideas and technology with everyone else. "We think NationsBank's brand name and overall leadership in the market will differentiate us," I was told. I mentioned how IBM had thought this, too, when it first entered the PC market. Grumbles, nasty expressions on faces. Woops, they must have thought I was out of line. There was a brief pause before the speaker asked if there were any other questions.

I couldn't help but wonder that even with all the potential benefits of the Internet, if once again the pundits and analysts were overreaching with their standard answers and recommended quick-fixes. Based on all their hype, it seemed like everybody was starting to speculate in Internet stocks that had not as yet turned a profit and didn't look like they would any time soon. Consultants were telling companies they could expect to reduce head count when e-commerce could actually increase required follow-up sales and the volume of call center requests for additional information. I was convinced there needed to be more than a cool-looking Web portal to do this e-commerce business right. There needed to be people and infrastructure that could support the new electronic channels. The behind-the-scenes engine would help. I for one thought this was more important than partnerships with other banks and sitting on committees.

It seemed to me that, even if we were able to build a collaborative Internet-based approach to banking, there was still work to be done in the far less visible, but vitally important back office. What good was a new front-end delivery system if the back-office processing remained virtually the same? Faster cart, same horse. The ability to handle payments efficiently and effectively on the back end was critical for banks. The financial institution that could provide a complete soup-to-nuts solution where it appeared "seamless" to the user and improved responsiveness could capture market share and emerge as the new heavy weight contender in electronic banking. There would be nothing "me, too" about that.

There was also a very primal motivational force at work. It would be important to me, personally, as the project manager to make the engine project a success. There was nothing I feared more than failure. The name Andersen Consulting may have brought a sense of security for my senior management—the insurance policy for minimizing personal risk in making decisions. I didn't feel, however, that this insurance extended to me. As always, if there needed to be a fall guy, it would be the client project manager, not Andersen. Consequently, I was prepared to work hard at making this work.

Since the first day we met, I felt I hit it off with the Andersen project manager who would be sharing my responsibilities on a day-to-day basis. Unlike so many of the others, Jay Kittles didn't take himself too seriously. He was a Texan, but was unmistakably lacking in the usual bravado. Kittles had a quick wit and had been working for Andersen long enough to have developed a real-world roll-up-your-sleeves-and-get-it-done approach to business. He combined this with a healthy touch of skepticism and sarcastic wit that projects sometimes require to break up the tension. It also helped in maintaining a grip on the political realities. I had a theory that a carefully controlled degree of skepticism could be turned into a barometer for anticipating "what ifs" and preventing failures that the eternal optimist would never anticipate. Jay had worked on the Model Bank project during the early years, so he brought some understanding of the Model Bank systems supporting our largest division, General Bank. He turned out to be a student of NationsBank's acquisition history who savored the details as if they were the building blocks that created Western civilization. No wonder he was placed in the project management role.

As it turned out, my copartner also had several years of experience in the electronic side of the banking business and seemed to understand the competitive exposures facing financial institutions. He wasn't the check-processing bigot that I suspected. I shared with him some of the internal research work my swat team from the Transaction Services strategy group had developed, independent from any external consulting activities. It showed the cost projections associated with running the current routing and settlement systems and the risks and dependencies in implementing change.

An article in *American Banker* was referenced as part of the analysis. It pointed out that based on industry data, conversion from checks to electronic methods should save eighty cents in processing costs per transaction. It went on to say that pending legislation would mandate that government payments be made electronically by 1999, which was expected to accelerate the demise of checks.[4] We would have to do something. A mere 3 percent decline in our paper volume could mean as much as a 30 percent increase in electronic processing. Sooner or later the gentle drift away from paper could turn into Niagara Falls. Boatmen's electronic requirement was initially projected to be 40 percent of our current electronic volume. This increased volume alone could push us beyond the breaking point. Given NationsBank's history, we all knew Boatmen's would probably not be the last acquisition.

If something wasn't done to address the electronic system expansion and new requirements issues, it could be lights out. If NationsBank internal systems couldn't handle *real-time* electronic banking, someone else would. Real time referred to the capability of updating a customer account as soon as the customer initiates the transaction, as opposed to the overnight updating process we were using at the time. Banks blew it on credit cards where they could have cornered the market if they had acted more decisively earlier in the game. Instead, nonbanks moved in and took advantage of the open opportunity left by slow-moving banks. How many of these kinds of losses could be sustained?

Our message was simple—don't muck with the paper. As one of my consultant friends once said, "No customer ever picked a bank because of the way they process checks." We argued that the key was to fix electronic systems with a new solution that could satisfy requirements for increased volumes and also provide real-time processing. Then, over time, we could create incentives for our check-writing customers to move to the new and more efficient electronic forms of banking. Checks would never completely disappear, but this needed to be a "maintain" versus "rebuild" strategy. If we were going to keep customers while electronic payment eventually replaced checks, we needed to have the right system in place. It might have sounded callous, but I was a firm believer, based on past experiences, that sometimes you really did have to eat your own children before somebody else did.

As our customers became increasingly more sophisticated, demanding real-time access to their accounts, float from checks would surely decline. The worst possible position to be in when this happened would be a react mode with no viable alternative. As noted in *Bank Management* magazine, "In large measure, the fortunes of the banking industry hinge on the evolution of transaction processing . . . moving from back-office processors of cash and checks, banks are emphasizing electronically enhanced processing."[5]

Our research suggested that there was a high probability we could implement a new electronic routing system in time for Boatmen's consolidation efforts. Andersen project manager Kittles said he supported this position and was willing to help promote it with NationsBank management. We met with Andersen's sponsor, Denny Billings, who also agreed with these conclusions, or at least that was his indication at the time. He agreed that this approach was a way of increasing our chances for success while still making an important contribution to the Boatmen's transition effort.

No doubt, having an Andersen consultant with me added the necessary credibility for influencing this senior executive's support. We also talked briefly about the project status. During the meeting, Billings referred all questions to Jay Kittles. It was not so surprising at this point. I had come to realize that when it came to projects, employee involvement like mine was only window dressing.

Denny Billings was the highest-ranking NationsBank officer on the engine project, represented as part of the program leadership on the organization chart.[6] During the project, Billings remained very aloof. It was as if he had removed himself from the process after helping to get the Andersen contract approved. Andersen was now in charge. Billings would call in for weekly status meetings, but it was obvious he was not concerned about the particular details and was looking for Andersen to push things forward.

Dave Gibbons, the Andersen partner, was meeting with Billings separately, giving him updates. I had learned that the large consulting firms often use this tactic of buffering the executive as a means of maintaining control. By placing themselves in between employees and executives, consultants can put their own spin on progress and filter out any potential negative noise or damaging information. When I met with Billings separately on a few occasions to discuss the project, he was obviously uncomfortable and his responses were curt. Carrying mail was apparently not my job. It was becoming obvious that I was expected to play along and not make waves. Had not everything so far pointed to this? I gave it my best shot.

We were several weeks into the project when Jay Kittles came to see me. "Steve, our nerd has arrived." Kittles was referring to the Andersen consultant who would head up the technology review. According to Kittles, he was rarely used as a consultant and was being called out of

Andersen internal operations for our project. He slipped by admitting that they couldn't get anyone else. When I met him, the new technology team leader went off into a dump of techno information, no doubt trying to impress us with his expertise for throwing around all the right clichés. He sounded as if he already knew the right solution—a bigger, better, faster float system. He may not have been the best possible choice, but he already had Dave Gibbons's party line down cold. He was also one of those IT (information technology) consulting types who would explain everything in the most complete, technically correct way down to the last minute detail—everything that was of little use to anyone.

"What about electronic payments?" I asked.

"Electronic? From everything I've learned so far, that's the least of our problems. We need to figure out how to handle the float."

He would blend in perfectly with the most of the other Andersen guys.

In spite of my efforts to try and bring the team together, there continued to be problems. There seemed to be a lot of "we" and "them" between the NationsBank associates and the Andersen and Alltel participants. The representatives from the Strategic Technology Group now working in an advisory role on the project argued that it would be impossible to complete all the work committed to in the Andersen proposal on time. They also said that they felt the Andersen consultants assigned to the project didn't have the right qualifications. Not that I needed advisors to tell me this. Even Darlene Wittington, a big fan of Andersen, had complaints.

She had also told me that I had an open invitation to move into her organization if things got too hot working for Barbara. Although Darlene presented this in an offhanded, teasing manner, it seemed obvious she was feeling me out. Stealing people away from Barbara may have been a way of evening the score after Barbara had so successfully done it to her. I wasn't interested. The rivalry between Darlene and Barbara was well known within the bank and a topic of continuous gossip. In spite of some reservations about Barbara's style and the issues around Gemini, I wasn't interested in jumping ship. Going over to Darlene would have been the equivalent of dumping the Mets and jumping on the New York Yankees bandwagon. You pick your team and you stick with them through good and bad. Sometimes I felt as if NationsBank senior executives liked pitting managers against each other for their own viewing pleasure, a modern adaptation of the Roman Coliseum. If that was the case, the battles between Barbara and Darlene provided lots of entertainment for the upper echelons.

"I'm hearing a lot of negative feedback from my people on the engine team," Darlene said.

"What kind of feedback?"

"I hear that Andersen and NationsBank employees aren't getting along."

"Says who?"

"Says some of my people assigned to the project. I think we need a bitch session to get it all out on the table."

This was a thankless job, I thought, fending off arrows in every direction—and Darlene's organization was supposedly the group that had a great working relationship with Andersen. I tried to point out that these issues could be addressed without involving the whole team in a bitch session. It took some arm-twisting by me, capped off with a phone call from her nemesis Barbara Albrecht, but Darlene finally agreed to limit it to the ones who were bitching. She had another issue, too.

"I don't think we have spelled how this process is going to work."

Darlene was on to the same issue I had tried to raise early on. Simple answer, I felt. Not that I liked it. Andersen assumed it would make recommendations based on the information collected. They had a successful track record at NationsBank. Whatever they recommended would probably get approved. They had been hired because of their consulting expertise, and no one had the credibility that they did.

Darlene kept pressing on with her concern. "Everybody has a list like mine of what we think the engine will need to do. You could paper the walls with them," she said.

Kittles's response did little to increase my comfort level. "Well, obviously we can't be expected to do everything all at once. We'll continue to add required function in future releases . . . that's how we handled it with Model Bank."

No wonder Model Bank was so far behind in converting branches. This was the standard "the customer is always right" approach to business. It ignored the fact that some needs may not be in the best interest of the bank, perhaps not worth the effort to implement, or in conflict with other needs. Needs had to be prioritized. Low-priority feature and function requirements could become an endless list of mutual exclusives if not managed through some kind of process. On this score, Darlene was right on target.

Trying to add all kinds of functions to make everybody happy would mean a lot more work, or as they say in the project management business, "scope creep." This was a big problem, unless you are the consultant billing by the hour. Why say no when you could say later instead? "We'll catch it in the next release." The longer the list of requirements, the longer consultants and integrators could feed off the project. At least for the first phase, thanks to Billings, the contract was based on a fixed price.

We had hardly kicked off the engine project, and I was already tired of hearing about how great the Model Bank project was and how all we really needed to do was to emulate the proven methods of Model. Jay wasn't as bad as some of the others, but he, too, seemed blinded by Model Bank propaganda.

There was something very strange about Darlene raising these issues. Why was Darlene of all people getting testy about Andersen? She had always been so high on them in the past. Why were her people having so many problems working with the consultants when they frequently worked together on other projects? Had these problems only surfaced now? Kittles and I scrambled to reassure her that we would address the issues she was raising, but I was left scratching my head.

I agreed with the points Darlene had made, just as I did with the gripes raised by the STG. There needed to be agreement on how requirements would be handled. I didn't like the implicit idea of leaving it up to the consultants just because they were consultants. If Andersen Consulting would always make the call, why were we as NationsBank associates involved at all? Was it simply so they could borrow our watch and then tell us what time it was?

It was all about the consultants. The steering committee would provide credibility with upper management. The rest of us were there to function as indentured servants, to assist Andersen in furthering its own cause. If this was their intention, they may have underestimated the tenacity of some of us working on the project from NationsBank.

It continued to puzzle me why the people from Integration Services who worked for Darlene had so many negative things to say about Andersen. This undercurrent of hostility from Darlene and her organization was completely unexpected. Until now Darlene Wittington had always given high praise to Andersen for the bottom-up review. She also said that unlike Gemini, "we can control Andersen." Things just didn't add up.

One of my guys brought back some interesting feedback that helped clue me in. As the earlier bottom-up phase run by Darlene was winding down, Andersen had circulated a draft of the final document to subject experts from NationsBank. These were people who had participated in the fact-gathering interviews. There were many inaccuracies and invalid conclusions, according to the information he had received. Andersen had promised to make the changes before final publication, but the changes were never made. He told me there were people within Integration Services who were livid. Darlene Wittington had apparently ignored the protests. That was until now.

As I tried to piece it together, I decided that Darlene had been sitting on a pressure cooker with her people ready to erupt regarding the Andersen relationship. Was it possible that in the past, Darlene didn't want to make waves? Upper management liked Andersen and she was too far invested with them in her organization to turn on them herself. Andersen consultants had infiltrated Integration Services and were indistinguishable from her regular employees. For a brief period of time, someone else was in charge of a major Andersen project. Now was the time to air all those festering complaints. Just my rotten luck that it would be now.

The lack of process for establishing priorities and addressing issues continued to be a problem. Andersen wanted to rely exclusively on its collection of interviews for developing the business requirements. There were serious issues with this approach and lots of questions left unanswered. With no synthesizing component built into the Andersen project, there were no guarantees that issues and requirements would be adequately addressed. And there was no consensus building. If our final output was simply a large list of functional and business requirements, composed primarily from internal interviews, couldn't we be drawn to inaccurate conclusions? Andersen consultants on the project were already saying things like the following: "There are no products on the market that can meet all of the needs we have uncovered; consequently, we will have to build the engine from scratch."

How did they know there was nothing on the market? We had not started the vendor reviews. How could we possibly address all perceived needs, especially if some were mutually exclusive? It was as if all identified needs would be addressed in the new solution design, regardless of their relative importance. The only issues would be determining what release would include the new functional requirements. Unlike me, they didn't seem concerned if it happened in time for Boatmen's, or at some later time, many billable hours away. This was one hell of a way to get everybody's buy-in.

There was also that other little problem. The identified needs were still not coming from customers. They were primarily coming from people responsible for operating the current systems with limited knowledge outside their sphere and no vested interest to change that comfort zone. There would have been no motorized cars, electronic calculators, or quartz watches if the focus of product creation was on building a bigger, better, faster product based on the same assumptions as the old. Imagine if the original design engineers locked themselves in a back room with nothing but a horse and buggy, a tabulating machine, or a mechanical watch and never received input from customers or other sources. I was afraid that rather than carefully understanding priority requirements and looking for a new solution, we would end up rebuilding the same old system, only with bigger and more expensive features. How quickly we could get it on the market and helping customers wasn't even on the list. "Late for Boatmen's? Not our problem." That little unfortunate occurrence would be a problem exclusively for me as the "client" project manager.

After much discussion among the NationsBank folks about the "processless" project, Dan Price offered a suggestion.

"You know. We've used something before that we might be able to apply here."

Here we go again, I thought. Just like Dan to look for an alternative to avoid rolling up sleeves and slugging it out.

Dan continued, "It's called *PowerPlus* and it can help resolve conflict and establish priorities. PowerPlus is also a great way of building consensus from different groups."

After checking it out, I decided Dan was right. It was already a de facto standard in NationsBank. The bank had purchased the rights to use it from PowerPlus Systems Corporation of America Inc.[7] The people who had used it before were raving about it. The PowerPlus Method, as noted in a PowerPlus flyer, demonstrates that, "when you use the PowerPlus Agile Modeling approach to requirement analysis, you will get *results* like you've never seen before." They boasted a track record of speeding up conventional analysis methods by as much as 400 percent.

This, I became convinced, was what we needed to get things right and speed things up.

We presented PowerPlus as a possible alternative to members of the steering committee. This did not please Andersen. Dave Gibbons was furious and took immediate issue with this approach. "I don't see why this is needed. We already have a plan in place," he said. He looked like he was about to explode in a tantrum. Gibbons was short and heavy with carrot red hair on top of a pudgy kidlike freckled face. Other Andersen consultants called him "Dennis the Menace," but only behind his back.

If Andersen did have a plan in place, it was a big secret to the rest of us. Perhaps Gibbons and the rest of the Andersen management team were reacting to the "results" thing. I was starting to believe it really was one of the most dreaded words a consultant could hear. It seemed to send those agonizing spasms straight up the spine, like kryptonite did to

Superman. Analysis, problem solving, OK, results . . . not if it can be avoided, and only when the client demands it.

Over the objections of Dave Gibbons, the steering committee approved using PowerPlus, and, in spite of Andersen's lukewarm reception, we were able to implement it. We used trained PowerPlus moderators from the bank and invited representatives from various business units within the Services Company to the engine PowerPlus session. It helped resolve some of the most contentious issues and helped get concurrence on what core functions the engine would need to provide—all within a couple days. No one wanted to appear to be too parochial in the open forum of PowerPlus. Participants, as well as several of our senior managers who made cameo appearances during the session, would later say that this was the most productive element of the engine project. I also brought in two of my reserves as a swat team to share some of their analysis and add critical assessment to the session.

The problem with the more conventional analysis approach Andersen Consulting was using wasn't only the amount of time required to complete it. The Andersen approach revolved around one-on-one interviews over a good portion of the three-month contract with clients considered subject experts and people representing many different parts of NationsBank. The problem was that there was no education taking place where different groups could begin to understand requirements from the perspective of others with different responsibilities. No one was made aware of the potential trade-offs involved in setting priorities. There were also no collective "buy-in," or acceptance, and no agreement on why some requirements would be giving higher priority than others. After information was collected, it would be written up in a report with Andersen recommendations for next steps. "Sounds like my interview was a waste of time. They're going with what that other group has always wanted to do." Why would we assume that our consultants, many of whom looked like they had just walked off the college campus, could take all this information and come up with the best solution for moving forward, when we at the bank couldn't come to agreement among ourselves? Conventional wisdom accepted this approach as business as usual. They were the consultants.

With PowerPlus, all parties spent five days together, sorting through issues, educating each other based on their knowledge and experience and, eventually, by using the PowerPlus method, coming to consensus on next steps. Technologists within the group gained a better understanding of how different business operations needed to work. Business specialists became more aware of what technology could and could not do. Names that had previously only popped up in e-mails or phone calls were put to faces. There was legitimate team buy-in and knowledge was shared. People left motivated to work together and make the project successful. Why? They now had a broader perspective and better understanding of requirements from the collective group. They were made aware of the trade-offs and worked collectively in making the tough decisions. They felt they had contributed. It was collaborative. The other major advantage of PowerPlus was that when they walked out the door, it wasn't over. Participants left motivated to help make this work. They now had "skin in the game."

Among the requirements validated through the PowerPlus process, the entire group of participants approved two very important priorities:

1. The transaction engine must support real-time processing.
2. The transaction engine must be inclusive.

Performance won out over function. "Real time" as a top priority implied that electronic processing was a top priority. The session output also indicated that speed and reliability would be key. Check processing would not be ignored, but it would have to take a backseat to electronic transactions in terms of priorities. The possibility of continuing to use the current check-processing system for the time being while we concentrated on building a new electronic-transaction system was the consensus. This was just fine with me.

Building the engine to be inclusive implied that it could not become just another component of the Model Bank program, or any other NationsBank initiative for that matter. Some groups within NationsBank might choose not to use the engine, at least not right away, but in our efforts to design the system, we should not exclude any groups from participating. It would need to be developed with all this in mind.

PowerPlus turned out to be a huge success in resolving conflicts and establishing priorities. It also was key in getting people with very different views to agree to the same common priorities.

So why didn't our consultants embrace this kind of approach? I suspected that in addition to the results problem, "rapid analysis" and resolution could demystify consulting activities and potentially expose the lack of business knowledge. It could also make it more difficult to steer the process in a direction to the consultant's best interest. Not to mention, if companies used the PowerPlus process it would mean less time running interviews and more time getting real business accomplished.

Requirements could be identified and prioritized in a few days as opposed to week after week of interviews with no way to resolve conflicting points of view until the consultant weighs in with a recommendation.

Gibbons would continue to minimize the importance of the results-oriented PowerPlus session and attempted to emphasize the value of the personalized interviews conducted by Andersen throughout the remaining weeks of the project. Many of the interviews emphasized were with NationsBank operational managers responsible for check processing and Model Bank. This I surmised was a pretty good indication of the direction in which our friends from Andersen wanted to take us, PowerPlus notwithstanding.

I didn't think Kittles was completely on board here, but it was obvious he wasn't going to cross Gibbons. The engine project, when used to gather requirements and develop a system design, was just a warm-up for a potentially large implementation contract. Gibbons was attempting to hook the big tuna with a larger follow-on contract, and Kittles didn't want to be perceived as the spoiler, regardless of his personal sympathies. This first phase was an investment, and Gibbons was determined to make the most of it. PowerPlus was an inconvenience, but I had the feeling it would still be business as usual for Andersen.

Shortly after completing the PowerPlus session, Peter Miles came storming into the engine project office, cornering Jay Kittles and me. Miles was the Andersen consultant reporting full-time to Darlene Wittington while serving as a liaison to the engine project. He was definitely a check bigot. The steering committee had just met to review the output from PowerPlus. They had been overwhelmingly supportive of the information presented. PowerPlus had given us the plan for moving forward. Miles had heard about it and was furious.

He wanted to know how the engine would handle check processing. Both Jay Kittles and Peter Miles had worked as Andersen consultants on the Model Bank program. Jay decided to give Miles the standard response that had worked so well for Model Bank.

"We can address it in a future release of the engine."

Miles did not look so happy as he turned and left. This was not going to enhance his list of accomplishments needed for fast tracking to a partner. Kittles looked like he wanted to take the words back. He may have been project manager, but Miles seemed to exhibit more control with the Andersen members of the team.

The Global Finance organization, which handled our largest corporate customers, was elated with the results of PowerPlus. Yet it had almost prophetic concerns that the consultants wouldn't accept it. I told Global Finance that we would be fighting tooth and nail to keep real-time capability a major priority, and we now had the PowerPlus conclusions to help push this forward. My belief was that what the Global Finance customers wanted today, General Bank customers would be demanding within a few short years. That was the way it usually happened. Boatmen's or no Boatmen's, we could lose customers if we didn't have the horsepower for supporting online transactions.

While Model Bank advocates from General Bank said they recognized the importance of real-time computing, they were not shy pointing out that real time wasn't going to fix the immediate performance issues of their pet project—checks and floats. Nevertheless, they had participated in PowerPlus as good corporate citizens and said they saw the value of a new payments engine. It just wasn't as big a deal for participants from Model Bank. Yet, this was the major competitive advantage we had according to the consultants and Wall Street analysts, which allowed us to acquire other banks in rapid succession and achieve huge cost savings with consolidation. It was Model Bank that was consistently billed as an advanced-technology solution.

Model Bank was based on mainframe communication and products such as IBM's IMS database, as well as proprietary application software from Alltel Information Systems. In spite of all "the mainframe is dead" talk mainframes were still viable for meeting many large-scale corporate requirements. What concerned me was the choice of software. In *Fundamental of Database Systems*, considered an authoritative book on the subject of databases, authors Ramez Elmasri and Shamkant Navathe point out that IMS, originally introduced by IBM in 1968, was based on a hierarchical data model, making it complex and less easy for users than more recent technological advances such as relational or object-based databases. As they noted, "IMS has no built-in query language, which can be seen as a major shortcoming."[8] In other words, there was no easy way to search and sort out data. This would seriously undermine flexibility, responsiveness, and ease of use. It was one thing to be running mainframes while mainframes still had a place, but to be running a thirty-year-old software program and calling it innovative technology? There were serious limitations for a project as large and as important as Model Bank.

In addition to all this, Model Bank was combining mainframes for back-office connected to front-end personal computers. To use client/server terminology, the mainframes could be viewed as servers. The personal computers were "fat" clients that required a whole other layer of heavy-duty software. Not exactly an efficient architecture. If we hadn't learned anything else in the client/server revolution, it was that companies wanted to exploit networking with efficient "thin" clients where less could go wrong—more like the old mainframe architecture were software was centralized and controlled on powerful servers, not spread out across individual workstations that were difficult to manage and support.

Making the technology choices even more questionable, they were using OS/2 for teller workstations and servers, the IBM operating system that lost the software *War of the Worlds* to Microsoft's Windows. Before Windows, Microsoft received a contract and the technical specifications from IBM to develop a "multitasking" operating system for PCs called OS/2. Amazingly, Microsoft built Windows with similar characteristics to OS/2 in a parallel development effort. Not surprisingly, Windows, with scaled down OS/2 specs, was first out the door. It became the dominant multitasking operating system of choice while OS/2 was still in development. In the end, OS/2 lost. Windows quickly became the de facto standard with 90 percent market share.[9] So why OS/2? Was there sill bitter feelings over Gates's dinosaur comment? No, couldn't be that.

NationsBank must have gotten a great deal on OS/2, but it begged the question: what about long-term support for a product that IBM was de-emphasizing? There had been much speculation by the trade press that IBM was planning to reduce future development efforts and support for OS/2.[10] How this kind of an approach of combining a legacy mainframe with OS/2 workstations could help NationsBank address the "10-to-1" cost disadvantages that banks were reported to be facing from nonbanks was beyond me. Like the plantation mansions of the Old South, Model Bank was very impressive from a distance. Up close, you realized that the Romanesque pillars were made of pinewood, not marble.

Attempting to absorb all the Model Bank problems within the scope of the engine project was the equivalent of trying to hide an elephant behind a telephone pole. Based on accepted standards of the day, the Model platform had to be considered antiquated, and yet we were still working hard to implement it across all branches. Besides, I had heard there was a whole other effort being quietly launched dedicated to replacing the current Model Bank with a more up-to-date technical architecture. Given the tight time frames for implementing Model Bank, the plan was to implement the current program and then switch to the new one sometime in the future—implying at least two highly disruptive conversions. Yet, in spite of all this, there were still advocates from the Model Bank program telling us that we should build the engine based on the same technology that they were currently using, "capitalizing on the success of Model." After PowerPlus, only the consultants still mouthed this mantra, at least publicly.

All the major questions seemed to have been addressed. Shouldn't we be building the transaction engine to support new customer needs versus supporting old infrastructure assumptions? How could we claim that we were building a strategic solution for the future if we merely continued business as usual? Thanks to PowerPlus, I was convinced we could now move from analysis and start making real progress.

In talking with a steering committee representative from the Corporate Strategic Technology Group named Vincent Porter, I told him that I had a big concern that Andersen Consulting kept trying to push us back to checks. Porter said he could keep them under control. At the time, I was very appreciative of his willingness to "step up" and take an active role. This seemed to be so rare, particularly from our corporate strategy organization.

It was obvious that Vincent Porter was not pleased with Andersen's work on our project. He came from one of the old and now defunct New York banks swallowed up in the merger frenzy. He was average build, had dark hair, dark eyes, a golden brown tan, and usually dressed in bright, loud colors. No doubt his wardrobe had been replenished from his days in New York banking. I soon began to realize that he wasn't interested in getting rid of Andersen, but changing to another group within Andersen for continuing the project. As one of his people had said, "Vincent and I think your guys are mainframe biased." According to her, Porter liked working with another Andersen group that specialized in client/server. It just so happened that this was a primary focus area for Andersen. We just happened to hook up with an Andersen team that had a mainframe basis. Client/server was still a huge moneymaker for consultants. Porter assured me that he would get us on the right track.

There was another Andersen initiative within NationsBank linking telephone banking with extensive customer and product data via client/server technology to significantly extend our current telephone-banking capability. This was called the Direct Bank project. Initial plans for Direct Bank were to provide extensive financial services around the clock for pilots in Washington, D.C., and Florida.[11] At one point we scheduled a meeting with Porter to discuss the transaction engine design. The Andersen partner responsible for the Direct Bank initiative showed up instead. "Vince was busy and asked me to attend for him."

His name was Ken Pollack. Porter must have had lots of confidence in this consultant to use him as his replacement. Pollack came to our meeting as Mr. Business Casual. At least in appearance, the two Andersen partners, Gibbons and Pollack, were Yin and Yang. Pollack looked more like a computer programmer than a consulting partner. Gibbons's custom-tailored suits did little to enhance his short and round physique. Pollack's blend of casual was custom, too, but seemed a better fit for his skin. Pollack was built thin and had pointed facial features and fuzzy gray blue eyes. Some people are name droppers. Pollack dropped technical acronyms within every series of comments as he bragged about all Andersen was doing with Direct Bank. He already knew what we on the engine project team needed to do—follow his lead.

Whereas the current Andersen team talked only of mainframes and using an approach "just like we did with Model," Pollack's take on Direct Bank was all about client/server and distributed computing. As was the case with many large consulting firms, Andersen had groups dedicated to different areas of technology. While we had been working with a group of Andersen consultants with mainframe experience, I had a feeling we would now be seeing some of their client/server people. Andersen appeared to have all the bases covered. "You want mainframe, we'll give you mainframe. You want client/server, we can give you that, too."

Many corporate managers were still operating under the assumption that consultants could point them in the right direction, helping to chart the best possible course. Consultants were expected to provide expertise to address complex issues and sort through the vast array of possible solutions. Instead, it was apparent that Andersen wasn't about to let anything stand in the way of landing the next NationsBank contract—even if it meant playing all the angles and steering different groups down separate, nonconverging paths, keeping all options open. I could tell that the fun was just beginning.

The prevailing joke became How many consultants does it take to change a light bulb? We don't know. They never get past the feasibility study.[12]

SUMMARY OF OBSERVATIONS

- Expectations surrounding a project can be set unrealistically when consultants and other vendors establish them in the pre-engagement selling phase. Corporate Management responsible for the project must be responsible for setting realistic expectations, testing them periodically, and controlling them through all phases of the project.

- Before contracts are signed, consultants should be asked to explain their process for determining priorities and resolving issues.

- In most contracts there is generally no incentive for the consultant to provide rapid analysis of requirements. It takes more than a fixed contract to create an incentive to accelerate the consulting engagement. Rapid analysis demystifies the process of consulting, potentially exposing weaknesses, such as lack of knowledge.

- Consultant contracts are often front-end loaded with analysis-paralysis. Without strong skills and knowledge, consultants will need to pick the brains of employees and other knowledgeable subject matter experts before they can consult. This approach increases time delays in projects. Corporate management needs to find new alternatives and be on guard against those consultants who are "churning the business" to maximize the length of contracts, versus working to achieve results. Time to market and execution should be major objectives of most projects. Look for alternatives that can reduce unnecessary times wasted in analysis.

- The typical requirements-gathering approach used by consultants can result in identification of mutually exclusive needs and requirements. There may be no effective method for prioritizing and/or eliminating requirements.

- A process like PowerPlus Agile Modeling from PowerPlus Systems of America can accelerate time-to-market by resolving conflicts, establishing priorities, and gaining buy-in. It is the antithesis of consulting "analysis-paralysis."

- Large consulting firms may have different competitive groups advocating different approaches with the same client. This is further evidence that hiring consultants to provide an "objective, third-party" view is at least suspect.

NOTES

1. "Quotations—Work and Recreation," http://bovis.gyuvet.ch/92varia/9243quo3.htm.
2. Brian Hellauer, "Andersen Shaping Bank Technology with it's Vision of What the Future Holds," *American Banker*, 13 December 1993, 18.
3. Ronald Henkoff, "Inside Andersen's Army of Advice," *Fortune*, 4 October 1993, 78–79.
4. Steven Marjanovic, "Electronic Payment Law May Hasten End of Checks," *American Banker*, 1 May 1996, 1.
5. Gregory A. Crandell and Richard K. Crane, "The Safest Place is the Cutting Edge," *Bank Management* (May/June 1996): 8.

6. See figure 2, p. 239.

7. PowerPlus is a trademark product from PowerPlus Systems of America Inc., www.powerplussystems.com.

8. Ramez Elmasri and Shamkant Navathe, *Fundamentals of Database Systems* (Redwood City, Calif.: The Benjamin/Cummings, 1994), 370–71.

9. Paul Carroll, *Big Blues: The Unmaking of IBM* (New York: Crown Publishers, 1993), 86–88.

10. Michelle Singletary, "Is OS/2 on Cruise Control?" *Software Magazine* (December 1996): 126–28.

11. "Banks Branch Out over the Phone-Electronic Options and Users Multiply," *Washington Post*, 21 June 1996, D1-2.

12. Elmar Ludwig, "Light Bulb Jokes," University of Osnabruck, Germany, http://www.informatik.uni-osnabrueck.de/elmar/Fun/light2.html.

CHAPTER TEN

CONSULTINGSPEAK

The Global Finance organization within NationsBank acquired a trading firm out of Chicago with a small high-tech support group. The manager of this group, John Turner, invited Denny Billings and me to visit. Billings decided we should go.

John Turner and his organization were using a "transaction engine" for supporting the traders. Prior to the trip, he had confided in me about his intent. Turner felt his organization could provide some of the integration work needed for developing the new transaction engine that could support all banking and trading applications for NationsBank.

Turner asked, "Why would you use outside consultants when we have the right kind of talent right here within the bank?"

NationsBank had a thing about tall buildings. We were the biggest in Charlotte, Atlanta, and, if not the biggest in Dallas, close to it. So it really didn't surprise me that NationsBank had space in the Sears Tower. No longer the world's tallest building, it still loomed over the rest of the lakefront city where softballs and pizzas were also oversized. It was still early morning when we arrived, and the landmark tower bathed in shadow a large part of the cold, blustery streets below. Chicagoans didn't seem to mind. It was the pride of their skyline.

In keeping with tradition, if and when NationsBank was ready to get serious about Global, I figured we'd have to build something taller than that new Malaysian skyscraper in Kuala Lamur. That, or acquire it.

Just about every large corporation with different lines of business had a technology group like Turner's organization. These were the guys who suffered from a serious case of "not invented here" disease. If they didn't think of it themselves, it wasn't a very good idea. When vendors pedaled new products, they could have invented something better themselves and had already thought of it years before, but they were always so busy doing all these other things on their plate, all of which were absolutely crucial to advancing technology—whether it was good for the business or not. It didn't really matter to them whether employees from other less prestigious groups or outside vendors understood the significance of their work. Nonetheless, they sometimes really did have good "hands-on" technical expertise.

The key was being a little deferential and cutting through all the arrogant crap that clouded discussions. In this case, I felt the timing of our visit could help. Global Finance had reason to be less arrogant these days. The newly acquired trading business was racking up poor quarterly earnings, one after another. Upper management was demanding action: "If they can't make profitability targets on revenue, they better start cutting costs." Until things turned around, Turner needed to find some temporary project work for his people in other places within the bank. If he didn't, he might be forced to lay off at least some of them.

Denny Billings, who came out of General Bank, seemed to harbor a negative perception of the entire Global Finance line of business. "These people have no reason—none whatsoever—for acting so superior," he said. After all, he pointed out, the major corporate account division was a rounding error, compared to the revenue generated by the retail accounts run by General Bank.

Billings and Turner made for interesting contrast. Billings was older and almost completely bald. Turner needed a haircut and seemed like a playful kid next to Billings, scheming to see what he could get away with. Billings spoke slowly and deliberately. Turner's speech pattern sputtered in fast-flowing streams of conscience.

During the meeting in Chicago, the Global Finance team launched into a presentation on their capabilities. These guys were out there—way out there. As Turner took over, the presentation became more grounded. He seemed to really know his stuff. Turner talked about the new technology his team was employing to support the traders. He told us that this was the same technology that was transforming businesses on Wall Street.

The transaction system they were using came from a company called Tibco Inc., one more of the numerous high-tech start-ups that were growing exponentially. Of course his team had souped it up and made it better. This solution had proven ideal for handling trading transactions for their group. Turner felt that, with some modification, it could also be applied to standard banking transactions. We had trampled all over Europe in search of a transaction engine when we had something that might work right in our own backyard. They had my attention. Billings, too, but not for the same reasons. Less than halfway into the presentation, Denny Billings stopped Turner, who was presenting.

"I have no idea what you are talking about . . . or . . . how this applies . . . to what we are trying to do."

As Turner stepped aside, Billings walked over to a chalkboard in the front of the room and sketched out his view of Model Bank. He was very proud of this mammoth bank operation he had helped turn over to Andersen and Alltel. Billings drew lots of boxes and arrows. It wasn't the first time he had sketched this diagram. In fact, I don't think I could remember a meeting where he didn't find some excuse to sketch it.

"We spent $500 million on this . . . and . . . we are not going to throw it away," Billings emphatically insisted.

Five hundred million dollars and still counting. This helped reaffirm my suspicions. From Billings's perspective, the transaction engine we were proposing was the answer to the performance problems that were impacting the Model Bank rollout. He couldn't go back and ask for more money to fix the Model Bank, which had been billed as one of the great technology success stories in banking. Neither could Andersen and Alltel. That's why he was so eager to get involved. Although he never said a word to me about it, Billings couldn't have been too happy about the PowerPlus conclusions. It delayed things.

Thanks to PowerPlus, the engine wasn't in his pocket, not yet.

After Billings had driven his stake in the ground, there were several awkward moments of silence. We were all looking around the room waiting for someone else to speak. No one had mentioned anything about throwing Model Bank away, yet Billings had become embarrassingly defensive on this point. Finally, the previous presenter looked over from Turner.

"Should I continue?"

Turner shook his head. What was the point?

The speakers from Global Finance believed they had a solution that could be applied to help all areas of the bank move to real-time processing, including the Model Bank program. This was obviously not important for Billings. He would be the first to argue that Model Bank and check processing would be around for years to come. Model Bank in its current form was as advanced as he was prepared to get. I for one thought the Global Finance solution deserved further consideration. That's what I thought the engine project was all about.

The original proposal from Andersen Consulting had stated: "A critical component of this work includes assessing the feasibility of and selecting possible industry solutions/best practices, vendor solutions, *as well as evaluation of internal capabilities* to form the core technical infrastructure." Forget about short and concise phrasing. Sometimes you almost needed a "Consulting to English Dictionary" to understand what they were saying. In English: "An important part of this project is finding the right solution, and we will look at what others are doing, both in other parts of the bank and elsewhere." In my mind at least, that meant looking at what these guys were doing in their area of the business.

During the taxi ride back to O'Hare Airport, Billings and I began discussing the progress on the engine project. I mentioned that the technical team was now in the process of evaluating several different vendors to determine the best product fit.

"I don't want to play musical chairs with vendors," Billings abruptly interjected, in a loud and clipped tone that reverberated over the Latin music coming from the radio in the front of the cab. He then shifted his pitch back to its normal cadence, adding, "I really don't care what the vendor solution is. I'm just tired . . . tired of all this . . . this . . . studying of this."

He added his favorite refrain, "We need to get on with this." For the rest of the ride to the airport, we both sat quietly as the driver bobbed up and down to throbbing brassy sounds as the cab weaved its way through dense lines of traffic.

Nobody wanted to accelerate things more than I did. I just didn't want to get shot by trying to implement something that was doomed to fail. By now what scared me most was that it seemed the consultants had their fingers on the trigger. My fate was in their hands. Not a pretty thought.

It stood to reason that not only Andersen, but the Model Bank people including Billings, wanted the transaction engine to handle checks because so much of the Model business was based on checks. This was true of NationsBank in general. Probably even more important to guys like Billings, the engine could be used as a front for funneling more money into the Model Bank. Best of all, this could be done without admitting anything about the performance problems with NationsBank's most respected program. This was the best explanation I could conjure up for why Denny Billings had become so interested in the transaction engine—interested enough to join the engine project and leave his prized $500 million pet project. Or did he?

In spite of problems, Billings and his buddies from Andersen and Alltel shared a common need to preserve and foster the Model Bank myth. The engine could provide relief while keeping the myth alive. By all counts, the performance problems with the Model needed to be addressed as soon as possible. They were becoming more obvious as the program continued to expand. I was hearing about Model Bank problems on a more regular basis from all kinds of sources within the bank.

Billings was the executive sponsor and highest-ranking NationsBank manager on the engine project. He still had his reputation to maintain with Model Bank. Andersen and Alltel wanted additional business. If the vendors were to be successful, at a minimum they needed to help keep Billings happy. As long as they continued to take care of each other, there was little to worry about. He would get them lucrative follow-on business. They would let him and other members of the NationsBank management team take credit for the ongoing success of Model Bank, the transaction engine, and so on. Public acclaim usually went to the client, as long as the consultants got paid. On the flip side, if things went badly, blame also went to the client. One way or the other, the consultants got paid and, if need be, they started looking for a new sponsor.

It was now obvious that Andersen and Alltel were getting their marching orders from Billings. His agenda was their agenda. The end game was already mapped out. It was only hidden from the rest of us. I was convinced this was why things like the Global Finance meeting were so irritating to Billings. If an alternative solution captured interest and caught on, it would eliminate the ability of his consulting partners to steer things in the agreed-upon, predetermined direction.

They must have also figured that no one on the inside would be stupid enough to get in their way, particularly someone with major strikes already against him. I was the guy who had met with Al Johnson and stirred everything up. While nothing had been directly said, it had obviously not gone without notice. Billings never said anything, but other people within my area of the business joked about my being "unpredictable," and the need to get back in the good graces of the "powers that be." In not so many words, I figured I was being given one more chance to show I could play ball.

My responsibility was to do a job regardless of what hidden agendas might have been in play. I was determined to complete that assignment to the best of my ability. Given all that had transpired, it would also be important to follow NationsBank management directives and avoid any potential actions that would be viewed as insubordinate. This was walking a tight rope in this highly political environment. I rationalized that as long as hidden agendas were not directly communicated, I was not violating any management directives by carrying out the original project plan. The adrenaline was really starting to flow now.

While Billings had not told me to stop the vendor review, he clearly indicated that he wanted to accelerate things. This I would attempt to do. With Andersen management's assistance, I worked with the project team to move things along at a faster pace, developing a short list of potential vendors. Different points of view were becoming very obvious. Impassioned advocates of one vendor over another were getting more emotional as the project rolled on.

There was another internal solution several of us from the strategy group felt should also be considered. It was a newly purchased software solution running on a Tandem computer. Tandem hardware was highly reliable and a proven technology in the Automated Teller Machine (ATM) and Point of Sale (POS) markets where stability was critical. The new electronic-payments solution was for NationsBank's Automated Clearinghouse (ACH). This was an important electronic product NationsBank offered to customers. It handled customer payrolls and other bulk payments, processing them in machine-readable form. Businesses would use the ACH to make payroll and dividend payments. Individuals would use the ACH to pay recurring bills such as utility, mortgage, and insurance bills.

In addition to my engine project assignment, I had also been put in charge of a task group to identify the best product fit for the ACH, which was out of gas and couldn't wait for the completed transaction engine to get on line. In a sense, part of the ACH solution was a transaction engine. If that engine turned out to be a good solution for the ACH electronic payments, why not let it become *the* transaction engine and expand its use for other bank applications?

As noted by Kristen Wells of the Federal Reserve, "The ACH network was designed to accommodate several types of fund transfers, including business payments to consumers and other businesses, consumer payments to businesses, and government payments to consumers and businesses. Therefore, ACH payments may be viewed as a close substitute for several types of check payments."[1]

Tandem had a proven track record in implementing large, complex solutions. Tandem claimed over 80 percent share of the ATM market and 65 percent of all credit card transactions. The top 125 regional and national electronic funds transfer networks were also using Tandem.[2] Historically, the knockoff with Tandem was the high cost. Their prices were going down dramatically, based on increased competition from vendors selling other solutions, such as *UNIX*—another of those open systems, where every vendor had its own unique version, often incompatible with all the other "open" versions. Utilizing the same Tandem solution for the transaction engine could reduce costs and potentially eliminate the creation of multiple solutions to perform similar tasks. If we already had potential transaction engines in-house, why buy or build a new one?

The Andersen team was unfamiliar with Tandem, so we set up sessions to provide education. We also set up a conference call with Tibco Inc., the vendor being used by Global Finance. That's another of those crazy things when working with consultants who have clout but limited business knowledge or technology skills. In an effort to drive the project in the best interest of the bank, we felt we had to educate Andersen, not only on our business, but also on potential vendor solutions.

How could Andersen recommend a vendor they knew nothing about? It was a backward way of doing business, but there didn't seem to be any other alternatives. At the same time, Andersen kept promising some of its business partners and other contacts, setting up meetings with potential providers. While we continued to look for electronic payment solutions, Andersen emphasized check-processing providers. PowerPlus conclusions were not about to get in their way. It was as if we were working on separate projects.

One vendor that Andersen immediately put at the top of the list was Hogan Systems. It was the Andersen consultant who doubled as a NationsBank manager who made the initial contact with Hogan Systems, my "good ol' bud," Peter Miles. He made his home in Dallas, which coincidentally was the headquarters for Hogan. Miles met with them in advance and told me, "They have a plan to build an engine that is very similar to what we need to do. It will handle both check and electronic." Miles also told me that Andersen had worked with them in the past.

During a Hogan presentation to the combined Andersen and NationsBank engine project team, it became apparent that Hogan had a partnership with a smaller Midwestern bank to build a check-processing system. If we joined as the third partner for this effort, they would solicit our input for product requirements, but they could make no commitment that our requirements would be satisfied, at least not immediately. As unbelievable as this sounded, it was explained that the agreement with the other bank specified that they would receive top priority over everybody else. We also learned that this other bank was only handling about 30 percent of our total workload. Miles squirmed as they mentioned this point, as if they had ventured off of a prerehearsed script. On top of this, some of the presentation charts looked a lot like ones we at NationsBank had previously developed as part of our very own engine project. I wasn't the only NationsBank employee to notice.

There was a subsequent meeting involving Denny Billings, Andersen partner Dave Gibbons, and me to discuss the status of the engine project. Despite Hogan's obvious mismatch, Gibbons unbelievably said, "Clearly, after reviewing various vendor options, Hogan is the front runner." I bit down on my tongue. Maybe I should have said something, but I didn't. My feeling at the time was that it would not be a good idea to appear eager to take issue with comments from an Andersen partner in front of Billings, an obviously devoted Andersen supporter from way back. One has to pick the battles worth fighting, not to mention the time and place. Not here, not now. Not yet.

Internal squabbles continued through the end of 1996. One of my biggest frustrations was that Peter Miles worked clandestinely around the outer fringes of the project team. I knew that Andersen subordinates assigned to the engine were in close contact with Miles. Kittles admitted this, as it was an ongoing source of frustration for him as well. He really didn't have to tell me; it was obvious to all of us on the NationsBank side. Acting as a NationsBank manager, Miles had developed more clout than Kittles, who was looking more like a mere figurehead all the time. Every so often Andersen would attempt to stuff information into steering committee presentations emphasizing the importance of check processing. It always conflicted with the priorities established in the PowerPlus session and the overall thrust of the engine project. It was starting to really irk me.

I concluded that my best strategy was to keep as much of the decision making out in the open as possible. The steering committee was capable of making the right decisions, provided its members were given the right information. I knew I would have to support whatever that final decision turned out to be—even if I didn't like it. Until then, I would work like hell to keep this thing from being railroaded.

Miles had a decided advantage. I was an employee assigned a management role on the project where everything I did was open to review. I had to play fair. There were too many people, both consultants and NationsBank senior managers, looking over my shoulder. As a consultant operating as a "liaison," Miles was below the radar screen. He could play any way he wanted. Operating with guerilla warrior efficiency, Miles was launching surprise offensives at the engine project whenever he felt the need. He also proved masterful at getting the "wet behind the ears" contingent of consultants assigned to the project to help promote his agenda while he remained hidden in the shadows.

Kittles was powerless to help with Miles. I had confronted Miles on several occasions about issues resulting from mixed signals caused by him telling people to do things that conflicted with agreed-upon tasks. It was obvious he was only paying lip service and had no intention of changing his game plan. Finally, in complete frustration at getting nowhere on this, I took my grievances to Dave Gibbons, the Andersen partner. He didn't seem overly concerned either.

"Dave, there continues to be a communications problem. I'm hoping you can help."

"Oh, how so?"

"People on the team keep getting different directives. As I've said before, it would help if Miles worked through me and Jay, like we originally agreed."

"Well, I know we are all running pretty hard. Peter's just trying to help, but I'll talk to him."

"There's another issue. Global Finance is ready to walk. They say they keep hearing all this talk about a new float-management system as the final solution. The talk is coming from Andersen consultants. Global Finance is afraid the engine won't address their requirements for real time-processing . . . the same concerns they expressed in PowerPlus."

"Of course it will. You know, I've heard from several NationsBank executives that those guys just like complaining."

Needless to say, not much ever happened to improve communications. Apparently, a split in the alliance was not an issue with the Andersen Consulting leadership.

Looking at it cynically, disparate views from different employee groups could help consultants get more work. A divided bank meant increased dependency on consultants to arbitrate with their renowned "objective" view. The more divisiveness in the corporation, the more opportunity for consulting. Why reduce redundancy and get different groups within NationsBank working together if it meant fewer consulting contracts? When I mentioned to Denny Billings my concerns about Global Finance pulling out, he reminded me that they contributed less in revenue than General Bank, as if anybody working for Nations-Bank didn't already know this. "I've about had it with those people anyway," he said. "They're the tail wagging the dog."

In spite of numerous discussions with Andersen's senior management on the project, they continued to communicate different signals to team members, thus creating all kinds of confusion. The confusion provided additional cover. While he started to keep an even lower profile working out of his NationsBank office in Dallas, Miles continued to provide direction through phone contact with Andersen members of the project team. Just trying to keep these consultants in line became a full-time job. It was like trying to herd cats. If nothing else, it did create more of a bond between Kittles and me. Without ever talking about it, I think we both realized that the guy creating the most problems, namely Miles, could easily turn around and blame any fallout on weak project management—us.

We increasingly shared notes. On several occasions Kittles would tell me that Miles was in Atlanta, meeting with select members of the team. It was always behind closed doors. While I was disappointed that Kittles wasn't doing anything about it, at least he kept me abreast of these kinds of things. I guess he figured I would try and do something. There were several times after getting the tip from Kittles that Miles was in the building, I would do my best to run him down. Miles appeared uneasy whenever I successfully stumbled into him slithering down a hall. If I were really lucky, I'd catch him leaving a closed-door office with junior Andersen consultants assigned to the project. This happened on more than one occasion.

"Hey Pete, what's up?"

"Oh, not much. Here to work on some Model Bank stuff. Thought while I was here, I'd check in with some of our people . . . see how they're doing."

"Any feedback on the project that might help?"

"No, not really. Sounds like things are moving along."

Never for a moment did I doubt that he was working for the Model Bank project team. In addition to all his other responsibilities at NationsBank, Miles was still very active with this Andersen monument to technological innovation. From the beginning, Andersen and Alltel had packaged Model Bank as a competitive weapon, using advanced technology. This, they claimed, gave a unique advantage to NationsBank for further expansion and consolidation, or so they always said. It also gave both Andersen and Alltel a unique advantage in credibility with management. There was always lots of public backslapping. I had a feeling that in between the "feel-good" meetings, there was lots of scrambling behind the scenes to keep all the holes plugged in this advanced-technology system.

As I had surmised, Model Bank needed relief, and the engine presented an opportunity to absorb some of the problems under a new budget, avoiding public scrutiny. Miles seemed more determined than ever to set up the engine project so it could be added to Model.

One day Jay Kittles told me that Dave Gibbons was coming down hard on him. Because things weren't going as smoothly as Gibbons would have liked, Jay was becoming a victim of more and more micromanagement. He apparently felt he was not in a position to challenge either Gibbons or Peter Miles. As Kittles was deciding to back off even further, I knew I would have to become more assertive. Things seemed headed to that unavoidable train wreck I kept worrying about. There was no doubt in my mind who would be straddling the cow plow when the train finally plunged off the track.

Before the end of 1996, the project was extended into February of the next year. Consulting projects never seemed to finish on time and everybody seemed used to it. By now Andersen management must have had enough of the interviews and design work. They had to be itching for the follow-on contract to start building. This was when the big bucks would start to flow. Even with all the politics and miscues, there was a feeling of accomplishment as the year wound down. In spite of all the backdoor maneuvering and squabbling, we had brought the steering committee to consensus on the engine's requirements. There was still much to do and not enough time to get it done. Andersen had badly underestimated the required time for completion.

As was the case with Gemini, Andersen decided to use me as its pitchman. This was in meetings with the steering committee as well as progress update meetings with our more contentious constituents such as Global Finance and the Strategic Technology Group. I had become the transaction engine guy. One would have thought I would have been the last person they would want advocating for the engine. The problem was that the Andersen team was even weaker than the Gemini team. There was no one else who could get up, present the material, and handle the questions that were sure to follow. I'm sure it would have been different if the Andersen "A" team had been assigned.

Like Gemini, they were stuck. As the presentation guy, I could emphasize electronic transactions and do my best to neutralize some of the noise about checks. The interesting thing was that it didn't seem to bother Andersen management. I wondered, was it because the group meetings were considered nothing more than public relations? If need be, they could always disavow things that I was saying as never having the Andersen endorsement. In the meantime, it was one less area for them to worry about. Lots of the major decisions at NationsBank seemed to be made behind closed doors. In this particular case, where our project was so visible, and had so many different groups in the loop, I didn't quite see how they could pull off such a backroom deal, dropping the nonsense about electronic processing and using the funds instead to slam a new float-management system into the back of the Model Bank program. Surely, if all else failed, the steering committee would keep all of us honest.

At a lunch meeting before year-end with the engine project team, Denny Billings announced that a technology survey conducted by the brokerage firm Dean Witter had placed NationsBank as the number one bank in technology. [3] He passed out copies of the report. The survey had evaluated twenty-five of the top national banks. Based on what I knew about NationsBank, as well as other major financial institutions, this was astounding, to say the least. We were, in fact, making new technology investments in PC banking, client/server ventures, and funding numerous consulting reviews. These were minimal investments compared to the large amount we were spending on antiquated systems.

"This points to the success of Model Bank. . . . We've set a standard and . . . we intend to continue our leadership . . . with the transaction engine," said Billings.

Somehow Model Bank was always included as an example of innovative technology. Yet, compared to other banks where I had previously done consulting, NationsBank was still in the Dark Ages. It seemed to me that most of our systems were in desperate need of being revamped, including the Model Bank program. The acquisition of Boatmen's with considerably more old technology coming under the NationsBank umbrella didn't help. Either these other financial institutions reviewed in the survey had fallen under serious disrepair, or we had one heck of a public relations department. Of course the report was slim on details as to how the conclusions were determined. That NationsBank and Dean Witter had formed a partnership and jointly owned a national securities company probably didn't hurt in getting a favorable report.[4] Believing our own PR could be dangerous when there was so much left to do.

Continuing his comments, Billings said, "I think . . . all of us . . . here at NationsBank . . . should be very proud . . . of what we have accomplished."

That sense of bullishness was prevalent throughout the economy, too. We were in the middle of one of the longest economic expansions in history and the stock market was soaring. There were those advocating a more cautious approach. On December 5, 1996, Federal Reserve Chairman Alan Greenspan spoke at a dinner meeting for the American Enterprise Institute for Public Policy Research, about "the Challenge of Central Banking in a Democratic Society." He said the following:

"But how do we know when irrational exuberance has unduly escalated asset values, which then become subject to unexpected and prolonged contractions as they have in Japan over the past decade?"[5]

Five days before Christmas I received a stock option bonus from Al Johnson, president of the Services Company. It was one of the most prestigious awards available at my level in the corporation. A senior manager in the Strategic Technology Group (STG) told me that Johnson liked me and was impressed with my aggressiveness. Good news—my meeting with him had not completely burned the bridge, at least not yet. The notification letter said, "This reflects our confidence in your ability to carry out your responsibilities at NationsBank and we hope you accept the award and the challenges we all face together." Denny Billings and his wife invited me to a holiday party at their home. I took a little time off during the Christmas holidays, spending a few days with my mom and sister in Connecticut. For the first time, I was starting to feel like things were coming together.

Over the holidays I got together with a friend who was a construction worker in New York City. He is a college graduate and one of the smartest guys I know. After a prolonged phase of living the life of a barroom drinker and sometimes brawler, always paying cash, he had settled down, married, and had a beautiful baby daughter. He now had a house of his own, and even more surprisingly, a credit card in his own name. I had never seen him so happy, so mellow. When I started talking about work, he stopped me.

"I'll never understand how guys like you put up with all the crap. At 3:00 in the afternoon I take off my tool belt and never think of work again until the next morning."

The next morning started by climbing out of bed by 4:30 and catching the early train while carrying a workman's bag with a handful of gray flannel suits, but he had a point.

There was another noticeable difference. He burned up the pages of the newspaper to get to the section where he could check on his stocks. In the past he had always turned first to the sports pages. It was strange seeing a die-hard union man rooting for the bubble market to continue bubbling. Companies were downsizing. His stocks were up. We had all bought in.

The beginning of 1997 brought organizational change. Denny Billings was taking on a new role in developing a customer data repository. "Guess I'll learn what this data . . .warehousing . . . stuff is all about . . . I guess," he said. Replacing him as the senior level manager for the engine project was a veteran of the Model campaign, Don Mangrove. The new senior manager on the project had been a regional manager for the Model Bank and reported to Denny Billings when he was running the program. Mangrove would now be responsible for completing the current phase as well as managing the follow-on implementation phase.

My Andersen counterpart, Jay Kittles, told me that our new leader had a very close relationship with Denny Billings. He also had the reputation of being a good company man. Jay told me Mangrove was a stickler for process, managing everything based on a weekly status report log called the Task Action Report (TAR). "It's really not so bad, once you get used to it," he said. Not so bad? I think I'd rather go to the dentist for root canal than attend anymore weekly status meetings to review reports.

The changes taking place in management for the engine project did not please me. What was even more disturbing at the time was the announcement of a new strategy group manager for Transaction Services. Barbara Albrecht was taking on an operational management assignment. There had been a few bumps along the way, but I felt we had survived the skids and were on our way to developing a reasonably good working relationship. When things got tough, she stuck by her people, including me. She was being replaced by the manager who was previously responsible for electronic operations within Transaction Services, Harvey Kraft.

While Kraft was in charge of electronic processing, he always struck me as a closet check bigot. Electronic banking for Harvey was scanning checks with the use of technology such as *imaging*. Using imaging to convert to electronics after the check was already received was like treating the symptoms as opposed to stopping the disease; but there were benefits. It helped preserve float. Kraft was never in any big hurry to implement electronic-banking solutions, but he loved meetings to talk about it. The only positive item I could think of concerning this change was that Kraft worked out of Charlotte. My immediate manager would still be remote from my work location in Atlanta.

Harvey Kraft was a large man with small beady eyes. As our paths frequently crossed and I had an opportunity to watch him in meetings, he would inevitably wait for others to speak first before entering into the discussion. When Harvey began, he generally started by asserting that he wanted to ask a few simple questions to help himself get up to speed. A standard disclaimer followed this: "You know, I'm just a good old country boy from Georgia." One had the feeling he was letting out the drag on his line until he hooked an unsuspecting fish. Better to keep your mouth shut when Harvey had his tackle out.

Harvey had played a crucial role in the Automated Clearinghouse replacement project that eventually went to Tandem. I thought his behavior had been peculiar. When I had presented the recommendation for the Tandem solution to an advisory committee, which included Harvey, he suggested we sign a "letter of intent" with the vendors of choice.

"Why?" I asked. "Why not just sign the contract?"

Harvey responded, "A letter of intent will give us a little more time to evaluate this. We don't need to do anything rash here."

His recommendation to proceed this way was approved by the committee. I had concerns about this approach. I believed that a letter of intent would neutralize our ability to negotiate for further concessions, essentially freezing early discussion on terms and conditions. At first I thought the letter of intent was an ill-conceived idea. I was wrong. It was a classic Harvey Kraft maneuver.

After the letter of intent was signed with Tandem, Harvey Kraft continued to meet with the other major vendor competing for the contract. Unlike the Tandem proposal, which was essentially neutralized by the letter of intent, this other vendor was still free to make changes to its offer. One day this other vendor called me saying that they had received suggestions from Harvey on how to restructure the bid, and they were in the process of making the necessary adjustments to their initial proposal. They would get it to NationsBank shortly. "Please, don't do anything until you see our latest offer," he said.

It started to smell like a backdoor marketing strategy. My suspicions were that the other vendor was preparing an outsourcing proposal. What was in it for Harvey to help these other guys out?

Outsourcing had been previously reviewed as an alternative for this project and rejected. I felt it was only fair to create a little discomfort for Tandem. Without my directly saying anything, they needed to know that, in spite of the letter of intent, they could lose the business. Without mentioning names or the circumstances precipitating my call, I talked to Tandem about the potential risk of losing the business if they didn't reduce their price.

"But we gave you our best price in the letter of intent. We both agreed."

"All I'm saying is that if you want to make sure the letter becomes a contract, you better come down some more."

At first I wasn't sure Tandem would do it. The next day the Tandem salesman called back. He told me that he knew his competitor was friends with Harvey Kraft and was continuing to meet with him regularly. He said that his calls to Harvey to schedule an appointment were never returned. No additional conversation was necessary. He got it. Tandem's prices went down.

An outsourcing proposal from the other competitor was introduced at the last moment. Tandem had already produced its new discounts, significantly below the estimated outsourcing costs. This saved the deal from going south, so to speak. Harvey stated publicly that he was impressed with my ability to negotiate. I was impressed with his ability to play politics. He always made me feel as if he had been on the winning side all along, in spite of all the evidence to the contrary. Not only that, it was as if he was the MVP. As another manager in Transaction Services once said about him, "He's the kind of guy who will start a fire in one place to get something going in another." Harvey never failed to take credit for putting out all the fires he started. "This is exactly the deal I wanted." Thanks for all your help, Steve." Part of me couldn't help but wonder if Harvey had been orchestrating this all along? Did I do exactly what he expected me to do? Nah. He couldn't have been that smart.

Shortly after it was announced that Harvey Kraft would be the new manager running the strategy group for Transaction Services, Harvey met with me to discuss his plans. He told me that he had struck a deal with Don Mangrove, the new senior manager responsible for running the engine project. I would continue on for a month reporting to Mangrove, while a replacement was recruited, and then return to the strategy group to work for Harvey. "This company has plenty of people who can do project management," he said. So I noticed. He went on to tell me that I was needed to develop an architecture plan for Transaction Services. "I want a technology blueprint we can use in the future to help us in building new systems." New check-processing systems? I was afraid to ask.

Harvey also indicated that Darlene Wittington from Integration Services had suggested that I could provide much more value back in strategy than in my current role as engine project manager. Not surprising—Darlene also wanted more emphasis on checks. Getting me out of the program could only help. In the interim, Harvey wanted me to keep him informed on developments related to the engine. For that matter, so did Barbara Albrecht, who said she would remain an advocate for a strategic-based transaction engine. Barbara also told me that I had developed a good reputation and could expect both Mangrove and Kraft to try to eventually win me over to work exclusively for them on a permanent basis.

During a trip to Charlotte, I met with Don Mangrove, who was just getting the lay of the land on the engine project he would now be running. Now in a new job, his former mentor from Model Bank, Denny Billings, would have only a figurehead advisory position, with minimal active involvement—as if his previous role had changed. Mangrove was tall and lanky with an upbeat disposition. His movements were noticeably awkward as he lumbered into the room where we were meeting alone for the first time. Once he had successfully pulled out a pad and pencil, the awkwardness appeared to dissipate, replaced by a projected aura of self-confidence. He arched back erect in his chair, scribbled something on his note pad, and then glanced at me from across the table.

"There are a few things I wanted to meet with you about," he said as he glanced down at the pad.

My first impressions were that Jay Kittles was right. Don was the kind of guy who lived for status meetings. "My style is to be very frank," he said. Like Harvey, Don Mangrove was also originally from Georgia. It was good to hear that he tended to be up-front, although I suspected we were not talking the in-your-face, New York City style of up-front. I suggested that my style was direct as well and that this should provide for good, candid discussion. Don told me he wanted to explore the idea of my staying on as project manager at the conclusion of the current project and during the engine implementation phase.

I shared with him that I felt my skills were best suited to developing technical strategy rather than implementing projects. I didn't have any interest in playing out my career as a monitor for status meetings. Given that he was new and would need to recruit someone to replace me, I was willing to stay on to ensure a successful transition and provide whatever help I could during the transition. He continued to press on the benefits of staying with the engine project. It was the visibility thing again. Don pointed out, "This could be good for your future at the bank." He could press all he wanted; the idea of working for him or for Harvey Kraft was not very appealing. I wasn't in the mood for picking my poison.

He then asked for my reaction to one of his ideas. It was to replace Jay Kittles, the current Andersen project manager, with Peter Miles. He implied that while he liked Jay, he didn't think he had all the necessary "tools" for driving the project forward. He felt that Miles was a better fit. I told him that I had some reservations regarding the change based on experiences with the project and my dealings with this particular manager from Andersen. He wanted to know why.

"I'm not sure he always operates in the best interest of the bank."

"Really? I've worked with him before and I think he does."

During our discussion, I also raised some general concerns about Andersen. Don brushed them off, suggesting that dealing with consultants was a management issue and that under his leadership these issues would go away. He also told me that Al Johnson, president of the Service Company for NationsBank, liked using Andersen and that this was important for me to keep in mind. He appeared annoyed. Maybe he was already having second thoughts about my working for him full time.

His decision to replace Jay Kittles as Andersen project manager was made public almost immediately upon returning to Charlotte. Jay would stay on through the end of this phase of the project and then assume other responsibilities during the next phase. It wasn't made clear if this would be on the same project or moving on to another one within the bank, or with a different client. In any case, Kittles had been swiftly relegated to a lame duck position.

In spite of the fact that Jay Kittles had been effectively neutralized, I still felt we had developed a good working relationship. While neither of us had as much clout in the project manager role as we would have liked, we had figured out pragmatic ways for working together and getting things done. We both had a vested interest in making this thing successful. We confided in each other. I shared with him some of my personal thoughts about technology becoming a commodity business and losing some of its appeal from both marketing and consulting perspectives. He shared with me some of his personal feelings about Andersen, the good and the bad. While he never said so, it was obvious that he was no big fan of Peter Miles, either.

At one point, Jay showed me an internal e-mail message he and some of his buddies in Andersen were passing around, each adding his own input under an assumed identity.

The message started by asking one of the greatest unsolved mysteries of all time: "Why did the chicken cross the road?" It was followed by pages of responses attributed to all kinds of famous people, such as the following:

Nietzsche: Because if you gaze too long across the Road, the Road gazes also across at you.

Ernest Hemingway: To die. In the rain.

Mark Twain: The news of its crossing has been grossly exaggerated.

Salvador Dali: The Fish.

Andersen Consultant: Deregulation of the chicken's side of the road was threatening its dominant market position. The chicken was faced with significant challenges to create and develop the competencies required for the newly competitive market. Andersen Consulting, in a partnering relationship with the client, helped the chicken by rethinking its physical distribution strategy and implementation processes. Using the Poultry Integration Model (PIM) Andersen helped the chicken use its skills, methodologies, knowledge capital, and experiences to align the chicken's people, processes, and technology in support of its overall strategy within a Program Management framework. Andersen Consulting convened a diverse cross section of road analysts and best chicken practices along with Andersen consultants with deep skills in the transportation industry to engage in a two-day itinerary of meetings in order to leverage their personal knowledge capital, both tacit and explicit, and to enable them to synergize with each other in order to achieve the implicit goals of delivering and successfully architecting and implementing an enterprise-wide value framework across the continuum of poultry cross-median processes. The meeting was held in a park-like setting enabling and creating an impactful environment which was strategically based, industry-focused, and built upon a consistent, clear, and unified market message and aligned with the chicken's mission, vision, and

> core values. This was conducive toward the creation of a total business integration solution. Andersen Consulting helped the chicken change to become more successful.

As the new senior manager for the engine, Don Mangrove began to place considerable emphasis on the final presentation to the engine steering committee. He said he wanted to meet once a week and review progress on the overhead slides. More kodachrome, I thought. The meetings would include Don, Dave Gibbons, Jay Kittles, Peter Miles, Larry Rogers—the senior Alltel manager on the project—and me.

Mangrove also planned "prebriefing" meetings with some of the key steering committee members in advance of the final presentation. Everything was to be carefully choreographed to avoid potential last-minute roadblocks. The key to being successful as a manager responsible for a consulting project at NationsBank was producing charts as the "deliverable." Andersen charts weren't quite as good as Gemini's, but they made Mangrove happy.

Mangrove's other early contribution as the new senior manager responsible for the engine was in facility management. Efforts were initiated to look for space to house at least fifty NationsBank associates and consultants for the next phase of the project. Why let the solution decision get in the way of gearing up for the implementation? It became more and more obvious that Andersen and Alltel were being positioned to play a key role in the next phase, regardless of what products or services were needed. No one seemed too terribly concerned about assessing the quality of work from the current phase before moving straight into the next.

It was hard to believe. The decision to secure space was independent and actually preceding the product decision. Questions and concerns rattled around in my head. Wasn't this just possibly a little premature, given we didn't know much about the solution or the personnel skills required to implement it? Couldn't we, in effect, be adding an additional, potentially unnecessary layer, depending on the final recommendations? If we decided on a solution where most of the products could be purchased versus built, did we need a large project management team? There was an underlying assumption that we were playing out the same approach that worked so well for Model Bank—a traditional, long-term development approach. There was another underlying assumption: too many questions and you run the risk of being perceived as someone who is not a team player.

In the beginning of 1997, NationsBank was facing some serious budget constraints that could impact the project, making it more difficult to justify. Hugh McColl had announced a 2 percent across-the-board budget cut early in 1997. With everyone scrambling to protect turf, getting approval for a new follow-on project to develop and implement a new transaction engine would now require a bulletproof justification.

Early on I had volunteered to assume responsibility for developing the financial justification for proceeding with the development of a new payments engine. I felt it was an important control lever, and I didn't think it would be prudent to turn it over to the consultants. We needed to avoid the fox in the henhouse scenario. At that time no one from Andersen appeared too concerned about the financial justification. Maybe they felt it was already a lock. At one point, two of my peer managers from the strategy group told me they realized I was spread thin. They offered to assist me in developing the business case justification. I told them I would get back after we had collected some of the hard data. When I approached them again and reminded them of their offer, they told me that Harvey Kraft, our new strategy group manager, didn't want them getting involved. "Why?" I asked. "Harvey says the engine is too political. We were told to hold back until things were sorted out."

Nice. I would be out there in the minefield on my own.

With the change in engine project management, Don Mangrove asked me to accelerate the financial case development. I explained to Don that the business case for financially justifying the engine would depend on determining the costs associated with the proposed technical solution. This was the area currently taking up most of our time. There was still work to be done before we could start putting all the numbers together for the business case. Apparently my answer was unacceptable.

Don asked Andersen and Alltel to take over. The financial justification became merely an expense budget with no projections or cost savings or impact on revenue included in the analysis. Not having the cost numbers on the proposed solution didn't stand in the way either. Andersen and Alltel came back within a week with a project expense budget of $30 million for the first two years. This number reflected project management and programmer development and support costs, excluding the hardware and software. Were they serious, $30 million? Needless to say, the hardware and software could add megabucks to the final cost. Without hardware and software, we could spend all we wanted on consultants and professional support services; there could be no engine. Was I the only one bothered by this? Apparently so.

Just as was the case with Gemini, no one publicly questioned these numbers. Finally, I just couldn't take it anymore. "How did we arrive at $30 million?" I asked. Peter Miles said with a bit of a smirk, "Didn't Gemini come up with $100 million for five years?" I reminded Miles that these numbers included more than the transaction engine and had never been validated. I'm sure in the minds of many I was becoming a real pain in the butt, and not exactly solidifying a good relationship with my new boss either.

I knew there had to be talented, hard-working people at Andersen Consulting. It was just that when a big-name firm doesn't have to work too hard at driving business with a particular client, it's easy to become complacent. It starts by cutting a few corners, reallocating the talented people someplace else. Before you know it, the consultants become fat, dumb, and happy. The quality of work for the client can start to deteriorate. Unfortunately for the client, this can often go on for some time before the problems become apparent—especially when the client views the prestigious company name of the consulting firm as the most important element in the arrangement, the insurance policy that insulates him from the potential repercussions from making a bad decision. Nobody was noticing that it was rarely the consultants who got fired.

"Who's going to question hiring Andersen?" The assumption is that they will do high-quality work, given the firm's reputation and instant name recognition, which back then was still impeccable and the envy of others. It's a huge mistake for management to think it can turn over critical work and never worry again—no matter whom they give it to.

Back in the days when I was peddling for IBM, if one of my customers gave me an open checkbook, I'm sure there would have been no limits to my creativity in helping them spend it. Nevertheless, in close to ten years of selling for IBM and three years as a consultant, no customer ever asked me to do a budget. Provide input, yes. Give them the numbers with no detail or validation, I don't think so.

The difference was that even though Andersen did much the same work as vendors offering technology services, such as contract programming, integration, and outsourcing, they also wore the hat of consultant. This gave them a more exalted position with clients and allowed them to get in earlier than the nonconsultant vendors. They had the inside track, helping to define requirements and determine how much the client would need to spend.

In other words, after interviewing dozens of people, all with diverse views on what needed to be done, Andersen had created this huge wish list of what they were now calling requirements. Of course there was no product on the market that could do all these things. Who in their right mind would want it?

The proposed implementation approach seemed to be moving closer to a "build versus buy" solution. This ran contrary to the standard technology assumption of the day that it was almost always better to buy versus build, if at all possible. Time and cost factors generally tipped the balance to buy. As pointed out by Randall K. Fields in *Chief Executive* magazine, companies need to avoid the trap of developing software where often only 70 percent of the function as promised is actually delivered. Instead, he argued that companies should opt for packaged software.[6]

Andersen continued telling upper management that "buy" was not an option, given the unique requirements uncovered by interviews during the engine project. Its consultants suggested that while some of the base technology could be purchased from a Hogan or possibly Tandem, there was considerable development work required to build all the necessary function. In other words, Andersen and Alltel would have to provide project management, additional software development, and integration—even if they had little or no expertise in transaction engines. Andersen and Alltel would be sunk costs, regardless of the vendor product specifics. These costs would be applied across the board on top of any proposed solution. Reality was slipping away. The technical solution was merely a line item on the "TAR" status report. Thanks to Don Mangrove, process management was now king . . . and to think I was the guy who complained early on about the lack of process.

That lame duck feeling started creeping into my belly. Jay Kittles was not alone on that score. A full court of Andersen consultants constantly surrounded Don Mangrove. They were in the middle of every meeting. Many of the meetings were focused on the problems in recruiting NationsBank associates for the engine implementation project and the need to find space for all the NationsBank, Andersen, and Alltel personnel who would be assigned for the next phase. Apparently it never occurred to anyone that Andersen and Alltel involvement had anything to do with the problem of recruiting NationsBank people. The only NationsBank personnel still working full time on the project were those associates from strategy who reported directly to me on a regular basis. The others had left once we passed the originally committed deadline for finishing the project. All were asked to continue on. With no exceptions, they all declined. I knew better than to give the people who worked for me a choice. Status meetings run by Don Mangrove continued as if there wasn't a problem in the world. Man, I hate those things. The ancient poet Virgil once said that status was "a mighty pomp, but made of little things."[7] Did the Romans of antiquity have to sit through these things, too?

One night I went for drinks with a woman who worked in public relations for the bank. She was attractive, with a pleasant face, a big beautiful smile, and blonde hair. She wanted to write a story on the transaction engine for a NationsBank newsletter.

"Isn't it amazing what NationsBank has been able to do in technology?" she commented.

"Sure is."

"When you think of Model Bank, our new bank-by-phone program, and now the transaction engine."

"Would you like another drink?"

She nodded affirmatively, much to my delight. The most amazing thing to me was that we had in effect replaced NationsBank employees wih Andersen and its business partners. Was this all it took to be a leader in technology? Andersen was now involved with the engine and it was sounding more and more each day like this, too, would go to our strategic business partners to run.

"So, tell me what you can about the transaction engine," she said.

"It provides a great opportunity for NationsBank. Once again we are leading the way. . . ." Sing the part line and keep smiling. I had learned the hard way.

SUMMARY OF OBSERVATIONS

- Consultants should be discouraged from making things sound more complex than they are—consultingspeak. Instead, they should be expected to "say what they mean," and use terms and language based on the culture of the client.

- Operational objectives can get in the way of meeting corporate goals. Consultants can thrive on operational conflict. They can play one business unit off against another.

- A client should not have to pay consultants fees for services while the client is educating the consultant.

- Using traditional development and project management approaches can add unneeded costs for new technology initiatives. Project scope and processes need to be determined based on the requirements of the specific project.

- Consultants need to be carefully managed. Proposed costs need to be validated.

- Consultants are masters at avoiding blame if things go south. Usually an employee becomes the fall guy. The fall guy usually does not have the same level of access or credibility to defend himself against this kind of assault.

NOTES

1. Kirstin E. Wells, "Are Checks Overused?" *Federal Reserve Bank of Minneapolis Quarterly Review* (fall 1996): 3.

2. "Tandem Conference Report, Embracing Change," *Banker* (November 1996): S1.

3. "Survey Says NationsBank Best at Using Technology," NationsBank Release, 29 October 1996, http://www.nationsbank.com/newsroom/press/1996/.

4. Hugh McColl, "Fulfilling the Vision: NationsBank, Our Region and Our Nation," NationsBank speech, 1 December 1992, www.nationsbank.com/s97is.v...y.

5. Allan Greenspan, "The Challenge of Central Banking in a Democratic Society" (Speech given at the Annual Dinner and Francis Boyer Lecture of the American Enterprise Institute for Public Policy Research, Washington, D.C., 5 December 1996) http://www.federalreserve.gov/boarddocs/speeches/1996/19961205.htm.

6. Randall Fields, "Build versus Buy: Resist the Seduction," *Chief Executive* (May 1995): 22.

7. Lewis Copeland and Faye Copeland, eds., *Ten Thousand Jokes, Toasts, and Stories* (New York: BantamDoubleday, 1965).

CHAPTER ELEVEN

BLAZING THE
ELECTRONIC TRAIL

The Model Bank migration program to convert all branches was running on a parallel path while we continued gearing up for the engine build project, sure to follow. We needed more space for all the people Andersen and Alltel wanted to bring in and all the focus now seemed to be on finding the right facilities. Like Model, as NationsBank personnel dropped off the engine project, they were slowly but surely being replaced by our business partners. I wondered if anyone here was concerned about the increasing amount of critical banking function and sensitive customer information that in essence was being handled by business partners as branches were "converted" to Model? If we ever did go live production with the payments engine, would Andersen and Alltel manage all customer transactions as our new payments engine caretakers?

Based on the numbers, things couldn't have been better. In the middle of January 1997, NationsBank announced its fourth-quarter earnings for 1996, and once again, they were very impressive. We reported a 24 percent increase in net income and the company stock was now hovering at around $100 per share. It was announced in the *Wall Street Journal* that NationsBank expected to cut $175 million in costs and generate $90 million in additional revenue as part of the Boatmen's acquisition. Buried in the announcement, it was also reported that there would be additional costs associated with the Boatmen's *transition*. It was estimated that these costs would be about $50 million more than originally expected." NationsBank said the money will be used for personnel and data processing expenses, and consulting fees associated with integrating Boatmen's into NationsBank."[1]

About this time it was also announced that Model Bank was finally rolling out in North Carolina—the hub of NationsBank. The plan called for unveiling it in Texas and Tennessee by the end of the year, and then in the new Midwest market acquired with Boatmen's in 1998. The *Business*

Journal, which served the Charlotte area, published the following about Model Bank: "In addition to differing fees, the program changes the bank's branch staffing, employee compensation, and computer network. Industry analysts say it helps the bank target profitable customers, while running off marginal ones. It's part of the reason for the bank's record profitability in 1996, pushing NationsBank's stock to unprecedented levels."[2] Working for NationsBank, most of us knew all too well that the changes to staffing included replacing employees with personnel from Andersen and Alltel. I wondered how customers would have felt about this.

While I tried my best to play the party line, there was this annoying notion that kept banging around in my head. Model or no Model, we were still a legacy bank buying other banks with lots of the same problems. Legacy meant old technology, labor-intensive systems, which were cumbersome to use. We would convert them to Model, but under the covers this was a tired old horse. Wall Street kept loving it, cheering us on for more. We weren't the only bank following this strategy of growth. Companies from other industries were doing it, too. Formerly tough-talking bank regulators were now rubber-stamping their approval. This wasn't about investing in the future or making us more competitive for the global market. This was about consolidation.

Was it possible that all this talk about using new technology as the engine for advancement was just talk? It was the acquisitions and ensuing layoffs—a cost-cutting strategy, not market growth—that had been the real engine behind our success. It was the employees who were still left working harder and longer, always trying to avoid having the consultants point a finger at them to join the next wave of layoffs. Sure, stocks were going up. But, somehow these mergers were supposed to be making the sum of the parts better. What if the megamergers were only temporarily masking the problems, kicking them out to some later day of reckoning? What if we were only creating a bigger dinosaur? I decided to stow these thoughts away. They were counterproductive, and they weren't going to help me continue doing what I thought needed to be done. McColl kept saying in speeches and press releases that we needed to exploit new technology to ensure future success. I would continue to focus on this important goal. It was what I had been hired to do.

One Saturday morning in January, I went to a local diner close to my home in Atlanta. It had become part of my regular routine. There was a newsstand close by that carried the *New York Times*. I sat in a booth close to the window. The waitress was a Generation Xer. She brought coffee and took my order. She had green hair, an earring through her eyebrow, and a tattoo on her shoulder. A headline on the front page also caught my attention, "A Clinton

Social with Bankers Included a Leading Regulator." White House Counsel Lanny J. Davis said there was nothing unusual or improper about the coffee hour, which included President Clinton, bankers, a bank regulator, and a top fundraiser for the Democratic Party. The bankers included senior executives from major U.S. banks, including Hugh McColl from NationsBank.

Participants at the meeting said that discussion included several issues important to banks, including the rollback of the Glass-Steagall Act. This law had been created as a safeguard after the Great Depression to restrict banks from underwriting securities. Boyden Gray, a former White House counsel from a previous Republican administration, was quoted: "It would be appropriate to discuss Glass-Steagall, but not appropriate to have political officials in the same meeting, especially during an election year."[3]

Top bankers such as McColl had been arguing for years that Glass-Steagall needed to be repealed. They would finally get their wish, but not until 1999 when noise about 1996 campaign-financing scandals had finally subsided. By then the planned merger of high-profile mega-multi-financial service companies was forcing regulators to abandon the "look the other way" approach and finally change the law. When they did reverse Glass-Steagall, there was almost a universal positive reaction from financial consultants and the mainstream press that this New Deal legislation had finally been dissolved.

The original intent of Glass-Steagall was to keep banks from making risky investments with depositors' money and avoid the kind of speculation that contributed to the Great Crash of 1929. It was no longer in touch with new global market conditions, or so it was said. The *Wall Street Journal* editorialized that "the repeal of these restrictions is long overdue."[4] It was reported in the *New York Times* that "after decades of trying, Congress finally repealed Depression-era laws that limited the ability of banks to enter securities and insurance industries. President Clinton is expected to sign the legislation shortly, ushering in a new era on Wall Street as leading institutions seek partners to become financial supermarkets."[5] It was sounding like the new banking model would create a super "Stop and Shop" for all kinds of financial products and services, including high-risk investments.

When the law was repealed in 1999, the banking industry was elated. In a speech he gave entitled "Main Street Rising," Hugh McColl would say: "Last week, President Clinton signed into law the Gramm-Leach-Bliley Act, also known as the financial modernization bill. Let me state for the record I'm glad Congress passed it and the president signed it. The bill removes the Depression-era restrictions on banks that have put us at a competitive disadvantage in the financial services industry. Regulatory relief has been a long time coming and, now that it's here, bankers across the country owe a round of applause and thanks to our 'partners' in government who made it happen." He went on to suggest that it was because of Glass-Steagall that "banks began to look more and more like—as Gates said a few years ago— dinosaurs."[6] Even in 1999, McColl was still talking about the Gates reference to dinosaurs. I also decided we needed a corallary to the Yeltsin theory: You could sit on a throne built with bayonets a little longer if you had some help.

No question, from a banking point of view the repeal of Glass-Steagall was a good thing. As a taxpayer, I wasn't so sure. If any of these new securities or other investments failed, the Federal Deposit Insurance Corporation (FDIC)—part of the Depression-era law that was not repealed— would still be there to protect the banks. In other words, taxpayer dollars would be used to underwrite the bad debt incurred. Banks were viewing the repeal as providing opportunity to take on riskier investments in the pursuit of higher profits.

Had we learned nothing from the $1 trillion Savings and Loan scandal of the 1980s?[7] Taxpayers were the silent "partner" who ended up footing most of the bill. Banks get an opportunity to make more money. Taxpayers absorb the risk if things went badly.

As the engine project continued, there seemed to be a direct correlation to the increased dependency on Andersen and Alltel and the lack of enthusiasm from NationsBank employees still working on the project. Mangrove was perplexed that employees weren't begging to be placed on the engine team.

It shouldn't have been so difficult to figure out. Several times I suggested that Mangrove spend time with some of the NationsBank people who had worked on the early phase of the project. It might help him understand why we were having so much trouble recruiting bank employees for the next phase. He indicated this would be a good idea, but other things continued to get in the way. Those other things were mostly his meetings with Andersen and Alltel. He always accepted their point of view, never listening to employees working the project. I couldn't help but think he could have taken a cue from New York City Mayor Rudy Giuliani. Even before September 11, 2001, he maintained direct lines of communication with police, fire, and other municipal workers, never letting political pressures or third parties get in the way. Giuliani was loyal to them, and they in turn to him. It was one of those intangibles, but I was sure it had much to do with improving morale with the uniforms and added to the amazing improvement in New York City quality of life during the Giuliani administration.

So where was all this going? I was feeling that I was being left in the dark. Don Mangrove and the Andersen entourage were now meeting regularly without including me or the rest of the team. There was an upside from my perspective. To begin with, I didn't need any more meetings of any kind. Meetings with Mangrove were especially intolerable. He relished his stature as moderating honcho, working laboriously down the line items from his TAR reports. "OK, next item. What is the status? . . . When will it be completed? . . . OK, next item. . . . " Already a lame duck who would soon be moving back to a strategy group, I wanted to concentrate on finishing up and getting the hell out. It would have been the prudent thing to do, but then no one ever accused me of being prudent. There was another part of me that wanted to hang on, and not because of any great love for project management.

In a sense, the engine had become my baby, and I didn't like the idea of watching it morph into something it was never intended to be. I probably would have been less inclined to get in the way, if at least I felt things were being done fairly. But then who decides what was in the best interest of NationsBank? Who the hell was I to speculate on what that might be? Was it fair to say I was trying to be consistent with publicly stated goals? Everyone had an agenda, and they could easily build arguments to support why they were right and I was wrong.

With Andersen management holding things closer to the vest, I decided the best way to figure out where all of this might be headed was to do a little more research. Consultants generally follow a pattern. Take a good look at what they're doing with other clients, and you can pretty much figure out what they will attempt to do with you and your company. From my experience, creativity and innovation is not a strong suit in the consulting profession. It seemed to me that it was more about taking what they've learned from one client and applying it to another. This was what they really meant when they talked about a "best practice" methodology. "Here's the way the best in your industry run their businesses. We can help you develop a comparable level of competency." "Me, too" was being institutionalized by the consulting profession. How long could they keep calling it "best" when they were selling it to everybody?

Sure, my unique experiences had contributed to my jaded view and led to the conclusions I was drawing, but plenty of my friends working for other corporations were sharing similar stories when we compared notes.

There is plenty of generally available information on consultants in almost any public library. The Internet has put even more information at your fingertips. Consulting Web sites, industry trade magazines, and general media Web sites can be most helpful in researching a consultant.

Ironically, thanks largely to the Internet, it didn't take a consultant to do research anymore. Yet corporations were continuing to hire high-priced consulting firms to research information that any college graduate could obtain. Consultants were being used to research just about everything. While there were a few cases of consultants being hired to research other consultants, the profession in general was continuing to get by without a lot of scrutiny from its corporate clients. They were the ones pointing the barrel at employees as they looked for ways to trim "fat." They had become senior management's hired guns.

Of course Andersen was rated as one of the top consulting and integration firms in the computer industry. No new news there. Areas of expertise included client/server technology and vertical-industry consulting. Client/server was still all the hype in almost every industry in spite of the fact that the Internet in many respects was making early client/server architecture obsolete. Why buy, install, and maintain all kinds of software licenses for your individual PC when it could be more cost effectively accessed and used via the Internet or private company networks using Internet technology "Intranets"? To paraphrase a Sun Microsystems Inc. slogan that was well ahead of its time, if the network was the computer, you didn't need souped-up software and high-powered workstations on everybody's desk.[8] By the end of the decade, Larry Ellison, Oracle's founder and chairman, and a major beneficiary of client/server technology, would admit: "We blew it in the 1990s. By running applications on the client, client/server was meant to put information at your fingertips. But all we did was create distributed complexity and fragmented data. CEOs have come to hate IT [information technology] because they can't get what they want from it."[9] The poor chief information officer. Damned if he did, damned if he didn't. So far Andersen had been pushing a mainframe solution with us, but there was also that client/server group lurking someplace in the background. They could play it several different ways. We still weren't hearing anything about the Internet or "thin" clients. Apparently, there was no one available for the project who had been trained in the latest technology wave. In this sense, consultants are always pushing clients to hire bodies off the bench in whatever they are trained in. This can potentially keep everybody in react mode, in spite of the accelerating pace of technological change.

A vertical-industry orientation implied an emphasis on industry expertise. Vertical industries would include specific business areas such as banking, retail, consumer goods, or manufacturing, for example. They set up "practices" to support each. This was very different from the Gemini Consulting approach that used a cross-industry model—the horizontal versus vertical view. The competitive information on Andersen stated that it focused on developing optimum solutions for specific industries and then attempted to replicate these solutions with the major industry leaders. This hit close to home and got me asking a lot of soul-searching questions. I had recently heard from one of the guys working for me that Andersen had been heavily involved with First Union Bank, one of our major competitors.

Weren't there risks and exposures in sharing information with consulting firms that were also helping the competition? With all the flack given to lawyers, at least they took an oath to operate within a professional code of ethics. In theory, a corporate law firm would not knowingly take a client that had a competitive relationship with another client. I had a friend who worked for the advertising firm of McCann-Erickson. He called me one day from his office in New York City. "Steve, so what exactly is it you do?"

Not being French, but a typical workaholic American, I launched into job talk. "I'm an 'oxymoron.' You know, like 'jumbo shrimp,' 'crisis management,' 'sure bet' . . . I'm a technology strategist."

He got a kick out of that and then told me he himself was working with a client who had hired a couple oxymoron consultants to work with them.

I couldn't resist. "You think 'truth in advertising' qualifies as an oxymoron?"

We both laughed. He then said something that really hit me. "Say what you will, but advertising isn't as bad as you think. You know, we handle the Coca Cola account here at McCann. We would never dream of going after business at Pepsi. That would be considered a conflict of interest in my business. Apparently it's not a problem for oxymoron consultants. Weren't you a consultant in your previous life?" He got me there.

There were no such restrictions for consultants. Take Dick Morris for example, who consulted for Sen. Jesse Helms and President Bill Clinton, not exactly bosom buddies. The online publication *Salon.com* reported: "Jesse Jackson has chastised Dick Morris for being 'amoral': a mercenary who serves both far-right Republicans like Jesse Helms and Democrats like Clinton."[10] Jackson was convinced it was Morris who persuaded President Clinton to sign the welfare reform bill, ending welfare as we know it. According to Jackson, this would push more than one million children into poverty. It was becoming difficult differentiating "New Democrats" from old Republicans. Jonathan Alter, a journalist from *Newsweek*, would applaud Dick Morris, calling him "brilliant."[11]

Couldn't one argue that the vertical-industry replication approach would lead to overall mediocrity and lack of differentiation? There were reputable firms that provided valuable knowledge in their industry and separated what was client confidential from what was industry shareable, but wasn't there always the possibility that sensitive information could be shared with competitors when consultants so frequently moved from one to another? Wouldn't it be better to restrict consultants working for you from double dipping with your competitors? I could already hear the chorus of rebuttal: "But everybody does it." Andersen had made vertical industry and the interchangeability of consultants between firms in the same industry the core of its "best practice" methodology. But of course, Andersen would argue it maintained strict confidentiality on all information considered sensitive by the client.

This was not to suggest that all vertical-industry consultants, or even that all Andersen consultants, operated without ethics or integrity. The corporate manager, however, should never assume that consultants left unattended would work in the best interest of the corporation employing them. It was up to the corporation hiring the consultants to implement safeguards and to monitor and manage the consultants on an ongoing basis throughout the engagement. Asking consultants to sign a nondisclosure statement was not enough. It was too easy to cheat.

A particular individual who worked for me said he had a friend employed at First Union where we heard they also used Andersen Consulting. I asked him to talk to his friend about Andersen. They went to lunch. According to his friend, First Union was cutting back on Andersen. First Union had concerns about increasing costs and reduced quality of workmanship of consultants in general, Andersen in particular. I was told by another source that the annual billing revenue for Andersen at First Union had declined dramatically from approximately $40 million down from the previous year to around $10 million. No doubt this could help explain the aggressive marketing efforts by Andersen's banking guys, and why they were targeting NationsBank for a big bump in consulting fees. There was a reduced revenue stream from First Union that they were trying to make up from that other little bank, just down the road a piece.

The other interesting piece of information, according to the competitive data, was that a major goal of Andersen was to expand outsourcing. According to a 1995 *Computerworld* article, Andersen Consulting's plan was to provide full-service outsourcing for information systems and to make itself the number one provider of outsourcing services in technology.[12] The outsourcing of data processing had grown significantly in the previous ten years and had become somewhat of a defacto standard for corporations in addressing the costs associated with ongoing technology operations.

Cost was another major factor leading to a decision to outsource, even though long-term assessments demonstrated that outsourcing could sometimes result in increased costs. Outsourcing companies sometimes lacked knowledge and experience in the specific business being outsourced.

Hadn't NationsBank learned this lesson in the past? The outsourcer might know technology, but not banking. Changes to the original contract due to establishment of new corporate directions, acquisitions, and/or divestitures could prove to be very expensive when the original contractual arrangements were inflexible and needed to be altered for accommodating change.

Outsourcing could potentially grandfather the currently installed systems and make changes or upgrades very expensive. As noted by the International Data Corporation (IDC), once a function was outsourced, it could become a captive market for the provider of outsourcing services. Future integration work or development for systems would become the responsibility of the outsourcer, potentially beyond the control of the client.[13] Nonetheless, IDC studies concluded that technology outsourcing had become one of the fastest-growing markets in the industry in 1996 and was expected to grow at a compound annual rate of 15 percent through the year 2001. Captive or not, it was a popular alternative that looked good on the books and based on conventional wisdom could minimize management's headaches, at least for the short term. It had become a standard remedy consultants often recommended to corporate management.

It was important to outsource only the right things and back-office less-important applications with minimal customer contact, repetitive processes not likely to change. Current projections indicated that the rate of change in technology had accelerated to the extent that technology products were becoming obsolete within an eighteen-month period.[14] In other words, hire an outsourcer on a long-term lease to take over an important business function and you could be locked out from taking advantage of late-breaking technological innovation. Make it a shorter-term lease and you pay through the nose. With everybody doing it, maybe it wasn't much of a concern. The only real threat would be from new market entrants who might not be as wedded to the old ways of doing business. They could exploit new technology solutions while everyone else's hands are tied with outsourcers. Barriers to entry might be the only hope, but how do you keep barriers in an ever increasing, deregulated "free market" environment?

On the flip side, I knew that NationsBank used outsourcing extensively in the past. Several key managers were very receptive to outsourcing proposals, even though it had produced at best mixed results. When the Perot outsourcing contract was terminated, management downplayed the transaction-processing issues and other related problems, which had been previously reported. Problems were eventually dismissed as cultural issues and growing pains—nothing that couldn't be remedied in the future.[15] Apparently, outsourcing was still a legitimate and well-regarded option at NationsBank for just about anything not tightly bolted down, particularly when recommended by reputable consultants.

I knew that outsourcing could be effectively marketed to certain managers of the bank as a way of reducing personal accountability and risk. "It was good when I had it." The flaw in this thinking was the assumption that if things went badly, NationsBank management would not take the blame.

I decided to share some of my research information on Andersen with several senior managers at NationsBank. Darlene Wittington, the manager responsible for running the Integration Services organization, was my first call. She had originally come to me to request a no-holds-barred "bitch" session for everybody. Now it was my turn. I took her to lunch. If routing and settlement were outsourced, it would be Darlene's people who would lose their jobs. We went to one of her favorite places, where South meets East. A local down-home, buffet-style, "all you can eat" Chinese restaurant.

After one or two extra trips back to the buffet table and some casual polite conversation, I suggested that a potential goal of Andersen and Alltel might be an outsourcing proposal for the transaction engine.

Darlene told me she thought I was mistaken, but she couldn't give me any explanation as to why, just that I was. I went on: "Darlene, you know all of your people are leaving the project. They can't get out of it fast enough. Several have expressed concerns about Andersen."

"I'm not aware of any concerns. I know they want to get back to their regular jobs."

"But you yourself expressed concerns early on."

"I was under the impression they were resolved."

It was like talking to a different person. As we continued the discussion, she pointed out to me that Andersen was needed at NationsBank because of its project management skills. Now I was really confused. If there was anything NationsBank had an abundance of it was employees with project management skills. She didn't specifically say it, but the impression she gave was that the skills Andersen brought to the bank were important enough to give it lots of slack. Finally, she offered some advice.

"Don't try and take on Andersen. Address each specific issue separately, that's OK, but you'd be making a big mistake if you go try to challenge Andersen."

As I drove her back to the office, Darlene told me that she felt I belonged in strategy, not in project management and encouraged me to move back to the strategy group. She thought I was doing a good job. It was just that she felt I could provide more help to NationsBank in the strategy group. This would also get me conveniently out of the way, but she didn't say it.

"We could really use your help in developing an overall architecture plan for Transaction Services," she said, adding, "that was what you were originally hired to do, wasn't it?"

Darlene wanted me off of the project. She was also obviously scared of Andersen, but why? On the organization chart they worked for her.

A few days later I asked Mangrove if he thought Andersen would propose an outsourcing arrangement for the engine.

"No. . . . I don't think so," he said.

"I'd also like to talk with you about Andersen's involvement with First Union."

"We don't have to worry about First Union. We are way ahead of them. Anything else?"

"Any luck in finding a replacement for me?"

"Not yet. . . . I'm still looking."

Since our first meeting, it was never a warm, friendly exchange. There wasn't time to discuss it further. Mangrove had another meeting to run. He didn't want to keep those Andersen guys waiting.

Shortly after these discussions, I received interesting feedback regarding a Boatmen's transition planning meeting in St. Louis. No doubt, another of those big yawn sessions. Peter Miles, who reported to Darlene, made an announcement of note during the meeting. In front of Model Bank people, he said that the new engine would not be available in time to handle the Boatmen's consolidation. He had just participated in an engine project meeting in which he was proposing a very aggressive time frame for the engine development to meet Boatmen's deadlines. So which was it? From the beginning I had been skeptical about Andersen's time frames for the engine, given all the requirements its people kept piling onto the project. I sent an e-mail message asking for clarification. He did not immediately answer the message. Darlene Wittington did, coming to his defense.

"Alternate plans needed to be made to accommodate tighter time frames than originally anticipated."

Later when I caught up with Miles, he told he that he was sorry for any confusion he might have created. He said he was in a Catch 22.

"Pete, answer me this. In your opinion can we have the engine done in time for Boatmen's?"

"It's possible," he said, "but a lot of things have to go right."

Yeah, sure. Like getting Romaine back to strategy.

The first phase of the engine project was winding down. It was time for me to become pitchman again. Mangrove had already laid out his strategy, trying to carefully choreograph things. He wanted to provide a private preview of the final presentation to all key members of the steering committee before the final extravaganza. If things went right, all the key managers would have already endorsed the next phase of the project and the final presentation would be nothing more than a formality. Andersen and Alltel would be positioned perfectly for getting the next contract. This was assuming the pitchman didn't screw up. Unfortunately, Mangrove had not yet found my replacement. The pitchman was still me.

One of the first meetings was with the new head of Transaction Services, Walt Shaw. Walt had just taken over from one of the good old boys who had recently retired. He was not the typical NationsBank senior executive. Walt had come over from one of the acquired Texas banks. With Shaw, I felt as if I had stumbled upon the last of the old-fashioned managers who demanded accountability from everyone, even the consultants. There was nothing indecisive about this guy. Also in attendance were Don Mangrove flanked by his Andersen compatriots, Dave Gibbons and Peter Miles.

Walt interrupted the canned presentation I was delivering with penetrating questions and pointed remarks. He talked about avoiding a rush to judgment, taking the time to do the job right, picking the right vendors, and also suggested that NationsBank partnerships worked best "when we are in control." Most important, he questioned their approach for selecting the appropriate vendors for the engine project. Andersen's plan, not surprisingly, was to conduct some additional interviews with the top two contenders and then write up a document with recommendations. "I think we should send out an RFI (request for information) instead and compare the responses," he said.

It was the best news I had heard on the subject, and it was coming from the head of our division. Dave Gibbons and Peter Miles looked less than pleased. I tried my best not to gloat. There had been a shift that had taken place in the Andersen management contingent. Whereas they wanted to painstakingly interview everybody who was anybody at NationsBank for defining "requirements," they now wanted to speed through the vendor selection. They had leveled the field like a cluster bomb.

The technical team had narrowed the vendor choices. There were a few other options that needed further investigation, but the primary choice was between Tandem and Hogan. Andersen was calling them "tier one" vendors. For the most part, NationsBank associates on the technical team still believed the Tandem option was the optimum solution while the Andersen members of the team continued to pull for Hogan. It didn't matter that the Hogan solution didn't meet our timelines or established requirements for electronic processing. Andersen management, with Mangrove's blessing, had kept the Hogan option alive. They had worn the rest of us down to the point where we were all about ready to pack it in.

There was a second group of potential vendors that was lumped into a "tier two" category. Andersen management wanted to close it out after one more site visit to Tandem and Hogan and then make a determination. Tier two didn't make the cut. They were already gearing up in anticipation of a much more lucrative implementation project, before this phase was completed. Additional facility space had been scouted, and Gibbons was on the phone recruiting additional Andersen people. An RFI threw a wrinkle into the plan as it would inevitably extend the time frame for the current fixed-payment contract. It would also afford the opportunity for a few more people to look a little closer at the proposed alternatives. I was still trying hard to keep my enthusiasm restrained. The odds were still with the consultants, but at least with Walt Shaw's direction, it wouldn't be a cakewalk.

One evening in early February 1997, before leaving to go home, Andersen partner Dave Gibbons said he wanted to meet with me first thing in the morning. He said he wanted to discuss a plan for accelerating completion of this phase of the project. I told him the meeting would be fine and went back to the project office to pack up my things. The project office was at the NationsBank Loop Road location in Atlanta, adjacent to the airport runway. It actually looked like a hangar from the parking lot, a perfect location for studying the Doppler effect. There was a large chalkboard in the office that was regularly used for conceptual engine drawings—before they were finalized in kodachrome. I spent most of my time outside of this office, working with team members and attending meetings. It was not one of my favorite places. I would arrive early, drop some things off, and very often not come back to the office until it was time to gather things up and head home. In contrast, Kittles liked camping out there. So did Gibbons, when he was on-site.

As I entered the office, I couldn't help but notice an organization chart on the board. It was a new organization to handle the RFI and finish off the vendor analysis. Much of it was consistent with the current structure, with one major exception. Peter Miles had been inserted as manager for the technical team. He would occupy a new box on the chart, between the current technical organization and the project management slots for Kittles and me—the two lame ducks who kept getting lamer. In other words, another layer of management was being created. I would be separated from the other NationsBank employees working on the project— the only NationsBank people left on the project. They were attempting to cut me off. These were people who worked for me on a regular basis in strategy, and the idea of them reporting up through Andersen instead of to me was infuriating. Andersen would be in a position to control the activities of the technical team evaluating vendors and influence the final decision. I guessed it would be positioned as a warm-up before Miles became the official top banana as project manager, an opportunity to help him hit the ground running. Now I knew why Gibbons wanted to meet.

Molten liquid raced through my swelling veins. It ruined the evening and kept me awake for most of the night. The situation was very bleak. It was not the first time I'd been in a dismal situation, but how could I possibly get out of this one? I was on my back with my eyes wide open, glued to the ceiling. Previous events began flashing in my brain. I remembered the fallout after the IBM executive briefing for Newport News Shipbuilding had cratered, and how my feelings back then were similar to now. I had somehow climbed out of that snake pit. There were parallels. As I lay there thinking, I rehashed some of my experience with IBM and Newport News Shipbuilding. Were there things I could now apply to my situation at NationsBank? Damn. I was starting to play back. Sleep? Forget about it.

IBM Time Capsule: Covering the Flank

Making quota was highly suspect with no business on the table and a customer increasingly more dissatisfied with IBM. There was more focus on internal reporting and many meetings to discuss forecasts. Executives from Newport News Shipbuilding were looking more and more to Gartner Group for advice and Digital Equipment Company for computers.

On top of all this, things had gotten very strange. My branch manager, Toby Hobson, continued to tell me that he thought I was doing a good job, yet the feedback from others in the IBM branch office was inconsistent with his ongoing pats on my back. One of the people who worked for me said that one day, when I was out of the office, Hobson was on the sales floor talking to the troops. He made a passing comment that he didn't think I was going to make it as a manager. "His rate of predicting these things is uncanny," she said. On another occasion my customer, Frank Nichols, the director of information services for Newport News, called me. He told me my branch manager had been to see him.

"Stay close to me and I will protect you," he said.

Frank Nichols wouldn't explain what he meant. Why would I need protection? I asked myself. Trying to set up that briefing with the chairman must have really aggravated him. Things were not looking good.

I decided that I was in a classic no-win situation. If I didn't make quota, I would be kicked out of the job. The only way I could make the numbers was to take a more active role in selling. If I did this, I could be accused of not managing. There was a series of conflicting requests that kept me looking over my shoulder. Sooner or later I was bound to step on a mine.

It was deeply ingrained in IBM that one needed to be a team player, which also meant being completely loyal to your immediate manager at all times. I decided to look for another job. There didn't appear to be any other options. One day I took a drive from Norfolk to Arlington to meet with a head-hunting company. I only knew two things about Arlington: it shared the banks of the Potomac with Washington, D.C., and it was home to the Arlington National Cemetery, the former home of Robert E. Lee, but better known for the Tomb of the Unknown Soldier. I could remember previous trips to the D.C. area, personifying the bumbling nameless tourist, immersed in the crowds. The Metro station for the National Cemetery was always busy. It was a must stop for tourists, definitely worth the hassle of crowds.

This head-hunting outfit was a fairly good sized firm, housed in one of the tall glass metallic buildings in downtown Arlington. I didn't have an appointment with any particular employment counselor. There was a guy filling in that day who told me he was friends with the owner of the firm. He had some kind of consulting business on the side. He and his wife owned a restaurant in Baltimore as well. My plan was to drop off a resume, try to make a good impression, and hope that at some point they would give me a call if something that looked like a reasonable fit got plopped into the incoming mail bin. The fill-in counselor had different ideas. He asked lots of probing questions. It occurred to me that within a few minutes he had stuck me on a pin and had formulated his own opinions regarding which box fit me best.

After the series of rifle-shot questions ended, he shared his thoughts, suggesting that before I could concentrate on finding the right kind of new position I needed to better understand some things about myself. This would ensure that I didn't just "rebound" in the wrong direction. Here we go, I thought to myself, pull up a couch and start the meter. He went on to say that he had a few ideas on how in the meantime I could stabilize things at work. He told me that he didn't think there was anything I could do that would ever make my branch manager like me. "But I can help you neutralize him," he said. His advice was to keep my cool and continue working as I had been. After every conversation with my branch manager, he suggested I should follow up with an e-mail confirming the conversation.

"You mentioned that whenever you talk he compliments you for doing a good job. It would be a good idea to end each message thanking him for his ongoing support."

"He'll know I'm leaving a paper trail," I said.

"That's precisely what we want."

We. I never forgot that he said "we." All of a sudden I didn't feel so all alone. The advice was brilliantly conceived and the consequences exceeded all expectations. Toby Hobson started to avoid conversations and left me to fend for myself. This gave me the window needed to focus my full attention on the territory, taking a much needed active role in the selling. I knew they could argue that I was relinquishing my role as a manager. So be it. We had been given little to no chance of making the numbers. I'd rather make the numbers and be accused of not managing than not make the numbers and be accused of being a manager who failed.

Without knowing where it would specifically come from, I decided to mount a campaign to make others in IBM aware that there were large business opportunities at Newport News Shipbuilding. It caused all kinds of trepidation with the sales team, as I knew it would:

"What, are you crazy? They'll increase our quota."

"You said yourself we don't have a prayer of making it anyway. What difference does it make?"

It also ran counter to standard business acumen. Nonetheless, my new forecasts to upper management were off the charts.

"$50 million opportunity at Newport News Shipbuilding."

The business was there, but getting it would be a huge stretch. We only did about $16 million the previous year and the competitive situation was getting more heated all the time.

Leveraging e-mail, I would copy my forecasts to support groups outside of my reporting structure, sending copies of the forecasts across multiple organizational lines. There was nothing to lose. The more eyes on this situation, the less opportunity for Toby Hobson to play Machiavelli at my expense. I rationalized that these other organization groups were support groups outside of my immediate chain of command, so I couldn't be accused of insubordination. It was a lateral move versus a vertical one. As if responding to an elephant whistle, my management in my immediate chain of command was incapable of hearing, IBM development managers and executives from other business units began taking an active interest in my customer. If Hobson tried playing any more games with either my customer or my head, there was a chance it could all be exposed to others.

Several IBM development managers met with executives from the shipyard to discuss new products they were responsible for building. The customer said it was quite different from the IBM product information they were getting second-hand from Gartner Group. They quickly put to bed most of the issues previously raised by our consulting friends. The customer loved talking directly with the people who actually built systems. We reestablished IBM—not the consultants—as the best source of information on IBM products and services. The chart maker from Poughkeepsie was sent packing.

Internal briefings were scheduled for me to present to IBM executives and their staffs on the potential business opportunities. When it came to interacting with me, Hobson became increasingly more aloof. He was spending a lot more time on the golf course with the other marketing managers who were all very devoted to Toby, and he obviously to them.

At one point, the president of the IBM Industrial Sector Division invited me to a meeting to present the business opportunity at Newport News. At the time I wondered if it was because of the $50 million opportunity or because someone up high asked him to intercede. Perhaps a little of both. His organization was responsible for expanding IBM's presence outside the traditional data center "glass house" into manufacturing and engineering environments. Toby Hobson couldn't understand why a division president wanted to hear about Newport News Shipbuilding. He told me that he believed his other territories had more business opportunities and there must be some kind of mistake. He was unable to make a switch and was annoyed.

"You know, Steve, this guy has a reputation of making mincemeat out of most people who present to him. You better be well prepared, 'cause you don't have such a great story to tell."

Hobson said he wanted me to "prebrief" him on the material first. He put me on his calendar. The day of our meeting I waited for an hour in Hobson's office. His secretary finally came into the room and told me that Toby Hobson had decided to play golf with the other managers instead. There was no time to reschedule. I needed to catch a plane. My meeting with the IBM division president went well, and his organization agreed to provide additional support for my customer. This helped us compete more effectively against Digital Equipment Company on the manufacturing shop floors and win more business away from several competitors in engineering.

I tried to call my new friend, the consultant, part-time career counselor, and restaurateur, to tell him how the plan had been successfully executed and that things had improved greatly. I thought maybe we could hook up on his own turf in Baltimore, and I could buy him a beer or two in one of the harbor gin mills. There was no answer at the number he had left. Finally, I called the Arlington office where we had first met. I was informed by one of the headhunters in the office, with waves of emotion breaking up her voice, that my friend had died a few days before. Why him? Why the good guys? It was a fluke that we met. In the short time I knew him, he had provided some of the best advice I had ever received— thank God he had been there the day I stumbled into the Arlington office. He had saved my butt and I never got to say thanks.

Years later, I had lunch with Frank Nichols, the former director of information services for Newport News Shipbuilding. He had become the CIO of Allied Signal. He told me that he and his management team at the shipyard were very aware of the problems I was having with my branch manager. He informed me that what impressed them the most was that I had never said anything negative about my personal relationship with my manager, and apparently never let it affect my work attitude.

Nevertheless, I still had a file cabinet full of documentation from my days in Virginia. So did several of my friends, for backup. I never used it, but that's how paranoid I had become by the time my tour there was up. One of those friends joked that if I didn't find a job working for people I trusted, before long he and his wife were going to have to add an extension to their house. Oh, well.

A faint stream of light was starting to crack through the shade on my window. I had hardly slept a wink. After lying awake through most of the night and thinking about the important lessons I had learned, I realized something: now more than ever, I couldn't let my frustration with the engine project impact my work attitude at NationsBank. There were ways to get the job done while protecting myself. I needed to be careful not to let my emotions get the best of me. It would be a big mistake to let them spill over in my dealings with NationsBank senior management, or with Andersen Consulting.

I could understand Andersen trying to push its own agenda, but I was beginning to understand that the problem was more than Andersen. Keeping my emotions under control would be one of the greatest challenges. I would keep an electronic record—names, dates, people, conversations. I would send notes confirming key conversations. It would also be important to maintain the transaction engine as a high-visibility project and to enlist support from groups outside of Transaction Services. I hoped this would make it more difficult for the engine's fate to be carved out behind closed doors. This was the best alternative therapy I could think of to alleviate my desire to rave on. I hadn't come up with it on my own.

The next day, February 6, 1997, I got in early to the NationsBank Loop Road location. The final steering committee meeting was one day away. I typed out a note via e-mail to Don Mangrove. It was the best way I could think of to make my points while keeping my emotions under control. It was also an attempt to preempt the plan I was convinced Gibbons was about to spring. The note referenced the proposed new organization chart on the project office chalkboard with Peter Miles heading up the technical team. I stated firmly that, as long as I was on the project, I did not want this particular individual from Andersen separating the reporting chain between me and the people from NationsBank who reported to me on a regular basis. The note stated the following reasons for my concerns:

> From the beginning, I have felt that there have been too many managers from Andersen trying to manage the process and not enough worker bees doing the day-to-day. Yesterday was the last day for most of the remaining worker bees from Andersen. It appears the brunt of the work for the duration of this phase of the project will be placed on the shoulders of NationsBank associates who have continued to get conflicting messages and continue to express deep reservations about the Andersen approach and agenda.
>
> In my opinion, *Miles* has been part of the problem, not the solution. He has continued to operate on the outskirts of the process. I have had numerous conversations with him as well as *Gibbons* regarding the need for integrity and a united management front. *Miles* has not honored this request, descending on the project on an irregular basis, sending conflicting messages, and asking associates to do things that were directly conflicting with management directives from me. As I have suggested before, feel free to contact people on the project to get their feedback as well.

I listed some of the other issues from past experiences and suggested that if additional management needed to be inserted more directly into the technical team to help move things forward, that it would be more appropriate for me to take on this role. After all, I had done this early on before Andersen had provided a technical manager for the project. I suggested using Miles for heading up the implementation team, an ad hoc group that at this point was on paper only.

The e-mail concluded by my indication that my intent was to continue working as a "team player" for as long as I was on the project. I pointed out that my preference would be to leave the team at the conclusion of this phase of the project. Not that my leaving would upset Mangrove now that we had gotten acquainted. I hit the send key releasing the message to the network just a few minutes before Dave Gibbons showed up for our meeting. He was wearing one of those dark blue power suits.

After we sat down, Gibbons started to take me through the recommended changes in organization. He had decided that the technology team leader from Andersen was weak and not providing the necessary stewardship. This was too much like my recent experience with Gemini.

I was starting to believe that all consulting firms shared the same weakness. He wanted to insert a new level Andersen manager to "accelerate" the review process and take over for the previous technologist who wasn't cutting it. Probably not the last time I'd see it, either.

"What an interesting coincidence," I said, trying my best to display a nonchalant attitude. I shared with him that I had just written an e-mail to Don Mangrove on this subject and read an excerpt that pointed out my interest in providing more "personal" leadership for the technology team. I told him I was willing to do it, even if it meant relinquishing the overall project management position. He said he didn't see how I could do both. "I know I can do both, and this will go over a lot better with the team than bringing a new manager in," I said, adding, "It would be much less disruptive." Gibbons looked a little uncomfortable, but said that he would go along with my suggestion.

Gibbons corralled Mangrove as soon as he entered the building and shuffled him off to a meeting room. Gibbons shut the door with a thud. I went on with my own business.

Shortly after his meeting with Gibbons broke up, Mangrove tracked me down and asked me to meet him in the main conference room. Again, the door was slammed shut, this time by Mangrove. His face was red and there was a rapid pace of heavy breathing. I swore I could hear the echo of his heart pounding loudly throughout the room, straight out of Edgar Allan Poe.

"You blind-sided me."

Imagine, they were trying to take my team away, but I was the one doing the "blind-siding." Next, they would probably argue that I was "bullying" Andersen into submission.

"I don't understand what you mean," I said. "Are you referring to the e-mail? I sent it only to you and didn't copy it to anyone else. I did read part of it to Dave . . . that's all."

I asked him why he felt blind-sided. After all, it was not the first time I had raised issues concerning Peter Miles and his firm. Mangrove said that he preferred discussion rather than exchanging messages. From this point on he said he wanted me to schedule biweekly conference calls where I would talk with the Andersen management team as well as Alltel management to ensure that we were all "on the same page." One more set of meetings. They were the cure-all.

"You sure you can handle two jobs at the same time?"

"Yes, I'm sure."

Mangrove nodded, but he was still very annoyed. He said he would intensify efforts to find my replacement. Before the meeting concluded, he asked me for my advice on how I would handle the project differently if I were in his shoes. This was the last thing in the world I would have expected him to ask. It was completely out of character. In the short time we had been working together, he rarely asked for advice from me. He looked concerned and actually sounded sincere.

"Andersen gave us the 'B' team for this project. The only way to avoid this in the future is to force them into a competitive bid situation. It's our best shot of getting the 'A' team, not to mention the best possible price."

They had us in the bag and were taking it for granted. That was my heartfelt belief.

Making no additional comments, he got up and left. It was agreed in a subsequent meeting of the management group that I would have primary responsibility for the technical team.

Jay Kittles would help in an advisory role. Jay was still serving as Andersen project manager for the duration of this phase of the effort. A small concession I was all too glad to accept.

Peter Miles, as I had suggested, would begin to manage implementation planning for the next phase of the project. Obviously, the implementation plan would be dependent on the final technical recommendations. "We pitch, you catch." I assigned one of my original swat team members to assist in the implementation planning and keep it from veering too far off track.

It was sending the e-mail to a senior NationsBank manager prior to meeting with Andersen management that helped me win this particular round. In spite of the fallout, it was, in my opinion, one of those critical junctures for pulling out all the stops. Sometimes a little blind-siding is necessary before they blind-side you. As one of my former managers use to say, "Every once in a while you have to show the steel."

I knew I would continue to be outgunned in numbers of votes during engine project management meetings by the consultants and vendors who had become almost indistinguishable from NationsBank staff. If used correctly, e-mail could be an effective weapon to level the playing field when you're outranked, outflanked, and outnumbered. The key was to let them know there was a record—it could make them think twice before ramming through things. If possible, it was always good to be subtle about it, not that this was a strong point for me. Past experience had provided a great training ground for leveraging e-mail as a defense against good-old-boy backroom politics.

The day of the final steering committee presentation arrived, February 7, 1997. Right up to when the final slides were ready, charts showing the importance of fixing check-processing operational issues mysteriously found their way into the draft versions, only to be edited out by me and a few other NationsBank people. During all the prebriefings in which I presented, the recommended approach of starting with electronic processing was proposed. We received positive support that was made official with the consensus of the steering committee during the final meeting.

After all the prebriefings, it was merely a rehash for most of the committee members. We would send out a request for information (RFI) and extend the project through February and into March. It was never made clear to me if Andersen would receive additional compensation based on the latest extension, but my assumption was that they could have built an argument with their friends in senior management that the extension was based on forces beyond their control. There were obviously managers sympathetic to the Andersen cause. The problem was that there was another guy not playing ball. Those sympathetic could potentially be persuaded to approve more funding. There were also ways to deal with problem employees. It would not have been the first time.

Just before heading home, my pager went off. I had guessed it would, and who would be calling. With all my acquired battle scars and phobias, had I now fallen victim to the "Pavlov's Dog" syndrome?[16] It was Mangrove who wanted more rehashing on the next steps.

Summary of Observations

- Vertical-industry consultants attempt to build an optimum solution and replicate it within a vertical industry. This can lead to lack of competitive differentiation within an industry where customers might end up seeing little difference from one company's offerings to the next.

- E-mail can provide a valuable tool for documentation and leaving a paper trail in business areas where there appears to be questionable activities and potential conflicts of interest.

- Talking up success can become a self-fulfilling prophecy.

- Keeping other groups apprised of project activities can provide new insights, allow for the sharing of similar experiences working with various third parties, minimize decisions being made in a vacuum, and help a group learn what works, what doesn't, and what to watch out for.

- Corporate manager have lots on their plate these days and can become insular and trapped in old approaches to doing business. It is important to keep in mind that "business as usual produces business as usual results." There is a need to get more than opinions from internal operational folks and consultants on projects. Talking with managers from other business units and other companies that are not direct competitors on a regular basis is helpful. Simply monitoring the trade press and listening to consultants and other third parties is not enough.

NOTES

1. Eleena De Lissner and Stephen E. Frank, "Major Banks Show Strength in Earnings," *Wall Street Journal*, 14 January 1997, A3.

2. David Mildenberg, "New NB Fees a Bottom Line," *Business Journal*, 21 February 1997, http://charlotte.bcentral.com/charlotte/stories/1997/02/24/story4.html.

3. Stephen Labaton, "A Clinton Social with Bankers Included a Leading Regulator," *New York Times*, 25 January 1997, 1.

4. John Steel Gordon, "May Glass-Steagall Rest in Peace," *Wall Street Journal*, 26 October 1999, A26.

5. Stephen Labaton, "Congress Eases Bank Laws," *New York Times*, 7 November 1999, Sec 4, 2.

6. Hugh McColl, "Main Street Rising," speech given by the Bank of America chairman at the Oklahoma State University Executive Management Briefing, 17 November 1999, www.bankofamerica.com/ newsroom.

7. Gabriella Stern, "S and L Hell: The People and the Politics Behind the $1 Trillion Savings and Loan Scandal," *Wall Street Journal*, 30 April 1993, A8.

8. Loosely based on an original Sun Microsystems Inc. slogan which early on described the increased importance of network connectivity in computing.

9. "ERP RIP?" *Economist*, 26 June 1999, http://www.economist. com/displayStory.cfm?Story_ID=322811.

10. Fred Bronfman, "Politics Unzipped," *Salon.com*, 9 September 1996, http:// www.salon.com/news/news960904.html.

11. Ibid.

12. Julia King, "Andersen Jumps into Full-Service Outsourcing," *Computerworld*, 1 May 1995, 28.

13. "1997 Worldwide and U.S. Systems Integration Markets and Trends," *IDC: Consulting and Management Services* (Framingham, Mass.: 1997), 28.

14. David P. Hamilton and Dean Takahashi, "Scientists are Battling to Surmount Barriers in Microchip Advances," *Wall Street Journal*, 10 December 1996, A1.

15. "NationsBank Sidelines Perot as Its Outsourcer," *American Banker*, 11 April 1995, 1.

16. Dr. Ivan Pavlov ran experiments in which he timed a series of bell rings to coincide with feeding his dog. Eventually the dog would hear the ring and salivate in anticipation of being fed. For more information, see Lester M. Sdorow, *Psychology* (Madison, Wisc.: Brown & Benchmark, 1993), 282–86.

CHAPTER TWELVE

STALKING-HORSES

Just because I was told that I could focus on running the technology group of the engine project didn't mean that the Andersen management team would start taking a hands-off approach. Future consulting dollars were at stake, and it was obvious Gibbons and Miles wanted them to go a certain way. Now there was also this other Andersen partner, Pollack, someplace out there in the high grass. The biggest question on my mind was not whether they would interfere with my activities again, but where and how.

It was the second week of February 1997, the first day in my new capacity as the manager for the engine technical team. While sitting in a status meeting with Andersen and Alltel management, I noticed that one of my NationsBank team members was at the door. She was trying desperately to get my attention. I excused myself and left the room. She appeared to be upset. Actually, I appreciated an excuse to get out of the meeting. I hated status meetings, especially when there was never much progress from the last one.

"We are having a discussion right now and you need to be in on it. It's very disturbing," she said.

"What's going on?"

"We are being told to send out an RFI today. Andersen did the RFI without our involvement. This is the first I've seen of it." She handed me a copy.

"Who told you to send it out?"

"Guess."

"Miles?"

"He's not at the meeting, but he was behind it. I asked one of the Andersen guys and that's what he told me."

This was Peter Miles's signature approach to business. Another potential feather in his cap for becoming partner on the fast track. He had given direction to the Andersen consultants assigned to the Technical Team on how to play it before slithering back to some hole in the ground. The meeting had been scheduled on short notice. They knew I had a conflict. Was it intentional that I should be excluded? Based on recent experiences, probably.

So much for my new role responsible for managing the technical evaluation team. No longer could I pass it off as my own special brand of paranoia. This was a blatant move to subvert our efforts. Luckily, one of my people had the good sense to pull me out of my other meeting. She didn't like what was going on but didn't think she had the clout to stop it. For some reason, most of the people who had been around Nations-Bank for a while acted like they needed permission to breathe. There was no doubt that this emboldened the consultants.

Following her back to the meeting, I walked in and immediately took a seat at the head of the big round table everyone else was surrounding. You could have drawn a line across the middle of the table separating the Andersen people from the NationsBank people. Andersen was on my right, NationsBank on my left. The Andersen people were doing all the talking. The Andersen consultants looked pumped. They had grown in confidence over the last few weeks. NationsBank people looked sleepy. Too many joint consulting projects over the years.

There was no fire left in the belly on that side of the table. It was the "don't make waves" mentality that had come to be a critical survival mechanism.

I still harbored the unconventional idea that this was a megamistake. Consolidations, downsizing, restructuring, all the things that gave power to consultants had taken their toll. Employees punched in, punched out, and minded their own business. We might as well have given the con-sultants a license to do whatever they wanted. Employees were actually helping to make themselves expendable.

The consultants on the project were young and didn't have anywhere near the experience of their NationsBank counterparts. In spite of the experience gap in their favor, the NationsBank people were playing the part of doormats while Andersen trampled forward. I would have liked to have seen a little backbone on the NationsBank side of the table, but that would have been asking for a lot. These people had been beaten down, especially over the last few years as the acquisitions kept coming faster and faster. I guess I should have been happy that at least one of them was enterprising enough to yell for a lifeline.

As I took a seat, an Andersen consultant was discussing the RFI they wanted to send to Tandem and Hogan. He looked a little shook up, a little off stride. I placed my elbows on the table and listened. His words became measured.

"So, what are we talking about here?" I asked, finally interrupting.

"Well, as you know we have to send out an RFI." This response came from another consultant who looked like a campus letterman.

"Who prepared it?"

"We did . . . last night," said the guy who had originally been speaking.

"When you say 'we,' are you talking 'we' as in team or 'we' as in you and somebody else?"

"Well . . . yes . . . Jim and I did most of it with help from Mary Lou." Like Joe College, Jim and Mary Lou were Andersen consultants assigned to the technical team.

Mary Lou jumped in. "It's just a stalking-horse," she said. "We can make revisions. It was done to help accelerate things so we meet the new timetable." There was a little more consultingspeak from both Jim and Mary Lou.

"We wanted you guys to see it before it went out."

"Right."

I looked down at my copy. It was as thick as a term paper. Leafing through, it was a compilation of almost all the material we had produced as part of the engine project. Composed primarily of copied charts from several internal presentations, it was big on pictures and weak on specifications. There was some written documentation, but it had been spliced together haphazardly and didn't make a lot of sense. If it didn't make sense to me, how was an uninvolved vendor going to get it? Was that the intent? It talked about electronic processing. It talked about checks. The implication was that we wanted one system that could do it all, but it didn't explain much more than that.

"I don't think we're ready to send out the RFI," I said. For an instant the room fell silent, but only an instant. They didn't work for me. I was just being a pain-in-the-neck client.

Explaining that it was important to do this right, I rifled through a list of concerns. There was too much confusing and contradictory information. Unless the vendors had been involved in the project, they could not understand what the RFI was all about—unless of course they were coached. I skipped the comment about coached, but that was exactly what I was thinking.

I said that I wanted to take a few extra days to ensure that the RFI we planned to send to vendors was professionally prepared and was consistent with the requirements approved by the steering committee.

One of the NationsBank members of the technical team joined the conversation. "We have a standard approach for doing RFIs, and they must meet certain NationsBank guidelines before we can send them out."

Another piped in, "That's right. We need to get a sign-off from our Contracts and Standards Department. The way this looks now, no way it should be going out with NationsBank's name on it."

"This is an embarrassment," said the woman who had pulled me into the meeting as she paged through the document. "Contracts and Standards would surely reject it."

It was as if the NationsBank side of the table was finally coming alive with newfound chutzpah. They were now punching and counter-punching. Given Andersen's position of strength at NationsBank, this could be viewed by some as reckless behavior, but I was loving it. It was like watching the Mets beat up on the Braves for a change.

A heated round of exchange followed while I sat numb. Finally, one of the NationsBank people said, "I think this needs to be completely rewritten. We should state the business problem we are trying to solve and see how the vendors would address it. If we sent it out like it is now, they could just parrot back a bunch of meaningless information . . . like the stuff presented in here."

I really liked this suggested approach, but I figured Andersen management would not. Why do you need consultants to solve business problems if you were now asking the vendors to come up with fresh ideas for solving the same problems? How embarrassing could it be if the vendors came up with a better solution completely missed by the consultants? Come to think of fit, probably not much. I didn't know too many consultants who stayed embarrassed for long. The business-savvy consultant would probably put his energy into figuring out a way to get paid on the new solution.

There was agreement around the table, even from the Andersen side. The combination of staying up all night preparing a stalking-horse, and an unexpected offensive siege from employees was now starting to turn the worm. They were the ones looking worn down. The client had trashed what they had pulled together after working late into the night. The RFI would be reworked. We would follow NationBank's preestablished guidelines.

"We all agree?" I asked.

They did. Heads nodded halfheartedly on the Andersen side of the table, but good enough for me. We had reached agreement.

In three days we prepared a well-thought-out RFI that stated the business problems and asked the vendors to provide a solution. They were given several options: they could bid on all or part, and they could also use other firms as subcontractors, as long as the subcontractors were properly identified and their roles clearly explained. This version did adhere to the Bank's RFI standard format. Also included was a request for total cost estimates. While it did meet NationsBank standards for an RFI, by adding a request for price quotes in addition to a migration plan, the RFI essentially became a RFP (request for proposal).

As part of the request for total cost estimates, we asked for information on project management costs. In other words, we were asking for a one-stop shopping proposal. I never thought this would slip by the Andersen censors. They continued to assume that they would do the project management, regardless of the vendor solution we selected. It was also assumed that Alltel would add "peripheral" product content, and additional consultants for the integration. Andersen and Alltel had already gone on record that they would provide project management and some ancillary resources for $30 million. It didn't matter how well they knew the selected products that would make up the core of the engine. It also didn't seem to matter whether we built it or we went with an off-the-shelf product. Add $30 million to it.

I shared the RFI with both Don Mangrove from NationsBank and Dave Gibbons from Andersen, fully expecting them to nix a few things. They spent several minutes giving it a cursory review before giving me thumbs up to send it out. Not one question about pricing or project management. Nothing about emphasizing electronic processing over checks. We only had a limited window of time for getting the engine project on track, and they were all for moving forward aggressively. This was great. I could now say I had the approval of my management. As Billings would have said, we needed to get on with things, and I completely concurred. Not only would we have project management numbers to compare with Andersen and Alltel estimates, the RFI could be the knockout blow for the new float-management system.

In spite of the heated politics, as outgoing project manager from Andersen, Jay Kittles was still taking an active interest in the project. He continued to provide insights and suggestions, while maintaining a management focus. I had a sense he wanted to do things right, even if it meant problems with Gibbons or any of the others, like Miles, who had been designated to replace him in the next phase. I wondered if part of Jay's motivation was based on being constantly criticized and eventually sidelined by Gibbons.

Jay had been involved in the development of the short list of vendors. It was actually two lists, a "tier one" list that had narrowed choices to Hogan and Tandem, and a "tier two" list that had included several other vendor options. Tier two was considered a list of viable alternatives, but not as strong as tier one. In reality, with all the distractions, we simply had not had as much time to review these other options. At this point, too, tier one was more about popularity than best product fit. It was still divided, with NationsBank people pulling for Tandem and Andersen emphasizing Hogan. Gibbons and Miles consistently referred to only Hogan and Tandem—a much more controllable list. Jay Kittles always talked about an extended list, including both tiers, and insisted that there was more work to be done.

"I don't think any one of these vendors can meet all our needs," he would say. "It will probably take a combination of vendors to build the engine if we're going to do it right."

There was a meeting of the entire technical team, which included both NationsBank and Andersen. During the meeting Kittles, completely out of the blue, made a pronouncement: "I think we should send the RFI, not only to Hogan and Tandem, but to the tier two vendors as well."

I could have hugged him.

Up until this point all of the discussion regarding the RFI was based on requesting information from Hogan and Tandem only. Everyone assumed a shoot-out between the two. I had never been comfortable with tier one vendors as the only viable options. Kittles may have been a lame duck, but he was still the Andersen project manager. No one, including Mangrove, could accuse us of not getting buy-in from Andersen management. We would be in a position to say that we had done the full due diligence and had kept Andersen management fully involved. When brought to task on this, and I was sure I would be, I could point out that not only was Andersen in the loop on this, but it was Andersen management that had recommended sending it to the extended list. Kittles had to have known that the other Andersen managers would not be pleased. I had this feeling he wasn't about to lose any sleep over it. Besides, no one had ever said we shouldn't send it to all vendors on both lists.

While perhaps less important, from the bank perspective, this would also help in public relations. Vendors were also bank customers. We could say that we gave each of the vendors involved in the process serious consideration and a fair shot at winning the business. If the vendor made either of our short lists, it deserved a shot at it. Maybe there was a solution that could meet all requirements that we had previously overlooked. It simply made no sense to exclude them.

From the beginning I knew there was an underlying assumption on the part of both Don Mangrove and Dave Gibbons that the RFI would only go to Hogan and Tandem. I had no intention of changing that assumption, unless I was specifically asked about it. There was an old adage I remembered from my days of selling for IBM: "It's easier to ask for forgiveness than to ask management for permission."

While all along I wanted to send it to a more inclusive list of vendors, I was already on thin ice. I wanted to avoid even the appearance of insubordination. Jay Kittles had provided me with plenty of cover. I wanted to thank him, but decided the less said to him, or anybody else, the better.

Eventually it would come out. I was hoping later versus sooner. There was always the possibility that Kittles would say something to upper management, but in his lame duck role as co-project manager, he never did. This was not a career-enhancing decision and he could only get hurt. For some reason, that didn't seem to matter. Someone else on the Andersen technical team could also spill the beans early on, and in my judgment this was the bigger threat. The only hope was that they might assume Kittles was speaking for all of Andersen management, with Gibbons and Miles already in the loop. Here, too, we lucked out.

So far, all the efforts to shift the focus to a long-term project for rebuilding check-processing systems had not worked. If it had only gone to Tandem and Hogan, all they really needed was to eliminate Tandem and the solution would be check processing. Now the RFI was going to an extended list of vendors and requested that the responses emphasize capabilities in electronic processing. An electronic focus had been emphasized all along in spite of Andersen's efforts to substitute a focus on checks. Based on the way the RFI had been written, vendors would need to respond with an electronic payments engine solution. How could we change directions now without raising a few eyebrows? Score one for the NationsBank team. Yet still, for some reason, I was uneasy. Up to now, Gibbons and Miles showed little indication of playing fair. There was no reason to think this would change. I figured they were still looking to make the engine part of Model Bank, and to hell with Global Finance and all those other less important organizations that wanted to share.

Model Bank was starting to run into some capacity-constraint issues prior to the Texas conversion, yet the Model Bank myth was alive and well. Senior management was continuing to extol the virtues of Model Bank as the common platform that could reach across the entire franchise and make future expansion possible from coast to coast, when it was impossible for almost everybody else. Knowing enough to be dangerous about systems architecture, I believed this was impossible given the limitations of the older technology being used. In spite of the public relations statements implying that Model Bank helped us accelerate bank consolidation, the conversion process was time consuming and extremely laborious. Employees continued working long hours without missing a beat while the consultants scrambled for new options to fix Model Bank performance problems. Model Bank was like an old boat. No matter how much money was sunk into it, it still needed more. Absorbing the engine as part of Model would mean an infusion of additional funding available, helping to feed the beast. Soon, they'd need to find more.

NationsBank was the kind of place where almost all associates seemed to work very hard. But did we work smart? You couldn't help but wonder why we seemed to cover the same ground over and over again. From what I could see, actual progress never quite lived up to reports. A Dave Matthews Band song was popular at the time and kept playing in my head:

> People in every direction
> No words exchanged,
> No time to exchange when
> All the little ants are marching
> Red and black antennae waving
> They all do it the same
> They all do it the same[1]

Was commitment to change merely a public relations ploy while we continued to grow by acquiring legacy banks? There was no question we continued to grow in size. We were spending lots of money in operations and technology, but were we growing in capability? What happens when we run out of acquisitions and need to rely on our competitiveness in the marketplace to extend and maintain leadership? Could we grow revenue without making buy-out deals? Maybe it didn't really matter. By then the fat cats would be retired. Andersen and Alltel would have made a killing.

I came in early one day prior to a status meeting. While pouring my first coffee of the day at the community breakfast nook, one of the managers in the Integration Services organization who worked for Darlene Wittington struck up a conversation. She mentioned that Peter Miles had asked her what she would do if the money allocated for the transaction engine was given to her instead.

"You know, we could do some 'interim' repair work for our current routing and settlement systems."

When she told me she had sent him an e-mail outlining an "alternative" plan, I asked her to give me a copy. She was reluctant to do so and looked like she wished she had kept her mouth shut.

After being at NationsBank for a while, I had a greater appreciation for why Dan Price hated going out of our group to collect information. Getting information from people working for other NationsBank organizations was often like trying to dislodge a computer game from one of the new generation of techno-savvy adolescents, the "Y" Generation. It didn't matter that I was a senior vice president. In contrast, when consultants asked for information, NationsBank people fell over backward trying to help them. There was this misplaced assumption that keeping the consultants on your side could help you solidify your position and tip the balance in your favor. There was sure to be rounds of downsizing to come, and the consultants were the ones who would influence management on where to cut. better to stay on good terms with them. If at some point in the future the consultants were asked by upper management which group should go first, you had better make sure you helped versus hindered. It took some prodding, but she finally agreed to give me a copy.

During the engine project status meeting, Miles launched into a presentation he prepared on the financial case. It was essentially a recap of previously disclosed information on the two-year, $30 million budget for project management, with one exception. It included an alternative plan for fixing the current systems. He said it was based on Andersen's research. He handed out a sheet. It was the same information copied verbatim from the memo I already had in my hand. It was that classic watch-borrowing stunt which by now had become so painfully familiar.

Nothing like creating a groundswell with the people who had a vested interest in the status quo. "How would you like it if we could throw more money into your budget to fix all those little annoying things?" Miles was launching a new offensive, playing one more group of employees against another.

I was entrenched in the other camp. Interim repair meant no real-time capability. It meant electronic processing was taking a backseat to the current check-processing system. Business units of the bank that required real-time routing and settlement would have to find their own solution. This would produce more system redundancy, more silos, and more consulting contracts. When I asked why we were exploring this kind of stalking-horse, Mangrove, the faithful protector of the consultants, barged into the discussion.

"*Because,* I asked Andersen to look into this."

His tone immediately softened, as he suggested that I shouldn't be overly concerned. This alternative merely represented a fallback position if we could not secure sufficient funding for the engine.

"We'll revisit this," Mangrove insisted, "after we look at the RFI responses and get a better handle on the available budget. We may not need to use it. Think of it as Plan B, kind of like insurance."

That was exactly what I was thinking. It was insurance all right, insurance for Andersen maximizing revenue for Andersen and maintaining tight control.

After the RFIs went out to the vendors, I prepared a white paper on what I thought the engine needed to address and a proposed plan for doing this. It was something I thought could be used as a "benchmark" for evaluating vendor responses we were about to receive. I used the output of PowerPlus as the basis of my assumptions. In the executive summary of the document, I quoted comments from Ken Lewis, president of NationsBank, which had appeared in a NationsBank internal publication in January 1997 called *NationsBank Times*:

> To serve customers the way they want to be served, we have to have a seamless approach—no boundaries. We have to make it easier for customers to do business with us, to think of the customer first, rather than of any one individual or any profit center. Creative teamwork will be even more important in the future. I want all of us to recognize that our destinies are intertwined, and then on behalf of our customers make declarations of interdependence. [2]

I sent copies of the white paper along with the RFI to several managers in NationsBank. One of them was John Turner, the manager responsible for the Global Finance Software Group. He was also an advisory member of the engine project. Turner called shortly after receiving it. He said he was interested in bidding on the engine.

"To be honest, I'm not sure you can. You're not on the short list of vendors."

"No, but I know that Tibco is and we could partner with them."

He had a point. Tibco, the vendor Turner had told me and Denny Billings about during our trip to Chicago, was on the tier two list. Turner knew this from steering committee meetings. He asked me to keep his interest in responding under wraps until he was able to get formal approval from his management. I told him I would and then need to get approval from mine. It was agreed. He would check first.

One of the people working for John Turner also called and said he really liked the thrust of the white paper. He said it provided useful information for better understanding the routing and settlement environment. "No outside consultant would write anything that passionate about our systems," he said.

There was a Corporate Strategy Technology Group board of directors meeting in Charlotte on February 27. As a division "strategist," I was on the board, but since taking over the engine project, I had missed most of the meetings. This one I decided to attend. Taking advantage of the time in Charlotte, I scheduled a meeting with Betsy Fields, the director responsible for managing the STG organization. For some reason she was not planning on going to the board meeting and had time on her schedule later that day.

It was the typical STG board meeting, lots of people, lots of reports, and no action required. During a meeting break, I successfully cornered the STG manager who was a member of the engine steering committee, Vincent Porter. Porter reported to Fields. I shared with him my concerns regarding the latest twist in the engine saga. He was from New York, so I felt I could talk candidly, as one New Yorker to another.

"We got problems . . . there seems to be a lot of discussion about an interim repair strategy versus doing the engine."

"I think it's a good idea. . . . It will give us the time needed to build a new engine the right way."

My gut flipped over and fell into an uncontrollable nosedive. Here was a senior manager in the corporate strategic organization for Nations-Bank saying business as usual was OK. Unless there was something I didn't know, with budgets being cut, there wasn't enough money to do both—not in the short term. But then . . . if there was . . . what a boon for Andersen. Maybe that was it. Gibbons, the Andersen partner for the engine was maneuvering to get a new float-management system. Pollack, the Andersen partner working on the client/server project for Direct Bank, gets the new engine. Everybody wins, except NationsBank's pocketbook. There was now another potential angle: Andersen was throwing a fallback option into the mix. If it lost on a new float system and also lost on client/server, it could still get consulting dollars by recommending a repair versus build solution. It seemed to have all the bases covered.

NationsBank Chairman Hugh McColl was continually beating the drum that a new breed of competitors, the technology providers, threatened banks. Maybe there was an even greater threat from within. Several months before, in the *Wall Street Journal*, senior executives from NationsBank expressed differing views on the importance of technology. McColl said technology filled him with trepidation. "He is convinced that if he makes the wrong bet, or the right bet at the wrong time, the company he nursed from a regional bank to a player on the national stage will fade into obscurity."[3]

In the very same article, Ken Lewis, president of the bank, who reported to the chairman and was slated to be his successor, was also quoted. Lewis said that changes in technology "may not be an issue of survival. . . . I don't think the changes will be so dramatic."[4] Lewis was the number one cheerleader for Model Bank. With Model, what's to worry?

The article went on to say that Hugh McColl relied on STG executives to assist him in making the right technology decisions and acting as internal consultants. If the people he relied on were content with the status quo,

McColl had good reason to be bursting with trepidation. Not only that, his internal consultants were taking cues from external consultants who might not have been as committed to NationsBank's long-term success.

I left the board meeting's off-site hotel location and drove my rental car to the NationsBank Independence Center in downtown Charlotte to meet with Betsy Fields. She was running a few minutes late, so I entertained myself browsing through most of the waiting room high-tech magazines while the other half of my brain played out various discussion scenarios.

According to the grapevine, and contrary to the positive press, the STG was starting to come under some heat. The company had invested lots of money in technology initiatives. The annual technology budget was reported as $1.4 billion.[5] In spite of all the hype, much of this was on traditional, legacy systems. The STG was to play a stewardship role in technology investments to assist the business units in moving ahead. Determining their effectiveness was difficult at best. I knew that Betsy Fields had a good rapport with Hugh McColl. She had told me this herself when we had met for lunch a few months ago. While I had turned down a job in her organization before agreeing to work for Barbara Albrecht, she had remained cordial. Betsy and Barbara didn't get along much better than Darlene and Barbara.

She explained that her relationship with Al Johnson, the president of the Services Company, was tenuous at best. She reported to him and told me that in the beginning she had similar problems with him that I was apparently having with senior executives in my area of the business. I hadn't said anything yet about concerns, but I guess it was common knowledge. Everybody knew about my end run to Johnson, she said. This was not a good thing, according to Betsy. It gave me a black eye at NationsBank.

"It's important here to be perceived as a team player first . . . not an agent of change," she said.

A few years later I would take up reading *Fast Company*, a monthly magazine that was filled with stories about "change agents." Sounded to me like there were plenty of people in this category who also knew something about team play. Nonetheless, Betsy was simply trying to give some career advice for NationsBank: "play ball."

Being a closet agent of change, however, did not hold a lot of appeal. Somehow, in my head change was inescapably linked as a prerequisite for competing in the emerging world of e-commerce. Time was of the essence. As McColl had said, there was a major "paradigm shift" taking place in banking. The rules of the game were changing. Former advantages such as size could become a liability when competing against the fleet of foot. Size could impact a bank's ability to respond. How much brand loyalty could be expected as e-commerce turned banking into a commodity business? What would hold customers back from better, easier-to-use options? "It's that friendly neighborhood personal touch." "And we just love the way you guys process checks."

Bill Gates was no longer alone in warning that banks could be shut out if they did not seize the moment. At a conference sponsored by the consulting firm Gartner Group, Gates was joined by other technology leaders warning banks about being complacent and not embracing change.[6] The change they were talking about wasn't getting bigger by acquiring more check-processing banks. If checks were a problem, why increase the problem's volume?

The ability to respond to new challenges would require swift, aggressive action. Competing effectively meant more than creating new front-end delivery channels such as home banking and Web-based interfaces while the rest of the bank remained virtually the same. In the long run these front-end additions were purely cosmetic. Customer responsiveness didn't stop with the graphic user interface and a stylish Web page. I still didn't see how being a team player and raising questions or alternative recommendations prior to a final decision as inconsistent. After the decision is made, a good team player does need to fall in line, but until then, I felt I had a responsibility to point out the issues and possible alternatives as I saw them. Call me a politically incorrect lemming, if I had to jump, I was determined to pick my very own cliff. I hoped it wouldn't come to that.

I wondered if Betsy was on board with Vincent Porter concerning the engine. Porter kept referring to the success of Andersen, General Bank, and the STG on the Direct Bank project. He was now talking up a plan to put a similar approach in place for the engine while we sunk additional bucks in the old systems. One of his people had recently told me that there was speculation that Betsy Fields might move into a new slot reporting directly to the chairman.

Most recently, she had become somewhat of a celebrity with lots of trade press exposure.[7] Porter would be the likely replacement. It occurred to me that Porter might be getting real aggressive in hopes of actualizing these potential changes on an accelerated time frame. He had certainly become a lot more active in all kinds of places. He was getting lots of visibility with executives. There was added pomp in his strut.

Betsy looked more like a college professor than an executive from a bank. She wore thick, wide cubes for glasses and her hair must have been carefully teased to achieve the waves of thickly packed curls rolling out in all conceivable directions. As our meeting began, she was pleasant and gracious, asking me to give her some background on how the project was going. After filling her in, I raised my concerns regarding Andersen, suggesting that they had not allocated the right kind of talent for the project. I pointed out that Andersen had not delivered on its commitments and yet it seemed inevitable that they would play a major role in the next phase as well.

She confided in me that several of her people had told her that the Andersen team assigned to this project was weak. Betsy went on to explain that I needed to keep in mind that both Ken Lewis and Al Johnson were very big fans of Andersen Consulting.

"There are two vendors they like to use for business: Andersen and IBM."

Of course, I said to myself. Not so surprising. Trying my best at being subtle, an art form I never completely mastered, I told the STG director that Vincent Porter seemed to be intimately involved with Andersen and was suggesting that the interim repair strategy might be the best way to go.

"I'm glad to hear that Vinny is now taking a more active role with business units projects," she said. "That's what I've told him to do."

"But an interim plan to dump more money into old systems at the cost of building something strategic, something we obviously need . . . I don't get it. Doesn't that run counter to our need for building strategic solutions?"

"Sometimes we have to take action to address short-term tactical needs," was her response.

Betsy had been told that the pressing payment issues that needed to be addressed related to check processing. They had gotten to her, too. I took the opportunity to explain how the paper-based routing system was not the problem and how this system had a sustainable architecture and didn't need a lot of fixing: Y2K checks and some other changes, but not much else—and that was from the guy who helped build it and was still running it.

"Model Bank may need fixing, but the float-management systems are sound and can handle additional capacity."

I shared with her how the major issues were related to electronic processing and that it would require a new engine to solve these problems. My comments shifted to the consultants.

"In my mind, there were two apparent reasons we used consultants within the services company at NationsBank. The first was for research. Consulting research assists management in decision making. Seems to me most of the information consultants gather is now available on the Internet, or from talking directly with employees. The other reason was corporate politics and the inability of different groups to get along."

As I had learned from experience, it wasn't only the case in Nations-Bank. Consultants are often hired to resolve internal political conflict within a company as opposed to gaining access to their knowledge and expertise. If corporate people could get along better, fewer consultants could be used in more productive ways.

"Reduce the conflict and we can reduce dependency on these kinds of consultants," I said.

I suggested that we had better talent in NationsBank than what Andersen had provided for the project. With the combined efforts of the STG, Transaction Services, and other business groups within the bank, I was convinced we could minimize the need for outside consulting and project management. "Let's use outside talent only where it makes sense," I added.

"To be perfectly honest, I'm not a big fan of Andersen's, either," she replied.

Betsy was starting to open up. She confided in me that she was meeting with Services Company President Al Johnson the following Monday at his office in Atlanta. She said she would be willing to talk with him about the engine, provided I gave her some detailed background information so she could get up to speed in a hurry.

What an opportunity. Someone else would take it to Johnson. I could continue playing the role of the born-again "play by the rules" bureaucrat. I told her that I would. I also offered to pick her up the day of her meeting at the Atlanta airport and drive her to the Plaza building. It would give me additional time at lobbying and filling her head with bullets on the engine. She decided to take me up on the offer. Her meeting was scheduled for the next Monday, March 3. Coincidentally, it was also the day the RFI responses were due from the vendors.

Monday morning there was no wait time when I arrived at the airport because her flight was a few minutes early. Betsy spotted me first. I had rented a full-size car for the occasion rather than using my beat-up personal set of wheels in desperate need of a tune up. Imagine if it broke down while transporting her to a meeting with a division president. As we approached midtown Atlanta, the casual small talk receded into NationsBank business and my preoccupation with keeping the engine on track. She mentioned that she had read the material I provided and said that it helped clarify things.

I suggested that there was a potential conflict of interest with Andersen involved in the RFI review. They had been very open about their intention to play an active role in the development and implementation of the new engine.

"Don't see how they can legitimately do both," I said.

"Steve, you need to be very careful here. You do not want to be perceived as being anti-Andersen. It could severely hurt your career."

Not so good for a born-again bureaucrat. Raising the conflict-of-interest card had swiftly impacted her mood. Betsy continued, pointing out that she could make no guarantees as to what might happen in her meeting with Johnson. "But I will suggest that we look at other options," she added. Betsy then offered some additional advice. She told me she read a lot of psychology books.

"If you think of people as being fundamentally good, you will find that in general they really are," she said.

Did I hear her right? Was she really that Pollyannaish? Or did she just recognize a wacko when she saw one? I was sure that's what she had said. In my efforts to present the facts within a limited window of time, it was quite possible that I had portrayed an air of cynicism and a touch of the neurotic. This was topped off by my unfortunate reference to the conflict issue, conjuring up potential "legalese" ramifications to the corporate executive types. The level of frustration as the engine project continued to unravel was probably getting the best of me. I blew it again.

I thanked Betsy for her willingness to help as we pulled up in front of the NationsBank Plaza building, with its impressive edifice capped off by its steeple of whickered mesh, resembling a gigantic birdcage. At one time the building belonged to C&S Sovran. Legend had it that as ground was broken and new skyscrapers rose in Charlotte and other cities, the steeple on the Plaza was a more recent edition to maintain C&S Sovran's distinction as owning one of the largest bank buildings in the Southeast. With the new steeple, it became the eighth largest building in the United States, and it didn't belong to Hugh McColl. His monument to himself in Charlotte was no longer best in class in the Southeast. Some believed it was this edition that prompted McColl to accelerate plans for acquiring C&S.

The story goes that McColl was so furious when he learned of the new edition that he paced up and down the corporate jet, saying, "We don't need separate banks towering above every cow path."

The Charlotte NationsBank building, by itself, could not sustain his pride and joy for long. It was a dog-eat-dog war for building dominance. The Charlotte NationsBank used to count for something back in the days when being the best in town was still important. Back then, McColl had beat out First Union to claim the biggest tower in town. First Union was also headquartered in the Tar Heel capital of high finance—the banking Mecca that some were saying would soon rival New York and Chicago, some from North Carolina that is. It seemed nothing could stand in the way of NationsBank and First Union breaking new heights in either revenue generation or office altitude.

Just prior to kicking construction off, Hugh unexpectedly held up plans. Ground breaking would force his hand in an announcement as to the planned height of the new structure. He wanted to prevent his competition from knowing for as long as he could. People from the bank said the NationsBank plan became public only after rival First Union had begun construction for its new building, a few blocks away from McColl's proposed site. As noted in a cover story in *Fortune* on Hugh McColl, he and his celebrated adversary, Edward Crutchfield at First Union, fought for a while over who would have the tallest building. They, "like kids trading 'does to's' and 'does not's,' have been trying to out-shine each other by seeing who can build the taller headquarters in Char-lotte."[8] Hugh eventually won with his sixty-story complex. As First Union started falling into bad times, it seemed McColl would win hands down on the business growth contest, too.

We pulled up in front of the building.

"Steve, can't thank you enough for the lift."

"What you've agreed to do is thanks enough."

"Remember, I said no guarantees. We'll see how it goes."

Betsy and I agreed that I would meet her in the afternoon and pro-vide her transport back to the airport. In the meantime, there was plenty to do with the vendor RFI responses rolling in. I had left strict orders that only those individuals who had worked on the technology team in devel-oping the RFI should be given access to the responses. This included just a handful of NationsBank employees and Andersen consultants. I left one of the bank people who worked for me in charge of collecting the responses as they came in.

A new project manager for Alltel was being introduced as I walked through the bullpen surrounding the project office. His name was Jack Tooms. We shook hands. I then organized a brief meeting of the tech-nology team, including Andersen consultants and NationsBank associ-ates, to review our plan of action. There were several interruptions and another brief meeting with Kittles. If I was going to retrieve Betsy, I only had a few minutes to get some things done and maybe grab a sandwich and some chips for the road.

I was getting ready to leave when one of the NationsBank members of the technology team came to see me. This was the guy collecting the incoming bids. He had just gotten back from an earlier lunch with Jack Tooms, the new Alltel manager who was being transitioned in for the next phase of the engine project—what Andersen and Alltel were calling the "build" phase. Tooms would eventually replace Larry Rogers, the senior Alltel manager who had worked with us so far. Tooms had explained to him over lunch that due to NationsBank budget cuts, Alltel and Andersen planned on delivering an alternative outsourcing proposal for the engine. It would be based on the client/server technology. They would also promote a partnership approach with other banks as a way of reducing the development costs and risks to NationsBank. "Coopetition," banking style. No doubt, this kind of argument could be very appealing to risk-averse bankers. "If wrong, at least we'll all be wrong together."

During the last phase of the project, I had had numerous conversations with Larry Rodgers from Alltel. On several of those occasions, he had taken the opportunity to tell me about the capabilities of his company. While he would point out that Alltel did not have the necessary technology for building the base for the transaction engine, Larry would always quickly assert that they did have technology that could be added to provide "additional functionality." They had done this with Model Bank. They could do it again with the transaction engine. "You might think of us as a mainframe company, but we can now do client/server at Alltel, too," Rodgers informed me. Never in any of the conversations with Larry Rogers, or the Andersen managers, did anyone suggest that they planned to provide a bid to outsource the entire engine. Several of us had suspected this, research suggested it, but nothing had been mentioned before the other vendor bids had started rolling in. The NationsBank associate who brought this to my attention was fuming.

"How can we let them shop around our design work to other banks? Isn't this proprietary NationsBank material?" he asked.

In my mind, he had an excellent point. Not to mention the obvious conflict of interest in evaluating other proposals while presenting your own. This revelation was just in time to prevent us from being railroaded into another phase where Andersen and Alltel held all the cards. I asked him if he would mind collecting his thoughts regarding the comments he had just made and sending me a note recapping the conversation. I told him I wanted to forward it to select members of upper management.

"If that makes you uncomfortable, you can say no," I said.

"I'd be happy to do it," he said.

The NationsBank team was no longer just punching in.

"Do me one other favor. You're still collecting the bids as they come in?"

"Yeah. They're all still sealed."

"Good. Keep it that way. I've got to run out, but when I get back you and I will put a game plan in place."

"No problem, boss."

Better than being called "Sir."

He knocked it out quickly. It seemed to hit the key points we discussed. His note, dated March 3, said the following:

Had lunch today with *Jack Tooms* from ALLTEL. He mentioned that he was going to participate in meetings this week between Andersen Consulting and ALLTEL regarding a bid to develop an "Engine" independently, which they would lease back to NationsBank. He also said that they planned to talk at these meetings about other bank clients of both Andersen and ALLTEL to which they would market it.

> This surprised me, because I believed that they were both partners of ours on this effort going forward. And more important, I thought that all the "Engine" work that we have done to date was proprietary property of NationsBank and that these vendors had signed nondisclosure agreements with us. I do not see how legally (or ethically) these two vendors of ours can simply take our specifications now and use them to develop their own product to sell to our competitors or even to sell back to us. What I find most surprising is that they have long-term relationships with NationsBank and are acting like this.

I would use it later. In the meantime, I tried calling Don Mangrove, but it rang through to his voice mail. I was now running late and decided to forgo grabbing lunch and head straight over to pick up Betsy. Before leaving, I stopped by to see Jay Kittles, explaining the situation based on the information that had recently come to my attention. With the RFI responses rolling in, a decision needed to be made.

"I want to hold off on Andersen and Alltel involvement in the review until I have a chance to talk with Don. Haven't been able to reach him yet."

He replied, "I understand. Let me know what he says, as soon as you can."

Jay then dropped the bomb with his patented understated approach. He told me that it was the Andersen partner from Direct Bank, Ken Pollack, along with Vincent Porter, the NationsBank manager from the STG serving on the steering committee, who had started the discussions around outsourcing the engine and shopping it to other banks.

I picked up Betsy Fields to take her back to the Atlanta airport.

"I want you to know right away, I didn't get a chance to discuss the transaction engine."

Betsy explained that she and Al Johnson had gotten into a lengthy conversation on e-commerce which dominated the entire conversation.

"E-commerce, as you know, is very important for our future."

She said she was sorry but that she would be seeing him again in the near future and would try to broach the subject then. I couldn't believe it. A lot of effort had been expended trying to get her pumped up, preparing information to make her more knowledgeable about the importance of the transaction engine, providing supporting documentation—not to mention becoming her personal chauffer to and from airports to meetings. All this for a "so sorry, maybe next time."

Betsy was sounding as if we had already completely embraced e-commerce at NationsBank. We had a Web site. We had a home-banking program. Never mind that less than three percent of our customers were using it at the time and, in itself, this wasn't even close to being the total solution for all of our customers' electronic-banking needs. To hear Betsy explain it, NationsBank was already fully exploiting the Internet for business. We were a strategic-technology leader, much to her credit and her organization. What more could we do? Customers had an option and they kept choosing checks. Our job was to give them the option and not much more.

She continued, pointing out, "Al Johnson and I are in agreement. What we need to do now is to leverage and build on our early success in this exciting new area."

Needless to say, I was deeply disappointed. If we were going to keep this moving in a strategic direction and avoid an end run, it would be totally up to my team and me. I tried to hide my feelings with an air of lightheartiness, though I'm not quite sure the ruse worked. I told Betsy that, after some thought, I had come to the conclusion that she was right about trusting people and that perhaps I had been a little too judgmental, suggesting that in the future I would give people the benefit of the doubt. She said she was delighted to hear about my change of heart and thought my taking a new approach would make working at the bank more enjoyable. So would a lobotomy.

The conversation managed to shift in several different directions, including Atlanta living, latest technology trends in the bank, recent organization changes, and a summary of world news and events. Eventually it looped back to the engine. I mentioned that the thing that kept me going was the belief that the engine was a critical "must do" business initiative. I mentioned that in spite of all the hard work and frustration, I was glad to be a part of it. The STG director said that she was happy that she was only responsible for strategy and not having a hand in implementing systems was just fine with her. If not the knowledge and skills, she certainly had the right temperament to become a successful management consultant.

As we proceeded down I-85 toward the airport, I could contain myself no longer. With my best attempt at an offhanded delivery, I shared with Betsy the conversation with Jay Kittles regarding outsourcing and the connection with her manager, Vincent Porter. I explained how he was working directly with Andersen on developing a completely different alternative for the transaction engine without involving other members of project team. He was also involved in discussions to let Andersen shop it around to other banks. She slid from a relaxed, perched position into a more crouched one as her eyes immediately dropped to the floor, as if looking for something that had fallen close to her feet.

She quickly introduced another topic into the conversation. I couldn't tell if her lapse into an apparently uncomfortable position signaled prior knowledge, possible collaboration, or genuine surprise. I decided to give her the benefit of the doubt. It was in keeping with my new resolution to think about the positive side. As I pulled up to the curb for departing flights, Betsy said that the members of her organization told her that they enjoyed working with me. She thanked me again for the lift as she stepped out of the car.

"Remember what I said. Stay positive, be a team player, and don't come on like you've got a grudge against Andersen. It's all going to work out fine."

Speaking of team, Mangrove had said that the management team should make all decisions on the engine. The current management team included Andersen and Alltel management along with Don Mangrove and me. Assuming the question of Andersen and Alltel involvement was put to a vote, and if the senior NationsBank manager Mangrove abstained, Andersen and Alltel involvement would continue. They had more votes. I had an even more disturbing thought, based on everything I had observed. I was willing to bet that if Mangrove didn't abstain—and nothing based on experience suggested that he might—no way could I count on his vote.

While other vendors had been requested to submit a bid for the implementation of a transaction engine, Andersen and Alltel had never submitted one. As stated in the RFI, all bids were due this day. Now, at the last moment, Andersen and Alltel said they planned to present an outsourcing alternative. Maybe the plan was to go to senior management after reviewing the other vendor bids. "None of these will meet your total requirements. As an alternative, we recommend you outsource to us." It might have worked if Tooms didn't fall victim to diarrhea of the mouth. It still could work if we didn't do something fast to stop it.

How could this be objective if Andersen and Alltel were reviewing other responses while planning to come in the back door with their own proposal, or proposals? What was the potential fallout if other vendors found this out and decided to make an issue of it? At the very least, I was convinced it could damage our credibility.

In addition, there was a second level of potential conflict of interest that could prove even more detrimental. The employee who brought this to my attention had it right. It was now becoming obvious that the intent was to create a partnership between potentially competitive banks. Consultants and vendors could hide behind the banner of client confidentiality to disguise that they were working for competitors in the same industry. We had learned, for example, that in addition to working for NationsBank, Andersen Consulting also worked for one of our primary competitors, First Union, the guys with the next biggest building in Charlotte. We had learned this from talking with First Union personnel, not Andersen Consulting.

Consultants rarely disclosed these potential conflicts of interest, except when brokering partnerships. Consultants such as Andersen could benefit greatly by convincing major players within industries such as banking that there was strength in partnerships and that the real competition was from new market entrants from other industries—just another example of playing off of "Fear, Uncertainty, and Doubt" to their own best interests and creating lucrative "me, too" engagements where one solution fits all. It no longer mattered if it was the best choice if everyone was using it. There was a sense of security in being one of many. It was "best practice" by default.

Returning to the project office, I found a private area and tried calling Mangrove again. Once more, it immediately rang through to his voice mail. I didn't want to leave a message, so I waited a few more minutes and called a third time. Again, only his recorded greeting. In addition to all my other neuroses, I was obsessive-compulsive. I felt compelled to do something immediate. I couldn't bring myself to wait any longer for a live voice on the other end of the line. Jay Kittles and the whole technology team were frozen until this issue was resolved. It was either a voice mail message or an e-mail. I began to rationalize myself into thinking that sending a message was the best way to go. No record with a voice mail. As much as I knew Mangrove wouldn't like it, I decided it was the best course for protecting myself in the long run, or was I simply delusional, too? The short run would get very ugly, but I'd been there before.

I had to leave a trail. Documentation, while not a preferred communication tool by Mangrove, had proven to be a powerful weapon in winning internal battles—at least this far. Without it, this would have ended a long time ago with Andersen and Alltel just going through the motions. I had no false pretenses of ever being part of the inner circle at Nations-Bank. If the decision reverted to the good ol' boys in the back room, there was no contest. Andersen and Alltel had established themselves as very successful in the back-parlor politics of NationsBank. The potential consequences of an Andersen-Alltel grand slam outweighed the risk, at least in my increasingly jaded perspective. Sending a message would make it harder to bury my concerns and ignore them.

With that settled, there was one more dilemma. Should I copy it to Walt Shaw or not? I knew Mangrove would see this as more egregious than anything else I could do. After bursting a vessel or two, I could be in some very serious trouble. By pulling Andersen off the review team, I already was.

Shaw was the executive who said we should send out the RFI. It was also Shaw who said it was important for NationsBank to maintain control. As the new executive running Transaction Services, he needed to know what was going on before his wishes were subverted. Unless he was copied on the message, Mangrove could bury it. By copying it to his boss, the options to dismiss my concerns would be more limited. Shaw read all his e-mails. I had gone this far. Oh well, what the hell.

My note got Mangrove's immediate attention. Within minutes of executing the "send" command, my electronic leash went off.

"I need to know, why did you do this? We are suppose to make these decisions as a group," he said, in a hostile, reprimanding tone.

I tried to lessen the sting, suggesting that it required immediate action as the bids were arriving that day and he had been unavailable by phone. I explained that in my judgment I needed to make a "tentative" decision on the spot. My intent was to only temporarily suspend their participation until he and I talked. It was a unique situation involving Andersen and Alltel, where their ability to provide a purely objective view was suspect at best.

"I just wanted to hold off on their involvement in the review until I could get ahold of you."

Mangrove wasn't buying it. He said that he wanted an engine management committee meeting in the afternoon of the following day to sort this out. The management committee was Mangrove, me, Andersen, and Alltel. He rarely conducted meetings without them. Why should it be any different now, even if the subject was to discuss whether they should stay involved?

He concluded his remarks, saying, "That's all I had on my list. How about yours?"

"I think it has been covered," I replied, as if I, too, was a devout disciple of his brand of project management, methodically reviewing the "to do" lists and status reports that were under constant revision as we traveled from one meeting to the next.

My effort to lessen the sting had been unsuccessful. A few seconds of dead air. I could hear his heavy breathing once again over the line.

"I'll see you tomorrow," Mangrove said, and he hung up abruptly.

I sent the message I had received regarding the lunch conversation between Tooms and the NationsBank employee to other select NationsBank managers as a "For Your Information" update. At this point, there was no need to worry about damaging rapport with Mangrove. I did have to restrain myself from the urge to editorialize. These were senior managers who were not in my direct chain of command for the engine project, but had asked me to keep them informed on progress. After all, as part of the engine project mandate, we were supposed to be working together across organizational boundaries, providing ongoing communication, and leveraging cross-functional assistance. In addition, bank president Ken Lewis had challenged us to recognize that "our destinies are intertwined" and to utilize "creative teamwork."

For a critical and highly visible project like the engine, I believed it was in the interest of all of us at NationsBank to do it right. I would gladly welcome all the additional help that I could get, from anywhere. The new engine would not merely belong to Model Bank, or Transaction Services for that matter, but to the entire bank. That's why the steering committee was cross-organizational. It was what the engine was all about. PowerPlus had identified cross-organizational objectives. We had received buy-in across the board. Senior executive feedback had confirmed that we were on the right path. I didn't think anyone with management responsibility at the bank could just sit back and let vendors run away with it, changing the course to better suit their own objectives. I rationalized my decision to enlist support from other groups. What a day it had been. It was still only Monday, and it was not over yet.

Jay Kittles came by. "There you are."

He wanted to know if I had talked with Mangrove and whether a decision had been reached on Andersen's participation in the RFI review. He was no dummy, and he must have wondered if I would be the one no longer participating.

"I'm good with it either way," he declared. "I just need to know."

Jay explained that if we weren't going to use Andersen for the review, he had people he wanted to cut loose for other projects. I told him that the final decision on this subject would be made in a joint meeting the following day. Until then, I suggested we proceed under the assumption that Andersen and Alltel would not be part of the review process.

Jay then shared that he could understand the concern on the part of NationsBank about a "perceived" conflict of interest.

"I was uncomfortable with us being involved in this from the beginning," he said.

He went on to say that he had raised concerns about Andersen evaluating responses while also submitting its own proposal. Jay had talked this over with Peter Miles, who had told him not to worry. He said a "Chinese Wall" would be constructed separating the review team from the consultants working on the outsourcing project.

Jay added, "I've never seen a Chinese Wall work very effectively."

The "Chinese Wall" argument was a typical consultant response to the potential conflict of interest issue. It was based on an accepted premise that the sales and implementation groups would be somehow partitioned from the group responsible for providing "objective" review and analysis, as if they were working for completely separate and independent companies. This was the same kind of argument that had been made when the large accounting firms such as Andersen first entered the consulting business. Organizational boundaries would ensure that auditing, which needed to remain independent and objective, would not be compromised by offering clients consulting services. Security and Exchange Chairman Arthur Levitt would argue in the year 2000 for the separation of auditing and consulting, but most would scoff at the idea. The arguments for separation would pick up steam again after the Enron bankruptcy at the end of 2001. It seemed that the reason they were so successful in getting consulting contracts was because of ties to successful auditing and accounting services. It was what gave them instant credibility. It was the reason they were hired by clients in the first place. I couldn't help but wonder how successful these firms would be, now that there was talk about Andersen and several others breaking away from auditing and accounting. Wouldn't this jeopardize whatever credibility was still left?

Evaluating other vendor solutions when they themselves were offering a solution was not just an aberration involving the Andersen Consulting team at NationsBank. In an article that appeared in *CMA Magazine* in February 1992, it was noted that Andersen Consulting believed that independence could be maintained by creating organizational divisions within a consulting firm.[9] Andersen Consulting was suggesting that just because it was involved in evaluating and recommending solutions, its credibility was not necessarily compromised by offering a competing alternative. With so much money involved in this kind of business, how could anyone expect a consulting firm to "objectively" police itself? Did corporate clients really think that intradepartmental collaboration in consulting firms could be avoided?

Although a "Chinese Wall" was highly implausible for handling this particular situation, I felt the analogy to this great two-thousand-year-old structure had merit. If Dave Gibbons and Peter Miles had their way, we would be concentrating all our efforts on protecting the old as opposed to building for the future. The entire project had been completed behind a Chinese Wall, concentrated on by back-office operational people, exploring their needs and wants. Customers? Seemed like their wishes came last.

What was even more disturbing was that Vincent Porter from the STG organization was apparently working behind the scenes, not only to help

Andersen secure an outsourcing contract for the engine, but to share it with the operational folks in other banks. It certainly appeared as if he was working with and for Andersen, while trying to keep the rest of us in the dark.

I wondered how much upper management knew. Did the president of the Services Company tell Betsy Fields to back off? Was she behind Porter's actions from the beginning? My mind was running wild with all kinds of scenarios. In the meantime, people from various organizations, including Betsy's own, were tripping over themselves doing everything possible to help Andersen. It didn't really matter that their performance during the last phase of the engine project was less than adequate, with work left incomplete. In addition to Porter, they had the best possible advocate in Don Mangrove, the highest-level NationsBank manager on the project. He always made it sound like Andersen had saved the day, under his direction, of course.

It was sometimes hard trying to figure out if Andersen was working for Mangrove, or if he was working for them. Mangrove was a strong proponent of Model Bank and wanted to tightly couple the engine with Model. Porter, one of those who reported directly to Betsy Fields and who had a client/server bias, was working with Andersen to construct an out-sourcing approach for building a different kind of engine. On top of all this, Andersen had been slated to evaluate all possible alternatives, including their own. Through it all, no one seemed too concerned about potential conflicts of interest. The bigger concern seemed to be pre-venting the "c-word" from ever being said. Whether it was a new pay-ments engine, or a part of Model Bank which was already outsourced to Andersen and Alltel, it was becoming clearer that the recommended Andersen solution would favor outsourcing. It was a good bet that even their Plan B for interim repair was also evolving into a solution to out-source to Anderson and Alltel personnel.

At first, bankers thought the ability to capture transactions electroni-cally would reduce the need for tellers, decreasing overhead expenses. Why stop with the teller? Electronic banking could also lead to *disinter-mediation*, which was to say, the elimination of the brokers or middlemen in trading and investment banking. Now they were talking about out-sourcing the technology. Why not eliminate the back-office processing and all the steps in between as well?

What they had failed to anticipate was the introduction of a whole new set of brokers leveraging technology either as Internet service providers (ISPs) or technology outsourcers. There was a major risk involved. The new technology broker could potentially take control of the customer relationship and relegate the bank to just one of many pop-up, point-and-click options on the menu screen. Didn't NationsBank people read what Hugh McColl had said about this? How could we tell customers in good faith that we were protecting their interests if we let mercenaries handle their financial transactions? What about a customer's right to privacy? What would prevent the mercenaries from selling customer information to others for the right price? They seemed to be brokering everything else. Could that be one of the reasons we get calls from so many telemarketing people who seemed to know so much about our credit ratings and purchase preferences? You couldn't assume anymore it was handled strictly by bankers.

Outsourcing cafeteria services for providing lunch and other meals to corporate employees, rather than having other corporate employees running the kitchen and taking food orders was one thing. In my mind at least, one didn't outsource pieces of the business that represented core competencies. If the handling of financial transactions isn't a core competency of a bank, I'm not sure what is. The banks participating in this venture would be operating in a shell. Somebody else would be running the store. In some cases partnering to solve a problem with an outsourcing solution made sense. In the case of routing and settlement, where each bank had its own complex homegrown systems that could not be easily replaced, a combined outsourcing solution with many banks would be the equivalent of dragging a larger boat anchor. It was playing into the hands of the new breed of competitors who were starting with a clean slate when it came to e-commerce. Why did we have to carry everybody else's baggage with us into that mother of battles the experts were predicting was just around the corner?

The next phase of the project would be collecting information for decision support systems, or as they say in the technology business, data warehousing. Andersen and Alltel could potentially be in a position to broker customer relationship management (CRM) information, not only back to the bank that essentially owned the information, but also to all its competitors. Just think about how the consumer goods industry was changed when retailers started collecting transaction information at the checkout Point of Sale (POS) registers. The major consumer goods companies used to dictate what shelf space they wanted from many of the retailers for their products. With POS, the retailers gained back control in determining what product gets what shelf space. This was because they had better information on customer-buying patterns than the consumer goods companies—information at the source. If Andersen and Alltel owned the routing and settlement system, they would be in a position to capture and replicate the event transactional information, just like the retailer. It begged many questions: Who really owns the customer information? What will they charge us to get it back? Who else will they sell it to? Who owns the customer?

The Bankers' Handbook, regarded as a bible by those in the banking profession, had pointed out almost ten years ago that cash management needed to move "from an emphasis on float management to an emphasis on information management."[10] Control of the information associated with the financial transaction would be critical to the corporate banker. Over time, this information could, in effect, prove more useful than the value of the transaction. The bank could determine customer-buying and retention patterns. It could also sell additional products and services tailored to the specific customer needs and wants. This was not news, but very little had actually been done in the traditional banking industry to exploit the potential benefits. Leave it to the consultants; they'd gladly take care of it for us. They might even be able to capitalize on the new deregulation in banking and the growing interest in cross selling customers to buy various products and services. Customer privacy was surely at risk. Banks would give customers the chance to *opt out* from having their personal account information used for additional marketing. The onus was on the customer to not miss the mailing and to fill it out to opt out. How did you opt out from the consultants using it after capturing it from the transaction?

While worrying about where this was all going, and trying my best not to let my acute case of paranoia start spreading to the others, one of the team members came into my office. He wanted to tell me that IBM had submitted an RFI response, but it was missing the requested financial information. Previoiusly, IBM had made the cut for the tier two list. "You think they're just kicking the tire, but not really interested in the business?" he asked. I placed a call to the IBM relationship manager, Jim Schiller. We had worked together as marketing managers in the Norfolk branch office. Small world. In spite of my best efforts to put it behind me, my past kept creeping up and smacking me like a two-by-four to the head.

When he had first learned that I had taken a position at NationsBank, Schiller had invited me to lunch. That had been almost a year ago. Jim had left the branch with a major promotion only a few months after I had been hired as a new marketing manager. During the short time we had worked together, he had been one of the more cordial members of the management team and had provided me with some very good advice for dealing with a tough customer situation. From my perspective, he struck me as a decent enough guy with good business sense. Jim had been a fast tracker in the IBM Mid-Atlantic area destined for big things. Just before his customer

C&S Sovran was taken over by NationsBank, Jim was promoted to the area office. He was now the NationsBank national account manager for IBM.

Jim was a throwback to the '50s. A good-looking guy, just a little strange in appearance. He was wearing a brown pin-striped suit with a pencil-thin tie. His hair was thick and slicked back without a part. His pompadour-like hairstyle added a few more inches to his six-foot-two-inch height. Trading his retro business attire for a white jump suit with a smattering of sequin trimming, Jim could have passed as an oversized Elvis Presley impersonator. In spite of the appearance, he was the kind of guy who took himself very seriously.

As we waited for our sandwiches, he gave me a collapsed version of his recent history.

"Did you know I became a branch manager? After that, they wanted to promote me to a vice president job in New York. I asked myself, 'Now Jim, what is it you really want to do?' . . . I like working with customers . . . that's what I like best. Besides, I hate New York."

This had been the same speech, verbatim, I had received from Toby Hobson, the Norfolk branch manager. When I first arrived in Norfolk, Hobson had told me how he had left a regional manager job to assume a lower-level position managing the branch. The grapevine version went that Toby was caught doing some bad things and should have been not only demoted, but fired. Friends in high places had saved him—this had become a big part of the problem in the pre-Gerstner IBM. Toby's version was exactly like Jim's. He decided to go back to a branch manager's job because "I like working with customers." Like Jim, Toby had also said he hated New York. I seemed to remember more emphasis on the word "hate" when Hobson relayed it. Even former New Yorkers can be sensitive to those kinds of things. Before lunch had concluded, Jim Schiller extended an invitation.

"One day when you're up in Charlotte, Louise and I will have you over for dinner. By the way, you'll never guess who also lives in Charlotte. Toby Hobson. We see quite a bit of each other. Great guy and one of the best managers that I ever worked for."

The good news was that I didn't expect an actual dinner invitation. Not in this life. It was a standard line I had heard several times from my peer managers while working for IBM in Virginia, usually with a cavalier intonation. After rolling in the jowls, it would casually slip off the lips. These were peculiar sounds to my ear. While it connoted high breeding, it was a very different speech pattern than the typical soft nasal inflection I had become familiar with over the years, connoting Northeastern class and distinction. I had deduced that these offers from the other managers were a reflex reaction of required politeness that were completely devoid of any meaning. It must have been a cultural thing. As Jim rambled on about the good life in Charlotte, I smiled to myself as my thoughts wandered back to my days in Virginia's Tidewater Basin. Some of those memories were good ones.

I could think of only one business-related dinner invitation while I was working for IBM in Norfolk where I actually did get a free meal.

IBM TIME CAPSULE: ESTABLISHING THE MARK

It was late spring 1990. The invitation came from one of my customers, Paul Young, the operations manager at Newport News Shipbuilding. Paul was a big man who had a reputation of being tough on vendors. Even his own people seemed to be afraid of him. Dinner would be followed by his favorite pastime, hunting—hunting for nocturnal animals late into the night. Most customers wanted to play golf. Not Paul.

I left my car at the shipyard and climbed up into his pickup truck. It was nosebleed high. Conversation didn't open up until we had gotten by the traffic jam leaving the shipyard. Paul then said, "Now these boys we're goin' be with tonight are a little rough. If I were you, I wouldn't talk too much." He had a unique sense of humor. He then told me that for supper we were having bear steak and wild boar. Paul wasn't kidding about dinner. After telling his very pleasant wife that the gamy tasting meal I had just eaten "was delicious" (I was still a salesman), we headed off to collect several dogs from their kennels and meet up with "the boys." As the trucks stopped on a hilly dirt road with dusk settling in, Paul pulled on a pair of waders that went up to his waist. He had told me to bring boots, which I did—New England hiking boots that ended around my ankles.

"What are those for?" I asked, pointing to his boots.

"That so when we're running through the swamp, the snakes won't bite."

Like his comment about dinner, he wasn't kidding about the swamp, either. As we let the dogs loose, they raced down the bluff and disappeared in the brush. I could hear a cascade of thunderous splashing. We eventually caught up to the dogs and leashed them. My dog pulled me through the swamp where he wanted to go.

I had somehow passed the ritual of initiation and gained his trust. Paul told me the only way to build trust on the team was for everyone to work together in support of a common goal. His idea of team included the incumbent vendors. Paul wanted to work with a team he could count on, especially when he was in the ditch. Years later, Paul would tell me that I was one of the few salespeople he never caught in a lie. Good thing, or I might never have come out of the swamp. While in the swamp, he shared his thoughts.

"Before I go running from the trench, I want to look to my right and look to my left. Don't wannta see nobody there who's gonna shoot me in the back."

He just continued to stare at me for a while. It created a bit of discomfort, which I tried not to show. The darkness helped. We came from very different backgrounds. None of the other managers within the IBM branch in Norfolk could understand this newly forged relationship, but I believe the answer was very simple. Paul was trying to do the right thing for his company, and I was trying to do the right thing for mine. Paul needed to understand IBM's commitment to support ongoing operations at the shipyard. He also unabashedly expected personal support for him. There had been support problems in the past, and he wanted to make sure they would not be repeated. Spending time with Paul also gave me an opportunity to present the IBM case. I remember telling him, "You can't have it both ways. You can squeeze me on price, but you can't then expect the same level of support and service . . . not without paying for it, one way or another."

Paul replied, "It's OK to talk to me like that in the office, but don't try it in the swamp."

Paul already knew this. If the buying and selling of technology products and services became nothing more than a commodity business, guys like Paul would be the ones who suffered most. He would be left trying to figure out how to make all of those low-price, multivendor products and support groups work together. Not even the consultants could make all his problems go away. It was his butt on the line, not theirs. I couldn't imagine him dealing with an 800-number and customer service reps whose performance was measured on how quickly they got you off the phone. Fortunately for me, Paul was not the kind of person to take consultant recommendations at face value. They, too, were invited to hunt, but according to Paul they always respectfully declined.

In subsequent meetings I convinced Paul Young to put all of the data-center business up all at once for competitive bid. It was a high-risk, all or nothing gamble. The alternative was a slow death with competitors continuing to nibble away, one limb at a time. Before the bid went out, I needed to learn as much as possible about Paul's business and how best to leverage IBM skills and technology. It was critical information for winning the bid. For example, Paul pointed out that vendors could win business when they demonstrated that they could provide products and services with unique benefits. Of course, they would also need to demonstrate that these unique benefits were important for Newport News Shipbuilding. Due to serious 1990 budget constraints, proposals would have to be cost justified, but if we could build a case based on unique, tangible benefits, it did not necessarily have to be the lowest-priced proposal. That information was worth the trip to the swamps. Previously, we on the IBM team believed the only way to win business from this government contractor was to have the lowest bid.

I knew that once Newport News Shipbuilding sent out a competitive bid, a "request for proposal," to numerous vendors, Paul would not talk to me again until his company had made a final decision. There were rules governing the RFP developed by Newport News Shipbuilding. It was part of an effort to maintain integrity in the vendor review process and comply with government regulations for defense contractors.

I went on one other hunt with Paul and "the boys" in early fall 1990. By then, I had purchased my own pair of waders.

* * *

As my thoughts drifted back to the lunch conversation with Jim Schiller, I thought about how those boots could come in handy running through the swamps at NationsBank. That had been the last time I had met with Schiller.

When Schiller answered the phone, he was his usual effusive self: "Hey, Steve, bud, how's life there at NationsBank treating you?"

"Couldn't be better." I still remembered salesman-to-salesman talk.

I asked him why he had not presented the financials as part of the RFI response. He told me he wasn't comfortable providing numbers. At first I assumed this might have been because IBM was one of the losing vendors on the Automated Clearinghouse (ACH) bid won by Tandem. He also knew Harvey Kraft had a relationship with another vendor and was very surprised when the business went to Tandem instead of the other guy. If not the other guy, then surely IBM should have won out over Tandem. He had told this to one of my guys when the Tandem deal was first announced. Maybe he didn't want to get burned twice.

"Everybody knows that Andersen is in control on this and our chances of winning this late in the game are not so great. We're not comfortable presenting any numbers, particularly when we don't have all the information needed to appropriately size a configuration."

This was a problem. If vendors felt Andersen consultants were in control of NationsBank and were reluctant to share information, how could this be good for our business?

As best I could and without revealing any of the current outsourcing controversy, I tried to assure him that IBM had a fair shot at winning the business. "All we want is your best-guess estimates based on the information we provided," I said. IBM had been given the same information as everybody else for developing preliminary configurations—no more, no less.

Schiller agreed to provide numbers but asked again for my word that IBM would receive serious consideration and that the numbers would not be shared with anyone outside the bank. I could certainly understand his concern. He didn't want to put his people through a drill when the end result might only be a proposal used for negotiation purposes with another preferred vendor. It wouldn't have been the first time one vendor's prices were used as a club to reduce prices for the preferred vendor of choice.

"You have my word, Jim. I will do my best to ensure that IBM gets a fair shot and that the numbers are between IBM and NationsBank."

March 3 was one of the most frustrating days I could remember. It had been filled with tension and a growing sense that the die was already cast. A series of unanticipated events combined with forces beyond our control seemed to be dragging us along, as if Paul Young's dogs were pulling us down to the swamp.

SUMMARY OF OBSERVATIONS

- As companies attempt to eliminate costs and operational complexities through outsourcing, technology vendors could potentially take control of the customer relationship, thereby distancing the customer from the company.

- There is risk of a potential conflict of interest when consultants who evaluate vendors also plan to compete for the same business. Management must set ground rules up front and ensure that full intentions of consultants doing evaluation of vendors are properly disclosed with "no surprises."

- Many consultants have prior, well-established relationships with certain vendors, which influence their ability to be objective.

- Consultants often hide behind the banner of client confidentiality to disguise that they are working for competitors in the same industry. These potential conflicts of interest are rarely disclosed, except when negotiating partnerships with other consultants.

- Outsource those activities that are ancillary, but not core to your business. In other words, if you are a financial-service provider, you should not outsource financial transactions with customers to a third party. You might want to outsource maintenance of back-office applications that do not impact the customer.

- Companies need to determine what is core competency and what is not before making an outsourcing decision.

NOTES

1. Dave Matthews, "Ants Marching," *Under the Table and Dreaming,* performed by Dave Matthews Band, Colden Grey, RCA, BMG Music, Produced by Steve Lillywhite (1994).

2. "A Winning Team," *NationsBank Times* (January 1997): 3.

3. Nikhil Deogun, "A Tough Bank Boss Takes on Computers With Real Trepidation," *Wall Street Journal*, 25 July 1996, A1.

4. Ibid., A2.

5. Liz Moyer, "Charting NationsBank's Future Systematically," *American Banker*, 3 October 1996, 14.

6. Jennifer Kingson Bloom and Karen Epper, "Bankers Told to Get On-line or Be Left Behind," *American Banker*, 29 March 1996, 13.

7. Moyer, "Charting NationsBank's Future Systematically,"14.

8. "Open Season on Banks," *Fortune*, 21 August 1995, 45.

9. Lawrence Walkin, "The Conflict of Interest Controversy," *CMA Magazine* (February 1992): 14.

10. William H. Baughn, Thomas I. Storrs, and Charles E. Walker, eds., *The Bankers' Handbook* (Homewood, Ill.: Dow Jones-Irwin, 1988), 973.

CHAPTER THIRTEEN

CHECK,
CHECKMATE

I was not looking forward to the next day, either. I would be meeting with the senior managers from Andersen and Alltel, and Don Mangrove. This was the meeting to decide whether Andersen and Alltel should participate in the vendor review process, given that we had established that they were also developing their own proposal. Now, with Don Mangrove's blessing, they would be part of the management team assembled to decide if they could do both. Calculating probabilities of winning my argument if it came to a vote did not require a high proficiency in quantitative math. They'd give better odds for an opposition candidate winning a fixed election against the controlling party machine. I could imagine the conversation in the upcoming meeting.

"After careful review, we representing Andersen have looked carefully at this and see no conflict of interest in our evaluating our own proposal along with all the others. We do this all the time. Our plan is to leverage our exclusive 'Chinese Wall' methodology, conforming to Andersen's best practices. This will ensure the highest level of objectivity in our review. The methodology has worked successfully in the past, withstanding all kinds of ill-advised challenges. The proven wall that we at Andersen will construct between our two separate teams evaluating proposals and preparing proposals, respectively, will be sufficient to ensure a completely fair and impartial review. How about Alltel?"

"Like Andersen, we feel deeply that there should be not the slightest concern of a potential conflict of interest. In fact, we have worked closely with Andersen in selling comparable solutions throughout the banking industry since 1991, and we can vouch for Andersen always maintaining an objective view, both in vendor analysis and in the subsequent implementation of the best available solution. Coincidentally, the solution often happens to be an Andersen/Alltel joint venture. As for us, we at Alltel always work as if we are employees of NationsBank. We have spent considerable time with NationsBank employees learning how to do their jobs. In fact, today people often mistake us for bankers. Who suggested there is a conflict of interest? Don Mangrove, as the highest-ranking NationsBank manager on this project, would you like to add anything?"

"There is nothing on my list that points to a conflict. When is our next meeting?"

The meeting was scheduled to take place in the middle of the afternoon. Prior to this, I was scheduled to have lunch with my other manager, Harvey Kraft. At times it became difficult remembering all of the reporting connections. Matrix management must have been invented by a football coach with an overly active chalkboard. I was still working for Kraft, technically speaking, even though our contact was minimal. When we did talk, it was because Harvey wanted an update on the engine project.

Kraft simply kept extending the period during which I was on loan to Mangrove so that I could continue to assist on the project. He had told his other people that the engine project was too political and to keep a distance, but it was OK having me immersed in the thick of it.

The current phase saw one extension after another as we continued to go whooshing by the agressive deadlines established by Andersen. As the completion date was moved back once again, there seemed little hope that I would rejoin the strategy group any time soon. I think Kraft liked the idea of having someone on the inside track who reported directly to him. This was a highly visible effort that had been called a priority by top executives at NationsBank. It made for coffee room conversation, if not sport.

"How long do you think before Andersen locks up the next phase to build the engine?"

This would only be our second one-on-one session since Kraft took over in this role as head of the strategy group. From my past experience, I had learned that he tended to be a little slippery and always seemed to have a hidden agenda. At least with Barbara Albrecht, when she was mad at you, you knew it. Kraft was very cagey and impossible for me to read.

Kraft and I met in my office in the Plaza building and decided to have lunch in the NationsBank cafeteria on the first floor. Harvey told me he had just come from a meeting with Al Johnson, president of the NationsBank Services Company, and Don Mangrove, my other boss. They had met to discuss the transaction engine. This was news to me. My discussion with Harvey began with him asking me how things were going with Don.

As I relayed to him the series of events leading up to the vendor request for information (RFI) controversy, he acted as if he was completely unaware of the situation and asked several open-ended questions, listening attentively to my responses. When I had finished sharing the most recent series of events, he told me that he had a chance to talk with Mangrove about my situation right after the meeting with Johnson. He said that Mangrove was very upset with me. Kraft had been aware of everything. He explained that he was now convinced that I needed to learn a few things about NationsBank.

"First," Kraft said, "you need to be a little less direct."

He offered to help me in developing a less aggressive style.

"Your style might work well in the New York, but things are a little different here."

Kraft pointed out that when he disagreed with someone, he would never directly challenge him. Instead, he would say something like, "Let's discuss this a little more."

"They don't have to know when you disagree," he said. "Let them win a few. It's very important to appear agreeable in all meetings."

I couldn't believe Kraft had let down his guard long enough to display his secret to survival, or should I say, his secret to success in the bank. It sounded like a public affirmation from Kraft was more an extension of cultural politeness, not a definitive yes. His style apparently worked, since he was an important member of the circle of good ol' boys who continued to hang on through all the restructuring at NationsBank.

But who was he kidding? Kraft wasn't the type to just hang on and not make waves. He loved casting a fishing line and watching the ensuing frenzy. Kraft was just subtle and never got his hands dirty. He was the kind of guy who would always have somebody else bait his hook and then clean up after he had his fun.

Harvey Kraft went on to indicate that I was getting a reputation of being anti-Andersen. This was certainly not the first time I had heard this.

"You better be careful when dealing with Andersen around here . . . or . . . IBM, too, for that matter. Someone is likely to hand your bowels to you."

Bowels? Was this a threat? It sure sounded like one. It was as direct as I had ever heard Kraft before. I tried to explain that I wasn't anti-Andersen but simply trying to be pro-NationsBank. He appeared unmoved.

"You know I used to work for Andersen. I was the guy who got them in here originally."

My stomach was turning again, and it wasn't simply from eating a tuna fish sandwich. Was there no end to Andersen connections within NationsBank? Come to think of it, Kraft looked, sounded, and acted like an Andersen consultant. The only difference was that he didn't appear to have missed too many meals lately. He was no longer lean and mean, but he still had the consultant jabber in his talk and swagger in his walk. Kraft then went on to share with me the results of his meeting with Johnson and Mangrove. The discussion had taken place earlier that day.

He told me that Johnson had come down very hard. As head of the NationsBank Services Company, Johnson wanted to make sure that the engine maintained a strategic focus and that this could not be compromised. NationsBank had proven to be a political jungle. Why hadn't he just come out and told us before that the engine had to be strategic? It would have saved months of political infighting. Was this, too, part of the sport?

As I thought about it, I realized that Johnson actually had told us before. The president of the Services Company had emphasized the importance of a new strategic transaction engine back in the beginning of the Gemini project, almost a year ago. Johnson had provided a favorable reaction to the PowerPlus recommendations with emphasis on an engine that could support e-commerce. He had talked about the strategic importance of the transaction engine at a recent off-site NationsBank managers meeting, where engine priorities such as real-time processing were presented. Somehow all this was clouded by all the noise surrounding the project.

Model Bank people like Denny Billings and Don Mangrove had constantly tried to change the direction to check processing. They had employed the services of Andersen and Alltel to help. Numerous interviews with check-processing people had served to emphasize the importance of meeting check-processing requirements. It was the consulting process under the direction of Billings and Mangrove that kept trying to shift our focus and muddle things up.

The consultants had turned an important project into a political football game where groups with a vested interest could fight and maneuver to assert their own agenda. Did consultants care if we made the best decision for the bank, or were they just looking for more lucrative contracts from their friends in NationsBank? What did they bring to the table to build consensus, or didn't they care about that, either?

The other major piece of the meeting Kraft shared with me was that budgets were tight and somehow we would have to find a way to do the transaction engine for less than what Andersen and Alltel were initially proposing. He added that during the meeting Al Johnson seemed comfortable with Andersen and Alltel as part of the implementation team. He just thought that another $30 million for two years was too steep. Did this mean that Al Johnson viewed Andersen and Alltel as providing a de facto strategic solution?

"And that $30 million is primarily project management," I interjected. "The hardware, software, and maintenance are still to be determined." I had blurted it out with a little too much emotion, and right after Kraft's lecture. . . . He had just advised me on being more controlled.

"Well, project management is very important. It needs to be done," Kraft retorted.

Blurting anything more to Kraft wasn't going to help.

At first Andersen and Alltel had been emphasizing a mainframe to handle checks—not exactly the most strategic of solutions. Now they were talking client/server. Everyone seemed to be operating from the premise that Andersen and Alltel would be involved in project management or some other capacity, regardless of the solution selected for the engine. Worst of all, Johnson was buying it, too. Not only that, but with an outsourcing proposal, Andersen could now take responsibility for all of it. Wouldn't it be nice to have all this messy business off your hands and let Andersen and Alltel worry about it? It worked for Model Bank.

Before the lunch meeting ended, Harvey Kraft reverted to a coaching role, making suggestions on how I could work more effectively with Don Mangrove. "Remember that he comes from the Model Bank project and has developed a strong relationship with Andersen," he said.

"Given all that's happened, do you think I'm still salvageable?" I was trying to be politically expedient. Admit my perceived mistakes; fall on my sword, so to speak; and live for the next battle.

"Yes, I think you're salvageable," Kraft replied. "I think you can benefit a lot by working for me in strategy. That's why I want to get you back here as soon as we can make that happen."

He also made a recommendation for handling the request for information. Kraft said that I should try a compromising approach. "Separate the technical from the financial sections of the proposal. Let Andersen get involved in the technical evaluation only, and don't let them see the numbers." He told me this could help repair some of the damage I might have caused with Andersen as well as cultivate a better relationship with Mangrove. By letting them in halfway to help on the technical evaluation, Harvey felt it would be the equivalent of extending an olive branch and showing that I could be flexible.

I wasn't pleased with any kind of compromise that had Andersen still involved in RFI reviews, but I decided I would keep this in my back pocket as a fallback strategy if all else failed. I was hearing the same kind of things from various senior managers. "You need to repair your image. You need to fix your anti-Andersen attitude. It could impact your career at NationsBank." Maybe Kraft was right. My "company-first" style was probably a little old-fashioned. Team playing with free agents was a whole new animal. Maybe I was the dinosaur. Highly evolved thinking had progressed from "The customer is always right," to "The consultant can do no wrong."

I also wanted to talk with Kraft about the people working for me because I had heard rumors that he and Mangrove were having conversations about splitting them up. Some of it could have been ego, but I felt pretty strongly that as a senior vice president who had direct management responsibility for people, I should be part of the process. No one else had been close enough to see firsthand who was doing what. This could also have been the problem they were looking to remedy by breaking the team up. I didn't think either Kraft or Mangrove wanted Steve Romaine rubbing off on too many others.

Several members of the team had told me they wanted to stay with me, whether it was on the engine project or in the strategy group. What they lacked in judgment, they were making up for in guts.

The employees working for me had been very dedicated, traveling every week, working remotely from home, racking up unbelievable hours, overcoming lots of political obstacles, and all of it with few pats on the back. Most recently, they had rekindled a take-charge attitude. It was the consultants who were getting pushed around for a change. If I needed to crash into a few walls for them, so be it.

Unfortunately, however, Kraft said he had another meeting and didn't have time to discuss these personnel concerns, now. Personnel never seemed to be a major concern with guys like Kraft, except in public relations campaigns. It would be even less with an outsourcing solution. Kraft had already shown his bias toward outsourcing during my first dealings with him. He'd probably outsource his own family if he thought it would reduce risk or save a buck.

I followed up with an e-mail that addressed my interest in staying in the loop on decisions involving my people. I mentioned that, with the exception of one person who had some very good personal reasons, none of them wanted to stay on the engine project team. If, however, the decision was to keep them on this project, then I wanted to stay there as well.

What was I thinking? I guess it really didn't matter anymore whether I was working for Mangrove or Kraft. At least I felt good about my team. Still trying to play the political animal, I also took the opportunity to thank Kraft for his help and advice and to confirm some of our conversation. Pointing out once again that I was not anti-Andersen as he had suggested, I added the following:

> Sometimes in strong partnership arrangements, vendors assume they
> can take advantage of the situation, particularly if no one calls them on

discretion's [*sic*] and they can command high-dollar contracts via sole-source arrangements. In this last phase, there has clearly been a double standard and no accountability for the vendors. NBK associates have done all the real work and have received no recognition. Andersen has not met the deliverables on a timely basis, and yet we are talking about giving them a de facto follow-on contract and potentially an outsource arrangement where they could lease back the by-product of our propri-etary functional and design specs to us as well as other interested "clients" as a way of offsetting costs (which are inflated because they developed them from a sole-source assumption).

With bad grammar and run on sentences, I must have still been pretty upset about the "bowels" comment. Kraft joined an ever expanding list of NationsBank officers who never responded to the issues I was raising about our management, or, more accurately, our lack of management, concerning the consultants. As was the case with most of the others, Kraft's only feedback was to warn me about my attitude.

My next meeting was at the engine project office in the Loop Road location. We met in a large conference room, next door to the project office. Attendees included Don Mangrove from NationsBank; Peter Miles, Dave Gibbons, and Jay Kittles from Andersen Consulting; the senior manager from Alltel, Larry Rodgers; and me. Jack Tooms, the guy who had made the original gaffe by announcing intentions to develop an outsourcing proposal, was conspicuously absent.

Peter Miles spoke first. He had now officially stepped out of his man-agement role with NationsBank Integration Services to work on the Boatmen's transition. He would stay part-time on the engine project until the implementation was approved. Then he would become project man-ager for Andersen. All of Mangrove's searching for a replacement for me as the comanager from the bank had failed to turn up a candidate. Most employees probably didn't want to work more closely with Andersen and Alltel than they already were. I had heard lots of that type of feed-back since I had started at NationsBank. In addition, the project manager position was a thankless job in which there was so much working against you, failing would be like falling off a log.

I remembered a story I had once heard. A project manager walks into his boss's office and says, "Here is the bottom-line budget needed for the success of the project."

The boss says, "What can you do at half the cost?"

The project manager says, "Fail."

The boss says, "When can you get started?"

The project manager says, "I think I just did."

Miles said, "The last thing we want is to create a *perception* of a potential conflict of interest." All Andersen and Alltel heads were nodding, like bobble head dolls in the rear window of a passing car. A plane took off from the nearby airport, forcing us to sit quietly for a moment or so, letting his comments sink in.

Naturally, it was only a perception—no real conflict of interest here. Never in my wildest dreams did I expect them to back off completely. I guess Andersen and Alltel didn't want anyone looking too closely at their methods; or should I say, the perception of their methods. Copying my e-mail message to Walt Shaw may have helped. It had sent up a flare. I liked thinking there were still senior executives like Shaw trying to do the right thing. Guys who weren't in bed with consultants and other business partners. Guys who were still thinking NationsBank first. They made life annoying for people like Mangrove.

Both Andersen and Alltel were willing to remove themselves from this part of the process, provided it was made clear that the responsibilities for this phase were now solely on my shoulders. They agreed to submit a bid response to the RFI, although it would take them close to two weeks to complete—two weeks after we had already received the rest of the proposals. Peter Miles sat slumped over in a corner. From his lifeless, dark-eyed stare across the table, I had a premonition of grenades being thrown over the transom for the entire two-week period. Nothing, however, could have squelched my jubilance over this major concession.

It was difficult maintaining a stoic presence. I knew no one would expect us to come through in the evaluation phase without the assistance of these vendors. It just wasn't done at NationsBank. I felt that now we had the best shot ever of doing a quality review. Andersen and Alltel would be competing for the business, just like everybody else—or almost. They had the inside track of an incumbent and two extra weeks. They also had high-level contacts helping as much as possible to tip the balance their way.

"Are you still thinking of getting other banks involved in the project to help reduce the costs?" I asked.

"Given the current budget constraints facing NationsBank, we think it makes a lot of sense," Miles replied defiantly.

So much for competitive advantage, that catchall phrase Andersen kept using. They were proposing to take NationsBank confidential information to other banks. I thought this, but I didn't say anything. Instead, I smiled and nodded. A Harvey Kraft success story in the making.

We agreed that in the meantime my NationsBank team would review the other proposals. Once we received the Andersen-Alltel bid, we would review their response based on the same criteria. No question, Andersen and Alltel had a decided advantage. Not only were they being given a longer window of time to respond, after having participated in the process to date, but they had helped to develop the criteria and weighting system for making the vendor decision.

It would be critical to avoid leaks. I knew this would be the only way to ensure a fair process. The meeting ended with Mangrove stating that he wanted to see regular progress reports during this entire phase of the project. Based on everything that had happened, I couldn't help feeling a little suspicious. Would Mangrove leak information to Andersen? I wasn't about to bet against it.

As I drove back to the NationsBank Plaza building, I reflected on the NationsBank team that would be working for me on the RFI review process. I had prepared a list of their skills and accomplishments in the event questions were raised regarding team qualifications. They were an elite group of NationsBank associates, and I could not have handpicked a better bunch.

One member had worked in banking for over twenty years and had a Ph.D. from Michigan State. "Doc," as we called her, had been involved as a manager in many areas of the bank and had participated in several vendor review processes in the past. Another had worked for a high-tech consultant prior to joining the bank. Much of his previous experience had been working as a contractor to high-tech divisions of the federal government such as NASA. He was very intelligent and had extensive experience in system-integration and modernization initiatives. One other member of the team had over twenty-five years banking experience and had managed request for proposal (RFP) initiatives for other banks. The team also included a highly respected former project manager from check processing as well as a former project manager from the Automated Clearinghouse, one of our major electronic-processing applications. There was also Dan Price, an additional project manager who had been with me from the beginning. Dan had surprised me, showing increasing signs of taking more personal initiative, especially now as we entered the latest gauntlet. Combined, we had over eighty years of experience in banking. It was important to keep in mind that no matter how good our combined credentials were, we as a team had one major liability. We were employees, not outside consultants.

Later that day I shared a summary of the meeting regarding Andersen-Alltel involvement with my team. It was difficult keeping my sentiments under control, but I tried my best. Upon hearing the news that Andersen had backed down, they erupted with a round of euphoric howls. Still, they were well aware that we would be working headlong for the duration and that every piece of work that we produced would be scrutinized under a microscope.

They were also smart enough to know that there would probably be plenty of hazards along the way.

We had received bid responses from everyone on the final two-tiered list, with the exception of the Global Finance Software Group of Nations-Bank. I have to admit that the idea of keeping the integration work within the bank had lots of appeal. My mind wasn't completely made up, but I was thinking either Tandem and the ACH solution, or John Turner's crew from Global Finance. This internal group still wanted to bid, and they seemed to have all the right qualifications, except that, like my team, they, too, were employees. Global Finance had requested a one-day extension, as they were late in getting the RFI in the first place. John Turner said he still needed to talk more with the vendors who would function as subcontractors on his bid. They were planning on proposing Tibco for software and Hewlett Packard 9000s for the hardware.

I apprised Mangrove of the situation. He said he didn't have a problem with Turner's organization responding to the RFI. "But I seriously doubt they could handle it," he confided. Mangrove was another of those guys who didn't view Global Finance as very credible. It occurred to me that Mangrove was still operating from the assumption that besides Global Finance and Andersen-Alltel, the only others that would be responding to the bid were Hogan and Tandem. I did nothing to indicate otherwise and was frankly glad nothing more was asked or said.

I went back to join my team. We worked through the evening. We took turns reading each proposal and then passing them around to other team members. I had instructed the team to try and keep individual opinions and comments to themselves until we met formally as a group. We had to avoid leaks on how we as a group were leaning. Not even members of the group would know. No one could say, "The consensus so far seems to be. . . ." My thought was, the longer we could extend the evaluation without showing our cards, the better our shot at conducting a fair and balanced review. There was no question we were trying to get away with something—preventing the consultants from railroading our process. This had become a great motivator.

It was late when we finally broke off. I was still feeling restless and decided to go for a drink. One of my team members decided to join me. His name was Sam Ritter. Like Will Logan, Sam was a Vietnam veteran with sad, Irish eyes. He didn't drink, but liked hanging out in bars as opposed to watching mindless TV shows from his hotel room. Sam was the one

NationsBank employee who actually wanted to stay on with the engine after this phase of the project was over. It was by default since the only other option for him was Harvey Kraft's strategy group. Everybody knew he and Harvey didn't get along. There had been some kind of problem in the past. I once asked him about it. "I don't like the way he does business," was all Sam would say. Sam hadn't had as much exposure to Mangrove.

We went to an Irish pub in Buckhead, one of the hot spots in Atlanta. This pub wasn't the kind of place you would find in New York City or Boston. It was more like Disney does Ireland. The walls were supposed to look rustic with drab, dark brown coloring and what appeared to be occasional wood knots and other imperfections. Up close it became obvious the walls were covered in plastic. On one wall there was a map of Ireland with several coats of arms boasting familiar names from ye'old country clans. There were placards with tired, clichéd Irish wit. There was no dust on the top of the picture frames and no smudge marks on the glass enclosures surrounding the pictures. The face of the bar was completely devoid of any scratches or other imperfections that were real or made to look real.

"Whad'ull ya have dare?" the waiter asked. He was a perfect fit for the establishment. His fake brogue sounded more like a cross between a drawl and Pennsylvania Dutch.

"Give me a Guinness and a club soda."

It took several minutes for the drinks to arrive. My Guinness was half foam. I probably should have ordered a beer that took less skill pouring from the tap. It was a friendly crowd. A combination of college kids and yuppies. We struck up a conversation with a couple from the Northeast who had moved to Atlanta a few years ago. Like many transplanted Atlanta residents I had met, they were trying a little too hard to convince us how great it was living here. As a Mets fan, I was never too comfortable. I felt I always had to be on my guard. Braves fans cherished New York scalps most of all. No kidding. They took extra pleasure slicing up the air with those tacky big foam tomahawk chops when playing the Mets. Not much Southern hospitality displayed for Metskies. Not much of a burning passion for political correctness, either.

"Oh, you guys work for NationsBank. That's where we do our banking."

Not such a surprise. There were fewer and fewer choices. The couple eventually moved on. Sam Ritter turned to me and said, "You don't look too happy. I think you should be feeling pretty good about what we've accomplished."

"You're right, but I'm still worried. Andersen gave up too easily. There's something going on that we don't know about. I keep wondering where they'll strike next."

"So far, we've been able to head it off . . . keeping them honest. . . . I think we're in good shape. We just need to keep the pressure on . . . and our eyes open."

Yeah, easy for him to say. It occurred to me that if I was pushed out, my buddy here sipping the club soda and egging me on might have thought it would improve his chances of becoming the new project manager. Never trust a man who doesn't drink, especially when you were pounding a few yourself. Sam had expressed an interest in succeeding me on several occasions: "That is, given . . . you want out of the job anyway . . . right?"

There I go again. I had already recommended him as my replacement, and he knew it. At the time Sam seemed surprised. He had thanked me, even though nothing came from it. In spite of Mangrove's unsuccessful efforts to find a new project manager, he was cool to my suggestion and never let me present the full case for promoting from within the ranks. Perhaps it was because of where the recommendation was coming from. If Sam Ritter were smart, he would be separating himself from me, trying an end run or something. He had ambition, but he didn't strike me as a backstabber. If you couldn't trust your own team, whom could you trust?

NationsBank was making me crazy. Too much thinking for one day. It was time to clear the tab, go home, and get some sleep. If only I could.

The next day we received the RFI response from Global Finance. We were all very amazed. They had essentially taken the white paper that I had previously written along with the graphics produced by my team and had changed a few words and added some Tibco and Hewlett Packard product information to an appendix in the back of the proposal. Essentially their RFI response was the work we had produced as part of the engine team. Turner of Global Finance asked me to hold this within our group. He still did not have formal permission from his chain of command to bid.

It was Wednesday, March 6, 1997, and we were two days into the review process. I received a call from Tony Alvarez, one of the sales reps from Tandem. I was reluctant to talk with him in the middle of the review, but he insisted.

Tony said, "I need some guidance, and it is an urgent matter."

I assumed he was going to try to pump me for some additional information that could help give Tandem a leg up on winning the engine business. Tandem had submitted its engine RFI response on time, partnering with another vendor called Applied Communications Inc. (ACI), the same partner Tandem most often used for running ATM systems and a big reason why together they had cornered most of the ATM market.

The conversation started with Tony telling me that he was confused.

He explained that a few weeks ago Vincent Porter, the STG manager still serving on the engine project steering committee, had been to see him. During the conversation, Porter suggested that Tandem call Ken Pollack, the Andersen partner for the Direct Bank initiative, to talk about the engine project. Porter was working overtime to help his friend at Andersen. Tony admitted that they had tried to call Pollack, leaving several messages but had not heard back until the day before.

According to Tony, Ken Pollack had called yesterday and had said that it was the opinion of Andersen that Tandem was the only viable vendor to partner with for the engine business. Tony said that this Andersen partner told him that he didn't believe any of the other vendors responding to the bid were viable options. Tandem combined with Andersen could be an unbeatable partnership. He invited Tandem to a meeting with Andersen to discuss this in more detail. Tony said that he was uncomfortable on the best way to proceed.

"They are probably saying the same thing to all the others. We really need your guidance on what to do."

I told him that my initial reaction was that Tandem had already submitted a bid with ACI. Changing the bid after the deadline had passed would probably not be acceptable, but I explained that it was only my opinion. I had to bite my tongue from expressing any further opinions about Andersen's latest antics.

Andersen was now attempting to hedge bets with even more options. After failing to provide direction that could have led us to the best possible solution, they were now attempting to load the dice. Whatever the ultimate solution became, Andersen seemed determined to be a part of it—even if it meant a complete about-face from their previous position; even if it meant cutting backstreet deals with all the other players. There was too much money to be made.

My next move was to meet with Mangrove. He was, after all, the highest-ranking NationsBank manager on the engine project. On the elevator ride to the fifty-fourth floor, I prerehearsed my comments. I needed to temper my feelings.

After I shared with him the conversation with Tandem, he said, "You did the right thing coming to me first." Yeah, no doubt.

With me in the room, Mangrove put his phone on speaker and called Gibbons, the Andersen partner who had been pushing a mainframe for the engine project. Gibbons acted surprised and said he was unaware of any calls to vendors. He apologized for any confusion it might have caused and said it was probably Pollack, the other Andersen partner, who had instigated the call to Tandem.

"I'll talk to him," Gibbons promised. He reassured Mangrove that this would be addressed.

"Fine, thanks Dave," Mangrove responded, as if the issue had been put to bed.

After Mangrove hung up the phone, he suggested that I call Hogan to tell them that they should also expect a call from Andersen.

"I'm not sure that's a good idea," I said. "What if they never get a call?"

We agreed to scrap this approach. It was a good thing, or I would have to have come clean that there were other vendors to call. Mangrove told me that he would get in touch with Tandem to discuss the situation. He thanked me again for bringing it to his attention.

Later that day I shared the latest series of events with Sam Ritter. He had been around the block a few times and usually had good suggestions. In the last few weeks he had become more comfortable sharing them. He recommended that I place a call to NationsBank Contracts and Standards Department. Contracts and Standards was the department at NationsBank responsible for overseeing vendor negotiations and contracts. They set the standards for vendor approval; provided help with proposal request and responses; and helped negotiate contracts, vendor discounts, and additional terms and conditions for contracts. The problem at NationsBank was that there were several executives who did their own thing without ever involving this department. Contracts and Standards could advise us on the best way of handling Andersen in this situation. I set up a conference call and asked Sam Ritter to join me.

"If they don't get the business, Tandem has good grounds for calling foul play," we were told. They could argue that because they didn't play ball with Andersen, who obviously had significant influence and came to them—thanks to Vincent Porter—as if they were acting in behalf of NationsBank, they were not given a fair shot at the business. Contracts and Standards said that this could become a bid protest. They also told us that this was the third contract-related issue in the last few months involving Andersen.

"Andersen Consulting has a lot of pull with senior management around here. Unfortunately, there isn't a lot we can do."

The next day Tony the Tandem rep contacted me again. He said that Don Mangrove had followed up and now he was even more confused. Mangrove had informed him that Andersen had contacted Tandem because he had personally asked them to explore this option. If this were true, why hadn't he mentioned this to me when I first brought it to his attention? Tony also mentioned that he had received another call from Ken Pollack. He told Tony that their conversation concerning Andersen and Tandem was supposed to have been confidential. "Pollack was angry and said I had no business sharing this with NationsBank. He told me that our conversation was supposed to be off the record. Maybe for him, but it wasn't for me. I never agreed to that," Tony said.

According to Tony, he informed the Andersen partners that he felt it would be inappropriate for the team covering NationsBank and bidding with ACI to work with Andersen on a competitive alternative for the same business. He said he was taking himself out of the loop and referred Pollack to senior executive management at Tandem, "if you want to discuss this any further."

After some thought, I decided to call Vincent Porter, the manager from the Strategic Technology Group. It was Porter who had originally encouraged Tony to call Andersen. He was also the one who, according to Kittles, had started the conversations with Andersen about outsourcing the engine and taking it to other banks without cluing any of the rest of us in.

The STG people working for Porter had been very supportive during my tenure at the bank, helping to steer things related to Transaction Services in a more strategic direction. The STG was not popular. I may have been one of the few employees who seriously appreciated their efforts. In addition, I was still hoping to leverage some assistance from Betsy Fields, the director of the STG organization. Her access to senior executives could be useful if we needed to launch a counteroffensive. She had not completely shut the door on going back to Al Johnson. It appeared to me that Porter was operating from a different agenda than the other folks in the STG, one that was more in the interest of Andersen. I knew his people weren't on board with him. I hoped Betsy wasn't, either.

There was certainly a large number of Andersen advocates coming from different organizations within the bank. These organizations had a history of being at odds with each other and appeared on the surface at least to have conflicting objectives regarding the direction we should be taking on the transaction engine. It seemed Andersen was prepared to provide as many different solutions as there were different groups within the bank. It didn't matter that each group had different and often conflicting sets of objectives. Andersen was willing to help each of them. In the end, the odds were good Andersen would get the follow-on contract, regardless of which internal group won.

This strengthened my belief that many consultants tell prospective clients whatever they think the particular client wants to hear. The bigger firms like Andersen could spread out across a company like NationsBank, covering lots of different groups with conflicting agendas. They had no incentive to bring these groups to a common resolution. Conflict brought more consulting revenue.

Porter was in a meeting when I called. I told the administrative assistant that it was important and asked that he be pulled from the meeting. When Vincent Porter finally came to the phone, he sounded surprised to find me on the line. Who the hell did this guy Romaine think he was pulling him out of a meeting?

I told him about the conversation with Tandem. I also told him that I was aware that he had initiated conversations with Andersen to outsource the transaction engine and shop it around. This I told him from my perspective was inappropriate, given that he had obviously done this without first discussing his plan with the steering committee or the engine project team.

"I don't know what you are talking about."

"Look . . . this is between you and me."

"Oh, OK . . . I think I understand."

Porter immediately shifted gears, telling me that he had been to an IBM briefing in Toronto with the IBM team supporting NationsBank.

"IBM told me that they had responded to the RFI. Have you seen it? Do you know how much it would cost?"

I told Porter that I had not had a chance to review all the vendor bids. Thanking him for the support of the STG, the conversation ended on what seemed to be a positive note. I hoped Porter would back off, knowing that someone from the bank was aware of his collaboration with Andersen. My assumption was that the matter was closed.

His comments about IBM were disturbing. I feared that we were about to lose our wild card, the proposals from the tier two vendors. I knew Porter rarely talked with Mangrove, but they both talked with Andersen. In addition to all of its other functions, Andersen Consulting sometimes served as a communications mechanism between different organizations within NationsBank who didn't always talk among themselves. Surely Porter would tell his buddies from Andersen that the bid didn't just go to Tandem and Hogan. This would eliminate the element of surprise I had been counting on. Porter's main contact at Andersen was Ken Pollack. It was Pollack who had called Tandem after Porter had greased the skids.

Would the team of Porter and Pollack also call IBM to try and cut a deal? Would they try and find out who else received the RFI and attempt to cut deals with all of them? At the very least, Porter, Mangrove, and potentially others from NationsBank were doing nothing to discourage Andersen's playing outside the rules.

Assuming Pollack would find out about IBM and the others getting a chance to bid, there was another question that started bouncing around and giving me a splitting headache. Would Pollack share this information with Gibbons? Gibbons did seem genuinely surprised when Mangrove called him about the Tandem situation, either that or he was one very talented actor.

Perhaps there was no sharing at all. My guess was that these two Andersen partners were competing against each other as separate profit centers trying to win the business at hand. At this point, Andersen was still not a publicly held company worried about return to stockholders. It was a partnership, not a public corporation. Apparently there were no team-based incentives. Every partner was probably trying his best to increase personal commission, or as they say in the business, "wallet-share," but not much more than that.

Pollack might not say anything. If I was right, then in the Andersen consulting model, knowledge was a competitive advantage since it increased the chances of personal gain. It was not to be shared with other consultants at the risk of losing one's edge. Why help another competitor, even if the other competitor worked for Andersen? Better to keep it to yourself and work to use this information for your own benefit. It was that zero-sum thing again.

For the time being, at least Jay Kittles and I were safe. Mangrove didn't seem to have learned about us sending the bid out to a larger list of vendors.

Like me, Jay had taken the position that, unless asked, the less said about the RFI, the better. We had been given primary responsibility to comanage the process. While Jay and I never talked about it, I had the feeling the RFI was a little gift Kittles wanted to leave for his management before moving on. No love lost there.

On the NationsBank side, Mangrove would have another excuse to ream me. I knew this would eventually happen once things played out. Helping Andersen seemed to be his passion, as if it were career enhancing. I still hoped Mangrove would find out later rather than sooner. The closer to when we were ready to make final recommendations, the better. We needed less time for Andersen and the friends of Andersen to react. Surely they would put additional countermeasures in place.

I had a call from a woman who had worked for Andersen but was now a NationsBank employee working in another area. At one point Mangrove had asked her if she would consider taking over for me. He was now vigilant in his pursuit of a new project manager. Anybody else, please. I had heard she turned it down. Smart lady. Even with all of her Andersen contacts to fall back on, it was still the job from hell.

"I was talking with Peter Miles about some of the problems getting NationsBank people to sign up for the engine project," she said. "We both agreed that part of the problem might be Dave Gibbons. Did you know he has no previous banking experience?"

"Oh?" This was another sales technique I had learned to keep the faucet going. She continued, spilling the following: "Peter and I both think Ken Pollack would be a much better fit."

Having a partner in charge who knew nothing about our business was just another example of why management needs to keep a tight leash on consultants. Nevertheless, I wasn't sure what the lack of Gibbons's banking experience had to do with recruitment of NationsBank employees. Did they really think if we got rid of Gibbons and substituted some other Andersen partner they'd be banging down the door to come on board?

Man, this Peter Miles was something. He was now stabbing the partner still in charge of the engine project in the back. As if he himself had nothing to do with the problems. Miles must have been apprised of Pollack's chances of winning and decided to cast his lot with him. But what about all that maneuvering to steer us to a check-processing solution? Wasn't Pollack a client/server guy and Miles a mainframe bigot? Would these consultants flip that easily when there was a change in the winds? I guess anything goes when it comes to winning the next contract and getting ahead.

A devious thought popped up. Many may have felt that the culture of greed died with the '80s. No so. In the consulting world at least, I kept running into more Gordon Gecko types than Ghandis. Perhaps it was less ostentatious, and a little more covert form of greed. Surely the 1990s version of greed was still creating dissension between partners in the same consulting firm. By now there was a lot of talk about the consulting partners at Andersen trying to break away from the auditors.[1] It was getting very nasty. Assuming Andersen won the business, whether the Nations-Bank decision went client/server or mainframe would determine which Andersen partner got paid. If it went client/server, wouldn't that also mean Alltel would lose out as well?

Larry Rodgers, the manager from Alltel, was still involved in the engine project. He had always struck me as being a stand-up guy, playing faithful partner with Andersen while remaining on the level with us. I decided to call him.

"Hey Larry, did you know Andersen contacted Tandem to see if they wanted to partner on the engine?"

There was dead silence for a few moments. He apparently didn't know. Andersen and Alltel were supposed to be partnering on this. I could almost hear him thinking, "What were they doing with Tandem? How come this was never mentioned to me? Those bastards are cutting me out." Larry said he was not aware of Andersen contacting anyone else.

"If that is what happened . . . that would really surprise me. It would appear almost . . . somewhat . . . unethical. Let me check in to it. . . . I'll keep your name out if it. I'll let you know what I find out."

He sounded furious. No way any of this would inflict a knockout blow, but it might create enough of a distraction to slow down the powerful Andersen machine. Perhaps my favorite Andersen partners would now be forced to spend time fending off internal disputes and covering their own butts. There would probably be some finger pointing between Pollack and Gibbons. There might even be some fallout for Miles, the golden boy with jet black hair. They'd definitely have some explaining to do with Alltel. As a proven outsource provider for financial institutions, Alltel was an important revenue source for Andersen, the kind of business partner they couldn't afford to lose. It really didn't matter if he kept my name out of it or not. I knew I was already a pariah for not rolling over. That didn't bother me, but I was getting concerned about what this experience was doing to my attitude. It's not the way I wanted to do business. It wasn't the way I was trained.

In the meantime, the technology team, absent the Andersen contingent, was hard at work evaluating the respondent bids. Breaking from the status quo was not something that was encouraged in this kind of environment. There were jokes about getting someone to start our cars for us and the need to watch for bricks falling off of buildings. It was a macabre way of dealing with the stress, but it helped break the tension we were all feeling.

Throwing myself into the process, I hoped to add at least something from my previous experience. Vendor analysis had been a major focus in my former life with Informed Technology Decisions. We were working long hours, starting around 7:00 in the morning and working through 10:00 at night, and sometimes even later. We drank lots of coffee. About midway through the review process, I went for a coffee run with one of the guys assigned to work for me on the project. On our way to the elevator, we walked by a slew of people busy behind their desks. It seemed as if we were completely oblivious to this army of desk jockeys. While waiting for the elevator, he turned to me, commenting in a discreet, low whisper, "You know, we really have no idea whether those people work for NationsBank, or work for somebody else. They could be consultants or vendors, for all we know."

"Imagine how our customers would like knowing that."

One night in the middle of the review, we decided to break early. This time a bunch of us went out for drinks. We went to one of those trendy Atlanta bars close to my apartment, called the Martini Club. I'm sure we stood out from the beautiful people who came to be seen. A piano banged out a crisp medley of early classical jazz in a simple and honest delivery. I didn't see a piano. A few cocktails, and I wouldn't be seeing anything. At least I still had long-range goals. It must have been piped-in music, but it sounded really good. I was hearing too much bar noise coming in all directions from a maze of crowded interconnected rooms to know for sure. There were two very attractive women lounging around on deep, low-hanging couches that must have been designed to highlight the extended contours of their calves. The chiseled legs rode high off of narrow, angular heels that were longer than the legs of the furniture. They were wearing expensive, tight dresses with no shoulders and were puffing away on long, lean cigars with plastic tips. They occasionally spoke to each other, but their demeanor never varied, and they appeared completely devoid of any emotion. The entire place gave me the feeling that I was on the set of a 1920s Hollywood production, except it was now the fairer sex smoking most of the cigars.

After ordering a round of cocktails, Sam Ritter raised his club soda and proposed a toast. "Here's to our success," he said. "So tell me, are we good, or just lucky?" Sam had become a little too cocky of late. It was amazing though that we had been successful in getting as far as we had in influencing the engine project and keeping things on track. There was still an uneasy feeling that at any minute the floorboards could crumble. Unfortunately we had edged too far out of the safe zone to contemplate retreat. Some of us had edged out farther than others.

"It might be a little premature for celebrating," one of the other guys said, knocking the rest of us back, like a shot of aged whiskey.

"I don't know, I'm starting to fell pretty lucky." Sam took one more swig of his fizzling nonalcoholic drink and smiled as if he had already read the ending.

Who could question the value of luck? It certainly had been there for me and my team as pieces of information had fallen into our laps at the most opportune times. It had been there for me before, at IBM in 1990.

IBM TIME CAPSULE: COMPETITIVE POSITIONING

It was the middle of autumn, but for me that year, working in the Hampton Roads area of Virginia, it still seemed like the long, hot summer had never ended. Saddam Hussein's Iraqi troops had invaded Kuwait in August 1990. American military forces were concentrated in the Persian Gulf as part of the early stages of Operation Desert Shield. We had no idea at the time it would lead to Desert Storm, but we did know that the situation was very serious. The U.S. forces were in the Gulf to protect against further aggression from Hussein and to impose economic sanctions on his country as an attempt to force him to release his stranglehold on Kuwait and order his troops back to Iraq. Sanctions versus military action was the raging debate. Several months had past. Kuwait remained occupied. The tension was still mounting in what was looking like a test of wills between Iraq and the United States.

It was a few weeks before Newport News Shipbuilding planned to send out a major competitive request for proposal to replace most of the equipment in their data center, which was one of the largest data centers in the Mid-Atlantic area. There were strict government guidelines for RFPs and the people managing it at Newport News went by the book. My very own management expected us to lose our shirt on the bid. Even with price discounts, IBM was always more expensive.

This particular day started with early morning meetings at Newport News. I had meetings with several managers. As a defense contractor, Newport News built aircraft carriers and submarines. Employees at the shipyard took great pride in their relationship with the United States government and the importance of their role as a major supplier to the U.S. Navy. Security at the shipyard, which had always been tight, seemed even tighter in fall 1990. The Persian Gulf crisis was on everyone's minds. The managers I met with at the shipyard were very concerned about the situation. Getting them focused on IBM-related business was difficult at best.

My first meeting had just finished. I was walking through one of the great hallways that separated different wings for the main facility at the shipyard. There were large framed photographs symmetrically lined across the wall of just about every U.S. president of the twentieth century looking on as their wives or some other important female dignitary was christening a ship built by Newport News. A few months before on a sun-drenched beautiful day I had attended the christening of the aircraft carrier, the U.S.S. *George Washington*. President George Herbert Walker Bush, a World War II Navy fighter pilot, and his wife, Barbara, participated in the ceremonies. Secretary of Defense Dick Cheney and all the top Navy brass looked on. A fly-by of F-14s at the end of the national anthem put a lump the size of a grapefruit in my throat. It would have made even the most cynical critic of the military-industrial complex feel a tinge of patriotism.

Kevin Jones, a data center manager who worked for Paul Young the operations manager who had previously taken me hunting, stopped me as I passed around the corner at the end of the hall. "Hey Romaine," he said. "You'll never guess who Paul is meeting with right now . . . it's good news, bad news." My first thought was of my branch manager, Toby Hobson. After everything I had learned about Hobson, what could have been worse than that?

"The bad news is that he's meeting with the salesman from one of your competitors, Amdahl." Amdahl in those days was taking lots of IBM business away. It was very bad news.

Kevin continued, "The good news is that I overheard some of the conversation as I was walking by. The salesman was telling Paul that he thought President Bush was making a big mistake in the Persian Gulf." Kevin howled with laughter. "Bush should leave it alone. That's what he told Paul." Grabbing his gut, Kevin continued to laugh. "Can you imagine 'leave it alone'? Next thing you know, they'll be marching through the oil fields of Saudi Arabia. I thought Paul was going to have a stroke."

I had really lucked out. Poor guy, that Amdahl salesman. I didn't think he would be getting an invitation to go hunting with Paul Young with talk like that. Amdahl, which was half-owned by Fujitsu Ltd., had become a worldwide leader in selling IBM mainframe-compatible products. They were just one of IBM's competitors that were swarming all over Newport News Shipbuilding that year, waiting to feed off discarded scraps from a weakened and failing IBM. To expand their presence in the United States and other markets, Amdahl was investing in new business partnerships, both outsourcing and consulting. They were also hiring a lot of ex-IBMers to provide increased customer coverage and engineering support. Those wanting to take a package and leave IBM didn't have to settle for consulting. They could become an IBM clone maker where they didn't have to learn a completely new drill.

Some of the top consultants in technology were giving lots of attention to Amdahl and writing positive reviews. Amdahl was viewed by many as a cost-effective substitute for the IBM mainframe. Gartner Group was predicting that along with Hitachi, they would begin taking larger chunks of market share of the IBM plug-compatible business. Adding to IBM's dismay at the time, according to a widely publicized independent survey conducted by DataPro Research Corporation, Amdahl had surpassed IBM as the number one mainframe vendor in providing customer support. Amdahl was using published consultant information to establish credibility and take more customers away from IBM.

The DataPro survey also had a devastating effect within IBM. It became a recurring example used by IBM senior management during internal meetings to flog the troops and help demonstrate how marketing reps and system engineers had taken their eyes off the ball. Never mind that the cutbacks had already started, and we who were left in the field were spread very thin. Various groups within IBM were now using consultants to provide advice on how to turn things around. I could not recall any efforts to counteract the issues raised by the DataPro survey, except the calls for more "Quality Training"—another 1990s opportunity for consultants. Internal political battles raged as finger pointing between different IBM groups escalated and a plethora of overhead presentations on the subject were created. While IBM fiddled away with internal presentations, customers were looking elsewhere for help. They looked to consultants and other vendors. Alternative vendors increased their foothold with traditional "Big Blue Only" customers, accelerating the slippage in IBM's leadership and market share.

Not surprisingly, the word had gotten out to other vendors such as Amdahl that managers at Newport News were not very pleased with IBM support, which had diminished of late, after all those years of business. Amdahl was just one of the many new vendors invited to the shipyard to sell their wares. Management at the shipyard had us from IBM on our toes and looking over our shoulders. I was convinced some of our major customer's were following Gartner Group's advice on how to manage the IBM relationship. There continued to be talk about mixing the pot by creating a "multi-vendor shop," and the need for IBM to increase support while reducing both the total number of IBM products on the floor and the cost of what was left.

Kevin seemed to be waiting for me to reply after relating the "good news, bad news." Part of the IBM culture was to never disparage the competition. In my view, given the right opening, it wasn't disparaging to present the facts.

"Kevin, did you know that Gene Amdahl was once one of IBM's top computer designers? It's true. When his plans to build a new computer were turned down by the IBM Management Committee, he quit IBM, started his own company, and went to the Germans and the Japanese for funding. I know there were a lot of upset people around after you did the design work for the Seawolf and then lost the construction contract to Electric Boat. I couldn't imagine Newport News Shipbuilding taking its design work to a competitive government." I had always been a student of history. A few days later I saw Kevin again at the yard. "You don't have to worry about those guys anymore. As Paul would say, 'dat dag ain't gonna hunt.'"

It wasn't unusual for Paul to draw comparisons between people and "dags." I don't think it was intended as a bad thing coming from Paul. Dogs were a big part of his life. Almost family. No hunt in a dag, now that was a bad thing.

Every once in a while, with a little luck, you caught a break.

✳ ✳ ✳

The key was to capitalize on your good luck, particularly when the competition gave you an opening. It also helped having a team of talented, hard-working people you could trust. Luck or no luck, NationsBank presented a different kind of problem in attempting to conduct "transaction engine" business in 1997. The vendor review process had been compromised by a consultant with special privileges within the bank.

People who worked for the bank were well aware of the problems with Andersen Consulting. As I had learned, these extended beyond the engine project. Unfortunately, most had decided to "leave it alone," and Andersen had continued to capitalize on the political infighting and apparent indifference, expanding its influence at the expense of NationsBank associates. Andersen's success had been based on a lot more than good luck. I wanted to believe we could somehow prevail with a recommended solution based on best product fit versus consultant manipulation. The reality was rather bleak. Andersen had a lot more pieces on the board, and in spite of a few minor setbacks, it was still best positioned to win.

One morning I was cornered by another of the NationsBank people working for me on the project who said, "I can understand your level of frustration with everything going on around here." This particular person went on to explain that a personal friend had left the bank because "he couldn't stand the politics at NationsBank." He had left shortly after the first phase of the Model Bank project, the large effort to standardize branch offices, spearheaded by Andersen and Alltel. "Somebody from the bank had gotten property on a golf course for helping to make the deal with Andersen and Alltel possible. That was why he left." At the time, I thought this was ridiculous hearsay and not to be taken seriously. I decided to dismiss it, although I never could quite forget what I had heard.

During the evaluation process, Don Mangrove called and asked me to schedule time for him to meet with the NationsBank technology team and me. He said he wanted to apologize for not explaining earlier about the outsourcing proposal. In addition, he said he wanted the team to present the process they were planning to use for evaluating the different vendors.

The meeting began with his apology. Mangrove explained that he had asked Andersen and Alltel to look into the possibility of outsourcing and that they were doing this under his direction. When I had first met Mangrove, he told me he was very up-front. On a separate occasion, he had told me he didn't think Andersen would propose an outsourcing solution.

When I talked with him about Andersen trying to cut a deal with Tandem after their bid was already submitted, Mangrove didn't seem to know anything about it. He had called Gibbons with me in the room to run it down. He later claimed that he had prompted Andersen to contact Tandem. What was I to believe? Oh, well. This guy probably would have laid down in front of an approaching steamroller for his buddies at Andersen and Alltel. I guess this was not so surprising. Without them, he was just another regular employee waiting for the ax to fall. With them, he figured he'd always be on the dull side of the blade, remaining alive to run another status meeting or two.

After he had finished his remarks covering Andersen, different members of the team took turns presenting the vendor evaluation approach and the status of the process. I was particularly impressed with Dan Price, not only what he said, but how he said it. It was the U.S. Marine again. The focus was intentionally on process and not on the results of our evaluation so far. Mangrove said that it looked good. Of course, he was a process guy. We were lucky he didn't ask about specifics.

Mangrove and I left the meeting, walking side by side down the hall.

"Thought your team did pretty well. You got some pretty sharp people there."

He told me again that he wanted to meet on a regular basis to review the status of the evaluation. He also said that it was his hope that the final by-product of the evaluation would have some explanation on how we had arrived at our conclusions.

"That's the plan," I said.

Our intent was to produce a thorough analysis of all of the submitted alternatives, highlighting the pros and cons associated with each. It would probably provide more information than Mangrove or other members of the steering committee were used to getting from their consultants before making decisions. That's because consultant reports, at least at NationsBank, were hardly ever questioned. Our report would be carefully scrutinized for holes—especially if it didn't go the way Mangrove and company wanted it to go. We as a team had hoped to complete an in-depth piece of work. We planned on giving it our best shot.

Mangrove then asked me to tell the team members he wanted to meet with each one of them on an individual basis, "to get better acquainted." While I agreed to do so, I was feeling uncomfortable. Was he about to embark on some kind of witch-hunt? My branch manager from IBM in Norfolk had turned one-on-one meetings with my direct reports into a kind of fishing expedition.

"So, tell me, what do you think of your manager, Steve? . . . you think he's all right? No one else seemed to feel that way. Do you think he plays favorites?"

Similar to "Did you beat your wife today?" An innocuous reply could easily be turned into the accusatory, if they were looking to get something. Good thing I had a team of people I trusted. It didn't work when Hobson had tried it. I didn't think it would work now.

Mangrove ended the conversation saying that the meeting with those who reported directly to me would have to wait until he was back from his vacation. In the meantime, how about a few rounds of club sodas to keep 'em happy? I was a little surprised that Mangrove would be taking a vacation at this time, given that we were in a critical stage of the project. He must have felt pretty confident that his buddies from Andersen and Alltel could take care of things while he was gone. They were certainly acting like they had the deal all sewn up. I wanted to believe we had a shot to pull it out and choose a vendor for the right reasons, but there had been curves thrown all over the place.

Before leaving for the evening, I pulled Dan Price aside.

"Danny, I've just got one thing to say. 'Welcome back to the fight.'"

"Thanks, sir."

He said "Sir,"knowing he'd get a rise out of me.

As I left the NationsBank Plaza building, I was still going over in my head the events of the day and trying to figure out what might happen next. Things seemed to be falling into place a little too easily. Mangrove and his Andersen buddies seemed unusually relaxed, given all that had transpired and all that still needed to be done. The more I thought about it, the less relaxed I became.

> Checkmate is a unique characteristic. In other board games *sacrifice* is justified only if material can be regained later; but in chess any number of pieces may be sacrificed, all kinds of advantage ceded, provided only that checkmate may be achieved.[2]

SUMMARY OF OBSERVATIONS

- Sometimes employees will assist consultants to the detriment of the employer. They may feel that consultants with access to senior management could potentially help their careers.

- Companies need to avoid potential conflicts of interest with consultants involved in review processes where these consultants have pre-existing vendor relationships or plan to provide their own proposal.

- Consultants should be forced to disclose any preexisting or contemporaneous arrangements they have or plan to explore with potential suppliers or bidders for the client's business on which they are consulting.

NOTES

1. Bruce Caldwell, "Andersen Stalls," *Informationweek*, 7 October 1996, 97.

2. David Hooper and Kenneth Whyld, *The Oxford Companion to Chess* (Oxford: Oxford University Press, 1984), 63.

CHAPTER FOURTEEN

DENOUEMENT

While Don Mangrove was on vacation, things began to unravel at an accelerating rate. Back when the engine project had first kicked off, I had tried to enlist the help of Vincent Porter's people from the Corporate Strategic Technology Group. They could help me keep the engine on track and avoid getting swallowed up by the check-processing monster. Hands-on help, I was told, was out of the question. Porter had instructed his people that they could help in an advisory role only. None of this getting down in the trenches and helping us slug it out.

Two of those people were now offering their services to review the vendor proposals.

When I declined the offer, they warned me that I could lose support from Vincent Porter. "He'll definitely want to talk with you about this. Vinny wants us to be part of it. We can help you here." All of a sudden Vincent Porter had changed his mind regarding the kind of help to render. No longer hands-off, he now wanted his people's hands all over our vendor RFI responses.

I decided to strike first, calling Porter before he called me. I wrote down discussion points for the conversation in memo form. It was my hope that writing it down would help keep my emotions restrained. I would call him after creating the memo and attempt to keep our talk as professional as possible. Inside, I was steaming with rage. Porter was obviously attempting to assist Andersen in winning the business any way he could. I needed to build an argument to prevent STG involvement in the vendor review. The argument would need to stand up under scrutiny. More important, given the pro-Andersen climate at NationsBank, it couldn't be perceived as disparaging this highly respected consulting firm.

I wanted to explain to Porter that we intended to continue using his organization in an advisory role. At this point it would be counterproductive to get new people involved in the review process that was currently in midstream. Hopeful of adding some more credence to my argument, I called back Contracts and Standards before talking with him.

"We now have another NationsBank group that wants to be included in the vendor review."

"My recommendation is that you keep the review limited to the people on your original team."

"OK to ask why?" I was hoping to add this to my arsenal of reasons for keeping Porter and his people at arms length. I wanted to be as accurate as possible in explaining the rationale behind Contracts and Standards's recommendation.

After a pregnant pause he responded, "It's the only hope you have of maintaining some integrity in the process."

"Thanks, you made my day. You don't mind if I quote you on that?"

"Not sure it will do you much good, but go ahead."

Once I had finished developing the memo, I called Porter. It was still early morning. He listened to my arguments as I rattled down the list. At first he refused to give in, arguing that we still needed his people in order to do the evaluation right.

"It's the STG that can give you the credibility you need," he insisted. "How else are you goin' to get 'buy-in' from other groups?"

"That's why we have a steering committee."

"They're just figureheads. I'm talking about real buy-in. You need us for that."

Porter himself was a member of the committee. I restrained myself from asking if this meant he was only a figurehead, too. Instead, I reminded him of our previous conversation and how I had learned of his involvement with Andersen in plotting an outsourcing solution. I was firm, never raised my voice, and stuck to my script.

"You should also know that we've got Contracts and Standards involved in this as well," I added.

"Now, look . . ." Porter started to say something, but stopped abruptly. He almost lost it. He suspended his speech just before blurting out something nasty. I had him going, which I knew was dangerous. It was like teasing a rotweiler.

Continuing, I said, "They've been giving us advice on how to manage the process. They told us we should stick with the original evaluation group and resist any pressure to expand the review team this late in the process." I went on to tell him, given everything that had already happened, Contracts and Standards told us that we needed to operate by the book and avoid the possibility of a vendor protest. "Sorry, Vincent, but that's the advice I was given." He finally backed down. "OK . . . OK . . . but, just don't be surprised when the skies start filling above you, buddy boy."

Another one. A second threat, all within one week's time. The most disturbing part about it was that the threats were coming from two completely different sources. Life would have been so much less stressful as a yes-man.

Within minutes after the conversation, I forwarded the memo I had prepared to Porter. It restated my arguments. There were only a few edits, reflecting the conversation we had just had. It also highlighted some of his feedback. I thanked him for the warning about skies filling above me. The note concluded, "Thank you for your ongoing support and assistance." I braced myself, waiting for the hailstorm sure to follow.

I left a message with Mangrove, who was still on vacation, explaining why in my opinion this situation required an immediate response. This time I left a voice mail instead of sending a note, conforming to Mangrove's indicated preference.

John Turner, the manager from Global Finance, called me. It was during our last conversation that he had asked me to hold off on including his bid response with the others until he had talked with his senior management. "Just keep it under wraps until I get the official OK from my boss."

To say the least, it was ironic that this guy who acted so entrepreneurial was all of a sudden so concerned about protocol. It didn't fit. I should have been more concerned. I passed it off that this was new territory for all of us. It wasn't often that one group within NationsBank bid against outside vendors on a NationsBank business opportunity. Besides, as a relatively new employee, he, too, was probably coming under pressure to conform to the "process." As the conversation continued, I started to realize that there was a lot more to this than I had suspected.

"Vinny Porter came to see me," Turner said. "I told him about my proposal. He asked for a copy. Hope you don't mind, but I gave him one."

"You gave it to him? I thought you hadn't gotten approval from your boss yet? I thought you didn't want anyone else to know about it until you did."

"Well, yeah. Like with you, I told Porter to keep it under wraps for the time being. He knows it's not official. Not yet. I figured he could help grease the skids once we made our intentions known to upper management."

Turner went on to inform me that Ken Pollack, the Andersen partner from Direct Bank, was coming to see him tomorrow.

That's what you mean by keeping it under wraps? Here we go again, I thought. Pollack and Porter seemed to have this down cold. The same pattern had happened with Tandem. First Porter smelled it out. He then opened the door for Pollack to try and cut a deal for Andersen. I was feeling really nauseous now. When I expressed some concern, Turner assured me that there was nothing to worry about.

"I'm not getting in bed with Andersen, if that's what you're thinking."

A day or so passed. It was March 14, a day before the Ides of March. I had another call from John Turner. He told me he had great news. His boss had read his proposal for the engine. This was the proposal he had lifted almost word for word from the white paper I had previously written.

"He loved my proposal. He said it was the best thing he'd seen on the engine."

Turner's boss not only liked it. According to Turner, he decided to take it to Al Johnson, president of the Services Company. What a knucklehead I had been. While I was holding his proposal under wraps, Turner was circulating our ideas all over the bank as if they were his, drumming up high-level support.

"I'm telling you this in confidence," he said. Of course. I'm supposed to continue sitting here until things unfold. You had to give him credit. It was a great way of neutralizing me, the rest of the evaluation team, and the other vendor proposals while he worked "his" proposed solution up the line.

Turner added, "You know, Al Johnson isn't real pleased with Betsy and her staff. Between us, there is a plan to dissolve the STG and make us a replacement organization with similar responsibility . . . except that we would be more hands-on. We'd start getting some things done for a change." So while Turner was playing Porter, using him to grease the skids, he was also planning on stabbing him and the whole STG organization in the back. These people deserved each other.

Turner was using the anti-STG sentiment prevalent throughout NationsBank for his personal gain. There were many who seemed to have had their fill of the STG's advisory-only approach. So that was why Betsy Fields was pushing her organization to get more involved with the line organizations, and why she was pleased to hear about Porter getting more involved. The STG was under the gun. If Al Johnson felt this way, too, the STG was in big trouble. Turner hadn't been at the bank very long, but he had become quite adept at the NationsBank way of doing business. He knew how to break through the gridlock when another group stumbled. It sounded like he wouldn't be hesitant about helping to trip them up to get things started.

Rather than confronting problems openly, successful managers seemed to operate within the shadows of smoke-filled rooms. It was ground zero for zero-sum manipulation. To gain an advantage, you had to take something from another manager. Preferably, with no one else having a clue what was about to happen until it was done. Few would be crying over the STG being trampled. Betsy, Vinny, and the rest of their organization hadn't made many friends.

Turner continued, "Al Johnson likes the idea of us using the engine as our first prototype . . . to show what we can do. You gotta admit, it would be a great project to show proof of concept. You know, with it already being a cross-organization project and all . . . don't you think? . . . and, you gotta know . . . you'd obviously be part of this too, Steve."

"Mmmm . . . thanks."

I wondered if Al Johnson was completely on board with Turner taking over corporate technology strategy. As I had discovered, there was a habit of embellishing the facts around here. Talk was cheap. It would take more than Turner's assurances to convince me he had a hard commitment from Johnson.

What Turner said next sent me reeling. Even though he would prefer not to, he said he was being asked to work with Andersen on this venture. He must have sensed my revulsion.

"You know if it was up to me, that wouldn't be the case."

"Who told you to work with Andersen?" I asked.

"Let me put it this way. It was critical in getting Al Johnson's approval."

Who could I confide in or trust? Andersen had gotten to just about everybody. It was *Invasion of the Body Snatchers*. Now, in almost every possible scenario, Andersen still gets the business.

I remembered an expression a friend of mine was fond of using. We had become friends while we were both working as independent consultants. My friend had plenty of battle scars from the consulting wars and loved sharing what he had learned the hard way.

"Just like General Custer. We have them right were we want them. Out in the open, and all around us."

By now Mangrove had returned from his vacation. I scheduled a face-to-face meeting.

"I got you're your voice mail," he said. He wanted more detail on my conversation with Porter concerning STG involvement in the vendor review.

As I began to fill him in, Mangrove became visibly annoyed. At first I wasn't sure if he was more annoyed at me or about Porter's effort to muscle in on the review while he was gone. He finally chimed in, indicating that he agreed with me on turning down STG involvement in the RFI reviews.

"No way we want them involved." Mangrove agreeing with me—that didn't happen very often. "I will not let the STG into the evaluation process," he insisted.

"You should also know that Porter seems to be working closely with Ken Pollack from Andersen. In fact, they've both been talking to John Turner about doing a client/server prototype for the engine. Turner says Al Johnson is already on board."

Mangrove's lantern jaw usually tightened when talking with me. I could now see his lower mouth gripped tighter than usual. His Adam's apple sank to the bottom of his throat. The last thing he wanted was some souped-up client/server solution. From day one Mangrove was looking for a mainframe-based check-processing engine. Up until now, this had been the end game for the Model Bank cabal.

It seemed my theory was dead on. Mangrove was working to help Dave Gibbons win the NationsBank engine business, not so much for Andersen, but for Gibbons and his area of the business, which was focused on extending Model Bank. Porter was working for Pollack. They were pushing client/server. Gibbons and Pollack were both partners for Andersen, but they were also competitors. Given Andersen's dominant position at NationsBank, probably the only competition they feared in winning the engine business was from each other.

"I'll talk to Al Johnson," he said.

"Perhaps we should talk to Porter and Tuner, too. I would think at the very least, they . . ."

"I . . . will talk to them . . . also . . ." Anger over these developments did nothing to alleviate the annoyance in his tone when addressing me.

Unfortunately, I didn't hold much hope for Mangrove resolving anything. If he were true to form, he'd probably come back insisting that the whole thing had been his idea, and he had asked Porter and Pollack to contact Turner.

At this point I had no idea what kind of proposal, or how many proposals, to expect from Andersen. The only thing for certain was to expect the unexpected. As foolish as this seemed to be now, I had tried my best to stay one step ahead and to keep them a little off balance. It was no contest. I was feeling like a drunken sailor. Andersen was everywhere and acting as if it was its divine right to the business. There were more than a few people working for the bank who were helping to reenforce this kind of thinking. My team and I were simply a minor distraction.

It was early in the morning March 15. When I first got to the office, I logged on to check my e-mail. There was an invitation to attend a meeting at the Andersen office in Charlotte. Before reading the content, I knew we were about to enter the next phase of the consulting wars.

Steering committee members had also been invited. The purpose of the meeting was to overview Andersen's transaction engine solution. The invitation came from Ken Pollack, the client/server bigot. Based on this incredibly overt action of sending a note to the entire steering committee, it appeared that Pollack was now in the catbird seat.

Whether there had been any confrontation between him and Gibbons was unclear, but it now appeared that they must have reached an accommodation on how revenue would be split between them. Andersen would be proposing client/server, at least in its RFI response. What other "covert" actions it might be planned still remained to be seen. I already knew, for example, that Al Johnson had hinted that the $30 million for a new solution was too high. Wasn't interim repair thrown out as Plan B, in case we didn't get enough funding? Was there a Plan C?

I immediately sent a reply suggesting that, given I was running the evaluation process, I felt it would be inappropriate to attend the meeting. If I attended a meeting like this for Andersen, shouldn't I also do the same for everybody else who had responded to our bid?

I stated, "Contracts and Standards has advised that we attempt as best as we can to keep the playing field even among vendors responding to our recent RFI. Consequently, given my role in the review process, I feel it would be inappropriate for me to attend."

I took the liberty of sending the message to all the members of the steering committee who had been invited to the session. It didn't do any good. I found out later that almost all of the invitees attended. Guess I was the only one concerned about the playing field being even. Consensus was that it was a very good meeting. Pollack had wowed them with a new version of kodachrome.

A day or so after the Andersen meeting was over, I went to see Mangrove. He had attended the meeting in Charlotte and said he was disappointed that I had not. "You could have learned some things," he said.

Elaborating, Mangrove explained that Andersen had presented information on the success of the Direct Bank initiative. By now there was talk within the bank about performance and support issues with the Direct Bank client/server pilot. I guess that part was "out of scope," to coin a consulting phrase. Mangrove noted in passing that the possibly of partnering with Turner's organization was also mentioned.

"You know, I'm going to have to learn about this client/server stuff," Mangrove quipped.

After highlighting some of the other key items covered during the meeting, Mangrove related to me how he had made a pronouncement, "I told everybody that from now on everything related to the engine is supposed to go through me first . . . and everybody agreed."

Way to go. He sat there arching his shoulders back, like the big man on campus. Andersen had changed the direction on him; they had partnered with other groups with different agendas, and they had subverted his management on the project. If that didn't get to him, on top of all this, with the help of a NationsBank manager ready to cut down anyone standing in the way of furthering his own career objectives, they had already sold this completely different approach to his boss. The best he could hope for was that in the future they would stop to say hello. That was the extent of his exercising control. Things had changed. Mangrove needed them more than they needed him.

"I have a question for you, Steve. When you spoke with Vincent Porter, did you get emotional with him?"

"No, I didn't. I stuck to my guns, but I did not get emotional."

I then asked him if Andersen was still planning on submitting its proposal to my technical evaluation team.

"Yes, of course. I can share with you a preview of what you can expect. It's really quite good."

Mangrove gave me a copy of the Andersen presentation from the Charlotte meeting. It was a complete 180 degrees from what they had been advocating in the past. I couldn't help but wonder if the client/server solution Andersen was now proposing was just another smoke screen. The proposal to repair the current systems could easily be used as a "backdoor" strategy—a proposal only upper senior management would see. It could be that Pollack and Gibbons were both working it from different angles. Pollack was now doing the frontal assault. Perhaps Gibbons was flanking with the repair work as a counterproposal. Maybe their agreement was to split revenue regardless of which proposal flew. I felt like I was about to earn my Ph.D. in the school of diversified portfolios and hidden agendas.

Imagine if the Lewis and Clark Expedition had to deal with a team whose various members were working hidden agendas. How could they have possibly ever completed successful passage to and from the previously unchartered Northwest? As NationsBank associates, our inability to work together played right into Andersen's hands. If we kept splitting apart into smaller, more vulnerable search parties, and hiking across the same trails over and over again, it was no skin off the back of our consultants. They still got paid. If we never made it back out of the woods, that probably wouldn't have bothered them, either. They had different objectives. So much for looking to consultants for guidance. More like the blind leading the blind.

I went back to my office and shared the Andersen presentation I had received from Mangrove with the rest of my team. As expected, Andersen was proposing an outsourcing solution. The presentation highlighted the benefits of multivendor client/server technology. It was to be patterned after Andersen's Direct Bank initiative. The big difference was that one of the vendors would be Alltel, our mainframe vendor for Model Bank. As

Larry Rodgers had suggested early on, they would add Alltel peripherals to the base system. NationsBank management liked Alltel, so put them in the client/server solution, too. I guess after the Tandem incident, Andersen had reached a new accommodation with them as well. There was another big surprise. The client/server solution they were proposing could do everything, including check processing.

As we flipped through the presentation, we noticed a familiar chart. It was an engine design chart that we the NationsBank team had created early on, with no assistance from Andersen, Alltel, or anybody else. We had placed a NationsBank copyright insignia on the diagram. The same diagram now displayed an Andersen copyright insignia, as if it belonged exclusively to them.

As one of my guys said: "Guess we should be flattered. Our work has become part of Andersen's 'best practice' for payments engines."

Once again I called Contracts and Standards for NationsBank. I told them that I had concerns regarding a potential bid protest and misuse of proprietary information.

"It looks like we may now have a NationsBank group partnering with Andersen on this bid," I said. "What happens if they win the business and we get a bid protest from one of the other vendors?"

"Not sure. I'll have to check," was the reply.

"My second question is about potential copyright infringement. What about Andersen using one of our copyrighted charts as if it belonged to them? They took off our copyright and are now showing it with their own. They have explicitly told us they plan to take this to other banks to explore partnership arrangements."

"I'm afraid you're not going to like the answer."

"What do you mean?"

"Well, . . . the initial contract with Andersen? . . . It was pretty much written so they own whatever they work on."

"You can't be serious."

As the contract specialist indicated, all future contracts were treated as an addendum to an original agreement signed several years ago. In other words, the substance of the initial agreement was still in effect. Andersen owned material derived from projects they worked on at NationsBank.

I had never heard of anything like this before, not at IBM, not at Chase, nowhere. If it were true, Andersen wasn't doing work for hire. It was as if we were working for Andersen and paying them for the privilege.

"I liked to see a copy of the original Andersen contract. Could you fax it to me?"

"What's your fax number?"

I also asked if I could talk with one of the corporate attorneys to ensure that we avoided doing anything that could lead to a bid protest. "We still needed a clear definition of what was proprietary and what was not," I said. They told me that a conference call would be scheduled with one of the attorneys. I was subsequently faxed a copy of the contract. It arrived on March 17.

Andersen appeared to have a sweet deal. The agreement was signed April 17, 1995, by an officer of the bank and the managing partner from Andersen. The bank officer was a senior vice president at the time.

There was a section of the contract indicating that nothing within the agreement precluded Andersen Consulting from developing for itself or others materials "irrespective of their similarity" to work pertaining to the agreement. Andersen was free to use for itself, or others, ideas, concepts, methods, expressions, know-how, and techniques used by Andersen during its course of performing services under the agreement.

Now how could this be in the best interest of the NationsBank stockholders?

It was starting to sink in. Andersen had played a critical role in our expansion. They would continue to be instrumental in our efforts to become the number one bank in the United States. If they managed to carve out a few extra scraps along the way, so be it. An agreement had definitely been struck. This seemed to be the NationsBank way of doing business.

NationsBank had grown from the consolidation of smaller banks and would continue to do so until they fulfilled Hugh McColl's goal of becoming number one. Most members of the senior management team came from those smaller banks. Working for a large institution such as NationsBank, which was constantly getting larger, must have been a new experience for most, and fraught with risk. As I had learned, these bankers hated risk. Andersen became the security blanket. The bankers could pound their chests at stockholder meetings and in front of the press knowing they had Andersen backing them up. Having Andersen in the loop helped senior management sleep at night. In return, Andersen got its "hooks" into banking like it had so desperately craved.

Whether we went with what was being billed as client/server, or with something more like Model Bank, Andersen was being positioned to share in the spoils. Client/server was sounding more and more like a diversionary tactic. If it included Alltel and could handle checks, then it was really being set up as a Model Bank add-on.

In spite of the rhetoric, we were still trying to grow the bank by acquiring additional old, legacy banks. It was still a business-as-usual approach. Like Robert E. Lee who relied on Napoleonic open field tactics at Gettysburg and ignored the impact of technological advancements, we continued to operate the same way banks had been working for the last thirty years.

But who fought to protect the best interests of the customer? Who was keeping an eye out for the real competition, outside the Bank? Who was the referee deciding what was really in the best interest of Nations-Bank? The problem was that once you sorted through the complex web of organization, internal bank rivalries, and different agendas, we were highly vulnerable to the whims of our consulting partners. There was no "independent, objective third party" that had any vested interest in driving things to consensus. Multiple agendas meant more consulting opportunities. Every group wanted its own consultants to champion its own cause.

I wondered if our organizational structure had been built to encourage a contentious managerial environment. It sure operated this way. A confrontational structure may have been based on the premise that NationsBank was in a strong market position, combined with friends in the right places. With no major pressing external forces to contend with other than absorbing occasional acquisitions, internal management could turn to survival of the fittest, corporate style. The assumption is that the people and proposals that can endure all the infighting and bubble to the top were the ones that should be embraced.

The former champion of "no surprises," IBM had employed a similar structure when it was arrogant enough to think that it was the only formidable competition in the marketplace. It created competition with IBM divisions. These divisions would compete for the same dollar pool. Back in the early '80s when it appeared IBM could do nothing wrong, *In Search of Excellence*, the 1982 best-seller, praised IBM's management philosophy and practices. It stated, "IBM is the acknowledged master in fostering competition among would-be product lines." It went on to suggest that the company encouraged innovative thinking and multiple approaches, culminating in "real performance comparisons" and "shoot-outs" among competing groups—as if IBM always championed the adoption of innovative technologies from various business units.[1]

Claiming to provide lessons from America's best run companies, *In Search of Excellence* suggested that good management practice was not only resident in Japan. Back then, American businesses were still looking with envy upon companies from the Land of the Rising Sun. At the time of publication, author Thomas J. Peters was running his own consulting business, after several years at McKinsey & Company. Coauthor Robert H. Waterman Jr. was still working as a director with McKinsey. The book was celebrated for providing new insights.

Why was it that consultants usually never saw the problems until after things started falling apart at the seams? Once a company was obviously broke or went into a dip, consultants could always tell you why. Just look at all the case studies that were written about General Motors, IBM, and Japan after they got into trouble.

Ten years later, an article in *Business Week* pointed out that it was the IBM mainframe guys who almost always won the "shoot-outs." As indicated in the article, the IBM management committee, packed with mainframe people, was the final arbiter and helped maintain the status quo. Historically, the mainframe contributed the most to profit, and "increasingly IBM's minicomputer and microcomputer divisions were fighting with one hand tied behind their backs."[2] In addition to its contribution to near-term profits, mainframes provided a certain comfort level and familiarity that detracted from other options. And IBM was becoming increasingly more detached, losing its customer focus and nobody saw it—except its customers.

Just five years after the publication of *In Search of Excellence*, Tom Peters would write another best-selling book. It was after a downturn in the economy when several of the companies, like IBM, he had described as "excellent" in his previous book were running into trouble. These companies were now confronted by a "chaotic new world in which new competitors spring up overnight and old ones disappear." The book was titled, *Thriving on Chaos*. "There are no excellent companies," Peters was now saying. "No company is safe. IBM is declared dead in 1979, the best of the best in 1982, and dead again in 1986."[3] It was as if someone else had written about excellence in IBM and other corporate giants. Chaos, it seemed, wasn't so surprising to Peters in 1987. His sequel talked all about its causes, effects, and how to handle the "new" world order.

There seemed to be a lot of striking similarities between the old pre-Gerstner IBM and the new NationsBank. The apparent "survival of the fittest" organizational structure actually was window dressing and protected the "do nothing new" culture where big business units dominated and maintained the status quo. I talked with a friend who had worked in IBM human resources in the Mid-Atlantic area. She had recently retired from IBM. When she asked me what I thought of NationsBank, I suggested that it appeared to me that NationsBank had taken a page from the old IBM playbook.

"It wouldn't surprise me," she said. "In the old days we had several of the banks now part of NationsBank coming to see us to better understand our organization as well as our human resource policies."

That was it. The people running NationsBank were check-processing people and were dead set on preventing change. Everything else was public relations, as they continued doing what they knew how to do and were comfortable doing. Bankers were making money the old fashioned way—interest from loans, fees for service, and float. A new acquisition now and then didn't hurt either. It was always positioned as strategic. Never mind that the acquired banks would have qualified by Bill Gates's criteria as a dinosaur. So much for the talk about improving business through strategic technology. Sure, there were a few highly publicized ventures and partnerships to show some commitment to new initiatives. Most of these, however, were fairly superficial compared to the traditional investments and ongoing operational efforts.

After all the internal jousting and grandstanding was done, the NationsBank "no surprises" culture would remain intact. Status quo would prevail. It was a sure bet. The problem was that we were only temporarily masking the issue concerning the reduced market share of banking. We were still losing our shirts to mutual funds, stocks, and other nonbanking alternatives. We masked it through one acquisition after another. Sure we were growing with each acquisition, but we were actually stagnant in terms of real progress, immersed in political dog fights. All the buzz about e-commerce was just buzz. Most of our efforts were converting someone else's legacy systems to our legacy systems. Sooner or later there had to be a day of reckoning.

Thinking of "the customer first" wasn't the same as thinking about how we could preserve our float income from checks. Similar to IBM, before it fell on hard times in the early 1990s, managers were protecting the traditional "cash cow." For IBM it was the mainframe, for NationsBank it was check processing, which, of course, ran on mainframes.

The consultants surrounding management weren't there to advise on strategy or to implement groundbreaking ideas. They were there to help push management's agenda. In the case of NationsBank, this meant facilitating merger "transitions" and handling the increasing volume of checks that went with them. They would help protect checks because it represented important business to their client. If that's what the client wanted, that's what the consultant would do. It didn't hurt that checks represented opportunity for long-term consulting contracts, either. It could also create a high degree of client dependency on large numbers of contractual workers as traditional workforces were being reduced, especially after acquisitions. Check processing supported lots of billable hours with minimal exposure from a consulting perspective. It was a perfect marriage.

Why did NationsBank acquire other retail banks with the same legacy infrastructure if NationsBank executives were really committed to change?

Either there was a hidden agenda to maintain the status quo as we continued to grow through acquisition, or there was somewhere one big misunderstanding about what was advanced technology and what we were doing. The publicly stated objectives of NationsBank were inconsistent with the actual plan of action, or the plan of action was not being followed.

As much as I tried to stretch my brain, there was no other viable explanation. This logic could be extended to our relationship with the consultants. Either Andersen was receiving special directives from senior management, or they were operating with reckless abandon. Neither scenario was very pretty. A deal that appeared mutually beneficial had been struck. Actually, it was beginning to sound like several deals had been made.

In the meantime, while the organizational infighting played out to an inevitable conclusion to outsource, consultants could feed off of several patches.

A report in *Forbes* magazine, for example, would identify at least $500 million in assets that had been lost to local St. Louis institutions within only a few months of taking over Boatmen's. They estimated that there was probably a lot more. Although this amount may have been insignificant when compared to the total asset value, it could indicate a disturbing trend. Was bigger really better or, as the article suggested, would customers flee as personal service went out the window? Were we wasting too much time on the infighting and not enough on trying to retain customers from acquired banks? Nonetheless, infighting appeared to be reaching new heights at NationsBank as we acquired new banks and continued to grow. "Buying your way to bigness is the strategy du jour."[4]

For the consultants, getting bigger was definitely better. Downsized employees were replaced with more consultants. They could play the remaining groups off one another and turn it all into a series of lucrative annuity streams. There were significant dollars spent on analysis and pilot tests with very little new and tangible ever getting implemented in a timely fashion. If the intent was to foster an organization with the help of consultants to protect the status quo, the mission had been accomplished. The saddest revelation of all was that the blame was not with the consultants.

When all else failed, I would always call on a higher level of management. In this case, I was now convinced it wouldn't do any good. Still, I wasn't going to quit. If I was going down, I'd go down swinging.

Contracts and Standards kept dragging its feet on setting up a meeting with the attorney. One of my neighbors who had come to my holiday housewarming party was a lawyer in a local Atlanta firm. Her name was Sue Loggins and she was a very attractive Southern belle. We had talked briefly at the party. She had indigo blue eyes, a terrific sense of humor, and pulled no punches. She saw through my lines and let me know it. She must be an atypical belle, I thought. Sometimes on my way home from work I would run into Sue walking her dog, Lloyd. We would chat for a while, while I competed with Lloyd for a little eye contact from Sue.

One day in the course of conversation, Sue told me that her mother was a descendant of the Austrian Hapsburgs, one of Europe's controlling families before World War I. There was something regal about her, maybe this was true.

I decided it might be a good idea to ask her for some advice. There weren't too many people around NationsBank who I felt I could confide in anymore. Sue was a lawyer with class. I asked her to join me for a bite to eat at a local Thai restaurant. After relating some of the events that had unfolded, she interrupted, asking, "Would you rather be right or happy?"

"If I couldn't be both? Right . . . I guess."

"Thought so. I have that same problem."

When I had finished, Sue told me she thought I needed to be careful. Her advice was to get out. Leave the bank. Find another job. By now the peppers from the hot and sour soup had really kicked in. I tried not to let it show.

"I can't. I can't just walk away."

"You realize, you can't win."

"But what's the alternative. Roll over?"

The rolling over reflex had somehow never materialized in my family gene pool. Sue said that she hoped, if faced with a similar situation, she would have the same kind of courage. Stupidity is often mistaken for courage. Hemingway viewed courage as "grace under pressure."[5] I certainly wasn't feeling very graceful.

Something inside made me want to stick it out and see what happened. From the beginning, I knew I was playing a high-risk game. Andersen seemed to have a Svengali-like influence with the senior managers of NationsBank. After some thought I concluded, worst case, I get fired. Finishing the rest of my career at NationsBank had probably never really been in the cards for me anyway. Might as well play it out. When it was over, I would need to live with myself.

It was March 20. Larry Rogers from Alltel invited me to lunch to discuss the plan for delivering the Andersen-Alltel proposal. We agreed to meet out at the original project office where Andersen and Alltel were working on their RFI response. There was an army of consultants working on the proposal. Both Gibbons and Pollack were there, running around with opened lap top computers and their sleeves rolled up. I had to give one to Mangrove because he actually had them working together on the same proposal. I wondered how often that happened on Andersen client projects. The two Andersen teams were now collaborating as one. I couldn't help but wonder if they were billing us for time and materials in developing the proposal.

During lunch there was a definite spirit of uneasiness in Larry Rodger's behavior. The Alltel manager avoided eye contact as he spoke. Larry said he had checked into the issue I had raised regarding Andersen's contacting vendors to develop an alternate bid. He assured me it wouldn't happen again. Let's hope not, given that the bid was due in a few days.

What Larry said next was surprisingly candid.

"When you get our bid response, it won't include costs. They won't be submitted until Don Mangrove has a chance to see the costs associated with the other vendor responses."

Did I hear him right? If so, why was he sharing this with me? Maybe he was fed up with the questionable gamesmanship himself. He did seem to be a decent enough guy. I tried to get him to expand on his comments, but he quickly changed the subject. It was obvious Larry didn't care to say anything more.

In spite of everything that had already transpired, the implication of what Larry Rodgers had said was startling. Not that I had come to expect fair play. It was as if Mangrove had completely forgotten that it was NationsBank that signed his paycheck.

Larry added that rather than submitting a RFI response like the other vendors had done, Andersen and Alltel had prepared a presentation. They wanted to present it to the review team and wanted to schedule it for next Monday—the day their bid was due. It sounded like we would get at best a slight variation of the presentation I had already seen. Two additional weeks and the best they could do was an overhead presentation? I didn't like it, but what was I going to do? Create more confrontation?

"Thanks for the information, Larry."

"No problem. I've enjoyed working with you."

I didn't like the way he said it. Did he know something I didn't? I was beyond paranoid.

When I mentioned that the Andersen-Alltel response would be in presentation format to the team, they came unglued. Several suggested that we disqualify them for not adhering to the specified guidelines. I told them that while I didn't like this myself, we needed to go out of our way in demonstrating that we could be open-minded. I suggested that given Andersen's established rapport with NationsBank senior management, we needed to give them some slack.

"Romaine, you starting to get soft all of a sudden?"

"Maybe."

The meeting was scheduled for the following Monday. With limited success, I tried to minimize rumblings from the team. A few of them looked about ready to cave in from the stress. I talked with them individually about taking some time if needed. They insisted on staying with the evaluation process through to the end. The rumblings continued.

"Kind of sad after all this time working with us they can't put out a proposal like the ones we have received from the other vendors."

"I don't think they're capable of developing a proposal without outside help."

"Look at what we've been able to do in our analysis document in the same amount of time . . . and we're not getting paid the same kind of fees that they are."

"Do you really think management will listen to us if we recommend anyone else besides Andersen and Alltel? "

That Friday, March 21, I met with Don Mangrove in his office in the NationsBank Plaza building. The air was thick with tension. The tone of his voice was a few notches deeper than usual.

"You said early on that your preference was to go back to the strategy group."

"That's true," I said.

"I think this might be a good time to make that transition."

"But we're only one week away from completing this phase of the project. At this point, I would prefer to stay on until the vendor reviews are completed." By now, I had made up my mind I would hang in and take my lumps wherever they fell.

The conversation took several turns. Our final recommendation was due the next Friday, four days after receiving Andersen's proposal without costs. In the interim, he emphasized that he wanted me to meet with him every day until then.

"I want you to discuss progress, and I also need you to get me up to speed on what you've been doing."

Because Mangrove was incapable of finding a replacement for me, he had decided to fill it himself. He would juggle the dual role of project manager as well as the one he was currently filling. Who in their right mind would want to be a project manager on this? We drifted back to the same subject initially discussed.

"You did say you wanted to go back to the strategy group. If you have a problem with that, you better speak now."

It was as if the previous discussion from just a few minutes ago had never taken place. I replied, "Like I said before, I would rather stay on until we complete this phase of the project."

"I'm thinking we may need to form another team to review the work that has been done so that we can get the proper buy-in. I'm thinking of some people from General Bank and from the STG, possibly Global Finance as well."

Buy-in. The same term used by Porter.

I responded, "Once we complete our work and present it, I think you'll be in a good position to assess what needs to be done next. I would like to suggest that we prebrief select members of the steering committee, prior to any formal meetings, like we have done successfully in the past."

"I always try to prebrief the key people."

For some strange reason, I got a kick out of Mangrove constantly correcting my "we," and replacing it with "I."

Mangrove asked me again about whether I had gotten emotional with Porter when we had talked about STG participation in the RFI reviews. With this being the second time he asked this question, I now surmised that there must have been another version to what had transpired during the discussion—Porter's version. It was probably circulating with other key senior managers besides Mangrove.

"I was just trying to offer some help. Romaine was out of control. Overly aggressive and irrational. He obviously doesn't understand our politics here at the bank. . . ."

"Anything else?" Mangrove was done.

"Not that I can think of," I said.

On Saturday, March 22, I went into the office to clean off the desk and fill in some expense reimbursement forms. There was a voice mail message from Tony Alvarez, the Tandem rep, asking me to please call him at home over the weekend.

"Steve, thanks for calling. Listen . . . I had another strange conversation with Don Mangrove. I want to share it with you."

Tony said the call started with Mangrove thanking him for coming to the bank with the information on Andersen. He told me that Mangrove had said once again that they should have made it clearer, but that Andersen had called Tandem based on his request. He felt that this was an approach to help solve the budget issue and had instructed this course of action.

The Tandem rep then told me that the mood of Mangrove shifted dramatically. It was as if Mangrove began to chastise him for bringing information related to Andersen's initial call to the wrong person. The wrong person was me.

Tony said that he was told by Mangrove, "You should keep working with Romaine on the day-to-day stuff, but on anything 'sticky,' I want you to come to me."

He then related what he thought was rather amusing. Tony reminded me that it was Mangrove who initiated the call. After Mangrove finished speaking, he asked, "Anything else?"

"That's a common response he uses when discussing business," I said.

"It was very strange. Hey Steve . . . my advice . . . watch you back."

He also told me that he had another call from Ken Pollack from Andersen. According to Tony, Pollack apologized for not calling back sooner. He explained that Andersen was busy responding to the RFI. Tony said he didn't sound pleased. Once they had finished this, Pollack said Andersen would be sending out their own RFP (request for proposal) for developing the transaction engine for NationsBank and would follow up again with Tandem.

Cocky, even if it was for good reason. He worked for Andersen and was assigned to NationsBank. Pollack was employing a new tactic, trying to discredit the evaluation process currently under way. It would take a follow-on Andersen-led effort to get it right. I was finding that I was less and less astonished by these kinds of developments.

My biggest concern was that based on the information they had already obtained, if they didn't get the business, Tandem could develop a case for a bid protest. It wasn't difficult to speculate on the kinds of questions that the Tandem team must have been formulating. Why was Andersen not on the same timetable for completing the RFI? Why after all the work in responding to this RFI would they have to do it again for Andersen? More important, why was Andersen assuming it could send out a separate bid response to vendors on behalf of NationsBank? Did our being forthright in sharing information with the bank damage our ability to win the bid, given Andersen's apparent position of control? Did we hurt our chances by blowing Andersen off when it first came to us to partner?

On Sunday morning, March 23, I went back to the office. I sent an e-mail to Mangrove confirming our conversation from last Friday, pointing out that "I am more than happy to assist you in becoming more intimate in the technology associated with the transaction engine and sharing with you the vendor analysis work in progress." I ended the note by typing, "Thanks for your ongoing support." From now on, I was making sure that I had his concurrence for every step I took the rest of the way. I just needed to hold out a few more days until we presented our vendor recommendations.

The next day I called back Contracts and Standards, imploring them to put me in touch with the corporate attorney. "I don't know how much longer they will keep me in this job," I said. They called back with a time for a conference call, that very same day, March 24. It was the same day that Andersen-Alltel would be presenting their proposal.

Contracts and Standards initiated the call and stayed on the line. I put the attorney on speaker and had Sam Ritter listen in. As I began to relate the details of the situation, the attorney became annoyed.

"I'm working another situation involving Andersen. These guys continue to overstep their bounds. Unfortunately, senior management has a tight yoke on the choke chain when it comes to Andersen."

Counsel for the bank agreed that there was potential for a bid protest. She went on to suggest that based on the events that had taken place "there could potentially be grounds for a vendor to initiate legal action against NationsBank." This was unlikely, she said, since most vendors do not want to jeopardize future business opportunities with a major customer like NationsBank. Now there's a good reason not to worry.

When I asked her for advice, she suggested that I send a letter to Andersen pointing out their various transgressions while working on the project.

"If I could document this information and send it to you, would you send the letter?"

"No, I'm sorry. That would be inappropriate."

"Inappropriate" was a favorite word for corporate attorneys and other bureaucrats. I remembered it being slung around during my executive briefing fiasco with IBM.

"Isn't there anything else that can be done? Just so you know, there is a strong possibility I might be pulled off the project."

"It's unfortunate when good people get hurt, but there is nothing we can do."

When I tried to get advice on handling the remainder of the project as best we could, she said, "Andersen has already tainted your process."

She then asked me if I had any idea who in the ranks of executive management at NationsBank was assisting or encouraging Andersen in playing outside the rules.

"How far up do you think this goes?" she asked.

"I don't know," I said, "and frankly, I would rather not know."

The call ended with me promising to keep Contracts and Standards informed on future developments.

"I can't believe what she was saying," Ritter said. "Do you think there's a professional courtesy between consultants and corporate lawyers?

"If there is . . . God help the rest of us."

The next time I saw my neighbor Sue Loggins, I shared with her the conversation I had with the NationsBank corporate attorney.

"She seemed more interested in finding out how much I knew than in giving me advice," I said.

"Remember, she doesn't work for you. She works for NationsBank."

After speaking with the NationBank corporate attorney, I couldn't help wondering how high up it really went. Did it go up all the way to the top? My friend Paul Young from Newport News Shipbuilding once said that executives need to audit their own internal operations and not rely merely on the packaged information received from staff assistants and consultants.

"It's no excuse to say they didn't know," he said. "The buck stops with them."

From Paul's perspective, if they took credit when things went right, then they should also be held accountable.

After several rounds of debate, Andersen and Alltel finally agreed to submit the proposal prior to their presentation. We wanted to get a look at it in advance so we could be prepared with questions. Andersen would drop it off in the early afternoon followed up with a late afternoon presentation. As expected, it was primarily a graphic presentation similar to the one Mangrove had handed to me after the meeting in Charlotte.

There was a brief executive overview that talked about the great relationship with Andersen-Alltel and NationsBank. After highlighting the great relationship, the overview framed a question: "What changed?" A subliminal message? It went on to say that they would do their best to work with my team and me. What changed is that we have to deal with Romaine and his team.

Finally, it talked about the proposed solution. After an exhaustive review, they had concluded that there was nothing in the marketplace that could meet all the needs they had uncovered. Ergo, Andersen and Alltel were proposing to "build" the solution from scratch. They would, however, use other vendors like Alltel and Tibco to supply some of the parts.

As my team got together to discuss our preliminary reactions to the proposal, it was as if the home team had just been stripped of the title. There was a lot of anger and frustration over a long list of things. Andersen was proposing a client/server-distributed solution for handling both paper and electronic processing. The presentation hyped the latest new technology jargon, object-oriented standards, reuse, and encapsulation. It talked about "best of breed" open systems. Yet the interfaces they were planning to use were proprietary interfaces from Alltel. The presentation also talked about a "float-management component." Combining object-oriented technology, a new approach to building systems, with float management for check processing would be a real feat. It was as if a client/server proposal had been smashed together with a mainframe proposal. If you couldn't decide, why not a hybrid solution? Include something for everybody.

As Larry Rodgers had forewarned, it did not include costs. We were told "more information on costs" would be submitted at the end of the week. Just as the Tandem rep had said, the Andersen-Alltel proposal indicated that an additional RFP would go to vendors for the hardware and software—the core components of the engine.

This had become theater of the absurd. Never mind that selection of the engine was a deliverable Andersen had committed to as part of the current contract. They could potentially blame me and my team for altering the process and slowing things down. Even so, we were now being asked to buy the car with nothing under the hood. Why let the engine decision get in the way of future consulting fees?

While there were no specifics on the costs, the RFI response did hint to a method of payment. They were suggesting payment based on number of transactions. In other words, a meter approach. NationsBank could pay a usage fee for every transaction that was handled by the Andersen-Alltel transaction engine. According to their proposal, this could help with "deferral of costs to better match the timing of the engine investment with the delivered benefits of the new engine capabilities."

More consultingspeak. In other words, Andersen would build the front end as an investment and we could pay later, as the benefits kicked in. Somehow, they had the audacity to suggest that, not only would the engine handle any and all payments, it would achieve significant financial benefits over time (reduce costs, make money) and we could pay later rather than sooner. Here was the rub. They were suggesting that we pay on a per-transaction basis once the payments engine was running in full production. There was a major flaw in this way of thinking.

It was not the first time Andersen had proposed pay by meter. Andersen consultants had been contracted to do integration work at Chicago's O'Hare International Airport. I first heard about it from a friend who was a senior partner from another Big Five firm. He explained to me that Andersen was getting paid a small percentage for every passenger who traveled through the airport. The small percentage was not so bad. O'Hare was one the busiest airports in the world, accommodating over sixty million airline passengers per year.[6] When I expressed disbelief, he told me, "Lots of people in the business know about this. It was a real coup d'état in consulting."

An article published in *Marketing Computers* referred to this deal in a piece about marketing "vision": "More compelling is Arthur Andersen's outrageously clever software development deal with O'Hare Airport: Andersen developed the FAA arrival/departure tracking software for 'free' in exchange for getting a few pennies per flight tracked. Given that O'Hare remains the world's busiest airport, reliable sources insist that this is one of the system integrator's most profitable contracts."[7] Wouldn't that annuity stream of revenue to Andersen Consulting have been better spent in other areas? Like airport security? We at Nations-Bank were now being offered an opportunity to challenge for the top spot as the new most profitable contract.

A little closer to home, I was told that Andersen's contract for the Direct Bank project was also based on a pay-per-transaction basis. This cost-deferral approach for development might be attractive to guys like Mangrove who were responsible for the front-end procurement and implementation, but not necessarily the ongoing operational budget. It worked because lots of times the purchasing organization is different than the organization responsible for ongoing support. They have different budgets. The problem was that it could result in significant ongoing costs that could blow all budgets combined.

Andersen indicated that it could not be more clear about the total costs as there was still much to be determined. Yes, they still needed to figure out what hardware and software to use before they could estimate the costs. Details. Even if they charged less than a penny per transaction, this could really add up given that we were talking about NationsBank daily averages of 100 million transactions. All of our assumptions related to the engine were based on running the system 24 hours a day, 365 days a year. At a usage charge of a half-penny per transaction, the costs incurred by NationsBank could be as high as $500,000 a day, or $182,500,000 a year, with no end in sight. We could dwarf the O'Hare deal, not to mention the more than $500 million costs attributed to Nations-Bank's Model program. Four years of operation could cost $730 million.

The Andersen presentation actually went on to say that the solution would "reduce costs for NationsBank by being able to increase transaction volume, while maintaining the same cost per transaction." In other words, we could still pay the same usage charge, that is, a half-penny per transaction, whether our volume increased or stayed the same—such a deal. Where do we sign?

Reducing costs was obviously relative. The best and only true way to reduce costs was to reject the Andersen bid. The Andersen approach would significantly increase our costs as part of an ongoing annuity. They would be making an incredibly fantastic amount of money. In addition, they planned to market the proposed system to other banks to get them to "share" some of the costs with us. So how would this work? Would we pay less per transaction as the number of participating banks increased? What about performance degradation because of increased volumes? What about the costs associated with the loss of competitive advantage? The cost of being "me, too"?

As we had already learned, the Andersen proposal to NationsBank was for outsourcing the engine. This solution would be run out of Chicago with an option to bring it back in house at some later date. But whose house? NationsBank, or one of the other participating banks? Chicago was the headquarters for Andersen Consulting and also the location of the Nations-Bank Global Finance organization run by John Turner. The presentation indicated that the transaction engine would be built at Andersen Consulting's "Eagle" Project Center, which was at the Chicago headquarters.

Andersen had launched Project Eagle in 1991. It was a worldwide initiative to investigate how Andersen could develop new systems for reinventing client organizations, processes, and technologies. On the Internet Web site for Andersen Consulting, Project Eagle was defined as an "integrated set of tools, architectures, processes, patterns, and reusable components.[8]

According to the competitive research information we had collected on Andersen Consulting, the objective of Project Eagle was to accumulate libraries of reusable packaged knowledge and to quickly assemble "customized" solutions for clients. You had to give them credit. They appeared to be taking the reusable-software development concept and applying it to reusable everything from one client to the next. Project Eagle would help clients develop an "Enterprise Blueprint."[9] One blueprint with minimal modification could potentially fit all clients in one industry.

What seemed to irritate the team most was the condescending tone of the presentation. It pointed out that we, the members of the technology review team, could not be expected to understand the proposal and would need further education from Andersen and Alltel, given that this represented a brand-new technology approach. What technology? I thought Andersen needed to do another bid to figure this out. This seemed to be another tactic, discrediting the internal team with decision-making responsibility—deflecting any potential criticism of their change in tactics or of their own glaring weaknesses in competency.

A few members of the team looked like they were ready to start throwing chairs. "Look," I said, "there is nothing these guys would love more than to build an argument that we can't keep our cool and be objective. We'd be playing right into their hands."

As painful as it would be for all of us, I told the team that we needed to demonstrate interest, ask good questions, and stay positive. They had that junkyard dog look in their eyes. It occurred to me that in a short period of time they had turned into an aggressive, self-assured group with some of the same bad tendencies that it took me years to develop. I just knew NationsBank would have to do something about this.

I wanted them to ask lots of intelligent questions and avoid anything that could be construed as sarcastic or vindictive. In my own head I rationalized this course of action, given that Andersen and Alltel had already established themselves with senior management as the premier partners of choice. We had to give them a better than fair shot. It was also a matter of survival.

For the most part, the meeting with Andersen and Alltel went pretty well—at least for the home team. They showed up with Dave Gibbons and Jay Kittles from the first phase, Larry Rodgers from Alltel, and an individual who was apparently their technical guru on client/server. None of us had ever met him before. He reminded me of the architect used by Gemini, the so-called client/server expert who had a British accent. He would be the lead presenter. From his opening remarks it was pretty clear he suffered from an obvious case of "Love Thyself" disease. This guy was born thespian with great elocution—a '90s version of John Barrymore, patriarch of the famous family of actors. I remembered hearing once that Barrymore had said one of his chief regrets was that he never sat in the audience to watch himself perform. Technology terms such as *rules-based engine* have more of a ring when spoken in proper English as opposed to a bastardized American twang. Consulting firms must think it adds more credibility when one of the consultants has a foreign accent, particularly when they are proposing to burn another village in the King's English.

With the exception of the presenter straight from central casting, the contingent from Andersen and Alltel included mainframe guys who must have been recent converts to new technology, I assumed. Pollack, the Andersen partner assigned to Direct Bank, was conspicuously absent, even though the proposal had a client/server emphasis similar to the program he was responsible for implementing as part of Direct Bank.

Peter Miles was also absent. Was it possible he was still busy working on the interim repair strategy? Andersen could potentially make two sales. I knew from the rumor mill he desperately wanted to be an Andersen partner. If he proved instrumental in Andersen's sale of both the interim repair for the old systems and the new engine, that had to be a grand slam. It could potentially accelerate the partner-approval process. Partners approved other partners. Helping to line the pockets of preordained partners helped improve the chances of promotion. Line his pockets and even Gibbons might forget how Miles tried to shoot him in the back.

The first few charts gave the typical Andersen high-level industry view. The only question on the first set of charts came from Mangrove, NationsBank's top manager for the engine project and a highly regarded veteran of the Model Bank campaign.

"What do you mean in this box where it says 'electronic commerce'? . . . that's a new one for me."

I resisted the temptation of explaining that "electronic commerce" represented the replacement of banking as we know it today. Barbara Albrecht had been right. There still were people at NationsBank who had never heard of electronic commerce. It just never occurred to me that I would be working for one of them.

We, the technology team, were cordial and performed as well as could be expected, with one exception. At one point Andersen mentioned that it was using client/server technology at NationsBank today, in the Direct Bank project. When someone asked if it was being used anywhere else in the bank, one of my people jumped in with a loud and resounding NO!

A few very uncomfortable seconds followed before the Andersen technical consultant continued with the presentation. I watched Gibbons grin at Mangrove, as if to say, "I told you so." As part of the discrediting process, I'm sure they had also floated the balloon that our team could not possibly be fair in our evaluation of Andersen. I had already heard that I had a reputation of being anti-Andersen from both Harvey Kraft and Betsy Fields. Andersen had unlimited access with senior management, unlike NationsBank employees. If they wanted to discredit, they were in a great position to do so.

During the presentation, the lead presenter with a British accent said that they would be sending out an RFP to vendors for the hardware and software components of the engine the next day. He was incapable of adequately addressing several of the questions that were being asked, even some of the softballs my team had thrown in an effort to honor my request to "ask good questions and stay positive." They shouldn't have been so terribly difficult for someone familiar with client/server architectures. Members of my team answered some of the questions for him. They actually had to hold the keynote presenter up for the last few rounds, reminiscent of what a prizefighter does when sparring with a poorly matched contender.

Toward the end of the presentation, I asked Andersen and Alltel to refrain from doing any additional RFPs to vendors until our process was completed as this could confuse the vendors and would be counterproductive. They agreed. At the conclusion, we graciously thanked them for all their efforts.

Just to make sure, I called Ken Pollack, leaving a voice mail. I wanted to make sure he got the info and couldn't claim ignorance on the matter. He sent back a response via e-mail suggesting that he was very sorry for any apparent miscommunications or misinterpretations of his past actions. Pollack said he had no intention of sending anything out to vendors regarding the engine at this time.

The fun was over. The real work for us was just starting. We still had to finish evaluating all of the other vendor responses in addition to adding the Andersen-Alltel response into the mix. We knew that people from the bank would be expecting a few overhead slides. We were actually preparing a lengthy document that had various sections, including a business case; vendor analysis with explanation; and a narrative that discussed the strengths, overall risks, and general assessment of each of the individual responses. If someone wanted to change the recommendations at a later date, it would require more than shifting "weights" for an evaluation matrix on an overhead slide.

Putting this kind of a document together given our limited window of time was no small task. It would, however, be our only hope of receiving any serious consideration. There would also be an attempt to leverage the element of surprise.

In addition to the other vendors, we would review the response received from Turner. Paradoxically, in one sense we were evaluating our own work, given that Global Finance had used my white paper and the conceptual design charts that my team had created. Our review was less than favorable. The Tibco product they recommended offered a proven technology for the trading environment. It had not as of yet established much of a presence in high-volume banking.

Global Finance had also proposed using their own homegrown monitoring system for network management—the same solution proposed in the Andersen-Alltel submission. The name was appropriate, Global Alarm System, or GAS. For distributed client/server solutions disbursed across a network, these kinds of monitoring systems with diagnostic and management tools were critical. We questioned the viability of using a homegrown proprietary product in supporting Transaction Services—we were a lot bigger than Global Finance and a totally different environment. According to most of the technology research analysts like Gartner Group, homegrown was rarely the optimal solution. Major vendors like Hewlett Packard and IBM offered better alternatives, and they could invest more over time to keep them current and viable.

In the back of my head, I couldn't help but wonder if my team had been right and the work we were engaged in would have minimal if any impact. It had become a most frustrating assignment. We were going through the motions of a structured review while all kinds of chaotic and disruptive things that were happening in the background were beyond our control.

The recommendations were due to Mangrove on Thursday, March 27. The plan was to distribute this work to the steering committee the following day. I had already met with Mangrove several times, going over the process for the review and showing samples of the summary matrix.

I was scheduled to meet with him again on Tuesday, March 25. I would have to show something more.

We met at the original project office. What I ended up showing during the meeting was another status report with a summary of the evaluations. It reflected evaluation of all vendors with the exception of Andersen-Alltel, which as I pointed out, there had not been a chance to add as yet. I told him the information was only preliminary, representing the total of individual raw scores and was subject to change. We still needed to meet collectively to develop the relative ratings and validate our initial scores. The summary showed Tandem and IBM neck and neck, with Tandem ahead by a nose.

"This is just preliminary. There is still more to evaluate for each of the vendors," I said.

The evaluation didn't show costs. I thought for sure he'd ask about them, but he never did. Instead, Mangrove only expressed concern when he noticed additional names on the summary matrix. The cover was now blown. Tier two had been exposed.

"I thought this only went to Hogan and Tandem," he said, adding, "You mean this went to others? . . . It went to IBM?"

"They made the cut as a second-tier vendor. We sent it to all the vendors who made the cut."

"I didn't know that this was being sent to IBM."

Somehow Mangrove had not heard about IBM submitting a bid. I had decided not to say anything unless asked, but I thought for sure he would have heard by now. Porter had known for some time. I would have bet the ranch Porter shared this information with his buddies at Andersen, and one way or another Mangrove would have been clued in. They were supposed to have regrouped as one team with all information passing through Mangrove. I guess they still needed to get some kinks out of the new process.

In any case, it really bothered Mangrove that it went to IBM. I had a flashback to a conversation with Betsy Fields.

"There are two vendors Al Johnson likes to use for business: Andersen and IBM."

I found his concern about IBM as somewhat ironic. Andersen and Alltel had never asked to be considered as an RFI candidate. They had participated in the process and had plenty of advance time to announce their intentions to provide an alternative solution. Did they really expect us to believe their solution was merely an afterthought? Why wasn't it a problem including them? At least IBM was on the original list as a viable option, albeit immediately relegated to the tier two list; possibly because even after all those years of consultant bashing, they were still the biggest threat to the game plan. An evaluation process that involved Andersen and Alltel had come up with a list of best vendor alternatives with the "Itsy Bitsy Machine" (IBM) Company hanging by the skin of its teeth at the very bottom. Someone would raise the issue if they didn't say they had evaluated IBM. Relegating them to "tier two" was a great way to dismiss them early on. Or so they thought. Neither Andersen nor Alltel was on the list they had helped to create. Why were they the only ones always getting special treatment?

That the bid went to IBM was a source of major anguish for Mangrove. I realized that we had stumbled onto something. Al Johnson liked IBM. Granted it was a low probability at this point with Andersen so entrenched, but IBM had the firepower to compete at the same level as Andersen. It was also obvious Mangrove wasn't buying my explanation and was getting ready to pounce once again.

"This was only supposed to go to Tandem and Hogan," repeating his earlier comments.

Luckily, I had a good excuse for sending the RFI to IBM and the other tier two vendors. Maybe not much, but this time I had some cover:

"Andersen management knew about this going to the tier two vendors. In fact, it was Andersen management that had recommended this in the first place," I said.

Andersen had come up with the tier concept. It was Jay Kittles from Andersen who had recommended sending it to both tiers one and two. I went on to explain that part of the rationale was to demonstrate that we had given each of the vendors a "fair chance." Mangrove's silence created an uncomfortable few moments. I added one more.

"We had no good reason not to include them. The original ranking with Tandem and Hogan on top was only preliminary . . . not based on a lot of detailed analysis. IBM is a major vendor for NationsBank. They could have made an issue of it if they weren't seriously considered."

While he did not look pleased, Mangrove gave an affirmative shake of the head and was apparently comfortable with the rest of the information presented. I overviewed the current status of the evaluation process. Mangrove seemed preoccupied and never asked about the financial estimates received from the vendors.

"Looks pretty good," he said.

As I was leaving the project office, I ran into Darlene Wittington. It had been several months since I had taken her to lunch. At that time I had mentioned my suspicion that Andersen and Alltel would submit an outsourcing bid for the engine.

"Hey, Darlene . . . the proposal from Andersen and Alltel? It is for outsourcing the engine."

I said it matter of factly, devoid of emotion. Just then, Don Mangrove strolled around the corner. Darlene said nothing, staring back with an equally bland lack of emotion. She turned and continued to walk in the direction she was originally going. I left for my office.

Minutes later my pager went off again. I didn't expect it this time. It was Mangrove. He said he was concerned that IBM might try to do an "end run" on the engine project.

Imagine, a vendor not playing by the rules? I explained that IBM had been involved early on in the review process, and it appeared that there would be at least some IBM content in almost all of the bids we received.

"They were not a tier one vendor, isn't that correct?"

"Yes, but we all agreed that they had enough to offer to give them a closer look. That included both NationsBank and Andersen people on the original evaluation team."

I added once again that we didn't want any of the vendors complaining that they didn't receive a full and fair review. We seemed to be going around and around on the same argument. After discussing a few additional concerns, he thanked me and hung up.

I spent the rest of the day with the technical evaluation team, reevaluating each of the vendor responses. This time, however, we discussed them as a group. We evaluated all of the vendors from a relative perspective, measuring one response versus the others. The evaluation was based on their ability to meet our weighted criteria.

We used the preliminary cost projections from Andersen that indicated a $30 million investment over two years. They had thrown this number around almost since the project started. Given they were now talking "meter," where costs would have been even greater, we felt we gave them a break. The $30 million figure, which didn't include the hardware and software, was still significantly higher than most of the other bids. In general, the other bids attempted to estimate total costs, hardware, software, integration, and project management. As we totaled up the revised scores, IBM just barely edged out Tandem as the most optimum solution.

Betting with my heart, I would have picked Tandem—I had enjoyed working with them, and they had been forthright in their dealings with us. Their solution for real-time routing and settlement, however, was suspect. They had proposed a combination of ACI legacy software and a product fresh from the Tandem labs that was unproven in the marketplace. It would require a significant amount of programming and integration to make it work. Bottom line: there was a lot of risk here.

From the head, the solution had to be IBM, which was rated highest because of its ability to provide the most complete and comprehensive of all the solutions. While all costs were just estimates, projected cost estimates for the first year—which included all hardware, software, and services—were less than 50 percent of Andersen-Alltel's incomplete costs. Needless to say, as part of the qualitative analysis, we hammered hard on the problems with Andersen's suggestion of a pay-per-transaction approach. You would have to have been delusional to have thought this was in the best interest of the bank, especially when compared with proposed solutions from IBM—or any of the other vendors for that matter.

There was a lot less to build with an IBM-based solution. It had one of the leading transaction engines in the business, which they referred to as a "transaction monitor." It was called MQ Series. This, combined with other IBM products, stood out from the pack as a viable solution. Less smoke, less mirrors. Reasserting itself as a technology leader, IBM was helping to influence future directions. It was less in react mode when it came to technology, thinking future versus "how do we get these people trained in mainframe and client/server off the bench?" IBM was still committed to skills transfer and keeping people current—both employees and clients.

Several months before, NationsBank had formed a coalition with IBM and fifteen other banks, called the Integrion Financial Network, for developing a common network standard for electronic banking services.[10] There could be some synergies between the engine and the Integrion project. Given that NationsBank had made a major commitment to use IBM's Integrion standards, didn't it make sense to coordinate the engine with this effort? Otherwise another separate transaction engine would need to be built to support this initiative—more silo processing. Integrion never really went anywhere, in spite of all the hype. In NationsBank alone, there were too many competing forces working against it.

IBM's proposal addressed all of our requirements. It was network-based as opposed to client/server or mainframe—the type of solution that could run more effectively and exploit the Internet and the latest in networking architectures. Its transaction engine would be Y2K ready. Their network-based solution was flexible enough to support whatever architecture made the most sense for the business. The IBM transaction system could run on all kinds of hardware—IBM as well as non-IBM. It could even run on Tandem hardware. Not only did IBM offer one of the best solutions for handling financial transactions, it was also a leader in providing security technologies, another critical component in e-commerce.

Ironically, the IBM solution was also the only proposed solution that conformed to the STG's recently published architecture standards. This was a recent document the STG had developed using Gartner Group material. It was one of the STG's more practical contributions. It wasn't just boilerplate. It evaluated products used at NationsBank in the context of Gartner Group product analysis. At NationsBank, the best way to fend off a consultant was with another consultant. They had a hell of a lot more credibility than employees. Maybe it was time to dispel the idea of consulting "full service provider" and begin segmenting them into separate boxes based on their "core competencies" and areas where most of their revenue was generated. "Segment them, or they will segment you."

As noted in the STG's *Technical Architecture Strategies* document, the MQ Series product IBM proposed as the basis of the transaction engine "is very nearly the de facto standard for message queuing in the industry, and as a result many vendors have built utilities specifically to enhance the functionality of MQ. MQ can be used in combination with many other types of middleware. . . . MQ is available on most of the NationsBank platforms."[11] Using the STG documents to recommend someone other than Andersen would not make Vincent Porter's day.

Another selling point of the IBM proposal was that it was willing to commit to building a prototype that could be up and running within a few months, very different than the Andersen-Alltel two-year plan, with the first prototype over a year out. This was not the typical consulting approach with a linear path with hand-offs, from one step to the next. The IBM approach would be collaborative with strategy working hand in hand with implementation. With IBM, we could test, make changes as necessary, and accelerate the implementation cycle. We could build off of the incremental gains. If nothing else, we had a chance of getting in the game a lot earlier. This was critical if we were going to have any chance at all of meeting Boatmen's transition schedule. What I probably liked best about the IBM proposal ran completely counter to the typical consultant recommendation for multivendor solutions. It represented pretty close to one-stop shopping for the hardware, software, and services, with no middleman hiking the price. Just one vendor to call if something broke.

Although not much was said about it, in the back of each of our minds somewhere I'm sure was the thought that IBM was the only competitor in a position at NationsBank to have anywhere near a fighting chance of succeeding against Andersen—that is if anyone could. NationsBank was definitely in the Andersen camp, but it was also an IBM shop. I kept remembering what Betsy Fields had said about Johnson. She had told me that IBM and Andersen were his favorites.

We ranked each vendor. After IBM was Tandem, followed by the NationsBank Global Finance solution and then by Andersen and Alltel and the other vendors. We listed strengths and weaknesses of each proposed solution. Collectively, we all felt, if anything, we had given Andersen and Alltel a huge break in rating them as high as we did. Their response to our bid was that they would have to do their own bid to determine the right solution.

Several of the items listed as strengths for Andersen required a real stretch. The following summarizes the strengths and weaknesses of the Andersen response:

STRENGTHS	WEAKNESSES
Partnership with NationsBank	Requires Major Development
Understanding of Environment	Implementation Timeline
Process Management	Ongoing System Support Risks
Integration	Platform Decisions Still to Be Determined
Architecture Framework	Outsourcing Core Competency for Bank
	Inconsistent with Previous Recommendations
	Overall Costs

That evening I received a call from Andersen partner Dave Gibbons. He said that he had an 8:00 A.M. meeting with Don Mangrove to go over the "preliminary financials" for the proposal. He said I could join him if I wanted, or he could drop off my copy on his way to the meeting. I told him that I had something else on my calendar and it would be preferable if he could drop it off. He said he would stop by around quarter of eight.

"I'll drop a copy off before the meeting."

I mentioned this to one of my team members who told me that he felt pretty strongly that I needed to be in the meeting with the Gibbons and Mangrove. All of a sudden I was the one who needed coaching. Of course, I knew he was right. This process had drained me. It was becoming very painful sitting through this unending succession of meetings. "OK, next item for discussion. . . ." Not to mention, we had a hard stop for producing the final deliverable on vendor evaluations. I decided to sleep on it.

The next morning, Wednesday, March 26, when Dave Gibbons arrived, I told him that I was able to free up my schedule and could now attend his meeting with Don Mangrove. At first he seemed a little taken back, but quickly recovered and said that would it be fine. We spent a few minutes together prior to the meeting. I asked Gibbons to take me through the numbers.

The costs in the proposal were over $60 million for three years. This included Andersen and Alltel products and services. Gibbons pointed out that additional costs would still need to be added for the engine hardware and software, presumably after another RFP process, or leveraging the one just completed. Not to worry, I thought to myself, these were the costs that could be deferred with the usage concept. Just turn on the meter. I listened politely and thanked him for sharing the information. We left for the 8:00 o'clock meeting.

Don Mangrove was not pleased when I walked through the door. I was obviously not expected. There was a financial analyst from Alltel already in the room. As we sat down to discuss the proposed finances, it became obvious that the financial analyst had no idea who I was; he seemed to assume he could talk candidly with friends sympathetic to the Andersen/Alltel cause. As Gibbons began to wade through the proposed budget, the financial analyst consistently interrupted with off-the-cuff comments. Mangrove looked annoyed as the financial analyst from Alltel said: "The key is that we need people from finance who will be friendly to us . . . just like we had with Model."

He had definitely mistaken me for one of the good ol' boys party to the NationsBank way of doing business with partners. Darlene's comments from when I first joined NationsBank came roaring back into my thoughts: Follow the money.

Mangrove watched as I scribbled notes. His face was ashen. After the overall costs were explained, Mangrove pointed out that with this year's budget cutbacks, it would be difficult getting it approved. He said the numbers seemed to be going in the wrong direction.

"At first we were talking $30 million for two, now we are talking $60 million for three."

"We're already deferring some costs," said Gibbons, "I'm sure there are a few other things we can do."

Like Plan B? Sitting quietly, I personified the good team player, except for the note writing. The meeting concluded with Mangrove leaving us behind as he walked out of his own office and down the hall. He was walking with his typical awkward gate, but a little faster than usual.

I met briefly with Gibbons after the meeting. We sat in the lounge chairs on the ground floor of the Plaza building as NationsBank associates marched across the lobby on their way to work. He asked me to debrief him on the status of the RFI analysis and the planned next steps. I summarized briefly where we were without getting into the specifics on vendor analysis. I told him the plan was to present recommendations the following day.

"Didn't you once tell me you worked for IBM?" Gibbons asked.

"Yes, I did."

"I thought so. You remind me of other guys I knew who also worked for IBM. You operate the same way they did."

"Thanks," I said as if he had just paid me an enormous compliment. I wondered if Gibbons was beginning to formulate a new argument about me having IBM biases.

My team spent the rest of Wednesday morning working on the finishing touches of the vendor evaluation document. The document included over eighty pages of analysis. How many hired consultants would it take to produce this kind of work developed by employees? I wondered how many would have been capable of delivering it in within a two-week time period. What would they have charged?

I had my final status meeting with Mangrove scheduled for late in the afternoon. It was early afternoon when Mangrove called down to the conference room where we were working. He said he wanted to see me right away. He was breathing hard again. Not good.

Mangrove motioned for me to sit down as soon as I entered his office. His face was red, and he was still having trouble catching his breath. He told me that effective right now he was assuming my position as project manager for the engine project. I was to leave the premises immediately.

"Harvey Kraft from the strategy group will meet with you first thing tomorrow morning."

"I don't understand. Why?"

"You discussed outsourcing with Darlene Wittington."

"Well, yes, but I don't see . . ."

He cut me off. "I don't want to discuss this anymore. Now I want you to leave, and I don't want you to talk to anyone on your way out."

My luck had run out.

As the senior manager of Integration Services, Darlene Wittington was higher in the organization than I was. She had just received an award from the chairman for her outstanding contributions and her reputation as a leader in technology in the industry. Her organization was responsible for routing and settlement. She was on the steering committee. Andersen had previously discussed its outsourcing proposal with the steering committee. She was also the manager who had originally engaged Andersen to evaluate routing and settlement.

Why, I thought to myself, was it so terribly wrong to mention the word outsourcing to a senior manager? Particularly when Andersen and Alltel were talking it up with senior management and had discussed it with my team, the steering committee, and others on several occasions. In fact, Mangrove had discussed outsourcing publicly as well. Surely Darlene was professional enough to handle hearing it again from me.

A couple of my people saw me as I was walking out.

"Steve, what's up. Where you going?"

"Sorry, I have to leave and I was instructed to not talk."

I walked out the door of the NationsBank Plaza building and for a moment couldn't help but enjoy the sardonic humor in it all. I was being pulled out of the job the day before the final recommendation was due. A year when budgets were being slashed, the politically correct answer was a solution that would blow the numbers away. As I was walking from the building, I looked up to the sky.

> *"A bank is a place where they lend you an umbrella in fair weather and ask for it back when it begins to rain."*
>
> —Robert Frost[12]

SUMMARY OF OBSERVATIONS

- Many consulting firms today claim to be "full-service providers," but few really are. They should be segmented based on areas of specific expertise and also based on where most of their revenue comes, that is, if most revenue is from contract programming, they are a vendor, and should be segmented accordingly.

- Companies need to carefully consider the total implications of outsourcing and avoid outsourcing areas of core competency.

- Indifference in addressing issues provides fertile ground for consultants to increase their penetration and control.

- Consultants will change the rules of the game to protect their interests.

- At times, consultants will discredit internal decision makers to further their cause.

- Validate proposed solutions from consultants. Do not assume they are objective or that they are the subject experts.

NOTES

1. Thomas J. Peters and Robert H. Waterman Jr., *In Search of Excellence* (New York: Harper and Row, 1982), 217.

2. John W. Verity, "It's PCs vs. Mainframes—Even at IBM," *Business Week*, 21 September 1992, 66.

3. Tom Peters, *Thriving on Chaos* (New York: Alfred A. Knopf, 1987), 3.

4. Gretchen Morgenson, "Binge and Purge," *Forbes*, 3 November 1997, 54.

5. Carlos Baker, ed., *Ernest Hemingway: Selected Letters, 1917–1961* (New York: Charles Scribner's Sons, 1981), 200.

6. Gary Washburn, "O'Hare Retains Title as Busiest Airport," *Chicago Tribune*, 16 February 1996, Sec. 2C, p. 3.

7. Michael Schrage, "The Return of Vision," *Marketing Computers* (January 1996): 30.

8. Andersen Consulting Web site, http://www.ac.com/aboutus/tech/eagle/.

9. Darryl K. Taft, "Andersen Sets Enterprise Blueprint," *Computer Reseller News*, 28 October 1996, 132.

10. "Major Banks, IBM Launch Network for PC Banking," *American Banker*, 10 September 1996, 1.

11. "Technical Architecture Strategies," NationsBank Strategic Technology Group, 25 February 1997, 60.

12. "Robert Frost," http://www.geocities.com/fire-hazzard/people/rfrost.html.

CHAPTER FIFTEEN

PUNT, PASS, SAFE

Deep fragrant smells of spring filled the air. The cruelest of months was about to arrive. By the time I reached home, I had made up my mind that I would go for a run and try and clear my head. It was probably a better alternative than killing any more brain cells at the Martini Club.

There were two messages on my answering machine from guys who had worked for me on the engine project. The first said that everyone was continuing to work, business as usual, making the best of things under the circumstances. Don Mangrove had made an announcement that I was returning to the strategy group. He said in the long run he felt certain things would work out for the best. "I guess the rest of us will keep working on this for a while," he said. "Don't worry, I'm sure things will be fine."

The second message was in stark contrast to the first. This was from Sam Ritter, who had actively campaigned for my job. He had really come on strong in the last few weeks in helping to produce the analysis work and in driving the process forward. He said the team was in disarray.

"Everyone seems a little confused and a little scared. We ended early without finishing the document. I tried to take over and press on but they wouldn't listen. They think there is no point to finishing it now."

As I had been instructed, I showed up first thing in the morning, Thursday, March 27, at my office on the seventeenth floor of the Nations-Bank Plaza building. I sat at my desk overlooking the Georgia Dome and Fulton County Stadium, the place where Hank Aaron had played.

The home opener for the Braves would be in just a few days, but not at Fulton County Stadium. The Braves would play at their new stadium, built and utilized for the 1996 Summer Olympics. That was part of the deal that was cut to justify building the new stadium for the Olympics. Fulton County was to be torn down and used for a parking lot. I looked at a picture on my wall. It was a going away present from the IBM team that I worked with on the Newport News Shipbuilding account. It was a picture of the nuclear aircraft carrier, the USS *Abraham Lincoln*. I would always treasure it. My mind was spinning. Once again, I remembered the past.

IBM TIME CAPSULE: CLOSING THE SALE

My entire focus was on two simple things: trying to make the numbers, and staying out of trouble. Achieving either of those objectives seemed improbable, but I was determined to give it my best shot.

One day Toby Hobson invited me to lunch. This was a rare occurrence. Something had to be up. As we finished lunch, he said, "You know, Steve, there is not a bigoted bone in my body. By the way, have you ever been to my house?"

Of course I had not.

"I want to give you something. Let's take a ride. We won't be gone long."

Toby did all the talking as he drove. It was all about him, and what a terrific guy he was, and all the personal challenges he had overcome. I wondered what he would give me.

What kind of Faustian deal was he contemplating? It had to be some kind of deal.

His home was beautiful. Toby asked me to sit in his living room while he went to fetch what he had in mind. I remember the room was crowded with stuff, but my head was spinning and I was too uptight to notice any of the particulars surrounding me as I sat in the corner of a long, wide couch. He came back and handed me a cased hunting knife.

"This is my favorite. Take it out. Have a good look. Pretty impressive, huh? I want you to give it to your friend over there at the shipyard, Paul Young. I hear he likes to hunt, right?"

I took the knife, but I had no intention of ever giving it to Paul. Providing gifts to customers, especially government defense contractors, was prohibited. I put the knife in my briefcase and decided to store it away for posterity.

After Toby dropped me off in the parking lot, I got in my car and drove to the shipyard. Several of the members of my team were working out of the branch office that day. I later heard from one of the women on the IBM shipyard team that Toby had called several of them together that very afternoon. He instructed them that if they heard of any IBM employees giving gifts to Newport News Shipbuilding employees to let him know. She said he warned them that there were strict regulations against this. Unbelievable. He must have been really desperate to try and nail me with something this contrived, but why?

I found out later that an employee sent an unsigned letter to the chairman complaining that Toby Hobson was a racist. Toby must have thought it came from me, or that I was somehow involved. I wasn't, and no one who worked for me was, either. There would be an investigation. Several employees would be interviewed, including the few minorities in the branch and all managers. Was the knife incident simply to get something on me to try and influence what I might say in the interviews?

An interview with IBM Human Resources about Toby was the last thing I needed, especially now. I agonized over what I would say. There was loyalty to the IBM chain of command thing, and then there were my personal feelings about the man. During my time working in Norfolk, Toby had said plenty of things that I felt were offensive and in particularly poor taste for an IBM branch manager. I decided that I would truthfully answer the questions I was asked, stick to the facts, and refrain from emotional outbursts.

"How do you feel about Toby as a manager?"

"He gives me a lot of rope. I'm kind of entrepreneurial, so that's OK."

Good thing they didn't ask how I felt about him as a person.

Toby weathered the storm. He eventually said he figured out who sent the letter and talked openly about it. At first I was convinced he was mistaken. According to Toby, it was a systems engineering manager, someone I never would have guessed would have done anything like sending an anonymous complaint letter to the chairman. He just happened to be an African American. Like me, he wasn't included in manager golf with Toby. When he first came to the branch, I remembered this guy demonstrated a lot of class and poise. A few times he had confided in me that he didn't like working for Hobson. On that score, we both agreed. We were busy working different territories and I wasn't aware of much else, but come to think of it, over time his self-assurance seemed to evaporate. But to do this? Send a complaint letter? It seemed out of character and a desperate move. Then it dawned on me. While I was obsessing on how bad things were for me, I had missed that it was probably even worse for others. At least I got to spend most of my time at Newport News or in a Hampton suboffice close to my customer. He was in Norfolk, in constant proximity to Hobson. Whereas in my territory I was playing the dual role of marketing manager and systems engineering manager, he was paired up in a territory with a marketing manager who was "buds" with Toby. It must have been hell. Toby gave him rope, too, but it was a lot shorter.

Officially, IBM policy was that letters to the chairman were to be handled discreetly, without repercussions to those employees who reached over their immediate manager's head. It was called "the Open Door Policy." It was one of those things that made IBM a great company. Part of the "Respect for the Individual" mantra. This didn't matter to Toby. Once he had covertly discovered who sent it, he had him shipped straight out the door, to be buried in an obscure staff assignment. "The people who work with him, the customers, they all keep telling me, he just ain't doin' the job."

In the meantime, Newport News Shipbuilding was reviewing responses to its data center RFP that included IBM's. I was in suspended animation waiting to hear the final word. Newport News was a defense contractor, and anybody who met minimum requirements could bid on the business. Anything could happen and anyone could win. My team really needed to win and if we didn't, I was assured of losing my job. One of the people who worked for me tried to help: "This is the way it always goes. Unless they need to clarify something in the response, they can't talk to any of the vendors until the final decision is made."

Toby called to ask about it. "So Steve, bud, you heard anything yet? By the way, you ever give that knife to Paul?"

"Haven't heard, yet. I haven't had a chance to see Paul, either . . ."

Man, it was almost as if he was hoping someone else would win the business so he could take me out. Come on Romaine, you're getting paranoid again. Keep it together.

Finally, we got the word. My team won the year-end RFP from Newport News Shipbuilding. It was to replace the entire data center with new IBM equipment, bringing our year-end revenue total to $37 million. We had grown the business 130 percent over the previous year. If not the best, one of the top increases for any major IBM account territory for 1990—and it was real business, contracts signed, the whole bit.

It turned out that while the briefing with the IBM chairman had fallen through, the executive assistant I had originally talked with had played a crucial behind-the-scenes role. He was the reason we started getting the attention of important IBM executives who decided to lend their personal assistance with Newport News Shipbuilding. He continued to grease our skids. His name was Sam Palmisano. Sam would come up through the ranks to turn IBM Global Services into a huge success story, and eventually replace Lou Gerstner as the new chairman of IBM.

I found out later from Paul that most other vendors had opted out with a "no bid" response. They couldn't meet the requirements to provide the comprehensive solution as described in the RFP. It wasn't even close; according to Paul, IBM was the clear winner.

Socialism, which I had been told was "dead" in IBM, raised mystically from the crypt. The quota for the IBM team assigned to the shipyard was increased by Toby Hobson to help other territories within the branch make the percentages and avoid what had turned into a disastrous year for most of the Mid-Atlantic area. After the game had been played, the rules had been changed. When all was said and done, we had merely squeaked over our revised quota objectives. In the old IBM "no surprises" culture, large increases in "dead" territories could be dismissed as a quota-allocation issue and readjusted to ensure that the world as projected materialized as planned. A "no surprises" view allowed IBM management to keep up the pretense that the universe still revolved around Big Blue long after the consultants had usurped IBM's leadership in most of the top Fortune 500 companies. It was as if the "lost cause" had not yet been lost. The pretense continued for a few more years. The real focus had turned to cutting costs and reducing head count. "Customer driven" continued to be the slogan.

Even though our accomplishments along with sizable commission checks were voided out by the revised quota allocation, it couldn't diminish a very deep personal feeling of satisfaction. They would never take that away. If it had not been so great for my career, at least I could try and think of it as a character-building experience. Isn't that what they call it? Maybe this time I could get it to work.

I had grown very fond of my customer and the IBM team. Not only did they really come through on the business side, they had stuck with me and covered my back when I needed it most. Nevertheless, at the beginning of 1991, I decided to make looking for another job my top priority. I didn't say anything to Toby or anyone else. Tired of constantly looking over my shoulder, leaving the Norfolk branch had become an easy decision to make. I accepted a staff job in White Plains, New York.

When I finally told Toby about my decision to leave, he didn't seem the least bit surprised, even though I had once again taken an unusual step. In the IBM culture designed for mentoring and team building, managers usually campaigned for their employees and helped place them in new jobs, once they were deemed ready to move on.

There was a gleam in his eye as he said, "Well, Steve, hate to see you go, but I certainly understand. To be honest, I never thought you fit in around here . . . you know, being from New York and all. . . ."

No sooner had I left than he was back out on the branch office floor expounding upon his accurate prediction from a year ago. "I told you, Romaine just wasn't goin' to make it. Too bad, but I had to let him go."

A year or so later Toby Hobson would leave IBM. Naturally he became a consultant. He was contracted by IBM on a retainer to provide advice for a period of time before embarking on a new career with a new company out of Charlotte. He bought a new house next to Jim Schiller. They would stay "buds." Jim, too, would eventually leave IBM.

The Mid-Atlantic area manager who told me to make it "his business" missed his quota again in 1990 and would go on to miss it a few more times before receiving a promotion. The "good ol' boy network" would hang on for a few more years.

I left the field to work for the IBM Consultant Relations Department. My job would be to manage consultant relationships for IBM, instead of customers. Coming from the field, I figured I could help fix what I saw as a growing problem in IBM's handling of consultants. "Keep your friends close and your enemies closer."

One of the technical team members from the NationsBank engine project walked into my office. He wanted to share with me some of the events that transpired after I left and Mangrove had stopped by to announce that he was taking over for me as project manager. I told him I really didn't want to hear it. No doubt, it was a third variation of what was going on. It was probably not a good idea for him to be seen with me at this time, anyway, I said. Before he could take a seat, I pointed him to the door.

He started to walk out, stopped, grabbed the doorframe, and swung back around.

"There is one thing you need to know. I'm behind you. We all are."

"Thanks, man. Now get the hell out of here."

After waiting for some time, the phone rang. I was told to come to the fifty-fourth floor.

Sitting in a corner office was Harvey Kraft. Next to him was Patti Conden, a storm trooper from human resources. I often wondered how people like her ended up in personnel. She had that "I knew I'd get you sooner or later" look conspicuously pasted on her face. I was in it deep. Harvey had flown in from Charlotte the night before. I was invited in as he finished a story about his expanding waistline. He beat around the bush for a while, in gentlemanly southern style, before honing in on the issue at hand.

"My problem is this . . . no one questions your technical ability, but as much as I might like to, I cannot bring you back to strategy. I am told there are problems with your getting along with some of our most important constituents."

The constituents, according to him, included Don Mangrove, Darlene Wittington, and the Strategic Technology Group. Funny, Betsy Fields,

Director of the STG, had told me just a few weeks before that her people liked working with me. It had to be Porter from the STG group who was spreading the negative stuff. Incredible how those skies really did fill. Coincidentally, Mangrove, Wittington, and Porter all had strong ties to Andersen. So did Harvey Kraft.

Patti Conden threw in that I was walking around the bank expressing my opinions on things. I assumed this referred to the comment I had made to Darlene Wittington. She mentioned that I had also developed a negative image with Alan Johnson, the president of the Services Company. This was because I had met with him when I had no authority to do this. Patti had never been a big Steve Romaine fan.

"That was early last year. Since then, I thought things were going pretty well. In fact, he gave me a stock option award and praised my efforts in the letter he sent. That was well after my meeting. . . ."

Ironically, the congratulatory letter from Al Johnson was the only written comments I had received regarding my performance during my tenure at the bank. It flashed through my head that the bonus mentioned in the letter may have been some subtle attempt at cutting a deal if I would just play along. The executive vice president from Model Bank, Denny Billings, had recommended this award that had been approved by the management committee for the Services Company.

It would not have been the first time that subtlety was lost on me. I also mentioned that I had followed the advice Harvey had given me on how to work more effectively with Don Mangrove and thought that things had improved significantly. In fact, I mentioned that I had received concurrence from Mangrove on all the activities that I was spearheading as project manager for the engine project.

"Just the other day he told me he thought the work I was managing looked pretty good. This is very surprising," I said.

There was no response to my comments. They had laid out their whole case against me. As terrible as all this sounded, there was one big bright spot from my perspective. None of my people who worked for me had turned against me, or surely they would have thrown that in, too. There had been times I wasn't so sure, but they had really hung in there in spite of it all.

"So, we are going to give you thirty days to find another job. You can continue to use your own office, send out resumes, and use the telephone. I also have a project I would like you to work on during those thirty days."

In my head, I had already made a decision that I would leave the first night I could sneak in discretely, pack up my stuff, and get the hell out of Dodge. The poor bastards, they looked very uncomfortable about all of this.

"What about the team?"

"Some will come over to strategy, some will stay on the engine project."

IBM TIME CAPSULE: DEBRIEFING

On my way home after being dismissed, I remembered an incident that had happened with U.S. Tobacco, one of my customers when I was a rookie IBM salesman. Probably, the only kind of company that could be more politically incorrect by 1990 standards than a defense contractor like Newport News Shipbuilding. I was at the customer site when one of the technology managers stopped me to ask if I had received the letter he had sent to my attention the other day. He was smiling ear to ear. When I told him not yet, he asked me to follow him back to his office. He rummaged through a pile on his desk, pulled out a copy, and handed it to me with a closed-mouth cynical smirk.

It was a complaint letter regarding a topic that seemed quite trivial at the time. The content of the letter didn't bother me. It was an issue that could be resolved fairly easily. What galled at me was that he had sent a copy to my marketing manager as well as my branch manager. He was escalating a complaint that he had never discussed with me, as if I had been unresponsive.

I left his office and was bouncing off the walls when another manager stopped me. It was the operations manager who had been instrumental in my recent sale of an IBM mainframe computer to U.S. Tobacco. It was the first new purchase from IBM in many years. He asked me to explain why I looked angry. I related the details, while he sat patiently appearing completely detached.

As I concluded the story he asked "Ever wonder why the Italians run New York and not the Irish?"

I shrugged my shoulders, having no idea where this was going.

"You guys swing first and think later. Hold you powder. Don't do a thing until you've had time to calm down and work some of the anger out. Think on it a while. If after you calm down you still want to do something, have at it."

It sounded like good advice, but I was still fuming and probably would be for a long time.

Summary of Observations

- Consultants with access to senior management can distort facts and neutralize threats from employees.

- Employees protecting turf will assist consultants, even when they are not operating in the best interest of the corporation.

- Disagreeing with and taking on an entrenched consultant can be detrimental to your career.

- Consultants cannot be expected to self-manage without creating an environment with potential for serious abuses.

- Companies take the risk of relinquishing their fiduciary responsibility when consultants control corporate decision making.

AFTERMATH

As I packed up my office, I picked up a copy of the most recent NationsBank annual report and added it to a box with my personal files. The annual report was hot off the press. The NationsBank chairman was quoted as saying:

> In many ways, your company is only five years old. Yet, as I have described, there is as much that is new about NationsBank today as there was when it was created in 1991. I believe this highlights two characteristics that distinguish your company. First, yours is a growth company. It has rarely—if ever—finished one year looking the same as when it began that year. Second, despite its size, yours is a dynamic and increasingly entrepreneurial company. It will never shy away from recreating itself in order to evolve one step ahead of our customers' needs. These two characteristics reflect our true competitive advantage—our people. Every day, the people of NationsBank demonstrate the innovation, entrepreneurial spirit and passion for finding a better way that our customers seek and our industry demands. Just as important, they do the right thing—for our customers, for our communities, and for each other.[1]

A few days after I had left, each of the members of the engine steering committee received a large envelope through internal mail. It was the evaluation document for the transaction engine. An employee of NationsBank who had worked with me on the project had sent it out anonymously. It discussed strengths and weaknesses of each vendor. It was critical of the Andersen client/server proposal with a meter for paying per transaction. The final recommendation was for IBM.

During the next steering committee meeting, the corporate chief information officer of NationsBank said that it was one of the best analysis documents he had seen while working for the bank. Several other members of the committee concurred, including, of all people, Darlene Wittington.

The Andersen client/server proposal for the engine had been based on the same concept as the Andersen home-banking project for Nations-Bank called Direct Bank. The Direct Bank pilot was now up and running in Florida. Two sources from separate organizations within NationsBank confirmed that it required 117 servers to support 200 users.

Based on performance issues with the Direct Bank initiative, combined with concerns over the pay-by-meter costs, the Andersen proposal for a new routing and settlement engine was rejected. Don Mangrove insisted that there needed to be more study—always a safe and acceptable answer in the new approach to business. A new vendor evaluation group was established. By now NationsBank had spent close to $2 million on consulting fees and expenses in transaction engine–related activities.

The new evaluation group rejected IBM's recommendation. All of the other proposed solutions received during the initial request for information (RFI) process were rejected as well. Five months after I was released from NationsBank, a decision was made by the new vendor evaluation group to repair and consolidate the current paper and electronic routing and settlement systems as opposed to implementing a new solution. The plan was to renovate and expand the batch-based paper system used for check processing and float management. It called for adding new capability to handle "electronic" workload in a future release. There were no provisions for implementing real-time routing and settlement. The electronic workload would be handled with overnight batch window processing, just like checks. The current electronic system would eventually be shut down. The Corporate Strategic Technology Group (STG) was disbanded. Harvey Kraft would continue to run the strategy group for Transaction Services.

Andersen Consulting received a new contract to assist in the interim repair and consolidation effort for routing and settlement. Andersen would provide ongoing support for repair and maintenance of the current systems. Peter Miles from Andersen Consulting was named manager for the initiative. He had still not gotten his partner stripes. Don Mangrove took over the role of project manager. Check processing would remain the top priority for routing and settlement. The transaction engine would be treated as if it was an extension to the Model Bank program, the program where Andersen and Alltel played critical, behind-the-scenes roles.

NationsBank would continue to rely on thirty-year-old technology for routing and settling the bulk of its banking transactions. The bank would continue to receive great press and Wall Street analyst praise about its technologically advanced systems. This was critical to its expansion strategy and the eventual acquisition of Bank of America. Business would continue to be outsourced to Andersen and Alltel.

The bulk of payment transactions for Bank of America are still in check. Increased pressures of trying to meet check-based processing requirements for a national bank in different time zones has intensified problems associated with the Model Bank program. Check processing requires that scheduled deadlines be met (windows). Friends from the bank have told me that there have been two subsequent efforts to implement an electronic payments engine. Both initiatives have been scrapped. For the last one, Bank of America contracted with another Big Five firm. Budgets were set at around three million dollars. Approximately eight subcontractors were invited to participate. The effort was disbanded after exceeding over twelve million dollars in expenditures. As one friend, who recently left Bank of America, said, "If they had implemented a payments engine the right way, they wouldn't be in such a mess today with Model Bank."

The Rise of a National Superbank

The following highlights subsequent events of note, tracing the steps leading to the acquisition of Bank of America and the establishment of a new bank. It became the largest bank of the United States, based on numbers of deposits and branches.[2]

A May 8, 1997, article in *American Banker* quoted NationsBank Executive Vice President Rusty Rainey saying that Model Bank "gives us an incredible competitive advantage . . . this is the foundation piece for our future. . . . The core technology architecture and development of common processes and products will allow NationsBank to become truly national." In the same article, David Hilder, an analyst from Morgan Stanley & Company, said that while it was difficult to calculate the contribution of Model Bank to NationsBank earnings, its goals of common systems and customer-relationship information are beyond reproach. He said, "Ultimately, the results of this will show up in higher income levels, a better efficiency ratio, and probably better returns on assets and equity."[3]

On August 29, 1997, NationsBank announced its intentions to acquire Barnett Bank. This would make NationsBank the third largest bank in the

United States and one step closer to fulfilling the chairman's goal of becoming the number one banking institution in the country. As noted in the *Wall Street Journal*, "The value of the transaction, initially pegged at $15.5 billion, or $75.18 a share, was a lofty four times book value, at a time when paying 2.5 times book value is considered expensive. . . . Barnett offers NationsBank, based in Charlotte, North Carolina, another bulwark in its aggressive drive to become a truly national bank."[4] According to the article, a major concern that led Barnett officials to consider a buy-out was the high costs associated with the necessary technology investments to effectively compete in the future.

It was reported that to make the Barnett acquisition possible, a NationsBank team using the project code name "Ohio" sprung into action, locking up Merrill Lynch & Co. and Goldman Sachs & Co. as advisers. After hand delivering his offer to the chief executive of Barnett, the NationsBank chairman "went to Morgan Stanley, Dean Witter Discover & Co. and, along with a team of advisers, hammered out the merger in a few hours. Later that day, they shook hands on the deal."[5]

NationsBank officials said that they projected $915 million in annual cost savings, representing a 55 percent cost reduction in Barnett's expense base. It was subsequently reported that as part of the deal, NationsBank had agreed to sell 124 branches in Florida. It would close another 200, and expected to trim at least 6,000 positions in the Florida workforce.

After the deal was announced, NationsBank Chairman Hugh McColl said that the consolidation of Barnett would take time, and he would not contemplate any additional acquisitions in the near future. A few analysts suggested that the acquisition could pose a big risk if economic conditions changed. Yet bank officials and Wall Street in general continued to be bullish on the future of the consolidation and future earnings potential. Three years later, the *Daily Deal* reported: "Under pressure to cut costs and make the Barnett franchise worth their price, the North Carolinians mishandled the consolidation. Customers of Barnett branches left in droves, causing deep Florida losses."[6]

NationsBank and BankAmerica Corporation announced a merger on April 13, 1998, which would create the largest national bank in the United States. It would be largest in terms of both deposits and branches, with close to 200,000 employees serving approximately 30 million customers. The NationsBank-BankAmerica merger, valued at approximately $60 billion, established a company with $570 billion in assets. Robert Albertson, an analyst with Goldman Sachs, said, "This is going to be the best franchise in the country, both in terms of their retail and wholesale businesses."[7]

Similar to the Barnett acquisition, Merrill Lynch and Goldman Sachs were employed to assist as advisers on the deal. It was reported in August 1998 by *American Banker* that NationsBank and BankAmerica Corp. had used a compensation formula based on the ability of their advisers to promote stocks for both banks. "The firms in that $60 billion deal, Merrill Lynch & Co. and Goldman Sachs & Co., not only would collect at least $25 million each in traditional advisory fees, but also would get 0.2 percent of the increase in market valuations of NationsBank and BankAmerica between the announcement date and the last trading day before the closing. The investment banks could pocket $50 million apiece. For obvious reasons, sales forces at Merrill and Goldman are touting the stocks fervently this summer."[8]

Not surprisingly, the deal was overwhelmingly hailed on Wall Street where stocks for both banks went up on the day of the announcement as the Dow Jones Industrial continued its historic upward trend. While it was called a "merger of equals," and the new holding company would be called BankAmerica Corporation, a careful look clearly revealed that NationsBank was the big winner. NationsBank was essentially acquiring one more bank as part of its aggressive acquisition strategy. NationsBank would hold a greater portion of shares outstanding and have more directors with seats on the new corporate board. The chairman of Nations-Bank, Hugh McColl was named chairman and CEO for the new bank and planned to maintain the principal office for the new BankAmerica in his hometown of Charlotte, North Carolina. Prior to all this, the former chief executive for BankAmerica, who had reneged on previous merger discussions with NationsBank, had retired. The current CEO for BankAmerica, David Coulter, was named president for the new company. McColl was expected to retire within a year or so, and it was expected that Coulter would replace Ken Lewis as the new heir apparent.

In many ways, NationsBank and BankAmerica were very similar. Both banks had close to 2,000 branches, a heavy base of check processing, and in spite of a few innovative technology ventures, they were each saddled with a preponderance of old technology systems within their infrastructures. Like NationsBank, in the last ten years BankAmerica (formerly called Bank of America) had grown through acquisitions. They had laid off thousands of workers as part of merger efforts. They also had a history of relying on consultants for various activities.[9]

The former CEO for BankAmerica was quoted as saying, "Both banks created a rich legacy of customer service, innovation, and a keen sense of competition. The scale we will achieve together means we will hold market leadership positions in the majority of our business lines, including strong market share in nine of the ten largest and fastest-growing states in the country. That will create earnings growth that can fuel the future investments necessary in both our people and technology in ways not possible for either company alone." He went on to say that both he and the chairman of NationsBank believed they would set a new standard for customer service, capabilities, and efficiencies. In his own remarks, Hugh McColl added that while expense reductions were not the prime objective of the merger, the potential existed for efficiencies in the combined expense base.[10] A NationsBank spokesperson said that they anticipated 5,000 to 8,000 layoffs.

During the merger announcement meeting with journalists, Hugh McColl said, "I call it a showstopper. In other words, everybody else becomes, basically, irrelevant."[11]

Diane Glossman, an analyst from Lehman Brothers, said that in one fell swoop the merger would create a national banking franchise. "It would create a company that reached from the consumer up through large corporate America, contemplating its essentially national scope," Glossman explained.[12]

Following the announced merger, it was reported that a "corporate identity consulting firm" was hired to determine what brand name would have the most appeal.[13] Choices included BankAmerica, the most currently used name, as well as the old "Bank of America" name. The final decision was that while the new company would remain "BankAmerica," the nod went to the old "Bank of America" name for the moniker.

Commenting on the Bank of America logo, Hugh McColl said, "We are confident that the selection of Bank of America will position our company for success in today's—and tomorrow's — swiftly changing and intensely competitive financial services industry. We also know, based on months of working together since our merger announcement, that the people of the new Bank of America strongly share the values it will take to succeed going forward. That is where the great potential of this company lies—in our people, who know we have the opportunity to make banking work in ways it never has before. . . . While it is the name of a country, America also stands for a powerful idea to people around the world. America means freedom to pursue ideas and ideals. It means opportunity to reap rewards of ingenuity, optimism, and hard work, and it means a pioneering spirit that can carry people as far as they want to go."[14] In his remarks at a national press conference, Hugh McColl called the new brand name decision "one of the most important decisions we had to make."[15] There was no mention of people from Anderson and Alltel who would also continue to play critical roles in bank operations.

Not everyone was quite as positive about the merger. There was some criticism from both the right and the left. With tongue in cheek, shortly after the announcement, *New York Times* columnist William Safire wrote, "When a big bank from the West Coast decides to merge with a big East Coast bank, that doesn't bother me. All the stuff about synergies and cost-saving layoffs and global reach will be meaningless soon enough; future banking will be done on the Internet, every home a branch, and today's giants will be undercut by speedy cyberbankers unencumbered by overhead." Safire went on to point out that "'Mere Size' can be a virtue when it reduces prices. But the fewer the competitors, the more collusive the pricing." What was really bothering Safire, according to his editorial, was the emergence of "keiretsu in America."[16]

Consumer advocate Ralph Nader also worried about the rash of banking megamergers. He argued that creating these behemoth, omnivorous corporations would ultimately reduce customer choices and lead to higher service fees.[17] On the Public Broadcasting Service television show the *News Hour with Jim Lehrer*, April 13, 1998, Nader suggested that it could increase exposure for the taxpayer, creating an unfair burden should any of the large banking institutions get into trouble. Without a major overhaul to the FDIC, the sheer size of the combined banks would dwarf currently available deposit insurance from the federal government.

On May 10, 1998, the *Atlanta Journal and Constitution* reported, "For years, bankers have been demanding more regulatory freedom, but consumer groups have been warning the powerful industry must be carefully curbed. Now NationsBank—the South's most dominant bank—has given its critics ammunition. Federal regulators hit the bank with $6.75 million in fines and gave it a good tongue-lashing for lying to poor, elderly customers to lure them into risky bond funds in 1993 and 1994. NationsBank consented to the fine and censure from regulators. It also paid about $30 million in 1995 to settle a class-action suit in Texas that alleged similar violations."[18] The article went on to say that the penalties were shocking because NationsBank was not a "fly-by-night" operation. It also referenced the plan to acquire BankAmerica and recent deregulation of the industry, which in the past had protected consumers against bank abuses. A question was posed: "Do customers really understand what is happening in the banking industry?"

NationsBank's acquisition of BankAmerica was approved by the regulators and became official by the end of September 1998. On Thursday, October 15, 1998, it was noted by the *Wall Street Journal* that third-quarter earnings for the new BankAmerica plunged 78 percent to $374 million. Net losses were attributed to a securities trading account shared by the old BankAmerica with a New York investment firm, volatile global markets, and from the costs of restructuring associated with the merger.[19] It was suggested that NationsBank's management team tended to be more conservative in its financing and trading business dealings than the old BankAmerica team.

The next day, the *Wall Street Journal* reported that executives from both NationsBank and BankAmerica had been aware of the losses at the high-risk trading company as early as August. As noted, "The merger closed on Sept. 30 without any public disclosure about the extent of the losses."[20] Chief Financial Officer Jim Hance said, "There was no way to preannounce this without totally jeopardizing the loan amount to the customer. It would have been totally irresponsible and exacerbated the loss, jeopardizing the customers. We are talking about a moving target of the highest order." Hance had been CFO for NationsBank prior to the merger.

According to the *Wall Street Journal* article, many accountants argue that any event or news that might affect a company's earnings, positively or negatively, anywhere from 5 percent to 10 percent, should be considered "material" and disclosed by corporate management. "Mr. Hance disagreed that the disclosure was large enough to be considered material. 'It's a big number but it's not material to a company that is as big as BankAmerica,' he said." The article went on to point out that "analysts, who were as surprised as investors by Wednesday's announcement, criticized the bank's handling of the situation. 'In terms of earnings-expectation management, this is not a great case study, to put it mildly,' said Judith Kraushaar, a banking analyst at Merrill Lynch & Co."[21]

The next day, David Coulter, the former chairman of BankAmerica who had become president for the combined operation, resigned, with an estimated $30 million buyout package. There was speculation that the former NationsBank chairman had asked for his resignation. Ken Lewis's name was floated once again as McColl's replacement upon the current chairman's imminent retirement. Additional layoffs to address the third-quarter decline in profits were also expected. Analysts surmised that NationsBank executives would solidify their positions further with the new company. As noted in the *New York Times*, rift between the different management teams had become increasingly more apparent as the merger unfolded: "When a senior executive at the old BankAmerica asked to meet his new boss from NationsBank before being reassigned, he was told no and chided for not being a team player."[22]

On November 3, 1998, *American Banker* reported that the new

BankAmerica was facing at least sixteen lawsuits filed by shareholders alleging a failure to disclose the extent of third-quarter losses. Litigation attorney Jonathan Albert was quoted as saying, "There is a positive goal of responsible corporate behavior that these lawsuits tend to generate. By filing them, one would encourage a more responsible corporate ethic than is the case here."[23] Bank of America would eventually settle the suit from shareholders for an estimated $490 million.[24]

On November 6, 1998, the *Wall Street Journal* reported that 150 jobs would be eliminated as BankAmerica reduced its trading and derivative operations. "We did an analysis which showed that the returns were not (high) enough to justify our being in this business," a BankAmerica spokeswoman said."[25] It was also announced that BankAmerica was reviewing its other trading businesses as a result of the merger and trading losses tied to the recent turmoil. More cutbacks were expected. Consultants to help with the analysis and restructuring initiatives were also a good bet.

The new BankAmerica Corporation reported a 20 percent decline in 1998 profits, citing a slowdown in the global market and losses in investment banking. For the most part, these problems were attributed to policies and investments made by the old BankAmerica prior to the merger.[26] More layoffs were expected. On March 8, 1999, it was reported in the *Wall Street Journal* that the three top executives from the new BankAmerica were voted a 29 percent cut in bonuses by the board of directors as a result of reduced operating earnings.[27]

A December 6, 2000, press release from Bank of America warned of reduced earnings estimates for the fourth quarter of 2000 due to bad loans, deterioration of credit quality, and overall growth in nonperforming assets. Loan losses were expected to more than double in the fourth quarter. Vice Chairman and CFO James Hance added, "Bank of America is budgeting for significantly higher loan losses and credit losses in 2001." In printed remarks from the December 6, 2000, Goldman Sachs and Financial Services Conference, President Ken Lewis indicated that Bank of America was moving from an acquisition-expense driven model to a customer-focused revenue driven model. "The transition period produced some hiccups," he said. He added, "We are moving at Internet speed in the e-commerce area."[28] The announcement set off a big retreat on Wall Street.[29] Net income eventually dropped 27 percent in the forth quarter of 2000, but it still surpassed Wall Street's significantly lowered expectations.[30]

Hugh McColl addressed the Little Rock Regional Chamber of Commerce at their annual meeting on December 7, 2000. He was introduced by his good friend and hunting partner Joe Ford, the Chairman and CEO of Alltel Inc. Ford's Alltel had previously donated a million dollars to the

Clinton Presidential Library.[31] McColl announced that Bank of America was donating $500,000 to the Clinton Library.[32] On December 22, 2000, NASCAR team owner and Charlotte car dealer Rick Hendrick received a presidential pardon. Hendrick had been convicted of mail fraud. According to Robert F. Moore of the *Charlotte Observer*, Hugh McColl had provided an affidavit requesting the pardon.[33]

Bank of America posted a 17 percent decline in first-quarter 2001 earnings. The *Wall Street Journal* headline read, "Bank of America, Bank of New York Meet Expectations." Lori Appelbaum from Goldman Sachs said, the "Bank of America first quarter wasn't bad," and suggested that there were encouraging trends.[34] The firm of Goldman Sachs was a paid "advisor" on the NationsBank-Bank of America merger, as well as other matters.

In spite of some initial "hiccups," based on the accumulation of bricks and mortar, Hugh McColl had accomplished his goal of building the number one bank. One could argue that in the dawning age of e-commerce and virtual banking, Bank of America had become the largest dinosaur. Hugh's consulting friends and advisors played their part in birthing the beast.

✷ ✷ ✷

THE MYTH OF TECHNOLOGY

Another important aspect to mergers that should not be taken lightly is the challenge associated with technology integration. Many have attributed the success of the U.S. economy in the 1990s to new technology. Yet, studies indicate that anywhere between 70 and 90 percent of corporate information technology projects of the 1990s failed.[35] Many of these projects were cancelled before completion. Those completed often ran well beyond projected timelines, and came in significantly overbudget. Most of these projects involved consultants, in either a recommendation or an implementation role. More important, they point to failure on the part of management. No one wants to admit the patient is dead: not the consultant, not the manager who hired the consultant, and not the employee who puts his job at risk if he speaks up.

There is a distinction that needs to be made between technology spending and investments. While many companies like Bank of America have spent heavily in technology, much of it has been on the integration of legacy systems, rather than the migration to innovative solutions. There is a major difference, for example, between "Web-enabled" and "Web-based." Connecting old legacy systems to a Web portal can be inefficient.

It is often only a short-term solution. It can significantly add to costs over time, as traditional back-office operations remain in tact. Front-end Web-enabled access now requires around-the-clock customer service. Many companies that boast of technology investments have only added window dressing. It was still business as usual in the back office. They have not affected their competitiveness with technology.

Corporate executives who often hype "technology improvements" have learned that layoffs have more of an immediate impact on reducing expenses and improving profitability. As noted in a April 13, 1998, article in the *New York Times*, concerning technology involved with a proposed Citicorp-Travelers merger, "The synergies that Citicorp and Travelers promise will result from the huge merger the two companies announced last week may be a while coming. That is because it is likely to be a decade, at least, before their computer systems can be fully integrated. Citicorp itself has tried for ten years to merge the computers in its banks in 100 countries into one happy family, a task that remains far from complete. Meanwhile, the computers holding Travelers insurance policies are barely on speaking terms with those at the company's brokerage and credit units."[36] In December 2001, Citicorp would announce plans to spin-off Travelers.

Often the technology platform used for consolidation is antiquated and incapable of meeting long-term needs. Unfortunately, company employees in the know who come forward to raise potential issues or suggest alternatives different from the party line put themselves at considerable risk. It was only speaking on a condition of anonymity that, back when plans for the Citicorp-Travelers merger were first announced, a technology executive from one of the companies said with regard to the people and technology resources proposed for making the Citicorp-Travelers merger possible, "We just don't have the bandwidth to look at a new deal."[37]

While NationsBank and BankAmerica share more of a similar business portfolio, both of these institutions were still in the process of integrating and streamlining systems prior to the merger. NationsBank was still trying to digest business acquired from both Boatmen's and Barnett. In an April 20, 1998, article in *Computerworld*, it was pointed out that a NationsBank spokesperson said most of the BankAmerica systems would be rolled into "a NationsBank computing model." This was not so surprising, considering the commanding position of NationsBank leadership within the new organization and all the hype around Model Bank.[38]

In addition to holding the top management role and a controlling number of board members, the former president of NationsBank, a major proponent of Model Bank, was named head of global retail banking for the new BankAmerica. The article also suggested that "although Nations-Bank has already standardized its branches on a single retail banking platform, BankAmerica will have to consolidate four disparate retail banking systems into the NationsBank architecture." When asked about this, a NationsBank spokesperson said, "It would not be an issue merging NationsBank and BankAmerica systems simultaneously.[39] While NationsBank and BankAmerica had been cooperating on various technology initiatives in the past, these comments were made a week after the announced merger, well before any comprehensive, detailed analysis for integrating systems could possibly have been done.

On November 18, 1998, the *Wall Street Journal* noted that many major banks involved in growth through acquisition were raising their estimates as to integration expenses as well as costs associated with Y2K compliance: "Part of the reason the cost has risen, some analysts say, is that banks have underestimated the sheer size of the problem. BankAmerica, for instance, has identified 24,000 separate business operations that may need to be fixed. In addition, banks not only have to reprogram their own computers, they have to make sure many of their corporate clients are addressing the problem as well. Regulators have been pressing banks for months to assess the potential credit risk of borrowers that aren't prepared. 'Banks really didn't realize all the things they'd have to coordinate,' said Lou Marcoccio, research director for Gartner Group, a consulting firm in Stamford, Connecticut." BankAmerica's revised estimate for Y2K programming fixes alone were reported to have increased 10 percent, to $550 million.[40] Instead of investing these funds in new technology, they were needed for integrating and fixing legacy systems.

From the beginning, technology had been touted as a critical element for making the BankAmerica-NationsBank merger possible. In his remarks to shareholders, just prior to the merger becoming official, Hugh McColl said, "Our customers are the defining element of this merger. In all our markets, we'll be the convenience leader, with 4,800 banking centers, almost 14,000 ATMs, and the most advanced telephone and computer banking products and services in the industry. Our customers also will experience the true value of interstate banking. With our combined financial and technological strength, customers will have access to the best products and services when they want . . . where they want . . . and how they want. At the same time, our business customers will benefit from the capital they need to grow . . . a full range of traditional and investment banking products and services . . . advanced technology that is increasing speed, efficiency and value in managing investments as well as collections and payment systems. . . ."[41]

As in the past, Model Bank received considerable credit for much of the advanced technological capabilities required for the merger. It was suggested by senior executives that Model Bank would provide the necessary infrastructure for making comprehensive interstate banking a reality. As stated in *American Banker*, October 26, 1998, "A senior executive of BankAmerica Corp. used a slogan reminiscent of the 1992 presidential campaign to stress the importance of having a strong technological backbone. 'It's the infrastructure.'" The article went on to point out that according to this executive, who also came from NationsBank, Model Bank was the linchpin for making a complete integration of NationsBank and BankAmerica possible within two years. As noted by the article "The merger partners will benefit from NationsBank's work on the retail banking infrastructure it called Model Banking." The executive compared it to the interstate highway system built in the 1950s. Having Model Bank in place, he suggested, made it possible for bank executives to focus on other pressing requirements. "We spend a lot of time thinking about what will make maximum use of what we create," he said.[42]

It was as if the NationsBank's Model Bank program with major components outsourced to Andersen-Alltel was highly adaptable, infinitely scalable, and completely capable of meeting banking customer needs from coast to coast for years to come. Who from NationsBank would dare say otherwise? The inherent performance and capacity issues associated with Model Bank could be funneled into funding requests for yet another new project—"the BankAmerica Transition Project." When third-quarter 1998 losses were reported, it was the problems inherited from the old BankAmerica that were highlighted, leading to the abrupt resignation of the former chairman. Also buried in those reported losses was a $519 million after-tax charge to cover additional transition costs.[43]

As noted in *Computerworld*, "It could take years before the players in last week's spectacular bank mergers reap any cost savings from systems consolidation, according to battle-scarred CIOs and industry analysts."[44] They argued that there was too much risk involved attempting to merge systems. This of course is a much different slant than the public statements issued by NationsBank officials and other personnel. In spite of assurances from NationsBank executives regarding the capabilities of the Model Bank program, the size and complexity of combined operations significantly stretched the capabilities of Model Bank.

As part of the merger public relations campaign, Model Bank was hailed as the advanced technology solution critical for making the merger economics work. NationsBank, according to analysts, could absorb Bank of America in an accelerated timeframe, making it a truly nationwide bank, while at the same time eliminating costs.

Bank of America announced in late 1999 that it was delaying the conversion of the newly acquired Bank of America systems to Model Bank until 2001. "Then it announced another delay two years ago (2000), and industry watchers called that a setback for the company."[45] The bank predictably turned to other proven methods of cost savings. Another round of layoffs were announced in early July 2000. The target was an additional 10,000 people. It was reported by the *New York Times* that savings from the layoffs were expected to be used to improve Internet offerings, promote brand name, and improve services.[46] Bank President Ken Lewis announced that electronic banking would become a top priority. Elaborating, he pointed out that in addition to Internet focus, there would be emphasis on imaging technology for scanning checks. The president of the Service Company was named head of BankofAmerica.com. During the April 25, 2001, Annual Meeting for the new Bank of America, Hugh McColl retired and Ken Lewis, the father of Model Bank, the engine credited for making the new Bank of America possible, succeeded him as chairman.[47] In his comments, Lewis signaled major changes to come in the redesign of banking processes and in the building of new systems. At the same time, he indicated that company would maintain its traditional values and work ethic:

> But I still believe there are some things about this company that will never change. These are the things that got us to where we are today. Aggressiveness and a fierce desire to win. A strong bias for action and a knack for creating solutions—in the marketplace and in the many communities where we do business. A spirit of innovation and ingenuity, always searching for and finding a better way to get things done. A solemn commitment to looking after the desires of our customers, the interests of our shareholders, and the needs of our associates.[48]

On April Fools Day, April 1, 2002, Bank of America announced that Model Bank conversion of the West Coast branches would be put off indefinitely. "A spokesman for Bank of America said executives had decided that a conversion would be too expensive and that the money could be used elsewhere."[49]

There was a deafening silence from Wall Street. Is "deafening silence" an oxymoron? Perhaps by now they had been desensitized after all the previous false starts and postponements. Yet Model Bank was critical in the justification of the merger between NationsBank and Bank of America, which had received considerable Wall Street support at the time. As Ruchi Madan, PaineWebber's top banking analyst had said in August 1998, "We expect (NationsBank) management to illustrate that it will move aggressively to integrate BankAmerica—including moving up the installation of 'Model Bank.'"[50] According to the *San Francisco Business Times*, Madan had also stated in a research report that the Model Bank anticipated cost-savings were as much as $500 million, and a significant factor in prompting the merger.[51]

Even with Bank of America applying funds elsewhere, it was a good bet that a major portion would go to the consultants. The behind-the-scenes role that consultants will play in ongoing consolidation, integration, and day-to day-operations at Bank of America cannot be overlooked. They are not alone. Are we mortgaging our future to the mercenaries?

NOTES

1. NationsBank Annual Report 1996.

2. "NationsBank and BankAmerica to Merge," Joint Release from Nations-Bank and BankAmerica, 13 April 1998, http://www.nations bank.com/news-room/press/1998/.

3. Carey Gillam, "NationsBank: $500M 'Model Bank' Paying Off," *American Banker*, 8 May 1997, 8.

4. Martha Brannigan, Nikhil Deogun, and Eleena de Lisser, "NationsBank Wins Bidding for Barnett," *Wall Street Journal*, 2 September 1997, A3, A5.

5. Ibid., A5.

6. "Over 20% of Branches in Florida to Be Shuttered," *Wall Street Journal*, 24 February 1998, B4; "Awaiting Results," *TheDailyDeal.com*, 24 May 2000, http://www.thedailydeal.com/features/special/A22952-2000May24.html.

7. Laura M. Holson, "Hands in a Lot of Markets and a Foot on Each Coast," *New York Times*, 14 April 1998, D10.

8. Aaron Elstein, "NationsBank and B of A Tie Advisors Fees to Stock Prices," *American Banker*, 5 August 1998, 1.

9. Robert L. Glass, *Software Runaways: Lessons Learned from Massive Software Project Failures* (Upper Saddle River, N.J.: Prentice-Hall, 1998), 171. Glass reviews a technology development effort at BankAmerica that failed for various reasons, including the consultants involved in the project. See also "BofA and Coopers & Lybrand Consulting Form Alliance On Purchasing Card System," BankAmerica Release, 5 February 1996, http://www.bankamerica.com/batoday/news52.html. Coopers & Lybrand would help promote the program to prospective bank customers, in addition to offering their own professional consulting services to revamp customer purchasing processes.

"BankAmerica Hires Consultant to Set Up Bad-Assets Subsidiary," *Wall Street Journal*, 12 August 1992, B2. Financial consultant was hired to help

BankAmerica absorb its $4.2 billion acquisition of Security Pacific Corporation. "BankAmerica Finds It Got a Lot of Woe With Security Pacific," *Wall Street Journal,* 22 July 1993, A6. While slashing close to 10,000 jobs, BankAmerica was accused of trying to avoid severance by forcing Security Pacific personnel department employees to take temporary jobs with a consulting firm. According to the article, the bank relented after protests.

10. "NationsBank and BankAmerica to Merge," Joint Release from Nations-Bank and BankAmerica, 13 April 1998, http://www.nationsbank.com/newsroom/press/1998/.

11. "CBS Evening News April 13, 1998," CBS, Inc. Transcript prepared by Burrelle's Information Services 13 April 1998, 2, http://www.burrelles.com/transcripts.

12. "2 Major Mergers Expected Today in Bank Industry," *New York Times*, 13 April 1998, A22.

13. Gary Gillam, "Brand Name to Be Unveiled in Ads Tonight," *American Banker*, 30 September 1998, 4.

14. "Nation's Largest Bank Chooses 'Bank of America," NationsBank press release, 1 October 1998, www.nationsbank.com/newsroom/press/1998.

15. "Remarks at National Press Conference Bank of America, Day One," 1 October 1998, www.nationsbank.com/newsroom/speeches.

16. William Safire, "Don't Bank On It," *New York Times*, 16 April 1998, A23.

17. Stephen E. Frank, "Consumers Wonder if Deals Will Deliver Better Service," *Wall Street Journal*, 14 April 1998, A3, A14.

18. Marilyn Geewax, "NationsBank Story Offers Chilling Reminder," *Atlanta Journal and Constitution*, 10 May 1998, R2.

19. Rich Brooks and Mitchell Pacelle, "BankAmerica Net Slides Unexpected 78%," *Wall Street Journal*, 15 October 1998, A3.

20. Rich Brooks and Mitchell Pacelle, "BankAmerica Knew in August of Trading Woes," *Wall Street Journal*, 16 October 1998), A3.

21. Ibid., A3.

22. Laura M. Holson, "BankAmerica President Says He Will Quit," *New York Times*, 21 October 1998, C1.

23. Carey Gillam, "BankAmerica Sued Over Hedge Fund Losses," *American Banker*, 3 November 1998, 6.

24. Carrick Mollenkamp, "Bank of America to Settle Shareholder Suits," *Wall Street Journal*, 11 February 2002, A11.

25. "BankAmerica Will Cut 150 Jobs as It Reduces Derivatives Operations," *Wall Street Journal*, 6 November 1998, A9.

26. Matt Murphy, Rick Brooks, and Joseph B. Cahill, "BankAmerica Profit Slides 20% Amid Turbulent Markets," *Wall Street Journal*, 20 January 1999, B4.

27. Rich Brooks, "BankAmerica Cuts Bonuses of 3 Executives, *Wall Street Journal*, 8 March 1999, B12.

28. "Bank of America Provides Earnings Guidance for Fourth Quarter and 2001," 6 December 2000, www.bankofamerica.com/newsroom/press; "Bank of

America Presentation at the 11th Annual Goldman Sachs CEO Conference," 6 December 2000, www.bankofamerica.com/news room/press.

29. Robert D. Hershey Jr., "Profit Warnings By Bank of America Sets Off Big Retreat," *New York Times*, 7 December 2000, B1, http://www.nytimes.com.

30. "Three Big Bank Report Mixed Fourth-Quarter Results," *Wall Street Journal*, 17 January 2001, B4.

31. John Brummett, "Ethics of a Presidential Library," *Morning News*, 13 February 2002, www.nwaonline.net/pdfarchive/2001/February13/2-13-0/%20A8.pdf.

32. "Remarks to the Little Rock Regional Chamber of Commerce 2000 Annual Meeting," 7 December 2000, http://www.bankofamerica. com/newsroom.

33. Robert F. Moore, "Hendrick receives pardon in federal case," *That's Racing*, 22 December 2000, http://www.thatsracin.com/00/docs/1223 pardon.htm.

34. "Bank of America, Bank of New York Meet Expectations," *Wall Street Journal*, 17 April 2001, A4.

35. "To Hell and Back," 1 December 1998; "When Bad Things Happen to Good People," 15 October 1997; "Software as Socialware," 1 March 1996; *CIO Magazine*, http://www.cio.com/archive

36. Saul Hansell, "Citicorp and Travelers Face A Tangle of Technology," *New York Times*, 13 April 1998), D1.

37. "Clash of Technologies in Merger," *New York Times*, 13 April 1998, D4.

38. Thomas Hoffman, "Y2K fixes will hold up bank merger payoffs," *Computerworld*, 20 April 1998, 16.

39. Ibid., 16.

40 "Many Banks Are Raising Estimates For Costs of Year-2000 Computer Fixes," *Wall Street Journal*, 18 November 1998, A3.

41. "Remarks at the Special Meeting of Shareholders," NationsBank, 24 September 1998, www.nationsbank.com/newsroom/speeches

42. Drew Clark, "B of A Says It's on the Fast Track to Systems Integration, *American Banker*, 26 October 1998, 20.

43. "BankAmerica Net Slides Unexpected 78%," *Wall Street Journal*, 15 October 1998, A3.

44. "Y2K fixes will hold up bank merger payoffs," *Computerworld*, 20 April 1998, 1.

45. "Bank of America Defers Western Plans, *Charlotte Observer*, 1 April 2002.

46. Diana B. Henriques, "BankAmerica to Cut Up to 6.7% of Work Force, or 10,000 Jobs," *New York Times*, 29 July 2000, http://search.nytimes.com.

47. "Media Advisory—Bank of America Annual Meeting of Shareholders," 25 April 2001, http://www.bankofamerica.com/newsroom/.

48. "2001 Annual Meeting of Shareholders, Kenneth D. Lewis, Bank of America, Remarks upon assuming office of chairman and chief executive officer," 25 April 2001, http://www.bankofamerica.com/newsroom/speeches/speech.cfm?SpeechID=speech.20010425.04.htm.

49. "Bank of America Defers Western Plans," *Charlotte Observer*, 1 April 2002, http://www.Charlotte.com/mld/Charlotte/need_to_map/2979175.htm.

50. Mark Calvey, "Paine Webber: Time to Take Stock in NationsBank, Norwest," *San Francisco Business Times*, 14 August 2002, http://sanfrancisco.bizjournals.com/san-francisco/stories/1998/08/17/newscolumn5.html.

51. Ibid.

EPILOGUE

SUMMARY AND RECOMMENDATIONS

The Enron scandal that broke at the end of 2001 provided the final deathblow to the "irrational exuberance" associated with the American business economy of the late 1990s.[1] There was a general sense that things were amiss. A May 6, 2002, John A. Byrne cover story article in *Business Week*, "Crisis in Corporate Governance," highlighted issues such as "excessive pay, weak leadership, corrupt analysis, and questionable accounting." Faith in American corporations, the article suggested, "hasn't been so strained since the early 1900s, when the public's furor over the monopoly powers of big business led to years of trust-busting by Theodore Roosevelt."[2]

Corporate greed, unscrupulous business practices, and insider cronyism were back, or perhaps they never left. Gordon Gekko, the Michael Douglas character in Oliver Stone's 1987 movie, *Wall Street*, who proclaimed, "Greed is good," had gotten a face-lift. It was a kinder, gentler form of greed in the 1990s. One of the new wrinkles in the market expansion that took place was the increased reliance on consultants in almost every aspect of American business. Corporate decision makers made more money as independent consultants, who helped create a buffer between them and corporate employees, "validated" executive decisions and usually proclaimed them in the best interest of the stockholder. Wall Street analysts agreed. Things seemed to be working great while the stock market soared. Some of those decisions appear questionable now.

As noted by David Maister in his May 2002 interview with *Fast Company* cofounder Alan Webber, consultants played a central role at Enron, as well as other major corporations racked by problems. "If there is a common thread in the scandals of the day, it is the central role played by the nation's elite professional services firms. McKinsey & Co., the bluest of blue-chip consulting firms, gave Enron its strategy—and even its former CEO, Jeffrey Skilling's model for Enron was to pattern it after a professional-services firm, to elevate the company above the lesser status of an energy company to the more rarified air of a knowledge-based, asset-light company. Andersen, among the most respected accounting firms, vouched for Enron's books. Enron was chock-full of MBAs and refugees from accounting and consulting firms."[3]

Previously, much of the success of the boom economy of the 1990s had been attributed to technology combined with globalization. In a feature article in the July 1997 issue of *Wired*, editors Peter Leyden and Peter Schwartz, of Global Business Network, predicted that the boom would continue well into the new millennium. "These two metatrends—fundamental technological change and a new ethos of openness—will transform our world into the beginnings of a global civilization, a new civilization of civilizations, that will blossom through the coming century."[4]

Yet, as noted by Peter Passell in the *New York Times*, December 25, 1997, issue, "Yes microprocessors are ubiquitous, revolutionizing everything from inventory control to movie animation. Yes, the globalization of trade and investment has left America's service industries at the top of the heap. Yes, Wall Street leads the world in financing invention and spreading risk. But all that gee-whiz technology and organizational change has yet to make a dent in the measured growth in output per hour of work. Productivity growth in the sustained boom of the 1990s has averaged a bit more than 1 percent, about the same as the sustained sluggish 1970s and 1980s and less than half the pace of the 1950s and 1960s."[5]

It is important to keep in mind is that there is a distinction between technology spending and technology investment. No question lots of dollars were spent on technology in the 1990s. We only need to look at what happened with the dot-coms to recognize that much of the spending didn't pay off. Wasted dollars spent in technology were not exclusively limited to dot-com ventures. A significant amount of the dollars spent in technology were spent in corporations to employ consultants, or based on consultant recommendations on where to "invest." It now is almost certain that a good portion of those investments will never pay off as expected. Hiring consultants does not guarantee success, even when they bring expert knowledge and skills in specialized areas like technology.

The purpose for writing *Soldier of Fortune 500* is not to advocate getting rid of consultants. There are consultants who continue to give good and balanced advice and provide excellent services to clients. Whether you like consultants or not, American business today cannot make it without them. What business leaders need to learn is how to more effectively manage consultants and how to avoid the pitfalls that can occur when consulting agendas play out to the detriment of the corporate client. Correct this, and business will be better for it.

As I think my experiences help demonstrate, several accepted business assumptions of the past decade concerning consultants are no longer valid. In my opinion, before consultants can be more effectively managed, three basic myths that represent major themes within this book must be dispelled. The first myth is that "consultants consult." By definition, consulting is the service of advising.[6] An increasingly fewer number of individuals and firms calling themselves "consultants" strictly consult.

The problem is that just as auditors expanded their offerings into consulting in the pursuit of higher fees, consultants have expanded their services beyond advising. Since the early 1990s, they have become the de facto answer for solving business problems—not only recommending solutions, but also often implementing them. Some no longer advise at all. In those cases, where advising services are still offered, the advice is simply the means for gaining a foot in the door. It becomes a mechanism for gaining an unfair competitive advantage for winning follow-on business, such as lucrative integration projects, contract programming, or outsourcing. The front-end analysis allows the "consultants" to get in early and gain an immense advantage in winning future contracts over other vendors—they in essence set the table for themselves. For example, Accenture, Ltd., formerly Andersen Consulting, reported $9.8 billion in new bookings for the first half of its fiscal year 2002, noting that nearly half of this represented "transformation outsourcing engagements." Joe W. Forehand, chairman and CEO of Accenture, said that the revenue from outsourcing was "demonstrating the strong demand for our unique ability to help clients improve business performance and bring their ideas to life."[7] Advising on ideas may be considered consulting. Implementing them is something else.

These firms are not consultants. Their core business is implementation. Corporate managers would be better off reclassifying them as vendors and treating them accordingly. Allowing them to play an advisory role in defining requirements and evaluating vendor alternatives, while at the same time the consultant plans to compete for follow-on contracts, is setting the client up for potential problems and abuses. Most business managers would rarely ask a firm classified strictly as a vendor to help define requirements. It would be the equivalent of giving a salesperson your checkbook and asking her to help you determine how much you need to spend.

Yet vendors operating under the label of consultants are often hired to do just this. We should not be surprised if the lion's share of recommendations benefits the consultants and their "friendly" business partners. Vendors unaligned with consultants may be more inclined to file a "bid protest" with the corporate client as prospects for future business continue to diminish. They can argue that this represents an unfair business practice fraught with conflicts of interest.

The second myth, closely related to the first, is that consultants are objective. Even those firms providing strictly advice and analysis are rarely objective. Conultants often become preoccupied with extending current contracts or winning the next one. If the consultant's primary goal is to secure additional billable hours, then it can become more important to provide recommendations that the sponsoring executive would like, versus being objective.

Almost all consultants have a bias. If the consultant previously worked for a vendor, say IBM, as in my case, you can bet that certain biases based on the IBM experience come with me. It might be pro-IBM; it might be negative, depending on my personal experiences or the circumstances under which I left. Nonetheless, my experience colors my perspective. A person trained as an Oracle specialist might be less inclined to recommend a database from Sybase, or IBM's DB2. As suggested in the book, having a bias is not necessarily a bad thing. Bias represents opinion. If consultants have no opinion, why hire them?

The key is for management to solicit information about the consultants and to get them to "lay their cards on the table." Understanding their background, for example, can tell you much about where they are coming from and where they may want to go with the project at hand. Is their inclination to provide analysis or contract programming? Are they formerly aligned with certain business partners, and who are they? What have they identified in their recent literature, press releases, and Web site as their business goals and areas they specialize in? If a firm begins to identify themselves in their literature as specializing in "outsourcing," this might be a good indication where they will want to take recommendations for the project.

The third myth is that hiring a consultant can increase your chances of success in conducting major business initiatives. Consultants are often hired because it is believed that they can bring specialized skills and knowledge to augment the current employee work force. They often can and do, but there appears to be no correlation between hiring a consultant and increasing the win rate on completing successful projects. In fact, the opposite may be true. As previously noted, today consultants are involved in almost all major IT project initiatives at major companies, and yet over 70 percent of those projects fail when classified as missing deadlines, missing budgets, or failing to meet objectives. [8]

Consultants are also involved in almost all corporate mergers. Studies indicate that almost 50 percent of corporate mergers and acquisitions fail to achieve the anticipated benefits, which often becomes the justification for the merger.[9] A study by McKinsey & Company concluded, "Making mergers work is an acid test for any executive team. Study after study has shown that up to 80 percent of M&A deals completed during the 1990s failed to justify the equity that funded them."[10] In my opinion, there are several reasons for this. The first is that consultants often set expectations in the preengagement selling phase. Marketing hype obscures reality. Gaining market and regulatory acceptance for a proposed client merger may lead to aggressive claims based on questionable assumptions regarding savings from consolidations or new market strength.

There are generally little or no consequences for the consultant if expectations aren't met, either on mergers or other projects. Furthermore, failing to meet expectations can actually work to the advantage of consultants in the form of more prolonged contracts and follow-on engagements. Because engagements, primarily for the benefit of the consultants, are under nondisclosure, there is little risk of a failed endeavor blemishing the consultant's track record and impacting his ability to secure future work with other clients.

Increasing the success rate on consulting projects and initiatives requires making their goals and objectives more consistent with yours. Requiring written commitment on objectives from consultants, ongoing evaluation of performance, and making no follow-on financial commitments until objectives for each phase of the project are met can help restore accountability and improve results. It also helps to let them know there will be consequences—one way or the other—with all appropriate management within your organization and theirs receiving performance evaluations of the consulting manager and her team.

Getting consultants to work more as a team is only part of the problem. As noted by the International Data Corporation, the employee relationship with the company employer and sense of commitment changed considerably in the 1990s. Trust, loyalty, and commitment had all but disappeared between employees and employer.[11] Outsourcing jobs to consultants and other third parties has further eroded the relationship and negatively impacted morale. Employees who have survived the rounds of layoffs see consultants as a threat. Some consultants, as described in this book, have become very adept at playing one employee group off of another, taking on the role of an "independent" arbiter, and deciding which will be next to go.

Even more disturbing, for fear of losing their jobs, employees are reluctant to point out consulting abuses that can put sensitive assets or private customer information at risk. Employees turn a blind eye, claiming to have "heard nothing and seen nothing" while abuses are allowed to occur. This represents a major security risk, especially in today's world. In spite of all this, today's employees are probably still the most undervalued assets in the corporation. Management must work hard to get their "skin back in the game."

One way to start to do this is to mingle more, and to provide more formal and informal channels of communication. Audit the system (for lack of better terminology) by periodically talking with different employees, rather than relying on the filtered information about what is going on from consultants and corporate gatekeepers. Employees, based on their time and experience with the corporation, are often inherently more qualified to give advice than the consultants hired to provide "an independent," objective view.

As one corporate manager at First Union Bank recently said to me, "There is nothing that infuriates us more than when the executives hire these 'six-figure suits' to spend months coming up with an answer we could have given them over a cup of coffee." Before the consultants are engaged, start by asking the employees. At least try. If it turns out to be good advice, recognize the employee who provided it. If nothing comes from the exchange, that's OK, too. Simply asking can pay dividends in building back employee morale and eliminating unnecessary "analysis-paralysis" as information is transfered from employee to consultant.

You can further audit the system by hiring a "swat team" of consultants to evaluate your other consultants. It would need to be made clear on the front end that this is a short-term one-time-only project and the consultant hired to evaluate other consultants must also be charged with training employees with the skills to do this on an ongoing basis. It would need to be contracted to consultants with skills for doing the evaluation and auditing. Have them audit as to whether the consultants you contract with are complying with their contractual obligations, and ensure that they are not engaged in activities that represent conflict of interest for them or you. Corporations usually do a fairly thorough screening of employees, but not consultants. It is a mistake to assume the consulting firm has done this for you. Have the swat team do background checks to make sure the other consultants working for you are who they say they are and not underqualified, inexperienced, or, as preposterous as this might have once sounded, not some misguided "hacker" or worse bent on destruction who can gain easier access as a third-party business partner to sensitive data and other assets. The swat team consultants auditing other consultants should also check to make sure they have identified all standing business partnership arrangements that could impact their ability to evaluate analysis projects and provide the most appropriate service for your specific needs. Also be sure that you are getting the most qualified personnel possible, not someone who was previously warming the bench at their consulting firm.

You should tailor the engagement based on the industry you are in and your most pressing needs. A consultant with technology skills and strong in vendor analysis could be engaged to evaluate if you are making the right technology investments, versus merely spending technology dollars. She should audit projects and determine if there are some that should be taken off the life-support machines. If, for example, you are in banking, you may be faced with new federal regulations for detecting and protecting against money-laundering activities. You might want to utilize the swat team approach to make sure that all individuals involved in critical areas (both employees and third parties) have been properly vetted and understand all of the important aspects of doing the job right. In fact, you need to ensure that people with proper credentials and the right skills are handling all activities that involve critical banking functions and sensitive customer information appropriately, whether they be employees or consultants.

In too many companies, projects are managed by consultants. In some cases there is a figurehead executive sponsor on the organizational chart, but it is really the consultant project manager running the show. Consultants love figureheads, because as high level, bright, and well educated as they may be, they often don't have a clue about how the underpinnings of the business really works. Why? They didn't come up from the ranks. They may be business unit executives who don't understand technology—a ploy sometimes used by consultants on technology projects to shore up control and corporate dependency on the consultants. Every major corporate project should have an informed and experienced corporate manager at the helm—someone who really manages and is accountable for day-to-day execution, and someone who knows how things really work. Even if the project is run remotely with an outsourcing firm, an employee manager must be responsible for running the show and ensuring that things stay on track. It needs to be someone the consultants can't schmooze or work around.

The job must be one where the project manager has "responsibility with authority." This project manager should be the one who sets expectations and manages all participants, employees and consultants alike, before and during the project. The project manager should be the one person who reports on the project to higher-level managers—never the consultants. If consultants try to avoid responsibility and work around to another agenda, they should be reprimanded to first go to the project manager. Make these project managers the "Commanding Officers of Projects" (COPs). The COP position should be given to only qualified employee managers who can motivate and kick butt when necessary.

If after downsizing and reorganizations, no employees like this exist, then they need to be trained. The best place to look for trainers if they don't exist "in-house" is within your recently retired employee group. Samurais learn their skills from older, experienced warriors, committed to the cause, not mercenaries. Retirees on the pension plan have a vested interest in the future success of the business. If I haven't learned "nuttin" else, it's that the skills that count don't ever age. That's why all of the most successful military (real military) generals in the field to this day (even Japanese Samurais) still read *The Art of War* by Sun Tzu, a Chinese military genius who lived thousands of years ago. These skills are not a commodity. Samurais, in all cultures, know the best thing they can ever, ever do, is not about paying you back, in kind, as a "transaction" for services rendered. You never can pay your Samari mentors back. Take what you've learned from them, the best of them, and pass it on.

You can always augment the training with the latest and greatest understanding of the newest business, newest market conditions understanding, as well as the latest and greatest newest and most incredible "this is it that will blow away all the others" technology breakthroughs. I've been hearing that one since I was an IBM marketing trainee in the middle 1980s. Demand "skills transfer" as a primary deliverable in all consulting engagements. The COPs need to be given important and meaningful new status within the company. You can "Beta" test on a limited trial basis, and if it works for your company, get on with it.

The position of COP must become a position of status, recognized by employees and executives as the linkage, the person with management responsibility in the field who is approachable to employees and communicates regularly with executives. There should also be consequences. "Commanding Officer of Project" should not be a position created for the faint-hearted. Use attaining the position of COP for providing incentive to lower-level employees looking for new career opportunities within your company. In addition to standard project management responsibilities such as developing the budget, gaining and maintaining upper-management support, creating a communications program, holding people accountable to meet defined deliverables on a specific timeline, and approving all changes (all those mundane but important things), the project manager should also be responsible for providing on-the-job training to other employees. Not that I've put it in a financial analysis model, it's just I believe the cost of doing it this way will be significantly less than the cost of continuing to run failed projects.

The only way to ensure that the consultant is operating in the best interest of the company is vigilant management of the relationship and ensuring good communication between all affected levels of management, employees, and consultants. It is only when this is effectively done that exposures are minimized and consultants can be expected to provide services in the best interest of the company. Employees provide valuable knowledge of the business and need to be incented to work in concert with consultants—and vice versa. Corporate management must put provisions in place like those discussed here before it is too late.

One of the first things the new project managers need to do before engaging the consultants is to develop a very good understanding of what kind of service is required. Are there requirements for developing a strategy, increasing industry knowledge, technical skills for contract programming, or integration of legacy systems to new technology? It could conceivably be a combination of several services. Many consulting firms now claim to provide a comprehensive set of offerings from strategy through implementation, and sometimes for managing ongoing operations. What the company manager needs to understand is that consulting firms, with few exceptions and in spite of what they may claim, tend to specialize in one or two very specific areas and bring certain predictable strengths and weaknesses to the engagement. Company managers also need to remember that they have a fiduciary responsibility, and hiring a consultant does not eliminate their responsibility for the decisions that are made. The manager hiring a consultant is ultimately responsible for decisions the consultant makes in his behalf.

In the appendix, there is a Consultant Matrix. When companies look to engage consulting firms, it becomes critical to understand what kind of consulting firm it is, whether it is specialized in management consulting, vertical-industry consulting, or process consulting. The type of specialty will have an impact on the kinds of output and deliverables the client can expect.

Representative firms that fall into each of these categories are presented below as well as an assessment of strengths and weaknesses of these different types of consulting firms. The matrix represents general opinions of the author and may not hold as completely accurate in all sit-

uations. Today, there is a growing effort for consulting practices to provide more of a soup-to-nuts comprehensive set of offerings, from strategy
to systems integration. This has led to acquisitions and some organizational changes. Nevertheless, most of these firms still specialize in one of
the following categories and have only experienced limited success in
expanding into other areas. This is because of the inherent weaknesses
associated with the consulting methodology they employ.

Management Consultants

This group of consultants attempts to provide high-level strategy assessment and analysis. Representative firms would include McKinsey &
Company and Booz Allan. They provide fairly good in-depth analysis
and generally operate with high-level executive sponsorship. The weakness with some management-consulting firms is the difficulty in transferring the high-level strategies they devise to a workable implementation plan. Often, the client must contract with other firms for implementation of these strategies. These other firms may have completely
different objectives and limited ability to understand and execute the
strategic plan as devised by the management consultants. With increased
demand to accelerate time to market, management consultant firms can
no longer operate in a vacuum, assuming that strategy can then be
handed off to implementers. Advancements in technology need to be
considered as the strategy is developed. A more collaborative approach
between strategists and implementers is needed.

Process Consultants

Process firms attempt to use a model approach to produce deliverables.
For example, in the case of Gemini Consulting, a "Transformation
Model" is used to help a client develop a business process reengineering
strategy. The Monitor Company uses a model based on the work of
Michael Porter from the Harvard Business School, developed in the 1980s
on "Competitive Differentiation."[12] One of the unique characteristics of
the Monitor Company is that it tells its clients that it will not engage in
consulting activities with organizations having a competitive relationship with the client. Theoretically, if AT&T were a client, the Monitor
Company would not accept engagements with MCI. As hard to believe as
this might be, such a policy, though found in other professions, is uncharacteristic in consulting.

Process consultants specialize in "packaging" their materials and often argue that they can apply the model approach across various industries. A potential weakness is that the model can be inflexible and time consuming before it can be completed. Relevance to specific business requirements of the client can also be an issue.

Research Analysts

This group evaluates industry trends and specializes in writing in-depth analysis reports. Representative firms in the computer industry would include Gartner Group and Forrester Research. They attempt to provide an objective review of vendors and have significant influence on buying patterns. The analysis can sometimes assume a one-size-fits-all approach.

The research information is generally very technically oriented, with minimal business orientation. In technology, for example, it has become highly specialized and compartmentalized. A major weakness with some of these firms is the inability to recommend comprehensive solutions that address specific client needs. Instead, they present the "pluses" and "minuses" of various alternatives. "You could do this, however, you have to worry about that. If you do that, there is always the danger of this."

Vertical-Industry Consultants

Consultants in this grouping attempt to focus on specific industries such as banking or retail. The Big Five and IBM have initiated vertical-industry practices. These firms specialize in "best practice" methodologies, which they say are based on their previous experience in the industry. The weakness of this approach can be a "me, too" orientation that limits client differentiation. These firms will also claim to provide an "objective view," but most either sell products and services, or have partnerships with other firms that can provide these kinds of offerings. This seriously damages the possibility of an objective analysis. They are focused on gaining implementation contracts, which can make the alleged objective view suspect. There are often no team-based incentives and the culture may be one where getting ahead is based on maximizing the benefit to the partner in your chain of command. Cutting someone else's legs out from under him may be viewed as unavoidable collateral damage. This is a major cultural issue with some of these firms. Comparing partnership firms to stock-holding entities will not necessarily impact the culture. Another weakness is that they are reactive in selling. Vertical-industry consultants often sell based on the skills sitting on the bench versus proactive strategic consulting, attempting to exploit new market trends and technologies. Whereas some vertical-industry firms like the old Andersen Consulting model sold "the bright, innovative kids," others argue that they have consultants with "a minimum of thirteen years experience." This translates into much higher billing rates. The concept of a balanced team, with a smattering of rookies and veterans, similar to the baseball teams that usually win, seems to have been lost by most. In fact, in many of these firms, the concept of team itself is lacking.

Vertical-industry consultants will sometimes propose partnership arrangements with competitors within a particular industry. They argue that the real problem is "out there" in the form of new competitive market entrants, and there is much to be gained through collaboration to minimize this threat and pool costs of implementing their proposed solutions. A major weakness in this approach is that while it might temporarily insulate traditional companies from change, it can help improve the position of new, more nimble entrepreneurial competitors who are not burdened by traditional business assumptions or protecting the current infrastructure. Most of the benefits are for the consultants who can broker the partnerships and market one solution to multiple clients. Imitation replaces creativity and innovation.

There are two major weaknesses that all categories of consultants generally share. The first is the inability to synthesize strategy and technical implementation. Today, given our dependence on technology, it is hard to imagine implementing a strategic plan or a major reengineering effort without some technology content. Strategists, business process consultants and technical integrators generally have very different skill sets. Even when they come from the same firm, there is usually a significant communications gap.

Developing technology architectures, the ability to "operationalize" a strategy into a technical implementation plan, is still a glaring weakness in most of these firms. Yet they all claim to provide it. In a dynamic environment with so much importance placed on time to market and profitability, there is a need to employ collaborative approaches versus the typical linear paths where strategist's hand off to technology implementers, and never the twain shall meet. Collaborative projects also require strong coordinated management and the use of real-time online management tools. Management must foster buy-in from all team members, employees and consultants alike, for meeting milestones, objectives, and goals. Keeping honest and direct communication throughout the process is also critical for success.

A second major weakness in all categories as listed is the lack of "skills transfer." A major objective of most consulting firms is to increase client dependency. Very often, as I have noted, this can lead to outsourcing contracts that eliminate company employees and replace them with consultants or other vendors. While outsourcing ancillary programs, functions, and operations can make good business sense, it should never be the de facto solution, regardless of what some consultants might say, for core business activities. Consultants will provide education on specific technical topics or projected future industry directions when asked to do so. They generally do not attempt to transfer the skills of the consultant to the employee unless required by the client. Consultant studies are often filled with "FUD" (Fear, Uncertainty, and Doubt) to create an environment that will spawn ongoing consultant dependencies and future contracts.

SO WHAT TO DO?

As suggested in this book, no consultants can be completely objective, certainly not this author. It is my opinion, based on experience, that there are two firms who clearly break from the pack. They are PowerPlus of America and IBM. They provide solutions with emphasis on achieving business results and encouraging teamwork and consensus building.

These are critical elements for improving the success rate of projects. Obviously, there are other firms that can provide high value. PowerPlus Systems Corporation of America and IBM are the ones that I am most familiar with, and most comfortable recommending to clients.

PowerPlus Agile Modeling from PowerPlus of America

PowerStart can resolve conflict, establish priorities, and accelerate results with a proven methodology that makes the typical front-end-loaded "analysis-paralysis" approach used by most consulting firms obsolete. They are very effective at bringing employees and consultants together by establishing common objectives aligned to corporate goals, improving shared knowledge, and producing cross-organizational team-based action plans. This approach is one of the most effective ways of gaining buy-in from the various groups impacted by proposed recommendations. Employees are today one of the most undervalued assets in the corporation. With the advent of consulting playing such a central role in projects, employees are rarely fully utilized or properly motivated to make project output successful for the long term. PowerPlus Agile Modeling can accelerate time to market and provide the framework for ongoing management of the project, benchmarking progress to preestablished goals and objectives. Beginning with PowerPlus and following the game plan it produces has proven to increase the win rate in implementing projects and new corporate initiatives.

IBM Professional Services

Managers looking to contract with a firm that emphasizes education and skills transfer as part of its culture, provides team incentives versus maximizing partner "wallet share," and is proactive in technology leadership, as opposed to reactive marketing of whatever skills happen to be on the bench, should give special consideration to IBM Global Services Consulting. IBM combines business knowledge with technology to provide comprehensive solutions that work. Collaborative management of complex projects is a major IBM strength. Given the emphasis in IBM on a rigorous certification process for consultants, and a track record in completing successful projects, few others can match IBM in performance and capabilities. They have consistently been best of breed for implementing major corporate initiatives and integration projects. "Respect for the individual" continues to be a core belief and practice at IBM.

* * *

TIPS ON MANAGING CONSULTANTS

The following represents some general recommendations that will prove effective in managing consultants, regardless of the type of firm the client plans to engage:

1. Consultants need to understand that as an agent of the corporation they must operate in the best interest of the corporate client. This needs to be clearly spelled out in the contract and periodic reviews should also be conducted to ensure compliance.

2. Potential competitive exposures need to be minimized. It can be very difficult to determine potential conflicts of interest resulting from consultants engaged with other clients. (In fact, many technology projects fail,

but they are hidden under the umbrella of "client confidentiality." Consultants will use confidentiality agreements to avoid disclosing potential conflicts of interest as they often sign contracts with firms engaging in direct competition within the same industry. If during the engagement they are willing to share confidential information from your competitors, you can be sure they will do the same with yours.) Contracts with consultants should be drawn as clearly spelled out work-for-hire arrangements. As part of contract negotiations, consultants should be asked to disclose any potential conflicts with competitors and the contract should prohibit disclosure of confidential information to others without expressed written consent. Proprietary, confidential information needs to be carefully safeguarded, and consultants need to be warned that they must comply with the corporate guidelines for confidentiality. All information viewed as sensitive by the client needs to be carefully established as proprietary property of the client. Material provided to consultants or developed as part of consultant contracts should be owned and copyrighted by the client. When in doubt, copyright the material and make it confidential. Failure to comply with confidentiality agreements should result in forfeiting both current and future contracts. The risk of potential legal action can also be used as a club. (See the sample confidentiality agreement in appendix E.)

3. Try to identify requirements prior to engaging the consultants. This may not always be possible, but get as much information as you can from your employees prior to bringing consultants in and letting them "repackage" information already available. "Joint application design" (JAD) sessions can help define requirements and gain group consensus. PowePlus is excellent here with its own unique approach. When consultants are engaged, management needs to be very specific as to what is expected in deliverables. Deliverables should be expected in phases throughout the project. Milestones based on specific timetables and results-oriented deliverables need to be put in place to measure the ongoing basis the effectiveness of consultants. Employees are measured. Consultants should be, too—and not by their own standards but by those of the client corporation.

4. Senior management needs to implement their own internal auditing processes to ensure that the packaged information received from consultants and staff assistants accurately reflects business conditions and requirements. One manager (or "Cop") should be appointed as a point person. The consultants must debrief this person on all activities. The

point person should provide ongoing communication with employees to ensure accuracy and consistency with the information provided by the consultants. This will help avoid consultants playing one group off against another for political gain.

5. Always implement a competitive bid process, even if you already have a strong preference for a particular firm and are planning to use it for all phases of a project. The government General Services Administration (GSA) provides guidelines for government contractors, and these guidelines can also be applied to private industry for building more integrity and safeguards into request for proposal (RFP) procedures. Competitive bid processes force consultants to think on their time as opposed to yours on how they will deliver their services. It can also help in keeping the costs more realistic and market sensitive, which will almost always be in the client's best interest. In cases where there is minimal in-house expertise, hiring an independent consultant to "validate" large consulting or integration proposals can help avoid long-term exposures. A short-term analysis contract by a qualified individual or firm who discloses in advance potential affiliations can minimize unnecessary problems and costs down the road that can result from sole-source engagements where the analysts who recommend solutions are also the solution implementers or affiliated with the implementers.

6. Consultants are often employed to resolve organizational conflict. Given that in these kinds of engagements most of the up-front analysis information comes from employees, in most cases it makes more sense to hire a facilitator with arbitration skills as opposed to a traditional consultant. A qualified facilitator can run a series of meetings with all relevant employees participating. At the conclusion of the session, the facilitator provides a report to all participants as well as executive management. If there are still conflicts that have not been resolved, executive management has information to make a final decision. This can save money and time, given that there is no longer a requirement to transfer considerable knowledge and skills from employees to consultants. This approach can minimize manipulation of the process and lead to consensus that is often missing at the end of consulting engagements. Again, JAD sessions and PowerPlus of America provide effective models for facilitation.

7. Clients should argue that if up-front education is needed so contractual consultants can perform duties, it should be performed "pro bono," since essentially the client is training the consultant. Otherwise, they are billing

you for on-the-job training that benefits them and may also benefit your competitors. This will also level the playing field for the competitive bid. Consultants will argue that once the client has employed them, they have an advantage in that they understand the client environment. They will argue that hiring a new firm will require additional investments in time and money to get the new firm up to speed. If a consulting firm can bring unique skills to the project, then it may be worth a few additional weeks for getting them up to speed, at their own cost, as opposed to relying on the incumbent firm. Consultants often benchmark clients and their competitors. Essentially, clients need to benchmark consultants on an ongoing basis.

8. Consultants should not be placed in a position to broker vendor deals for the client without strict rules and supervision. In most cases, using a consultant, as the middle person should be avoided. The consulting firm will almost always attempt to structure vendor contractual arrangements in its own best interest. This can result in higher costs and considerably more risk for the client.

9. Background, credentials, and references of consultants should be thoroughly checked for all consultants assigned to a project. Ask references about the core competencies and weaknesses they have observed first-hand so that contracts can be put in place to maximize benefit and reduce exposures. Corporate management should insist on reference contacts, not only for firms, but also for all individual consultants proposed for the assignment. It may be impractical to check all, but spot checks are a good way to ensure that you're not getting a complete complement of the "B" team. Make the consulting firm identify in advance the names and backgrounds of the individual consultants who will be assigned to the engagement and spell out what their job responsibilities will be. This will avoid common bait-and-switch tactics. It will also provide a good indication as to whom they have really worked for in the past, and the types of assignments.

10. Partners in consulting firms are generally responsible for "hooking" the client. Their primary focus during an engagement is securing the next contract. Nevertheless, clients pay high fees for partners during this process. Clients should not be paying for the consultants selling activities and this needs to be clearly spelled out. Many times consultants assigned to the engagement are often junior and middle level. Clients must remember that consultants recommend and sell what they know. If, for

example, consultants have client/server backgrounds and guidelines and requirements are not carefully spelled out, they will almost always recommend a client/server solution. Clients should always challenge consultant recommendations to ensure validity. No follow-on commitments should be made until work of the current engagement is satisfactorily completed. This will help keep their heads on the project versus focusing on selling the next one.

11. In technology procurement, the consultant often advises clients to implement a multivendor strategy. Clients should look to minimize the number of vendors they plan to use to reduce integration complexity and support issues. A one-vendor shop may be impossible to implement today, but clients should keep the number to a minimum and strive to select vendors that have good working relationships. One vendor should have primary responsibility for providing seamless support and service. For example, if Sun is a major incumbent vendor and part of the client's future plans, other vendors that have technology exchange alliances and long-standing service agreements with Sun should be given first priority. This can minimize costly integration work with incompatible products.

12. Do not be tempted to shift management decisions to consultants, and do not let them disparage or alienate employees. Employees can provide useful insights and hidden treasures that are overlooked, often until they are put in use by consultants to exploit their own ends. Don't let consultants "cherry-pick" your best employees. Contractual arrangements should be put in place to avoid letting consultant firms hire employees for a specified period of time extending after their contract is completed without written consent from the client.

13. Skills transfer should be considered as a required component for most consulting contracts. Change the dynamics from consultants learning from employees and create a more collaborative environment where consultants must provide training and education in areas where they are skilled. Most often employees know the business better than the consultant. The consultant must have some skills and knowledge, for example, Web-based technologies that can be shared. If they don't have skills and knowledge that can be shared, there is no reason for hiring them.

14. Question in advance consulting processes and methodologies. Employ processes that can bring people together—management, employees, and consultants—to establish priorities and drive results.

15. One last suggestion. When paying for consultant travel expenses, stipulate that they must fly coach. It will force them to mix with the real people.

Remember, say what you mean and always think team. Manage them, or they will manage you.

Steve Romaine

NOTES

1. "The Challenge of Central Banking in a Democratic Society," Remarks by Chairman Alan Greenspan at the Annual Dinner and Francis Boyer Lecture of the American Enterprise Institute for Public Policy Research, Washington, D.C., 5 December 1996 http://www.federalreserve.gov/boarddocs/speeches/1996/19961205.htm.

2. John A. Byrne, with Louis Lavelle, Nanette Byrnes, Marcia Vickers, and Amy Borrus, "The Crisis in Corporate Governance," *Business Week*, 6 May 2002, 69.

3. Alan M. Webber, "Are All Consultants Corrupt?" *Fast Company* (May 2002): 132.

4. Peter Schwartz and Peter Leyden, "The Long Boom: A History of the Future, 1980–2020," *Wired* (July 1997), http://www.wired.com/wired/archive/5.07/longboom.html.

5. Peter Passell, "Hidden in the Glitter of a Bountiful Economy, Problems Remain," *New York Times*, 25 December 1997, D1.

6. *Webster's New Universal Unabridged Dictionary*, s.v. "consultant."

7. "Accenture Reports Second-Quarter Results," 11 April 2002, http://www.accenture.com/xd/xd.asp?it=enweb&xd=_dyn/dynamicpressrelease_468.xml.

8. Tom Field, David Pearson, and Polly Schneider, "To Hell and Back," *CIO Magazine*, 1 December 1998, http://www.cio.com/archive/120198/turk.html; Tom Field, "When Bad Things Happen to Good People," *CIO Magazine*, 15 October 1997, http://www.cio.com/archive/101597/bad.html; Thomas H. Davenport, "Software as Socialware," 1 March 1996; *CIO Magazine*, http://www.cio.com/ archive/030196/dave.html.

9. Freda Turner, "Reasons why mergers and acquisitions can fail," *Business Journal of Jacksonville*, 25 August 2000, http://jacksonville.bcentral.com/jacksonville/stories/2000/08/28/smallb2.html; Rick Mauer, "Why Half of All Mergers Fail after the Honeymoon Ends," Mauer & Associates, http://www.beyondresistance.com/htm/2article/honeymoons.html; "How to Make Mergers Work?" *Economist*, 9 January 1999, 15, http://www.cio.com/archive.

10. Matthias M. Bekier, Anna J. Bogardus, and Timothy Oldham, "Mastering Revenue Growth in M&A," *McKinsey on Finance* (summer 2001): 1.

11. "1997 Worldwide and U.S. Consulting Marketing and Trends," *IDC: Consulting and Management Services* (Framingham, Mass.: IDC, 1997), 34.

12. Michael Porter, *Competitive Strategy: Techniques for Analyzing Industries and Competitors* (New York: Free Press, 1980)

APPENDIX

APPENDIX A:
CHECK LIST FOR HIRING A CONSULTANT

* Determine what you need. Create a list of your requirements, or utilize a firm such as PowerPlus of America to help in identifying and prioritizing. This will eliminate front-end loaded "analysis-paralysis" as part of consulting engagements.

* Identify what kind of project(s) is (are) required to meet your requirements. For example, will it require strategic planning, process reengineering, integration, contract programming, or something else?

* Determine what kind of consulting firm can best meet your needs: management consulting, process consulting, industry analysts, or vertical-industry integrators. The "Determining Best Consultant Fit" chart which follows may help.

* Contact a minimum of two or three firms that you believe have the necessary skills. Explain the scope, or send a request for proposal and ask them to submit a written response, including costs, time-frames, personnel, and the skills of personnel to be assigned. For large complex projects guidelines similar to those used by the U.S. General Services Administration (GSA) can help.

* Also ask for verifiable references.

* Evaluate responses compared to your needs and to the other responses.

* Create a list of questions based on responses. Clarify questions and potential issues, and seek missing information.

* Rank responses. Select your number-one choice and follow steps below. If you run into a showstopper, then start here with your next choice.

❊ Check references.

❊ Interview representative personnel who will be assigned to the project. Consulting firms may argue that this cannot be completely determined until contracts are finalized. Make sure they understand that the final contract will be contingent on your approval of assigned personnel. Make sure that all assigned personnel are carefully screened prior to final approval to avoid "bait and switch" tactics.

❊ Review contractual obligations, stressing the importance of compliance with corporate standards and confidentiality requirements.

❊ Ask the consulting firm to disclose any potential competitive conflicts of interest with other clients, as well as identifying subcontractors (if any) to be used on the engagement, as well as partnership arrangements with potential suppliers.

❊ Assign a strong corporate manager as program manager with both responsibility and authority. Strong management is required to ensure that consultants collaborate with employees and other consultants. This can minimize rework and accelerate the timeline for project completion. It is essential that consultants understand that the corporate manager will be in charge. The best case would include a program manager skilled in the specific project area.

❊ Review rules of the road to avoid surprises. For example, what is considered a workweek? For an integration project, when are personnel expected to arrive on site, when will they leave? (Firms will often employ consultants from out of town with travel time, Mondays and Fridays for example, are not always clearly identified within workweek assumptions.)

❊ Make sure consulting partners and senior personnel are focused on successful completion of project versus securing the sale of the follow-on project. If they want to sell, this time should not be subsidized as part of contract.

❊ Develop a list of deliverables expected at various milestones and upon completion of the project. Request periodic written status reports.

❊ Include skills transfer to employees as a required deliverable.

❊ Schedule a kick-off meeting prior to commencing the project and have the program manager schedule ongoing group meetings with both consultants and employees to avoid communications issues.

❊ Understand core competencies and potential exposures of consulting from the "Consultant Matrix" chart which follows "Determining Best Consultant Fit." Managers should maximize advantages and minimize exposures. Corporate management is the key to making projects that employ consultants successful.

APPENDIX B: Determining Best Consultant Fit

Representative Consulting Projects

Consulting Categories	Strategic Planning	Market Analysis	Requirements Identification	Program Management	Operational Resource Allocation	Process Re-engineering	Systems Planning	Vendor Analysis	Integration	Contract Programming	New Build
Management Consultants	✓	✓	✓								
Process Consultants				✓	✓	✓	✓				
Technology Research Analysts		✓	✓					✓			
Vertical Industry Consultants			✓	✓			✓		✓	✓	✓

The above chart reflects the point of view of the author based on his experiences and research and reflects generalities that could be open to other interpretations. Corporate managers need to create their own "firm specific" chart based on experiences and research, or hire for a limited engagement consultants who analyze other consultants, who will work with your team to help them pick the most appropriate firms for the projects at hand.

APPENDIX C: CONSULTANT MATRIX

Consultant Categories	Core Competency	Potential Exposures
Management Consultants	• Strategic Planning • Business Requirements Analysis • Operational Assessment • Executive Sponsorship	• Problem Assessment vs. Tangible Results • Limited Success in Operational & Technical Implementations • Expensive • Limited Skills Transfer
Process Consultants	• Process Reengineering • Modeling Helps Neutralize "Business as Usual" Biases • Applying Cross-Industry Knowledge • Graphic Presentation	• Methodologies Can Prove Inflexible • Time-consuming Process • Gaining Buy-in to New Methods • Limited Skills Transfer
Technology Research Analysts	• Forecasting Technology Trends • Market Analysis • Vendor Analysis • Perceived Objectivity • Influencing Buying Patterns	• Generally Not Tailored to Specific Client Needs • Techno Speak • Limited Business Orientation • Limited Skills Transfer
Vertical Consultants	• Industry Specific Knowledge • Systems Planning • Critical Mass • Best Practice Methodologies • Contract Programming • Integration	• Limited Objectivity • Tactical Implementation Focus • Limited Differentiation • Often Front End Loaded with Analysis-Paralysis • Long Development Cycles • Reactive Bench Selling • Limited Skills Transfer

The above chart reflects the point of view of the author based on his experiences and research and reflects generalities that could be open to other interpretations.

APPENDIX D:

Applying Traditional Management Assumptions to Consultants

(when most of their revenue comes from non-consulting, consider reclassifying)

The Conventional Vendor		The Consultant
Engaged after requirements have been defined	vs.	Often engaged to help determine requirements
Is hired after extensive checks of references, research	vs.	Often hired based on strength of brand name, relationship
Is usually hired with consensus	vs.	Hired by executive sponsor or subject expert
Limited access and closely managed, monitored	vs.	Is given a great deal of freedom by management

APPENDIX E:
CONFIDENTIALITY AGREEMENT FOR CONSULTANTS, CONTRACTORS, AND OUTSOURCED PROFESSIONALS

(printed with permission from donphin.com *)

This Confidentiality Agreement ("Agreement") is executed effective between _____, its subsidiaries, parents, successors and assigns ("Company") and _____, his/her/its, spouse, heirs, subsidiaries, parents, successors, assigns or other legal representative ("Signator"), as consideration for the establishment and/or continuation of their employment relationship and sharing of Confidential Material. The parties agree as follows:

Length of Agreement. This Agreement begins retroactively to the beginning of Signator's relationship with Company and remains in effect at all times during any consulting, partnering, or other business relationship between the parties and for the periods of time specified thereafter as set forth below. This Agreement does not create any form of continued business relationship other than as set forth in a separate written agreement signed and dated by all parties.

Representation and Warranties. Signator represents and warrants that their relationship with Company will not cause or require he/she/it to breach any obligation to, agreement, or confidence related to confidential, trade secret and proprietary information with any other person, company or entity. Further, Signator acknowledges that a condition of this relationship is that he/she/it has not brought and will not bring or use in the performance of his/her/its duties at Company any proprietary or confidential information, whether or not in writing, of a former employer without that employer's written authorization. Breach of this condition results in automatic termination of the relationship as of the time of breach. Except as may be noted on the back of the signature page hereof, there are no inventions of Signator heretofore made or conceived by Signator that Signator deems to be excluded from the scope of this Agreement, and Signator hereby releases Company from any and all claims by the Signator by reason of any use by Company of any invention heretofore made or conceived by Signator.

---

*The above confidentiality agreement for consultants, contractors, and outsourced professionals was created by Donald A. Phin, Esq., www.donphin.com, 1-800-234-3304.

Confidentiality. Signator hereby acknowledges that Company has made, or may make, available to Signator certain customer lists, pricing data, supply sources, techniques, computerized data, maps, methods, product design information, market information, technical information, benchmarks, performance standards and other confidential and/or Proprietary Information of, or licensed to, the Company or its clients/customers ("Customers"), including without limitation, trade secrets, inventions, patents, and copyrighted materials (collectively, the "Confidential Material"). Signator acknowledges that this information has independent economic value, actual or potential, that is not generally known to the public or to others who could obtain economic value from their disclosure or use, and that this information is subject to a reasonable effort by the Company to maintain its secrecy and confidentiality. Except as essential to Signator's obligation under this Agreement, Signator shall not make any disclosure of this Agreement, the terms of this Agreement, or any of the Confidential

Material. Except as essential to Signator's obligations pursuant to their relationship with the Company, Signator shall not make any duplication or other copy of the Confidential Material. Signator shall not remove Confidential Material or proprietary property or documents without written authorization. Immediately upon request from Company, Signator shall return to Company all Confidential Material or proprietary property or documents. Signator shall notify each person to whom any disclosure is made that such disclosure is made in confidence, that the Confidential Material shall be kept in confidence by such persons, and that such persons shall be bound by the provisions of this Agreement. Signator further promises and agrees not solicit Customers or potential Customers of the Company, after the termination of this Agreement, while making use of Company's Confidentiality Material.

Proprietary Information. For the purpose of this Agreement, "Proprietary Information" shall include, but not limited to any information, observation, data, written material, record, document, drawing, photograph, layout, computer program, software, multimedia, firmware, invention, discovery, improvement, development, tool, machine, apparatus, appliance, design, work of authorship, logo, system, promotional idea, customer list, customer need, practice, pricing information, process, test, concept, formula, method, market information, technique, trade secret, product and/or research related to the actual or anticipated research development, products, organization, marketing, advertising, business or finances of Company, its affiliates or related entities.

All right, title, and interest of every kind and nature whatsoever in and to the Proprietary Information made, written, discussed, developed, secured, obtained or learned by Signator during the term of the relationship with the Company or the_____[time] period immediately following termination of that relationship, shall be the sole and exclusive property of Company for any purpose or use whatsoever, and shall be disclosed promptly by Signator to Company. The covenants set forth in the preceding sentence shall apply regardless of whether any Propriety Information is made, written, discussed, developed, secured, obtained or learned (a) solely or jointly with others, (b) during the usual hours of work or otherwise, (c) at the request and upon the suggestion of Company or otherwise, (d) with Company's materials, tools, instruments, or (e) on Company's premises or otherwise.

Signator shall comply with any reasonable rules established from time to time by Company for the protection of the confidentiality of any Proprietary Information. Signator irrevocably appoints the President and all Vice Presidents of the Company to act as Signator's agent and attorney-in-fact to perform all acts necessary to obtain and/or maintain patents, copyrights and similar rights to any Proprietary Information assigned by Signator to Company under this Agreement if (a) Signator refuses to perform those acts, or (b) is unavailable, within the meaning of any applicable laws. Signator acknowledges that the grant of the foregoing power of attorney is coupled with an interest and shall survive the death or disability of Signator.

Signator shall promptly and fully disclose to Company, in confidence (a) all Proprietary Information that Signator creates, conceives or reduces to practice in writing either alone or with others during the term of this Agreement, and (b) all patent applications and copyright registrations filed by Signator within one year after termination of this Agreement, including but not limited to materials and methodologies involved.

Any application for a patent, copyright registration or similar right filed by Signator within one year after termination of this Agreement shall be presumed to relate to Proprietary Information created by Signator during the term of this Agreement, unless Signator can prove otherwise with reasonable certainty.

Nothing contained in this Agreement shall be construed to preclude Company from exercising all of its rights and privileges as sole and exclusive owner of all of the Proprietary Information owned by or assigned to Company under this Agreement. Company, in exercising such rights and privileges with respect to any particular item of Proprietary Information, may decide not to file any patent application or any copyright registration on such Proprietary Information, may decide to maintain such Proprietary

Information as secret and confidential, or may decide to abandon such Propriety Information, or dedicate it to the public. Signator shall have no authority to exercise any rights or privileges with respect to the Proprietary Information owned by or assigned to Company under this Agreement.

Works for Hire. Signator acknowledges that all works of authorship performed for Company are subject to Company's direction and control and that such works constitute a work for hire pursuant to Title 17, United States Code, Sections 101 and 201(b).

All Propriety Information developed, created, invented, devised, conceived or discovered by Signator that is subject to copyright are explicitly considered by Signator and Company to be "works made for hire" and the property of Company.

Assignment. Company shall own as its sole and exclusive property, and Signator agrees to assign, transfer, and convey and or its authorized nominees all of his or her right, title and interest in and to any and all said "ideas" that related generally to Company's business, including but not limited to any inventions, processes, improvements, ideas, copyrightable works of art, trademarks, copyrights, formulas, manufacturing technology, developments, writings, discoveries, and trade secrets that Signator may make, conceive, or reduce to practice, whether solely or jointly with others, copyrightable, patentable or unpatentable, from the date of this Agreement or the date of first employment with Company if earlier, until the termination of Signator's employment. Signator is not required to assign any invention where no Company equipment, supplies, facilities or trade secret information was used and that was developed entirely on Signator's own time and: that does not relate to Company's business or to Company's actual demonstrably anticipated research or development or; that does not result from work performed for Company.

Signator hereby assigns to Company all releases and discharges Company, any affiliate of Company and their respective officers, directors and employees, from and against any and all claims, demands, liabilities, costs, and expenses of Signator arising out of, or relating to, any Propriety Information.

Execution of Instruments. During employment by Company, upon request and without compensation other than as herein provided but at no expense to Signator, Signator shall execute any documents and take any action Company may deem necessary or appropriate to effectuate the provisions of this Agreement, including without limitation assisting

Company in obtaining and/or maintaining patents, copyrights or similar rights to any Proprietary Information assigned to Company.

Signator further agrees that the obligations and undertakings stated in this paragraph will continue beyond termination of employment for any reason by the Company, but if Signator is called upon for such assistance after termination of employment, Signator is entitled to fair and reasonable fee in addition to reimbursement of any expenses incurred at the request of the Company.

Patent Application. Company agrees to pay all expenses in connection with the preparation and prosecution of patent applications in the United States of America and all foreign countries wherein Company may desire to obtain patents.

Company agrees to pay Signator a cash award of_____upon execution by Signator of application for United States Letters Patent for such invention or improvement and issuance of a patent on said application, together with an assignment thereof to Company.

Excepted from this Agreement are inventions or improvements relating to Company business made by Signator before commencement of this employment by Company which are:

embodied in the United States Letters Patent or an application for United States Letters Patent filed prior to commencement of this employment; or

in the possession of a former Company who owns the invention; or

set forth in an attachment hereto.

Non-Compete. Signator agrees not to engage in any activity that is competitive with any activity of Company during the course of their relationship and for a period of_____after termination of the Agreement. For purposes of this paragraph, competitive activity encompasses forming or making plans to form a business entity that may be deemed to be competitive with any business of Company. This does not prevent Signator from seeking or obtaining employment or other forms of business relationships with a competitor after termination of employment with Company so long as such competitor was in existence prior to the termination of relationship with Company and Signator was in no way involved with the organization or formation of such competitor.

Business Opportunities. During the terms of this Agreement, if Signator becomes aware of any project, investment, venture, business or other opportunity (any of the preceding, collectively referred to as an "Opportunity") that is similar to, competitive with, related to, or in the same field as Company, or any project, investment, venture, or business of Company, then Signator shall so notify Company immediately in writing of such Opportunity and shall use Signator's good-faith efforts to cause Company to have the opportunity to explore, invest in, participate in, or otherwise become affiliated with such Opportunity.

No Ownership. Neither Signator nor any of their agents or principals shall become or be deemed an owner, partner, joint venture or agent of or with Company or any of its affiliates or related companies or businesses by reason of this Agreement or his/her relationship with Company unless set forth in a separate written agreement signed and dated by the parties. Neither Company nor Signator nor any agent, Signator, officer or independent contractor of or retained by Signator shall have any authority to bind the other in any respect unless set forth in a separate written agreement signed and dated by the parties.

Solicitation of Employees. Signator agrees that he/she will not, either during the period of this Agreement, or for a period of one year after this Agreement has terminated, solicit any of Company's employees for a competing business or otherwise induce or attempt to induce such employees to terminate their employment with Company.

Soliciting Customers After Termination of Agreement. For a period of _____, following the termination of the relationship with the Company, Signator shall not, directly or indirectly, make known to any person, firm or corporation the names or addresses of any of the customers of Company or any other information pertaining to them, or call on, solicit, take away, or attempt to call on, solicit, or take away any customer of Company on whom Signator called or with whom Signator became acquainted during the time of this Agreement, for either himself/herself/itself or for any other person, firm, or corporation.

Injunctive Relief. Signator hereby acknowledges (1) the unique nature of the protections and provisions set forth in this Agreement, (2) that Company will suffer irreparable harm if Signator breaches any of said protections or provisions, and (3) that monetary damages will be inadequate to compensate Company for such breach. Therefore, if Signator breaches any of such provisions, then Company shall be entitled to injunctive relief, in addition to any other remedies at law or equity, to enforce such provisions.

Continuing Effects. Signator's obligations regarding trade secrets and confidential information shall continue in effect beyond the period of the relationship as stated above, and said obligation shall be binding upon Signator's spouse, affiliates, assigns, heirs, executors, administrators, or other legal representatives.

Subsidiaries And Parents. For the purposes of this Agreement, the term "Company" shall also be deemed to include any affiliated organization that owns fifty percent (50%) or more of the voting stock, whether or not Signator is directly employed by such other organization.

Non-Filing. Signator specifically agrees that Company's rights granted hereunder shall include the right not to file for copyrights or domestic or foreign patents when such is considered by Company in its sole discretion appropriate for the business objectives of Company.

Notice to Signator. This Agreement does not apply to any invention for which no equipment, supplies, facility, or trade secret information of Company was used and that was developed entirely on Signator's own time and:

> That does not relate (1) to Company's business or (2) to the actual or anticipated research or development work of Company; or

> That does not result from any work performed by Signator or Company. The burden of proof is on the Signator with respect to the exceptions of this Paragraph.

Counterparts. This Agreement may be executed in counterparts, each of which shall be deemed an original and all of which together shall constitute a single integrated document.

Severable Provisions. The provisions of this Agreement are severable, and if any one or more provisions may be determined to be illegal or otherwise unenforceable, in whole or in part, the remaining provisions and any partially unenforceable provisions to the extent enforceable shall nevertheless be binding and enforceable.

Attorneys' Fees. In the event any litigation, arbitration, mediation or other proceeding ("Proceeding") is initiated by any party against any other party to enforce, interpret or otherwise obtain judicial or quasi-judicial relief in connection with this Agreement, the prevailing party in such Proceeding shall be entitled to recover from the unsuccessful party all costs, expenses and actual attorney's fees relating to or arising out of (a) such proceeding, whether or not such proceeding proceeds to judgment, and (b) any post-judgment or post-award proceeding, including without limitation one to enforce any judgment or award resulting from any such Proceeding. Any such judgment or award shall contain a specific provision for the recovery of all such attorneys' fees, costs, and expenses. Any such judgment or award shall contain a specific provision for the recovery of all such subsequently incurred costs, expenses and actual attorney's fees.

Modifications. This Agreement may be modified only by a contract in writing executed by the party to this Agreement against whom enforcement of such modification is sought.

Prior Understandings. This Agreement contains the entire agreement between the parties to this Agreement with respect to the subject matter of the Agreement, is intended as a final expression of such parties' agreement with respect to such terms as are included in this Agreement is intended as a complete and exclusive statement of the terms of such agreement, and supersedes all negotiations, stipulations, understanding, agreements, representations and warranties. If any, with respect to such subject matter, which precede or accompany the execution of this Agreement.

Waiver. Any waiver of a default under this Agreement must be made in writing and shall not be a waiver of any other default concerning the same or any other provision of this Agreement. No delay or omission in the exercise of any right or remedy shall impair such right or remedy or be constructed as a waiver. A consent to or approval of any act shall not be deemed to waive or render unnecessary consent to or approval of any other or subsequent act.

Drafting Ambiguities. Each party to this Agreement has reviewed and had the opportunity to revise this Agreement. Each party to this Agreement has had the opportunity to have legal counsel review and revise this Agreement. The rule of construction that any ambiguities are to be resolved against the drafting party shall not be employed in the interpretation of this Agreement or of any amendments or exhibits to this Agreement.

Jurisdiction and Venue. This Agreement is to be construed pursuant to Laws of the State of _____. Jurisdiction and venue for any claim arising out of this Agreement shall be made in the State of _____, County of _____.

Receipt of Copy. Signator hereby acknowledges that he/she/it has received a signed copy of this Agreement.

By: By:

Title   Title

Signator   Company

Date   Date

---

donphin.com materials and services presented are designed with the philosophy that the only way to manage today's workforce is through strategies and tools that generate trust, a shared direction, effective communication and deep commitment – "the building blocks of all powerful relationships."

—3304

GLOSSARY

ACH. Automated Clearinghouse. Facility used by banks and other depository institutions to assist corporate customers by processing payment orders, such as payroll checks, into machine-readable form.

Application. Specific functions made available, generally via a technology implementation, to support a business need. In the past, many of the technology functions were hard coded into the application. New technology advancements now allow applications to share logic and create a more seamless "view" for customers and business users. For example, today separate applications can share the same database. Applications would include specific functions for order entry, inventory, accounts receivable, and payroll. Banking specific applications would include, ACH, Lock Box, or Fed Wire.

Application development. The building of processes, generally via a technology implementation, to support an application. For example, the building of a new order-entry system might be referred to as "a new order-entry application development initiative."

Architecture. A system of design for building. Technology or systems architecture is a blueprint or methodology that attempts to align technology to address business goals by offering standard services and common functions that can provide seamless integration for all technologies within an enterprise, including hardware, software, networks, interfaces, and management tools.

Assembler. Machine-level computing language used to execute programs. It is sometimes referred to as a hard-coded program language as it is tightly coupled to computer hardware.

ATM. Automated teller machine. Machine capable of processing banking transactions between a customer and a depository institution.

Backplane. The shelf board within a hardware computer product that may hold programmable modules, circuits, and/or switches. "The guts" within the product. Sometimes referred to as "the interconnection topology."

BAI. Bank Administration Institute. Advisory counsel for banking industry.

Batch processing. Transactions are assembled into groups (batches) and processed at one time. The batch is used to update a master file within a specific window. No further changes are made until the next group of transactions are processed. It is considered "off-line" as opposed to "on-line" processing were updates can be made immediately.

Benchmarking. Evaluating competitive systems or processes. Consultants will "benchmark" various companies within an industry and attempt to come up with a best-practices approach based on the systems and processes that appear to work best.

Benchmarking (the competition). Evaluating competitive vendors based on a preestablished criteria and possible weighting system to determine a relative ranking of each vendor. This can be done across various categories, such as product capability and performance, support and service, costs, financial performance of parent company, compatibility with previously installed products, and professional ethics and standards.

Best practices. An approach for conducting business that is viewed as "best of breed" based on a cumulative analysis of various techniques. Generally confined to a specific industry such as banking, retail, or manufacturing. Consultants pass it from one client to another.

Beta version. An early version of a computer hardware or software product that has not been sufficiently tested for general release to the public. Beta versions are sometimes released to a select group of customers to be tested and observed in a production environment prior to general release.

Big Blue. Nickname given to IBM.

Broadband. A relatively new networking technology that provides multimedia transmission of data, voice, and video. It is an extremely wide and fast bandwidth so it can simultaneously handle large numbers of users.

Broadcast technology. A one-to-many communications transmission.

Business process reengineering. The redesign of the workflow processes that supports a current business function. As opposed to new application development, business process reengineering is the rebuilding of a current application or business function.

Byte. A single character of information.

Cafeteria services. On-site meal services provided to employees. For most companies, this is not a core competency. Meal services may represent a potential opportunity for outsourcing to reduce costs without impacting major business activities.

Cash cow. Business or product that is highly profitable, generating a continuing flow of cash.

Churning business. Method used by some consultants to maximize billable hours versus driving a project to completion.

CIO. Chief information officer. The senior technology executive within the corporation. Some companies have a STO (senior technology officer).

Client/Server. Technology approach that provides intelligence and functional capability at a "client" workstation that can access data from a "server" engine as opposed to a hierarchical approach with a "dumb" terminal accessing information from a traditional mainframe processor.

Clustering. A distributed architecture. An early approach of parallel processing.

Computer. A piece of equipment capable of executing functions such as arithmetic and other logical manipulations of data, such as transfer data to another computer.

Configuration. Bringing together computer equipment and software so that it all works together for running systems.

Coopetition. When competitors decide to cooperate for mutual advantage. An example is the cross-licensing of patents between competitors. Another example is when one rival company decides to buy parts from another or agrees under contract to sell a competitor's product under its own label. One company reduces its manufacturing costs. The other reduces selling costs by selling "wholesale" to its competitor.

CORBA. Common object request broker. Specifications for distributed object-oriented computing.

Core competency. Specialized abilities that are critical success factors for conducting primary business functions. For example, a core competency of a bank might be the ability to accept, route, and settle financial transactions.

Credit card. An interest-bearing electronic-payment card.

CRM. Customer relationship management. Tools, products, and services used to help companies better know, support, and administer to customers.

.com. E-business entity using Internet infrastructure to create a virtual business. Clicks vs. bricks.

Cross-team buy-in. Gaining broad acceptance and support from employees within different business units within a large corporate structure.

Customized on-site consulting. Providing the service of advising, or other consultant-related activities, at a specific client location, tailored to specific requirements. This contrasts with consulting services that are broader in scope, based on industry analysis, for example, and not specific to one client.

Database. A collection of data elements or records that can be accessed based on relationship to other data elements. For example, information extracted from a database might include, customer name, address and social security number.

Data warehouse. Collection of large amounts of corporate data from various operational sources to provide decision support information to business managers.

Debit card. Electronic-payment card, similar to a credit card, but with funds deducted and transferred immediately from the customer's bank account to the merchant's account. The advantage to the consumer is avoiding interest charges. The advantage to the merchant is instant access to funds.

Decision support system. A system that provides data for managerial decision making. Generally a subset of data warehouse information; not as inclusive.

De facto standards. When a dominant technology company uses its market position and product penetration to establish precedence in buying patterns. This contrasts with "open-systems" standards which are established through vendor collaboration.

Deliverables. Tangible products or services. In many consultant contracts, the deliverables are the agreed-to output of a project. A deliverable may include a document, a new application, or a reengineered system. For measuring if a project is on track, deliverables are sometimes broken into component parts of a product or service. Deliverable A might be the functional design. Deliverable B is the completion of the build phase. The final deliverable may be the new product or service, up and running in full-production mode.

DCE. Distributed computing environment. Standards for Networked Applications from Open Systems Foundation. It has created multi-vendor standards for distributed networking, processing, synchronization, security, and other services.

Direct bank. NationsBank initiative providing new ways for customers to gain access "anytime and anywhere" through technology-supported delivery channels, such as PC banking and enhanced telephone call centers.

Direct report. Someone within the corporate chain of command who works for a manager, with no other managers in between on the organizational-reporting structure.

Disintermediation. Elimination of the middleman in the buying and selling process.

Distributed computing. Decentralized computing services that can be shared by multiple users across a network.

Drill down. Diving into the details for more information. For example, the drill down on a demographic report on percentages of whites and nonwhites in a community might break down to white and nonwhite males and females, or nonwhites into specific minority groups, etc.

Due diligence. Investigating all reasonable means available to thoroughly understand an organization, situation, condition, or problem.

e-business. Companies buying and selling products via the Internet.

Economies of scale. Developing more efficient and less costly output by maximizing the best proportional effectiveness in input factors such as labor, raw materials, plant capacity, and geographic proximity to suppliers and/or distribution outlets.

Electronic "over check". An alternative to paper checks for paying bills. Customers can use the Internet, credit cards, debit cards, and smart cards, which are electronic methods of payments versus checks. It is an immediate transfer and eliminates "float," which is exclusive to check. When checks are in float, banks on both ends of the transaction can "double count" the money and continue to use it for earning interest until it clears. If the payee receiving the check is not a bank, he cannot use the check until it clears. For an electronic payment, payees can use immediately.

e-mail. Electronic messaging and mail system via communications network facilities. Examples of information exchanged and stored may include interoffice correspondence, calendars, and schedules.

e-commerce. Electronic commerce. Adds flexibility and convenience of networking technology to the traditional buying, selling, and service aspects of commerce. Generally used to describe buying and selling of products and services on the Internet.

EFTS. Electronic funds transfer system. A system used for financial transactions that takes advantage of electronic computing and networking.

Engine. In technology discussion usually refers to a computer system or set of software applications that work together to perform specific functions.

Encapsulation. Database object-oriented concept where the internal structure of the object is hidden and the object is only accessible through predefined operations.

ERP. Enterprise resource planning. Back-office applications such as inventory, logistics, and accounting.

FAX. Facsimile. Transmission of images over a communications system.

FDIC. Federal Deposit Insurance Corporation. Enacted with Glass-Steagall Act which the federal government guaranteed bank deposits.

Federal Reserve. Established in 1913 to regulate the monetary and banking systems of the United States.

Float. When credit is extended to an institution before payment is obtained from another institution. Essentially, for a period of time there is "double counting" of system deposits.

Float management. A repository for warehoused check information that runs interest calculations.

Front-end solution. The customer interface. The components of the application provider closest to the customer. An example is the GUI (graphical user interface) or a Web page that the customer views when accessing the Internet site of a vendor.

General Bank. Business unit within NationsBank responsible for providing retail and commercial banking services for individuals and small and medium-sized businesses.

Glass house. Term used to describe the technology data center within large companies.

Glass-Steagall Act. New Deal legislation that restricted banks from investing in securities.

GFSE. Global Finance Software Engineering. NationsBank organization providing technical support for large corporate customers. They are part of the Global Finance business unit within the Services Company.

Global Finance. NationsBank business unit responsible for providing financial products and services for domestic and international corporations and institutions.

Groupware. Network software that allows users to share data and collaborate on projects, potentially increasing productivity. E-mail and calendaring are generally considered components of groupware.

GUI. Graphical user interface. The user screen view to the application(s). In early computer programs this was done with text. Today, graphics are used to help guide the person using the system in such areas as how to enter information, where to click to get more information, and how to navigate through the application or program

Hardware. Computer and peripheral equipment that run programs.

Imaging. Conversion of documents from a physical medium to electronic digital form.

Image archiving. A process of converting received checks into an electronic database for future queries and analysis.

IMS. Hierarchical database and data communications system from IBM.

Infrastructure. The underlying foundation.

Integrating the back office. Building the interface that connects the front end (the Web interface) to the back office. Often done with "middleware" that provides the connection between the front-end and back-office systems. Examples of back-office systems are inventory, accounts payable, and accounts receivable.

Integration. Ability of separate systems to access and manipulate common data through a seamless connection.

Integration Services. NationsBank organization within the Transaction Services business unit responsible for managing back-office technology systems, such as the routing and settlement operations.

Internet. "World Wide Web," serving tens of millions of people via network communications. It was originally funded by the U.S. Department of Defense. The Internet is an internetwork of many networks and computers.

Internetworking. Local and wide-area networks connected by data linking devices and services. Devices may include routers, switches, and hubs.

IS. Information services. Common name given to technology organizations within large companies.

Keiretsu. Japanese system in which groups of companies have interlocking financial interests. This system can lock out potential competition.

LAN. Local area network. Connects separate computers within a work group through a public or private communications link.

Legacy systems. Traditional, older technology. Generally used to refer to mainframe computers.

Lock box. Service by which banks act as an agent in directly receiving and collecting a corporate customer's incoming payments.

Macro business view. A high-level conceptual view of a business process or processes, independent of the underlying technologies or specific business, functions required to implement this process or processes.

Mainframe. Large centralized computer. Sometimes referred to as a legacy system. There are established processes and procedures for handling business and work sessions cannot be disrupted.

Management Consultants. Consults who provide advice and counsel to senior management in companies. Their primary focus is to provide strategic plans and problem assessment on major corporate issues.

Mercenary. Hired for pay. Soldier hired to fight for pay.

Micro business view. A detailed, granular-technology and business function–specific view of a business process or processes.

Middleware. Acts as a weigh station where data is transmitted, reformatted, and sent on between host databases and users. Insulates users from communication and data access complexities.

Model Bank. Major NationsBank project for General Bank customers that encompassed a streamlining of technology to provide common products and services for more than two hundred branch functions.

MPP. Massively parallel processing. "Share Nothing" architecture for parallel-processing systems.

MQ Series. IBM transaction monitor that provides messaging and queuing services that ensures delivery, integrity, and recovery functions for transactional business activities.

Multimedia. Combining voice, video, and graphics. For making this possible, networking technology requires the ability to move large amounts of data over very fast communication lines.

Multitasking. Concurrent execution of multiple tasks.

Net. Slang term for Internet. The worldwide network highway for computers.

Networking. When computers and workstations are connected together by a communication facility that includes communication lines, software, and hardware devices.

NT. Operating system for distributed computing developed and marketed by Microsoft Corp.

Object-based databases. A collection of data, or pieces of information, that are represented by predefined modules or "objects," where data is merged together. This allows for faster assembly and ease of use as information can be retrieved without initiating complex programming calls or understanding all the underlying details of syntax.

Object-oriented programming. New programming technique that uses semiautonomous modules, fostering structured design and the ability to reuse code, reducing time and complexity in building systems.

Opt out. Customer can fill out a form to ensure that her private financial information is not used or sold for marketing purposes by the financial service provider. The onus is on the customer to decline, otherwise it is assumed it's OK to use this information.

OEM. Other equipment manufacturer. Company makes product for another company to sell under the label of the company selling the product to consumers. Sometimes the product is altered or changed prior to distribution.

OMG. Open management group. An open-systems advocacy group that emphasizes object-based programming. It aims at defining standards for information sharing in widely distributed, heterogeneous networks to support reusability and portability.

Open systems. Technology specifications that are published and made generally available.

Operating system. A critical software program for controlling basic computer operations.

Operationalize. Ability to take a strategic plan and implement it.

OS/2. IBM PC-based operating system for individual workstations and client/server networks.

Outsourcing. When a company turns over responsibly for running a specific department to an outside firm. This is generally done to reduce costs in areas that are considered ancillary functions as opposed to critical business functions. An example would be the "outsourcing" of cafeteria services. In the 1990s the "outsourcing" of technology departments became very common.

Paradigm. A model or pattern. Consultants often refer to "paradigm" shifts to describe dramatic changes within an industry.

Parallel processing. When separate components related to a unit of work are broken down into discrete units and handled concurrently by separate processors. The separate processors operate as if the unit of work was handled by one processor. Final output is reassembled as one unit of work. A DEC VAX cluster would be an early example of parallel-processing. The IBM SP2 Risc/6000 is a more recent example of a parallel processing architecture.

Partnering arrangements. When firms agree to work collaboratively to achieve common goals. For example, a banking consultant might partner with a software vendor to maximize billings for both within a banking client. The vendor gets paid for use of its products. The consultant gets paid for installing these products.

PC. Personal Computer. A desktop computing system that gained popularity in the 1980s.

Performance metrics. Tangible measurements for evaluating the progress in achieving an agreed-upon goal. For example, a corporate manager might measure consultants based on the actual time and cost in producing phased deliverables, versus the projected timeline and budget as previously established.

Peripherals. Ancillary parts or components to a product. For example, peripherals to a personal computer might be an auxiliary printer, an external disk drive, and a mouse.

Plug-compatible. Ability to interchange computer equipment parts from different vendors.

POS. Point of sale system that permits customer to transfer funds at a retail cash register, bar code scanner, or other retail-based system.

Process consultants. Consultants who operate with a "model" methodology that can be applied across various industries.

Proprietary. Equipment or programs that are owned by a particular organization. For example, a program that can be purchased in executable from, but not in source form (the language that the program is written in).

Protocol. Characteristics of network that define how hardware and software will interoperate.

Publish subscribe. "Push" technology that can eliminate bottlenecks via a broadcasting distribution technology as opposed to a "pull" technology where individual applications need to invoke a structured sequence of events to retrieve specific information from other applications.

Real time. Processing updates take place during the actual occurrence of an event. The event that triggers the process can be immediately affected by the transaction.

Redeploys. Employees of a company who are transferred from one area of the business where they performed a specific function to another area of the business where they will perform a different function. For example, manufacturing personnel from a closed plant may be redeployed into sales.

Relational-based databases. Information is organized between tables to "relate" from one table to another through the use of common identifiers. For instance, one table might be items sold, the other organized by regional sales organization. The user could search to determine what products were sold by a particular region by invoking a relational request of product sales by region. Relational is easier to use than older databases, but not as easy as object-oriented, which is a more recent database approach.

Relational database. Data is stored in two-dimensional tables for improved access versus the hierarchical model.

Research analysts. Consultants who assess industry trends and evaluate industry-specific companies. In the technology industry, these firms write reports that influence vendor buying patterns.

Research subscription business. A practice of industry-analyst consulting firms that sell reports to clients. These reports are generally monthly and review specific industry trends, provide vendor analysis, competitive analysis, and forecast future industry events.

Retail banking. Banks or divisions within banks that concentrate on the individual consumer. In some bank organizations, retail may also include small commercial establishments.

Reverse engineer. To take a finished product built by a competitor apart in an effort to determine how it was developed and the feasibility for building a clone.

RFI. Request for information. When a company asks multiple vendors to supply information to assist it in evaluating various alternatives.

RFP. Request for proposal. When a company asks multiple vendors to respond to a competitive bid with their best offer and prices to meet a specific business need.

Rounding error. When the exact detailed (decimal) value is insignificant and is approximated by a nondecimal number. For example $10,

000.01, would become $10,000. Used in text sarcastically, to suggest a major discrepancy is a "rounding error."

Routing & settlement. Process in which financial records or transactions are moved either physically or electronically from the point of origination to the organization that keeps the account and expects to collect. The settlement function completes the process by clearing and "settling" among the various parties involved in the transaction.

Rules based. Technology concept where changes can be made to a system by executing a series of commands as opposed to having to reprogram code within the system. The system conforms to a predefined set of rules.

Scalability. Ability to grow a system in size. There are several different metric systems used such as the ability to grow the number of concurrent users, or amount of data capacity a system can handle. For a network, scalability generally refers to growth capacity in bandwidth.

Server. Computer program that provides shared resources for users.

Services company. NationsBank organization that provides operational and technical support to other NationsBank lines of business.

Silo. A closed pit where fodder, grain, or food is stored. In the technology business, the silo analogy is often used to describe individualized processing, tightly coupled to a very specific application that cannot be shared with other applications or programs.

Skills transfer. Phrase often used by consultants to describe the service of providing education to clients. "Consultingspeak" for training.

Smart card. A electronic payment card that contains a computer chip that stores financial information. It performs functions like an electronic check book.

SMP. Symmetrically multiprocessing. Multiprocessing parallel systems that share memory and common input and output devices.

Software. Computer programs and data.

Stalking-horse. A prototype to be tested to determine if it is a viable alternative. For example, if no one is sure what kind of document should be created, a stalking-horse might be created containing a hypothetical argument, so others can "shoot holes at it" and see if it can stand up to critical scrutiny.

STG. Strategic technology group. NationsBank organization within the Services Company responsible for advising on new technology directions and technology investments.

Strategy Group (NBK). A new organization created within Nations-Bank's Transaction Services business unit to develop a more strategic focus for this line of business. This is a different organization than the strategic technology group that provides strategic support across all lines of business.

System. This word has several meanings. It is most frequently used to refer to a complete application of programs working together. It is also sometimes used to refer to the computer and its peripherals.

System integration. The process of combining or joining disparate systems by creating new programs, or the use of middleware technologies. This process often requires some type of translation from one computing language, format, and/or protocol to another.

Systems management. The set of procedures, disciplines, tools, and products for operating and managing all components associated with the technology environment within a company. Systems management provides critical services to keep technology systems up and running, as well as providing backup and recovery functions in the event of a failure.

TAR. Task action report. Status report used by NationsBank and Andersen Consulting for large NationsBank projects such as Model Bank.

TAS. Technical architecture strategies. Document published by Nations-Bank Strategic Technology Group.

Thin client. A user workstation or platform with minimal overhead required. Architectures using thin clients leverage high-speed networks to access required data from distributed servers.

Three-tier client/server. Modularized architecture that separates (1) graphical front-end presentation for the user from (2) specific business logic for applications or functions and (3) database information. Decoupling into separate layers adds a high degree of flexibility for user responsiveness and making changes. This contrasts with hard-coded applications of the past in which changes could impact all aspects of the application. These changes were time consuming, costly, and could not be leveraged across multiple business applications.

Throughput. Ability to perform specific units of work in a designated time frame.

Transaction engine. A payments engine for handling the acceptance, routing, and settlement of banking customer financial transactions. When a payment is made, it needs to be accepted, the payer account (within same bank or another bank) debited, the payee account credited, and the posting systems of both the bank and the Fed updated on a regular basis to reflect new balances of payments. This represents a critical function in banking.

Transaction monitor. Provides the logic and services for handling transactions from different applications. Transaction monitors provide services required for maintaining transactional integrity to be offloaded from computer operating systems, databases, and application logic. They are considered "middleware" and can reduce redundant functions that previously had to run separately for each business application.

Transaction Services. Organization within NationsBank Services Company responsible for handling back-office operations and technology systems to support both electronic and check-based financial transactions.

UNIX. A operating system originally developed by AT&T that is hardware independent.

Vendor strategies. Competitive marketing plans to increase revenue, market share, and reduce exposure from other vendors and additional market forces. Industry-analyst consultants often share their opinions regarding vendor strategies with clients.

Virtual bank Internet-only bank, providing services with less overhead than traditional banks.

Vertical-industry consultants. Consultants who provide a specific expertise based on industry knowledge, such as banking, retail, or manufacturing. They apply a "best-practice" methodology that attempts to package the best information obtained from previous client engagements.

Web. Slang name for Internet.

Web browser. An Internet-based technology that is invoked on a client workstation and initiates an interactive "conversation" with a Web server. It provides a easy to use process that reduces client software overhead. In addition, the browser can communicate with central Web servers, where applications can be written and executed. The browser then becomes the primary interface between the user and the application.

White paper. A document that states a position on a particular subject and attempts to defend it.

Wholesale banking. Banks or divisions within large banks that provide services to large corporate customers.

Window. In check-processing, the time required to meet preestablished daily posting deadlines from when checks are received until posted.

Windows. Microsoft operating system for workstations and client/server networks.

Y2K. Term used to refer to the issue facing legacy-based computer technology that employed a two digit convention to track annual dates. If this situation is not corrected, in the year 2000, programs will generate inaccurate data and numeric calculations.

Zero-sum. To make more money, you have to take it from somebody else. The aggregate sum remains the same in spite of changes in ownership.

Note: Some of the terms in this glossary may have other definitions. The definitions provided relate to the information provided within the book and are intended to assist the reader for clarification purposes.

BIBLIOGRAPHY

Alsop, Ronald. "The Best Corporations in America." *Wall Street Journal*, 23 September 1999, B1, B6.

Anderson, Jack, and Michael Binstein. "Special Treatment or Great Deal." *Washington Post*, 1 August 1994, B8.

Baker, Carlos, ed. *Ernest Hemingway Selected Letters* 1917–1961. New York: Charles Scribner's Sons, 1981.

"BankAmerica Hires Consultant to Set up Bad-Assets Subsidiary." *Wall Street Journal*, 12 August 1992, B2.

"BankAmerica Will Cut 150 Jobs as It Reduces Derivatives Operations." *Wall Street Journal*, 6 November 1998, A9.

"Bank of America, Bank of New York Meet Expectations." *Wall Street Journal*, 17 April 2001, A4.

"Bank of America Defers Western Plans." *Charlotte Observer*, 1 April 2002, http://www.charlotte.com/mld/charlotte/need_to_map/2979175.htm.

Bank of America Presentation at the Eleventh Annual Goldman Sachs CEO Conference, 6 December 2000, www.bankofamerica.com/newsroom/press.

"Bank of America Provides Earnings Guidance for Fourth Quarter and 2001." 6 December 2000, www.bankofamerica.com/newsroom/press.

"Banks Branch over the Phone." *Washington Post*, 21 June1996, D1–2.

Barthel, Matt. "Cost Savings Pegged at $335 Million a Year by '99." *American Banker*, 3 September 1996, 21.

Bauer, Roy A., Emilio Collar, and Victor Tang. *The Silverlake Project*. Oxford: Oxford University Press, 1992.

Baughn, William H., Thomas I. Storrs, and Charles E. Walker, eds. *The Bankers' Handbook*. Homewood: Dow Jones-Irwin, 1988.

Bekier, Matthias M., Anna J. Bogardus, and Timothy Oldman. "Mastering Revenue Growth in M&A." *McKinsey on Finance* (summer 2001): 1.

Berg, Lynn. "The Scoop on Client/Server Costs." *Computerworld*, 16 November 1992, 169–76.

Bloom, Jennifer Kingson, and Karen Epper. "Bankers Told to Get On-line or Be Left Behind." *American Banker*, 29 March 1996, 13.

"BofA and Coopers & Lybrand Consulting Form Alliance on Purchasing Card System."

BankAmerica release, 5 February 1996, www.bankamerica.com/batoday/news52.html.

"BofA Spent $600 Million on Model 'Cost Cutting Bridge Tech Gap." *Charlotte Observer*, 27 April 1998, http://charlotte.bcentral.com/charlotte/stories/1998/04/27/story6.html.

Boudette, Neal E. "How a Software Titan Missed the Internet Revolution," *Wall Street Journal*, 18 January 2000, B1, 4.

Branfman, Fred. "Politics Unzipped." *Salon.com*, 9 September 1996, http://www.salon.com/news/news960904.html.

Brannigan, Martha, Nikhil Deogun, and Eleena de Lisser. "NationsBank Wins Bidding for Barnett." *Wall Street Journal*, 2 September 1997, A3, A5.

Brzezinski, Zrbigniew. "Bombshells Lurk in the Russian Scandal." *Wall Street Journal*, 3 September 1999, A10.

"Bridging Today and Tomorrow: A Call for Evolution and Partnerships in the Banking Industry." NationsBank Chairman Speech, Bank Administration Retail Delivery Conference, 4 December 1995, http://www.nationsbank.com /newsroom/.

"Briefing.com Story Stocks: Accenture," Cnet.com, 19 July 19 2001, http://investor.cnet.com/investor/news/newsitem/0-9900-1028-6613330-0.html.

Brooks, Rick. "BankAmerica Cuts Bonuses of 3 Executives." *Wall Street Journal*, 8 March 1999, B12.

———. "Many Banks Are Raising Estimates for Costs of Year-2000 Computer Fixes." *Wall Street Journal*, 18 November 1998, A3.

Brooks, Rick, and Mitchell Pacelle. "BankAmerica Knew in August of Trading Woes." *Wall Street Journal*, 16 October 1998, A3, A10.

———. "BankAmerica Net Slides Unexpected 78%." *Wall Street Journal*, 15 October 1998, A3, A13.

Brummett, John, "Ethics of a Presidential Library." *Morning News*, 13 February 2002, http://www.nwaonline.net/pdfarchive/2001/February/13/2-13-01% 20A8.pdf.

Bulkeley, William. "These Days, Big Blue Is about Big Services Not Just Big Boxes."*Wall Street Journal*, 11 June 2001, 1,10.

Bull, Katherine. "Sybase off Base." *Informationweek*, 17 April 1995, 104.

Burgess, John. "IBM Chief Outlines Vision for the Future." *Washington Post*, 25 March 1994, B1, B10.

Byrne, John. "The Craze for Consultants." *Business Week*, 25 July 1994, 65.

Byrne, John A., with Louis Lavelle, Nanette Byrnes, Marcia Vickers, and Amy Borrus. "The Crisis in Corporate Governance," *Business Week*, 6 May 2002, 68–78.

Caldwell, Bruce. "Andersen Stalls." *Informationweek*, 7 October 1996, 97.

Calvey, Mark. "Executive of the Year: No Matter What You Think of Hugh McColl Jr., the Carolina Banker Rocked the Bay in 1998." *San Francisco Business Times*, 25 December 1998, http://www.bizjournals.com/sanfrancisco/stories /1998/12/28/story2.html.

———. "PaineWebber: Time to Take Stock in NationsBank, Norwest." *San Francisco Business Times*, 14 August 2002.

"Cap Gemini Is in Talks with Ernst & Young." *New York Times*, 7 December 1999, C14.

Caroll, Paul. Big Blues: *The Unmaking of IBM*. New York: Crown Publishers, 1993.

"Chase Is Turning to a Specialist To Help Sharpen Its Budget Ax." *New York Times*, 6 May 1995, A35, 37.

"Chase Reports Profit Dip in First Quarter." *New York Times*, 18 April 1995, D4.

Churchill, Winston . *While England Slept*. New York: G.P. Putnam's Sons, 1938.

"Citigroup to Sell up to 20% of Travelers Property Casualty Corp. in Initial Public Offering with Intention to Spring off Remainder of Company to Citigroup Shareholders." 19 December 2001, http://www.travelers.com/news/docs/12-19-`01.html.

Clark, Drew. "B of A Says It's on the Fast Track to Systems Integration." *American Banker*, 26 October 1998, 20.

Cline, Kenneth. "Momentum Builds." *Banking Strategies*, 1 March 1997, 46.

———. "NationsBank Sees Boatmen's Revenue Potential." *American Banker*, 25 September 1996, 4.

"Consultants Vie for Slice of Aid for Palestinians." *Wall Street Journal*, 25 January 1994, A9.

Copeland, Lewis, and Faye Copeland, eds. *Ten Thousand Jokes, Toasts & Stories*. New York: Bantam Doubleday Dell, 1965.

Cousteau, Jacques-Yves, and Philippe Cousteau. *The Shark: Splendid Savage of the Sea*. Garden City, N.J.: Doubleday, 1970.

Crandell Gregory A., and Richard K. Cvrane. "The Safest Place Is the Cutting Edge." *Bank Management* (May/June 1996): 8.

Crone, Richard. "Banking without Banks." *Bankers Magazine* (January/February 1996): 41.

Davenport, Tom. "Software as Socialware." CIO, 1 March 1996, www.cio.com.

Davey, Tom. "Three Bay Area Companies Lead Pack in Database Race." *San Francisco Business Times*, 17 June 1994, A4.

De Lesser, Eleena, and Stephen E. Frank. "Major Banks Show Strength in Earnings." *Wall Street Journal*, 14 January 1997, A3.

Deogun, Nikhil. "A Tough Bank Boss Takes on Computers with Real Trepidation." *Wall Street Journal*, 25 July 1996, A1, 2.

Der Hovanesian, Mara, Heather Timmons, and Chris Palmeri. "For Small Banks, It's a Wonderful Life." *Business Week*, 6 May 2002, 83–84.

"Digest of Earnings Reports." *Wall Street Journal*, 20 January 1993, 16.

"Digest of Earnings Report." *Wall Street Journal*, 1 February 1996, 20.

Duffy, Jim. "Cisco Rips Plum from IBM's Hand." *Network World*, 31 October 1994, 1, 9.

Dunaief, Daniel Cline, and Kenneth Cline. "NationsBank's Midwestern Deal: 7 New States, But Questions on Price." *American Banker*, 3 September 1996, 1

"Earnings, Andersen Consulting L.L.P." *Chicago Tribune*, 27 February 1996, 3.

Elkins, Ken. "Cost-Cutting, Bridging Tech Gaps Replaces Merger Mania." *Business Journal*, 24 April 1998, http://charlotte.bcentral.com/charlotte/stories/1998/04/27/story6.html.

Elmasri, Ramez, and Shamkant Navathe. *Fundamental of Database Systems*. Redwood City, Calif.: Benjamin/Cummings, 1994.

Elstein, Aaron. "Goldman Director Says Banks Have Edge in Consolidation Endgame." *American Banker*, 11 February 1997, 18.

———. "NationsBank and B of A Tie Advisors Fees to Stock Prices." *American Banker*, 5 August 1998, 1.

"Enron Invesors: Firms Fueled Fraud." *Charlotte Observer*, 8 April 2002, http://www.charlotte.com/mld/charlotte/news/3019874.htm.

Epper, Karen. "NationsBank Sidelines Perot as Its Outsourcer." *American Banker*, 11 April 1995, 1.

"ERP RIP?" *Economist*, 26 June 1999.

"Executive Decisions." *Multinational Monitor* (March 1998): 5.

"The Executive Pay Scam." *New York Times*, 14 April 2002, 12.

Ferril, Arthur. *The Fall of the Roman Empire*. London: Thames and Hudson, Ltd., 1986.

Fialka, John J. "Helping Ourselves: U.S. Aid to Russia Is Quite a Windfall for U.S. Consultants." *Wall Street Journal*, 24 February 1994, A1, 8.

Field, Tom."When Bad Things Happen to Good People." *CIO*, 15 October 15 1997, http://www.cio.com/archive.

Field, Tom, David Pearson, and Polly Schneider. "To Hell and Back." *CIO*, 1 December 1998, http://www.cio.com/archive/120198/turk.html.

Fields, Randall K. "Build versus Buy: Resist the Seduction." *Chief Executive* (May 1995): 22.

Foley, Mary Jo. "Service with Smiles, Thanks to OS/2." *PC Week*, 19 June 1995, 25.

Frank, Stephen E. "Consumers Wonder If Deals Will Deliver Better Service." *Wall Street Journal*, 14 April 1998, A3, A14.

Frezza, Bill. "Conspiracies Afloat: Keeping Tabs on the Inslaw Affair," *CommunicationsWeek*, 11 August 1997, 28.

Friedman, David H. *Money & Banking*. Washington D.C.: American Bankers Association, 1985.

McColl, Hugh. "Fulfilling the Vision: NationsBank, Our Region and Our Nation." speech given 1 December 1992, www.nationsbank.com/s97is.v...y.

Gage, Deborah, and Darrly K. Taft. "Justice Says, 'No!'" *Computer Reseller News*, 20 February 1995, 1.

Gates, Bill. *The Road Ahead*. (New York: Viking Penguin Books, 1995).

Gearino, G. D. "Rebel Yell." *News and Observer of Raleigh*, January 1999, 36.

Geewax, Marilyn. "NationsBank Story Offers Chilling Reminder." *Atlanta Journal and Constitution*, 10 May 1998, R2.

Gillam, Carey. "BankAmerica Sued over Hedge Fund Losses." *American Banker*,3 November 1998, 6.

———. "NationsBank: $500M 'Model Bank' Paying Off." *American Banker*,8 May 1997, 8.

Gillam, Gary. "Brand Name to Be Unveiled in Ads Tonight." *American Banker*, 30 September 1998, 4.

Glass, Robert L. *Software Runaways: Lessons Learned from Massive Software Project Failures*.Upper Saddle River, N.J.: Prentice-Hall, 1998.

Gordon, John Steele. "MayGlass-Steagall Rest in Peace." *Wall Street Journal*, 26 October 1999, A26.

Grant, Linda. "Here Comes Hugh." *Fortune*, 21 August 1995, 43–55.

Greenspan, Alan. "The Challenge of Central Banking in a Democratic Society."

remarks at the Annual Dinner and Francis Boyer Lecture of The American Enterprise Institute for Public Policy Research, Washington, D.C., 5 December 1996, http://www.federalreserve.gov/boarddocs/speeches/1996/19961205.htm.

Greising, David, Kelley Holland, and Nancy. "BankAmerica and NationsBank: No White Smoke Yet." *Business Week*, 6 November 1995, 42.

Gullo, Karen. "Andersen, Systematics Join to Offer Technology Services." *American Banke*r, 18 September 1991, 2.

Hamilton, David P., and Dean Takahashi. "Scientists Are Battling to Surmount Barriers in Microchip Advances." *Wall Street Journal*, 10 December 1996, A1.

Hamilton, Rosemary. "Foggy Mainframe Picture Stalls User Plans." *Computerworld*, 27 August 1990, 25, 32

Hansell, Saul. "Citicorp and Travelers Face a Tangle of Technology." *New York Times*, 13 April 1998, D1.

———. "Clash of Technologies in Merger." *New York Times*, 13 April 1998, D4.

Harris, Catherine L. "Cashing in on Computer Confusion." *Business Week*, 20 April 1987, 85–86.

Hays, Laurie. "Big Banks Post Healthy Earnings for the Third Quarter." *Wall Street Journal*, 16 October 1996, B4.

Hedin, Marianne. "1997 Worldwide and U.S. Consulting Marketing and Trends." *IDC: Consulting and Management Services*. Framingham, Mass.: IDC, 1997.

Hellauer, Brian. "Andersen Shaping Bank Technology with It's Vision of What the Future Holds." *American Banker*, 13 December 1993, 18, 19.

Henkoff, Ronald. "Inside Andersen's Army of Advice." *Fortune*, 4 October 1993, 78–83.

Henriques, Diana B. "BankAmerica to Cut Up to 6.7% of Work Force, or 10,000 Jobs." *New York Times*, 29 July 2000, http://search.nytimes.com.

Hershey, Jr.,Robert D. "Profit Warnings by Bank of America Sets Off Big Retreat." *New York Times*, 7 December 2000, B1.

Hoffman, Thomas. "Y2K Fixes Will Hold Up Bank Merger Payoffs." *Computerworld*, 20 April 1998, 1, 16.

Hoffman, Thomas, and Julia King. "Chemical to Call Most Shots in Merger with Chase." *Computerworld*, 6 November 1995, 24.

Holmes, Steven A. "Huge Bank Mergers Worry Consumer Groups." *New York Times*,19 April 1998, 14.

Holson, Laura M. "BankAmerica President Says He Will Quit." *New York Times*, 21 October 1998, C1, 8.

———. "Hands in a Lot of Markets and a Foot on Each Coast." *New York Times*, 14 April 1998, D10.

Hooper, David, and Kenneth Whyld. *The Oxford Companion to Chess*. Oxford: Oxford University Press, 1984.

Hooper, Lawrence. "IBM Grants Gerstner Pay Package Valued at Up to $3.5 Million." *Wall Street Journal*, 31 March 1993, A3.

"How to Make Mergers Work?" *Economist*, 9 January 1999, 15.

"How a Software Giant Missed the Internet Revolution." *Wall Street Journal*, 18 January 2000, B1.

Huey, John. "The Year's 25 Most Fascinating Business People." *Fortune*, 2 January 1989, 63.

IBM Annual Report 1994

"IBM Chipcom Form Superhub Partnership." *Computerworld*, 27 July 1992, 49.

"IBM Customers Face Tough Networking Choices." *Business Communications Review* (November 1994): 22–24.

"IBM Forecast: Market Dominance (IBM PC Line)." *Byte* (fall 1984): 8.

"IBM Reaches Accord with Gartner Group over Trade Secrets." *Wall Street Journal*, 2 December 1983, 39.

"IBM's Personal Computer Spawns an Industry." *Business Week*, 15 August 1983, 88–90.

"IBM Tops U.S. Patent List for Eighth Consecutive Year." 10 January 2001, http://www.ibm.com/news/2001/01/10.phtml.

"Is AnyNet Going Anywhere?" *Business Communications Review* (October 1994): 22.

Johnston, David Cay. "U.S. Corporations Are Using Bermuda to Slash Tax Bills, Profits over Patriotism." *New York Times*, 18 February 2002, 1, 12.

Julekha, Dash. "Two Big Failures Cite Cap Gemini." *Computerworld*, 13 December 1999, 1.

King, Julia. "Andersen Jumps into Full-Service Outsourcing." *Computerworld*, 1 May 1995, 28.

———. "Consulting Conundrum." *Computerworld*, 27 May 1996, 45.

King, Mary L. *The Great American Banking Snafu*. Lexington: Lexington Books, 1985.

King, Jr., Ralph T. "BankAmerica Finds It Got a Lot of Woe with Security Pacific." *Wall Street Journal*, 22 July 1993, A1, 6.

Kirkpatrick, David. "Breaking Up IBM." *Fortune*, 27 July 1992, 44–58.

Kleege, Stephen. "Millions in Technology Needs Changed Craig's Mind." *American Banker*, 3 September 1996, 8.

Knowles, Anne. "Is OS/2 on Cruise Control?" *Software Magazine* (December 1996): 126–28.

Labaton, Stephen. "A Clinton Social with Bankers Included a Leading Regulator." *New York Times*, 25 January 1997, 1.

———. "Congress Eases Bank Laws." *New York Times*, 7 November 1999, Sec 4, 2.

Lindsay, Noel. "A Look at the New Networking Paradigm." *CommunicationsWeek*, 31 October 1994, 72.

Lipin, Steven. "Chemical and Chase Set $10 Billion Merger, Forming Biggest Bank." *Wall Street Journal*, 28 August 1995, A1, A6.

Lohr, Steve. "At Last, a Sneak Preview of Big Blue's Strategy." *New York Times*, 24 March 1994, D1, D6.

———. "What Lotus Got: Cash and Freedom." *New York Times*, 13 June 1995, D1.

Loomis, Carol J., and David Kirkpatrick. "The Hunt for Mr. X: Who Can Run IBM?" *Fortune*, 22 February 1993, 68.

Long, Larry. *Introduction to Computers and Information Processing.* Englewood Cliffs, N. J.: Prentice-Hall, 1984.

Lunday, Sarah. "Stock Options Lift BofA CEO's Pay to $17.5 Million." *Charlotte Observer*, 25 March 2002.

Lyons, Daniel. "IBM's Giant Gamble." *Forbes*, 4 October 1999, 91–95.

McColl, Hugh. "Main Street Rising." Speech given at the Oklahoma State University Executive Management Briefing, 17 November 1999, www.bankofamerica.com/newsroom.

"Major Banks, IBM Launch Network for PC Banking." *American Banker*, 10 September 1996, 1.

Manchester, William. *American Caesar*. Boston: Little, Brown & Company, 1978.

———. *The Last Lion, Alone 1932–1940*. Boston: Little, Brown & Company, 1988.

———. *The Last Lion, Visions of Glory 1874–1932*. Boston: Little, Brown & Company, 1983.

Markoff, John. "IBM's Chief Criticizes Staff Again." *New York Times*, 19 June 1991, D1.

Marjanovic, Steven. "Electronic Payment Law May Hasten End of Checks." *American Banker*, 1 May 1996, 1,12.

———. "Payments Inroads by Non-Banks Worry Bankers." *American Banker*, 16 October 1996, 13.

Markels, Alex. "Consulting Giant's Hot Offer: Jobs, Jobs, Jobs." *Wall Street Journal*, 6 March 1996, B1.

Matthews, Gordon. "Goldman Sachs No. 1 Last Year in Bank Merger Advice." *American Banker*, 31 January 1997, 18A.

McClean, Bethany. "The Enron Disaster, Lies, Arrogance, Betrayal." *Fortune*, 24 December 2001, 58–68.

"McColl: Approval of Interstate Banking Could Spark Greater Economic Activity across the Country." NationsBank release, 24 November 1992, www.nationsbank.com/newsroom/press/1992.

McFadden, Kay. "IBM Cuts 300 Jobs in Triangle." *Charlotte News & Observer*, 1 December 1994, A1.

"McKinsey & Company, Company Capsule." *Hoover's Online*, http://www.hoovers.com/co/capsule/4/0,2163,40304,00.html.

McNamee, Mike, Paula Dwyer, and Christopher H. Schmitt. "Accounting Wars, Powerful Auditor-Consultants Are the Targets of Arthur Levitt's Crusade." *Business Week*, 25 September 2000,cover story.

"Media Advisory—Bank of America Annual Meeting of Shareholders." 25 April 2001, www.bankofamerica.com/newsroom/.

Mildenberg, David. "NationsBank's Bid for Boatmen's Has Nationwide Implications." *Wichita Business Journal*, 30 September 1996.

———. "New NB Fees a Bottom Line." *Wichita Business* Journal, 21 February 1997.

Milligan, Jack. "Awaiting Results." *TheDailyDeal.com*, 24 May 2000, http://www.thedailydeal.com/features/special/A22952-2000May24.html.

Mills, D. Quinn, and G. Bruce Friesen. *Broken Promises*. Boston: Harvard Business School Press, 1996.

Mollenkamp, Carrick. "Bank of America to Settle Shareholder Suits." *Wall Street Journal*, 11 February 2002, A11.

Moody's Bank and Financial Manual 1996. New York: Moody Investor Services, 1996, 1824–29

Moore, Pamela L. "Bottom Line on the Line for Bank NationsBank Could Lose Contracts if Bias Proved." *Charlotte Observer*, 10 August 1997.

Moore, Robert F. "Hendrick Receives Pardon in Federal Case." *That's Racing*, 22 December 2000, http://www.thatsracin.com/00/docs/1223pardon.htm.

Moore, Thomas, and Michael Rogers. "Apple vs. IBM." *Fortune*, 18 February 1985, 8.

Morency, John, Nick Lippis, and Eric Hindin. "The Cost of Network Complexity." *Network World*, 31 July 1995, 44–46.

Morgenson, Gretchen. "Binge and Purge." *Forbes*, 3 November 1997, 54.

Morrall, Katherine. "Reengineering the Bank." *Bank Marketing* (February 1994): 67–71.

Moschella , David C. *Waves of Power*. New York: American Management Association, 1997.

Moyer, Liz. "Charting NationsBank's Future Systematically." *American Banker*, 3 October 1996, 14.

Mulqueen, John T. "Net Unit Sundered in Big Blue Reorg." *CommunicationsWeek*, 16 January 1995, 1.

Murphy, Matt, Rick Brooks, and Joseph B. Cahill. "BankAmerica Profit Slides 20% Amid Turbulent Markets." *Wall Street Journal*, 20 January 1999, B4.

Nash, Kim S. "Delta Ejects Sybase as Standard." *Computerworld*, 3 July 1995, 1, 103.

———. "Sybase Disputes Report Slamming System 10." *Computerworld*, 11 July 1994, 7.

"NationsBank and BankAmerica to Merge." Joint Release from NationsBank and BankAmerica, 13 April 1998, http://www.nationsbank.com/newsroom/press/1998/.

NationsBank Annual Report 1996

"NationsBank Chairman Hugh McColl Says Deregulation of the Banking Industry Could Provide Powerful Nationwide Economic Stimulus." NationsBank release, 24 February 1993, www.nationsbank.com.

"NationsBank Merger." *Atlanta Journal Constitution*, 31 August 1996, D4.

"NationsBank Merger Analysts Agree: It's McColl's Bank." *Atlanta Journal and Constitution*, 31 August 1996, D4

"Nation's Largest Bank Chooses 'Bank of America." Press release, 1 October 1998, www.nationsbank.com/newsroom/press/1998.

"Offerings in the Offing." *Barrons*, 27 September 1993, 44.

O'Leary, Meghan. "Work in Progress." *CIO*, 1 November 1992, 52–60.

"Open Season on Banks." *Fortune*, 21 August 1995, cover story.

O'Toole, James. "Spreading the Blame at Andersen." *New York Times*, 26 March 2002, A25.

"Over 20% of Branches in Florida to Be Shuttered." *Wall Street Journal*, 24 February 1998, B4.

Paley, Norton, "When Everyone Is Good, You Need a New Strategy." *Marketing News*, 29 April 1991, 12.

Passell, Peter. "Hidden in the Glitter of a Bountiful Economy, Problems Remain." *New York Times*, 25 December 1997, D1, 2.

Pelton, Robert Young, and Coskun Aral. *The World's Most Dangerous Places.* Redondo Beach, Calif.: Fielding Worldwide, 1995.

"Personal Computers: And the Winner Is IBM." *Business Week*, 3 October 1983, 76–80.

Peters, Thomas J., and Robert J. Waterman, Jr. *In Search of Excellenc.* New York: Harper and Row, 1982.

Peters, Tom. *Thriving On Chaos.* New York: Alfred A. Knopf, 1987.

Petre, Peter D. "Meet The Lean, Mean New IBM." *Fortune*, 13 June 1983, 69–82.

Pitney Bowes 1991 Annual Report .

Porter, Michael. *Competitive Strategy: Techniques for Analyzing Industries and Competitors.* New York: Free Press, 1980.

Prince, Cheryl J. "BAI Study Calls Banks to Action on the Electronic Frontier." *Bank Systems & Technology* (October 1995): 18–20.

"Remarks at National Press Conference Bank of America, Day One." 1 October 1998, www.nationsbank.com/newsroom/speeches.

"Remarks at the Special Meeting of Shareholders." 24 September 1998, www.nationsbank.com/newsroom/speeches.

"Remarks to the Little Rock Regional Chamber of Commerce 2000 Annual Meeting." 7 December 2000, http://www.bankofamerica.com/newsroom.

"Retraining, Outsourcing Rule the Roost at Chase." *Computerworld*, 2 October 1995, 93.

Ricciuti, Mike. "Sybase Steps Up to the Enterprise," *Datamation*, 1 July 1993, 18–22.

Rogers, David. *The Future of American Banking.* New York: McGraw-Hill, 1993.

Safire, William. "Don't Bank On It." *New York Times*, 16 April 1998, A23.

Sapsford, Jathan. "Bank of America Profit Falls 54%, Highlighting Loan-Market Problems." *Wall Street Journal*, 16 October 2001, C1.

Schlosberg, Jeremy. "Gideon Gartner: Building an Empire." *High-Tech Marketing* (May 1987): 10–15.

Schrage, Michael. "The Return of Vision." *Marketing Computers* (January 1996): 30.

"Shareholders Demand IBM Make Changes." *USA Today*, 25 January 1993, B1.

Sherrin, Ned, ed. *Oxford Dictionary of Humorous Quotations.* Oxford; Oxford University Press, 2001.

Singletary, Michelle. "Banks Branch Out over the Phone." *Washington Post*, 21 June 1996, D1, 3.

"Smithsonian: After the Shouting." *Washington Post*, 7 May 1995, C6.

Sobel, Robert. *IBM Colossus in Transition.* New York: Times Books, 1981.

Stern, Gabriella. "S and L Hell: The People and the Politics behind the $1 Trillion Savings and Loan Scandal." *Wall Street Journal*, 30 April 1993, A8.

"Survey Says NationsBank Best at Using Technology." NationsBank release, 29 October 1996, http://www.nationsbank.com/newsroom/press/1996/.

Taft, Darryl K. "Andersen Sets Enterprise Blueprint." *Computer Reseller News*, 28 October 1996, 132.

"Tandem Conference Report, Embracing Change." *Banker* (November 1996): S1.

"Technical Architecture Strategies." NationsBank Strategic Technology Group release, 25 February 1997.

"Three Big Bank Report Mixed Fourth-Quarter Results." *Wall Street Journal*, 17 January 2001, B4.

"Tom Labrecque, Left for Dead in a Merger, Found Alive and Well." *Wall Street Journal*, 25 November 1998, A6.

Lewis, Kenneth D. "2001 Annual Meeting of Shareholders Bank of America." Remarks upon assuming office of chairman and chief executive officer, 25 April 2001, http://www.bankofamerica.com/newsroom/speeches/speech.cfm?SpeechID= speech.20010425.04.htm.

"2 Major Mergers Expected Today in Bank Industry." *New York Times*, 13 April 1998, A22.

Verity, John W. "It's PCs vs. Mainframes—Even at IBM." *Business Week*, 21 September 1992, 66, 67.

Vogel, Todd. "Gideon Gartner Wants His Baby Back." *Business Week*, 4 December1989, 108, 110.

Walkin, Lawrence. "The Conflict of Interest Controversy." *CMA Magazine* (February 1992): 14.

Washburn, Gary. "O'Hare Retains Title as Busiest Airport." *Chicago Tribune*, 16 February 1996, Sec. 2C, 3.

Webber, Alan M., "Are All Consultants Corrupt?" *Fast Company* (May 2002): 130–34.

Wells, Kirstin E. "Are Checks Overused?" *Federal Reserve Bank of Minneapolis Quarterly Review* (fall 1996): 2–12.

Welsh, Jack, with John A. Byrne. *Jack Straight from the Gut*. New York: WarnerBusiness Books: 2001.

"We're on the Same Team...and the Customer Benefits!" *NationsBank Times* (January 1997): 2.

"When Bad Things Happen to Good People." *CIO*, 15 October 1997.

Williamson, Mickey, and Law McCreary. "Consulting Services: Making the Numbers." *CIO*, 15 November 1993, 48.

Willy Stern, and Gail Edmondson. "Memo to Gemini: Read This Book." *Business Week*, 26 June 1995, 40–42.

"A Winning Team." *NationsBank Times* (January 1997): 3.

For additional information on managing consultants, see www.Sof500.com, a resource for management, employees, and ethical consultants.

INDEX